Mead's Unfair Dismissal

Mead's Unfair Dismissal

Fifth Edition

M A Rich, LL M

Regional Chairman of Industrial Tribunals

I A Edwards, LL B, LL M

Full-time Chairman of Industrial Tribunals

Edited by Helen Mead, LL B, LL M

Solicitor

LONGMAN

© Longman Group Ltd 1983
© Longman Group UK Ltd 1987, 1991
© Longman Group Ltd 1994

ISBN 0 752000 640

Published by
Longman Law, Tax and Finance
Longman Group Ltd
21–27 Lamb's Conduit Street
London WC1N 3NJ

Associated offices
Australia, Hong Kong, Malaysia, Singapore, USA

A CIP catalogue record for this book is available from the British Library.

Printed and bound in Great Britain by
Bell & Bain Ltd, Glasgow

Contents

Foreword

My predecessor as President of the Industrial Tribunals, His Honour Judge Sir David West-Russell, described Malcolm Mead as 'the most outstanding candidate [for part-time Chairmanship] I have ever interviewed'. The Lord Chancellor appointed Mead a part-time Chairman of Industrial Tribunals in 1989 but he was already an established expert in the field of Employment Law with a record of teaching at Exeter University and as a partner specialising in the subject in a major West Country practice. Great promise was tragically cut short by his sudden death in 1993 at the age of 44.

The fifth edition of his important work on unfair dismissal has been brought up-to-date by Michael A Rich, a Regional Chairman of Industrial Tribunals and Ian A Edwards, a full-time Chairman, with the assistance of Malcolm Mead's widow, herself a lawyer, as editor.

Unfair dismissal is the largest portion of Employment Law which itself is undoubtedly one of the fastest-growing areas of law and of litigation. It is a field of law that stands at the interface between Westminster and Brussels. This new edition takes account of the changes brought about by the Trade Union Reform and Employment Rights Act 1993, the Sunday Trading Act 1994 and the many important decisions that affect the Transfers of Undertakings with implications for tendering and opting out. The new edition is clear, concise and readily accessible to all who need an authoritative but user-friendly book as a companion for their work. The experience of the authors underwrites the importance and integrity of this work. Those who feel that they can survive in the field of unfair dismissal without it are taking a chance—and those who take a chance in such a complicated and important area of law, usually come unstuck!

His Honour Judge Timothy Lawrence
President of the Industrial Tribunals
    for England and Wales

Preface

For many years the common law afforded, and still affords, to a dismissed employee an action for wrongful dismissal; that is a claim for damages where the employer, without lawful cause, has terminated a fixed-term contract during its term, or an indefinite contract with incorrect or no notice. The common law has never been concerned with the concept of the fairness of the employer's actions. Apart from cases where there is a dispute as to whether a contract could be terminated forthwith because of the employee's conduct, the common law concerned itself with the method of dismissal rather than the reason for it.

The first statutory incursion into this territory arose from the Redundancy Payments Act 1965, which gave some financial redress to employees dismissed by reason of redundancy.

The International Labour Organisation Recommendation 1963 suggested that termination of employment should not occur unless there was a valid reason connected with the capacity or conduct of the employee, or based upon the operational requirement of the employer. This theme was taken up by the Royal Commission on Trade Unions and Employers' Associations 1968 (known as the Donovan Commission) and eventually the concept found its way onto the Statute Book in the Industrial Relations Act 1971. It was that Act that introduced what it described as the right not to be unfairly dismissed.

Inevitably, a subject as politically sensitive as this has been the subject of numerous statutory amendments and innovations. Its development during a little over 20 years has been dramatic, not only by reason of the statutory alterations, but also the judicial interpretation of those statutes and the ever-growing influence of European law. In 1981, Munday in *Tribunal Lore* (1981) 10 ILJ 159 described employment law as 'possessing all the major attributes of other subjects, possibly in a more dynamic form'. Browne-Wilkinson J (as he then was), when President of the Employment Appeal Tribunal, described that tribunal as 'over-reported'—*The Role of the Employment Appeal Tribunal in the 1980s* (1982) 11 ILJ 69. It is, therefore, something of a daunting task to attempt a textbook on the subject of unfair dismissal.

The bulk of the legislation is now contained in the Employment

Protection (Consolidation) Act 1978, a commendable effort at codification of what had gone before. Regrettably, amendments have been made almost annually to that Act, such that it is now rumoured that another consolidation act is in the pipeline.

Claims for unfair dismissal are considered in the first instance by industrial tribunals, which were again foreseen in the Donovan Commission Report as forums which will be easy of access and relatively informal. That is difficult to achieve in the light of the background just described and also the fact that some claims involve important issues for either the employer or the employee which can have effects beyond the specific case. Increasingly, both employees and employers rely on professional advice of some sort. Those who proffer such advice not only have to bear in mind the common law, but the exceedingly complex and diverse statutory provisions, as well as the wealth of case law.

The first edition of this book was written primarily for those who are required to advise upon unfair dismissal, although, obviously, it was of interest to law students and others. That was the theme which the late Malcolm Mead continued in the next three editions.

Our intention with this edition has been to continue with that aim, to make a comprehensive examination of the law with appropriate references to reported cases. Some of the facets are so new that there are no reported cases on them. The law is as stated as at October 1994.

We are privileged to have been invited by Malcolm Mead's widow to prepare this edition. Malcolm Mead had been our respected colleague in the tribunal and we were deeply shocked by his sudden and untimely death.

Our thanks are due to our publishers for their advice and help but, above all, to Helen Mead as our Editor. Without her knowledge and information of her late husband's work on the earlier editions, our task would have been impossible. She assisted in the first four editions and so she is able to provide a continuity which is essential when dealing with such a fluid and dynamic subject.

Michael Rich
Ian Edwards   October 1994

Table of Cases

Table of Statutes

Table of Statutory Instruments

Table of Abbreviations

EP(C)A 1978	Employment Protection (Consolidation) Act 1978
TULR(C)A 1992	Trade Union and Labour Relations (Consolidation) Act 1992
PAYE	Pay As You Earn
EAT	Employment Appeal Tribunal
MSC	Manpower Services Commission
DHSS	Department of Health and Social Security
NIRC	National Industrial Relations Court
TURERA 1993	Trade Union Reform and Employment Rights Act 1993
STA 1994	Sunday Trading Act 1994
EOC	Equal Opportunities Commission
SDA 1975	Sex Discrimination Act 1975
RRA 1976	Race Relations Act 1976
TUPE 1981	Transfer of Undertakings (Protection of Employment) Regulations 1981
EPA 1975	Employment Protection Act 1975
EA 1990	Employment Act 1990
SSA 1985	Social Security Act 1985
SSA 1990	Social Security Act 1990

Table of Amendments to the Employment Protection (Consolidation) Act 1978

References throughout the text to sections or paragraphs in schedules are as amended. Only those amendments to the EP(C)A as are directly relevant to the contents of this book are detailed hereunder.

Sections 1–160 of the EP(C)A 1978

Sections 1–6 are inserted by s 26 and Sched 4 to the TURERA 1993.

Section 22A Act is inserted by s 28 and Sched 5 to the TURERA 1993.

Section 22B is inserted by s 28 and Sched 5 to the TURERA 1993.

Section 22C is inserted by s 28 and Sched 5 to the TURERA 1993.

Section 23 is repealed by s 300(1) and Sched 1 to the TULR(C)A 1992.

Section 27 is repealed by s 300(1) and Sched 1 to the TULR(C)A 1992.

Sections 33–44 are inserted by s 23 and Sched 2 to the TURERA 1993.

Sections 45–47 are inserted by s 25 and Sched 3 to the TURERA 1993.

Section 49 is amended by s 20 and para 3 of Sched 2 to the 1982 Act.

Section 49(4A) is inserted by s 20 and para 3 of Sched 2 to the 1982 Act.

Section 53 is amended by s 20 and para 4 of Sched 2 to the 1982 Act: s 15(1) of the 1989 Act: s 49(2) and para 11 of Sched 8 to the TURERA 1993: s 51 and Sched 10 to the TURERA 1993.

Section 53(2A) is inserted by s 24(4) of the TURERA 1993.

Section 55 is amended by s 21 and para 1 of Sched 3 to the 1982 Act: s 51 and Sched 10 to the TURERA 1993.

Section 56 is amended by s 20(2) and para 11 of Sched 1 to the 1980 Act: s 49(2) and para 12 of Sched 8 to the TURERA 1993.

Section 56A is inserted by s 12 of the 1980 Act and amended by s 49(2) and para 13 of Sched 8 to the TURERA 1993.

Section 57 is amended by s 6 of the 1980 Act: s 300(2) and para 14 of Sched 2 to the TULR(C)A 1992: s 28 of and para 2 of Sched 5 to the TURERA 1993.

Section 57A is inserted by s 28 and Sched 5 to the TURERA 1993.

Section 58 is repealed by s 300(1) and Sched 1 to the TULR(C)A 1992.
Section 59 is amended by s 21(2) and para 17 of Sched 3 to the 1982 Act: s 300(1) and Sched 1 to the TULR(C)A 1992: s 24(2) of the TURERA 1993: s 28 and para 4 of Sched 5 to the TURERA: s 29(2) to the TURERA 1993: s 49(2) and para 14 of Sched 8 to the TURERA.
Section 60 is inserted by s 24 of the TURERA 1993.
Section 60A is inserted by s 29(1) of the TURERA 1993.
Section 61 is amended by s 49(2) of and para 15 of Sched 8 to the TURERA 1993.
Sections 62 and 62A are repealed by s 300(1) of and Sched 1 to the TULR(C)A 1992.
Section 64 is amended by s 3(1) of the SDA 1986: s 21(2) and para 19 of Sched 3 to the 1982 Act: The Unfair Dismissal (Variation of Qualifying Period) Order 1985 (SI 1985 No 782): s 300(1) and Sched 1 to the TULR(C)A 1992: s 28 and para 5 of Sched 5 to the TURERA 1993: s 29(3) of the TURERA 1993.
Section 64(3) is inserted by s 24(3) of the TURERA 1993.
Section 64A is repealed by s 49(1) and para 2 of Sched 7 to the TURERA 1993.
Section 65 is amended by s 49(2) and para 16 of Sched 8 to the TURERA 1993.
Section 66 is amended by s 20(2) and para 13 of Sched 1 and Sched 2 to the 1980 Act.
Section 67(3) is repealed by s 300(1) and Sched 1 to the TULR(C)A 1992.
Section 68 is amended by s 21(3) and para 21 of Sched 3 to the 1982 Act.
Section 71 is amended by ss 5(1) and 21(3) and para 22 of Sched 3 and Sched 4 to the 1982 Act: s 300(2) and para 15 of Sched 2 to the TULR(C)A 1992: s 28 and para 6 of Sched 5 to the TURERA 1993: s 30(1) and (2) of the TURERA 1993.
Section 72 is inserted by s 300(2) and para 16 of Sched 2 to the TULR(C)A 1992: s 28 and para 7 of Sched 5 to the TURERA 1993.
Section 72A is repealed by s 300(1) and Sched 1 to the TULR(C)A 1992.
Section 73 is amended by ss 9 and 20 and Sched 2 to the 1980 Act: ss 4, 20(1) and 21 and para 5 of Sched 2 and Sched 4 to the 1982 Act: s 3(2) of the SDA 1986: the Unfair Dismissal (Increase of Limits of Basic and Special Awards) Order 1992 (SI 1992 No 313): s 300(2) and para 17 of Sched 2 to the TULR(C)A 1992: s 28 and para 8 of Sched 5 to the TURERA 1993.
Section 74 is amended by s 21(2) and para 23 of Sched 3 to the 1982 Act: s 30(1) and (3) of the TURERA 1993.
Section 75 is amended by the Unfair Dismissal (Increase of Compensation Limits) Order 1993 (SI 1993 No 1348): s 30(1) and (4) of the TURERA 1993.
Section 75A is inserted by s 28 and para 9 of Sched 5 to the TURERA 1993.

Section 76 is amended by the Sex Discrimination and Equal Pay (Remedies) Regulations 1993 (SI 1993 No 2798).

Section 77 is inserted by s 28 and para 10 of Sched 5 to the TURERA 1993.

Section 77A is inserted by s 28 and para 10 of Sched 5 to the TURERA 1993.

Section 78 is inserted by s 28 and para 10 of Sched 5 to the TURERA 1993.

Section 78A is inserted by s 28 and para 10 of Sched 5 to the TURERA 1993.

Section 79 is inserted by s 28 and para 10 of Sched 5 to the TURERA 1993.

Section 80 is amended by s 1(3) and para 30 of Sched 1 to the Education Act 1980.

Section 81 is amended by ss 20(1) and 21(2) an para 6(2) of Sched 2 and para 2(1) of Sched 3 and Sched 4 to the 1982 Act.

Section 82 is inserted by s 16(1) and para 3(1) of Sched 9 to the 1989 Act.

Section 86 is amended by s 49(2) and para 17 of Sched 8 to the TURERA 1993.

Section 132 is amended by s 20 and Sched 4 to the Social Security Act 1980: s 86 and Sched 11 to the Social Security Act 1986: para 50 and Sched 2 to the Social Security (Consequential Provisions) Act 1992: s 86 and para 50 of Sched 10 to the TULR(C)A 1992: s 300(1) and Sched 1 to the TULR(C)A: s 300(2) and para 19 of Sched 2 to the TULR(C)A 1992.

Section 133 is amended by s 20(2) and para 17 of Sched 1 to the 1980 Act: s 32(1) and para 9 of Sched 4 to the Wages Act 1986: s 86 and Sched 11 to the Social Security Act 1986: s 300(1) and Sched 1 to the TULR(C)A 1992: s 49(2) and para 20(a) and Sched 8 to the TURERA 1993: s 51 and Sched 10 to the TURERA 1993.

Section 134 is amended by s 20(2) and para 18 of Sched 1 to the 1980 Act.

Section 136 is amended by s 32(1) and para 10 of Sched 4 to the Wages Act 1986: s 300(1) and Sched 1 to the TULR(C)A 1992.

Section 138 is amended by s 28 and Sched 5 to the Armed Forces Act 1981: s 157 and Sched 9 to the Reserve Forces Act 1980: s 86(2) and Sched 11 to the Social Security Act 1986: s 66(2) and Sched 10 to the National Health Service and Community Care Act 1990: s 31 of the TURERA 1993: s 49(1) and para 3 of Sched 7 to the TURERA 1993: s 51 and Sched 10 to the TURERA 1993.

Section 138A is inserted by s 31(2) to the TURERA 1993.

Section 139 is amended by s 86(2) and Sched 11 to the Social Security Act 1986: s 49(1) and para 4 of Sched 7 to the TURERA 1993: s 51 and Sched 10 to the TURERA 1993.

Section 139A is inserted by s 49(1) of and para 11 of Sched 7 to the TURERA 1993.

Section 140 is amended by s 20 and para 20 of Sched 1 and Sched 2 to the 1980 Act: s 39(1) of TURERA 1993: s 49(2) para 21 of Sched 8 to the TURERA 1993.

Section 141 is amended by the Insolvency of Employer (Excluded Classes) Regulations 1983 (SI 1983 No 624): s 49(2) and para 22 of Sched 8 to the TURERA 1993.

Section 142 is amended by s 8(2) of the 1980 Act.

Section 144 is amended by s 49(2) and para 23 of Sched 8 to the TURERA 1993.

Section 146 is amended by ss 20 and 21 and para 8(5) of Sched 2 and para 6 of Sched 3 and Sched 4 to the 1982 Act: the Insolvency of Employer (Excluded Classes) Regulations 1983 (SI 1983 No 624): s 300(1) and Sched 1 to the TULR(C)A 1992: ss 27 and 51 and Sched 10 to the TURERA 1993.

Section 146A is inserted by s 49(1) and para 5 of Sched 7 to the TURERA 1993.

Section 149 is amended by s 20 and para 9 of Sched 2 to the 1982 Act: s 21(3) and Sched 4 to the 1982 Act: s 7 and Sched 1 to the Dock Work Act 1989: s 15(2) of the 1989 Act: s 51 and Sched 10 to the TURERA 1993: s 49(2) and para 24 of Sched 8 to the TURERA 1993: s 300(1) and Sched 1 to the TULR(C)A 1992: s 66(2) and Sched 10 to the National Health Service and Community Care Act 1990: s 49(1) and para 13 of Sched 7 to the TURERA 1993: s 49(1) and para 16 of Sched 7 to the TURERA 1993.

Section 149(2a) is inserted by s 49(1) and para 13 of Sched 7 to the TURERA 1993.

Section 151 is amended by s 20 and para 7(1) of Sched 2 to the 1982 Act: para 1(3) of Sched 4 to the STA.

Section 153 is amended by s 23(4) and Sched 7 to the Nurses, Midwives and Health Visitors Act 1979: s 21 and para 26 of Sched 3 and Sched 4 to the 1982 Act: s 29(3) and para 24 of Sched 6 to the 1989 Act: s 86(2) and Sched 11 of the Social Security Act 1986: s 29(4) and Sched 7 to the 1989 Act: s 33 and Sched 4 to the 1988 Act: s 16(2) and Sched 3 to the 1990 Act: s 300(2) and para 21 of Sched 2 to the TULR(C)A 1992: s 49(2) and para 25 of Sched 8 to the TURERA 1993: s 51 and para 10 to the TURERA 1993.

Schedule 2 of the EP(C)A 1978

Paragraph 2(1) is amended by s 20(2) and para 23 of Sched 1 to the 1980 Act: s 300(2) and para 22 of Sched 2 to the TULR(C)A 1992: s 49(2) and para 26 of Sched 8 to the TURERA 1993.

Paragraph 2(2) is amended by s 300(1) and Sched 1 to the TULR(C)A 1992: s 49(2) and para 26 of Sched 8 to the TURERA 1993.

Paragraph 2(4) is amended by s 20(2) and para 24 of Sched 1 to the 1980 Act: s 21 and para 27(2) of Sched 3 to the 1982 Act: s 7(4) of the Dock Work Act 1989: s 300(1) and Sched 1 to the TULR(C)A 1992.

Paragraph 2(5) is amended by s 49(2) and para 26 of Sched 8 to the TURERA 1993.
Paragraph 4 is amended by s 49(2) and para 26 of Sched 8 to the TURERA 1993.
Paragraph 5 is amended by s 49(2) and para 26 of Sched 8 to the TURERA 1993.
Paragraph 6 is amended by s 49(2) and para 26 of Sched 8 to the TURERA 1993.
Paragraph 7 is amended by s 49(2) and para 26 of Sched 8 to the TURERA 1993.

Schedule 3 of the EP(C)A 1978

Paragraph 2(2) is amended by s 10 and para 13 of Sched 2 to the Social Security and Housing Benefits Act 1982: s 49(2) and para 27 of Sched 8 to the TURERA 1993.
Paragraph 3(3) is amended by s 10 and para 13 of Sched 2 to the Social Security and Housing Benefits Act 1982: s 49(2) and para 27 of Sched 8 to the TURERA 1993.
Paragraph 5 is amended by s 300(2) and para 23 of Sched 2 to the TULR(C)A 1992.

Schedule 9 of the EP(C)A 1978

Paragraph 2 is amended by s 300(2) and Sched 2 to the TULR(C)A 1992: s 49(1) and para 6 of Sched 7 to the TURERA 1993.
Paragraph 6A is amended by s 21 and para 7 of Sched 3 to the 1982 Act.

Schedule 12 of the EP(C)A 1978

Paragraph 9 is amended by s 21(2) and para 28 of Sched 3 to the 1982 Act.

Schedule 13 of the EP(C)A 1978

Paragraph 1 is amended by s 20 and para 7(2) of Sched 2 to the 1982 Act; para 1(3) of Sched 4 to the STA.
Paragraph 3 is amended by para 1(3) of Sched 4 to the STA.
Paragraph 4 is amended by para 1(3) of Sched 4 to the STA.
Paragraph 8 is amended by s 20 and para 7(3) of Sched 2 to the 1982 Act.
Paragraph 9(1)(*d*) is amended by s 49(2) and para 31 of Sched 8 to the TURERA 1993.
Paragraph 10 is amended by s 20(2) and para 31 of Sched 1 to the 1980 Act: s 49(2) and para 31 of Sched 8 to the TURERA 1993.

Paragraph 11 is amended by s 20 and para 32 of Sched 1 to the 1980 Act: s 21 and para 29 of Sched 3 to the 1982 Act: s 51 and Sched 10 to the TURERA 1993.

Paragraph 14(1) and (4) is inserted by the Social Security (Consequential Provisions) Act 1992.

Paragraph 16(1) is amended by s 21 and para 6 of Sched 4 to the Reserve Forces (Safeguard of Employment) Act 1985.

Paragraph 17(1) is amended by s 21 and para 2(2) of Sched 3 to the 1982 Act.

Paragraph 18A is inserted by s 21 and para 3 of Sched 3 to the 1982 Act.

Paragraph 19 is amended by s 28 and Sched 5 to the Armed Forces Act 1981 and s 157 and Sched 9 of the Reserve Forces Act 1980.

Paragraph 20 is amended by s 49(1) and para 14 of Sched 7 to the TURERA 1993.

Schedule 14 of the EP(C)A 1978

Paragraph 7(1) is amended by s 20(2) and para 33 of Sched 1 to the 1980 Act: s 21 and para 30(2) of Sched 3 to the 1982 Act: s 86(2) and Sched 11 to the Social Security Act 1986: s 49(2) and para 32 of Sched 8 to the TURERA 1993.

Paragraph 8 is amended by s 21(2) and para 30(3) of Sched 3 to the 1982 Act: the Employment Protection (Variation of Limits) Order 1992 (SI 1992 No 312).

Chapter 1

Persons Protected Against Unfair Dismissal

Section 54 of the Employment Protection (Consolidation) Act 1978 (EP(C)A 1978) provides that every employee has the right not to be unfairly dismissed by his employer (except so far as is provided by ss 54–80 and 141–9 of the Act and ss 237–9 and 152–167 of the Trade Union and Labour Relations (Consolidation) Act 1992 (TULR(C)A 1992)). Protection against unfair dismissal is thus afforded only to *employees*.

'Employee' defined

An 'employee' is defined as an individual who has entered into or works under (or, where the employment has ceased, worked under) a contract of employment. A 'contract of employment' is defined as a contract of service or apprenticeship, whether express or implied and (if it is express) whether it is oral or in writing: s 153(1) of the EP(C)A 1978 and s 295 of the TULR(C)A 1992. Whether an individual is an employee and thus protected against unfair dismissal depends upon the existence of a contract of service or apprenticeship with the employer. The phrases *contract of service* and *contract of employment* are treated by the courts and tribunals as interchangeable expressions; but, strictly speaking, a contract of employment has a wider meaning than contract of service in that it includes a contract of apprenticeship.

Employees distinguished from independent contractors

A relationship which closely resembles that of the employer and the employee is that of hirer and independent contractor. This relationship has its foundation in a contract which is known as a *contract for services*. The independent contractor is not protected by the legislation when his contract is terminated. Therefore, the distinction between the contract *of* service and the contract *for* services is important. While it is easy to recognise the difference between the two, it is more difficult to say wherein that difference lies. The relationship of a chauffeur and his employer is that of employee and employer, and the contract is a

1

contract of service. The relationship between a fare and his taxi driver is that of hirer and independent contractor, and the contract is a contract for services. The distinction is apparent, but what are the differences? A contract under which a person provides services may be a contract *sui generis: Ironmonger v Movefield Ltd (t/a Deering Appointments)* [1988] IRLR 461.

In *WHPT Housing Association Ltd v Secretary of State for Social Services* [1981] ICR 737, Webster J thought that:

> the difference between a contract of service and one for services must reside, essentially, in the terms of the principal obligation agreed to be undertaken by the employee—a word which I use without begging the question. In a contract of service, it seems to me, the principal obligation undertaken by the employee is to provide himself to serve: whereas in a contract for services the principal obligation is not to provide himself to serve the employer but his services for the use of the employer.

The 'tests' or criteria

The following are some of the tests which have been suggested by the courts over the years, but no one test will necessarily be conclusive. Each case will have to be looked at in the light of the various tests, and the existence or otherwise of the following criteria.

Control

The *control* test is the oldest test. It was based on the proposition that the employer had the right to control the employee, both as to the work to be done, but more importantly as to the manner in which that work was to be done. If the 'employer' did not have the right to control the manner in which the work was to be done then the contract was not a contract of service. This test has become difficult to apply with changing economic and social conditions. Where skills were simple, it might well be possible for the employer to control the employee. With the increase in specialist skills (eg computing) it is no longer possible for the employer to control the employee, particularly as to the manner in which the work is done, although it is quite clear that the relationship between the parties is that of employer and employee. The courts, recognising these problems, have modified the test so that the power or residual right to control the employee is an important factor in determining whether or not the relationship between the parties is that of employer and employee. Thus, control remains relevant as a factor in deciding whether an individual is an employee or not: see *Ready Mixed Concrete (South East) Ltd v Minister of Pensions and National Insurance* [1968] 2 QB 497 and *Warner Holidays Ltd v Secretary of State for Social Services* [1983] ICR 440. In

Narich Pty Ltd v Commissioner of Pay-Roll Tax [1984] ICR 296, Lord Brandon, giving the decision of the Privy Council, held:

> while all relevant terms of the contract must be regarded, the most import-
> ant, and in most cases the decisive, criterion for determining the relation-
> ship between the parties is the extent to which the person, whose status
> as employee or independent contractor is in issue, is under the direction
> and control of the other party to the contract with regard to the manner
> in which he does his work under it.

Even where the individual has agreed to be subject to the control of the 'employer' the relationship between the parties can still be one of hirer and independent contractor.

Organisation

A second test, which has been little used, is the *organisation* or *integra-tion* test. In *Stevenson, Jordan and Harrison v Macdonald and Evans* [1952] 1 TLR 101, Denning LJ said:

> One factor which seems to run through the instances is that under a
> contract of service a man is employed as part of the business and his
> work is done as part of the business, whereas under a contract for services,
> his work, although done for the business, is not integrated into it but is
> only accessory to it.

This test was followed by Lord Denning in *Bank voor Handel en Scheepvaart NV v Slatford* [1953] 1 QB 279. This test may be of some assistance where, for instance, the control test is inapplicable because the employer is not able to control the employee in the way in which he performs his duties, but the employee is clearly an essential part of the organisation. It may be particularly relevant in the case of a doctor employed by a health authority (see *Cassidy v Ministry of Health* [1951] 1 All ER 574) or an employee who is a computer programmer within a commercial organisation.

Ungoed-Thomas J used this test in *Beloff v Pressdram Ltd* [1973] 1 All ER 241, to decide that Nora Beloff was an employee of *The Observer* newspaper.

Economic reality

More recently, the *economic reality* test has evolved; it was suggested by MacKenna J in *Ready Mixed Concrete (South East) Ltd v Minister of Pensions and National Insurance, above.* The issue before the court was whether or not the owner-driver of the lorry was an independent contractor. There was a complex agreement between the driver and the company which cast the driver as an independent contractor. Under the agreement the driver agreed to deliver the company's cement and not to haul for anyone else during the period of the agreement. The agreement provided that the driver should buy the lorry on hire-purchase from a company in the same group. The driver had to carry out orders given to him by the company as if he were an employee. He was under obligations as to repairs and maintenance of the vehicle, but was not subject to the company's instructions in driving the lorry. There were no provisions as to the hours of work, meal breaks and the times at which he took holidays; in these matters he was not subject to the control of the company. The driver could employ others who would be his employees, to drive the vehicle. He could not be asked to do work other than drive for the company, whereas drivers who were the company's employees could be asked to do work other than drive lorries. Moreover, at the expiration of the agreement, the driver was free to work elsewhere. The chance of profit from operating the vehicle and the risk of loss were the driver's.

MacKenna J examined the economic realities, the ownership of tools, investment, the use of skills, and particularly the chance of profit and the risk of loss to answer the question suggested by the earlier authorities: whose business is it? Was the driver carrying on business on his own behalf or on behalf of a superior, the company? It was held that the driver was carrying on business on his own account. He was a small businessman and not a servant.

Profit/risk

If the person who undertakes the work has a chance of profit and a risk of loss, and has the responsibility for investment in the business, it is an indication (but not conclusive evidence) that there is no contract of service. These factors are likely to be of increasing importance since the decision in the *Ready Mixed Concrete* case *above.*

Ownership of tools and the obligation to provide them

Where the tools (or *instrumentalia*) belong to the person who undertakes the work and are complex, specialised or expensive, it is an indication (but not conclusive evidence) that there is no contract of service. However, by custom, employees may be obliged to provide their own tools: *Challinor v Taylor* [1972] ICR 129 and see *Hitchcock v Post Office* [1980] ICR 100. The provision of clothing by the 'employer' may also be indicative of a contract of service.

The entitlement to exclusive service

Exclusive service is an indication (but not conclusive evidence) of a contract of service. If the person who agrees to undertake the work can substitute another to carry out the work, it is an indication (but not conclusive evidence) that there is no contract of service. If the person who undertakes the work has to engage helpers at his expense, it is again an indication (but not conclusive evidence) that there is no contract of service.

The payment of wages, sickness pay and holiday pay, and by whom payment is made

Payment of fixed remuneration for a specific period is an indication (but not conclusive evidence) that there is a contract of service. The renumeration may be calculated in various ways, such as on a piece-work or day-work basis. Payment for holidays or for absences caused by sickness or injury will also be an indication (but not conclusive evidence) that there is a contract of service. When payment is for a particular undertaking or task, it is an indication (but not conclusive evidence) that there is a contract for services: see *O'Kelly and Others v Trusthouse Forte plc* [1983] ICR 728. Payment by tips received from others or payment by commission may be consistent with the existence of a contract of service.

The power of selection and appointment

The courts and tribunals will pay particular attention to the circumstances at the time when the contract was made, and the way in which the individual was taken on. The unilateral imposition of contractual terms by one of the parties on the other may be an indication (but not conclusive evidence) that there is a contract of service.

The power to suspend and dismiss

In the contract of service it is usual for the employer to have the power to suspend the employee and to dismiss. In the contract for services there is no power to dismiss, but there may be a power to terminate the contract. In practice the effect may be the same, although the different nature of the provisions will be relevant. The power to dismiss is probably more important than the power of selection, although even where there is a power of dismissal, other elements may make the contract one for services.

The power to fix the place, time of work and the times at which holidays are taken

These matters may be seen as an element of control and the existence of this power in the contract may be an indication (but not conclusive evidence) of a contract of service.

The existence of a disciplinary and grievance procedure

The existence of a disciplinary and grievance procedure may be an indication (but not conclusive evidence) of a contract of service.

The deduction of PAYE etc

The deduction of income tax under the PAYE rules and the payment of national insurance contributions for an employed person may be indicative of (but not conclusive evidence of) a contract of service. Conversely, payment without deduction of tax to workers who hold a

715 Certificate does not necessarily mean a person is not employed. Payments of tax and national insurance contributions are not primarily employment matters, and method of payment is only one of the factors to be taken into account.

Intention of the parties
The intention of the parties to the contract or the label which they use to describe their relationship cannot alter or indeed decide the true relationship. The expression of their true intention is relevant but not conclusive in determining the relationship. Thus, a declaration by the parties in the contract that the person rendering the services is to be regarded as a self-employed person or as an independent contractor will be disregarded if the contract is consistent with the relationship of employer and employee. The legal relationship must be classified not by appearance but by reality: *Young and Woods Ltd v West* [1980] IRLR 201. In each case the tribunal will examine the agreement to discover its real nature. The intention of the parties may well be a relevant factor for consideration. While the parties cannot alter the true nature of the relationship between them by the label they give it, where there is doubt or ambiguity, their intentions and the agreement between them may be strong evidence as to the true nature of the relationship or, in some cases, decisive: see *Massey v Crown Life Insurance Co* [1978] ICR 590, in which the Court of Appeal distinguished its earlier decision in *Ferguson v John Dawson and Partners (Contractors) Ltd* [1976] 1 WLR 346. In *BSM (1257) Ltd v Secretary of State for Social Services* [1978] ICR 894, the High Court, following *Massey*'s case, held that effect should be given to the intentions of the parties unless the terms of the contract or the circumstances were inconsistent with their intentions.

The view of the ordinary person
In *Cassidy v The Ministry of Health* [1951] 2 KB 343, Somervell LJ quoting Buckley LJ in *Simmons v Heath Laundry Co* [1910] 1 KB 543, confirmed that a further element to be considered in determining whether the relationship between the parties was that of employer and employee was whether the contract was 'a contract of service within the meaning which an ordinary person would give to the words'. In *Thames Television Ltd v Wallace* [1979] IRLR 136, the EAT held that the tribunal in deciding whether or not there is a contract of service should consider whether, in the light of the members' own experience and qualifications, the contract is such that the ordinary person looking at it would say that it was a contract of service. This approach was applied in *Midland Sinfonia Concert Society Ltd v Secretary of State for Social Services* [1981] ICR 454.

A further variation was considered in *Withers v Flackwell Heath Football Supporters' Club* [1981] IRLR 307, where the issue was whether or not a steward was an employee or was self-employed. The EAT, following the decision of Cooke J in *Market Investigations Ltd v Minister of Social Security* [1968] 3 All ER 732, found that the ultimate question in deciding the relationship between the parties is to ask, 'Is he on his own business rather than the business of the party for whom the work is being done?' It considered that if Withers had been asked while acting as a steward of the club bar 'Are you your own boss?', then the answer would be 'No'. It followed he was an employee.

The need for mutual obligations

Recent cases involving casual employees have highlighted the need for mutuality of obligation between the employer and employee.

If the person providing the work is under no obligation to provide work on a regular basis and the individual who undertakes the work has the right to decide whether or not to accept the work, it is an indication (but not conclusive evidence) that there is no contract of service. In *O'Kelly and Others v Trusthouse Forte plc* [1983] ICR 728, mutuality of obligation was treated as an important factor in deciding whether or not the relationship was that of employer and employee. It was found to be missing in the case of regular casual workers at the Grosvenor Hotel.

Multiple or mixed test

Since no test is conclusive, the tribunals and courts will have to look at all the elements of the relationship. Each case must be considered on its own facts: see *Warner Holidays Ltd v Secretary of State for Social Services* [1983] ICR 440. The weight to be given to each of these elements will vary in each case. The *above* is not an exhaustive list. MacKenna J in *Ready Mixed Concrete (South East) Ltd v Minister of Pensions and National Insurance above*, summarised what could be called the multiple test as follows at p 515.

> A contract of service exists if these three conditions are fulfilled. (i) The servant agrees that, in consideration of a wage or other remuneration, he will provide his own work and skill in the performance of some service for his master. (ii) He agrees, expressly or impliedly, that in the performance of that service he will be subject to the other's control in a sufficient degree to make that other master. (iii) The other provisions of the contract are consistent with its being a contract of service.

Addison v London Philharmonic Orchestra Ltd [1981] ICR 261; *Midland Sinfonia Concert Society Ltd v Secretary of State for Social Services* [1981] ICR 454; *Warner Holidays Ltd v Secretary of State for Social Services* [1983] ICR 440; and *O'Kelly and Others v Trusthouse Forte plc* [1983] ICR 728, provide examples of cases where most of the elements as set out above have been considered in determining the nature of the relationship between the parties. However, as these cases make clear, each of these elements has to be considered in the circumstances of each case and the importance to be attached to them will vary from case to case. Usually the presence or absence of one or more of these elements will not be conclusive as to the question whether there is or is not a contract of service.

In *Hall (Inspector of Taxes) v Lorimer* [1994] IRLR 171, the Court of Appeal upheld the decision of the EAT that Lorimer, a freelance vision mixer, was self-employed and not an employee of the twenty or more companies with whom he engaged in contracts, most of which lasted for one day only. The Court of Appeal approved Mummery J in the EAT who took the view that: 'It is a matter of the evaluation of the overall effect of the detail, which is not necessarily the same as the sum total of the individual details'.

Whose employee?

It may be clear that an individual is an employee; but whose employee is he? Where one employer loans an employee to another employer, the elements set out *above* will need to be examined in relation to each potential employer in deciding who is the real employer. Some elements may be present in relation to both employers and the courts will have to decide the issue on balance. Some of the elements will be more appropriate than others as, for instance, who selected the employee and who may dismiss him?

Fact or law?

Is the question 'is a contract a contract of service or a contract for services?' one of law alone or a question of fact and law? An appeal from the decision of the tribunal can only be made to the EAT on a question of law. If it is a question of law then it is open to the EAT to substitute its findings for the findings of the tribunal. However, even if it is a question of law, then for an appeal to be made successfully against the decision of the tribunal on the issue, the EAT must find that the tribunal has misdirected itself as to the law or has misapplied the law to the facts, or the decision was such that no reasonable tribunal properly instructed as to the law could have properly reached the conclusion that that tribunal reached on the evidence available to it.

There is a wealth of authority as to whether or not the question is one of law or fact but, regrettably, the authorities are conflicting.

In *Young and Woods Ltd v West* [1980] IRLR 201, Stephenson LJ held that the true inference from the facts and the true construction or interpretation of an agreement, whether written or oral, is a matter of law and if the Court of Appeal considers the tribunal is wrong in its view of the agreement then it should find an error in law and reverse the tribunal's decision. See also the judgment of Sir David Cairns.

The view of Stephenson LJ was followed by the EAT in *Addison v London Philharmonic Orchestra Ltd* [1981] ICR 261, where the conflicting authorities were reviewed. In *Midland Sinfonia Concert Society Ltd v Secretary of State for Social Services* [1981] ICR 454, Glidewell J again reviewed the earlier authorities, and following the decision of Lord Radcliffe in *Edwards v Bairstow* [1956] AC 14, considered that he could interfere on appeal if 'the facts found are such that no person acting judicially and properly instructed as to the relevant law could have come to the determination under appeal', or to put it another way, 'the true and only reasonable conclusion contradicts the determination.' The powers of the appellate court to interfere with a decision at first instance were further considered in *WHPT Housing Association Ltd v Secretary of State for Social Services* [1981] ICR 737, where Webster J considered that an appellate court had jurisdiction to interfere only if it concluded that no reasonable body, on the facts found by it and the inferences reasonably to be drawn from those facts, and properly directing itself as to law, could have made the decision which was reached. 'In other words, if the validity of the decision in law depends on the nature of the inferences to be drawn from the primary facts found', then the appellate court 'should interfere with it only if it is wrong, as a matter of law, in the light of inferences which must inescapably be drawn'. The early authorities have been reviewed by the Court of Appeal in two further cases.

In *O'Kelly and Others v Trusthouse Forte plc* [1983] ICR 728, the Court of Appeal found that the EAT had interpreted a passage in the judgment of Stephenson LJ in *Young and Woods Ltd v West* [1980] IRLR 201, as authority for the proposition that the question was one of pure law. Donaldson MR referred to *Simmons v Heath Laundry Co* [1910] 1 KB 543, where the issue was described as 'one of fact with which an appellate court could not interfere in the absence of reason to believe that the arbitrator had misdirected himself'. The tribunal's findings and assessments of the facts will dictate the correct legal answer. He found 'it is only if the weight given to a particular factor shows a self-misdirection in law that an appellate court with a limited jurisdiction can interfere'.

In *Nethermere (St Neots) Ltd v Gardiner* [1984] ICR 612, Stephenson LJ accepted that in *Young and Woods Ltd v West, above,* he had suggested that whether a contract is a contract of service or for services was a question of pure law. That had been decided without reference to *Simmons v Heath Laundry Co, above.* In the present case the Court of Appeal held that whether the contract is a contract of service or contract for services is a question of law, but the answer includes questions of degree and fact which it is for the tribunal to determine. Applying the decision in *Edwards v Bairstow, above,* it was not open to the EAT 'to interfere with the industrial tribunal's decision unless the industrial tribunal had misdirected itself in law or its decision was one which no tribunal, properly directing itself on the relevant facts, could have reached'.

In *Catamaran Cruisers Ltd v Williams and others* [1994] IRLR 386, the EAT stated at p 388 'In our view, it is a question of fact in every case whether or not the contract in question is one of service or a contract for services'. In this case the worker had, at the employer's request, created a limited company for the purpose of raising invoices for payment for his work on river bus and pleasure cruises. It was held by the EAT that he was still an employee. They stated at p 388 'We accept that the formation of a company may be strong evidence of a change of status but the fact has to be evaluated in the context of all the other facts as found'.

Labour-only contracts

In the labour-only contract the main contractor provides the plant and materials, and arranges with a subcontractor to find the labour. The subcontractor is given a lump sum to remunerate those he engages. The subcontractor may engage employees who will remain his employees, unless it is clear that in reality they are the employees of the main contractor, or he may engage independent contractors who may be independent contractors in relation to the main contractor and/or the subcontractor. In *Ferguson v John Dawson and Partners (Contractors) Ltd* [1976] 1 WLR 346, a man taken on as a member of a 'lump' labour force was held by the Court of Appeal to be an employee.

Apprentices

A contract of apprenticeship is akin to a contract of service, but it has an essential difference. The apprentice agrees to serve his master for the purposes of learning and the master agrees to teach the apprentice. If these elements are not present or if they are incidental, the contract is not one of apprenticeship, but probably of service. If the apprentice is a minor, the contract must be substantially for his advantage, otherwise he may be free to repudiate it. As regards statutory protection the distinction is largely academic because an apprentice is afforded the rights given to employees.

A person on the government work experience programme

Whether or not a person on a work experience programme is an employee of the sponsoring company will be determined in the normal way. In *Hawley v Fieldcastle and Co Ltd* [1982] IRLR 223, the tribunal found the relationship between the parties was not that of employer and employee because the Manpower Services Commission (MSC) imposed some limitations or restrictions, which are not usually found in the employer-employee relationship; namely, on recruitment, the work to be done, discipline, termination and remuneration. In *Daley v Allied Suppliers Ltd* [1983] IRLR 14, it was held that a person working under the MSC work experience scheme was not employed either by the MSC or by the 'sponsoring employer'. In so far as there was a contract between the sponsoring employer and the individual, it was not a contract of service. The object was to enable the individual to obtain some work experience. There is nothing to prevent a trainee being regarded also, on the facts, as an employee, eg if he is paid additional money by the employer: see *Glaister v Burns* (1985) (unreported).

Agents

In *Tyne and Clyde Warehouses Ltd v Hamerton* [1978] ICR 661, it was held that an agent expressly engaged as 'self-employed', who paid Schedule D income tax and self-employed social security contributions, was an employee. It is unclear why *Massey*'s case was not regarded as applicable. See also *JC King Ltd v Valencia* (1966) 1 ITR 67.

Directors

Directors *qua* directors are office holders and not employees, although they may be agents of the company or have a dual capacity of agent and trustee. Most managing directors and directors with executive functions may well be employees of the company. In large companies it will usually be apparent from the circumstances and the existence of a service agreement that the director is an employee.

Difficulties have occurred in the case of smaller companies, particularly 'one-man companies'. The question has been considered in claims for redundancy payments where the tribunals regarded whether or not the director had a controlling interest as being important.

In *Ferguson v Telford Grier Mackay and Co Ltd* (1967) 2 ITR 387, Ferguson was a company director and also company secretary. He worked as a full-time executive and held 30 per cent of the share capital. The other director held 50 per cent of the share capital. It was held that Ferguson was an employee.

In *Robinson v George Sorby Ltd* (1967) 2 ITR 148, it was held that the managing director who held over 90 per cent of the shares and was in control of the board of directors was not an employee. The remainder of the shares were held by members of the family, and the director could devote such time and energies to the company as he thought fit. There was no control by the company over him because he was, in effect, the company. It is possible, however, for a controlling shareholder-director to be an employee if the position of the director *vis-à-vis* the company is consistent with that of an employee.

In *Margetts v Underwood (Zelah) Ltd* (1973) 8 ITR 478, directors were held not to be employees. The only functions they had were directorial ones supervising the running of the business, and there was no evidence from which a contract of service could be inferred.

In *Albert J Parsons and Sons Ltd v Parsons* [1979] IRLR 117, the Court of Appeal held that a full-time working director who received no salary but had his remuneration voted to him by way of director's fees and emoluments, and who was treated as being self-employed for the purpose of national insurance contributions, was not an employee. In *Eaton v (1) Robert Eaton Ltd and (2) Secretary of State for Employment* [1988] IRLR 83, Kilner-Brown J gave very helpful guidance at p 83.

Two more recent unreported decisions of the EAT have followed this guidance: *Wilson v Trenton Service Station Ltd* (1987) (unreported), and *McLean v Secretary of State for Employment* (1992) (unreported).

The position of a director who has some executive functions may be clarified by the existence of a service agreement. In marginal cases this may help to establish the director as an employee. See also *Stanbury v Overmass and Chapple Ltd* (1976) 11 ITR 7.

Office holders

In some circumstances, office holders may be both the holders of an office and employees. In *Social Club (102) and Institute Ltd v Bickerton* (1977) 12 ITR 442, the EAT held that the fact that a club secretary held an office from which he was removable by a two-thirds majority of the members, was irrelevant to the consideration of the question of whether he was an employee. The EAT held that in deciding whether a secretary to a club is an employee the following factors should be considered:

(1) whether the individual's payment was contractual and whether it was an honorarium or a salary;

(2) whether payment was fixed in advance or whether it was voted at the end of the year in token of the individual's work;

(3) whether the arrangements conferred upon the individual a right to payment or whether what was paid was a mere bounty;

(4) the size of the payment;

(5) whether the individual was exercising the functions of an independent office (somewhat in the way that a curate or police officer does) or was subject to the control and orders of the club;

(6) the extent and weight of the duties performed—the smaller they are the less likely he is to be an employee;

(7) the description given to the payment in the Minute or Resolution authorising it, and its treatment in the accounts for tax and national insurance purposes.

Ministers of religion

In *President of the Methodist Conference v Parfitt* [1984] IRLR 141, it was held that a Methodist minister was not an employee. Even if the relationship between such a minister and the Methodist Church were to be contractual it would not be a contract of employment. Again in *Davies v Presbyterian Church of Wales* [1986] ICR 280, the House of Lords held that a pastor of the Presbyterian Church of Wales was not employed under a contract of service. See also *Birmingham Mosque Trust Ltd v Alavi* [1992] ICR 435. Here, a Professor of Islamic Studies was appointed director and Khateeb of the Birmingham Central Mosque, his duties being both religious and administrative. The EAT held that where religious duties were concerned it had to be asked first of all whether there was any intention to enter into a contractual relationship at all, and then, if there were sufficient certainty that the parties were *ad idem*, to address the question of whether there was a contract of service.

Partners

A partner is generally not an employee but a self-employed person: see *Cowell v Quilter Goodison Co Ltd and QG Management Services Ltd* [1989] IRLR 392. However, the circumstances may show that a salaried partner is an employee, as may be an associate partner. Someone who is not described as a partner may in law be a partner and not an employee. See *Burgess v O'Brien* (1966) 1 ITR 164.

Outworkers

An outworker working from home may be an employee even though he or she is regarded as self-employed for tax purposes.

In *d'Ambrogio v Hyman Jacobs Ltd* [1978] IRLR 236, the employee, a machinist, who had worked at the company's premises, agreed to work from her own home instead. She worked at least 40 hours a week on equipment provided by the company. She was visited daily by a director who supplied her with materials and took away the completed garments. He also instructed her as to the method of work. Following the *Ready Mixed Concrete* case, above, the tribunal held that she was an employee.

In *Airfix Footwear Ltd v Cope* [1978] ICR 1210, the EAT also held that an employee who had worked for the company for seven years on work supplied to her on a daily basis five days a week and did her work in accordance with the company's instructions, was an employee.

In *Nethermere (St Neots) Ltd v Gardiner and Others* [1984] ICR 612, it was held that the two individuals who were machinists working at home on machines provided by the company were employees. The Court of Appeal accepted that there was an 'overall' or 'umbrella' contract obliging the company to continue to provide work, and the individuals to continue to accept and perform the work provided. The individuals were doing the same work for the same rate as employees in the factory. See p 7 *above*, for the importance of mutuality of obligations.

Casual employees

In *O'Kelly and Others v Trusthouse Forte plc* [1983] ICR 728, it was held that individuals who were regular but casual waiters in the company's banqueting department were not employees.

Diplomats

The doctrine of sovereign immunity originally prevented an industrial tribunal from considering a claim for unfair dismissal brought by an employee at a diplomatic mission who was engaged in carrying out the work of that mission: see *Sengupta v Republic of India* [1983] ICR 221. However, the State Immunity Act 1978 enables an employee to claim wrongful dismissal, provided the contract was made in the UK and the work is to be wholly or partly performed there; and to claim unfair dismissal; and also to take proceedings to enforce other statutory rights. The State Immunity Act 1978 does not apply to contracts made before the coming into force of that Act: see *Sengupta*'s case.

Workers' co-operative

A workers' co-operative registered with the Registrar of Friendly Societies as a limited company is an employer capable of employing and dismissing its workforce, so that an employee who is a member of the co-operative and a member of the workforce can bring a claim against the co-operative: *Drym Fabricators Ltd v Johnson* [1981] ICR 274. Although the point was not in issue the EAT appears to have considered that an unregistered co-operative could have a legal personality as distinct from its members so that the co-operative could employ and dismiss, allowing an individual to bring a claim against it.

Employees excluded from protection

Employees who lack the qualifying period of employment

See Chapter 3 for the normal requirements as to a qualifying period of service and its calculation, and see Chapter 10 as to the special rules in maternity. See also Chapter 11 for trade union cases, Chapter 13 for health and safety cases and Chapter 2 for shop workers.

Employees employed under illegal contracts

As a general principle the courts will not enforce illegal contracts entered into for purposes which are either forbidden by the law or which, while not forbidden by the general law, are immoral or contrary to public policy. It is for the tribunal to decide whether any illegality connected with the contract of employment renders it unenforceable. Where the contract is illegal then the employee is prevented from exercising his statutory rights: see *Tomlinson v Dick Evans 'U' Drive Ltd* [1978] ICR 639.

In *Hewcastle Catering Ltd v Ahmed and Elkamah* [1991] IRLR 473, two waiters were involved in the operation of a VAT fraud but they derived no personal benefit from it. They were subsequently called to give evidence at a trial in connection with the fraud and were dismissed by the club manager. The Court of Appeal held that the applicants' claims for unfair dismissal could not be precluded by public policy. They were involved by their employers in the fraud and were then dismissed for giving evidence to customs officers. Here the contracts of employment were not entered into on the basis that the employees would assist in the fraud and, in this type of case, if the employee could not bring a claim for unfair dismissal then that might well encourage employers to dismiss employees for giving evidence regarding fraud.

A contract may be illegal where it cannot be performed without illegality on the part of one or both of the parties to the contract, or it may be that the contract is on the face of it perfectly legal, but the parties intend to or subsequently do perform the contract illegally.

In *Corby v Morrison (t/a The Card Shop)* [1980] IRLR 218, the employee was paid in addition to his wages £5 a week which was not declared and upon which no tax was paid. This sum was roughly equivalent to the amount of tax and national insurance which was deducted from the employee's wage. The EAT held, following *Miller v Karlinski* (1945) 62 TLR 85, that the contract was a fraud on the Revenue and as such was illegal, and it made no difference whether or not the parties were ignorant that what they were doing was illegal. The EAT also held that if they were wrong in law and the contract was on the face of it legal so that 'the existence or otherwise of knowledge of its intended illegal performance by the employer and employee becomes relevant then the test must be subjective and not objective'. See also *Cole v Fred Stacey Ltd* [1974] IRLR 73, following *Napier v National Business Agency Ltd* [1951] 2 All ER 264. An agreement to understate earnings so as not to affect social security benefits will make the contract illegal: *Wilkinson v Lugg* [1990] ICR 599. In *Salvesen v Simons* [1994] IRLR 52, the EAT held that where an employee requested, and the employer agreed, that part of the employee's remuneration would be payable as a management fee without deductions for income tax and national insurance to a partnership operated by the employee and his wife, it was a fraud on the Revenue and the contract of employment was therefore illegal.

The employee as well as the employer must be guilty of an illegal act or intention: *Davidson v Pillay* [1979] IRLR 275. Failure by the employee, unknown to the employer, to declare to the Revenue a benefit which he has received from his employment does not necessarily render the contract illegal: *McConnell v Bolik* [1979] IRLR 422.

In *Newland v Simons and Willer (Hairdressers) Ltd* [1981] IRLR 359, the EAT found that if the contract of employment is one which, on the face of it, is lawful and the illegality consists of an illegal performance by the employer it is necessary to consider whether the employee was aware at the time she entered into the contract or became aware during the continuance of the contract of that illegality. The EAT further found that, if viewed subjectively, although the employee ought to have appreciated that the contract was being performed illegally but as a matter of fact she did not, then the fact that the employee ought to have known but did not know is insufficient to deprive the employee of her right to rely upon the statutory employment provisions.

The illegal part of a contract which is a fraud on the Revenue cannot be severed from the remainder: *Corby v Morrison (t/a The Card Shop), above.*

Illegality may be collateral to the contract in other ways. In *Coral Leisure Group Ltd v Barnett* [1981] IRLR 204, the employee alleged that after his employment commenced he was told by his employer that as part of his duties he was expected to obtain prostitutes for his employer's clients and pay for them out of funds provided by his employer. The EAT found that in deciding whether any taint of illegality affecting part of the contract necessarily rendered the whole contract unenforceable by a party who knew of the illegality, a distinction had to be drawn between '(a) cases in which there is a contractual obligation to do an act which is unlawful, and (b) cases where the contractual obligations are capable of being performed lawfully and were initially intended so to be performed, but which have in fact been performed by unlawful means.'

It found that in cases coming within category (a), it depends upon how far it is possible to separate the tainted contractual obligations from the untainted; in cases coming within category (b), it depends upon whether the performance of an unlawful act by a party to the contract precludes that party from further enforcing the contract. Where, in the course of performing a contract, an employee has committed an unlawful or an immoral act that does not by itself prevent him from further enforcing the contract, unless the contract was entered into with the purpose of doing an unlawful or immoral act, or the contact is prohibited by law. Since in this case the employee did not enter into employment with the intention of procuring prostitutes and there was no prohibition at law against the contract of employment, the employee was not precluded from asserting his contract against his employer. If an employee has been defrauding his employer, the employer cannot plead that the contract is therefore illegal: *Broaders v Kilkare Property Maintenance Ltd* [1990] IRLR 421. The EAT held that the extent to which the applicant was involved in the act of dishonesty and fraud on the employer may be relevant to issues under the EP(C)A 1978, but did not render the contract illegal.

In *Annandale Engineering v Sampson* [1994] IRLR 59, where a kennel hand received occasional payments without deduction of tax from the owners of winning greyhounds, the EAT held that this did not render the contract illegal or one which was being illegally performed and therefore unenforceable. The payments were not regular or part of the employee's remuneration.

An illegal contract cannot be taken into account in computing continuous employment. In *Hyland v JH Barker (North West) Ltd* [1985] IRLR 403, the employee received a tax-free lodging allowance for 4 weeks although he was not lodging away from home and this was known to his employer. The 4 weeks broke his continuous period of employment. Thus, although he had been employed for 16 years, since the 4-week period had occurred 11 months before his dismissal, he could not establish a year's continuous employment (the then qualifying period).

An overseas worker who works in this country without a work permit commits an offence and runs the risk of deportation. A dismissal in these circumstances would fall within s 57(2)(*d*) of the EP(C)A 1978.

Employees over retiring age

There is no lower age limit. However, an employee is precluded from bringing a claim for unfair dismissal if on or before the effective date of termination (see Chapter 5) he had attained the age which, in the undertaking where he was employed, was the normal retiring age for an employee holding such a position, and the age was the same whether the employee holding that position was a man or a woman, or where there is no normal retiring age in the undertaking, if he or she had attained the age of 65 (s 64(1)(*b*) of the EP(C)A 1978). If there is a normal retiring age, the employee may bring a claim if he or she is under the normal retiring age, notwithstanding that he or she is over the age of 65. Conversely, if there is a normal retiring age which the employee has attained which is below 65, the employee is precluded from claiming unfair dismissal: *Nothman v Barnet London Borough Council* [1978] ICR 336, upheld on appeal to the House of Lords; *Nothman v Barnet London Borough Council* [1979] ICR 111.

There is no double barrier. See the judgment of Lord Salmon at p 116.

Where the employee has been taken on over the age of 65 and there is no normal retiring age, the employee will not be able to claim unfair dismissal: see *Dixon v (1) London Production Tools Ltd and (2) Phildon Instrumentation (London) Ltd* [1980] IRLR 385.

The interpretation of normal retiring age has given rise to a difference of judicial opinion. The point was considered by the House of Lords in *Waite v Government Communications Headquarters* [1983] ICR 653, where Lord Fraser rejected the view that a contractual retiring age conclusively fixes the normal retiring age. He found there is a presumption that the contractual retiring age is the normal retiring age for the group but this can be rebutted by evidence that in practice there is a higher age at which employees holding the position are regularly retired. He said the proper test is to ascertain what would be the reasonable expectation or understanding of the employees holding that position at the relevant time.

This case was followed in *Mauldon v British Telecommunications plc* [1987] ICR 450, where the EAT held that the tribunal should have regard to both the statistical and the contractual situation. In *Whittle v Manpower Services Commission* [1987] IRLR 441, the EAT held that statistics are important. It further found that although Lord Fraser had referred to the abandonment of the contractual retiring age he had meant the regular departure from it. See also *Secretary of State for Scotland v Meikle* [1986] IRLR 208.

However, there are still difficulties as the decisions in *Hughes v Department of Health and Social Security; Coy v Department of Health and Social Security* and *Jarnell v Department of Environment* [1985] ICR 419, illustrate.

In 1948 Hughes and Coy were transferred from local government to the civil service subject to a proviso that they could be retired at any time after reaching the age of 60. Service would not normally be prolonged after 65, although temporary employment might be permitted after that age. Because in 1948 there were staff shortages it was the intention that both should be employed to 65 and this was incorporated in a DHSS circular. There was a primary code applicable to civil servants which set out, *inter alia*, terms and conditions relating to retirement. This code made it clear that the contractual retirement age was 60, but retirement could be postponed in certain circumstances. In reliance upon the code in 1981 the DHSS changed its policy in relation to retiring ages and the changes were set out in a circular. This change in practice was to be operative in two stages from 1 April 1982 and 1 April 1983. This circular provided that:

> officers aged 61 and over on 31 March 1982 will have to retire on that date; officers reaching age 61 between 1 April 1982 and 31 March 1983 will have to retire on their birthday in that year; officers over age 60 on 31 March 1983 will have to retire on that date and subsequently officers will retire on their 60th birthday.

Hughes, a senior executive officer, was retired on 31 March 1982 when he was aged just over 61. Coy, a higher executive officer, was retired on 2 May 1982, his 61st birthday. Had Hughes and Coy been dismissed before they reached normal retiring age? Lord Diplock held that the contractual retiring age throughout their employment was 60 although the head of each department could postpone this on a discretionary basis. If, because of administrative policy, a category of employees was allowed to retire at a stated higher age and that policy was communicated to those employees in a circular, those employees could reasonably expect their normal retiring age to be the higher age. The presumption in *Waite*'s case that the contractual retiring age of 60 constitutes the normal retiring age for the category of employees was rebutted.

Changes in administrative policy communicated to the employees would alter their expectations. He said the relevant circular in force in this case was D76/81 issued on 3 June 1981. The employees' reasonable expectations of the normal retirement age was the age set out in D76/81. The notices of termination had been strictly in accordance with the circular.

Therefore, neither Hughes nor Coy (nor Jarnell—the facts of his case were indistinguishable), were entitled to claim unfair dismissal because they had all attained normal retiring age.

Two other issues fell to be considered: first, the relevant time for determining the normal retiring age and secondly, in ascertaining the normal retiring age, the 'group' of employees to be considered.

Lord Diplock, referring to the decision of the House of Lords in *Waite*'s case, held that the word 'group' used by Lord Fraser is not referred to in the legislation. Lord Fraser had used it as an alternative to the word 'position' which is defined in the statute. An applicant's 'position' is ascertained at the date of termination of the employment and does not include prior employment history and he thought the Court of Appeal application of the word 'group' was wrong. Lord Fraser used the phrase 'the relevant time' at which to establish the reasonable expectation. The Court of Appeal thought he was referring to the effective date of termination under s 64(1)(b). Lord Diplock thought this was correct and he thus held that the relevant time for determining the normal retiring age is the effective date of termination and that the relevant employees were employees who were senior executive officers in the case of Hughes, and higher executive officers in the case of Coy. He did not accept that the relevant employees were restricted by reference to historical origin. The remainder of their Lordships concurred. See also *Highlands and Islands Development Board v MacGillivray* [1986] IRLR 210.

When an employee was expected to retire between the ages of 62 and 63 it was held that there was no normal retiring age: *Swaine v Health and Safety Executive* [1986] IRLR 205.

In *Brooks and Others v British Telecommunications plc* [1992] IRLR 66, the Court of Appeal held the question to be asked in determining the normal retiring age is 'What, at the effective date of termination of the claimant's employment, and on the basis of the facts then known, was the age which employees of all ages in the claimant's position could reasonably regard as the normal age of retirement applicable to the group?' It was not correct to ask what all the members of the relevant group could reasonably expect would happen to those members of the group who were approaching the alleged normal retiring age. In this case the normal retiring age was 60, even though previously employees over that age had been retained subject to their fitness and efficiency. The employer can change the normal retirement age by introducing a new specific age as part of its administrative policy properly communicated to the employees affected even though it might take immediate effect and destroy the employees previous expectation of working until they reached a higher age. This is always subject to there being no breach of contract of employment or suggestion that the policy is a sham or never properly implemented.

In *Barber v Thames Television plc* [1992] IRLR 410, Barber who had joined the company in 1968 when the policy was retirement at 65 elected in 1973 under a new policy to continue to have a retirement age of 65. Subsequently, the company sent a letter detailing a phased reduction of the retiring age. This was sent to Mr Barber in 1987 explaining that pre–1978 employees would be compulsorily retired at the age of 64 as from 1 November 1988.

The Court of Appeal held that 64 was the normal retiring age for employees holding the same position as Barber and he could not therefore claim unfair dismissal. In determining 'position', as defined by s 153(1) of the EP(C)A 1978, regard could be had to a term of employment which dealt only with retirement and differences in terms and conditions as to the normal retiring age could distinguish between groups or classes of employees. Although an employee's previous employment history is not relevant in considering 'position' under s 153(1) it is relevant to consider terms and conditions, including those as to retirement which currently apply even though they may derive from the history of the employment. There were two groups of employees, post 1 January 1978 employees whose normal retiring age was 60 and pre 1 January 1978 employees who, having been informed of the phased reduction in retirement age, could reasonably expect to be compelled to retire at 64. Mr Barber was therefore precluded by s 64(1)(*b*) from claiming unfair dismissal.

See also *Carter v Parkside Health Authority* (1992) (unreported) and *Fleur de Lys Automobile Manufacturing Ltd v Terry* (1994) (unreported), both decisions of the EAT.

Employees who ordinarily work outside Great Britain

Employees who, under their contracts of employment, ordinarily work outside Great Britain are excluded from protection against unfair dismissal: s 141(2) of the EP(C)A 1978. The phrase 'ordinarily works outside Great Britain' has given rise to difficulties.

In *Portec (UK) Ltd v Mogensen* [1976] ICR 396, the EAT held that under his contract of employment, an employee could ordinarily work both inside and outside Great Britain, and so could not claim unfair dismissal. The effect of this decision would have been to deprive many employees of their statutory rights.

In *Wilson v Maynard Shipbuilding Consultants AB* [1978] ICR 376, Wilson was employed by Maynard, a Swedish company, as a consultant from July 1973 until September 1975. His contract of employment contained no express provision as to where he was to work. It was found that he worked for 50 weeks in Italy and for 40 weeks in the UK. It was held that he could not ordinarily work both inside and outside Great Britain, and the decision in *Portec (UK) Ltd*, above, was wrong in law. The Court of Appeal gave some guidance in determining where the employee ordinarily works. It held that if the contract does not provide for the employee to work wholly or substantially in or out of Great Britain then one has to look at the express and implied terms of the contract to ascertain where, looking at the whole period contemplated by the contract, the employee's base is to be. The base would probably be the place where he is treated as ordinarily working under the contract of employment. In ascertaining the base one has to look at, for example, where the employee's home is, where his headquarters are, and in what currency he is to be paid. Each individual contract of employment will contain the relevant factors.

The Court of Appeal accepted that the tribunal should not just look at the position at the time of dismissal but the whole of the employment—a view first propounded by the NIRC in *Maulik v Air India* [1974] ICR 528.

The decision in *Wilson*'s case was followed by the Court of Appeal in *Todd v British Midland Airways Ltd* [1978] ICR 959. Todd was employed by the company which was a British company as a first officer on aircraft flying on international routes. Although he worked outside Great Britain for 53 per cent of his time, his base was in Great Britain. The contract of employment did not provide where the employee ordinarily worked. The Court of Appeal was influenced by the fact that his base was in Great Britain in reaching its conclusion that he ordinarily worked in Great Britain.

In *Janata Bank v Ahmed* [1981] ICR 791, the Court of Appeal followed the decision in *Wilson*'s case *above*. Ahmed was employed by the United Bank in Bangladesh which was then taken over by the respondent. In 1972 he was posted to London although under the terms of his contract of employment he could be recalled to Bangladesh at any time. He was posted to Brussels for a short period of time and then returned to London. He was then ordered to transfer to the bank's head office in Dakar. He did not move to Dakar. His employment was terminated. The Court of Appeal held that 'a broad brush' approach should be adopted. The starting point was the contract of employment. Although the place where the employee has been working may be a strong indication of where he was required to work under his contract of employment it is not determinative.

In *Wood v Cunard Line Ltd* [1989] IRLR 431, Wood, a seaman, was employed on a UK registered ship based in Puerto Rico, but which at no time entered UK territorial waters. His contract provided for each voyage to terminate in the UK. This did not happen in practice. The company's head office was at Southampton where he was recruited and from where he was paid. Wood argued that the proper test for determining where he ordinarily worked was the base test and his base was the company's head office in Southampton.

The EAT held that the proper test was where the employee would carry out his work under the contract rather than at the time of making the contract where it was contemplated his base would be. The base test is not the only test, nor is it always the appropriate test to determine where, under his contract, an employee ordinarily works.

In *Sonali Bank v Rahman Same v Chowdhury* [1989] ICR 314, both employees worked in Great Britain. Both had contracts with a mobility clause which required them to work abroad. Both employees were based in and worked exclusively in Great Britain and the fact that they had a contract with a mobility clause did not mean that they were employees ordinarily working outside Great Britain.

An employee only ordinarily works under the contract subsisting at the time of the dismissal. It is that contract of employment to which s 141(2) of the EP(C)A 1978 is directed. Thus, if under that contract the employee ordinarily works in Great Britain he is not excluded by s 141(2) of the EP(C)A 1978 Act, even if under a preceding contract he ordinarily worked outside Great Britain even within a period of two years prior to the dismissal: *Weston v Vega Space Systems Engineering Ltd* [1989] IRLR 429.

Special categories of employees

Employees on offshore installations

Pursuant to powers in the EP(C)A 1978, protection against unfair dismissal now applies to certain employees working on certain offshore installations: Employment Protection (Offshore Employment) Order 1976 (SI 1976 No 766) as amended by SI 1977 No 588, which, although made under earlier legislation, continues in force under the EP(C)A 1978 and is further amended by SI 1981 No 208 and SI 1984 No 1149. Employees working on offshore installations within British territorial waters are protected, provided they do not ordinarily work outside either those waters or Great Britain. Similarly, employees working on offshore installations in British designated areas of the continental shelf who are engaged on work connected with exploration of the sea bed or subsoil or the exploitation of their natural resources, are protected. Again those employees must neither be employed on other types of work in the British designated areas nor be ordinarily employed outside those areas, British territorial waters nor Great Britain. Under the 1981 Order employment for the purposes of activities connected with the exploration or exploitation of the Frigg Gas Field is covered if the employer is a company registered under the Companies Act 1985 or directs operations from Great Britain. The employment legislation may also be extended to cover activities relating to the exploration or exploitation of a cross-boundary petroleum field in a foreign sector of the continental shelf. See ss 22A–22C of the EP(C)A 1978 for rights not to suffer detriment in health and safety cases. This does not yet apply to offshore employment where the issue is sensitive but the provisions can be extended under s 49(1) and para 13 Sched 7 of the TURERA 1993.

Members of the armed forces

Section 138A of the EP(C)A 1978 (introduced by s 31 of the TURERA 1993) allows members of the armed forces new employment rights. They had previously been specifically excluded from protection against unfair dismissal. They will in future be able to claim unfair dismissal rights except under ss 57A and 80. The extension of the rights to the armed services may be modified by additions or omissions introduced by Order in Council: s 138A(2) of the EP(C)A 1978. However, those modifications are not to result in a position where an employee could not bring a claim for unfair dismissal because it would be out of time. Section 138A will come into force on a day to be appointed.

Police officers

Persons engaged under contracts of employment in police service cannot claim unfair dismissal: s 146(2) and (3) of the EP(C)A 1978. Police service means service as a member of any constabulary or service in any capacity 'by virtue of which the person has the powers or privileges of a constable'. Section 8 of the Prison Act 1952 provides that 'every prison officer while acting as such shall have all powers, authority, protection and privileges of a constable'. Therefore a prison officer could not claim unfair dismissal notwithstanding that the conduct complained of was while he was off duty and outside the prison: *Home Office v (1) Robinson and (2) Prison Officers Association* [1981] IRLR 524.

Share fishermen

The master and crew members of a fishing vessel who are remunerated only by shares in the profits or gross earnings of the vessel cannot claim unfair dismissal: s 144(2) of the EP(C)A 1978.

Seamen

A person employed to work on board a ship registered in the UK, which is not registered at a port outside Great Britain, is regarded as a person who under his contract ordinarily works in Great Britain: s 141(5) of the EP(C)A 1978. To this provision there are exceptions where the employment is wholly outside Great Britain or the person is not ordinarily resident in Great Britain. See *Wilson v Maynard Shipbuilding Consultants AB* [1978] ICR 376. See also under 'Employees who ordinarily work outside Great Britain', p 21.

In *Royle v Globtik Management Ltd* [1977] ICR 552. Royle was an engineer who was employed by a shipping company which managed three tankers, two of which were registered in England and one overseas. By his contract Royle was obliged to work on any of the ships owned, managed or submanaged by the employer, irrespective of the port of registration. Royle worked on the two tankers registered in London sailing between Japan and the Persian Gulf until he was dismissed. The EAT held that Royle was not employed only to work on board a ship registered in the UK and, further, that because he worked on a tanker registered in Great Britain, it was not sufficient to prevent him from ordinarily working outside Great Britain. A British ship was not part of Great Britain for these purposes. Thus what is now s 141 (2) of the EP(C)A 1978 applied. See also *Wood v Cunard Line Ltd* [1989] IRLR 431.

Crown employees

A Crown employee may claim unfair dismissal. The termination of Crown employment is treated as a dismissal for this purpose: s 138(1) of the EP(C)A 1978. The protection afforded may be removed where a Minister of the Crown issues a certificate certifying that the employment should be excepted from protection on the grounds of national security: s 138(4) of the EP(C)A 1978.

Section 49 of the EP(C)A 1978 (which relates to the minimum period of notice to which an employee is entitled) does not apply to Crown employees. Similarly, the provisions relating to redundancy payments (ss 81 *et seq* of the EP(C)A 1978) do not apply to Crown employees, but they are able to claim unfair dismissal in a redundancy situation, since the claim is one for unfair dismissal.

House of Lords and House of Commons staff

As with Crown employees, relevant members of the House of Commons staff may claim unfair dismissal, and the termination of their employment is treated as a dismissal: s 139(1) of the EP(C)A 1978. 'Relevant members of the House of Commons staff', are defined in s 139(3) as any person appointed by the House of Commons Commission or employed in the refreshment department, and any member of the Speaker's personal staff.

Section 139A of the EP(C)A 1978 (introduced by s 49(1) and Sched 7 of the TURERA 1993) provides that the unfair dismissal legislation contained in the Act shall apply to House of Lords staff who are now treated as employed under a contract with the House of Lords corporate officer. Under s 139A(2) nothing shall prevent a relevant member of the House of Lords staff from bringing proceedings before a tribunal which could be so brought by any other person.

Teachers in aided schools

Where a teacher in an aided school is dismissed by the governors of the school as a result of a requirement of a local authority, pursuant to s 24(2) of the Education Act 1944, the statutory provisions as to unfair dismissal apply as if the local authority were the employer and it had dismissed the teacher for the reason or principal reason that it had required his dismissal: s 80(1) of the EP(C)A 1978.

Part-time employees

See Chapter 3 and the decision of the House of Lords in *R v Secretary of State for Employment ex parte Equal Opportunities Commission* [1994] IRLR 176.

Contracting out of statutory protection

There is no general power to contract out of the provisions affording protection against unfair dismissal. Thus, any provision in an agreement is void insofar as it purports to exclude or limit the operation of the unfair dismissal provisions or in so far as it precludes any person from presenting a complaint to, or bringing any proceedings before a tribunal for unfair dismissal: s 140(1) of the EP(C)A 1978. In *Council of Engineering Institutions v Maddison* [1977] ICR 30, the EAT held that where any document or agreement purports to deprive the employee of his rights under what is now s 140(1) of the EP(C)A 1978, any uncertainty as to its meaning should be resolved in favour of the employee. Any agreement which deprived the employee of the right to claim unfair dismissal would be rendered void under s 140(1).

In *Naqvi v Stephens Jewellers Ltd* [1978] ICR 631, the EAT held that this section embraces an agreement to withdraw a complaint which has been made as well as to an agreement not to initiate proceedings. Where an employer settles a claim for unfair dismissal the settlement should be recorded on a form of settlement prepared by ACAS. The employer is thereby able to ensure that the employee is precluded from bringing a claim against the employer for unfair dismissal. See 'Conciliation' *below* at p 28.

However, there are certain limited exceptions to this provision.

Fixed-term contracts

The employee's protection against unfair dismissal does not apply where the employee is employed under a contract entered into after 1 October 1980 for a fixed term of one year or more, provided that the dismissal consists only of the expiry of the term without its being renewed, where before the term expires the employee has agreed in writing to exclude his right to claim unfair dismissal in relation to that contract. Any agreement excluding any such claim must be contained either in the contract of employment or in a separate agreement. The agreement may be made at any time before the term expires, but since in many cases where the employee agrees to exclude his right to claim unfair dismissal after the contract has been signed there would be no supporting consideration from his employer, the contract will be unenforceable unless it is in the form of a deed: s 142(1) and (3) of the EP(C)A 1978.

A contract is for a fixed term if it fixes the maximum duration of the period of employment, whether or not the contract contains a power for either party to bring the contract to an end by giving notice to the other party before the expiration of the period certain: *BBC v Dixon* [1979] IRLR 114; *BBC v Constanti* [1979] IRLR 114. A contract may be a fixed-term contract where the employee has to make herself available for a fixed period even though during that period she is not called upon to perform the work for which she is employed: *Wiltshire CC v NATFHE and Guy* [1980] IRLR 198. But for the contract to be a fixed-term contract, it must have a defined beginning and end, so that a contract which is to come to an end upon the happening of an uncertain future event, eg for the life of the present sovereign, is not a fixed-term contract: *Wiltshire CC v NATFHE and Guy, above*. Similarly, a contract for a specific task which has no defined end is not a contract for a fixed term: *Ryan v Shipboard Maintenance Ltd* [1980] IRLR 16.

In determining if there is a fixed-term contract of sufficient length to include the statutory protection, it must be the final contract which is for a fixed term of one year or more. It is not possible to amalgamate the cumulative total of all contracts of a fixed term so as to achieve the one year: *Open University v Triesman* [1978] ICR 524. Arguably, a distinction must be drawn between the extension or renewal of an existing fixed-term contract and a re-engagement under a new contract, so that whereas the former would count as part of the fixed-term contract the latter would not. See the judgments of Stephenson and Lane LJJ in *BBC v Ioannou* [1975] QB 781 and compare the judgment of Denning MR. In *Mulrine v University of Ulster* [1993] IRLR 545, the Court of Appeal held that the test in *BBC v Ioannou*, that it is only the period of the final contract which must be considered, should not be applied if it would produce an unfair and unreasonable result. Here Mulrine's two-year fixed term had been clearly extended by a further four months, and she had not been re-engaged under a new contract. During the extension she did the same work under the same terms and conditions and it could not be argued that she had been re-engaged on a new fixed-term contract for less than one year.

Dismissal procedures agreements

A dismissal procedures agreement is an agreement in writing with respect to procedures relating to dismissal made by or on behalf of one or more independent trade unions and one or more employers or employers' associations: s 153(1) of the EP(C)A 1978. An application may be made jointly to the Secretary of State by all the parties to the agreement for an order designating the agreement as one which will have effect in place of the statutory protection against unfair dismissal. In such cases the provisions of the agreement shall apply where the employee is dismissed or is in the course of being dismissed (otherwise than on the grounds of pregnancy): ss 65(1), (3) and (4) and 140(2)(c) of the EP(C)A 1978. The Secretary of State must be satisfied that certain requirements have been fulfilled before he makes an order under s 65: see s 65(2) of the EP(C)A 1978. For revocation, see s 66 of the EP(C)A 1978.

Conciliation

Section 140(1) does not apply to any agreement to refrain from presenting a complaint for unfair dismissal, where in compliance with a request under s 134(3) of the EP(C)A 1978 a conciliation officer has taken action in accordance with that subsection: s 140(2)(*d*) of the EP(C)A 1978; or to any agreement to refrain from proceeding with a complaint of unfair dismissal where a conciliation officer has taken action in accordance with s 134(1) and (2) of the EP(C)A 1978: s 140(2)(*e*) of the EP(C)A 1978.

Section 134(1) of the EP(C)A 1978 provides that where a complaint of unfair dismissal has been made to a tribunal, a copy of the originating application must be sent to the conciliation officer. It is the duty of the conciliation officer, if he is requested to do so by the employee and by the employer against whom it was presented, or in the absence of any such request, the conciliation officer considers that he could act with a reasonable prospect of success, to endeavour to promote a settlement of the unfair dismissal complaint without its being determined by the tribunal.

Section 134(2) of the EP(C)A 1978 provides that for the purpose of promoting such a settlement where the employee has ceased to be employed by the employer, the conciliation officer shall in particular seek to promote the reinstatement or re-engagement of the employee by the employer or by a successor of the employer or by an associated employer on terms appearing to him to be equitable, but where an employee does not wish to be reinstated or re-engaged or where reinstatement or re-engagement is not practicable and the parties desire the conciliation officer to act, he shall seek to promote agreement between them as to compensation to be paid by the employer to the employee.

Section 134(3) of the EP(C)A 1978 provides that where a person claims that action has been taken where a complaint for unfair dismissal could be presented to a tribunal and before a claim for unfair dismissal has been made, if a request is made to a conciliation officer, whether by that person or by the employer, to make his services available, then the conciliation officer shall act in accordance with s 134(1) and (2) as if a complaint of unfair dismissal had been presented.

The conciliation officer is under an obligation, where appropriate, to have regard to the desirability of encouraging the use of other procedures available for the settlement of grievances: see s 134(4) of the EP(C)A 1978.

Anything communicated to the conciliation officer in connection with the performance of his functions under s 134 of the EP(C)A 1978 shall not be admissible in evidence before a tribunal except with the consent of the person who communicated it to the conciliation officer: s 134(5) of the EP(C)A 1978.

In *Moore v Duport Furniture Products Ltd and others* [1982] IRLR 31, Moore was suspended by the employer on suspicion of theft. He was totally deaf but could read and write. At a meeting Moore was told by the employer that his job was at an end and he would not be re-employed. Under protest Moore accepted £300 and resigned. A conciliation officer was not present at that meeting but was then involved and asked to prepare a form of settlement on form COT3. He went through the form with both parties and they then signed it. Subsequently, Moore made a complaint of unfair dismissal. The House of Lords held that the duty of a conciliation officer to endeavour to promote a settlement does not necessarily involve any positive act. The words 'endeavour to promote a settlement' must be given a liberal construction capable of covering whatever action by way of such promotion is applicable in the circumstances of the particular case, so that ascertaining what the parties had agreed, and preparing a form of settlement recording the agreement, fell within the expression 'endeavouring to promote a settlement'. It was also held by the House of Lords that there is no obligation on the conciliation officer to see that the terms of settlement are fair for the employee.

In *Slack v Greenham (Plant Hire) Ltd* [1983] IRLR 271, the EAT held that there was no obligation upon a conciliation officer to advise or inform an employee of the framework of his rights under the relevant legislation, although if he thought it necessary he could do so but he should never advise as to the merits of the employee's case. The EAT went on to hold that if a conciliation officer were to act in bad faith or adopt unfair methods when promoting a settlement the agreement might be set aside.

Likewise a conciliation officer will not have failed to comply with s 134(4) of the EP(C)A 1978 by not encouraging the use of a grievance procedure where it is obvious that the only area for negotiation was as to compensation: *Hennessey and Another v (1) Craigmyle and Co Ltd (2) ACAS* [1985] ICR 879.

Where an offer made by one of the parties in a claim for unfair dismissal has been accepted by the other through the intermediary of a conciliation officer, so that there is a binding agreement, the conciliation officer has undertaken his duties pursuant to s 134(1) of the EP(C)A 1978 and the employee will be prevented from claiming unfair dismissal: *Gilbert v Kembridge Fibres Ltd* [1984] IRLR 52.

It has been held that the expression 'where a person claims that action has been taken' enabling him to make a complaint of unfair dismissal is to be construed as 'not referring only to some express or formal claim, but as including also in its meaning an implied claim to be inferred from the overt acts or attitudes of the employee concerned in the particular circumstances of the case': *Moore v Duport Furniture*

Products Ltd and others, above. In *Hennessey and Another v (1) Craig-myle and Co Ltd (2) ACAS, above,* it was held that where the employee asserts that action has been taken and the evidence supports that assertion, the conciliation officer is required to act. The employee was told that if he signed an agreement prepared by a conciliation officer he would be treated as redundant and paid a sum of money. He saw his solicitor. The solicitor contacted ACAS and the employee had a discussion with them. He subsequently signed the agreement. It was held that the employee was plainly asserting that action had been taken in respect of which a complaint could be presented, and that the conciliation officer was entitled to act before a complaint had been presented. In *Freeman v Sovereign Chicken Ltd* [1991] ICR 853, an employee's claim for unfair dismissal was settled and recorded on form COT3 under which she agreed not to make any claim to a tribunal. The form was signed by a CAB officer on the employee's behalf. The EAT confirmed the tribunal's decision that where an agreement is reached, as here between the CAB adviser and the other party under the auspices of a conciliation officer, the agreement will be binding on the client of the CAB as well as against the other party. The CAB client might have a separate claim against the CAB adviser if he had proceeded without due authority.

Economic duress is capable of making a conciliated settlement void-able, but it is likely that this will only arise in the most exceptional circumstances: *Hennessy and Another v (1) Craigmyle and Co Ltd (2) ACAS, above.*

The provisions of s 140(1)(*b*) of the EP(C)A 1978 apply equally to an agreement which is reached between the employer and the employee after a tribunal has found that the employee's dismissal was unfair, but before the remedy had been determined. Section 140(1)(*b*) renders void any provision in an agreement which precludes an employee from presenting a complaint to, or bringing any proceedings before, a tribunal. Bringing is not the same as 'presenting', and proceedings include a consideration of the employee's claim for reinstate-ment, re-engagement or compensation. Again, s 140(2) of the EP(C)A 1978 does not preclude a conciliation officer from taking action after proceedings have been commenced or after liability has been deter-mined. There is a continuing duty on the ACAS officer until all ques-tions of liability and remedy have been determined by the tribunal. Section 134(1) of the EP(C)A 1978 also makes it clear that the concili-ation officer is under a duty to promote a settlement without the matter being determined by a tribunal: *Courage Take Home Trade Ltd v Keys* and *Keys v Courage Take Home Trade Ltd* [1986] IRLR 427. In this case, after the tribunal had determined liability, the employer paid the employee the sum of £9,500.50 which was expressed to be in full and final settlement of his unfair dismissal claim. After he had accepted the money the employee asked the tribunal to assess compensation. The agreement was found to be void under s 140(1) of the EP(C)A 1978, but the tribunal refused to award compensation on the grounds that it would not be just and equitable in all the circumstances to make a compensatory award to the employee. He was 'taking advantage of a section of the statute'.

Other agreements

An agreement between the parties that an employee will not pursue his claim for unfair dismissal in consideration of a sum of money is void. Where there is such an agreement and payment is made, the agreement and payment cannot be pleaded as an accord and satisfaction in defence to a complaint for unfair dismissal. The tribunal will consider the case on its merits and may make an award accordingly. Depending on the nature of the payment, it may be taken into account by the tribunal if it makes an award of compensation.

Compromise Agreements under s 140(3) of the EP(C)A 1978

These have been introduced because ACAS officers have refused to act in settlements before the initiation of proceedings, and in doing this they have relied on legal advice that ACAS 'has no statutory role to become involved where the parties have already reached an agreement between themselves since there is no dispute outstanding' (Hansard, HL 6/5/93, col 904).

Section 140(3) of the EP(C)A 1978 (introduced by s 39 of the TURERA 1993) states that certain compromise agreements are effective provided they comply with certain conditions:

(a) the agreement is in writing;

(b) the agreement must relate to the particular complaint:

(c) the employee must have received independent legal advice from a qualified lawyer as to the terms and conditions of the proposed agreement and in particular its effect on his ability to pursue his rights before an industrial tribunal;

(d) there must be in force, when the adviser gives the advice, a policy of insurance covering the risk of a claim by the employee in respect of loss arising in consequence of the advice;

(e) the agreement must identify the adviser; and

(f) the agreement must state that the conditions regulating compromise agreements under the Act are satisfied.

Section 140(4) of the EP(C)A 1978 provides that 'independent', in relation to legal advice to the employee, means that it is given by a lawyer who is not acting in the matter for the employer or an associated employer and 'qualified lawyer' means a barrister or a solicitor with a practising certificate. See also s 288 (2A)-(2C), (4) and (5) of the

TULR(C)A 1992 for similar provisions relating to matters within the scope of the 1992 Act.

Doubt has been expressed as to whether the indemnity scheme can be classed as a 'policy of insurance' and this would effectively disqualify all practising solicitors, except insofar as they are covered by top-up insurance. See, however, the guidance to solicitors from the standards and guidance committee of the Law Society (*Law Society's Gazette*, 3 August 1994) where, as long as the law remains unclear, it will not be considered a breach of professional conduct by a solicitor to state that the statutory conditions regulating compromise agreements have been satisfied.

Consent Order Incorporated into Decision of Tribunal

Under rule 13(2)(*b*) of the Rules of Procedure 1993 (SI 1993 No 2687) a tribunal may 'if both or all the parties agree in writing upon the terms of a decision to be made by the tribunal, decide accordingly'. Thus if the parties to proceedings currently before a tribunal can agree a settlement in writing, the tribunal can immediately make a binding decision without reference to ACAS.

Chapter 2

Dismissal and Shop Workers

General

The Sunday Trading Act 1994 (STA 1994) came into force on 26 August 1994. It removes restrictions on shop staff working on Sundays, and introduces a new jurisdiction for tribunals whereby shop workers, who consider that they have been unfairly dismissed, or suffered other detriment for refusing to work on a Sunday, may complain to a tribunal.

It creates a new head of automatically unfair dismissal in respect of certain shop staff.

All the relevant provisions are contained in Sched 4 to the STA 1994, which divides the staff into three categories: a protected shop worker, an opted-out shop worker and an opted-in shop worker. In broad terms, a protected shop worker is one who was already working in the shop the day before the Schedule came into force; an opted-out worker is one who opts not to work on Sundays; and an opted-in worker is one who opts to work on Sundays. Again, in broad terms, it is automatically unfair for an employee who is protected or has opted-out to be dismissed for refusing to work on a Sunday.

The paragraphs referred to *below* are those contained in Sched 4 to the STA 1994, unless otherwise stated.

The statutory definitions

Paragraph 1 contains the general interpretation provisions, including the definitions of 'shop', 'shop worker', 'opted-out' etc. The relevant definitions are considered *below*.

'Shop' and 'retail trade or business'

'Shop' includes any premises where any retail trade or business is carried on, but excludes premises used primarily for:
  (a) the sale of meals, refreshments or intoxicating liquor for consumption on the premises; and/or

33

(b) the sale of meals or refreshments prepared to order for immediate consumption off the premises.

'Retail trade or business' is defined to include the businesses of a barber or hairdresser, the sale of refreshments or intoxicating liquor, lending books or periodicals when carried on for gain, and retail sales by auction. Specifically excluded is the sale of programmes and catalogues and other similar sales at theatres and places of amusement.

It should be noted that the effect of these definitions is that the provisions of Sched 4 do not apply to premises for the sale of intoxicating liquor for consumption off the premises, where the premises are used primarily for purposes falling within (a), *above*. Thus, the off-licence section of a supermarket would be included within the definition of a shop.

A shop worker

This is an employee who, under his contract of employment, is required or may be required, to work in or about a shop in England or Wales on a day on which the shop is opened for the serving of customers.

This definition is wide enough to include persons who would not immediately be regarded as shop workers. This is because a shop worker is defined as one who does shop work and the shop work is defined as work in or about a shop on a day when the shop is open for serving customers. It would thus apply to the cashier in the finance office in a store, the liftman in a department store and, as the definition says 'may be required', it could, perhaps, extend to a delivery driver. A security guard employed by a security company, who may be required to work in or about a shop when it is open for the serving of customers, would also be within this definition. Other categories to which it could extend would be the staff nurse, the catering staff of the staff canteen and, presumably, depending upon its proximity to the shop, a warehouseman. General maintenance staff, if they could be required to work in or about the shop when it is open to customers, would also be included.

A protected shop worker

A shop worker is to be regarded as protected if, and only if:
(a) on the day before the commencement date of Sched 4 to the STA 1994 he was employed as a shop worker;
(b) on that day he was not employed to work only on Sunday;
(c) he had been continuously employed during the period beginning with the day before the commencement date, and ending with the 'appropriate date'; and
(d) throughout that period, or throughout every part of it during which his relations with his employer were governed by a contract of employment, he was a shop worker: para 2(1).

The appropriate date for unfair dismissal purposes is the effective date of termination: see para 2(2) and Chapter 5.

Despite the words 'if, and only if' in para 2(1), there is, in fact, an additional category which is provided for by para 2(5). That applies to an individual whose relations with his or her employer on the day before the commencement date of Sched 4 are not governed by a contract of employment but, on the last day when they were so governed, he or she was a shop worker and was not employed to work only on a Sunday. If the reason for the relations not being governed by a contract is one of those covered by para 9 or 10 of Sched 13 to the EP(C)A 1978 (ie absence from work because of sickness or injury; temporary cessation of work in circumstances that by arrangement or custom the employee is regarded as continuing in employment; absence wholly or partly due to pregnancy or childbirth; or a return to work after pregnancy or childbirth in relation to an offer covered by s 39 of the EP(C)A 1978), then he or she is still considered a protected worker. There are thus no less than three separate provisions relating to maternity or childbirth covered by Sched 4 to the STA 1994. They are: the reference to para 9(*d*) of Sched 13 to the EP(C)A 1978; the reference to para 10 of Sched 13 to the EP(C)A 1978; and para 12(4) (see *below*).

A protected shop worker ceases to be protected if, on or after the commencement date of Sched 4 to the STA 1994 he has given to his employer a notice in writing, which he has signed and dated, expressly stating that he wishes to work on Sunday, or that he does not object to Sunday working, and, after giving such notice, has expressly agreed with his employer to do shop work on Sunday, or on a particular Sunday: para 3.

An opted-out shop worker

A shop worker is regarded as opted-out if, and only if:

(a) he has given his employer notice in writing, which he has signed and dated to the effect that he objects to Sunday working; and

(b) he has been continuously employed during the period beginning with the day on which that notice was given and ending with the appropriate date; and

(c) throughout that period, or throughout every part of it during which his relations with his employer were governed by a contract of employment, he was a shop worker: para 5(1).

Again, for unfair dismissal purposes, the appropriate date is the effective date of termination: para 5(2). An opted-out worker ceases to be such if, after giving the opting-out notice, he gives his employer an opting-in notice (see *above*) and, after giving the notice, he has expressly agreed with the employer to do shop work on Sunday, or on a particular Sunday: para 5(5).

As can be seen from the definitions, there can be difficulties where a shop worker ceases to be a shop worker for a temporary period, so that, under his contract of employment, he cannot be required to do such work, and then resumes work as a shop worker. Paragraph 4 covers the situation where any shop worker who under his contract is or may be required to work on Sunday (whether or not as a result of previously giving an opted-in notice) but is not employed to work only on Sunday, may at any time give an opting-out notice. This, presumably, is aimed at the category which has just been defined.

The statutory right

There are four rights concerned with dismissal in Sched 4. There is also the right (outside the scope of this work) in respect of the suffering of a detriment.

The right not to be dismissed

Paragraph 7(1) provides that the dismissal of a protected or opted-out shop worker is automatically unfair if the reason or, if more than one, the principal reason was that the shop worker refused or proposed to refuse, to do shop work on Sunday or on a particular Sunday: para 7(1). There is, however, an exclusion in para 7(2) whereby the protection afforded by para 7(1) does not apply to an opted-out shop worker where the refusal or proposed refusal to do shop work on Sunday applies to any Sunday or Sundays falling before the end of three months, beginning with the day on which the opting-out notice concerned was given. This appears to mean that a shop worker's opting-out notice is ineffective until three months after the date it is given.

This three-month period, however, may be reduced to one month by the provisions of para 11. If an employee *becomes* a shop worker who is, or may be, required to work on Sunday, but is not employed to work only on Sunday, the employer is required within two months to give him a written statement of his statutory right in the prescribed form set out in para 11(4). If the employer fails to do so and the shop worker gives an opting-out notice, the period of three months is reduced to one month. However, there is even an exclusion to this, for an employer is not to be taken as failing to comply with the provisions of giving notice where, in the first two months after becoming a shop worker, the employee gives an opting-out notice. The apparent effect of this is that, if the employer fails to provide the statutory right statement within two months and if the employee does not give an opting-out notice within two months, any subsequent opting-out notice can only be effective three months after the notice is given.

It has to be said that the draftsman has sought to put innumerable difficulties in the paths of both employer and employee in the requirements of the various notices. Not only are the periods themselves changed on the occurrence or non-occurrence of certain events, but on the employee there are very strict requirements. It should be noted that both in the case of an opting-out and opting-in notice not only does it have to be in writing, but it must be dated and signed by the employee. This will effectively prevent trade union officers from signing on behalf of their members and for collective agreements not to be able to effect opting-in and opting-out notices en-masse.

Paragraph 7(3) provides that the dismissal of a shop worker is automatically unfair if the reason or, if more than one, the principal reason, was that the shop worker gave, or proposed to give an opting-out notice to the employer.

Right not to be selected for redundancy

Where the reason, or principal reason, for the dismissal of a protected, or opted-out, shop worker was that he was redundant, and the reason for his selection for dismissal for redundancy was his refusal, or proposed refusal, to work on Sunday, or on a particular Sunday, then, the dismissal is automatically unfair: para 8(1). There is again the exemption from this provision where the refusal relates to a Sunday before the end of the notice period.

Where the reason, or principal reason, for the dismissal of a shop worker was that he was redundant and the reason for his selection for dismissal was that the shop worker gave or proposed to give an opting-out notice to the employer then the dismissal is automatically unfair: para 8(3).

Other matters

Where a fixed-term contract for one year or more expires without being renewed then, even if the shop worker has agreed in writing before the expiry of the fixed term to exclude any claim in respect of the right not to be unfairly dismissed given by s 54 of the EP(C)A 1978, the shop worker is still able to claim his dismissal is automatically unfair if it falls under para 7(1) or (3) (see *above*).

There is no qualifying period of employment or upper age limit in respect of unfair dismissal claims. As can be seen, the automatic dismissal provisions equate to those for trade union activities (see Chapter 11) and health and safety matters (see Chapter 13). There is a restriction on contracting out of the provisions of Sched 4 unless with the assistance of ACAS or a compromise agreement (see ss 133–134 and 140(2) and (3) EP(C)A): para 17.

Paragraph 19 amends s 60A of the EP(C)A 1978 (assertion of statutory rights (see Chapter 14)) by adding to the list in s 60A, Sched 4 to the STA 1994. It is difficult to contemplate a situation where an employee asserts his rights not to work on Sunday, which would fall within s 60A, but not within Sched 4 itself. It may, perhaps, arise where an employee indicates to his employer that he has a right to opt-out without actually saying he proposes to do so, and is thereupon dismissed. Even that is doubtful, for it is difficult to see how that would be asserting his right, rather than asserting that a general right exists.

The greatest problem appears likely to be in the notice provisions. Both the opting-in and opting-out notices are described as being written notices 'signed and dated by the shop worker'. The prescribed explanatory statement required to be given by the employer to new shop workers under para 11 specifies that notice must 'be in writing; be signed and dated by you; . . .' One can visualise disputes, where the notice is typed and signed by the employee, as to who actually typed the date. As has already been mentioned, the different time limits appear to be almost as difficult for an employee to follow as the erstwhile notices of maternity rights.

Mention must be made of para 12, which has an effect on current contracts of employment. By para 12 any contract of employment, in respect of a shop worker, who is employed immediately before the commencement date of Sched 4, and on the day before that day was not employed to work only on Sundays, is unenforceable to the extent that it requires the shop worker to do shop work on Sunday on or after the commencement date, or requires the employer to provide the shop worker with shop work on a Sunday after that date. Similarly, any agreement entered into after the commencement date between a protected shop worker (ie a pre-existing shop worker) and the employer is unenforceable to the same extent. The situation can, of course, be changed by an opting-in notice.

Special provision is given in para 12(4) to a female who is a protected shop worker on the day on which she returns to work after maternity absence.

Chapter 3

The Qualifying Period of Employment

Introduction

Subject to certain limited exceptions an employee cannot bring a claim for unfair dismissal unless he has been continuously employed for a period of not less than two years ending with the effective date of termination: s 64(1)(*a*) of the EP(C)A 1978.

There are certain exceptions to this provision, so that a claim for unfair dismissal can be brought by an employee with more than one month's continuous employment, where the employee is dismissed on medical grounds by reason of any requirement imposed by law or any recommendation in a code of practice issued and approved under s 16 of the Health and Safety at Work etc Act 1974: s 64(2) of the EP(C)A 1978. There is no minimum qualifying period of continuous employment where the reason or principal reason for dismissal, or in a redundancy case, for selecting the employee for dismissal was:
  (i) for an inadmissible reason defined in s 64(4) of the EP(C)A 1978 as a reason being one of those specified in:
     (*a*) s 57(A)(1) of the EP(C)A 1978 (read with (2) and (3)) (dismissal in health and safety cases),
     (*b*) s 60(*a*) to (*e*) of the EP(C)A 1978 (dismissal on grounds of pregnancy or childbirth);
     (*c*) s 60A(1) of the EP(C)A 1978 (read with (2) and (3)) (dismissal on grounds of assertion of statutory right);
  (ii) for an inadmissible reason defined in s 154(2) of the TULR(C)A 1992 as a reason being one of those specified in s 152(1) of the TULR(C)A 1992 (dismissal on the ground of trade union membership or activities);
  (iii) that the employee was a protected or opted-out shopworker who refused to work on a Sunday (See Chapter 2).
Section 64(1) does not apply to a case falling within s 60(*f*) of the EP(C)A 1978; s 64(5) of the EP(C)A 1978 (See Chapter 10).

Computation of the period of continuous employment

The general basis

Section 151(1) of the EP(C)A 1978 provides that references in the Act to a period of continuous employment, unless otherwise provided, are to a period of continuous employment computed in accordance with the provisions of s 151 of and Sched 13 to the EP(C)A 1978, and in any provision which refers to a period of continuous employment expressed in months or years, a month means a calendar month and a year means a year of 12 calendar months.

Schedule 13 provides a complete definition of what is meant by the term 'continuous employment': see *Wood v York City Council* [1978] ICR 840. It is not open to the parties to agree that one or more periods of employment shall be continuous employment within the meaning of continuous employment under Sched 13 unless the period or periods of employment are continuous periods of employment within Sched 13: see *Secretary of State for Employment v Globe Elastic Thread Co Ltd* [1979] IRLR 327. Conversely, it is not open to the parties to agree that a period of continuous employment shall not be continuous where continuity is preserved under Sched 13: see *Hanson v Fashion Industries (Hartlepool) Ltd* [1981] ICR 35.

An agreement reached between the parties whereby employment is to be treated as continuous, even though it is not continuous under the provisions of Sched 13 may give rise to rights under the contract between the parties.

Section 151(2) of the EP(C)A 1978 provides that in computing an employee's period of continuous employment any question as to whether or not the employee's employment is of a kind counting towards a period of continuous employment or whether periods, consecutive or otherwise, are to be treated as forming a single period of continuous employment, is to be determined in accordance with Sched 13, that is to say week by week, but the length of an employee's period of employment is to be computed in months and years of 12 months. The qualifying period for unfair dismissal is two years. However, the question whether or not a week counts as part of the employee's period of continuous employment, or whether it breaks the period of continuous employment, must be decided in terms of weeks. For these purposes a week is a week ending on a Saturday: para 24(1) of Sched 13. The effect is that a gap of up to 12 days may not operate to break the employee's continuity of employment. If an employee was dismissed on a Sunday, he may count that week as part of his period of continuous employment so that his continuity is preserved until midnight on the following Saturday. If he were re-engaged on the next following Saturday, he may count that week starting with the preceding Sunday as part of his period of continuous employment. Although in practice there has been a break, there has for the purposes of the legislation been no break in his continuity of employment. In *Roach v CSB (Moulds) Ltd* [1991] IRLR 200, the EAT appears to have put a gloss upon the statute. The case must be considered of doubtful authority. There may be statutory provision which effectively breaks the continuity—see *Gale v Northern General Hospital National Health Service Trust* [1994] IRLR 292, though this case probably turned on its own facts.

Continuity of employment will be broken if, during what would otherwise have been a period of continuous employment, the contract has become illegal, and that illegality will taint the whole of the contract of employment: *Hyland v J H Barker (North West) Ltd* [1985] ICR 861. 'Continuously employed' means continuously employed under a lawful contract of employment (see Chapter 1 as to illegality).

Date of starting and finishing work

Section 151(3) of the EP(C)A 1978 provides that an employee's period of continuous employment for the purposes of the Act begins with the day on which the employee starts work, and ends with the day by reference to which the length of his period of continuous employment falls to be ascertained for the purposes of the provision in question. In *General of the Salvation Army v Dewsbury* [1984] ICR 498, the EAT held that the phrase 'starts work' 'is intended to refer to the beginning of the employee's employment under the relevant contract of employment', so that in this case the employee who was offered a post as a teacher commencing on 1 May 1982, a Saturday, which she accepted, although she did not start work until Tuesday 4 May, had been continuously employed from Saturday 1 May.

The date upon which the employee starts work may be postponed if the employee is absent from work because he has been taking part in a strike or because he has been locked out by his employer. See under 'Industrial disputes', *below* at p 51.

The period of continuous employment ends with the date by reference to which the length of the employee's continuous employment falls to be ascertained. For the purposes of unfair dismissal this is the effective date of termination. See Chapter 5.

The effect of this provision is that the employee cannot count the whole of the week in which his employment begins or ends for the purposes of calculating the period of continuous employment. However, the provisions of s 55(5) and (6) of the EP(C)A 1978 may apply.

Presumption of continuity

Under para 1(3) of Sched 13 to the EP(C)A 1978, a person's employment during any period shall, unless the contrary is shown, be presumed to have been continuous.

In *Woolcott v Edwardes* (1966) 1 ITR 333, the employee was able to count the weeks, as it has not been shown that they did not count.

In practice, and as indicated by the EAT in *Nicholl v Nocorrode Ltd* [1981] ICR 348, all the employee need show is that he was an employee, that he was dismissed and that there was a week which counted under Sched 13 of the EP(C)A 1978. Thereafter he may rely upon the presumption. It is important to note that the presumption of continuity only applies to employment by one employer: see *Secretary of State for Employment v (1) Cohen and (2) Beaupress Ltd* [1987] IRLR 169. However, the employee's position may be protected by the provisions of paras 17, 18 and 18A of Sched 13 to the EP(C)A 1978 or the Transfer of Undertaking (Protection of Employment) Regulations 1981. See *below* and Chapter 15.

Miscellaneous provisions

Schedule 13 to the EP(C)A 1978 applies to a period of employment notwithstanding that during that period the employee was engaged in work wholly or mainly outside Great Britain or was excluded by or under the Act from any right conferred by the Act: see para 1(2) of Sched 13. Schedule 2 of the Employment Act 1982 as amended contains the detailed rules. See also *Weston v Vega Space Systems Engineering Ltd* [1989] IRLR 429. Under s 77A of the EP(C)A 1978 and s 163 of the TULR(C)A 1992 orders can be made by the tribunal in applications for interim relief so that the contract of employment continues in force for the purpose of, *inter alia*, determining for any purpose the period for which the employee has been continuously employed from the date of termination of the contract until the determination or settlement of the complaint. See also Chapter 16 as to remedies.

Weeks which count

The method of calculating those weeks which count as continuous employment is prescribed by Sched 13 to the EP(C)A 1978. Two aspects of the calculation must be looked at separately; the weeks which count in computing continuous employment, and the events which do not break the continuity of employment.

The basic principle of calculating the length of period of employment is, in Sched 13, concerned with weeks in which the employee's relationship with his employer is normally governed by a contract of employment which involves 16 hours per week or more or, in some circumstances, eight hours per week or more. This statutory provision has recently been overtaken by the House of Lord's decision in *R v Secretary of State for Employment ex p The Equal Opportunities Commission* [1994] IRLR 176.

The basis of the application by the Equal Opportunities Commission (EOC) for judicial review was that the thresholds in the EP(C)A 1978, in respect of hours necessary to qualify a week for continuous employment, were discriminatory against women. That the application by the EOC succeeded, there is no doubt, but it is the basis upon which it succeeded which is important. When the application was before the Court of Appeal, there was a finding that compensation for unfair dismissal was 'pay' within the meaning of art 119 of the Treaty of Rome. In the House of Lords, Lord Keith remarked that though there was much to be said in favour of the view, 'the European Court of Justice has not yet pronounced upon this issue, and there may be a question whether the answer to it can properly be held to be *acte clair*, or whether resolution of it would require a reference to the European Court under art 177 of the Treaty'.

Neither Lord Keith, nor any of the other three Law Lords who gave judgments said that the Court of Appeal was wrong, which one would have expected them to do had they felt that the finding of the Court of Appeal was incorrect. Therefore, until the House of Lords overturns that finding it is binding on tribunals. This situation has now been confirmed by the EAT in *Mediguard Services Ltd v Thame* [1994] IRLR 504. In the Court of Appeal it was argued on behalf of the Secretary of State for Employment that a threshold of eight hours per week was objectively justified on the grounds of administrative convenience. Reference was made to a draft Directive issued by the European Commission which provided for employees with less than eight hours employment per week to be excluded from certain rights. In fact the EOC's application was rejected by the Court of Appeal on the basis that the EOC had no standing to apply for judicial review. The House of Lords reversed that decision, but in the House of Lords hearing the Secretary of State for Employment did not pursue the matter of any objective justification for the 8 hour threshold. Lord Keith, in dealing with this, said 'the conclusion must be that no objective justification for the thresholds in the Act of 1978 has been established'. It will be noted that the word 'thresholds' is in the plural, which must refer to both the eight hour and 16-hour thresholds. It does seem that a draft Directive has no force and, in any event, could not derogate from the Treaty. That being so, then as long as in each week the employee's relations are governed by a contract of employment with the employer (whether or not the employee actually works in that week), there is no requirement that it should relate to a certain number of hours. This view was taken by a tribunal in *Warren v Wylie and Wylie* [1994] IRLR 316, from which there was no appeal.

If, however, at some future date a Directive in the form mentioned comes into force, or the Treaty is amended, there may be need to refer to the various previous cases concerning how a specific number of hours is to be calculated. As compensation for unfair dismissal was held to be pay within the Treaty and not under a Directive, the question of whether the employer was the State or an emanation of the State does not arise. Being a provision of the Treaty, it is applicable to all employers and employees as part of UK law.

A change from one job to another job or the termination of one contract and the entry into a new contract, provided it is with the same employer under a qualifying contract with no break, will not break the continuity of employment: *Wood v York City Council* [1978] IRLR 228; *Tipper v Roofdec Ltd* [1989] IRLR 419.

Weeks not governed by a contract of employment

Weeks in which the employee's relations with his employer are not governed by a contract of employment will (subject as *below*) not count and will break the continuous period of employment. Where a contract of employment subsists, periods of absence caused by holidays, sickness or otherwise, of whatever length, do not break the period of continuous employment and in fact form part of that period: para 4 of Sched 13 to the EP(C)A 1978.

The point is illustrated by taking as an example the two-year qualifying period for bringing a claim for unfair dismissal. If there is a contract of employment which subsists for two years, it does not matter that during the two years the employee takes holidays totalling six weeks. However, if there is no such contract, and the employee works in each week during the first year, but then takes three weeks' holiday when he does not work at all, those three weeks do not form part of the continuous period of employment and will break the continuity. It does not matter that the employee then works in each week for a further year.

However, there are limited exceptions. See under 'Weeks which count where there is no contract of employment' *below* at p 45.

In *Justfern Ltd v D'Ingerthorpe and others* [1994] IRLR 164, the applicant's employment ended due to the insolvency of the employer. The applicant then drew unemployment benefit. Over a week later he was re-employed by the new management. The EAT held that his employment was continuous by reason of the provisions of para 17(2) of Sched 13 to the EP(C)A 1978. In view of the wording of para 17(2), it is difficult understand the decision. Even the EAT admits it took a liberal construction of the paragraph.

Weeks governed by a contract of employment

In deciding whether or not there is a contract of employment, the starting point is to examine the contract itself. Does employment mean actual work or when the employee can be required to work? In *Bromsgrove Casting and Machining Ltd v Martin* [1977] ICR 417, Martin's contract of employment as a consultant was silent as to when he was required to work. It was held that he was only employed when he was actually performing services under his contract by giving advice to the employer, not when he was retained but not performing services. Similarly in *Suffolk County Council v Secretary of State for the Environment and Another* [1984] ICR 882, the House of Lords held that a retained fireman, while he was not on duty was under a contract to make himself available for employment if a fire occurred and he was called. Such a contract was not a contract of employment and the fireman did not become an employee until he was called.

Where the employee is required by the contract of employment to live on the premises where he works, the hours of employment are those hours when he is on duty or when his services may be required.

Both the *Martin* and *Suffolk County Council* cases were decided before the House of Lords decision in the EOC case, *above.* As in both the contract subsisted there may now be a distinction between contracts such as *Martin's* on the one hand and those similar to a retained fireman on the other. The latter contained an obligation to be available for call, so that the contract was not only subsisting, but operating. Thus, it could be that if Martin did not advise during a whole week the continuity would be broken, whereas if the fireman was not called for a week it would not break continuity.

The full effect of the EOC case on previous decisions remains to be seen.

Weeks which count where there is no contract of employment

It has been seen that where there is no contract of employment, a week in which the employee does not work will not form part of the continuous period of employment and will break the continuity. There are limited exceptions to this rule. Where there is no contract of employment and the employee is for the whole or part of the week:
  (*a*) incapable of working in consequence of sickness or injury; or
  (*b*) absent from work on account of a temporary cessation of work; or
  (*c*) absent from work in circumstances such that by arrangement or custom he is regarded as continuing in the employment of his employer for all or any purpose; or
  (*d*) absent from work wholly or partly because of pregnancy or confinement;

the whole of that week, although not caught under the earlier provisions, is counted as a week for computing a period of continuous employment: para 9(1) of Sched 13. Paragraph 9 will only apply when there is no contract of employment: *Ford v Warwickshire County Council* [1983] 1 All ER 753. Paragraph 9 covers a period between two contracts of employment.

In deciding whether or not there was no contract, and the reason why the employee was absent from work, the period has to be examined on a week-by-week basis.

Incapacity due to sickness or injury

Not more than 26 weeks will count under para 9(1)(*a*): para 9(2). The employee must be incapable of doing work which he is obliged to do under the terms of his contract of employment; it does not mean that he must be incapable of any work at all: see *Collins v Nats (Southend) Ltd* (1967) 2 ITR 423 and *Donnelly v Kelvin International Services* [1992] IRLR 496, where the applicant was working elsewhere. An absence for sickness arising out of a pregnancy or childbirth is within this provision, but not the pregnancy or childbirth itself, which is dealt with in para 9(1)(*d*). Under para 9(1)(*a*) the absence must be connected with sickness: see *Scarlett v Godfrey Abbott Group Ltd* [1978] ICR 1106. In *Pearson v Kent County Council* [1993] IRLR 165, the Court of Appeal held a gap of ten days when the employee retired on the grounds of ill health and then took up a less onerous position (there being the gap for reasons of pension arrangement) was not a period when he was 'incapable of work in consequence of sickness or injury', so the period could not count as a period of continuous employment under para 9(1)(*a*). There must be a causal link between the absence and the incapacity. Incapable of 'work' does not mean incapable of work generally, nor, however, does para 9(1)(*a*) refer to the particular work the employee was employed to do. The tribunal has to look backwards and decide what was the reason for the employee's absence week by week during the period of absence and consider the work on offer from the employer and if it was suitable for the employee. The tribunal would then have to decide whether the absence from that work was due to incapacity because of sickness or injury.

Temporary cessation of work

The test of temporary cessation has given rise to difficulties. In *Bentley Engineering Co Ltd v Crown and Miller* [1976] ICR 225, it was held that the decided cases have established that para 9(1)(*b*) poses three questions:

> Was there a cessation of the employee's work or job; was the employee absent on account of that cessation, and ... was the cessation a temporary one?

The EAT considered that these questions were a helpful guide in considering the wording of the statutory provision. Having considered these questions the tribunal must still look at the question in the round to see whether or not an employee was absent from work on account of a temporary cessation of work.

Absent from work   The employee must be absent from work. This means away from work. The matter has to be considered retrospectively: *Fitzgerald v Hall, Russell and Co Ltd* [1970] AC 984; *Ford v Warwickshire County Council, above*. An employee may be absent on account of a temporary cessation of work notwithstanding that he obtains work with another employer where that employment is intended to bridge the gap during the temporary cessation. He is absent from work: *Thompson v Bristol Channel Ship Repairers and Engineers Ltd* (1970) 5 ITR 85. The position would be the same if, following the employment intended to bridge the gap, the employee returned to work not with the original employer, but with an associated employer. An employee may be absent on account of a temporary cessation of work where he takes a job elsewhere, even though he assumes that job will be permanent: *Bentley Engineering Co Ltd v Crown and Miller above*, followed in *GW Stephens and Son v Fish* [1989] ICR 324, where it was held that absent from work does not necessarily mean physically absent. It means not performing in substance the contract that previously existed between the parties.

If, however, the employee leaves his employer and after a period of unemployment obtains a job with an employer which is an associated employer, the period of unemployment cannot be said to be an absence on account of a temporary cessation of work; rather it is an absence caused by the employee's resignation: *Wessex National Ltd v Long* (1978) 13 ITR 413. The position is the same if an employee is dismissed for misconduct and subsequently re-engaged: see *Clark v Blairs Ltd* (1966) 1 ITR 545.

Temporary   Whether or not the absence is caused by a temporary cessation of work is a matter of fact to be decided by the tribunal: see *Hunter v Smith's Dock Co Ltd* [1968] 2 All ER 81. Whether the cessation of work is temporary must be decided retrospectively. Broadly, temporary means a relatively short time compared with the period in work. See *Fitzgerald v Hall, Russell and Co Ltd* [1970] AC 984.

It is not possible to lay down what might be regarded as temporary but in *Bentley Engineering Co Ltd v Crown and Miller above*, Phillips J thought that two years could be temporary. See also *G W Stephens and Son v Fish, above*. In *Flack v Kodak Ltd* [1985] IRLR 443, Mrs Flack was first employed on 21 May 1979 and was dismissed and re-employed on several occasions. The tribunal found that the cessation of work was not a temporary cessation but a cessation of a more substantial nature. In reaching this conclusion it confined itself to the purely mathematical approach of comparing each gap in employment falling within the two years preceding the final dismissal with the period of employment immediately before and the period of employment immediately after the gap. The EAT held that, although in most cases the mathematical approach may well be the decisive factor, there may be cases where it is not and the whole period of intermittent employment, including the employment outside the two year period, should be considered, so that the tribunal can then decide if the gaps in the two year period are a temporary cessation.

The decision of the EAT was upheld on appeal: see *Flack v Kodak Ltd* [1986] IRLR 255. However, the Court of Appeal emphasised that in deciding whether or not there was a temporary cessation of work, regard must be had to all the circumstances over the whole period of employment, not simply the periods of work adjacent to the periods of absence. In *Sillars v Charrington Fuels Ltd* [1989] ICR 475, the Court of Appeal held that the tribunal was entitled to adopt the mathematical approach and to consider the length of the employee's last two periods of seasonal employment with the length of the last two periods of unemployment. The tribunal was not in error in failing to follow the broad approach of looking back over the entire period of the employment relationship. The last period was representative. See also *Berwick Salmon Fisheries Co Ltd v Rutherford and others* [1991] IRLR 203, where it was held that if a mathematical approach is adopted then a period out of work will not be temporary if it is longer than the period in work.

Cessation of work   A cessation of work may arise for a number of reasons, for instance, where the employer does not have orders; where the employer does not have supplies or where the employee cannot work at his employer's premises due to a serious fire, flood or explosion. In *Fitzgerald v Hall, Russell and Co Ltd above*, the issue arose as to what was a cessation of work. Lord Morris concluded that where the employee 'would have been at work but for the fact that his employer could not find work for him, but which period ended when the employer did find work for him, [the employee] ... was absent from work on account of a cessation of work even though the employer's business, or the particular department of it, had not completely closed down.'

In the same case Lord Upjohn equated a temporary cessation with the employee being laid off or dismissed and, following Lord Morris, found that the temporary cessation of work must refer to work available for a particular workman and not to workmen generally.

In *Ford v Warwickshire County Council* [1983] 1 All ER 753, a teacher had been employed under a series of successive fixed-term contracts between September and July for eight years. Between July and September she was on holiday and had no contract of employment. Was the holiday a temporary cessation of work? It was held that it was, and it did not matter that the employers had foreseen the unavailability of work and had made arrangements accordingly by entering into fixed-term contracts with the employee.

In *Byrne v City of Birmingham DC* [1987] IRLR 191, the employee was a member of a 'pool' of casual cleaners. The Court of Appeal held that when he was not allocated work under the pooling arrangement he was not absent on account of a temporary cessation of work within the meaning of para 9(1)(*b*). The expression cessation of work must denote that some 'quantum of work' had for the time being ceased to exist. Paragraph 9(1)(*b*) did not apply where work was available, but under the pooling arrangement it had been allocated by the employer to another employee. The decision was followed in *Letheby and Christopher Ltd v Bond* [1988] ICR 480.

Work means paid work for the employee to do: see *University of Aston in Birmingham v Malik* [1984] ICR 492, where it was held that the tribunal cannot consider the reason for the non-availability of work.

Special arrangement or custom—absent from work
The meaning of the phrase absent from work has been considered above.

Paragraph 9(1)(*c*) of Sched 13 only applies where there is no contract of employment. See *above* and *Ford v Warwickshire County Council* [1983] 1 All ER 753. In the light of the decision in *Ford*'s case the earlier decision in *Lloyds Bank Ltd v Secretary of State for Employment* [1979] ICR 258, must be considered wrong in law.

Although *Ford*'s case involved a consideration of para 9(1)(*b*), the same considerations must also apply to para 9(1)(*c*). However, the position is complicated by the fact that para 9(1)(*c*) refers to the employee being regarded as continuing in the employment of his employer. It may be difficult to establish an arrangement or custom where the employee is employed on a series of single separate contracts with no overall 'umbrella contract': *Letheby and Christopher Ltd v Bond* [1988] ICR 480. This provision is designed to cover a situation where an employee is loaned by one employer to another: see *Wishart v NCB* [1974] ICR 460. The reported cases show that whether or not there was a custom or arrangement, and whether or not the employee is regarded as continuing in employment during the period of absence, are matters of fact for the tribunal to decide.

It may be possible for an employee to rely upon the terms of a collective agreement and have his employment treated as continuous: see *Taylor v Triumph Motors, British Leyland (UK) Ltd and Secretary of State for Employment* [1975] IRLR 369.

Parties cannot retrospectively agree that the absence from work is such that by arrangement or custom the employee is regarded as continuing in the employment; the arrangement must exist at the time when the absence began: *Murphy v Birrell and Sons Ltd* [1978] IRLR 458.

In *Ingram v Foxon* [1984] ICR 685, the employee was dismissed and then reinstated by his employer without making a complaint to a tribunal. He was reinstated on the basis that his employment was regarded as having been continuous since the date when he first started work. It was held that this was an exception to the rule in *Murphy v Birrell and Sons Ltd, above,* and there was an arrangement, albeit retrospectively, that the employee's employment should be regarded as continuous. This decision must, however, be doubtful when compared with *Secretary of State for Employment v Globe Elastic Thread Co Ltd* [1980] AC 506.

The employee must establish the arrangement or the custom. Custom refers to a trade or professional custom going beyond the limits of a single employer's own practice. See the decision of the EAT in *Ford v Warwickshire County Council* (1980) (unreported).

It is open to argument that para 9(1)(*c*) applies without limitation as to time, although in *Southern Electricity Board v Collins* [1969] 2 All ER 1166, there is some support for the argument that it applies only where there is a temporary absence.

Paragraph (9)(1)(*c*) may apply to a period at the commencement of the employment, but it is essential that there should be clear evidence of such an arrangement: see *Brown v Southall and Knight* [1980] IRLR 130.

Pregnancy or childbirth — absent from work
The meaning of the phrase 'absent from work' has been considered above. Again, this provision only applies where there is no contract of employment, see *below.*

Subject to para 10 not more than 26 weeks' absence can count under para 9(1)(*d*): para 9(2). An example is where a woman is dismissed because of pregnancy before she has completed two years' service. If the woman returns to work within 26 weeks from the date when she was dismissed, the whole period of absence will count as part of her continuous period of employment. Where in accordance with s 39 of the EP(C)A 1978 or in pursuance of an offer made in the circumstances described in s 56A(2) of the EP(C)A 1978 she exercises her right to return to work following a period of absence from work, occasioned wholly or partly by pregnancy or childbirth, every week during that period of absence counts in computing a period of employment. The situation is as if the employee had not been absent; further, there is no break in the continuity of employment: para 10. If the employee returns to work but not in accordance with s 39 or s 56A(2), para (9)(1)(*d*), *above*, may apply.

In *Mitchell v British Legion Club* [1980] IRLR 425, the EAT held that if during a period when there is no contract of employment a woman is absent from work wholly or partly because of pregnancy then those weeks count in computing her period of employment and there is no break in continuity. It does not matter whether the contract comes to an end by resignation or dismissal.

Paragraph 9(1)(*d*) does not apply where the contract of employment has come to an end, before the beginning of the 11th week before the expected week of childbirth, so as to allow the employee to tack weeks on and extend the employment up to or beyond the beginning of the 11th week before the expected week of childbirth to claim the benefits conferred by (what was then) s 33 of the EP(C)A 1978. See: *Secretary of State for Employment v Doulton Sanitaryware Ltd* [1981] IRLR 365; and Chapter 10 on maternity, and for the effect of s 33 of the EP(C)A 1978 (maternity leave).

Where the employee is absent from work but the contract of employment continues, then the employee may be able to claim that the period of employment is continuous under one of the other provisions of Sched 13.

Events which do not break continuity

Industrial disputes

Strike
'Strike' is defined in para 24(1) of Sched 13 as:

> the cessation of work by a body of persons employed acting in combination, or a concerted refusal or a refusal under a common understanding of any number of persons employed to continue to work for an employer in consequence of a dispute, done as a means of compelling their employer or any person or body of persons employed, or to aid other employees in compelling their employer or any person or body of persons employed, to accept or not to accept terms or conditions of or affecting employment.

A week will not count for the purposes of paras 3, 4, 5, 9 or 10 of Sched 13 if the employee is on strike for the whole or any part of that week: para 15(1). However, a week beginning before 6 July 1964 will count if the employee was absent from work on strike for all or any part of the week: para 22. The continuity of employment is not broken by a week which does not count under Sched 13 and which begins after 5 July 1964 if in that week, or any part of that week, the employee is on strike, whether or not the week would (apart from para 15(1) of Sched 13) have counted: para 15(2) and (3).

The protection afforded by para 15 extends to dismissed employees: *Bloomfield v Springfield Hosiery Finishing Co Ltd* [1972] ICR 91. Note also that the definition of 'employee' contained in s 153(1) of the EP(C)A 1978 and s 295(1) of the TULR(C)A 1992 includes reference to a person whose employment has ceased. Thus a person or persons employed must, in relation to a strike, mean 'persons who, but for their action in ceasing or refusing to continue work, would be employees'. An employee has the benefit of this protection (per Sir John Donaldson):

> unless and until [the employer] engages other persons on a permanent basis to do the work which the strikers had been doing or he permanently discontinues the activity in which they were employed.

It is clear from the decision in *Bloomfield*, that where strikers take temporary employment pending a settlement of the dispute, they may still claim they are on strike. Continuity of employment is not preserved under this provision where there is a break between the end of the strike and when the 're-employed' employee starts work. Where there is a shortage of work after the strike is over, an employee may be treated as being absent on account of a temporary cessation of work: *Clarke Chapman—John Thompson Ltd v Walters* [1972] ICR 83. Again it may be that an employee is absent from work, in circumstances that by arrangement or by custom mean he is regarded as continuing in the employment of his employer. In both cases the period of absence will count and continuity of employment is not broken.

Paragraph 15 of Sched 13 applies, even though during the strike the employee has been dismissed, if following the strike he is re-engaged. An attempt on re-engagement to contract out of the continuity provisions contained in para 15(2) and (3) is void by virtue of s 140 of the EP(C)A 1978: see *Hanson v Fashion Industries (Hartlepool) Ltd* [1980] IRLR 393.

Section 151(5) and (6)(*b*) of the EP(C)A 1978 provides that if an employee's period of continuous employment includes one or more periods which under Sched 13 do not count in computing continuous employment but do not break the continuity of employment, the beginning of the period shall be treated as postponed by the number of days falling within that intervening period, or as the case may be by the aggregate number of days falling within those periods. Where para 15(2) of Sched 13 applies, the number of days falling within such an intervening period is the number of days between the last working day before the strike and the day on which work was resumed. The rationale for this provision is that only the days on which the employee was on strike are lost. However, on the wording of s 151(5) and (6)(*b*), the period of continuous employment is postponed by the total number of days during which the strike lasted, even though the employee was not on strike for the whole of that period. The beginning of the period of continuous employment is postponed by the number of days for which the strike lasts. Presumably, for these provisions to apply, the employee must have participated in the strike at some stage. The provision is not restricted to working days.

The period is calculated from the last working day before the strike. Thus, if a strike takes place on a Monday, the number of days is calculated from the preceding Friday where the working week is Monday to Friday. This is so even if the strike finishes on the Monday. If, however, the strike both starts and finishes on the same day (being any day other than a Monday) of the week, no days are lost.

Paragraph 15 only applies where an employee is actually taking part in a strike. (See Chapter 12 for a consideration of when an employee is taking part in a strike.)

It will be important for the employer to keep a record of when the strike started, when it finished and the names of employees involved in the strike.

Lock-outs

Lock-out is defined in para 24(1) of Sched 13 as:

the closing of a place of employment or the suspension of work, or the refusal by an employer to continue to employ any number of persons employed by him in consequence of a dispute, done with a view to compelling those persons, or to aid another employer in compelling persons employed by him, to accept terms or conditions of or affecting employment.

A week beginning before 6 July 1964 will count if the employee was absent from work due to a lock-out by the employer for all or any part of the week: para 22 of Sched 13.

The continuity of employment is not broken by a week which does not count under Sched 13 and which begins after 5 July 1964 if in that week, or any part of that week, the employee is absent due to a lock-out by the employer: para 15(4). Further, such weeks may count in computing the period of employment. Unlike the position where the employee is taking part in a strike, there is no statutory exclusion akin to para 15(1), applying only to strikes (see *above*), which prevents the employee who is locked out from counting a week where, during the week or part of the week, the employee is locked out.

Where the employee is locked out that period will count if it falls within one of the paragraphs of Sched 13. One example would be where the contract of employment still subsists. A lock-out does not automatically terminate the contract of employment: *E and J Davis Transport Ltd v Chattaway* [1972] ICR 267. If a week during which there is a lock-out is not caught by one of the other provisions of Sched 13 then continuity is preserved by para 15(4). Section 151(5) and (6)(*b*) apply, so that if an employee's period of continuous employment includes one or more periods which under Sched 13 do not count in computing continuous employment but do not break the continuity of employment, the beginning of the period shall be treated as postponed by the number of days falling within that intervening period, or as the case may be, by the aggregate number of days falling within those periods. Where para 15(4) of Sched 13 applies, the number of days falling within such an intervening period is the number of days between the last working day before the lock-out and the day on which work was resumed. (See *above* for the way in which this provision operates.)

It follows that the employee who is locked out, and whose contract of employment is terminated, will find himself in a worse position than the employee whose contract of employment continues, because in the latter case the continuity of employment is not only preserved but increases.

Absence on service with the armed forces

An employee who is entitled to apply to his former employer under the Reserve Forces (Safeguard of Employment) Act 1985 to be reinstated may, provided he complies with the provisions of that Act, aggregate the periods before and after his service with the armed forces so that the continuity of employment is not broken: para 16 of Sched 13.

Section 151(5) and (6)(*c*) of the EP(C)A 1978 provides that if an employee's period of continuous employment includes one or more periods which under Sched 13 do not count in computing continuous employment but do not break the continuity of employment, the beginning of the period shall be treated as postponed by the number of days falling within that intervening period or, as the case may be, by the aggregate number of days falling within those periods. Where para 16(1) applies, the number of days falling within such an intervening period is the number of days between the employee's last day of employment before service and the day on which he resumed employment, ie the period between the two contracts: see the Reserve Forces (Safeguard of Employment) Act 1985.

An accrued right

Where the employee has, at any time during the relevant periods of employment, been continuously employed for a period which qualifies him for a right, such as the right not to be unfairly dismissed or to claim a redundancy payment, he is regarded for the purposes of qualifying for that right, as continuing to satisfy the criteria for continuous employment until certain conditions occur: para 7(1) of Sched 13 to the EP(C)A 1978.

Following the House of Lord's decision in the EOC case, *above* at p 42, it is difficult to envisage circumstances in which this para will now have effect. It had particular application to a situation where an employee had worked for two years and thereby 'acquired' a right but his employment thereafter ceased to qualify by reason of a reduction in hours.

Reinstatement or re-engagement

Continuity of employment may be preserved under The Employment Protection (Continuity of Employment) Regulations 1993 (SI 1993 No 2165).

These regulations provide, in certain circumstances, for the preservation of continuity where the employee has been reinstated, or re-engaged, by his employer, or by a successor or an associated employer. They apply where as a result of:

(*a*) the employee having presented a complaint of dismissal under s 67 of the EP(C)A 1978, s 63 of the SDA 1975 or s 54 of the RRA 1976, or

(*b*) the employee having made a claim under a designated procedures agreement (s 65 of the EP(C)A 1978) (Note—there is but one, that for the Electrical Contracting Industry), or

(*c*) action by a conciliation officer under s 134(3) of the EP(C)A 1978, s 64(2) of the SDA 1975 or s 55(2) RRA 1976 (ie before a complaint has been presented), or

(*d*) a compromise contract under s 140(2)(*fb*) and (3) of the EP(C)A 1978, s 77(4)(*aa*) of the SDA 1975 or s 72(4)(*aa*) of the RRA 1976

the employee is reinstated or re-engaged as mentioned *above*. In such circumstances the continuity of that employee's period of employment is preserved and, accordingly, any week falling within the interval beginning with the effective date of termination and ending with the date of reinstatement or re-engagement, as the case may be, shall count in the computation of the employee's period of continuous employment. Note that even where a complaint is made to the tribunal, not every reinstatement or re-engagement may be in consequence of that complaint. See *Gardener v NCB* (1982) (unreported).

Change of employer

The general principle is that an employee will enjoy continuity of employment with only one employer: para 17(1) of Sched 13. However, there are certain circumstances in which a change of employer will not break the continuity of employment and the employee's period of employment at the time of the change counts as a period of employment with a new employer. These exceptions are set out in paras 17,

18, and 18A of Sched 13. Unless an employee can show that he falls within one of those exceptions his continuity of employment will be defeated.

The Transfer of Undertakings (Protection of Employment) Regulations 1981 (SI 1981 No 1794) (TUPE 1981) have made a significant change in the law in so far as they affect the employee's rights upon the transfer of an undertaking. For a detailed account of the effect of these regulations see Chapter 15. Broadly the effect of these regulations is to provide that on a transfer of an undertaking which comes within the regulations, the employee's contract of employment is automatically transferred from the transferor to the transferee. Nothing in these regulations affects para 17. It is arguable that since the employee's rights under the contract are transferred from the transferor to the transferee, the regulations operate to preserve continuity of employment. In any event, continuity will generally be preserved under Sched 13. The exceptions to para 17(1) are contained in para 17(2)–(5) and para 18 and are set out *below*.

Where a trade, business or undertaking is transferred from one employer to another

Paragraph 17(2) provides that if a trade, business or undertaking (whether or not it be an undertaking established by or under an Act of Parliament) is transferred from one person to another, the period of employment of an employee in the trade or business or undertaking at the time of the transfer shall count as a period of employment with the transferee, and the transfer, shall not break the continuity of the period of employment.

Section 153(1) of the EP(C)A 1978 provides that business includes a trade or profession and any activity carried on by a body of persons whether corporate or unincorporate. The use of the word activity in the definition of a business covers such operations as may be carried on by a charity and a college: see *Robinson v Council of the County Borough of Bournemouth* (1970) 5 ITR 100. Transfer in para 17(2) is to be construed as if it involved a change of ownership. See *Lord Advocate v de Rosa* [1974] 2 All ER 849.

It is a question of fact whether or not there has been a transfer of a trade, business or undertaking. In *Kenmir Ltd v Frizzell and Others* [1968] 1 WLR 329, Widgery J held:

> the vital consideration is whether the effect of the transaction was to put the transferee in possession of a going concern the activities of which he could carry on without interruption.

In *Woodhouse v Peter Brotherhood Ltd* [1972] 3 All ER 91, Crossleys manufactured diesel engines. This company sold its factory to Peter Brotherhood Ltd, together with some of the plant, machinery, equipment, fixtures and fittings. Peter Brotherhood Ltd purchased the factory to manufacture spinning machines and steam turbines. Some unfinished diesel engines remained in the factory and Peter Brotherhood Ltd agreed to complete the work on these diesel engines. It was held that the transfer was one of assets and not of a going concern. The Court of Appeal held that the fact that the employees continued to work in the same environment was not sufficient evidence of the transfer of a business. Buckley LJ held the test is simply whether B has become the proprietor of the trade, business or undertaking in succession to A.

In *Melon v Hector Powe Ltd* [1980] IRLR 477, where it was again held that there had been a transfer of assets, the House of Lords confirmed that it is for the tribunal to ascertain on the facts whether or not there has been the transfer of a business or part of a business or a transfer of physical assets. It did not matter that the individual employees may continue to do the same work in the same environment and that they are unaware that they are working in a different business.

In deciding whether or not there has been the transfer of a business as a going concern, the agreement between the transferor and the transferee will have to be considered. It is the substance of the agreement which will be determinative. Factors to be considered are has there been a transfer of assets, work in progress, the trading name, brand names or customer lists? The importance attaching to these factors will depend on the circumstances of each case. One aspect to consider is whether or not there has been a transfer of goodwill, perhaps supported by a restrictive covenant, though the absence of a transfer of goodwill will not be fatal. There may be little goodwill left in the business: see *Kenmir Ltd v Frizzell and Others above*; see also *Jeetle v Elster* [1985] ICR 389. The transfer of goodwill on its own may be the transfer of a business or part of a business: see *Ward v Haines Watts and Another* [1983] ICR 231, where an accountant agreed with the transferee to sell to the transferee a list of clients. The clients were then informed by circular letter of the change of practice and were asked whether or not they were prepared to transfer their affairs to the transferee. About half of the clients circularized were prepared to do so. There was a transfer of the appropriate files, but there was no transfer of any physical assets. It was held that there was a transfer of part of a business as a going concern. See also *Secretary of State for Employment v Spence and Others* [1986] IRLR 248, where there was a transfer of the assets and goodwill of a business by a receiver. The employees had all been dismissed at the time of the transfer. The Court of Appeal found that although there were no employees, none the less the transfer of the assets and the goodwill of the business, where the transferee had the option to continue the business as a going concern, was a transfer of a business. Needless to say this situation would be covered by TUPE 1981: see *Litster v Forth Dry Dock and Engineering Co Ltd* [1990] 1 AC 546.

The sale of farmland has been held to amount to the transfer of a business as a going concern: see *Lloyd v Brassey* [1969] 2 QB 98, as has the surrender of a tenancy of licensed premises: *Young v Daniel Thwaites and Co Ltd* [1977] ICR 877.

Paragraph 17(2) (although it is not specifically stated) may apply where there has been a transfer of part of a business: see *Melon v Hector Powe Ltd* [1980] IRLR 477. The part of the business may have been run separately before the transfer as in *Ault v Gregory* (1967) 2 ITR 301, but the part of the business transferred may not have been run as a separate entity before the transfer: see *Green v Wavertree Heating and Plumbing Co Ltd* [1978] ICR 928.

The transfer of part of the equity of a business by one of two partners to the other partner, whereby that other partner has the entire equity, was a transfer of a business within the meaning of para 17(2) because two partners as joint proprietors transferred the whole business to one: *Allen and Son v Coventry* [1979] IRLR 399.

There may be a transfer at the time of the employee's dismissal even though further steps are to take place which do not take place and the merger is subsequently called off: *Dabell v Vale Industrial Services (Nottingham) Ltd* [1988] IRLR 439. There may be a transfer of a trade or business or undertaking within para 17(2) if the business assets and goodwill of the transferor pass to the transferee, even though the transferor is insolvent at the time of the transfer and the business is no longer a going concern. The fact that the transferor is insolvent is a relevant factor, but it does not necessarily mean that there has been no transfer within this provision: *Teesside Times Ltd v Drury* [1978] ICR 822.

The meaning of the phrase 'at the time of the transfer' was considered in *Teesside Times Ltd v Drury* [1980] ICR 338. Drury worked for Champion Publications Ltd. A receiver was appointed on 15 October 1975. Drury was dismissed at 4pm on Friday 17 October. At 6.30pm on Friday 17 October the business of Champion Publications Ltd was transferred to Teesside Times Ltd. On Monday 20 October Drury went to work for Teesside Times Ltd. He was dismissed by Teesside Times Ltd that night. Teesside Times argued that continuity was broken because Drury was not employed at the time they took over. Goff LJ thought that phrase 'at the time of the transfer' meant moment (or as near as possible) of time. Stepehenson LJ found that it meant the period of transfer, but that a gap which broke the continuity of employment under what is now Sched 13 would be fatal. Eveleigh LJ found that the length of the gap was not material (but again see the TUPE 1981 and the cases decided on them).

In *Macer v Abafast Ltd* [1990] IRLR 137, Macer was employed by CTR Ltd. On 31 December 1986, Macer was told his employment with CTR Ltd had come to an end. It was intended to transfer the business to a subsidiary of Abafast, CTR (Recruitment) Ltd. The transfer took place in stages. On 21 January 1987 Abafast wrote to Macer offering him employment with effect from 12 January. Macer was subsequently dismissed. Did the gap between 31 December and 12 January break his continuous employment? The EAT held that para 17(2) can be construed as having four essentials:

> The first essential is the transfer and therefore the continuation of the business or undertaking. The second is employment by the owner before the transfer or change of ownership and by the owner after. The third essential is the period of service with the former must be continuous within paras 1 to 16 of Schedule 13, and likewise the periods of service with the latter. Fourthly, that the combined periods of service must satisfy the qualification period.

It construed para 17(2) as meaning:

> Provided that there has been a valid transfer of a business from A to B, then the continuous period of service of an employee with A may be added to the continuous period of service with B so as to establish a qualifying period of continuous employment . . .

The EAT rejected the view that the words 'at the time of the transfer' in para 17(2) referred to a moment in time. Macer's continuity of employment was not broken. The EAT was influenced by the view of Eveleigh LJ in *Drury*'s case *above* and by the purposive approach of the House of Lords in *Litster v Forth Dry Dock and Engineering Co Ltd* [1989] IRLR 161.

This principle has been endorsed in two more recent cases. In *A & G Tuck Ltd v Bartlett* and *A & G Tuck (Slough) Ltd* [1994] IRLR 162, the employee remained in the employ of the transferor until two weeks after the transfer, then moved to the transferee. The EAT held that continuity was not affected, apparently construing para 17(2) as covering a gap which related to the machinery of the transfer. In *Justfern Ltd v D'Ingerthorpe and others* [1994] IRLR 164, the same paragraph was held to operate where a college lecturer's employment ended due to the insolvency of the college and he was re-employed by new management over a week later, even though the lecturer had drawn unemployment benefit (being available for work) in the interim. The EAT concluded that *Macer's* case was not limited to a deliberate avoidance scheme and did apply where the termination was by virtue of insolvency rather than a step in the transfer machinery. It has to be said that both these cases do seem to put something of a gloss upon the statute and appear to be in conflict with para 1 Sched 13 which provides that a week which does not count breaks the continuity of employment. See the decision of Stephenson LJ in *Drury*'s case *above*. See also *Gibson*'s case, *above*.

If one body corporate is substituted for another body corporate as the employer

Paragraph 17(3) provides:

> If by or under an Act of Parliament whether public or local and whether passed before or after this Act a contract of employment between any body corporate and an employee is modified and some other body corporate is substituted as the employer, the employee's period of employment at the time when the modification takes effect shall count as a period of employment with the second mentioned body corporate, and the change of employer shall not break the continuity of the period of employment.

If the employer dies and his personal representatives or trustees keep the employee on in employment

Paragraph 17(4) provides:

> If on the death of an employer the employee is taken into the employment of the personal representatives or trustees of the deceased, the employee's period of employment at the time of the death shall count as a period of employment with the employer's personal representatives or trustees, and the death shall not break the continuity of the period of employment.

At common law the death of an employer automatically terminates the contract of employment. However, if the employee is employed by the deceased's personal representatives or trustees, continuity may be preserved. If the personal representatives or trustees continue to run the business in which the employee was employed then inevitably there is a transfer under para 17 and under TUPE 1981.

The employee may be his deceased employer's personal representative. As the personal representative he has power to contract with himself as an individual and continuity of employment will not be broken: *Rowley, Holmes, and Co v Barber* [1977] ICR 387. Where the employee, as well as being personal representative, is also beneficially entitled to the business, the position remains the same so long as the business remains part of the estate. If the employee sells the business as personal representative and continues in the employment of the purchaser, there will be no break under these provisions in the continuity of employment: *Rowley, Holmes and Co v Barber, above.*

If there is a change in the partners, personal representatives or trustees

Paragraph 17(5) provides:

> If there is a change in the partners, personal representatives or trustees who employ any person, the employee's period of employment at the time of the change shall count as a period of employment with the partners, personal representatives or trustees after the change, and the change shall not break the continuity of the period of employment.

At common law a change in the partnership is a change of employer. Although a partner leaving a partnership or dying might not affect the contracts of employment of the partnership employees, a major change in the partnership may have the effect of terminating the employee's contract of employment: see *Tunstall and Another v Condon and*

Another [1980] ICR 786, where the decision in *Brace v Calder* [1895] 2 QB 253 was considered.

Paragraph 17(5) is intended to deal with the situation where there is a change in the partnership. Where there is a change from employment by a partnership to employment by a sole partner, continuity of employment is not preserved under para 17(5) (see *Harold Fielding v Mansi* [1974] IRLR 79), unless it involves a transfer of a business. Where there is a change from employment by an individual to employment by a partnership where that individual becomes a partner, para 17(5) does not preserve continuity: *Wynne v Hair Control* [1978] ICR 870.

In *Allen and Son v Coventry* [1979] IRLR 399, the employee was employed by a partnership of two solicitors. The senior partner retired, leaving the junior partner as the sole proprietor. The employee was subsequently dismissed and the EAT had to consider whether or not para 17(5) preserved continuity. The EAT distinguished the cases of *Fielding v Mansi* and *Wynne v Hair Control, above,* finding that in each of these cases different businesses were involved, whereas this was the continuation of the same business. Therefore there was a transfer of the ownership of the business within para 17(2), hence continuity of employment was preserved under that provision.

In *Jeetle v Elster* [1985[ICR 389, Elster was employed by a partnership of four doctors. The partnership was dissolved and Dr Jeetle set up as a sole practitioner in one of the surgeries previously operated by the partnership. He kept the majority of the patients who had previously attended that surgery and some others transferred to him from the other surgery previously operated by the partnership. He also acquired certain assets of the partnership. Elster joined Dr Jeetle. Did she have continuity of employment? The EAT would if necessary have interpreted para 17(5) as preserving continuity. It found that the argument that ' "where one of two partners leaves the partnership, there are no partners but only a sole proprietor, after the change",... [was] correct in pure legal terminology ... The expression "sole partner" is no doubt legally inaccurate but is extensively used and everyone knows what it means.' Again the EAT found that para 17(2) preserved continuity because there was a transfer from one person to another within the meaning of para 17(2), the other being a partner in the firm at the time of the transfer.

If the employee of one employer is taken into the employment of another employer

Paragraph 18 provides that:

> if an employee of an employer is taken into the employment of another employer who, at the time when the employee enters his employment, is an associated employer of the first-mentioned employer, the employee's period of employment at that time shall count as a period of employment

with the second-mentioned employer and the change of employer shall not break the continuity of the period of employment.

Section 153(4) of the EP(C)A 1978 provides, for the purposes of that Act, that any two employers are to be treated as associated if one is a company of which the other (directly or indirectly) has control, or if both are companies of which a third person (directly or indirectly) has control; and the expression 'associated employer' shall be construed accordingly.

Section 153(4) was considered in *Gardiner v London Borough of Merton* [1980] IRLR 472, where it was held that this section applies only where at least one of the employers concerned is a company with limited liability. For the purposes of para 18, the definition of associated employer in s 153(4) is exhaustive. It follows that since a local authority is not a limited company local authorities could not be associated employers within s 153(4). See also *Southwood Hostel Management Committee v Taylor* [1979] IRLR 397.

Other forms of statutory bodies corporate are excluded: *Hasley v Fair Employment Agency* [1989] IRLR 106. A partnership of companies is within the definition: *Pinkney v Sandpiper Drilling Ltd* [1989] ICR 389. This case is difficult to reconcile with s 153(4) of the EP(C)A 1978. Likewise, a foreign company may be within the definition if it can be likened in its essentials to a company incorporated under the Companies Acts: *Hancill v Marcon Engineering Ltd* [1990] ICR 103.

'Control' in s 153(4) in the context of a limited company means control by the majority of votes attaching to shares exercised in general meetings. It is not control in the sense of how or by whom the enterprise is actually run: *Secretary of State for Employment v (1) Newbold and (2) Joint Liquidators of David Armstrong (Catering Services) Ltd* [1981] IRLR 305; and see also *Umar v Pliastar Ltd* [1981] ICR 727. However, see *Secretary of State for Employment v Chapman and Another* [1989] ICR 771, where it was suggested that, exceptionally, factors other than voting control could be considered.

In *Zarb and Samuels v British and Brazilian Produce Co Sales Ltd* [1978] IRLR 78, it was held that 'person' may include a group of people exercising control, provided they act as one. This approach was followed in *Harford v Swiftrim Ltd* [1987] ICR 439.

In *South West Launderettes Ltd v Laidler* [1986] IRLR 305, South West Launderettes Ltd was controlled by S who held 94 per cent of the shares, the remainder being held by his son. There were other companies in which S had 50 per cent of the shares and his wife held the other 50 per cent. The Court of Appeal held that the persons controlling the companies were different and although S was the controller of South West Launderettes Ltd the other companies were controlled by Mr and Mrs S. Therefore, South West Launderettes Ltd and the other companies were not associated employers, because the third person was not the same person in each case. It also found that an alternative argument that S controlled all the companies failed because there was no evidence that S had any control over his wife's shares, or that he could exercise the voting powers which attached to his wife's shares. In this case the Court of Appeal cast considerable doubt on whether two or more individuals acting in concert could be a third person for the purposes of s 153(4) of the EP(C)A 1978.

In *Chapman*'s case above, it was held that where A held 50 per cent of the shares and B held 50 per cent of the shares as nominee for A, A had control. In *Hair Colour Consultants Ltd v Mena* [1984] ICR 671, it was held that a 50 per cent holding on its own did not give control. Negative control was not sufficient. *Laidler*'s case was followed in *Strudwick v Iszatt Brothers Ltd* [1988] ICR 796, where it was held that even if the third person can be more than one individual, the same individual, and not a varying combination, must have voting control over each relevant company. In this case Wood J expressed the view, *obiter*, that *Harford*'s case, *above*, would create an enormous problem and if necessary he would adopt the view of Mustill LJ in *Laidler*'s case, *above*, who did not accept the concept of plural control at all. See also *Poparm Ltd v Weekes* [1984] IRLR 388. In *Russell v Elmdon Freight Terminal Ltd* [1989] ICR 629, *Laidler*'s case was followed where no one person had voting control over two relevant companies and there was insufficient evidence to establish *de facto* joint control by two persons. A 'dormant' company may be an associated employer: see *Charnock and Another v Barrie Muirhead Ltd* [1984] ICR 641. Charnock was dismissed by company A and was not taken on by company B until some two weeks later. Company B had not previously had any employees. The employee's continuity of employment was preserved by para 11 Sched 13—when the employee was dismissed he was entitled to three weeks' statutory notice which meant that the effective date of termination with company A was postponed by three weeks thereby bridging the gap. It was held that although company B had not previously been an employer it became an employer on the day when the employee entered its employment, and was an associated employer.

A gap between the employment with associated employers will not defeat the continuity of employment, provided it is preserved under Sched 13: see *Binns v Versil Ltd* [1975] IRLR 273 and *Charnock and Another v Barrie Muirhead Ltd, above.*

Continuity of employment in certain schools

Paragraph 18A provides that where an employee of one employer is taken into the employment of another employer, and either both those employers are governors of schools maintained by a local education authority or such governors are one and that authority the other, his period of employment at the time of the change shall count

as a period of employment with the second employer and shall not
break his continuity of employment.

Estoppel

At one stage it seemed that if, on a change of employer, the new
employer promised the employee that he would honour the former
employer's obligations to the employee, the new employer could be
estopped from alleging a break in the continuity of employment and so
defeating the employee's rights: *Evenden v Guildford City Association
Football Club* [1975] ICR 367, and *Secretary of State for Employment
v Globe Elastic Thread Co Ltd* [1978] ICR 1041. However, in *Secretary
of State for Employment v Globe Elastic Thread Co Ltd* [1979] ICR
706, the House of Lords overruled the earlier decisions and held that
continuity on a transfer of employment could only arise in accordance
with the statutory provisions, and that nothing in the nature of an
estoppel between the employer and the employee could confer jurisdiction on the tribunal beyond that given to it by statute. Where there is
an enforceable agreement between the employer and the employee
that the employer will honour the existing continuous period of
employment, its failure to do so may give rise to an action in damages
for breach of contract.

Effective date of termination

The provisions of s 55 of the EP(C)A 1978 as to the postponement of
the effective date of termination may prolong the period of continuous
employment in certain circumstances. See para 11(1) of Sched 13;
Charnock and Another v Barrie Muirhead Ltd [1984] ICR 641, and
Chapter 5 as to the effective date of termination. It is vital to note
that these provisions apply to calculating the length of service and not
to the date of termination for other purposes, especially they do
not apply to the commencement of any time limits.

Chapter 4

Dismissal

To claim unfair dismissal, an employee must have been dismissed. The onus of proving dismissal is on the employee.

The meaning of dismissal

The EP(C)A 1978 defines dismissal for the purposes of a claim for unfair dismissal in s 55(2). Dismissal may arise in the following cases.

Termination of employment by the employer

The employee is treated as dismissed where the contract under which he is employed is terminated by the employer whether with or without notice: s 55(2)(a) of the EP(C)A 1978. For the purpose of this provision, it is irrelevant that the contract is terminated by the employer with proper notice or with incorrect notice, or that it is terminated without notice whether with or without wages in lieu of notice.

With notice
The giving of notice by the employer or employee is a unilateral act, and once given, it can only be withdrawn with the agreement of the other, although, if the employer attempts to withdraw the notice, the withdrawal may be treated as an offer of new employment: *Riordan v War Office* [1959] 1 WLR 1046; see also *Harris and Russell Ltd v Slingsby* [1973] IRLR 221.

A possible exception arises where the employee is dismissed but successfully appeals against the decision to dismiss him under an internal disciplinary procedure resulting in an offer of reinstatement by the employer: see *Petch v Taunton Deane DC* (1977) (unreported), where the tribunal considered that the effect of the offer of reinstatement might be to render the notice null and void, because that was the intention of the parties under such an agreement, further, or in the alternative, that the notice in such a case is conditional, the employee impliedly agreeing that if his appeal is successful, the employer may withdraw the notice. See also *Savage v J Sainsbury Ltd* [1980] IRLR 109.

Notice, whether given by the employer or employee, must be specific. It should specify the date when it is to take effect, or if it does not specify the date, it must at least make it possible for the date to be deduced with certainty from what is said: *Morton Sundour Fabrics Ltd v Shaw* (1967) 1 ITR 84; see also *Hughes v Gwynedd Area Health Authority* [1978] ICR 161. It is not sufficient for the employer to tell the employee that the date of termination will be some specific date or such earlier date as the employer may select, whether or not it is coupled with a statement that the earlier date will not be earlier than the date upon which the contract could be brought to an end by the requisite period of notice: see *The Burton Group Ltd v Smith* [1977] IRLR 351.

In *Brown v Southall and Knight* [1980] IRLR 130, it was held that the summary dismissal of an employee by letter could not take effect until the employee had read the letter or had been granted a reasonable opportunity of reading it. In *Hindle Gears Ltd v McGinty and Others* [1984] IRLR 477, it was held that communication of a decision to dismiss an employee in terms which either bring it expressly to the attention of the employee, or give him at least a reasonable opportunity of learning of it, was essential.

An employee's contract of employment may be divisible into two distinct parts. The employer may by notice terminate part of the contract without bringing the contract to an end. In *Land and Wilson v West Yorkshire Metropolitan County Council* [1981] IRLR 87, the employee had initially been employed solely as a full-time fireman. Subsequently he had agreed to be available for work if required during his off-duty periods. The employer then terminated with notice the off-duty arrangement. It was held that it was open to the employer to terminate simply that part of the contract.

Where an employer gives notice to an employee but tells the employee that he does not require him to continue to perform his duties, and the employee does not return to work, the employer and not the employee has brought the contract to an end: *Springbank Sand and Gravel Co Ltd v Craig* [1973] IRLR 278. Where an employer has given notice it is always open to the employer during the period of notice to dismiss the employee summarily before the expiration of the period of notice: *Stapp v The Shaftesbury Society* [1982] IRLR 326.

The effect of warnings

A warning of dismissal as opposed to notice will not operate to determine the contract of employment. Whether a warning or notice of dismissal was given is a question of fact. An example of a warning arises where, in a redundancy situation, employees are told that they may be dismissed for redundancy in the future: *Morton Sundour Fab-*

rics Ltd v Shaw, above; see also *International Computers Ltd v Kennedy* [1981] IRLR 28. An employer may warn the employee against a repetition of a particular course of conduct or will seek through warnings to achieve an improvement in the employee's performance. Warnings of this nature will not amount to a dismissal in law except where the employer is not justified in giving a warning, or where the employer uses abusive language to the employee in administering the warning and the employer is thereby guilty of repudiatory conduct entitling the employee to resign and claim a constructive dismissal. See 'Constructive dismissal' at p 71.

In *Haseltine Lake and Co v Dowler* [1981] IRLR 25, the employee was told by a partner in the firm that he should seek a job elsewhere or be dismissed. He would have to be gone by the end of the summer. It was held that there was no dismissal because the employer did not specify the date for termination, nor was a date positively ascertainable. This was not a case of 'resign or you will be dismissed forthwith or at a specified or ascertainable date'. *East Sussex County Council v Walker* (1972) 7 ITR 280, was distinguished because in *Walker*'s case the employee was told that her job was to come to an end forthwith and she was invited to resign. See 'Forced resignation' at p 97.

Dismissal without notice

The employer may tell the employee that he is dismissed with immediate effect, or bring the contract to an end without notice by his use of words or actions.

The problems of language

It may not be clear from the employer's language whether or not he is terminating the contract. Abusive language by the employer may entitle the employee to resign and claim a constructive dismissal.

The problem is illustrated by the following cases. In *Kendrick v Aerduct Productions* [1974] IRLR 322, an employee, having told his employer that he was hoping to take a tenancy of an off-licence, was told to 'fuck off and play with your shop'. It was held that he had been dismissed. In *King v Webbs Poultry Products (Bradford) Ltd* [1975] IRLR 135, it was held that the use of the words 'piss off' and 'fuck off' could only mean the employee was being dismissed where the employer took the initiative in terminating the contract.

However, the employer's use of 'fuck off' does not necessarily amount to a dismissal. Among the fish filleters of Hull, the expression, 'if you do not like the job, fuck off' means 'if you don't like the work you are doing, clock off. You will receive no pay after you clock off. You can come back to work the next day when you are disposed to do some work.' If a dismissal is imminent 'unexpected formality seems to descend upon the parties': *Futty v Brekkes (D&D) Ltd* [1974] IRLR 130. See also *Davy v JE Collins (Builders) Ltd* [1974] IRLR 324.

What approach is to be adopted where ambiguous or indeed unambiguous words of dismissal are used? In *Tanner v DT Kean* [1978] IRLR 110, the employer had loaned Tanner a sum of money to enable him to purchase his own transport. He discovered Tanner was still using his (the employer's) van and said, 'What's my fucking van doing outside? ... That's it; you're finished with me.' The EAT held that, when it is uncertain whether words or actions constitute a dismissal or resignation or not, all the circumstances need to be considered, including events after the words spoken and before the employee's departure. Was it intended that the contract be terminated by the words spoken? 'Would a reasonable employee, in all the circumstances, have understood what the employer intended by what he said and did?' This is not quite the same question posed by the Court of Appeal in *Sothern*'s case (see *below*). The latter seems the better view.

The EAT envisaged that in the case of ambiguous words, the test to be applied was a subjective one: *Gale (GB) Ltd v Gilbert* [1978] ICR 1149. In *J and J Stern v Simpson* [1983] IRLR 52, there was a heated discussion during which one of the partners said to the employee, 'go, get out, get out'. The EAT followed the decision of the Court of Appeal in *Sothern v Franks Charlesly and Co* [1981] IRLR 278, see *below*. It held that it was necessary to construe the words in all the circumstances to determine whether an employee has resigned or been dismissed, and that only where the words used are ambiguous after considering them in their context must a further test be applied; whether any reasonable employer or employee might have understood the words to be tantamount to a dismissal or resignation.

The following cases all involving a resignation by the employee, but relevant to cases involving a dismissal, are of assistance in establishing the principles to be applied where unambiguous words are used.

In *Gale (GB) Ltd v Gilbert, above*, Gilbert lost his temper and said to the employer, 'I'm leaving, I want my cards.' The EAT found that the words were unambiguous and therefore the employee's resignation stood.

In *Sothern v Franks Charlesly and Co, above*, Sothern said 'I am resigning.' Fox LJ held that they were unambiguous words of resignation so understood by her employer. In both these cases it was held that where unambiguous words are used, what a reasonable employer might have understood was not relevant. Fox LJ said 'The non-disclosed intention of a person using language as to his intended meaning is not properly to be taken into account in determining what the true meaning is.' He did not find it inconsistent with the conclusion which he had reached that the employee returned to work and stayed on for some weeks after she had said that 'I am resigning'.

In *Barclay v City of Glasgow District Council* [1983] IRLR 313, the EAT accepted that there might be exceptions to the principle that where unambiguous words of resignation were used the employer is entitled to accept the resignation. These included cases of an immature employee, or where a decision was taken in the heat of the moment, or where the employee was jostled into the decision by the employer, or where idle words were used under emotional stress which the employer knew or ought to have known were not meant to be taken seriously.

In *Sovereign House Security Services Ltd v Savage* [1989] IRLR 115, the Court of Appeal, per May LJ, held that although at first sight there may appear to have been a real resignation there may have been something in the circumstances to entitle the tribunal to conclude otherwise.

It is difficult to extract guidelines from the reported cases. However, the following propositions can be put forward. The employer's intention will not generally be relevant, but see *Tanner*'s case, *above*. Unambiguous words must be construed at face value and given their ordinary meaning, unless the circumstances suggest otherwise. When ambiguous words are used, the question is what would a reasonable person have understood the words to mean. Thus, in interpreting the words used, whether the words used are ambiguous or unambiguous, an objective test must be adopted. There may be circumstances where unambiguous words are used which may not be binding on the employer, and he may be entitled to withdraw them.

In *Martin v Yeoman Aggregates Ltd* [1983] IRLR 49, the EAT found that unambiguous words of dismissal or resignation used in the heat of the moment did not bring the contract to an end if they were immediately withdrawn. The party using the words should have the opportunity of recanting. It is a question of degree. Furthermore, it must be seen as an exception to the rule that once notice has been given by either the employer or the employee it cannot be withdrawn without the consent of the other party.

Just as the employer's words may operate to terminate the contract, so may his conduct. The giving of a P45 does not of itself bring about the termination of the contract. Removing an employee's clock card may in certain circumstances amount to a dismissal, although where it is withdrawn pending investigation of some act of misconduct, it may be no more than an indication that management does not require the employee to work until the action has been investigated. The removal of the clock card may simply show that the employee is not wanted or is released from work for that particular day.

In *Kwik-Fit (GB) Ltd v Lineham* [1992] IRLR 156, the EAT held that unless there are special circumstances, eg personality conflicts or individual characteristics, then an employer is entitled to treat unambiguous words or actions of resignation as such and to accept the employee's repudiation immediately. However, if there are special circumstances then the employer should allow a reasonable time, such as a day or two, to elapse before accepting the resignation. During that time further facts may arise indicating that it was not correct to have interpreted the employee's words or actions as an intention to resign.

Expiry of fixed-term contracts

See also Chapter 1 at p 26. The employee is treated as dismissed when he is employed under a contract for a fixed term and that term expires without being renewed under the same contract: s 55(2)(b) of the EP(C)A 1978. A fixed-term contract is not defined by the legislation. If the contract is for a fixed term it fixes the maximum duration of the employment, whether or not the contract contains a power for either party to bring the contract to an end by giving notice to the other party before the expiration of the period certain: *BBC v Dixon* [1979] IRLR 114; *BBC v Constanti* [1979] IRLR 114. In *Wiltshire County Council v NATFHE and Guy* [1980] IRLR 198, the employee was engaged by the authority as a part-time teacher. It was held that she had a fixed-term contract starting at the beginning of the autumn term and ending on the last day of the summer term. Her hours and even her wages fluctuated but her contractual obligation continued for the whole of the session. The Court of Appeal distinguished the contract where the employee was simply employed for a specific task which is not a contract for a fixed term: see *Ryan v Shipboard Maintenance Ltd* [1980] IRLR 16. In this type of contract it is not possible to ascertain the precise date in the future when the contract will come to an end.

In *Brown and Others v Knowsley Borough Council* [1986] IRLR 102, Brown's employment was to last only as long as sufficient funds were provided by the Manpower Services Commission (MSC) or any other firms or sponsors. When the MSC funding ceased, the contract of employment came to an end. There was no fixed-term contract and so there was no dismissal.

In *Mulrine v University of Ulster* [1993] IRLR 545, Mulrine had a fixed-term contract for two years which excluded her right to claim unfair dismissal in relation to the contract. The term, however, was extended for a further four months and Mulrine claimed unfair dismissal arguing that the final fixed-term contract was only for four months and so any exclusion invalid. The NICA held that there was no new separate contract but the original one had been extended or renewed to make it for a fixed term of two years four months. It was not appropriate here to follow the test in *BBC v Ioannou* [1975] IRLR 184 (that it is solely the final contract which is to be taken into account), without regard to whether there had been any renewal or extension of a previous contract, and that test should not be applied if it would produce an unfair and unreasonable result.

Constructive dismissal

General

The employee is treated as dismissed where he terminates the contract with or without notice in circumstances such that he is entitled to terminate it without notice by reason of the employer's conduct: s 55(2)(*c*) of the EP(C)A 1978. The employee's termination of the contract in such circumstances is treated as a constructive dismissal.

Here, the contract test has to be applied—does the employer's conduct amount to a repudiation of the contract? See *Western Excavating (ECC) Ltd v Sharp* [1978] ICR 221.

For there to be a repudiation by the employer, he must by his act or omission be guilty of either a fundamental breach of the contract or a breach of a fundamental term of the contract. The term may be express or implied. The act or omission must go to the root of the contract. The employer must have evinced an intention no longer to be bound by the contract: *London Borough of Camden v Pedersen* [1979] IRLR 377; see on appeal *Pedersen v London Borough of Camden* [1981] IRLR 173. A unilateral alteration by the employer of a minor or inconsequential term will not amount to a repudiation: *Gillies v Richard Daniels and Co Ltd* [1979] IRLR 457.

In *Western Excavating (ECC) Ltd v Sharp, above,* Lord Denning MR held:

> If the employer is guilty of conduct which is a significant breach going to the root of the contract of employment; or which shows that the employer no longer intends to be bound by one or more of the essential terms of the contract; then the employee is entitled to treat himself as discharged from any further performance. If he does so, then he terminates the contract by reason of the employer's conduct. He is constructively dismissed. The employee is entitled in those circumstances to leave at the instant without giving any notice at all or, alternatively, he may give notice and say he is leaving at the end of the notice. But the conduct must in either case be sufficiently serious to entitle him to leave at once. Moreover, he must make up his mind soon after the conduct of which he complains: for, if he continues for any length of time without leaving, he will lose his right to treat himself as discharged. He will be regarded as having elected to affirm the contract.

Lord Denning adopted the common law test, but Lawton LJ adopted a different approach and held, simply, that sensible people can easily recognise the types of conduct which would bring a contract to an end and it is unnecessary to lay down what legal principles operate to terminate the contract by reason of the employer's conduct.

Although recognising the need for a breach of a contractual term, Lawton LJ's approach was much wider and has enabled tribunals to find new implied terms in a contract of employment so that the result may sometimes be very little different from the application of a test of reasonableness. See *'Terms of the contract'* at p 73. This case firmly establishes that the test to be applied is one based on contract.

In (1) *Spafax Ltd v Harrison* and (2) *Spafax Ltd v Taylor* [1980] IRLR 442, the Court of Appeal made it clear that in *Sharp's* case Lord Denning was not intending to distinguish between conduct which is a significant breach going to the root of the contract, and conduct which shows that the employer no longer intends to be bound by one or more of the essential terms of the contract, so that the latter course of conduct does not necessarily involve a breach of the contract. The Court of Appeal held that conduct which shows that the employer no longer intends to be bound by one or more essential terms *will* be a repudiation. Where the employer's action is lawful and does not involve a breach of contract it will not be a repudiation. The tribunal, having established the evidence, must decide whether or not there has been a constructive dismissal. There is no rule of law for determining whether a particular set of facts amounts to a fundamental breach of the contract by the employer entitling the employee to claim a constructive dismissal: *Woods v WM Car Services (Peterborough) Ltd* [1982] IRLR 413.

The fact that the employer neither intended to repudiate the contract nor that he did not reasonably believe that his conduct would be accepted as repudiatory, is not the proper test to apply. It is necessary to determine whether, viewed objectively, the employer's conduct evinced an intention no longer to be bound by the contract: *Lewis v Motorworld Garages Ltd* [1985] IRLR 465. See also *Post Office v Roberts* [1980] IRLR 347, where it was held that where the employer's conduct breaches the implied obligation of mutual trust and confidence, it does not matter that the employer did not intend his conduct to have that effect.

It is not relevant in examining the question of repudiation whether or not the employer can justify the steps which he took. This will be relevant in considering whether or not the dismissal was fair or unfair under s 57(3) of the EP(C)A 1978: *Wadham Stringer Commercials (London) Ltd and Wadham Stringer Vehicles Ltd v Brown* [1983] IRLR 46.

In *Courtaulds Northern Spinning Ltd v Sibson and Another* [1988] ICR 451, the employers required Sibson, an HGV driver, to transfer to a different depot a mile away to avoid conflict with the union. The Court of Appeal found there was an implied term that Sibson could be required to work at any place within reasonable daily reach of his home. There was no need or justification to import into the implied term a requirement that the request must be reasonable or for genuine operational reasons. In *Prestwick Circuits Ltd v McAndrew* [1990] IRLR 191, the Court of Session accepted there was an implied term that McAndrew could be required to change his workplace, but reasonable notice had to be given.

In *United Bank Ltd v Akhtar* [1989] IRLR 507, the bank insisted that Akhtar moved immediately under a contractual mobility clause. The EAT found that there was an implied term that reasonable notice would be given to Akhtar and that the employer's conduct in requiring an immediate move was a fundamental breach of the implied duty of trust. This implied duty may qualify a contractual right. Although this decision conflicts with the Court of Appeal's decision in *Sibson*'s case, none of these cases suggests that the test is other than a contractual test. In *White v Reflecting Road Studs Ltd* [1991] IRLR 331, the EAT stated that the decision in *Akhtar*'s case did not mean that where there is an express mobility clause there should be an implied term that the employer should act reasonably. They stated that this 'would be to re-introduce the reasonable test by the back door'.

See also *Bass Leisure Ltd v Thomas* [1994] IRLR 104, where the EAT held the employer's failure to consider the employee's domestic circumstances (which they were contractually obliged to do under a mobility clause) was a breach of contract which warranted her resigning.

Whether or not there has been a repudiation might appear to be essentially a question of law. Initially, that was the view of the EAT. However, in *Woods v WM Car Services (Peterborough) Ltd* [1981] IRLR 347, the EAT considered that in *Pedersen v London Borough of Camden, above*, the Court of Appeal had found 'that the questions whether there has been a breach of contract and, if so, whether such breach is fundamental are both mixed questions of fact and law so that the Employment Appeal Tribunal cannot substitute its decision for that of the Industrial Tribunal if there was evidence which would justify the Industrial Tribunal's decision'.

This was upheld by the Court of Appeal: see *Woods v WM Car Services (Peterborough) Ltd* [1982] IRLR 413.

While a unilateral change by the employer in a fundamental term of the contract will be a repudiation, if the parties agree to the change then there is a consensual variation and no repudiation. The employer may have reserved the right to make a change in the contract. A change made in accordance with the contractual right will not be repudiation. In *McClory and Others v The Post Office* [1993] IRLR 159, the High Court held that there is no implied term in the contract of employment that the rules of natural justice apply so that an employer must first inform the employee as to the reason for a decision that is to be made. There is, however, an implied term that an employer must not exercise contractual powers on unreasonable grounds.

Terms of the contract
The terms of the contract may be express or implied, and oral or written. Certain implied contractual terms have long been recognised, such as the obligation to pay agreed wages promptly; or to take reason-

able care for the employee's safety; but new implied contractual terms have been recognised by the courts and tribunals coincidentally with the acceptance that the strict common law test should apply in determining whether the employer has constructively dismissed the employee although the process has not gone so far as to recognise an implied contractual term that the employer will behave reasonably (see *Post Office v Roberts* [1980] IRLR 347), because such a term was too wide and too vague.

In *FC Gardner Ltd v Beresford* [1978] IRLR 63, Beresford had not received any pay increases for two years, although other employees had received pay increases. The EAT held it was an implied term of the contract of employment that the employer will not treat the employee arbitrarily, capriciously or inequitably in matters of remuneration. In *Murco Petroleum Ltd v Forge* [1987] IRLR 50, it was held that where the contract made no reference to pay increases it was impossible, as the tribunal had done, to imply a term in the contract that there would always be a yearly pay rise so that a failure to give a pay rise in one year amounted to a constructive dismissal. The EAT further held that if the tribunal had considered whether or not the employer had acted arbitrarily or capriciously so as to be in breach of the implied duty of mutual trust and confidence, it would have reached the conclusion that the employer's action was neither arbitrary nor capricious.

In *British Aircraft Corporation Ltd v Austin* [1978] IRLR 332, Austin was required to wear safety goggles but because of her spectacles these were uncomfortable and unsatisfactory. Despite her complaints to management nothing was done and because she was concerned that she might suffer injury to her eyes she left her employment. The EAT held that the employers were in breach of a general obligation to take reasonable care for the safety of their employees. As part of that general obligation they were also under an obligation to act reasonably in dealing with matters of safety. Because they had failed to investigate complaints made by Austin promptly they had failed to take reasonable care. The EAT also found that if an employer behaves in a way which is not in accordance with good industrial relations practice to such an extent that the situation is intolerable or the employee cannot be expected to put up with it any longer, the employer will be in breach of an implied term.

In *Courtaulds Northern Textiles Ltd v Andrew* [1979] IRLR 84, an assistant manager told the employee who had had 18 years with the company, 'You can't do the bloody job anyway.' The EAT held that he had been constructively dismissed and found that any conduct which is likely to destroy or seriously damage the relationship of confidence and trust between employer and employee is something which goes to the root of the contract and is a fundamental breach.

See *Bliss v South East Thames Regional Health Authority* [1985]

IRLR 308, and also *Lewis v Motorworld Garages Ltd* [1985] IRLR 465, where the Court of Appeal, following the decision of the EAT in *Woods v WM Car Services (Peterborough) Ltd* [1981] IRLR 347, held that it was now established that it was an 'implied term of the contract of employment that the employer will not, without reasonable and proper cause, conduct himself in a manner calculated or likely to destroy or seriously damage the relationship of confidence and trust between employer and employee'.

In *Wetherall (Bond Street W1) Ltd v Lynn* [1978] ICR 205, where a manager blackguarded the employee in the presence of his subordinates, there was a constructive dismissal. Accusations made by the employer to the employee that the latter has been dishonest without any basis for the accusations will also be a breach of the implied term of mutual trust and confidence: *Robinson v Crompton Parkinson Ltd* [1978] ICR 401. However, see *Pressurefast Ltd v Turner* (1994) (unreported).

In *Wigan Borough Council v Davies* [1979] ICR 411, the EAT held it was an implied term of the contract of employment that the employer should take reasonable steps to ensure that the employee could do her job without harassment from fellow employees. No such steps had been taken, and the onus was on the employer to show that there were no steps that they could reasonably have taken.

In *White v London Transport Executive* [1981] IRLR 261, it was held that there is an implied term in the contracts of employment of probationary employees that the employer will take reasonable steps to maintain an appraisal of the probationer during a trial period, giving guidance by advice or warning where necessary.

In *Woods v WM Car Services (Peterborough) Ltd* [1981] IRLR 347; see on appeal *Woods v WM Car Services (Peterborough) Ltd* [1982] IRLR 413, the EAT affirmed that there is an implied term that the employer will not, without reasonable and proper cause, conduct itself in a manner calculated or likely to destroy or seriously damage the relationship of confidence and trust between the employer and employee. It held that if an employer persistently attempts to vary an employee's conditions of service, whether the conditions are contractual or otherwise, with a view to getting rid of the employee, or in varying the conditions of service acts in a manner which is calculated or likely to destroy the relationship of confidence and trust, he will have breached an implied term of the contract. The EAT recognised that one effect of the contract test as laid down in *Western Excavating (EEC) Ltd v Sharp, above,* is that an employer who wishes to get rid of an employee or to change the terms of the contract without paying unfair dismissal compensation or a redundancy payment, may try to squeeze out the employee. While not committing any major breach of the contract, the employer attempts to make the employee's life uncomfortable so that the employee resigns or accepts the changed terms. For this reason the implied term that the employer will conduct himself reasonably and not do anything calculated or likely to destroy or damage the relationship of mutual confidence and trust is of great importance.

In *Lewis v Motorworld Garges Ltd, above,* the Court of Appeal held that there may be a series of incidents, some trivial, which cumulatively amount to a repudiatory breach of the implied term not to destroy or damage the relationship of confidence and trust.

In *Bracebridge Engineering Ltd v Darby* [1990] IRLR 3, it was held that an employer's failure to treat allegations of sexual harassment seriously was a breach of the implied term of mutual trust, confidence and support towards a female employee.

In *Hilton International Hotels (UK) Ltd v Protopapa* [1990] IRLR 316, it was held that an unjustified reprimand given by the employee's supervisor which had the effect of humiliating, intimidating and degrading the employee was a breach of the implied term of trust and confidence which went to the root of the contract.

When new implied contractual terms are relied on, it will be for the employee to establish them. Although there may be an express or implied term in some contracts allowing employees to have reasonable time off in an emergency, particularly where large employers are involved, there is no such term over the whole ambit of the employer and employee relationship, particularly where small employers are involved: *Warner v Barber's Stores* [1978] IRLR 109. If the new implied obligation has not been defined and established it is for the tribunal in the circumstances of each case to examine what would be reasonable in the general run of such cases: *Pepper and Hope v Daish* [1980] IRLR 13.

In *Dryden v Greater Glasgow Health Board* [1992] IRLR 469, the employee sought to treat the introduction of a no-smoking policy affecting all employees as a repudiatory breach of an implied term in relation to herself. The EAT held that 'an employer is entitled to make rules for the conduct of employees in their place of work, as he is entitled to give lawful orders, within the scope of the contract; ... once it has been held there is no implied term in the contract which entitled the employee to facilities for smoking, a rule against smoking is, in itself, a lawful rule'. Just because an employer introduces a general rule, with which a particular employee cannot comply, it does not follow the employer has repudiated the employee's contract.

In *Newns v British Airways plc* [1992] IRLR 575, the Court of Appeal held that an employee does not have an implied right enabling him to prevent a proposed transfer of the business in which he is employed, and the employee has no right to prevent the transfer of an undertaking because that transfer will bring about a change in the identity of the employer under reg 5 of the TUPE 1981. Regulation 5 provides for a statutory novation of the contract and the transfer does not in itself constitute a repudiatory breach by the employer. (See Chapter 15 as to Transfer of Undertakings.) But now see reg 5 (4A) and (4B), inserted as from 30 August 1993 by s 33 (1) of the TURERA 1993 whereby an employee can object to becoming an employee of the transferee. In this case the transfer will terminate the employee's contract, but it will not be treated as a dismissal by the transferor for any purpose. This would exclude the possibility of claiming unfair dismissal against a transferor.

Cases invovling allegations of repudiatory conduct by the employer
Some of the following cases were decided before *Western Excavating (ECC) Ltd v Sharp, above,* and although there is no specific reference to the contract test, the point in issue was whether or not there had been a fundamental breach of contract or a breach of a fundamental term by the employer.

Remuneration—non-payment   Generally the employer's failure to pay the employee's wages in accordance with the terms of the contract agreed between them will be a repudiation. This may arise where there is no right for the employer to suspend the employee without pay. Suspension without pay can only take place where there is a contractual term express or implied or such an implied contractual right arising from long usage or custom. Similarly the making of unauthorised deductions from wages may amount to a repudiation. In addition, the deduction may be in contravention of statute: see the Wages Act 1986. A unilateral reduction in the basic rate of pay, even for good reasons and even though it is small, may be a material breach of a fundamental term of the contract: *Industrial Rubber Products v Gillon* [1977] IRLR 389, where a reduction was made to regularise an inadvertent breach of the government's pay policy. However, not every reduction in remuneration will be a breach of a fundamental term. In *Gillies v Richard Daniels and Co Ltd* [1979] IRLR 457, the employer reduced payment made to Gillies for additional duties so that Gillies suffered a reduction of a maximum of £1.50 a week. It was held that although this was a unilateral change by the employer, it was not so fundamental as to strike at the root of the contract.

The employer's failure to give an employee overtime payment which was due to the employee, may also be a fundamental breach going to the root of the contract: *Stokes v Hampstead Wine Co Ltd* [1979] IRLR 298.

Remuneration – change in the method of computing wages   In *Graham v Glenrothes Time Switch Co* [1975] IRLR 43, the employer repudiated the contract where he insisted that a watchmaker should be paid on a piecework rather than a basic wage plus overtime basis.

The employer's unilateral change of an express contractual term as to the receipt of commission by the employee was a fundamental breach. It did not matter that subsequently the employer sought to justify it with figures which could not have been produced at the time of the change: *RF Hill Ltd v Mooney* [1981] IRLR 258.

A change which the employer is entitled to make which results in a reduction of commission may not be a fundamental breach of contract: see (*1*) *Spafax Ltd v Harrison* and (*2*) *Spafax Ltd v Taylor* [1980] IRLR 442.

Remuneration—failure to pay on the contractual date In *Hanlon v Allied Breweries (UK) Ltd* [1975] IRLR 321, a barmaid was suspended with pay following a dispute with her superior. She was not paid as she ought while on suspension in accordance with her contract. The tribunal held that there was a repudiation which entitled the employee to resign and have her resignation treated as constructive dismissal.

However see *Adams v Charles Zub Associates Ltd* [1978] IRLR 551, where the employee was told when he enquired about payment that it depended upon payment being made by a foreign client. There was no breach.

Remuneration—failure to pay an increment This may be a breach of an implied term of the contract where everybody else has an increment or is to be given one and the employee is excluded: *Pepper and Hope v Daish* [1980] IRLR 13. The failure to pay may mean that the employer is treating the employee arbitrarily, capriciously or inequitably in breach of an implied term in the contract: see *FC Gardner Ltd v Beresford* [1978] IRLR 63. Alternatively, the non-payment may amount to victimisation which of itself may be a breach of an implied term.

Remuneration—change in fringe benefits In *Durrant and Cheshire v Clariston Clothing Ltd* [1974] IRLR 360, it was a term of the employment that both employees would receive free transport from their homes to their place of work. The company then discontinued the benefit, and although other proposals for transport were made, no agreement was reached. Free transport was an essential element of the contract, and since there were no other suitable means of getting to work, they resigned. The tribunal held that they had been constructively dismissed. The position may be different where the emoluments or fringe benefits are not fundamental terms of the contract.

Hours of employment A substantial unilateral change in the hours of work or the times at which such hours are worked may amount to a repudiation. An employer insisted that two female employees who worked respectively from 8.00am to 4.00pm and 8.30am to 4.30pm five days a week should change their hours of work to 8.30am to 4.30pm in one week, and from 9.30am to 5.30pm in the next week. Because of family commitments both refused. A tribunal held that by demanding a unilateral revision of the hours under which these ladies were employed, the employer had breached their contracts of employment: *Muggridge and Slade v East Anglia Plastics Ltd* [1973] IRLR 163. Similarly, altering the employee's shifts from night to day shifts is a breach of contract: *Simmonds v Dowty Seals Ltd* [1978] IRLR 211. See also *Spencer Jones v Timmens Freeman* [1974] IRLR 325 and *Derby City Council v Marshall* [1979] IRLR 261.

Where the contractual terms on hours of work are varied by an agreement with the union, a change may be a repudiation of the individual's contract. In *Singh v British Steel Corporation* [1974] IRLR 131, Singh was required to change his shift system to one which involved regular weekend working. The change in the system had been agreed with the union although there were no provisions in any agreement with the employee that the employer could change the system unilaterally. Singh had been a member of the union but ceased to pay union dues, after which he no longer considered himself a member of the union, nor bound by its agreements. The agreement modifying the shift system was reached after Singh ceased to be a union member and was thus held not to be binding upon him. The tribunal was not prepared to imply a term in the contract that the employee should be bound by agreements reached between the union and the employer, since there was no evidence establishing incorporation of the agreement in the individual's contract of employment.

There must be a firm proposal to alter the employee's hours of work. A mere suggestion by the employer as a basis for discussion, however, is not a repudiation of the contract of employment.

Where the employer has a contractual right to alter unilaterally the hours of work or to alter the pattern of shiftworking, the exercise of that power cannot be regarded as a breach by the employer. See *Dal and Others v AS Orr* [1980] IRLR 413.

Duties A substantial unilateral change in the work that the employee is required to do which involves a change of duties and loss of prestige is likely to amount to a repudiation. In *Coleman v S and W Baldwin (t/a Baldwins)* [1977] IRLR 342, the employee's duties as a buyer were an important part of his job. His employer took these away and left him with humdrum duties which involved a loss of job satisfaction and prestige. It was held there was a repudiation by the employer. A change in emphasis in an employee's duties from bar steward to catering assistant, where under the terms of the contract he was required to perform both duties, although the catering duties were subsidiary duties, was a breach of contract: *Pedersen v London Borough of Camden* [1981] IRLR 173. A resolution to remove the secretarial part of a club steward's duties amounted to a fundamental breach, and the fact that the resolution was invalid under the club rules did not prevent a finding of constructive dismissal: *Warnes and Another v The Trustees of Cheriton Oddfellows Social Club* [1993] IRLR 58. However, the removal of part of the contractual duties which the employee enjoys doing most is unlikely to be a breach. The employee cannot insist on doing those duties which he likes most: *Peter Carnie and Son Ltd v Paton* [1979] IRLR 260. A change in the employee's duties may be a breach of the contract by the employer even though the employee is leaving the employer and the change is to protect the employer's business interest: *Ford v Milthorn Toleman Ltd* [1980] IRLR 30.

Where an employer requires an employee to transfer to less skilled employment for an indefinite although temporary duration this may be a constructive dismissal: *Millbrook Furnishing Industries Ltd v McIntosh* [1981] IRLR 309. In this case it was not clear whether or not the employees were, in addition, going to suffer a reduction in their pay. The EAT considered that a temporary transfer to a different department for a specified or short fixed period was unlikely to be a constructive dismissal. In *McNeill v Charles Crimin (Electrical Contractors) Ltd* [1984] IRLR 179, it was held that where the employer required the employee, a foreman electrician, to work on tools under the supervision or direction of an ordinary electrician, there had been a breach of the fundamental term of the contract. There was no evidence that this change was to be permanent. It is sufficient if there is any substantial alteration in the terms and conditions of employment.

The change in duties may be accompanied by other changes. The demotion of an executive to the status of clerk, the deprivation of discretion in the way in which she performed her new duties, and the taking away of a car for her own exclusive use were held to be a repudiation of the contract: *Moore v Rowland Winn (Batley) Ltd* [1975] IRLR 162.

A change of status unaccompanied by other changes may amount to a repudiation: see *Stephenson and Co (Oxford) Ltd v Austin* [1990] ICR 609.

The contract may provide for a change in duties and status following disciplinary action. Under the disciplinary procedure of British Rail, a reduction in grade is one of the disciplinary measures which can be imposed. It is accepted custom and practice by both sides in the industry as an implied term of the contract. In *Theedom v British Railways Board* [1976] IRLR 137, a change in the employee's grade from signalman to leading railwayman as a disciplinary measure was not a repudiation of the contract of service, though it might be if the punishment were grossly out of proportion to the offence or if it were imposed for improper motives. See also *Phillips v Glendale Cabinet Co Ltd* [1977] IRLR 307.

In *BBC v Beckett* [1983] IRLR 43, it was held that Beckett's contract had been repudiated by the employer. There was a contractual power to demote an employee who had been guilty of a disciplinary offence. However, there was an obligation on the employer to act reasonably in exercising the power and, in the circumstances of the case, disciplinary demotion involving a loss of status and pay was outside the band of reasonable penalties which a reasonable employer might impose. See also *Cawley v South Wales Electricity Board* [1985] IRLR 89.

Promotion A failure to upgrade an employee where there is no express or implied contractual right to be upgraded will not entitle the employee to claim a constructive dismissal: *Bridgen v Lancashire County Council* [1987] IRLR 58.

Place of employment A change in the place of the employee's employment may amount to a repudiation. Again the change will have to be fundamental.

In *Grace and Anderson v Northgate Group Ltd* [1972] IRLR 53, there was no repudiation when the two waitresses who worked in the directors' dining-room were asked to work in the executives' dining-room, but where a labourer refused to transfer from King's Lynn to Roxton and resigned, he was held to be dismissed, although he had worked away from King's Lynn, which was his home, on a previous occasion. The terms and conditions of his employment were governed by a working rule agreement covering the company's operations and the employee was not a mobile operative within that agreement: *Aldridge v Dredging and Construction Co Ltd* [1972] IRLR 67.

A change in the employee's place of employment where it has been agreed that he shall not be moved out of a certain area, will amount to a repudiation of the contract: *Hawker Siddeley Power Engineering Ltd v Rump* [1979] IRLR 425. In *Little v Charterhouse Magna Assurance Co Ltd* [1980] IRLR 19, Little was required to perform such duties as were necessary for the conduct and management of the company's affairs. There was no express term in the contract of employment as to location. It was held that there was an implied term that the employee could be required to move and there was no geographical limitation implied in the contract. There was no breach by the employer when the employee was required to move from Uxbridge to Bletchley. In *Jones v Associated Tunnelling Co Ltd* [1981] IRLR 477, it was held that the contract cannot be silent on the place of work. If there is no express term then the term may be implied from the surrounding circumstances. Here the employee could be required to work at any site within reasonable daily commuting distance from his home and there was no constructive dismissal on being so required.

If an employer wishes to rely on a mobility clause, he must make it clear that he is relying on it when the move is proposed. To rely on an alternative offer of suitable employment is a quite different course, and he cannot dodge between both hoping to adopt the most profitable at the end of the day: see Knox J in *Curling v Securicor Ltd* [1992] IRLR 549.

Assistance In *Associated Type Specialists (Eastern) Ltd v Waterhouse* [1976] ICR 218, the employee, a supervisor, had complaints made against her by her subordinates because she was too strict and she was given a warning by her employer. The employer than failed to tell her about further complaints which were made. She was given no guidance by her employer as to whether or not her efforts to improve were successful. The subordinates walked out and she resigned. It was held that the employer had breached an implied term of the contract in not giving her management support and assistance in carrying out her duties on their behalf. See also *Seligman and Latz Ltd v McHugh* [1979] IRLR 130.

Provision of work The employer's failure to provide the employee with work will not amount to a repudiation of the contract, except in certain cases, provided the employee is remunerated. If the employer suspends or lays-off the employee without pay where he has no contractual right to do so, it will amount to a repudiation of the contract of employment. Exceptions arise where it is a term of the contract, express or implied, that the employer will provide work, or where the employee is to have the opportunity of practising his skills, gaining experience, increasing his earnings or enhancing his reputation.

The overall circumstances of the contract may mean that the employer has to give the employee work, as where the employee is entitled to practise his skill etc. The contract must be looked at as a whole to decide whether the employer is obliged to provide the employee with work: *Breach v Epsylon Industries Ltd* [1976] ICR 316 and *Bosworth v Angus Jowett and Co Ltd* [1977] IRLR 374. The obligation to provide the employee with work may be greater where higher management is involved.

See, however, *Langston v Amalgamated Union of Engineering Workers* [1974] ICR 180, where Lord Denning MR said, *obiter*, that there might be an implied term in every contract that an employee has a right to work.

Safety At common law the employer is under a duty to take reasonable care to ensure that the plant, premises and system of work are safe. The Factories Act 1961, the Offices, Shops and Railway Premises Act 1963, and Health and Safety at Work etc Act 1974 as amended and regulations made thereunder have imposed considerable obligations on the employer to ensure the health, safety and welfare of his employees. The employer's failure to take reasonable steps to ensure the safety of his employees may be a fundamental breach of an implied term of the contract either that the employer will take reasonable steps to ensure the safety of employees or that the employer will observe the law.

In *Pagano v HGS* [1976] IRLR 9, Pagano had made numerous complaints about the condition of the company's vans. One which he considered unsafe was checked, found to have faults and a prohibition order was imposed. He made complaints about the van and the servicing and resigned. The tribunal found that because of his concern about the vans and the lack of concern by the employer Pagano was justified in terminating his employment.

In *Keys v Shoefayre Ltd* [1978] IRLR 476, the employer's failure to improve security following an armed robbery was held to be a breach of the employer's obligation to take reasonable care to operate a safe system of work and to take reasonable care to have reasonably safe premises. See also *Graham Oxley Tool Steels Ltd v Firth* [1980] IRLR 135.

It is likely that any serious failure by the employer to ensure his employee's safety will entitle the employee to resign and claim constructive dismissal: see *British Aircraft Corporation Ltd v Austin* [1978] IRLR 332; *Lindsay v Dunlop Ltd* [1980] IRLR 93; *Dutton and Clark Ltd v Daly* [1985] IRLR 363. See also Chapter 13 with regard to the new automatically unfair dismissal provisions introduced by the TURERA 1993.

Rudeness and abuse   The employer's use of rude or insulting language where it amounts to a repudiation of the contract entitles the employee to claim constructive dismissal: *Palmanor Ltd (t/a Chaplins Night Club) v Cedron* [1978] ICR 1008. In *Wares v Caithness Leather Products Ltd* [1974] IRLR 162, a female employee was constructively dismissed where foul language which was excessive and unreasonable was used in reprimanding her for taking time off. In *MacNeilage v Arthur Roye (Turf Accountants) Ltd* [1976] IRLR 88, a female assistant was constructively dismissed where a branch manager called her a 'bloody fat sod and stupid stuck up bitch', having earlier sworn at her in front of customers. In *Isle of Wight Tourist Board v Coombes* [1976] IRLR 413, a female secretary was constructively dismissed where her boss said of her in front of another employee 'She is an intolerable bitch on a Monday morning.' The mutual confidence and trust had been destroyed.

Disciplinary procedure   The employer's failure to follow a contractual disciplinary procedure may be a repudiation of the contract as in *The Post Office v Strange* [1981] IRLR 515, where the employer's failure to allow an appeal against a disciplinary penalty to the proper level of management led to the imposition of a penalty which was a nullity and the employer's requirement that the employee comply with the penalty was a breach of contract. The lesson for employers is not to make the disciplinary procedure contractual.

Warnings   The giving of a justified warning to an employee cannot amount to a breach of an implied term in the contract entitling the employee to claim constructive dismissal. The giving of a warning, even though objectively unfair, will not necessarily amount to a repudiation of the contract. An unjustified reprimand given in an officious and insensitive manner was held to be a repudiatory breach in *Protopapa*'s case, *above*. Further, the EAT has expressed the view that the giving of an unjustified warning or a series of warnings without legitimate complaint, aimed not at improving the employee's conduct or performance but at disheartening him and driving him out of employment, might amount to a constructive dismissal: *Walker v Josiah Wedgwood and Sons Ltd* [1978] ICR 744. See also *Woods v WM Car Services (Peterborough) Ltd* [1981] IRLR 347; on appeal *Woods v WM Car Services (Peterborough) Ltd* [1982] IRLR 413. The circumstances in each case have to be carefully investigated.

Strikes It has been suggested that if an employer provokes or engineers a strike or other industrial action in a gross manner, this may be conduct amounting to a repudiation of the contract. It is interesting to speculate whether it is a repudiation requiring acceptance or whether the contract comes to an end automatically. If it is the latter, the action of the employee going on strike would occur after the contract came to and end and could not therefore amount to a termination of the contract: *Thompson v Eaton Ltd* [1976] ICR 336.

Victimisation Victimisation of the employee by the employer will not entitle the employee to resign and claim constructive dismissal, unless it is a fundamental breach of the contract of employment or a breach of a fundamental term.

Failure to pay an award following a pay review, failure to include an employee in an annual pay review coupled with complaints about job performance, preferential treatment of other employees, warning of a redundancy situation with criticism of an employee's work, and advertising an employee's job while he is still employed, have been pleaded as acts of victimisation, but each have been held not to amount to a repudiation. For two cases where aggravation or victimisation were established see: *Bariamis v John Stephen of London Ltd* [1975] IRLR 237 and *Fanshaw v Robinsons and Sons Ltd* [1975] IRLR 165.

Repudiation and contracts generally

It is a general principle that the repudiation of a contract does not in itself terminate the contract, unless the circumstances of the repudiation are such that the continuance of the contract is totally impossible. Save where performance is totally impossible upon a repudiation, the innocent party is entitled to ignore the breach and insist upon the performance of the contract or alternatively to accept the repudiation. In the former case each party remains bound by the contract, and the innocent party is entitled to sue for damages for loss caused by the breach. In the latter case the contract is terminated from the time the innocent party elects to accept the repudiation. The rights and obligations of the parties under the contract to that time are preserved and the innocent party is entitled to sue for damages.

In *Hogan v ACP Heavy Fabrications Ltd* (1994) (unreported), the EAT held that where an employee resigns because of a fundamental breach by the employer, acceptance of the resignation is unnecessary. The resignation was effective and the employee was constructively dismissed.

Repudiation and the contract of employment There has been a considerable division of judicial opinion upon the question whether or not the contract of employment comes within the general principles outlined above or whether, in this respect, it is a contract *sui generis*. One of the difficulties about the contract of employment in practical terms is that where the employer repudiates the contract by wrongfully dismissing the employee, it is difficult to provide a remedy which will keep the contract alive. It is this practical problem which has often led to the finding that a repudiation by the employer automatically brings the contract to an end, so that the employee cannot elect to keep the contract alive.

Repudiation and wrongful dismissal Although this chapter is concerned with constructive dismissal for the purposes of unfair dismissal rather than wrongful dismissal, it is helpful to examine the way in which the courts have approached the problem of the need for acceptance in cases of wrongful dismissal.

Broadly, the traditional view has been that where the employer wrongfully dimisses the employee the employer's repudiation automatically terminates the contract of employment without the need for acceptance by the employee: see *Vine v National Dock Labour Board* [1956] 1 QB 658 and on appeal [1957] AC 488. It was recognised that the employee might suffer because wrongful dismissal brought the contract to an end without the need for acceptance and that the employee's remedy would usually be damages. Rarely can the employee keep the contract alive in practical terms, whether or not the contract exists in theory. Furthermore, since the employee's claim is for damages rather than remuneration and he is obliged to mitigate his loss, he is usually well advised to treat the contract as being at an end as quickly as possible: see *Denmark Productions Ltd v Boscobel Productions Ltd* [1969] 1 QB 699 and *Marsh v National Autistic Society* [1993] ICR 453.

In *Decro-Wall International SA v Practitioners in Marketing Ltd* [1971] 1 WLR 361, the Court of Appeal doubted whether wrongful dismissal brought a contract of service to an end in law although no doubt in practice it does. It considered that the contract remained alive in principle although no action could successfully be brought to preserve the contract in practical terms. What was limited was not the employee's right to elect to preserve the contract but the range of remedies available to the employee.

In *Hill v CA Parsons and Co Ltd* [1972] 1 Ch 305, Hill was granted an injunction against the employer preventing it from treating the contract as at an end. Here the confidential nature of the relationship between the employer and the employee had not been affected by the dismissal, and so it was possible for the relationship to continue. The majority of the Court of Appeal, while accepting that where the employer wrongfully terminates the contract of employment the employment relationship comes to an end, found that in special circumstances the court may grant a declaration that the relationship still exists and an injunction to prevent the employer treating it as at an end. In this case the employee did not accept the repudiation, the notice was too short and damages were an inadequate remedy. See also *GKN (Cwmbran) Ltd v Lloyd* [1972] ICR 214, and *Robb v Hammersmith and Fulham London Borough Council* [1991] ICR 514.

In *Sanders v Ernest A Neale Ltd* [1974] ICR 565, the National Industrial Relations Court (NIRC) held that where the employer has wrongfully dismissed the employee, acceptance of the employer's repudiation by the employee is not necessary: the contract will come to an end without acceptance. The employee's refusal to accept the repudiation cannot keep the contract alive. The NIRC accepted that there might be rare exceptions such as *Hill v CA Parsons and Co Ltd*, *above*.

In *Brown v Southall and Knight* [1980] IRLR 130, the EAT held, in a case involving unfair dismissal, that wrongful dismissal brought the contract of employment to an end without the need for acceptance by the employee. There will be a dismissal within s 55(2)(*a*) of the EP(C)A 1978, whether or not the repudiation is accepted.

In *Gunton v The Mayor Aldermen and Burgesses of the London Borough of Richmond-upon-Thames* [1980] IRLR 321, Gunton was held to have been wrongfully dismissed where the authority failed to follow the terms of a disciplinary procedure incorporated in Gunton's contract of employment. It was held that a wrongful dismissal does not automatically terminate the contract of employment and the repudiation on the part of the employer needs acceptance. Buckley LJ recognised that because of the nature of the contract of employment, in many cases it would be very difficult for the employee to do other than accept the employer's repudiation. In the absence of special circumstances, the court 'should easily infer that the innocent party has accepted the guilty party's repudiation of the contract'. Brightman LJ found that where the employee did not accept the wrongful dismissal the contract remained alive even though it put an end to the status or relationship of the parties. See also *Dietman v Brent London Borough Council* [1987] ICR 737 where the High Court followed *Gunton's* case.

In *Robert Cort and Son Ltd v Charman* [1981] ICR 816, it was held that in determining the effective date of termination under s 55(4) of the EP(C)A 1978, wrongful dismissal brings the contract of employment to an end without the need for acceptance. The EAT found that it was of the greatest importance that there should be no doubt or uncertainty as to the effective date of termination. Uncertainty could result if the identification of the effective date of termination depended upon the law of repudiation and acceptance of repudiation. In *BMK Ltd and BMK Holdings Ltd v Logue* [1993] ICR 601, Knox J said that to look at the employee's own understanding of when the contract had come to an end was wrong. He referred to *Charman's* case which showed that there is no single principle in constructive dismissal cases that there must be an acceptance by the employee. He held that for determining the effective date of termination in a constructive dismissal case the correct approach was to look at the wording of s 55(4)(*b*) of the EP(C)A 1978 which states that the effective date of termination is the date on which the termination takes effect.

If wrongful dismissal does not bring the contract to an end without the employee's acceptance, once the employee has accepted the employer's repudiation, is it the employer's initial repudiation which terminates the contract or the employee's acceptance? There is authority for the proposition that it is the employee's acceptance that terminates the contract: see *Western Excavating (ECC) Ltd v Sharp, above.* This produces a strange result in that it is the employee rather than the employer who terminates the contract. The statutory provisions have been drafted on the basis that wrongful dismissal brings the contract of employment to an end without the need for acceptance.

However, recent cases suggest that wrongful dismissal does not bring the contract to an end without acceptance. Indeed, cases in which injunctions have been granted are inconsistent with a view that repudiation does not require acceptance. See *Dietman's* case, *above.*

If the contract is brought to an end by repudiatory conduct without the need for acceptance, the guilty party may thereby relieve himself from performing his contractual obligations leaving the innocent party simply with a claim for damages: see *Evening Standard Co Ltd v Henderson* [1987] ICR 588.

Repudiation other than wrongful dismissal   Does a repudiation by the employer where there is no actual dismissal operate to determine the contract without the need for acceptance?

In *Thomas Marshall (Exports) Ltd v Guinle and Others* [1978] ICR 905, the employee was in breach of a term in his contract that during the continuance of his employment he was not to engage in any other business without the employer's consent. Megarry VC held that if employment cases are subject to the doctrine of automatic termination upon a fundamental breach of contract or breach of a fundamental term then there would be a termination of the contract, even though the innocent party did not know of the breach or, if he had known, would have elected to keep the contract in existence.

In *Rasool and Others v Hepworth Pipe Co Ltd* [1980] IRLR 88, the EAT, following the tribunal in *Sealey and Others v Avon Aluminium Co Ltd* [1978] IRLR 285, found:

> the cases support a cross division of fundamental breaches into (i) employer's and (ii) employee's breaches which:
> (*a*) being or entailing a deliberate curtailment of the contract, effectively terminate it without more, and those which
> (*b*) merely entitle the other party at his option to treat it as discharged, 'accepting' the repudiation, and thus lawfully terminating the contract without notice.

In *London Transport Executive v Clarke* [1981] IRLR 166, the majority of the Court of Appeal held that the repudiation requires acceptance by the innocent party, so the general rule of contract law applies to contracts of employment. See the judgment of Templeman LJ at p 170, where he said that in employment cases at common law 'self dismissal' and 'acceptance of repudiation' are usually simultaneous both being implied rather than express where affirmation of the contract would be meaningless. However, there may be cases where it is not clear whether an employee's breach of contract is repudiatory or not. The employee may expressly or impliedly try to persuade the employer to continue the contract and, if the employer refuses, the tribunal may first have to decide if the employee's breach is repudiatory or not. If it is, then the tribunal must next decide whether or not the repudiation amounts to a self-dismissal. If the breach was repudiatory and amounted to self dismissal then to be able to proceed to consider the question of fairness or unfairness the employee must establish conduct by the employer which turns the self dismissal into a constructive one. If, however, the employee's breach was not repudiatory, or if it were but did not amount to a self-dismissal, then the tribunal must assume the contract was terminated by the employer and consider fairness in the normal way. He said that these complications only arise if there is an exception in the case of contracts of employment to the common law rule that repudiation requires acceptance. He thought that the exception was contrary to principle. If the employee leaves work and does not claim to be entitled to return, that is a repudiation which is accepted by the employer taking no action to affirm the contract. He must claim constructive dismissal to be able to proceed on the question of whether the dismissal was fair or unfair. If, however, the employee leaves employment but then claims he is entitled to return then the contract is only terminated if the employer expressly or impliedly accepts the employee's repudiation, either by formal writing or refusing to allow the employee to return. If the contract is determined by the employer accepting the repudiation the tribunal then has to decide the question of unfair dismissal.

It is not clear from the judgment of Templeman LJ whether the employer who refuses to have the employee back dismisses the employee or not. In *Rigby v Ferodo Ltd* [1987] ICR 457, confirmed on appeal by the House of Lords [1988] ICR 29, it was held that a repudiatory breach of the contract of employment, being the employer's unilateral reduction in wages, did not bring the contract to an end without acceptance by the employee. Rigby continued in employment not accepting the breach and sued for the underpayment.

It is clear from these authorities that repudiation by the employer, (in a case other than where he wrongfully dismisses the employee), or by the employee, requires acceptance by the other to bring the contract to an end, except perhaps in exceptional circumstances.

If the employer's repudiation needs acceptance by the employee, and the employee's repudiation needs acceptance by the employer to bring the contract to an end, by whom is the contract terminated? In *Western Excavating (ECC) Ltd v Sharp, above*, Lord Denning MR held that where the employer repudiates one or more essential terms of the contract and the employee accepts the repudiation, the employee's acceptance results in the termination of the contract. This is consistent with s 55(2)(*c*) of the EP(C)A 1978. It must be borne in mind that this was not a case where the repudiation consisted of wrongful dismissal. Conversely, if it is the employee who has been guilty of repudiatory conduct, it must be the employer's acceptance which terminates the contract. Thus, there will be a dismissal in law, see s 55(2)(*a*) of the EP(C)A 1978. See also *Sealey v Avon Aluminium Co Ltd, above.* If, however, the acceptance of the repudiation results in the termination of the contract by the party repudiating the same, then in the case of the employee who repudiated the contract, the employer's acceptance of the repudiation would mean that it was the employee who had terminated the contract.

Notwithstanding the decision in *Western Excavating (ECC) Ltd v Sharp, above*, the EAT has, on occasions, reached a different conclusion. Thus in *Kallinos v London Electric Wire* [1980] IRLR 11, the EAT found 'that where there is a fundamental breach of contract the person who is guilty of the fundamental breach so that it amounts to a repudiation of that contract is the party to the contract who is bringing the contract to an end'. In this case it was the employee who brought the contract to an end when he was discovered asleep in the rest room when he should have been on duty.

In *Rasool and Others v Hepworth Pipe Co Ltd* [1980] IRLR 88, the EAT followed the decision in *Western Excavating (ECC) Ltd v Sharp, above*, and found that attendance at an unauthorised mass meeting was a repudiation of the contract of employment by the employee and it was open to the employer to accept the repudiation which it did. The employer's acceptance of the repudiation terminated the contract of employment and so the employee was dismissed. In this case Waterhouse J held that:

> it would be unfortunate if the impact of the unfair dismissal legislation were to depend in many cases on the whim of the employer (with or without legal advice) in deciding how to respond to a fundamental breach.... If a restrictive interpretation were to be applied to the word 'terminated' in ... [s 55(2)(a) of the EP(C)A 1978] the result would be that a large category of decisions to 'dismiss' by employers would be excluded from scrutiny by Industrial Tribunals, and it is most unlikely that this was the intention of Parliament.

It is submitted that in the vast majority of cases the authority in *Rasool v Hepworth Pipe Co Ltd, above*, will be preferred, although there may be certain exceptional cases where there can be a self-dismissal. The tribunal recognised this in *Sealey v Avon Aluminium Co Ltd above*, and it was recognised in a dissenting judgment of Lord Denning MR in *Clarke*'s case, *above*, and also it seems in the judgment of Templeman LJ in that case. The view that an employee may, by his repudiatory conduct, bring the contract of employment to an end, is the antithesis of the view that wrongful dismissal brings the contract to an end without the need for acceptance by the employee. If wrongful dismissal needs acceptance, then it would seem unlikely that the concept of self-dismissal can survive in any form.

The reason for leaving

The employer's breach of contract must be sufficiently serious to entitle the employee to leave and claim constructive dismissal. The employee must leave as a result of the breach and not as a result of any other circumstances. In *Logabax Ltd v Titherley* [1977] IRLR 97, the EAT held that the employee must clearly and unambiguously show that he claims a constructive dismissal.

In *Walker v Josiah Wedgwood and Sons Ltd* [1978] IRLR 105, Arnold J held that the employee must leave clearly because of the employer's breach of contract, rather than just leaving, and because of that breach rather than for some other ground.

This was approved by the EAT in *Norwest Holst Group Administration Ltd v Harrison* [1984] IRLR 419. Equivocal conduct which is consistent with the contract remaining in force will not amount to an acceptance: *Spencer v Marchington* [1988] IRLR 392.

Waiver of the breach

Where the employer has repudiated the contract and the employee wishes to rely upon the repudiation, he must not do anything which amounts to a waiver of the repudiation. Where the employer, for instance, unilaterally alters a fundamental term of the contract, the employee may reject the unilateral alteration expressly or, without making any express statement, he may seek employment elsewhere. However, he may expressly accept the unilateral alteration and remain in the employment or without any express statement he may remain in the employment. If so, he will acquiesce or waive the repudiation and he will have difficulty pleading the repudiation at a later date: *Betteridge v CA Parsons and Co Ltd and AUEW* [1973] IRLR 228; *Crapper v Butler Machine Tool Co Ltd* [1973] IRLR 194.

As Lord Denning said in *Western Excavating (ECC) Ltd v Sharp* [1978] ICR 221, 'he must make up his mind soon after the conduct of which he complains: for, if he continues for any length of time without leaving, he will lose his right to treat himself as discharged. He will be regarded as having elected to affirm the contract.'

Where the employee continues in the same employment, for any length of time he may, in exceptional circumstances, be taken not to have acquiesced in the change and therefore not to have affirmed the contract. However, he should make his position clear, otherwise it may be fatal. In *Marriott v Oxford and District Co-operative Society Ltd (No 2)* [1970] 1 QB 186, Marriott was an electrical maintenance foreman. The side of the business in which he worked declined and his services were no longer required. He was told by the society that it would continue to employ him as a supervisor with a reduction in wages. Marriott complained and never accepted the transfer, although he continued to work for three or four weeks for the society following the change, and he looked for work elsewhere. He subsequently left and claimed a dismissal. It was held that he had been dismissed following the repudiation of the contract by the society. By remaining in employment for three to four weeks after the repudiation, he had not accepted the repudiation. He had never concurred with the changed terms. He had protested about the terms, but he remained in employment so that he would not be unemployed while he looked elsewhere. See also *Air Canada v Lee* [1978] ICR 1202.

In *Bashir v Brillo Manufacturing Co* [1979] IRLR 295, an employee who fell sick following a change in the terms of his contract and accepted sick pay for two and a half months, and had made it clear that the change was not accepted, was able to claim a constructive dismissal. Here, the EAT distinguished the case where an employee actually performs his work from the case where he simply receives sick pay to which he might have been entitled in any event under the terms of his contract.

In *Hunt v British Railways Board* [1979] IRLR 379, Hunt, who claimed that he was constructively dismissed following disciplinary action taken against him by the Board, was still reporting to work at the time of the tribunal hearing. It was held that he had waived the breach. The concept of constructive dismissal does not allow the employee to go on acting as if he was employed when what the employee is trying to say is that he is no longer employed.

In *WE Cox Toner (International) Ltd v Crook* [1981] IRLR 443, the EAT held that Lord Denning's summary of the law in the *Western Excavating* case, *above*, was not intended to be a comprehensive statement of the whole law. It had to be seen in the context of the general principles of contract law. Once the innocent party affirms the contract, his right to accept the repudiation is at an end. However, he is not bound to make an election either within a reasonable time or any other time. Delay by itself does not constitute an affirmation of the contract unless there is express or implied affirmation of the contract. Prolonged delay may be evidence of an implied affirmation. Implied affirmation may arise where the innocent party requires the guilty party to perform the contract further. It may arise if the innocent party himself does something which is only consistent with the continued existence of the contract unless the innocent party, while further performing the contract to a limited extent, makes it clear that he is reserving his rights to accept the repudiation or is only performing the contract so as to allow the guilty party to remedy the breach. The EAT recognised that there was an obvious difference between a contract of employment and most other contracts in that if the employee, following a repudiation of the contract by the employer, reports to work the next day, he will be acting in a way which in one sense is only consistent with the continued existence of the contract. Similarly, when he accepts his next pay packet there is strong evidence that he is affirming the contract. Much depends upon the evidence. Delay in accepting the repudiation is only one factor which may be relevant.

In *Reid v Camphill Engravers* [1990] ICR 435, the employer failed to pay wages in accordance with a Wages Council Order for three years. It was held that this was a continuing breach, so that even if the employee had not reacted to the initial breach, he could refer to that initial breach where the employer committed further breaches. The facts were exceptional in that the employee could not in any event affirm a contract at a lower wage than that fixed by a Wages Council.

An employee will not be deemed to have acquiesced by waiting until the change takes place: *Simmonds v Dowty Seals Ltd* [1981] IRLR 211. Indeed there may be circumstances where the employee would be wise to await the change, particularly where changes in the contract are under negotiation. If an employee resigns and claims constructive dismissal before the results of the negotiations are clear, he may be unable to establish a constructive dismissal: *GC Machines Ltd v Forshaw and Malain* (1978) (unreported); see also *Genower v Ealing, Hammersmith and Hounslow Area Health Authority* [1980] IRLR 297.

Where the employer gives the employee an opportunity to make up his mind whether or not to accept the employer's repudiation or affirm the contract, and continues to pay the employee's salary while he is making up his mind, the employee cannot be taken to have waived the repudiation: *Bliss v South East Thames Regional Health Authority* [1985] IRLR 308. In this case Dillon LJ considered *Payman v Lanjani* [1985] 2 WLR 154, a case not involving employment law, where May LJ found that a party to a contract cannot be shown to have irrevocably chosen between rescission and affirmation unless he knew of the other party's serious breach and also knew of the fact that he had the right to make the choice.

In *Bliss*'s case Dillon LJ commented that the acceptance of this formidable argument could have considerable repercussions in employment law. The acceptance of a new contract will not necessarily mean the employee has waived a breach of the original contract: *Hogg v Dover College* [1990] ICR 39.

The employee must be careful as to the language which he uses when notifying his employer that he is resigning because of the employer's repudiatory conduct. A request by the employee to the employer to leave which is answered in the affirmative may well be a termination by mutual agreement and will not be treated as the employee's acceptance of the employer's repudiation. Whereas in the case of a termination by mutual agreement the employee may seek and obtain the employer's consent, in the case of a constructive dismissal the employee tells the employer that because of the employer's conduct he is going without a by-your-leave: *Lipton (L) Ltd v Marlborough* [1979] IRLR 179.

Anticipatory breach
The employer may give notice that he will not perform his obligations in the future or he may do something preventing the performance of the contract in the future. Such a breach is called an anticipatory breach. Generally, in the case of anticipatory breach, the innocent party may accept the repudiation and enforce the appropriate remedy, or wait until the time fixed for performance arrives. If the contract is then not performed the innocent party has the usual remedies. Where there is an anticipatory breach which is repudiatory of the contract of employment by the employer, the principles enunciated *above* as to acceptance apply. Where the employee does not accept the repudiation but waits until the time fixed for performance, the employer may perform the contract and, in effect, withdraw the repudiation and avoid a constructive dismissal situation.

In *Norwest Holst Group Administration Ltd v Harrison* [1985] IRLR 240, Harrison was employed as a director and manager in Derby. On 14 June 1982 the company wrote to him telling him that the design office would close on 30 June 1982, and that he would be based at Chesterfield but would no longer be a director. Harrison replied on 17 June in a letter headed 'without prejudice' saying he considered his contract had been terminated with effect from 30 June. On 18 June the company told Harrison that his salary would not be reduced and on 24 June told him that he could continue as a director although based at Chesterfield. On 25 June Harrison was offered employment with another company and he ceased work with Norwest Holst Group on 30 June. It was held that the employer's action on 14 June amounted to a repudiation of the employer's contract of employment. However, the letter of 17 June did not amount to an unequivocal acceptance of the repudiatory conduct, since it was headed 'without prejudice', the effect of which was to communicate to the company that Harrison was prepared to enter into discussions. Cumming-Bruce LJ quoted from the decision of Buckley LJ in *Gunton v The Mayor Aldermen and Burgesses of the London Borough of Richmond-upon-Thames* [1980] IRLR 321, where Buckley LJ held that where a party evinces an intention not to perform his part of the contract there is no breach until the date for performance arises, but the innocent party may treat the guilty party as having breached the contract in advance of the time for performance. Where some of the guilty party's obligations still remain to be performed, the time for performance of the other part already having arrived, the position is the same and the innocent party can elect to regard himself as relieved from all his own obligations under the contract.

Cumming-Bruce LJ held that these principles applied to the contract of employment. It could not be held that the employer's actions constituted an immediate repudiation of the contract. Harrison had a reasonable period to make up his mind whether or not to accept the repudiation and the company had an opportunity of repentance because there was a sufficient anticipatory element in their breach to confer on them a *locus poenitentiae*. See also *Greenaway Harrison Ltd v Wiles* [1994] IRLR 380.

It must be remembered that a contract of employment is not a contract for perpetual servitude. If the employer tells the employee the contract will come to an end in the future, there is not necessarily an anticipatory breach by the employer. There must be evidence of an inevitable breach of the contract by the employer. Therefore, if there is no suggestion that the contract will not be terminated by the employer in accordance with the terms of the contract then there is no anticipatory breach: *Haseltine Lake and Co v Dowler* [1981] IRLR 25, following the decision in *Universal Cargo Carriers Corporation v Citati* [1957] 2 QB 401.

The proper construction of a contract
Suppose the employer has repudiated the contract as a result of an erroneous interpretation or a genuine mistake of fact or law? In *Frank Wright and Co (Holdings) Ltd v Punch* [1980] IRLR 217, Punch resigned after the employer refused to pay him a cost of living increase

which they were contractually obliged to pay. The employer argued that on their interpretation of the contract they were not obliged to make such a payment. On appeal the employer argued that there was an error of interpretation or a mistake of both fact and law and that it was not to be taken as evincing an intention not to be bound by the contract of employment. The EAT, relying on *Chitty On Contracts*, 24th edn, vol 1, para 14.80, held

> that were there is a genuine dispute as to construction and one party intends to perform the contract on the basis of its mistaken interpretation of it then the courts are unwilling to hold there is a repudiation.

See also *Sweet and Maxwell Ltd v Universal News Services Ltd* [1964] 2 QB 699 and *Woodar Investment Development v Wimpey Construction UK Ltd* [1980] 1 WLR 277.

In *Financial Techniques (Planning Services) Ltd v Hughes* [1981] IRLR 32, there was a dispute between the parties as to the employee's entitlement under a profit sharing scheme. The Court of Appeal did not accept that there had been a repudiatory breach by the employer. The employers were doing no more than arguing their point of view. They had not yet evinced an intention no longer to be bound by the contract. Templeman LJ expressed caution against holding that where a party to a contract has a plausible but mistaken view of his rights under the contract and insists upon his rights, that insistence cannot amount to a repudiation. He further expressed doubt about the decision in *Punch*'s case *above*, in so far as that case lends support to the view that a genuine but mistaken belief as to the terms of the contract may prevent repudiation.

In *Blyth v Scottish Liberal Club* [1983] IRLR 245, the Court of Session found that the decisions in *Sweet and Maxwell* and *Woodar* applied solely to anticipatory and not to actual breaches of contract. In *BBC v Beckett* [1983] IRLR 43, the EAT refused to follow *Woodar*'s case, above, where the employer believed that under the contract of employment it had the power to impose a particular disciplinary sanction where on an objective construction of the contract it did not.

In *Bliss v South East Thames Regional Health Authority* [1985] IRLR 308, the Court of Appeal again distinguished the decision in *Woodar*'s case, *above*, and found that it was not open to the authority to argue that by requiring Bliss to undergo a psychiatric examination which it genuinely believed it was entitled to do, its actions could not be repudiatory since the authority did not indicate any intention not to be bound by the contract. The authority was not purporting to exercise any power in the contract. It had to be judged not by its intentions, but by objective standards.

The most recent re-statement of the law is in *Brown v JBD Engineering Ltd* [1993] IRLR 568, where the EAT held that the tribunal had misdirected itself in law in holding that where an employer acts upon a genuine, though mistaken, belief then the act cannot found a plea of constructive dismissal. However, in cases where the employer's belief was reasonable and was brought about wholly or in part by the employee's conduct, the fact the employer acted on the genuine though mistaken belief may be treated as a relevant factor in determining whether or not there has been a material breach of contract. A genuine belief is not on its own sufficient to prevent the employer's action amounting to a repudiation. The tribunal should have asked itself 'whether anything done by the respondents amounted to a breach of contract going to the root of the agreement between the parties given the whole circumstances of the case, including ... the fact that the appellant had not attended for work ... for some time, and the respondents' belief that he would not return to work there.'

For circumstances where a constructively dismissed employee can suffer a reduction in compensation because he has contributed to his dismissal, see *Polentarutti v Autokraft Ltd* [1991] IRLR 457, and Chapter 16.

Pregnant employee's right to return to work

For the special rules relating to this situation, see Chapter 10.

Employee resignation

An employee who resigns, whether with or without notice, is not dismissed unless there is a constructive dismissal or there is a forced resignation. In certain circumstances, the employer may not be able to rely upon the words of resignation and may find that in those circumstances there is a dismissal if the employment comes to an end: see *Gale (BG) Ltd v Gilbert* [1978] ICR 1149 and *Sothern v Franks Charlesly and Co* [1981] IRLR 278. Thus, where the employee resigns during the course of a heated argument or discussion, then it seems that provided he withdraws his words of resignation almost immediately, the resignation will not take effect: *Martin v Yeoman Aggregates Ltd* [1983] IRLR 49. Again, the employer may not be able to rely on the words of resignation if the employee is an immature employee, the decision was taken in the heat of the moment or the employee was jostled into the decision by the employer, or where idle words are used under emotional stress which the employer knew or ought to have known were not meant to be taken seriously. For a recent example, see *Kwik-Fit (GB) Ltd v Lineham* [1992] IRLR 156. See also *Ely v YKK Fasteners (UK) Ltd* [1993] IRLR 500, (discussed more fully in Chapter 6 at p 130) where the Court of Appeal held that the tribunal was right to attribute a reason in a case of constructive dismissal where resort could be had to a state of facts known and relied upon by the employer at the time of dismissal.

Forced resignation

An employer may give an employee the option of resigning or being dismissed. If the employee then resigns, does this amount to dismissal? In *East Sussex County Council v Walker* (1972) 7 ITR 280, the NIRC held 'in such circumstances there really can be no other conclusion than that the employer terminated the contract'.

Following this decision tribunals have consistently held that a forced resignation is a dismissal: see *Scott v Formica Ltd* [1975] IRLR 104; *Spencer Jones v Timmens Freeman* [1974] IRLR 325. In such cases, the resignation is in form only and in substance the resignation will be treated as a dismissal: *Robertson v Securicor Transport Ltd* [1972] IRLR 70. The use of persuasion by an employer to obtain an employee's resignation may also be a dismissal. The element of persuasion by the employer is important: *Pascoe v Hallen and Medway* [1975] IRLR 116. However, an ultimatum to perform the contract or resign may not amount to a dismissal and each case will depend upon the circumstances. In *Chapple v Andrew Antenna Systems* [1975] IRLR 7, the employer told the employees that he did not intend to recognise their union, and they were told that if they did not want to accept the position and preferred to resign, they would be given a severance payment. The applicant resigned and it was held that he had not been dismissed either expressly or constructively. He had been given an opportunity to resign with severance pay or to continue in his employment, but with the knowledge that the employer did not intend to recognise the union. He had chosen to resign.

It may be that even though the employee has been given the option of resigning or being dismissed there is no dismissal in law because the employee resigns in consideration of the financial inducement or other terms offered to him to resign: *Sheffield v Oxford Controls Co Ltd* [1979] ICR 396. Arnold J held that in some cases the resignation can only be a dismissal. The principle is one of causation and the causation is the threat. The threat of dismissal causes the employee to resign. However, in other cases the actual causation of the resignation is the employee's state of mind, ie that he is happy to resign on negotiated and satisfactory terms and here there can be no dismissal.

In *Martin v MBS Fastenings (Glynwed) Distribution Ltd* [1983] IRLR 198, the employee used the company's minibus on a Sunday to go and watch a company football match. He was involved in an accident and was breathalysed with positive results. He was told by the company that there would be an inquiry which would probably result in his dismissal and that it would be in his own interests to resign rather than to face an inquiry. It was held that the employee had resigned. He had been presented with an option and had chosen voluntarily to resign. The question of whether or not in such circumstances there is a dismissal in law is a question of fact for the tribunal.

See *Caledonian Mining Co Ltd v Bassett and Steel* [1987] IRLR 165, where the employees were 'inveigled' into resigning by the employer. They were in substance dismissed.

Again if an employee signs a letter of resignation as a result of a misrepresentation by the employer he may claim he had been dismissed: see *Makin v Greens Motors (Bridport) Ltd* (1986) *The Times*, 18 April.

An indication by the employer that the employee should look elsewhere for a job because his job would come to an end in the future would not in law amount to a dismissal, nor is it a case of enforced resignation: *Haseltine Lake and Co v Dowler* [1981] IRLR 25; see also *International Computers Ltd v Kennedy* [1981] IRLR 28.

Employee's resignation during notice

Where an employer gives notice to an employee to terminate the contract of employment, and within that period of notice the employee gives notice to the employer to terminate the contract on a date earlier than the date on which the employer's notice is due to expire, the employee is nevertheless taken to have been dismissed by the employer. The reason for the dismissal is the reason which the employer originally gave in terminating the contract: s 55(3) of the EP(C)A 1978. See *Thompson v GEC Avionics Ltd* [1991] IRLR 488, where the EAT held the effective date of termination was the date the employee ceased working in accordance with her own counter-notice.

See also *Marshall (Cambridge) Ltd v Hamblin* [1994] IRLR 260, which probably turns on its own peculiar facts.

Where the employer gives notice, and during the currency of the notice the employee walks out and does not return, is he protected under this provision? 'No'. The counter notice to terminate the contract by the employee must be a notice which, within reason, either specifies the date of termination or specifies sufficient facts from which the employer can reasonably work out the date of termination. While it is unlikely that this condition will be applied too strictly, some certainty is required: *Walker v Cotswold Chine Home School* (1977) 12 ITR 342. This case left open the question as to whether the notice had to be valid. However, in *Ready Case Ltd v Jackson* [1981] IRLR 312, the EAT found that it did not matter whether the notice given by the employee was shorter than the statutory minimum period or the contractual notice which the employee was required to give. In this case the EAT considered, but left open, the question whether notice could be immediate notice of termination.

Employee repudiation

The employee may repudiate the contract where he fundamentally breaches the contract or breaches a fundamental term of contract. The employee must have evinced an intention to be no longer bound by the contract.

Examples of employee repudiation have arisen where an employee refused to work under a rota system agreed between the employer and the union and incorporated into the employee's contract of employment: *Dudar v Leys Malleable Castings Co Ltd* [1973] IRLR 51; where an employee refused to work on a construction site because of rain, where there was a working rule agreement incorporated in the employee's contract that decisions as to stoppages for bad weather should only be made by the employer or his representative: *London v James Laidlaw and Sons Ltd* [1974] IRLR 136; calling a staff meeting during working hours despite the employer's instructions not to do so: *Johns and Bloomfield v Trust Houses Forte Ltd* [1975] IRLR 36. For disobedience to amount to a repudiation, it is likely that the disobedience must be wilful. Strikes, and possibly other industrial action, are further examples of employee repudiation. The essence of a strike is that the employee refuses to do any of the work which he is engaged to do, and so is in breach of his contract: *Simmons v Hoover Ltd* [1977] ICR 61; *Wilkins v Cantrell and Cochrane (GB) Ltd* [1978] IRLR 483. In *Ticehurst and Thompson v British Telecommunications plc* [1992] IRLR 219, the Court of Appeal held that where the employee clearly evinced an intention to continue taking part in industrial action amounting to a breach of an implied term of the contract, the employers, without bringing her contract to an end, were entitled to refuse to accept part performance of the contract. Gibson LJ held there was an implied duty of faithful service in the case, as here, of a manager who was entrusted to exercise judgment and discretion. Where the employee exercised the discretion in order to disrupt the employer's business or to cause inconvenience, then it would be open to the employer to treat that as a breach of contract and grounds for dismissal. However, there is no breach of contract if the employee only intends to respond to a strike call if and when that is issued.

Does the breach of the contract by the employee bring the contract to an end immediately without further action on the employer's part, or does it give the employer the right to treat the contract as ended so that he can dismiss the employee, the act of acceptance (the dismissal) bringing the contract to an end? The cases suggest that the repudiatory conduct on the part of the employee does not bring the contract to an end, unless and until the employer accepts the employee's repudiatory conduct: see *Howard v Pickford Tool Co Ltd* [1951] 1 KB 417 and *Thomas Marshall (Exports) Ltd v Guinle* [1978] ICR 905. Usually the employer will in practice commit some act evidencing his acceptance of the repudiation, for instance, either by giving the employee notice or by forwarding to him his P45 or other employment documents. If the repudiation of the contract of employment by the employee does not need acceptance, then the contract is at an end without the need for further action. Therefore, the forwarding of the P45 or other documents or property is not an act of dismissal, but a recognition of the fact that the employee has by his actions brought the employment to an end.

See *Rasool and Others v Hepworth Pipe Co Ltd* [1980] IRLR 88, where the EAT followed the decision of the tribunal in *Sealey and Others v Avon Aluminium Co Ltd* [1978] IRLR 285, discussed under *'Repudiation other than wrongful dismissal'* at p 87.

In *London Transport Executive v Clarke* [1981] IRLR 166, the Court of Appeal held that the contract of employment, like any other contract, is not brought to an end by an act of repudiation until the repudiation is accepted by the innocent party. Dunn LJ, while agreeing with Templeman LJ, (see *'Repudiation other than wrongful dismissal'* at p 87) conceived of circumstances where it was possible for the repudiation by the employee to bring about the termination of the contract without the need for acceptance. Referring to the decision in *Smith v Avana Bakeries Ltd* [1979] IRLR 423, he considered that where the company's rules were incorporated into the employee's contract of service and the rules provided that if an employee remained off work for more than three days without submitting a medical certificate he would dismiss himself, the failure to submit the medical certificate and remaining off work for more than three days would result in the contract being terminated by the employee in accordance with its terms. Denning MR dissented. The decision of Templeman LJ, supported in the main by the decision of Dunn LJ, although permitting of some exceptions, is to be preferred to that of Denning MR.

If the employer wishes to rely on an act of repudiation by the employee, he must not do anything which amounts to a waiver of the repudiatory act: *Allders International Ltd v Parkins* [1981] IRLR 68.

Where there is a fundamental breach of the contract by the employee which is accepted by the employer, the contract is terminated by the employer and consequently there is a dismissal within s 55(2)(*a*) of the EP(C)A 1978. See the decision of *Western Excavating (ECC) Ltd v Sharp* [1978] ICR 221 and the discussion above.

Constructive resignation or 'self-dismissal'

Associated with the repudiation of a contract by the employee and the need for acceptance by the employer is the concept of constructive resignation or self-dismissal. Implicit in this concept is the idea that the employee by his conduct 'dismisses' himself in that his misconduct is equivalent to giving his employer notice. The employee is repudiating the contract and the employer's acceptance of that repudiation is not required. The idea of constructive resignation arose in *Jones v Liverpool Corporation and Liverpool Polytechnic* [1974] IRLR 55. Jones refused to report to work when asked to do so, having been told that his failure would lead to the termination of his employment. It was argued that his conduct was equivalent to giving his employer notice and that the employer, by paying wages in lieu of notice, merely recognised the fact; so there was no dismissal but, rather, a constructive resignation. The NIRC held that the employee had by his conduct repudiated the employment and that, by paying wages in lieu of notice, the employer was in effect recognising that the employee had repudiated his contract by dismissing him. Support for the proposition was given by the cases of *Smith v Avana Bakeries Ltd* [1979] IRLR 423; and *Kallinos v London Electric Wire* [1980] IRLR 11. However, in *Rasool and Others v Hepworth Pipe Co Ltd* [1980] IRLR 88, another division of the EAT found that it is for the employer to decide whether or not to treat the employee's repudiation of the contract as discharging the employer from further performance. It is the employer rather than the employee who terminates the contract, although there may be circumstances where the employee's fundamental breach was such that it effectively terminated the contract without the need for anything more. If the employer accepts the repudiation so that the contract is terminated by the decision of the employer, then this is a dismissal: s 55(2)(*a*) of the EP(C)A 1978; see also *Fisher v York Trailer Co Ltd* [1979] IRLR 386. The employer told Fisher that if he failed to sign an undertaking to work at normal speed the company would consider that he had repudiated his contract. Fisher did not sign and his employment came to an end. It was held that although the employer regarded Fisher's conduct as repudiatory, since he had not indicated that he considered the contract to be at an end, the repudiatory conduct did not in itself determine the contract until it had been accepted by the employer. It was the acceptance which terminated the contract.

The line of reasoning in the cases of *Rasool* and *Fisher* was followed by the majority of the Court of Appeal (Denning MR dissenting) in *London Transport Executive v Clarke* [1981] IRLR 166, although whether Templeman LJ would have accepted that certain breaches effectively terminate the contract without more is open to doubt. In any event the ratio in the cases of *Smith* and *Kallinos* must be regarded as bad law, although see the views of Dunn LJ as to the decision in *Smith*'s case *above*.

Agreement

It is open to the parties to terminate the contract of employment by mutual agreement: *L Lipton Ltd v Marlborough* [1979] IRLR 179; but compare *Thames Television Ltd v Wallis* [1979] IRLR 136. Where an employee leaves employment in consideration of a financial inducement, in law that will amount to a termination by mutual agreement: *Sheffield v Oxford Controls Co Ltd* [1979] IRLR 133; see also *Staffordshire County Council v Donovan* [1981] IRLR 108.

The issue may arise where the employee is under notice and seeks to leave his employment before the expiration of the period of notice. The employee may comply with the provisions of s 55(3) of the EP(C)A 1978. See under Employee's resignation during notice at p 98 The parties may agree that the employment shall come to an end on a date earlier than the date of the employer's notice. This may constitute an agreement to bring the contract to an end, or it may be an agreement that the effective date of termination shall be brought forward or that the employee may not be required to work out the balance of his notice period. In the first case dismissal by the employer is superseded by an agreement that the contract should be brought to an end. In the latter two cases the employer's notice remains effective so that there is a dismissal in law.

In *McAlwane v Boughton Estates Ltd* [1973] ICR 470, Sir John Donaldson held that it would be very rare for an employer and employee to agree mutually to terminate a contract where there was a current notice of termination as the employee, particularly, would be financially disadvantaged. See also *Lees v Arthur Greaves (Lees) Ltd* [1974] IRLR 93; and consider *Harman v Flexible Lamps Ltd* [1980] IRLR 418. In *Hellyer Bros Ltd v Atkinson and Dickinson* [1992] IRLR 540, (confirmed by the Court of Appeal [1994] IRLR 88) the EAT held that there was a dismissal in law when the employee, a trawlerman, signed off a crew agreement because his ship was not going back to sea within a short time and he had been requested to sign off by the employer. He was not mutually agreeing to terminate the contract but merely filled in the appropriate form. The EAT held that there is no rule of law that in the absence of duress or pressurisation where an employee's voluntary act is the physical event which terminates a contract that that amounts to an agreement to terminate the contract.

Where the employee offers to retire and his offer is accepted by the employer the contract is brought to an end by mutual agreement and not by dismissal: *Birch and Humber v University of Liverpool* [1985] IRLR 165. See also *Scott and Others v Coalite Fuels and Chemicals Ltd* [1988] IRLR 131. This situation must be distinguished from the case where the employee has no objection to being dismissed or even volunteers to be dismissed in a redundancy: *Burton, Allton and Johnson Ltd v Peck* [1975] IRLR 87. The judgment in this case did not encroach 'upon the distinction which exists in law between a contract which is terminated unilaterally (albeit without objection, and perhaps even with encouragement from the other party) and a contract which is terminated by mutual agreement'.

Where there is a clear agreement as to termination there can be no claim for unfair dismissal.

The problems of termination by mutual agreement have arisen in connection with employees who have failed to return from leave by an agreed date.

In *Midland Electric Manufacturing Co Ltd v Kanji* [1980] IRLR 185, the employer gave Kanji unpaid leave to go to India. Kanji was told that if she failed to return to work on the due date for whatever reason, including sickness, the company would consider that she had terminated her own employment. She was two weeks late in reporting to work because of ill health. The employer argued that the employment had been terminated by mutual agreement. It was held that a unilateral statement by the employer that the employee's employment could come to an end amounted to a dismissal and that there was no consensual agreement to termination.

In *Tracey v Zest Equipment Co Ltd* [1982] IRLR 268, the EAT held that an employee's employment had not come to an end by mutual consent where he overstayed a leave of absence having signed a document that if he did not return by a stipulated date the employer 'will assume that you have terminated your employment with us'. The employee wished to return to work. The EAT held that very clear words are required in such circumstances to constitute an agreement that, in the event of a failure to comply with such a requirement, there is a mutual consent to the termination of the employment. The employee's failure to return may be a repudiation by him of the contract.

In *Igbo v Johnson Matthey Chemicals Ltd* [1986] ICR 505, Igbo was granted extended leave to go to Nigeria. She signed a document which required her to work her normal shift immediately after her return from her leave of absence. The document which she signed went on to say 'you have agreed to return to work on 28 September 1983. If you fail to do this your contract of employment will automatically terminate on that date.' She returned to England but failed to return to work on 28 September 1983 due to ill health. The employers wrote to her advising her that her employment had come to an end in accordance with the terms of the agreement. The Court of Appeal held that agreement was intended to exclude or limit ss 54 and 55 of the EP(C)A 1978 and was therefore void by virtue of s 140. See Chapter 1. The earlier decision in *British Leyland (UK) Ltd v Ashraf* [1978] ICR 979, where it was held that the contract of employment had come to an end where the employee had agreed that if he did not return from overseas leave by a certain date is, it is submitted, wrongly decided. In that case the effect of s 140 of the EP(C)A 1978 was not considered.

Dismissal at common law

There are certain events which at common law amount to a dismissal. Historically these events have been regarded as a repudiation of the contract of employment by the employer because the employer has by his actions, albeit that the actions may be involuntary, rendered it impossible for the employer to continue with the employment.

Dissolution of a partnership

At common law the dissolution of a partnership by the retirement of one or more of the partners and the transfer of the business to the remaining partners, in the absence of an express or implied term in the contract of employment to the contrary, brought the contract to an end: *Brace v Calder* [1895] 2 QB 253. However, such a transfer is now likely to be within the provisions of the TUPE 1981. In any event continuity of employment will probably be preserved under either para 17(2) or 17(5) of Sched 13 to the EP(C)A 1978. See Chapters 3 and 15.

The dissolution on the death of a partner will not automatically terminate the contract unless the contract is dependent upon the continued existence of that partner: see *Phillips v Hull Alhambra Palace Co* [1901] 1 QB 59. Again, if there is a transfer of the business to the surviving partners, the transfer will probably be within the TUPE 1981 and continuity will probably be preserved.

Bankruptcy and winding-up

The bankruptcy of an employer does not operate to terminate the contract of employment. As the contract is of a personal nature, it may be frustrated, although this is arguable.

The appointment of a receiver by the court will probably operate to terminate the contract: see *Re Foster Clark Ltd's Indenture Trust* [1966] 1 All ER 43 and *Reid v Explosives Co Ltd* (1887) 19 QBD 264, although the point is not free from all doubt. Where a receiver is appointed other than by the court, it will depend upon whether he is appointed as agent of the company or as agent for the creditors. If the former, the appointment will not necessarily be inconsistent with the continued existence of the contract of employment, unless it is clear from the circumstances that the contract must be terminated: *Deaway Trading Ltd v Calverley and Others* [1973] ICR 546; and *Re Mack Trucks (Britain) Ltd* [1967] 1 WLR 780. If the latter it is more likely that the contract will be terminated.

A winding-up order has been held to operate as a termination of the contract of employment: *Golding and Howard v Fire Auto and*

Marine Insurance Co Ltd (1968) 3 ITR 372; see also *McEwan v Upper Clyde Shipbuilders Ltd (in liquidation)* (1972) 7 ITR 296.

It has been held that a resolution for the voluntary winding-up of a company does not operate as a notice of dismissal: see *Midland Counties District Bank Ltd v Attwood* [1905] 1 Ch 357; but in *Reigate v Union Manufacturing Co (Ramsbottom)* [1918] 1 KB 592, it was held that although a voluntary winding-up will not always terminate the contract of employment, where it was not intended to carry on the business, it would. In *Fowler v Commercial Timber Co Ltd* [1930] 2 KB 1, it was held that a resolution for voluntary winding-up was likely to result in the termination of the managing director's contract. In *Fox Brothers (Clothes) Ltd (in liquidation) v Bryant* [1978] IRLR 485, it was held that the employees' contracts of employment did not automatically come to an end where the company went into voluntary liquidation. The EAT doubted if the employee could claim to have been unfairly dismissed.

Frustration

The common law doctrine of frustration applies to contracts of employment and is based upon the proposition that a contract of service is a contract of personal service. Consequently, it can only be performed by the contracting parties, and it will be discharged where either party is incapable of performing his contract due to circumstances beyond his control; ie the agreement as envisaged between the parties has become impossible and is frustrated. The contract is discharged and not avoided so that the parties' vested rights are preserved. See *Marshall v Harland and Wolff Ltd* (1972) 7 ITR 150.

Frustration is produced by events actually happening and not by the risk of such events in the future: *Converfoam (Darwen) Ltd v Bell* [1981] IRLR 195. Frustration puts an end to the contract independently of the conduct or intention of the parties. There is no dismissal.

In deciding whether the employee's incapacity due to sickness renders future performance impossible or radically different from that which the parties envisaged when entering into the contract, the NIRC in *Marshall's* case *above*, held that the tribunal should take into account the following:

The terms of the contract, including the provisions as to sickness pay
The whole basis of weekly employment may be destroyed more quickly than that of monthly employment and that in turn more quickly than annual employment. When the contract provides for sick pay, it is plain that the contract cannot be frustrated so long as the employee returns to work, or appears likely to return to work, within the period during which such sick pay is payable. But the converse is not necessarily true, for the right to sick pay may expire before the incapacity has

gone on, or appears likely to go on, for so long as to make a return to work impossible or radically different from the obligations undertaken under the contract of employment.

How long the employment was likely to last in the absence of sickness
The relationship is less likely to survive if the employment was inherently temporary in its nature or for the duration of a particular job, than if it was expected to be long term or even lifelong.

The nature of the employment
Where the employee is one of many in the same category, the relationship is more likely to survive the period of incapacity than if he occupies a key post which must be filled and filled on a permanent basis if his absence is prolonged.

The nature of the illness or injury and how long it has already continued and the prospects of recovery
The greater the degree of incapacity and the longer the period over which it has persisted and is likely to persist, the more likely it is that the relationship has been destroyed.

The period of past employment
A relationship which is of long standing is not so easily destroyed as one which has but a short history. The legal basis is that over a long period of service the parties must be assumed to have contemplated a longer period or periods of sickness than over a shorter period.

These factors are interrelated and cumulative, but not necessarily exhaustive. The question is and remains: 'Was the employee's incapacity, looked at before the purported dismissal, of such a nature, or did it appear likely to continue for such a period, that further performance of his obligations in the future would either be impossible, or would be a thing radically different from that undertaken by him and accepted by the employer under the agreed terms of his employment?'

The ending of the relationship of employer and employee by operation of law is, by definition, independent of the volition or intention of the parties. A tribunal is, however, entitled to treat the conduct of the parties as evidence to be considered in forming a judgment as to whether the changed circumstances were so fundamental as to strike at the root of the relationship.

In *Egg Stores (Stamford Hill) Ltd v Leibovici* [1977] ICR 260, the EAT held that an important but not the only question is 'has the time arrived when the employer can no longer reasonably be expected to keep the absent employee's post open for him?' There may be a dramatic event when it will be obvious the contract is at an end, or there may be, for example, a long illness where looking back it can be said that at some stage, even though it is not possible to pin-point the exact time, the contract could not be regarded as subsisting and then

> the matters to be taken into account in such a case in reaching a decision are these:
> (1) the length of the previous employment;
> (2) how long it had been expected that the employment would continue;
> (3) the nature of the job;
> (4) the nature, length and effect of the illness or disabling event;
> (5) the need of the employer for the work to be done, and the need for a replacement to do it;
> (6) the risk to the employer of acquiring obligations in respect of redundancy payments or compensation for unfair dismissal to the replacement employee;
> (7) whether wages have continued to be paid;
> (8) the acts and the statements of the employer in relation to the employment, including the dismissal of, or failure to dismiss, the employee; and
> (9) whether in all the circumstances a reasonable employer could be expected to wait any longer.

This approach was followed in *Williams v Watsons Luxury Coaches* [1990] IRLR 164. It was held other factors to be considered were the contractual terms as to sickness pay, if any, and the prospects of recovery.

The *Marshall* and *Leibovici* cases were also followed in *Hart v A R Marshall and Sons (Bulwell) Ltd* [1977] ICR 539, where the EAT again emphasised the importance of examining why the employer did not dismiss the employee. If he did not think he could, this may well be important in establishing that the contract has not been frustrated. It may be that he has not put his mind to the question whether he can dismiss and this may be consistent with frustration of the contract.

In *Notcutt v Universal Equipment Co (London) Ltd* [1986] ICR 414, Dillon LJ held:

> as a periodic contract of employment determinable by short, or relatively short, notice may none the less be intended in many cases by both parties to last for many years and as the power of the employer to terminate the contract by notice is subject to the provisions for the protection of employees against unfair dismissal now in the Act of 1978, I can see no reason in principle why such a periodic contract of employment should not in appropriate circumstances, be held to have been terminated without notice by frustration according to the accepted and long established doctrine of frustration in our law of contract. The mere fact that the contract can be terminated by the employer by relatively short notice cannot of itself render the doctrine of frustration inevitably inapplicable.

Notcutt suffered a coronary. His contract of employment was terminable by 12 weeks' notice. He was dismissed without notice and brought a claim for pay during the notice period under s 50 and para 3 of

Sched 3 to the EP(C)A 1978. It was held that the contract had been frustrated and therefore the notice was unnecessary.

The contract of employment may also be frustrated by a period of internment where it is likely that the internment is of a permanent rather than a temporary nature.

Military service may also frustrate the contract of employment. An employee may be entitled to apply to his former employer to be reinstated: see the Reserve Forces (Safeguard of Employment) Act 1985.

In *Harrington v Kent CC* [1980] IRLR 353, it was held that a prison sentence of 12 months imposed for offences of indecency operated to frustrate the contract of employment. The contract was frustrated from the moment the employee was sentenced, even though he was appealing against his sentence. See also *Hare v Murphy Bros Ltd* [1974] ICR 603.

In *FC Shepherd and Co Ltd v Jerrom* [1986] ICR 802, the Court of Appeal held that a Borstal sentence of between six months and two years frustrated Jerrom's apprenticeship agreement, even though it arose as a result of fault on the employee's part. Thus, *Norris v Southampton CC* [1982] IRLR 141, where it was held that a contract is not frustrated by the deliberate conduct or fault of one party, would appear to be wrongly decided. However, in such cases, there is a thin dividing line between frustration and repudiation.

Chapter 5

The Effective Date of Termination

It is important to ascertain the effective date of termination for the following reasons:

(1) to decide whether the employee has brought his claim for unfair dismissal within the limitation period;
(2) to calculate the continuous period of employment;
(3) to calculate the employee's pay and the amount of the basic award; and
(4) to ascertain whether or not the employee is within the upper age limit.

It must be borne in mind that if s 55(5) or (6) of the EP(C)A 1978 apply, the date for the purposes of points (1) and (4) can differ from the date for the purposes of points (2) and (3). See *below*.

Statutory definitions

Section 55(4) of the EP(C)A 1978 defines the 'effective date of termination' as follows:

(*a*) in relation to an employee whose contract of employment is terminated by notice, whether given by his employer or by the employee, the 'effective date of termination' means the date on which that notice expires;
(*b*) in relation to an employee whose contract of employment is terminated without notice, the 'effective date of termination' means the date on which the termination takes effect; and
(*c*) in relation to an employee who is employed under a contract for a fixed term, where that term expires without being renewed under the same contract, the 'effective date of termination' means the date on which the fixed term expires.

Thus, where the employee is dismissed without notice s 55(4)(*b*) applies; where the employee is dismissed with notice which is less than that specified in s 49, then s 55(4)(*a*) applies. Both, however, are subject to s 55(5).

That section contains a provision designed to prevent employers defeating employees' claims to various statutory rights, by dismissing them with no notice or less than the statutory period of notice. It provides that where the contract is terminated by the employer and the notice required by s 49 of the EP(C)A 1978 to be given by an employer would, if duly given on the material date, expire on a later date than the effective date of termination under s 55(4) then for the purposes of ss 53(2), 64(1)(a), 73(3) and para 8(3) of Sched 14 to the EP(C)A 1978, the later date shall be treated as the effective date of termination. The material date for this purpose is the date when notice of termination was given by the employer or, where no notice was given, the date when the contract of employment was terminated by the employer: s 55(7)(a) of the EP(C)A 1978. Suppose that A is continuously employed until one week short of two years and is dismissed without notice one week short of two years. Apart from s 55(5), the day that he was dismissed would be the effective date of termination. Under s 55(5), however, the effective date of termination is treated as the date when statutory notice would have expired. A is entitled to one week's statutory notice, and so has two years' employment. Provided that the two years are made up of continuous weeks of employment, he may bring a claim for unfair dismissal.

Section 55(6) of the EP(C)A 1978 provides where the contract of employment is terminated by the employee and:

(a) the material date does not fall during a period of notice given by the employer to terminate that contract; and

(b) had the contract been terminated not by the employee but by notice given on the material date by the employer, that notice would have been required by s 49 of the EP(C)A 1978 to expire on a date later than the effective date of termination under s 55(4) of the EP(C)A 1978,

then for the purposes of ss 64(1)(a) and 73(3) and para 8(3) of Sched 14, the later date shall be treated as the effective date of termination in relation to the dismissal. The material date means the date when notice of termination was given by the employee or, where no notice was given, the date when the contract of employment was terminated by the employee: s 55(7)(b) of the EP(C)A 1978.

The effect of this provision is to give the employee who is constructively dismissed the same protection as he would have enjoyed had he been actually dismissed by the employer.

Under s 55(5) and (6), and (7)(a) and (b) of the EP(C)A 1978, only the length of notice prescribed by s 49 of the EP(C)A 1978 can be considered and not the length of any contractual notice which the employee should have been given, so the effective date of termination can be postponed only by the length of the statutory notice: *Fox Maintenance Ltd v Jackson* [1978] ICR 110.

Does s 55(5) postpone the effective date of termination where the employee has been lawfully summarily dismissed by the employer?

It does not, by virtue of the provisions of s 49(5). But, in *Lanton*

Leisure Ltd v White and Gibson [1987] IRLR 119, it was held that the mere designation by the employer of the employee's conduct as gross misconduct was not decisive. Thus, a tribunal can find itself hearing and determining a wrongful dismissal action before it knows whether the employee has two years continuous service to enable him to claim that he was unfairly dismissed.

Unlike s 55(5), s 55(6) does not apply to s 53(2) which deals with the qualifying period for a written statement of reasons for dismissal.

An argument that an employer's wrongful dismissal did not terminate the contract until the breach was accepted by the employee, was rejected by the EAT in *Gunton v The Major Aldermen and Burgesses of London Borough of Richmond upon Thames* [1980] 3 WLR 714. The EAT also concluded that there is nothing in s 55(4)(*a*) to suggest that notice is limited to that complying with any contractual obligation. It is the notice which is actually given. In s 55(4)(*b*) the effective date of termination is the date on which the termination takes effect, and as the relationship of employer and employee comes to an end at the moment of dismissal, it is at that moment that the employee's rights under the contract are changed to a right to damages only.

The EAT held it was 'of the greatest importance that there should be no doubt or uncertainty as to the date which is the "effective date of termination." ' A claim for unfair dismissal must be brought within three months of the effective date of termination and so it is important the employee knows when this is, free from the 'subtle legalities of the law of repudiation and acceptance of repudiation': see also *Brown v Southall and Knight* [1980] IRLR 130. The EAT followed the decision in *Dedman v British Building and Engineering Appliances Ltd* [1973] ICR 82 and on appeal [1974] ICR 53. In *BMK and BMK Holdings Ltd v Logue* [1993] ICR 601, Knox J observed that it was remarkable that since the passing of the EP(C)A 1978, there had been no decision dealing with the precise method of ascertaining the effective date of termination in relation to constructive dismissal. However, he concluded that it is the date on which the termination takes effect which is the key, ie that turns on what the legal relationship between the parties was, or was not, and that it was wrong to apply a test relating to the employee's intellectual understanding of what had taken place.

Where an employee agrees to waive his right to statutory notice or to accept a payment in lieu thereof, this does not operate to defeat s 55(5) of the EP(C)A 1978 which still applies to postpone the effective date of termination until the date when the statutory notice would have expired had it been given in full: *Staffordshire County Council v Secretary of State for Employment* [1989] ICR 664. Nothing in s 55(5), (6) and (7) of the EP(C)A 1978 postpones the effective date of termination for the purposes of the statutory time limit.

Application of the statutory definitions

The statutory definition of the effective date of termination has given rise to difficulty in cases where: the employee is paid wages in lieu of notice; the employee is told during the period of notice that his services are no longer required; and the employee appeals against dismissal. In each case the question arises as to when the effective date of termination is.

Wages in lieu of notice

A distinction must be drawn between those cases where an employee is dismissed immediately with wages in lieu of notice and those cases where an employee is dismissed with notice but is given wages in lieu of working out the notice. In the former case the effective date of termination will usually be ascertained in accordance with s 55(4)(*b*) of the EP(C)A 1978—the effective date of termination will be the date upon which the termination takes place. In *Dedman v British Building and Engineering Appliances Ltd* [1974] ICR 53, Dedman was given a letter on 5 May 1972 terminating his employment immediately. With the letter was his salary for the month of May, plus one month in lieu of notice. The Court of Appeal found that the crucial words were 'terminate your employment immediately' and equally important was the fact that his national insurance card was only stamped up to 5 May. It held that the contract was terminated immediately, and the payment of salary was made as compensation for immediate dismissal and not by way of continuation of his employment. See also *Dixon v Stenor Ltd* [1973] ICR 157 and *Hackwood v Benross Trading Co Ltd* [1975] IRLR 2.

Where an employee is given notice and during the notice period is told in a letter 'to relinquish your duties . . . with effect from today . . . and remove yourself and your belongings at the same time', that letter was a letter of summary dismissal and therefore the effective date of termination was the date upon which the employee finished work. The effective date of termination in s 55(4) of the EP(C)A 1978 meant the actual date of termination: *Stapp v The Shaftesbury Society* [1982] IRLR 326.

In *London Borough of Newham v Ward* [1985] IRLR 509, it was held that the content of form P45 is one of the factors to be taken into account in determining the effective date of termination, but it is of no more importance than that. The employee had been summarily dismissed on 9 February 1983; that was the effective date of termination, notwithstanding the fact that form P45 showed the effective date of termination as 27 June 1983.

Where an employee receives notice but is not required to work out the notice and is paid wages in lieu, the effective date of termination will usually be ascertained in accordance with s 55(4)(*a*) of the EP(C)A 1978.

In *Brindle v HW Smith (Cabinets) Ltd* [1972] IRLR 125, Brindle was given one months' notice, but during the notice was told that she need not come in to work, but to go on holiday. She indicated that she would prefer to work out her notice but she never returned to work. Her national insurance card was stamped for the whole of the period of the notice. The Court of Appeal held that the effective date of termination was the date when the notice would have expired and not when Brindle was told that she need not come into work and could go on holiday. *Brindle*'s case was distinguished in *Stapp*'s case in that on the facts Brindle was not summarily dismissed whereas Stapp was.

In *Lees v Arthur Greaves (Lees) Ltd* [1974] ICR 501, Lees was given six months' notice orally on 1 October 1971 which was confirmed in writing on 7 October 1971 to expire on 31 March 1972. On 28 January 1972, it was alleged that the contract had terminated as at that date by agreement between the parties. As at that date Lees received all his monetary entitlements, his P45 and his national insurance card. The evidence was that Lees had agreed under pressure to leave on 28 January. The Court of Appeal, by a majority, refused to find an agreement whereby Lees consented to the termination of his employment as at that date, and concluded that after 28 January Lees was still employed but not required to work. As in *Brindle's* case, Lees was not summarily dismissed and therefore this case may be distinguished on its facts from *Stapp's* case. See *above*. Whilst neither of these decisions is without its problems they indicate that it is a question of fact, albeit against a legal background.

In both *Brindle* and *Lees*, notice had been given which straddled the introduction of the statutory protection against unfair dismissal. If the employee had been allowed to work out the notice it would have enabled the employee in each case to claim the benefit of the statutory protection and claim unfair dismissal.

In *Adams v GKN Sankey Ltd* [1980] IRLR 416, Adams was dismissed by letter dated 2 November 1979 which stated 'you are . . . given 12 weeks' notice of dismissal from this company with effect from Monday 5 November 1979.

'You will not be expected to work your notice but will receive monies in lieu of notice, and these, together with all other documentation, will be sent to you through the post.'

It was held on the evidence that this was a case where the employee was not required to work out the notice but would receive monies in lieu, and therefore the employment did not come to an end until the expiration of 12 weeks from 5 November 1979.

The ratio of the cases on this point indicates that if the words, or letter, of dismissal are ambiguous, the ambiguity will be resolved in favour of the employee.

Appeals against dismissal

The effective date of termination, where the dismissed employee has a right of appeal against his dismissal under the provisions of a domestic appeal procedure, was first considered in *McDonald v South Cambridgeshire RDC* [1973] ICR 611. It was held that the exercise of the right of appeal did not affect the effective date of termination. In *High v British Railways Board* [1979] IRLR 52, it was held that in such circumstances the provisions of the contract of employment relating to the appeal procedure continue to apply to that extent only.

In *J Sainsbury Ltd v Savage* [1980] IRLR 109, Savage was instantly dismissed on 21 February 1978. He exercised his right of appeal against dismissal under the terms of the company's disciplinary procedure, where, pending the decision of an appeal against dismissal, the employee was suspended without pay, but if the employee was reinstated he would receive full back pay for the period of his suspension. However the exercise of the right of appeal did not affect the effective date of termination. On the failure of the appeal he was treated as dismissed from 21 February 1978, which was the effective date of termination.

An exception would arise where, under the provisions of the appeal procedure, the contract continues in full force pending the appeal so that the employee has the right to work and to be paid, and the employer can call upon the employee to work. See also *Crown Agents for Overseas Governments and Administration v Lawal* [1978] IRLR 542.

In *The Board of Governors, The National Heart and Chest Hospitals v Nambiar* [1981] IRLR 196, Nambiar was dismissed on 16 January. He exercised his internal right of appeal. His appeal was allowed to the extent of recommending that he should be found suitable alternative employment. The employer paid Nambiar his arrears of salary and continued to pay him until it became apparent that they could not find him suitable alternative employment. It was held that the effective date of termination was 16 January, notwithstanding the fact that he was paid arrears of salary and salary was paid to him while alternative employment was being sought. The contract of employment did not continue in force. If an employee's contract does continue in force pending the determination of an appeal the effective date of termination may thereby be postponed.

Where the employee is successful in having the decision to dismiss him overruled on appeal, then the effect upon his employment will depend upon the facts of the case and his contract of employment. Where the employee is reinstated his continuity of employment will not be broken whether or not there is a term to that effect in his contract of employment: see the cases of *High* and *Savage, above,* and also *Howgate v Fane Acoustics Ltd* [1981] IRLR 161. Where the employee is successful the initial notice may be rendered null and void: see *Petch v Taunton Deane District Council* (1977) (unreported).

In *BBC v Beckett* [1983] IRLR 43, Beckett was dismissed and appealed against the penalty of dismissal. Following the appeal he was demoted. Beckett argued that once notice of dismissal had been given by the employer it was not open to the employer to withdraw that notice unilaterally and therefore he was being offered alternative employment under a new contract. This contention was rejected by the EAT, which found that the employee was being offered the chance to continue his employment with the employer but in a different post.

In *Batchelor v British Railways Board* [1987] IRLR 136, Batchelor was dismissed with immediate effect on 5 February. She appealed. On 25 February she was told that an appeal against her dismissal had been disallowed. It was held that the effective date of termination was 5 February. The fact that the Board were not entitled under the disciplinary procedure to dismiss summarily for the conduct in question did not alter the effective date of termination. It might enable the employee to bring an action for breach of contract.

Miscellaneous matters

The effective date of termination—a matter of evidence

Where an employee is given wages in lieu, usually in a lump sum, it is a matter of evidence whether or not the employee is employed for the period of the notice, albeit that he is not required to work out the notice. It may be quite clear that the effective date of termination is the date when the notice would have expired, although the employee will not be required to work during the notice period. The employee may, for instance, be treated as still in employment for all or some purposes. However, it is open to argument that where the employer pays wages in lieu, particularly in a lump sum, unless there is clear evidence that the effective date of termination is not until the end of the notice period in practice, the relationship ceases on the day when the employee leaves the place of work, and in such cases the effective date of termination is likely to be the date when the termination takes effect, which will be when the employee is actually dismissed.

Whether a letter of dismissal brings the contract to an end immediately or at a future date depends upon the construction of the letter: see *Adams v GKN Sankey Ltd* [1980] IRLR 416. In *Chapman v Letheby and Christopher Ltd* [1981] IRLR 440, it was held that a letter of dismissal must be construed in accordance with what an ordinary reasonable employee would understand the words to mean in the light of the facts known to him at the time. In *Stapp v The Shaftesbury Society* [1982] IRLR 326, Stephenson LJ said:

a notice to terminate employment must be construed strictly against the person who gives it, the employer, and if there is any ambiguity it must be resolved in favour of the person who receives it, the employee.

Where an employee has received oral notification of dismissal followed by a confirmatory letter, the oral and written words have to be read and construed together in order to resolve any ambiguity: see *Leech v Preston Borough Council* [1985] ICR 192.

The importance of exercising care is illustrated by *Hammerton Shipping Co Ltd v Borg* (1977) 12 ITR 54, where the company wrote to Borg on 28 October 1975 terminating his employment on 31 January 1976. Borg accepted the notice and suggested that he should take his holidays on 15 November 1975 for two weeks. No reply was made to the letter, but on 14 November 1975 the employee notified the employer that he would be on holiday from 17 November to 30 November 1975. The company's response was that if he took his holiday then he should not return to work again. Borg took the holiday and did not return to work, but the employers continued to pay him until 31 January 1976. The EAT upheld the decision of the tribunal that the effective date of termination of the employment was 31 January 1976, the date when the notice expired. See also *Goldsmith v RIBA Services Ltd* [1974] IRLR 176 and *IPC Business Press Ltd v Gray* [1977] ICR 858. Where an employee is sent a letter summarily dismissing him, the effective date of termination is the date when either the employee reads the letter or the date when he reasonably had the opportunity of knowing about it: see *Brown v Southall and Knight* [1980] ICR 617, see also *Hindle Gears Ltd v McGinty* [1984] IRLR 477.

An agreed change to the effective date of termination

In *TBA Industrial Products Ltd v Morland* [1982] IRLR 331, the employee was given a letter by his employer on 27 May terminating his employment on 2 August. At that date he was to be given a payment in lieu of the unexpired period of notice which would have continued until 30 August. He was told that if he wished to leave before 2 August he should fill in a blank letter and insert in that letter the date he wished to leave. The employee returned the letter and inserted 7 June. The employer accepted the employee's request and the agreed date when the employee was to leave was brought forward to 6 June. The majority of the Court of Appeal held that the effective date of termination was 2 August. Waller LJ held that, 'Termination by notice involves the notice being causative of the termination. The notice, in my opinion, has to be unconditional.' He found that the notice given by the employer was causative of the termination and unconditional and brought the employee's employment to an end on

2 August. The letter from the employee was simply an acceptance of the employer's invitation to leave before 2 August. Waller LJ also found that the letter did not produce a variation or waiver of the original notice. It was open to the employer if it wished to withdraw the original notice and serve a new notice complying with the date suggested by the employee. Support for this view was gained from the wording of s 55(4)(*a*) of the EP(C)A 1978. A variation would only be possible if after the words 'the date on which the notice expires' there were added 'or any variation thereof'.

In a dissenting judgment Ackner LJ clearly thought it was possible to vary by agreement the effective date of termination.

In *McAlwane v Boughton Estates Ltd* [1973] ICR 470, McAlwane was told in a letter that his employment was terminated with effect from 19 April. On 10 April he asked if he could leave his employment on 12 April to take up a new job and it was agreed that he could do so. It was held by the NIRC that in the circumstances the parties had agreed to vary the notice of dismissal by substituting an earlier date: that was the effective date of termination. The decision in *McAlwane v Boughton* was followed in *CPS Recruitment Ltd t/a Blackwood Associates v (1) Bowen and (2) Secretary of State for Employment* [1982] IRLR 54. As *TBA Industrial Products Ltd v Morland, above,* illustrates, much will depend on the facts. See also *Staffordshire County Council v Secretary of State for Employment* [1989] ICR 664.

However, in *Crank v Her Majesty's Stationery Office* [1985] ICR 1, the employers ceased trading at the premises where the employee worked. Crank was offered employment at the new premises. On 2 September 1983 he left the employers without telling them that he would not be moving to the new location. He subsequently obtained employment with different employers at the same premises. On 5 September he wrote to his employers asking for a redundancy payment. On 14 September in reply to a letter from his former employers asking why he was not working at the new location he wrote offering his resignation as from 2 September, which was accepted. It was held that it was open to the parties to agree retrospectively that 2 September was to be taken as the date of termination of the contract even though the contract was subsisting after that date. There was nothing in s 55(4) of the EP(C)A 1978 which required a later date to be taken. What is almost the converse situation arose in *Marshall (Cambridge) Ltd v Hamblin* [1994] IRLR 260. The employee gave three months' notice to terminate his contract. The employer, shortly after the notice had been given, told the employee that it did not require him to work his notice, and paid him 'in lieu' to the end of the notice period. The contract gave the employer the right to pay money in lieu of notice. The EAT held that the employer had waived its right to notice, that it was entitled to use the contractual term to bring the employment to an end at an earlier date, and that the employee had not been dismissed. It has to be admitted that the logic of this decision is difficult to follow. The first two conclusions, if correct, seem to exclude the possibility of the third.

The effective date of termination and the employee's counter notice

Section 55(3) of the EP(C)A 1978 enables an employee to whom an employer has given notice to terminate his contract of employment during the period of that notice to serve a counter notice upon the employer to terminate the contract of employment on an earlier date than that on which the employer's notice is due to expire. See Chapter 4. The Act is silent as to the effective date of termination in these circumstances. In *TBA Industrial Products Ltd v Morland* [1982] IRLR 331, it was argued before the EAT that the effective date of termination was the date specified in the employer's original notice. The EAT did not reach any decision. However, in *Thompson v GEC Avionics Ltd* [1991] IRLR 488, the EAT held that (*a*) where the employee had given counter notice the effective date of termination was the date that the employee ceased working in accordance with her own counter notice, and (*b*) where the employee's counter notice would terminate the contract on a date earlier than the date of expiry of the employer's notice, then the effective date of termination is the date upon which the employee's counter notice expires.

Constructive dismissal and the effective date of termination

Where the employee is constructively dismissed (see Chapter 4), the effective date of termination is the date when the employee accepts the employer's repudiation, ie the date the employee terminates the contract: see *Western Excavating (ECC) Ltd v Sharp* [1978] ICR 221. Usually this will be the date of the employee's departure. It is clear from the decision in *Crank*'s case, *above*, that the parties may agree the effective date of termination and the date may be a specified date. But consider *TBA Industrial Products v Morland, above*. See also now *BMK Ltd and BMK Holdings Ltd v Logue* [1993] ICR 601.

To this situation, the provisions of s 55(6) apply, so that for the purposes of s 64(1)(*a*) and 73(3) and para 8(3) of Sched 14, the date is postponed to the date of expiry of a deemed employer's statutory notice under s 49, as if given on the day upon which the employee terminated the contract.

Notice and effective date of termination

In *West v Kneels Ltd* [1986] IRLR 430, the employee was told on a Monday afternoon, 'We have made a decision: you are unsuitable for our kind of work and I am giving you a week's notice from now.' It was held that seven days' notice means seven days exclusive of the day on which work has been done. The EAT restricted its decision to cases where notice of termination is given orally. It is, however, very difficult, if not impossible, to see how the decision could have differed, if West had been handed a letter, in the same terms, on the Monday afternoon.

In *Octavius Atkinson and Sons Ltd v Morris* [1989] IRLR 158, Morris was summarily dismissed at lunchtime by reason of redundancy. He left the site on which he was working at 2.00pm. The Court of Appeal held that where an employee is summarily dismissed during the course of a working day and the employer's repudiation is accepted, the contract of employment and the status of employee cease at the moment when dismissal is communicated to the employee. The effective date of termination is determined in accordance with s 55(4)(*b*).

Strikes and lockouts

Section 238(5) of the TULR(C)A 1992 contains special provisions dealing with the 'date of dismissal' for the purposes of that section. They apply where at the 'date of dismissal' the employee was taking part in an official strike or official industrial action, or where the employer was conducting, or instituting a lock-out. In these circumstances, if the employer terminates the contract by notice (ie any length of notice) then, for the purposes of that section, the date of dismissal is the date upon which the employer gave notice. If the contract is terminated without notice then, for the purposes of that section, the date of dismissal is the effective date of termination.

Section 237 deals with the analogous situation where the strike or action is unofficial. Section 237(5) introduces, for the purposes of that section, yet another concept: the 'time of dismissal'. It is:

(*a*) where the contract is terminated by notice, when the notice is given,

(*b*) where it is terminated without notice, when the termination takes effect,

(*c*) where it terminates by effluxion of time, when the time expires.

Section 239(1) provides that ss 237 and 238 'shall be construed as one with Part V' of the EP(C)A 1978, ie the unfair dismissal provisions. In these circumstances, not only is there an 'effective date of termination', but also either a 'date of dismissal', or a 'time of dismissal'. In the former case, if there is no notice, or short notice, there can be a postponed 'effective date of termination'; in the latter case, there cannot.

As the starting date for the three month time limit under s 67(2) of the EP(C)A 1978 for presenting a claim for unfair dismissal is not affected by the postponement provisions of s 55(5) and (6), there is no conflict with the commencement of the six month time limit under s 239(2) of the TULR(C)A 1992.

Chapter 6

The Reason for Dismissal

In a claim for unfair dismissal, once the employee has established a dismissal or the employer has accepted that a dismissal has occurred, it is for the employer to show a reason for the dismissal which is within the EP(C)A 1978, s 57(1) and (2). There are certain exceptions which are considered later. (See Chapters 2, 10, 11, 13 and 14). The tribunal must then determine whether or not in the circumstances the employer has acted reasonably: s 57(3) of the EP(C)A 1978. Indeed, until the employer has established a reason, the tribunal should not consider reasonableness: *Post Office Counters Ltd v Heavey* [1989] IRLR 513.

Written reasons

Section 53(1) of the EP(C)A 1978, entitles every employee whose contract of employment is terminated by his employer, whether with or without notice or where his employment under a fixed-term contract expires without being renewed, to be given by his employer a written statement containing particulars of the reasons for his dismissal. The employee must ask the employer to give these written reasons and, once the request is made, the employer is obliged to supply the reasons within 14 days of the request. Section 139A of the EP(C)A 1978 provides that s 53 of the EP(C)A 1978 shall apply to House of Lords staff as from 30 November 1993 (SI 1993 No 2503). Section 138A (commencement to be announced in due course) provides that s 53 shall apply to members of the armed forces. An amendment made by s 24(4) of the TURERA 1993 brought into force on 10 January 1994 by SI 1994 No 1365 inserts s 53(2A) of the EP(C)A 1978 which states that an employee shall be entitled (without making any request and irrespective of whether or not she has been continuously employed for any period) to be provided by her employer with a written statement giving particulars of the reasons for her dismissal if she is dismissed (*a*) at any time while she is pregnant, or (*b*) after childbirth in circumstances in which her maternity leave period ends by reason of the dismissal. See Chapter 10.

If the employee claims constructive dismissal he is not entitled to a written statement. A written statement need not be supplied unless, on the effective date of termination, the employee has been or will have been, continuously employed for a period of not less than two years ending with that date: s 53(2) of the EP(C)A 1978. The qualifying period for an employee to claim written reasons and unfair dismissal is the same: see s 64(1)(*a*) of the EP(C)A 1978.

Section 53 does not apply to an employee who under his contract of employment ordinarily works outside Great Britain: s 141(2) of the EP(C)A 1978; a share fisherman: s 144(2) of the EP(C)A 1978; and the police service: s 146(2) of the EP(C)A 1978.

The employee has the right to make a complaint to a tribunal on the grounds that the employer has unreasonably failed to provide a written statement, or that the particulars of the reasons given by the employer are inadequate or untrue: s 54(4) of the EP(C)A 1978. If the tribunal finds the complaint well-founded it may make a declaration as to the employer's reason for dismissing the employee and it must order the employer to pay to the employee a sum equal to two weeks' gross pay: s 53(4)(*a*) and (*b*) of the EP(C)A 1978. The period for making a complaint to the tribunal is the same as in the case of a complaint for unfair dismissal: s 53(5) of the EP(C)A 1978.

The statement is admissible in evidence in any proceedings (see s 53(3) of the EP(C)A 1978) and will be of particular value in proceedings for unfair dismissal. In giving the reasons the employer must ensure accuracy and consistency. Nothing will be worse for the employer than to inform the employee of one reason for the dismissal, to give another in the written statement and to give yet another reason in his notice of appearance in a claim for unfair dismissal. If the written particulars of the reason given by the employer are inadequate or untrue the tribunal may make a declaration as to the reason. The employer will then be fixed with that reason in any claim for unfair dismissal and he will have difficulty in seeking to put forward another reason.

A complaint can only be made to a tribunal if the employee has requested written reasons: *Catherine Haigh Harlequin Hair Design v Seed* [1990] IRLR 175. However, there are now special rules where the employee is dismissed while she is pregnant. See Chapter 10.

Since the amendment on 30 August by the TURERA 1993 when the word 'failed' was substituted for the previous word 'refused', a tribunal will have to decide what amounts to an unreasonable failure. Previously, there was no 'unreasonable refusal' where the employer merely failed to comply with a request: see *Lowson v Percy Main and District Social Club and Institute Ltd* [1979] IRLR 227. However, this decision must now be ready in the light of the amendment.

It is a matter of degree so that the longer the period which elapses after the request the easier it is to construe the employer's failure as unreasonable: see *Newland v Simons and Willer (Hairdressers) Ltd* [1981] IRLR 359.

The employer may deny that the employee has been dismissed. It will be difficult for a tribunal although holding that there is a dismissal to find also that the employer unreasonably refused to give reasons for a dismissal where the employer genuinely believed that a dismissal had not occurred. It is a question of fact whether or not an employer genuinely honestly and reasonably believed that there had been no dismissal: see *Broomsgrove v Eagle Alexander Ltd* [1981] IRLR 127. A statement by the employer that there had been no dismissal is not a complete answer: see *Brown v Stuart Scott and Co* [1981] ICR 166, where the EAT held that the tribunal had to examine whether or not the employers were acting in bad faith in failing to produce written reasons relying upon an averment that there had been no dismissal.

No particular form is required for the written reasons but they must be adequate. The EAT in *Horsley Smith and Sherry Ltd v Dutton* [1977] ICR 594, suggested that 'The document must be of such a kind that the employee, or anyone to whom he may wish to show it, can know from reading the document itself why the employee has been dismissed.' The document can refer to other documents: see *Marchant v Earley Town Council* [1979] IRLR 311.

Much will depend upon whether the document to which reference is made clearly sets out what the EAT envisaged should be given to the employee in *Dutton's* case, *above.* In *Gilham and Others v Kent CC (No 1)* [1985] ICR 227, the Court of Appeal held that where an employer writes to the employee's solicitor stating that the reasons for dismissal have been set out in two earlier letters and enclosing copies of those letters, and confirming that the contents of those letters contain the reasons for the employee's dismissal, the employer will have complied with his statutory obligations. *Dutton's* case, *above,* was not overruled, each case turning upon its own particular facts. In that case the letter did not contain written reasons. The employer cannot rely upon a notice of appearance filed by him in an unfair dismissal claim for the purposes of s 53(1) of the EP(C)A 1978. This section requires the employer to provide the employee with an independent and separate document: *Rowan v Machinery Installations (South Wales) Ltd* [1981] IRLR 122.

An employee is entitled to have documentary proof of the reason and it is no excuse that he already knows the reason: *McBrearty v Thomson t/a Highfield Mini-Market* (1991) (unreported). Section 53(4) of the EP(C)A 1978 requires an employer to state truthfully the reason that he was relying upon. The section does not involve an examination of the justification for the dismissal.

'A reason has two elements: it has a factual basis of events that have occurred and which the employer considers to be the foundation for the dismissal and it has the consequences of those factual events which the employer, rightly or wrongly, relies on to justify his dismissal': *Harvard Securities plc v Younghusband* [1990] IRLR 17.

Statutory reasons

Under s 57(1) and (2) of the EP(C)A 1978, the employer has to establish the reason for the dismissal or, if there was more than one, the principal reason, and that the reason:

(*a*) related to the capability or qualifications of the employee for performing work of the kind which he was employed by the employer to do; or

(*b*) related to the conduct of the employee; or

(*c*) was that the employee was redundant; or

(*d*) was that the employee could not continue to work in the position which he held without contravention (either on his part or on that of his employer) of a duty or restriction imposed by or under an enactment; or

(*e*) was some other substantial reason of a kind such as to justify the dismissal of an employee holding the position which that employee held.

General approach

Under s 57(1) of the EP(C)A 1978 it is for the employer to establish the reason or principal reason and it is for the tribunal to see whether or not there is a reason and if so whether it is a valid one: see *Shannon v Michelin (Belfast) Ltd* [1981] IRLR 505. In *Carlin v St Cuthbert's Co-operative Association Ltd* [1974] IRLR 188, it was held that an employee may be dismissed for a number of reasons, all of which are equally important in the mind of the employer. If the employer seeks to rely on more than one reason, he must establish those reasons and that they entitle him to dismiss: see *Smith v Glasgow City District Council* [1987] ICR 796. The employer must specifically plead each reason upon which he relies and he must adduce evidence in support of each of them before the industrial tribunal: *Murphy v Epsom College* [1983] ICR 715, approved by the Court of Appeal [1985] ICR 80. If the employer only pleads one reason or only leads evidence in support of one reason he will fail if he cannot establish that reason, even if there is another reason which might have enabled him to succeed: *Barbar Indian Restaurant v Rawat* [1985] IRLR 57. The Court of Appeal has held that although it is not legally necessary for the tribunal to identify the precise reason for dismissal rather than finding it falls under one of the general headings, eg 'conduct', as a matter of practice it is usual for them to do so: see *British Railways Board v Jackson* [1994] IRLR 235.

It is not sufficient for the employer merely to establish that the employee has committed a dismissible offence. The employer must also show the reason why he decided to dismiss: see *Adams v Derby City Council* [1986] IRLR 163. The reason for a dismissal is made up of all sorts of reasons and sub-reasons. 'A construction ... which required one only to look at one reason would produce an absurdity': *Patterson v Messrs Bracketts* [1977] IRLR 137. See also *Bates Farms and Dairy Ltd v Scott* [1976] IRLR 214.

In *Abernethy v Mott, Hay and Anderson* [1974] ICR 323, Cairns LJ held: 'A reason for the dismissal of an employee is a set of facts known to the employer, or it may be of beliefs held by him which cause him to dismiss the employee.' This was re-emphasised by the EAT in *CGB Publishing v Killey* [1993] IRLR 520.

Therefore, as a general proposition the employer must show that at the time of the dismissal he honestly believed that the employee was dismissed for the reason expressed. Additionally, the employer's belief should be based on reasonable grounds.

In *Ferodo Ltd v Barnes* [1976] ICR 439, a case involving the employee's vandalism, the EAT held that the tribunal should not ask, 'Are we satisfied the offence was committed?', but 'Are we satisfied that the employers had, at the time of the dismissal, reasonable grounds for believing that the offence put against the applicant was in fact committed?'.

In *British Homes Stores Ltd v Burchell* [1978] IRLR 379, followed in *Weddel and Co Ltd v Tepper* [1980] IRLR 96, it was held that in the case of misconduct not necessarily involving dishonesty it is usually necessary for the employer to show that he:

> entertained a reasonable suspicion amounting to a belief in the guilt of the employee of that misconduct at that time. ... First of all, there must be established by the employer the fact of that belief; that the employer did believe it. Secondly, that the employer had in his mind reasonable grounds upon which to sustain that belief. And thirdly, we think, that the employer, at the stage at which he formed that belief on those grounds, at any rate at the final stage at which he formed that belief on those grounds, had carried out as much investigation into the matter as was reasonable in all the circumstances of the case.

See also *Pritchett and Dyjasek v J McIntyre Ltd* [1987] IRLR 18. In *The Distillers Company (Bottling Services) Ltd v Gardner* [1982] IRLR 47, the EAT considered *obiter* that this principle extended to cases of misconduct not involving dishonesty. However, the principle in *British Homes Stores Ltd* and *Weddel and Co Ltd*, *above*, is not of universal application. In some exceptional cases a reasonable suspicion is sufficient: *Monie v Coral Racing Ltd* [1980] IRLR 464, a case where the employer had a reasonable suspicion that one of two employees or possibly both had been guilty of dishonesty.

In *Parr v Whitbread and Co plc* [1990] ICR 427, the EAT held that where a group of employees could have committed an offence the employer may be entitled to dismiss all of them where he reasonably believes at the date of dismissal that one or more persons was guilty and that that belief was based on solid and sensible grounds. In *Whitbread and Co plc v Thomas and Others* [1988] ICR 135, the employer dismissed three employees from a shop which had had serious stock losses. The employer could not identify the cause of the stock losses or the persons responsible. It argued that its only option was to dismiss all three employees since they failed to prevent stock losses. The EAT found that the employers were able to establish a reason. The act or acts were committed by one or more of the group, all of whom were individually capable of having committed the act. The employers had been able to establish a reason at the time of the dismissal based upon conduct or capability.

Thus, the employer may be able to establish the reason notwithstanding the fact that he is mistaken in his belief, provided that the belief is genuinely held, although where the employer relies upon a genuine but mistaken belief, he may be in difficulty when it comes to considering the reasonableness of the dismissal: *The Maintenance Co Ltd v Dormer* [1982] IRLR 491, and see *Smith v City of Glasgow District Council* [1985] IRLR 79.

The approach in *Ferodo Ltd v Barnes, above,* has been adopted by tribunals in cases where the reason is a reason related to the employee's conduct, whether or not it involves the commission of a criminal offence, as well as cases where the reason is related to the employee's capability. In *Harper v National Coal Board* [1980] IRLR 260, the EAT held that 'an employer cannot claim the reason was "some other substantial reason" if it were whimsical or capricious, but he could if he genuinely believed the reason in his mind at the time of dismissal to be fair. If the belief is genuine and one which most employers might adopt that may be "some other substantial reason".'

Where the reason is 'some other substantial reason' the employer has to show that the reason is a justifiable one. The reason is one which can justify the dismissal but not necessarily one which does justify the dismissal. If the employer is able to establish some other substantial reason the tribunal will still have to examine the reasonableness of the dismissal.

The relationship between the burden of proof imposed upon the employer and the burden which may be placed upon the employee if he seeks to rebut the employer's reasons was considered by the Court of Appeal in *Maund v Penwith District Council* [1984] ICR 143. It was held that once the employer has produced evidence which appears to show the reason for the dismissal, 'then the employee has the lighter burden of producing evidence to cast doubt about the employer's reason. The employee does not have to prove the reason for his dismissal; the onus for doing that remains with the employer.'

Where the reason for dismissal results from a corporate decision it may not always be sufficient to look at the reason recorded in the minutes of the corporate body: see *Smith v Hayle Town Council* [1978] IRLR 413; *Maund v Penwith District Council, above.* The minuted decision will be strong *prima facie* evidence of the reason for the dismissal; per Griffiths LJ in *Maund's* case *above.* In *Smith's* case the issue was whether Smith had been dismissed by reason of misconduct or because of union activities. Sir David Cairns felt that in reaching a decision as to the reason or principal reason '... it would be permissible to look at what was said at the meeting in order to see what actuated the minds of those who voted in favour of the resolution'. It was clear that there was no compelling evidence that the reason for dismissal was Smith's trade union activities. The fact that one of the councillors was influenced by anti-union prejudice and that his vote was decisive did not affect the reason or principal reason for the dismissal.

The hurdle of establishing a fair reason is designed to deter employers from dismissing employees for some trivial or unworthy reason. See *Gilham and Others v Kent CC (No 2)* [1985] ICR 233.

Where the employer applies the wrong label
Where the evidence establishes that the employer has dismissed an employee but the employer has honestly although mistakenly given the wrong legal description to the reason, it will not prevent the tribunal from seeking the true reason and properly defining it. Thus, the employer is not estopped from relying on the true reason. It may be that the reason for the dismissal is clear and apparent in the employer's mind at the time of the dismissal, but that he is not aware of the correct legal description. In *Abernethy v Mott, Hay and Anderson* [1974] ICR 323, the employer thought that the reason for the dismissal was redundancy whereas there was no redundancy within the firm. The tribunal found that Abernethy was dismissed because of capability. There was work available, but Abernethy was not capable of doing it. Lord Denning held:

> I do not think that the reason has got to be correctly labelled at the time of dismissal. It may be that the employer is wrong in law as labelling it as dismissal for redundancy. In that case the wrong label can be set aside. The employer can only rely on the reason *in fact* for which he dismissed the man, if the facts are sufficiently known or made known to the man. The reason in this case was—on the facts—already known or sufficiently made known to Mr Abernethy. The wrong label of 'redundancy' does not affect the point.

The employer honestly thought that the facts constituted redundancy, but in law they did not. See also *Land and Wilson v West Yorkshire Metropolitan County Council* [1979] IRLR 174.

In *Trust Houses Forte Leisure Ltd v Aquilar* [1976] IRLR 251, it was held that the reason is a fact existing at the moment of dismissal.

It is necessary for a tribunal to distinguish those cases where the employer has applied an incorrect label and seeks to change the label, from those cases where the employer seeks to argue that the dismissal was for a reason other than that upon which the employer relied at the time of the dismissal. The reason given at the time of dismissal is evidence as to the real reason, but the description of the reason may be mistaken; the employer may have kindly labelled the real reason differently, or he may have difficulty in proving the facts leading to the dismissal: see *Cairns LJ* in *Abernethy v Mott, Hay and Anderson, above*, approved by Lord Bridge in *West Midlands Co-operative Society Ltd v Tipton* [1986] IRLR 112. It is open to the employer at the hearing to rely upon a different set of facts, however, he may have difficulty in persuading the tribunal that the real reason is a different reason from that put forward at the time of the dismissal, although he may prove that the reason put forward before the tribunal is the real one. The employer cannot rely upon facts which were subsequently discovered and which were not known to him at the time of the dismissal: see *W Devis and Sons Ltd v Atkins* [1977] AC 931 and under 'Reasonableness and subsequently discovered misconduct' at p 154.

On appeal to the EAT, the employer cannot rely upon reasons which were not pleaded by him in his notice of appearance to the tribunal and which were not canvassed by him before the tribunal: see *Nelson v BBC* [1977] ICR 649.

In *Murphy v Epsom College* [1983] ICR 715, (approved by the Court of Appeal [1985] ICR 80) Browne-Wilkinson J followed *Nelson's* case. At p723 he recalled that in *Nelson's* case the EAT had substituted 'some other substantial reason' for dismissal on the ground of redundancy, but that the Court of Appeal held that although the reason was not redundancy, since it was the only defence pleaded before the tribunal, the employers could not rely on a defence that there was some other substantial reason and the EAT was not '... entitled to apply facts found in relation to the fairness of the dismissal for the purpose of holding that the dismissal was for "some other substantial reason"'. He held that in the light of *Nelsons'* case '... it is probably necessary that the matter [as to some other substantial reason] should be expressly ventilated in the industrial tribunal before it reaches a decision on the matter so that the parties can have a full and proper opportunity to deploy their case on the matter'.

In *Hotson v Wisbech Conservative Club* [1984] ICR 859, the employee was dismissed by reason of gross inefficiency. At the tribunal hearing, as the result of questioning by the tribunal chairman, the club added, or substituted as the reason for dismissal, suspected dishonesty. On appeal the EAT held that although the employer is not tied to the label he puts upon the facts relied on, and the tribunal can declare the reason relied upon at the time of dismissal was not the real reason, and although 'some other substantial reason' may be put forward by the employer or found by the tribunal to be the real reason differing from that which may have been put forward at the time of dismissal the employer may not, however, change after the time of dismissal the facts which were relied upon at the time as the basis for dismissal. Even in cases involving only a change of label, it must be ensured that the employee is not procedurally or evidentially disadvantaged by that change, as is made plain in *Murphys'* case. In this case it is clear from the decision of the EAT that they did not feel that this was a case involving simply a change of label.

In *McCrory v Magee t/a Heatwell Heating Systems* [1983] ICR 414, the tribunal following the approach in *Abernethy*'s case, *above*, found that the employer's reason for dismissing the employee was his belief or suspicion in the employee's dishonesty notwithstanding that the employer did not put forward that suspicion of dishonesty as the justification for the dismissal, either in his notice of appearance or in evidence. The NICA held that although the tribunal could not 'pick out and substitute a reason which was neither given nor entertained by the employer merely because the tribunal thinks it a better reason or one which would justify dismissal (or summary dismissal) when the employer's stated reason would not' there was evidence to support the view that the employer's suspicion of dishonesty was the real reason for the employee's dismissal. Although the employer was not changing the label but relying upon a different reason the employee had been given the chance to deal with the allegations so that *Nelson v BBC, above*, is capable of being distinguished. None the less there is a difference in approach between the two cases.

In *Hannan v TNT-IPEC (UK) Ltd* [1986] 165, the EAT considered the earlier decisions. It held:

> It seems to us that one can summarise the distinction between the two lines of authority to which we have referred in this way, that where the different grounds are really different labels and nothing more, then there is no basis for saying that the late introduction, even without pleading or without argument, is a ground for interference on appeal; but that where the difference goes to facts and substance and there would or might have been some substantial or significant difference in the way the case is conducted, then of course an appeal will succeed if the Tribunal rely on a different ground without affording an opportunity for argument. For the reasons which we have endeavoured to express, we are persuaded that [in this case] ... the distinction is in truth one of labels and that there are no grounds for thinking the case would have been conducted in any significant way differently or more thoroughly investigated or the cross-examination or the evidence called would have been in any way significantly different had the case, as ultimately relied upon by the industrial tribunal, been pleaded or canvassed in evidence.

This case was applied in *Burkett v Pendletons (Sweets) Ltd* [1992] ICR 407, in which the EAT held that where the tribunal finds that the reason was different from that pleaded and the parties had not been given an opportunity to deal with that different reason the tribunal had erred in law. The employers had contended the reason for dismissal was redundancy but the tribunal had found the reason was some other substantial reason, namely a re-organisation, although that had not been pleaded or argued by the parties. The EAT held that this could not stand, and since the employers had failed to show a reason the dismissal was unfair. In *Clarke v Trimoco Group Ltd and Another* [1993] IRLR 148, the reason given at the time of dismissal and relied upon in the employer's notice of appearance was the post-dating of fuel vouchers although the real reason was a police investigation into a more serious fraud. The EAT held the dismissal was not unfair on that particular ground (although it possibly was on other grounds). The critical question was whether the employee was unaware of the real reason and whether he was able to challenge the facts in the tribunal. Although this was more than a labelling error the dominant consideration was that the reason why he was being dismissed was obvious to the employee. In *Abernethy* there was simply a true labelling error. In *Hotson*'s case a great deal more than a change of label was involved and the employee was deprived of a proper opportunity of dealing with a much more serious allegation of dishonesty and of being sufficiently prepared to state her answer at the hearing.

In the present case in the end 'the dominant consideration is that it was found that it was obvious to Mr Clarke ... what was the reason ... he was dismissed'. In *Ely v YKK Fasteners (UK) Ltd* [1993] IRLR 500, the Court of Appeal held the tribunal was correct in holding that the reason was some other substantial reason where the employers did not think that they had dismissed the employee, but that he had resigned. Waite LJ held that it would be illogical 'to adopt an interpretation of s 57 which would result in dismissals which have occurred through an erroneous insistence upon a supposed resignation being placed in a category of their own—in which every such dismissal, regardless of the merits, would be rendered automatically unfair because the employer could not supply reason for it. To outlaw such dismissals from the ordinary rules as to fairness affecting all other forms of dismissal (including constructive dismissal) would ... introduce an unnecessary complication into employment relations which would be more likely to confuse than to clarify resignation procedures in the work place.' He thought it was right to extend the principle in the *Abernethy* case so that resort could be had to a state of facts known and relied on by the employer at the time for the purpose of supplying him with a reason for dismissal which, because he had misunderstood the true nature of the circumstances, he had not been able to treat as a reason for dismissal at the time.

Facts discovered subsequent to the dismissal

The employer is only entitled to rely upon reasons which were known to him at the time of the dismissal. He cannot rely upon other grounds or reasons which subsequently came to his knowledge: *W Devis and Sons Ltd v Atkins* [1977] AC 931. The decision of the House of Lords in this case makes it clear that the common law authorities (*Boston Deep Sea Fishing and Ice Co v Ansell* (1888) 39 ChD 339, and *Cyril Leonard and Co v Simo Securities Trust Ltd* [1972] 1 WLR 80) have no application to the statutory jurisdiction.

Subsequently discovered facts may entitle the employer to reduce the amount of compensation. See Chapter 16.

The employee may have the right to appeal against his dismissal under the employer's internal disciplinary procedure. The employer's failure to allow the employee to appeal notwithstanding that that is something which happens after the dismissal, may render the dismissal unfair: see *West Midlands Co-operative Society Ltd v Tipton* [1986] IRLR 112. See Chapter 7.

An internal appeal may show that the original reasons relied upon by the employer cannot be supported by the evidence. In *Monie v Coral Racing Ltd* [1981] ICR 109, the Court of Appeal held that the fairness or otherwise of the dismissal depends upon the sufficiency of the reason given by the employer at the time of the dismissal. The hearing of an appeal when the dismissal was confirmed was not the time of dismissal. Therefore, the employer was not entitled to rely upon a subsequent and different reason given to the employee for his dismissal following the hearing of an internal appeal.

In *West Midlands Co-operative Society Ltd v Tipton* [1986] ICR 112, the House of Lords held that in determining whether the employer acted reasonably or unreasonably in treating his real reason for dismissal as sufficient, both the original and appeal decisions are to be taken into account. Thus, it may be that on appeal the employer will realise that he is acting unreasonably in dismissing the employee because of circumstances established in the course of the domestic appeal procedure. If the employer could not take into account those facts discovered on appeal injustice would result. In giving judgment Lord Bridge approved a passage from the judgment of Waterhouse J in *The Board of Governors, The National Heart and Chest Hospitals v Nambiar* [1981] IRLR 196, where it was held that where evidence at an internal appeal shows that a different reason from the one originally given would justify dismissal, then the original dismissal should not stand and the employer should reconsider the matter to decide whether a dismissal on the new evidence is appropriate. Usually, an employer confirms the original decision to dismiss following an appeal and it is right for the tribunal to look at evidence that arose during the course of the appeal. Lord Bridge held that 'a dismissal is unfair if the employer unreasonably treats his real reason as a sufficient reason to dismiss the employee, either when he makes his original decision to dismiss or when he maintains that decision at the conclusion of an internal appeal'.

Monie's case was not considered by the House of Lords in *Tipton*'s case *above*. The judgment of Lord Bridge does conflict with the decision in *Monie*'s case, *above*; see also *Whitbread and Co plc v Mills* [1988] IRLR 501.

The statutory reasons are now considered in the light of reported cases.

Capability and qualifications

The reason for dismissal may relate to the employee's capability, or qualifications. 'Capability' means capability assessed by reference to skill, aptitude, health or any other physical or mental quality: s 57(4)(*a*) of the EP(C)A 1978. (As to dismissal for health see Chapter 8.)

Skill
Skills may be executive or manual. In the case of executive skills, it may be the total inability of the manager to perform competently the whole ambit of duties which are entrusted to him. In *Kendrick v Concrete Pumping Ltd* [1975] IRLR 83, Kendrick, a depot manager, was dismissed because he was not able to organise the repair or maintenance of vehicles; he had difficulties with the control of spares, with the organisation of the depot and with controlling personnel. See also *Lewis Shops Group v Wiggins* [1973] ICR 335.

There may be criticism of a particular skill rather than the employee's overall capability. In *Duncan v Scottish Farmers Dairy Co Ltd* [1973] IRLR 48, Duncan placed too much faith in his staff to the extent that he had allowed one person unsupervised to be responsible for the money which had to be banked and so exposed his staff to temptations.

Capability may relate to manual skills. In *Davison v Kent Meters Ltd* [1975] IRLR 145, Davison failed to assemble 471 out of 500 components correctly. In *Day v Diemer and Reynolds Ltd* [1975] IRLR 298, Day, a gathering machine operator, failed to ensure that the sections of a book had been gathered together properly prior to binding.

Capability is assessed in relation to the employer's demands which may change.

In *Sutton and Gates (Luton) Ltd v Boxall* [1979] ICR 67, the EAT held that the tribunal, should distinguish whether the case was one of sheer incapability due to an inherent incapacity to function, or one of failure to exercise to the full such talent as the employee possessed. Where a person has not come up to standard through carelessness, negligence or idleness, the case should be dealt with as one of misconduct rather than incapability.

Aptitude

Lack of aptitude may be a failure to achieve a 'theoretical' or 'practical' standard. In *Blackman v Post Office* [1974] ICR 151, Blackman was capable at a practical level, but he had failed all three attempts at an aptitude test. The union was not prepared to waive a rule that the employee had to pass a written examination and so he was dismissed. The reason was one related to his capability.

In *Judge International v Moss* [1973] IRLR 208, lack of aptitude was the reason for the dismissal of a financial controller and group secretary. The employer felt in the long term he could not 'succeed in his job because we think the position is too big for him as he is not self-motivating and probably lacks leadership'.

In *Abernethy v Mott, Hay and Anderson* [1974] ICR 323, the employee's inflexibility and lack of adaptability was a reason which related to the employee's aptitude.

Physical health

Poor health (see also Chapter 8) may be physical or mental health. In *Finch v Betabake (Anglia) Ltd* [1977] IRLR 470, Finch, an apprentice motor mechanic, was dismissed because of defective eyesight. A report by an ophthalmic surgeon stated he could not be employed without undue danger to himself or others.

Ill health may have been caused by the nature of the work, as where an employee contracts dermatitis and is no longer able to work a machine which exposes him to oil, or where an employee suffers with a skin complaint through using a chain-saw, or where he sustains a knee injury in the course of his work. See *Grootcon (UK) Ltd v Keld* [1984] IRLR 302. Physical incapacity may also be compounded by the anxiety and strain of employment.

Where a disabled worker is dismissed because of his disability, the reason is one related to his capability, even though the disability existed and was known to the employer when the employee was first employed. Capability was the reason where a disabled worker was dismissed because of absences for prolonged periods which led to disruption in the employer's business: *Kerr v Atkinson Vehicles (Scotland) Ltd* [1974] IRLR 36; see also *Pascoe v Hallen and Medway* [1975] IRLR 116.

In exceptional circumstances it may not be necessary for the disability to interfere with the employee's actual performance of his job. In *Harper v National Coal Board* [1980] IRLR 260, Harper, an epileptic, while in an epileptic fit attacked fellow employees. The EAT found that if, because of ill health, an employee, however involuntarily, may be a source of danger to his fellow employees, this reflects upon his capability for performing work of the kind that he was employed to do. The tribunal had held that in the alternative the dismissal was for 'some other substantial reason' under 57(1)(*b*) of the EP(C)A 1978.

A novel point was raised in *Shook v London Borough of Ealing*

[1986] IRLR 46. Shook was appointed as a residential social worker in a home for handicapped children. She was dismissed due to problems with her back. It was contended that the tribunal had to look at 'the whole range of work not only being performed by the employee under the employment contract but which he or she might lawfully be required to do for the purpose of determining whether or not he or she has been dismissed for a reason relating to capability for performing such work'. It was contended on behalf of the employee that potentially she might have been obliged to work in a very wide range of activities and that she must be incapacitated from the performance of every such activity before the employer could establish that her dismissal was on the grounds of capability. The EAT held that the analogy was unsound. Under s 57(2)(a) of the EP(C)A 1978 the reason must have related to the employee's capability for performing the work. 'The matter thus has to be looked at as an exercise in relation when one is dealing with questions of incapability'.

Since Shook's disabilities related to the performance of her duties under the contract even though it may not have affected her performance of all of them, the tribunal had not erred in finding that the reason for dismissal fell within s 57(2)(a) of the EP(C)A 1978.

Mental health
This may include mental illness where the potential incapability is greater than the present. In *Singh-Deu v Chloride Metals Ltd* [1976] IRLR 56, an employee was diagnosed as having a susceptibility to paranoid schizophrenia. The job required him to have his wits about him and if he did not perform his duties properly it might cause serious consequences for his fellow employees. No assurances could be given by the doctor that he would not be subject to a recurrence of the illness. A catastrophic accident could have occurred.

Poor mental health may arise from the employment itself as where an employee suffers with a nervous breakdown due to the pressure and anxiety of his employment.

Where the reason for the dismissal is not merely the employee's mental illness but the fact that he has deliberately misled the employers by not disclosing the illness in order to obtain employment, the reason may be 'some other substantial reason': *O'Brien v Prudential Assurance Co Ltd* [1979] IRLR 140.

Qualifications
'Qualifications' means any degree, diploma or other academic, technical or professional qualification relevant to the position which the employee held: s 57(4)(b) of the EP(C)A 1978. In *Blackman v Post Office* [1974] ICR 151, the NIRC commented: 'the passing of the aptitude test gives a technical or professional qualification relevant to the position' which the employee held. The court left open the question

of whether qualification is something analogous to degree, diploma or other academic qualification but held, 'One answer to that may be that "qualifications", in relation to the statute, has to be construed in the light of the particular position which the employee held.'

In *Singh v London Country Bus Services Ltd* [1976] IRLR 176, Singh had been charged with theft. The tribunal had held: 'One of the qualifications for performing such work is trustworthiness', but the EAT held that qualifications are more than personal characteristics. Trustworthiness was not a qualification within the statutory definition.

In *Blue Star Ship Management Ltd v Williams* [1979] IRLR 16, the EAT held that the employee's lack of authorisation as a registered seafarer was not a 'qualification' within s 57(4)(*b*). The EAT held 'qualification has in mind matters relating to aptitude or ability, and that a mere licence, permit or authorisation is not such a qualification unless it is substantially concerned with the aptitude or ability of the person to do the job'.

In some cases the employee's lack of qualifications may mean that his continued employment will result in the infringement of legislative provisions.

Conduct

'Conduct' is not defined by s 57(2)(*b*) of the EP(C)A 1978 and it has been left to the tribunals and courts to decide what conduct includes.

Timekeeping and absenteeism

'Conduct' includes bad timekeeping and unauthorised absenteeism in one of its various forms. Bad timekeeping may be lateness in arriving for work as in *Hallet and Want v MAT Transport Ltd* [1976] IRLR 5, where an employee was late for work on 12 out of 80 days following a final warning for lateness. He had been late on 65 occasions in 2 years, and on at least half of those occasions, he had been late by more than 15 minutes. See also *Elliott Brothers (London) Ltd v Colverd* [1979] IRLR 92, where an employee falsified another employee's clocking in card by clocking in for that employee.

Absenteeism may arise when the employee leaves his place of employment during his working day without permission: see *Stewart v Western SMT Co Ltd* [1978] IRLR 553, where the employee was summarily dismissed for three incidents of leaving work early and claiming pay for hours not worked. Absenteeism may also arise where nightwatchmen absent themselves during the night from the building which they are employed to look after: *Ross v Aquascutum Ltd* [1973] IRLR 107; *City of Edinburgh DC v Stephen* [1977] IRLR 135.

In *Maxwell v Grimwood Heating Elements Ltd* [1972] IRLR 81, Maxwell left the factory during a dispute about bonuses and was dismissed. It was held that the reason was one related to his conduct.

In *Lindsay v Fife Forge Co Ltd* [1976] IRLR 47, a turner's labourer, whose duties included cleaning a lathe alleged that the lathe was dirty because his opposite number on the earlier shift had not carried out his duties properly. The employee clocked off, refusing to clean the machine. The reason related to his conduct.

Absences may be for the best reasons. An employee absented himself on Saturdays to fulfil religious obligations without permission. The reason for his dismissal was one related to conduct: *Esson v London Transport Executive* [1975] IRLR 48. The employee was also failing to co-operate.

Absenteeism may follow annual or public holidays where the employee fails to return to work promptly, particularly where the holiday is abroad: *British Leyland (UK) Ltd v Ashraf* [1978] IRLR 330; *Midland Electric Manufacturing Co Ltd v Kanji* [1980] IRLR 185. Where an employee takes time off without securing permission or where permission has been refused and he is dismissed, the reason is one related to his conduct.

Lastly, absenteeism may result because the employee is in custody pending trial on criminal charges. If he is dismissed, the reason for his dismissal is one related to his conduct.

Failure to co-operate
The employee's failure or refusal to co-operate with the lawful requests or directions of his employer is a reason related to 'conduct'. There may be one incident, as in *Lindsay v Dunlop Ltd* [1980] IRLR 93, where Lindsay was one of a number of employees working in an area affected by hot rubber fumes. They decided not to work in the area. The other employees then agreed to accept masks and resumed normal working as a temporary measure pending further action by the employer. Lindsay refused to work normally until the fumes were cleared, and was dismissed. Failure to co-operate may extend over several occasions or incidents and lead to a pattern of unwillingness to co-operate. That failure may arise in a broad sense as in *Rose v Leeds Metal Spinning Co Ltd* [1976] IRLR 142, where Rose refused to impart to the management any knowledge he had about offensive and derogatory graffiti which had been written on lavatory walls.

The failure or refusal to co-operate may arise because the employee has decided the way in which he will work irrespective of and in opposition to the way the management requires, or because the employee is unwilling to accept policy formulated by the employer and is prepared to make his dissension known: *Retarded Children's Aid Society Ltd v Day* [1978] ICR 437.

The employee's failure or refusal to co-operate may arise where he is requested to work overtime or to carry out special work or different duties, whether or not he is contractually bound. See *Martin v Solus Schall* [1979] IRLR 1.

The reason is one related to the employee's conduct if he is unwilling to accept a change in the terms of his contract of employment where the change is not a repudiation. In *Mordecai v Jacob Beatus Ltd* [1975] IRLR 170, an employee refused to move from a dispatch department to other operations in an adjoining factory even though his contract contained a flexibility clause. See also *Wilson v IDR Construction Ltd* [1975] IRLR 260.

There may be no power in the contract to alter its terms, but if the employer seeks an alteration for good reason, as where he wishes to make the operation more economical to benefit the employee, and the employee refuses to accede to the change and is dismissed, the reason for the dismissal is conduct—his failure to co-operate. See *Coward v John Menzies (Holdings) Ltd* [1977] IRLR 428, where the employer wished to transfer Coward from Letchworth to Swansea for training. Coward refused and was dismissed.

Where the employee refuses to accede to a change in the terms of the contract and there is no contractual power to alter those terms, the reason for the dismissal may also be treated as 'some other substantial reason' within s 57(1)(*b*) of the EP(C)A 1978. See also *St John of God (Care Services) Ltd v Brooks and Others* [1992] IRLR 546. The reason was 'some other substantial reason' where the company decided the only alternative to closure was to employ staff on less beneficial terms of employment. Under new proposed terms there was a reduction in holidays, the abolition of overtime rates, the replacement of a generous sick pay scheme with statutory sick pay only and a pay freeze.

Where the employee's failure to co-operate arises from some lack of ability on the part of the employee, the reason for the dismissal may be one related to the employee's capability: *AJ Dunning and Sons (Shopfitters) Ltd v Jacomb* [1973] ICR 448.

Refusal to obey an order
'Conduct' also includes the employee's failure to obey a lawful order given to him by his employer. This may also involve a failure to co-operate. The refusal may be a refusal to do a job, such as to work in a warehouse, to move concrete, to work in bad weather, to take out a loaded van, to undertake a night journey or to operate a new system. It may also relate to matters ancillary to the employment, for instance, a refusal to have one's hair cut, to wear a uniform or to go on a course of instruction.

Breach of the employer's rules
The employee's breach of the employer's rules, whether the rules are written or oral, is a reason related to conduct. The breach may be a failure to obey the employer's orders or the commission of a criminal offence. Examples are: drinking during working hours: *Gray Dunn and*

Co Ltd v Edwards [1980] IRLR 23; failing to ring up purchases on a till: *Laws Stores Ltd v Oliphant* [1978] IRLR 251; disclosing confidential information belonging to the employer: *Archer v Cheshire and North-wich Building Society* [1976] IRLR 424; failing to follow procedures for the transfer of money from the employer's vehicles to customer's premises: *Rigden-Murphy v Securicor Ltd* [1976] IRLR 106; dealing in another company's products: *McCall v Castleton Crafts* [1979] IRLR 218; and a breach of the employer's rules relating to hygiene: *Unkles v Milanda Bread Co Ltd* [1973] IRLR 76.

There may be a breach of the employer's safety rules. In *Bendall v Paine and Betteridge* [1973] IRLR 44, the employee was dismissed because he smoked on the employer's premises, despite a warning to the contrary. The premises were constructed of matchwood and there were additional fire risks of paint and timber. Other cases have involved the removal of guards or safety devices on machinery: see *Martin v Yorkshire Imperial Metals Ltd* [1978] IRLR 440.

Insubordination

Insubordination to superiors is a reason related to 'conduct'. It may arise out of a failure to obey an order or a failure to co-operate as in *Lambsdale v Her Majesty's Stationery Office* [1975] IRLR 239. Lambsdale refused to attend a meeting with his superior officers and failed to apologise for not attending. This failure was coupled with critical remarks about his employer.

Gross impertinence may be insubordination as in *McCabe v Ninth District Council of the County of Lanark* [1973] IRLR 75, where McCabe lost his temper on two occasions, and on the second occasion he was offensive and aggressive at an investigatory hearing.

In *King v Motorway and Tyres Accessories Ltd* [1975] IRLR 51, King told his branch manager to 'fuck off', was argumentative and abusive; in *Chantril v WF Shortland Ltd* [1974] IRLR 333, Chantrill an apprentice, on being told off by the managing director in front of two other apprentices, retorted, 'You couldn't have done any fucking better'; in *Rosenthal v Louis Butler Ltd* [1972] IRLR 39, the employee, a millinery trimmer and finisher, called the factory manager a 'stupid punk' when other staff were present.

Employee relationships

'Conduct' also includes cases where the employee is dismissed because of his relationship with the other employees. It may be potential, rather than actual, problems in the relationship which lead to the dismissal. Where there is a mere conflict or clash of personality leading to dishar-mony between employees and one employee is dismissed to restore harmony, the reason may be 'some other substantial reason'.

The problem may be of a general nature as where a foreman dis-played an attitude to his fellow workers which was aggressive, unpleasant and created a bad atmosphere in the works: *McKinney v Bieganek* [1973] IRLR 311. Another recent example is making nuisance telephone calls to fellow employees in a hospital: *East Berkshire Health Authority v Matadeen* [1992] IRLR 336.

There may be a specific incident as where an employee has a violent argument with a colleague and subsequently the relationship is tense and quarrelsome, leading to further arguments. An employee may assault another: *CA Parsons and Co Ltd v McLoughlin* [1978] IRLR 65; *Meyer Dunmore International Ltd v Rogers* [1978] IRLR 167. It does not matter that the violence arises outside the workplace if the tension arises within it.

'Conduct' may be the employee's sexual relationship with another employee. In *Newman v Alarmco Ltd* [1976] IRLR 45, Newman was dismissed because he formed an extra-marital relationship with his secretary and was living with her. The conduct was detrimental to the employer, was offensive and was something which was likely to be discussed to the detriment of the company. In *Grace v Harehills Working Men's Club and Institute* [1974] IRLR 68, a club steward was dismissed for his conduct when he formed a sexual liaison with a girl and allowed her to live with him on the club premises. In *Whitlow v Alkanet Construction Ltd* [1975] IRLR 321, Whitlow had a sexual relationship with the chief executive's wife and was dismissed.

However, a reason may not relate to the employee's conduct where it is extra-marital sexual activities carried on between the employee and another in private, but if sexual activities outside the place of employment involve a breach of criminal law resulting in dismissal, it is one related to conduct. In *Gardiner v Newport CBC* [1974] IRLR 262, a lecturer was convicted of an offence of gross indecency with another man in a public lavatory which followed other alleged incidents involving the employee and his sexual activities.

Lawful sexual activities, for instance lesbianism, detrimentally affecting the employment, may be a reason relating to conduct. However, it is probable that such activities must actually detrimentally affect the employment.

Criminal activities

'Conduct' is the reason where an employee is dismissed because he is suspected of or has been found guilty of a criminal act connected with the employment, or where an employee is dismissed for a criminal offence unconnected with the employment which has an effect on the employment: *Singh v London Country Bus Services Ltd* [1976] IRLR 176; *Nottinghamshire CC v Bowly* [1978] IRLR 252.

Examples of criminal activity which have been the reason for dismissal are theft: *Carr v Alexander Russell Ltd* [1975] IRLR 49; dishonesty: *Tesco Stores Ltd v Heap* (1978) 13 ITR 17; handling stolen property: *Jones v RM Douglas Construction Ltd* [1975] IRLR 175;

vandalism: *Ferodo Ltd v Barnes* [1976] ICR 439; indecent assault: *Creffield v BBC* [1975] IRLR 23; incest: *Bradshaw v Rugby Portland Cement Co Ltd* [1972] IRLR 46; gross indecency: *Gardiner v Newport CBC* [1974] IRLR 262 and *P v Nottinghamshire County Council* [1992] IRLR 362; possession of cannabis: *Norfolk CC v Bernard* [1979] IRLR 220; and embezzlement of club funds: *Secretary of State for Scotland v Campbell* [1992] IRLR 263.

Even where no criminal proceedings are taken, conduct by the employee which might justify criminal proceedings would be a matter of conduct: *Hotson v Wisbech Conservative Club* [1984] IRLR 422, where a reason for the employee's dismissal was suspected dishonesty, and *Royal Society for the Protection of Birds v Croucher* [1984] IRLR 425, where the employee had dishonestly submitted private petrol bills for reimbursement by the society and *Conlin v United Distillers* [1994] IRLR 169, where the employee overbooked an item on a payment by results system, an offence for which he had previously received a final written warning.

Redundancy

Redundancy is considered separately in Chapter 9.

Contravention of a statutory duty or restriction

The essence of this reason, under s 57(2)(*d*) of the EP(C)A 1978, is that the employee could not continue to work in the position which he held without contravention either by him or the employer of a duty or restriction imposed by or under an enactment. The contravention must affect the position which the employee held. In *Fearn v Tayford Motor Co Ltd* [1975] IRLR 336, Fearn, a vehicle supervisor, was required to drive vehicles as an essential and integral part of his duties. He lost his licence and could no longer legally do the job he was taken on to do.

However, in *Cordiner v Smith of Maddiston* (1975) (unreported), a yard foreman who was only required to drive occasionally was dismissed following his disqualification from driving. He could do his job without a driving licence, and there was no contravention of any legislation.

In *Tayside Regional Council v McIntosh* [1982] IRLR 272, McIntosh, a vehicle mechanic was disqualified from driving and dismissed. Although there was no specific provision in the contract, from the surrounding circumstances, the EAT considered it was an essential term of his contract that he should hold a driving licence, so he could not do his job without the contravention of legislation.

The continued employment itself may be a contravention of a statutory duty or restriction. It is for the employer to establish this. In

Myeza v Avon Area Health Authority (1977) (unreported), Myeza was dismissed when it was discovered that her work permit had expired. However, at the date of dismissal, the Home Office were considering renewal of the permit and had intimated to the authority that until a final decision had been reached, it would not be in breach of the immigration regulations to continue to employ Myeza. Further, it was not possible to establish an offence on the part of the authority by the continued employment of Myeza. The authority had acted with haste and had not made sufficient investigations.

Some other substantial reason

'Some other substantial reason' within s 57(1)(*b*) of the EP(C)A 1978, was considered by the NIRC in *RS Components Ltd v Irwin* [1973] ICR 535. The tribunal had interpreted the phrase 'some other substantial reason' as being *ejusdem generis* with the other reasons under s 57. The NIRC rejected this, finding that 'Parliament may well have intended to set out ... the common reasons for a dismissal but can hardly have hoped to produce an exhaustive catalogue of all the circumstances in which a company would be justified in terminating the services of an employee'.

In *Priddle v Dibble* [1978] ICR 148, the EAT followed *Irwin*'s case. This reason is intended as a safety net for the employer. In *Harper v National Coal Board* [1980] IRLR 260, the EAT held that a reason is not substantial if whimsical or capricious, but if the employer can show that he genuinely believed that the reason he had in his mind at the time of dismissal was a fair reason then this would be 'some other substantial reason'. See also *Saunders v Scottish National Camps Association Ltd* [1980] IRLR 174, upheld on appeal [1981] IRLR 277.

In *Dobie v Burns International Security Services (UK) Ltd* [1984] IRLR 329, Sir John Donaldson MR in the Court of Appeal held:

> I construe it [s 57(1)(*b*)] as requiring the tribunal to consider the reason established by the employer and to decide whether it falls within the category of reasons which could justify the dismissal of *an* employee—not *that* employee but *an* employee—holding the position which that employee held. Thus different types of reason *could* justify the dismissal of the office boy from those which *could* justify the dismissal of the managing director.

It is not possible to give an exhaustive catalogue of instances which will fall within this category. Some will suffice. In *Gorfin v Distressed Gentlefolks' Aid Association* [1973] IRLR 290, and *Treganowan v Robert Knee and Co Ltd* [1975] ICR 405, the tribunals found that the reason was 'some other substantial reason' where personality conflicts gave rise to hostility and tension between employees which were beginning to affect detrimentally the employer's business. In each case an employee was dismissed to stop dissension among the staff and to restore harmony.

The reason was 'some other substantial reason' where an employee was not prepared to abide by the terms and conditions generally prevailing for that category of employee within the company: *Tovey v F and F Robinson (Stockton-on-Tees) Ltd* [1975] IRLR 139.

This is also the case where the employee has been dismissed following his failure to accede to a request by the employer to work at times other than those provided in his contract. In *Knighton v Henry Rhodes Ltd* [1974] IRLR 71, Knighton's contract defined his normal working hours as day-time hours. He was asked to do a night shift working one week in six, but he refused and was dismissed. In *Martin v Automobile Proprietary Ltd* [1979] IRLR 64, a dismissal of three employees for refusing to accept a change in their contractual weekly hours of work from 31½ hours to 42 hours was for 'some other substantial reason'. Even where the employee has a contractual right not to be asked to undertake additional duties but refuses to take on new duties the reason may be 'some other substantial reason': *Bowater Containers Ltd v McCormack* [1980] IRLR 50.

In *Moreton v Selby Protective Clothing Co Ltd* [1974] IRLR 269, Moreton who refused to accept the termination of one contract of employment and the substitution of another which would place her under a new obligation to work during school holidays, was dismissed. It was essential for the employer's business that the employee should work during the school holidays and other employees in the same position had accepted the change. See also *Muggridge and Slade v East Anglia Plastics Ltd* [1973] IRLR 163. Similarly a failure to agree new terms and conditions of employment following a reorganisation of the employer's business is 'some other substantial reason': *Hollister v National Farmers Union* [1979] ICR 542. The reorganisation probably must be such that there was some good sound business reason for it. Whether the reorganisation was such that the only sensible thing to do was to terminate the employee's contract unless he would agree to a new arrangement consequent upon the reorganisation, would depend upon the circumstances. Compare *Ellis v Brighton Co-operative Society Ltd* [1976] IRLR 419; see also *Genower v Ealing, Hammersmith and Hounslow Area Health Authority* [1980] IRLR 297, and consider *Evans v Elemeta Holdings Ltd* [1982] IRLR 143.

Where an employee is offered a more menial position following a reorganisation at the same salary as he enjoyed previously, which he refuses to accept, the reason for his dismissal consequent upon his failure to accept the new position will be 'some other substantial reason': *Hannan v TNT-IPEC (UK) Ltd* [1986] IRLR 165.

The reason may be 'some other substantial reason' where the employee has breached his obligation of confidence to the employer. It may arise where the employee competes with his employer while his contract of employment subsists: see *Gray v Pembroke (CP) Ltd* (1972) (unreported); *Bergman v A Farr and Sons Ltd* (1972) (unreported), where an employee had an interest in another firm which might damage his employer's reputation for impartiality, and *Glendinning v Pilkington Bros Ltd* (1973) (unreported), where an employee refused to sign an undertaking that on leaving the employment he would not compete with the employer.

The reason may be 'some other substantial reason' where there is evidence that the employee is going to join some other firm: *Foster v Scaffolding (GB) Ltd* (1972) (unreported); see also *Davidson and Maillov v Comparisons* [1980] IRLR 360.

In *Marshall v Industrial Systems & Control Ltd* [1992] IRLR 294, the reason was held to be conduct justifying dismissal where Marshall, a managing director, had formed a plan with another important manager to try and persuade another to join them in order to deprive the respondent of their best client, but the EAT distinguished an earlier case, *Laughton and Hawley v Bapp Industrial Supplies Ltd* [1986] IRLR 245, where an employee had merely indicated his intention to set up in competition with his employer in the future. See Chapter 7 under 'Substantive reasonableness and the interests of the business' at p 207. A rumour that the employee is leaving to set up a rival business without evidence of an approach to customers was held not to be 'some other substantial reason' in *Betts v Beresford* [1974] IRLR 271. The fact that a member of the employee's family works for a rival firm is probably not 'some other substantial reason': *Cahill v Doulton Glass Industries Ltd* (1974) (unreported); *Ross v Holland House Electro Co Ltd* (1973) (unreported). Where an employee's wife is dismissed by the employer following her arrest on charges of theft from the employer, the dismissal of the employee on the grounds that consequent suspicions about the employee's involvement in the offence had resulted in the breakdown of the employer's confidence and trust in the employee was not 'some other substantial reason': *Wadley v Eager Electrical Ltd* [1986] IRLR 93. It was not an act of the employee which had caused the breakdown in confidence and trust, and the EAT considered that the act must be the act of the employee rather than of some third party. It expressed the view that the loss of confidence by customers in an employer if it continues to employ an employee might be 'some other substantial reason'. Marriage to an employee of a competitor may, however, constitute such a reason: *Foot v Eastern Counties Timber Co Ltd* [1972] IRLR 83; *Skyrail Oceanic Ltd (t/a Goodmos Tours) v Coleman* [1980] IRLR 226, overruled on appeal for different reasons, [1981] IRLR 398.

The reason may be 'some other substantial reason' where the employee is dismissed because the employer's best customers are not willing to accept him doing their work: *Scott Packing and Warehousing Co Ltd v Paterson* [1978] IRLR 166.

In *East African Airways Corporation v Foote* [1977] ICR 776, Foote, a white British citizen, was dismissed as a consequence of a policy directive from the African governments that employees who were not citizens of one of these countries were to be replaced by those who were. The EAT held the tribunal should have asked itself whether this particular policy, and its adoption, was such as to constitute 'some other substantial reason'. It also held 'That involves a finding of what the policy is . . ., consideration . . . of the ingredients of the policy, the reasons for the policy and the circumstances in which the employer decides to apply the policy. . . . it is then for the industrial tribunal to make a finding whether such facts constitute a substantial reason such as to justify dismissal.'

The employee's failure to live within a reasonable distance of his work may constitute 'some other substantial reason' where it is important that the employee should live near the place of his employment: *Farr v Hoveringham Gravels Ltd* [1972] IRLR 104.

The dismissal of an employee following his conviction for indecently assaulting a 13-year-old girl was a dismissal for 'some other substantial reason'. Because of the conviction he was no longer regarded as fit to carry out his duties and represent his employer: *Creffield v BBC* [1975] IRLR 23. Similarly, in *Bell v The Devon and Cornwall Police Authority* [1978] IRLR 283, the employee was dismissed because of his admission that he was a practising homosexual; see also *Saunders v Scottish National Camps Association Ltd* [1980] IRLR 174, confirmed on appeal [1981] IRLR 277. In *Kingston v British Railways Board* [1984] IRLR 147, the Court of Appeal upheld the decision of the tribunal that a sentence of three months' imprisonment was capable of being 'some other substantial reason'.

Failure to meet with the employer's requirements may also be 'some other substantial reason'. In *Flude v Post Office* [1975] IRLR 330, Flude was taken on for a trial period of one year. He received a written warning about being incapable of performing his duties because of drink. He was then involved in an argument with, and made allegations about, another employee. The tribunal held that because of these incidents it was apparent from the trial period that the employee was not up to the employer's requirements. The employee's inability to obtain a fidelity bond may amount to 'some other substantial reason': *Moody v Telefusion Ltd* [1978] IRLR 311.

In the case of joint contracts of employment with the same employer, where it is a condition of the wife's employment that the husband should remain in employment or *vice versa*, the dismissal of the wife because the husband's employment has come to an end for whatever reason will be 'some other substantial reason': *Hendry and Hendry v Scottish Liberal Club* [1977] IRLR 5.

In *North Yorkshire County Council v Fay* [1985] IRLR 247, the Court of Appeal found that where an employee had been engaged under a fixed-term contract for a genuine purpose which was known to the employee, and the purpose for which the fixed-term contract was designed had ceased to exist, then the reason for the employee's dismissal on the expiry of the fixed-term contract may be 'some other substantial reason'.

There may be some overlap between the different statutory reasons.

Failure to show a statutory reason

Having heard the employer's evidence, the tribunal may make a finding that the employer has failed to establish one of the statutory reasons within s 57(1) and (2) of the EP(C)A 1978. It may decline to hear evidence from the employee. Thus the dismissal will be unfair without the need to consider the reasonableness of the dismissal. In *Coral Squash Clubs Ltd v Matthews and Matthews* [1979] IRLR 390, the EAT held that normally the tribunal will need to hear evidence from both the employer and the employee. However, in exceptional cases, the tribunal can stop a case at the end of the case of the party whose evidence and submissions come first and upon whom the onus lies, where that party has clearly failed in law or in fact to establish what he has to establish. See also *Ridley v GEC Machines Ltd* (1978) 13 ITR 195.

There may be a total failure of evidence as in *Yates v British Leyland UK Ltd* [1974] IRLR 367. Here the employer was not able to establish that the reason for the dismissal was that the employee had been urinating over the workshop floor as was alleged. The only evidence the employer could produce was that the employee 'indulged in certain gymnastic exercises ... consistent with ... urinating and restoring himself to what one might call his personal comfort'.

The burden imposed upon the employer is not an onerous one. Thus, where there is some evidence to support the reason given by the employer, the tribunal will only find that the employer cannot show one of the statutory reasons where the evidence is not sufficient to establish the employer's genuine belief in the reason and that he had reasonable grounds for honestly believing the reason existed. In some cases a suspicion may be sufficient: see *Monie v Coral Racing Ltd* [1980] IRLR 464.

In *Gilham and Others v Kent CC (No 2)* [1985] ICR 233, Griffiths LJ held:

> The hurdle over which the employer has to jump at this stage of an inquiry into an unfair dismissal complaint is designed to deter employers from dismissing employees for some trivial or unworthy reason. If he does so, the dismissal is deemed unfair without the need to look further into its merits. But if on the face of it the reason *could* justify the dismissal, then it passes as a substantial reason, and the inquiry moves on to s 57(3) [of the EP(C)A 1978], and the question of reasonableness.

If the reason is not in dispute the tribunal will err in law in finding that the employer has failed to show a statutory reason: *Post Office Counters Ltd v Heavey* [1989] IRLR 513.

There may be a total failure of evidence where the evidence is not admissible, for instance where an employer seeks to rely on an employee's conviction which is a spent conviction under the Rehabilitation of Offenders Act 1974. Furthermore there is no obligation on the employee to disclose a spent offence: *Property Guards Ltd v Taylor and Kershaw* [1982] IRLR 175.

The employer will have difficulty in showing a reason where the reason for the dismissal is pressure brought about by a strike or other industrial action, or threats of a strike or other industrial action, because no account can be taken of such pressure in determining the reason or principal reason for a dismissal: s 63 of the EP(C)A 1978.

The employer will also be unable to establish a reason where he seeks to rely on facts relating solely to a prior employment. However, he may be able to rely on facts which predate the commencement of the employment where those facts affect the employment. In *Torr v British Railways Board* [1977] ICR 785, the employee made false statements in his application for employment. When asked if he had been found guilty of any offence, he replied, 'No'. After the employment had commenced the Board discovered that he had been convicted of a criminal offence and imprisoned. He was successfully prosecuted for dishonestly obtaining a pecuniary advantage by deception and was dismissed. The Board was able to establish a reason and it did not matter that the employee had discharged his duties as a guard satisfactorily for a period of 16 months.

The statutory reason where a dismissal is denied

The employer may also be unable to establish a reason for the dismissal where dismissal is disputed. This may arise where the employee claims a constructive dismissal or where the employee alleges he was dismissed, but this is denied by the employer. The difficulties where the employee alleges he has been constructively dismissed and succeeds, were highlighted by the EAT in *Associated Tyre Specialists (Eastern) Ltd v Waterhouse* [1977] ICR 218. An employer who fights a constructive dismissal claim:

> on the basis that there has been no dismissal at all is inevitably in the difficulty that it is really a very unhappy course to try to run in double harness with that [alternative] defence ... if we did, this was our reason for the dismissal which we say we didn't do; and it was fair.

The problems were highlighted in the decision of Slynn J in *Savoia v Chiltern Herb Farms Ltd* [1981] IRLR 65. He held:

> It is not entirely easy, as we have said recently in *Genower v Ealing, Hammersmith and Hounslow Area Health Authority* [1980] IRLR 297, to

apply s 57 of the 1978 Act to the case of constructive dismissal. Where the employer dismisses, it is easy to understand how he is to show the reason for the dismissal under ss 57(1) and 57(2) of the Act. The employer, having done that, is entitled to go on to show that the dismissal was fair. [But see Chapter 7 as to the onus of proof since the passing of the 1980 Act.] But where it is the employee who has terminated the contract by accepting a repudiation of the contract, it is clearly not easy to apply the words of ss 57(1) and 57(2). The onus appears, if the words are read literally, still to require the employer to show what was the reason for the dismissal and that it was one of the reasons relating to conduct or capability or was some other substantial reason of a kind such as to justify the dismissal. But in a constructive dismissal situation, the employer has not determined the contract for one of these reasons, and so it seems to us that, in a case like the present one, the Industrial Tribunal, having found that there was a fundamental breach, is entitled to consider the question posed in sub s 3 [of s 57] as adapted to a constructive dismissal situation and it must, applying those words to a constructive dismissal situation, ask itself whether, even though in fundamental breach of contract, the employer had, in all the circumstances, behaved fairly. It seems to us that that is the better approach rather than to seek to turn the words of ss 57(1) and 57(2) in such a way as to apply them to a constructive dismissal situation.

The decision of the EAT was upheld by the Court of Appeal: see *Savoia v Chiltern Herb Farms Ltd* [1982] IRLR 166, where Waller LJ held that under s 57 of the EP(C)A 1978 the onus is firmly put upon the employer to show what was the reason. He went on, 'This goes beyond the simple circumstances of the employer's conduct which amounted to dismissal and involves looking into the conduct of the employee and all the surrounding circumstances.'

In *Delabole Slate Ltd v Berriman* [1985] IRLR 305, the Court of Appeal held:

even in the case of constructive dismissal, s 57(1) of the 1978 Act imposes on the employer the burden of showing the reason for dismissal, notwithstanding that it was the employee, not the employer who actually decided to terminate the contract of employment. In our judgment, the only way in which the statutory requirements of the 1978 Act can be made to fit a case of constructive dismissal is to read s 57(1) as requiring the employer to show the reasons for his conduct which entitled the employee to terminate the contract thereby giving rise to a deemed dismissal by the employer. We can see nothing in the decision of *Savoia v Chiltern Herb Farms Ltd* [*above*] which conflicts with this view.

Where in a case involving a constructive dismissal the employer also puts forward a longstop defence that if the dismissal was for a particular reason it was fair, the tribunal must consider carefully the reason put forward for the dismissal: see *Derby City Council v Marshall* [1979] IRLR 261, and where the employer wishes to adopt the alternative defence that if there was a dismissal the dismissal was fair in all the circumstances, the employer must plead that defence: see *Post Office v Strange* [1981] IRLR 515.

In *Industrial Rubber Products v Gillon* [1977] IRLR 389, Gillon's basic rate of pay was unilaterally reduced to regularise a breach of the government's pay policy. It was a breach of a fundamental term of the contract enabling the employee to claim a constructive dismissal. However, it was held that the reduction to comply with the pay policy was 'some other substantial reason'. In *Genower v Ealing, Hammersmith and Hounslow Area Health Authority* [1980] IRLR 297, there was a change in the employee's job which entitled him to claim he had been dismissed. The reason for the change was a reorganisation— 'some other substantial reason'.

For dismissal in health and safety cases and on grounds of assertion of statutory rights, see Chapters 13 and 14.

Chapter 7

The Fairness of the Dismissal

General

Once a reason for dismissal within s 57(1) and (2) of the EP(C)A 1978 is established the tribunal must be satisfied that the employer has acted reasonably. There are certain exceptions, where a dismissal will be automatically fair or unfair. See Chapters 2, 10, 11, 13 and 14.

Section 57(3) of the EP(C)A 1978 provides that:

> The determination of the question whether the dismissal was fair or unfair, having regard to the reason shown by the employer, shall depend on whether in the curcumstances (including the size and administrative resources of the employer's undertaking) the employer acted reasonably or unreasonably in treating it as a sufficient reason for dismissing the employee; and that question shall be determined in accordance with equity and the substantial merits of the case.

The burden of proof is sometimes described as being neutral so that there is a balance between the employer and the employee. The tribunal has to look at the whole of the evidence in deciding whether or not the employer has acted reasonably or unreasonably. In the majority of cases coming before the tribunals it will be clear whether or not the employer has acted reasonably or unreasonably.

Tribunals have to have specific regard to the size and administrative resources of the employer's undertaking. What might be found to be unreasonable in the case of a large employer with perhaps a specialised personnel section might be reasonable in the case of a small employer with no more than, say, four employees.

However, the small size of the employer will not justify his failure to carry out a proper investigation: see *Henderson v Granville Tours Ltd* [1982] IRLR 494. Conversely a large employer may not succeed in circumstances where a small employer can. The EAT has held that 'while the size of the undertaking may affect the nature or formality of the consultation process, it cannot excuse the lack of any consultation at all. However informal the consultation may be, it should ordinarily take place': *De Grasse v Stockwell Tools Ltd* [1992] IRLR 269.

149

The tribunal will have to consider whether the employer acted reasonably both 'procedurally' and 'substantively' and is entitled to have regard to equity and the substantial merits of the case.

In *UCATT v Brain* [1981] ICR 542, the Court of Appeal held that in having regard to equity, ie common fairness, and the substantial merits, tribunals have to look at the question of reasonableness without involving legal technicalities, but rather in an employment and industrial relations context. Questions of law arising from s 57(3) of the EP(C)A 1978 should be rare. See also *Dillett v National Coal Board* [1988] ICR 218.

The fact that the employee may have acted reasonably does not mean that the employer must have acted unreasonably. See *Richmond Precision Engineering Ltd v Pearce* [1985] IRLR 179, where the original employer's business was taken over by the company. Pearce's employment continued but the company offered him less favourable terms and conditions to which he refused to agree. The EAT found that the dismissal was fair. It held 'Merely because there are disadvantages to the employee, it does not ... follow that the employer has acted unreasonably in treating his failure to accept the terms which they have offered as a reason to dismiss'. See also *Chubb Fire Security Ltd v Harper* [1983] IRLR 311.

However, injustice to the employee is one of the factors which has to be considered. In *Dobie v Burns International Security Services (UK) Ltd* [1984] IRLR 329, the Court of Appeal held that the employer must have regard to the question of injustice to the employee. He must take account of, eg, length of service, performance, the likelihood of obtaining new employment. The list of factors will differ not only according to the reason for the dismissal, but on the facts of the individual case. Thus, whatever the length of service, however good the performance, and whatever the chances of new employment, these factors are unlikely to weigh much, if at all, in a case where the reason for dismissal was some form of dishonesty.

The function of the tribunal is 'to decide, not what they would have done had they been the management, ... [but] whether or not the dismissal was fair or unfair, which depends on whether the employer acted reasonably in treating it as a sufficient reason for dismissing the employee': *Grundy (Teddington) Ltd v Willis* [1976] IRLR 118.

In deciding whether the dismissal was fair or unfair the tribunal must apply 'the objective standard of the way in which a reasonable employer in those circumstances, in that line of business, would have behaved ... The test is whether what has been done is something which "no reasonable management would have done ..." ' A tribunal must not try to decide what it would have done itself in the same circumstances: *NC Watling and Co Ltd v Richardson* [1978] IRLR 255; see also *Rolls Royce Ltd v Walpole* [1980] IRLR 343. In *Neale v County Council of Hereford and Worcester* [1985] IRLR 281, the EAT held that a tribunal should ask itself what range of response would have been acceptable to a reasonable hypothetical employer in the same situation. This is illustrated in *British Leyland UK Ltd v Swift* [1981] IRLR 91, where the Court of Appeal per Lord Denning MR held that 'if no reasonable employer would have dismissed him, then the dismissal was unfair. But if a reasonable employer might reasonably have dismissed him, then the dismissal was fair.' There is a band of reasonableness within which two employers might reasonably have different opinions.

In *Swift*'s case the issue was the employee's conduct. For a case involving a similar approach when the issue was capability, see *Bevan Harris Ltd (t/a The Clyde Leather Co) v Gair* [1981] IRLR 520.

In *Walton v TAC Construction Materials Ltd* [1981] IRLR 357, the employee was dismissed by the employer in accordance with their policy not to employ drug addicts. The EAT found that although a more lenient employer might have continued the employment it was within the range of reasonable responses for the employer to dismiss, particularly as the policy of not employing drug addicts was reasonable. The dismissal was fair.

In *United Distillers v Conlin* [1992] IRLR 503 (confirmed by the Court of Session [1994] IRLR 169), the EAT held that dismissal for dishonesty after a prior final warning for the same offence of deliberate fraud was within the range of reasonable responses for an employer to make notwithstanding the fraud involved did not exceed £3 in value.

In *Iceland Frozen Foods Ltd v Jones* [1982] IRLR 439, the EAT held that the correct approach for a tribunal when considering the test of reasonableness is as follows:

(1) the starting point should always be the words of s 57(3) [of the EP(C)A 1978] themselves;

(2) in applying the section a tribunal must consider the reasonableness of the employer's conduct, not simply whether they (the members of the tribunal) consider the dismissal to be fair;

(3) in judging the reasonableness of the employer's conduct a tribunal must not substitute its decision as to what was the right course to adopt for that of the employer;

(4) in many (though not all) cases there is a band of reasonable responses to the employee's conduct within which one employer might reasonably take one view, another quite reasonably take another;

(5) the function of the tribunal, as an industrial jury, is to determine whether in the particular circumstances of each case the decision to dismiss the employee fell within the band of reasonable responses which a reasonable employer might have adopted. If the dismissal falls outside the band it is unfair.

The higher courts and the EAT have been reluctant to lay down guidelines for the tribunal to follow in applying the test of reasonableness: see *Thomas and Betts Manufacturing Co Ltd v Harding* [1980] IRLR 255.

In *Rentokil Ltd v Mackin* [1989] IRLR 286, the EAT held that the tribunal, acting as an industrial jury, must determine whether the decision to dismiss falls within the band of reasonable responses which a reasonable employer might have adopted. 'That does not mean that such a high degree of unreasonableness be shown so that nothing short of a perverse decision to dismiss can be held to be unfair....' See also *Bailey v BP Oil Kent Refinery Ltd* [1980] IRLR 287.

In *Piggott Brothers & Co Ltd v Jackson* [1991] IRLR 309, employees who refused to work on a factory floor with material which gave off fumes were dismissed. The tribunal held that the dismissals were unfair because the employers never found a definitive answer to the problem with the material and the employees were reasonable in refusing to work with the materials because harmful long-term adverse effects on their health were unknown. The EAT found the decision perverse and considered that because the Health and Safety Executive had not been able to identify a cause of the problem it could not be unreasonable for the employers to fail to find a cause either. The Court of Appeal held the EAT had erred. A tribunal decision can only be perverse if it is not a permissible option. The EAT would have to identify a finding of fact unsupported by any evidence, or a misdirection in law by the tribunal. The factual element predominates in reasonableness. Here it was unreasonable to dismiss the employees before the answer to the problem had been found or it had become clear that nothing further could be done. See also *East Berkshire Health Authority v Matadeen* [1992] IRLR 336 (note that a case such as *Piggott Brothers & Co Ltd above* might now fall within s 57A of the EP(C)A 1978. See Chapter 14).

In *Anandarajah v Lord Chancellor's Department* [1984] IRLR 130, the EAT held: 'The authorities which will be found, ... to be the most helpful for the future are those recent decisions of the Court of Appeal—notably *O'Kelly v Trusthouse Forte Plc* [1983] IRLR 369 and *Kearney and Trecker Marwin Ltd v Varndell and Others* [1983] IRLR 335—which have upheld the right of industrial tribunals to be their own guide on issues of reasonableness'. Tribunals should be directed by the wording of the statute and should not rely upon judicial guidelines extracted from reported decisions even if certain decisions have attained a hallowed status.

See also *Siggs and Chapman (Contractors) Ltd v Knight* [1984] IRLR 83 and *Rolls Royce Motors Ltd v Dewhurst* [1985] IRLR 184.

Although there is a tendency illustrated by the foregoing cases to emphasise the importance of the statutory provisions without giving guidelines to the tribunal, this approach is by no means universal. In *Grundy (Teddington) Ltd v Plummer and Salt* [1983] IRLR 98, the EAT held: '... it should be proper in the absence of specific guidance in the statutory codes of practice for this Appeal Tribunal in a very limited number of cases to indicate in general terms how reasonable employers should approach the types of problems with which they are faced.'

One such case was *British Railways Board v Jackson* [1994] IRLR 235, where Jackson was dismissed because he was suspected of taking food onto a train and selling it, in breach of a BRB regulation. The Court of Appeal held that if a reason for dismissal, and into which category it fell, were established, then in the present case the tribunal must ask if it were reasonable for BRB to have found the employee intended to sell the food and if so was it reasonable in all the circumstances for BRB to treat their finding as a sufficient reason for dismissal. The Court of Appeal held that the answer to both questions was yes. There was a need to deal with the conduct severely as a deterrent to others and as Jackson had given evasive and conflicting explanations then it was within the range of reasonable responses to dismiss.

In deciding whether or not the employer has acted reasonably substantively and procedurally, it is for the tribunal to reach a decision as an industrial jury having regard to all the circumstances in deciding whether or not the employer's response was within a range of reasonable responses. In addition, it used to be entitled to have regard to the guidelines laid down in the Codes of Practice. See *below*. However, the Codes of Practice now have no statutory standing, but their influence undoubtedly lingers on, and much of their content has either become incorporated in disciplinary procedures, or is now viewed as employment 'common-sense'.

An appeal from a tribunal to the EAT can only be made on a point of law. The Court of Appeal has criticised dressing up points of fact so that they fall to be treated as points of law: see *Retarded Children's Aid Society Ltd v Day* [1978] ICR 437 and *Hollister v National Farmers Union* [1979] ICR 542. In *Kent County Council v Gilham* [1985] IRLR 18, it was recognised that since the question whether or not an employer has acted reasonably is one of fact, different tribunals might reach a different conclusion on not dissimilar facts. There is judicial authority for the view that a tribunal has no obligation to provide an analysis of the facts and arguments on both sides with reasons for rejecting those they did reject, and for accepting those relied upon in support of their conclusion: see *Kearney and Trecker Marwin Ltd v Varndell and Others* [1983] IRLR 335, but see also *Iggesund Converters Ltd v Lewis* [1984] ICR 544, where the EAT found in cases of misconduct: 'it will normally be desirable, and frequently essential, for the industrial tribunal to make specific findings as to what allegations were put by the employers at any accusatory interview preceding the dismissal, what opportunity the employee was given of learning the nature of the evidence relied on, what opportunity he was allowed of replying to it, and what his reply was'.

If the tribunal has not asked the right question or the evidence does not support the conclusion the tribunal has reached, or the decision is perverse, the EAT will intervene: see *Day*'s case *above*; *Earl v Slater and Wheeler (Airlyne) Ltd* [1972] IRLR 115; *Spook Erection v Thackray* [1984] IRLR 116, and *Dillett*'s case, *above*.

Reasonableness and subsequently discovered misconduct

The question whether or not the employer acted reasonably or unreasonably has to be answered with reference to the circumstances known to the employer at the moment of dismissal: *Earl v Slater and Wheeler (Airlyne) Ltd* [1972] ICR 508. The moment of dismissal is the time when the decision to dismiss was taken. The moment of dismissal and the effective date of termination will only coincide where the employee is dismissed instantly: see s 55(4) of the EP(C)A 1978. If the employer's action was unreasonable at the moment of dismissal, subsequently discovered facts which were unknown to the employer at the moment of dismissal cannot make the dismissal reasonable. For an interpretation of the moment of dismissal see *Stacey v Babcock Power Ltd (Construction Division)* [1986] IRLR 3 and see discussion below. The point was considered in *W Devis and Sons Ltd v Atkins* [1977] AC 931. Atkins was dismissed, was given salary in lieu of notice and offered £6,000 as an *ex-gratia* payment by way of compensation. Several weeks later the company discovered certain information which led it to believe Atkins was guilty of dishonesty and the *ex-gratia* payment was withdrawn. At the tribunal hearing the employer sought to adduce this evidence. The tribunal was not prepared to admit the evidence which was not known to the company at the time of the dismissal. It relied on the decision in *Earl v Slater and Wheeler (Airlyne) Ltd* [1972] ICR 508.

On appeal to the High Court, Phillips J referred to another decision of the High Court in *Merseyside and North Wales Electricity Board v Taylor* [1975] ICR 185, where it was held: 'the circumstances ... referred to are those applying at or prior to the date of dismissal. What happens subsequent to the date of dismissal cannot be relevant in considering whether the employer acted reasonably or unreasonably in treating the reason as sufficient for dismissing the employee.' Following this he found: 'it is quite clear that the ... matter ... is the reasonableness of the behaviour of the employer at and leading up to the time of dismissal'. The decision was upheld by the Court of Appeal and the House of Lords. Both found that in applying the test of reasonableness the tribunal must decide whether the employer acted reasonably in treating his actual reason as a sufficient reason and not merely whether he acted reasonably in all the circumstances, so that circumstances after the dismissal could not be taken into account. They may, of course, be material to remedy.

Phillips J did not accept that the common law principle as enunciated in *Boston Deep Sea Fishing and Ice Co v Ansell* (1888) 39 ChD 339, or *Cyril Leonard and Co v Simo Securities Trust Ltd* [1972] 1 WLR 80, applied to the statutory jurisdiction, confirmed by both the Court of Appeal and the House of Lords. The approach in *Devis*'s case was followed in *Polkey v AE Dayton Services Ltd* [1988] ICR 142. It may happen that where there is an internal appeal by the employee against the employer's decision to dismiss, new evidence may emerge. In *Board of Governors, The National Heart and Chest Hospitals v Nambiar* [1981] IRLR 196, the EAT held that where the employee appeals against his dismissal under an internal appeals procedure, the fairness of the dismissal is to be judged by the tribunal on the basis of all the information available to the employer by the conclusion of the appeal. It would be artificial to exclude any new material from consideration by the tribunal: 'When an internal appeal body decides or recommends that a dismissal shall stand, it has to consider whether the reason is sufficient to justify confirmation of the dismissal in the light of any new information about it, as well as the information available to the employer when the original decision was made; and it would be artificial to exclude the new material. . . .'.

The EAT distinguished the facts of this case where the appeal established and upheld the original reasons, and the case of *Monie v Coral Racing Ltd* [1980] IRLR 464, where the original reason was invalidated on appeal, although a new reason was established.

The employer cannot substitute a reason which was not in his mind at the time of the dismissal, for the reason which was in his mind at the time of the dismissal, to justify the original dismissal. In such a case the employer has to decide whether the new reason is one which can be a reason for a fresh dismissal.

The decision in *Nambiar*'s case was upheld in *Sillifant v Powell Duffryn Timber Ltd* [1983] IRLR 91, where Browne-Wilkinson J held:

> The commonsense of industrial relations demands that . . . account must be taken of information coming to [the employer's] knowledge on the hearing of the appeal: the appeal is part of the procedural structure established by the employer to ensure fair treatment. . . . In our judgment this apparent exception to the rule that one can only look at facts known at the date of dismissal does not run contrary to the underlying principle of *Devis v Atkins*.

See also *Greenall Whitley plc v Carr* [1985] IRLR 289.

The earlier authorities were reviewed by the House of Lords in *West Midlands Co-operative Society Ltd v Tipton* [1986] ICR 192, where Lord Bridge held:

> But there is nothing to mitigate the injustice to an employee which would result if he were unable to complain that his employer, though acting reasonably on the facts known to him when he summarily dismissed the

employee, acted quite unreasonably in maintaining his decision to dismiss in the face of mitigating circumstances established in the course of the domestic appeal procedure which a reasonable employer would have treated as sufficient to excuse the employee's offence on which the employer's real reason for the dismissal depended. Adopting the analysis which found favour in *J Sainsbury Ltd v Savage* [1981] ICR 1, if the domestic appeal succeeds the employee is reinstated with retrospective effect; if it fails the summary dismissal takes effect from the original date. Thus, in so far as the original dismissal and the decision on the domestic appeal are governed by the same consideration, the real reason for dismissal, there is no reason to treat the effect date of termination as a watershed which separates the one process from the other. Both the original and the appellate decision by the employer, in any case where the contract of employment provides for an appeal and the right of appeal is invoked by the employee, are necessary elements in the overall process of terminating the contract of employment. To separate them and to consider only one half of the process in determining whether the employer acted reasonably or unreasonably in treating his real reason for dismissal as sufficient is to introduce an unnecessary artificiality into proceedings on a claim of unfair dismissal calculated to defeat, rather than accord with, the 'equity and the substantial merits of the case' and for which the language of the statute affords no warrant.

This is the conclusion I should reach as a matter of construction, taking due account of the decision in the *Devis* case, if there were no other authority to guide me. But the conclusion is powerfully reinforced by the series of decisions of the Employment Appeal Tribunal, to which I have earlier referred, with which it is in full accord. The relevant cases are *Rank Zerox (UK) Ltd v Goodchild* [1979] IRLR 185; *Quantrill v Eastern Counties Omnibus Co Ltd* (unreported), 30 June 1980; *National Heart and Chest Hospitals Board of Governors v Nambiar* [1981] ICR 441; *Sillifant v Powell Duffryn Timber Ltd* [1983] IRLR 91 and *Greenall Whitley plc v Carr* [1985] ICR 451.

In *Whitbread and Co plc v Mills* [1988] IRLR 501, the EAT held that it is possible to remedy defects in disciplinary and dismissal procedures on appeal, since appeal procedures form an important part of the process of ensuring that a dismissal is fair. An appeal hearing, if it is a rehearing, not just a review, may correct any earlier deficiencies in the procedure. See also *Clark v Civil Aviation Authority* [1991] IRLR 412, where, although Clark was not fully aware of the charges made against her at the time of dismissal and had not been given an opportunity to explain, the defects had been rectified on a very comprehensive appeal and she had suffered no injustice. Fairness falls to be considered after the appeal procedure has been completed. There is nothing in *Devis*'s case which is inconsistent with this approach. It is clear from *Tipton*'s case that matters which come to light during the appeal procedure can be taken into account when considering equity and the substantial merits of the case.

Between the date when the employer gives the employee notice to terminate the employment and the date when the notice expires, certain facts may come to the attention of the employer.

In *Williamson v Alcan (UK) Ltd* [1978] ICR 104, Phillips J suggested that where an employer acquired information after the moment of dismissal and before the effective date of termination which indicated that they should not have dismissed the employee, the dismissal could well become unfair if they did not then do that which they obviously had the power to do, namely, to withdraw the notice. However, the giving notice is a unilateral act and can only be withdrawn by consent. If the employee is unwilling to agree to the notice being withdrawn in these circumstances, will the dismissal still be unfair? In *Stacey v Babcock Power Ltd (Construction Division)* [1986] IRLR 3, the EAT found that where an employee is given notice of dismissal, the process of dismissal is not complete until the notice period has expired. 'Dismissal' in the EP(C)A 1978 is applied solely to cases where the contract is terminated by the employer and in the case of a dismissal on notice the contract does not terminate until the notice has expired. 'Dismissal' in s 57(3) of the EP(C)A 1978 is the whole process initiated by the giving of the notice and completed by its expiry. Although the language used in earlier authorities was consistent with the view that the date of notice rather than the effective date of termination, where the two were different, was the point at which the reasonableness of the dismissal fell to be determined, those cases were ones where either there was no or virtually no notice given and where it was immaterial to draw any distinction between the date of notice and the effective date of termination as representing the moment of dismissal, or the point was not raised. Therefore, since in this case there was a substantial period between the giving of the notice and the effective date of termination, the tribunal was entitled to take into account events occuring during the period of notice in deciding whether the employer's decision to dismiss was reasonable in all the circumstances. The reason for giving Stacey notice was redundancy, which at the time notice was given was a good and genuine reason. During the notice more work arrived. The EAT found that a tribunal was entitled to take into account in deciding if the employer had acted reasonably, whether or not the employer had offered to renew the employee's contract. This approach overcomes the technical problem of the employer being unable unilaterally to withdraw the notice. This case does not involve an exception to the rule in *W Devis and Sons Ltd v Atkins, above*. The EAT simply found that the dismissal was not complete until the notice expired.

It is arguable that if the employer acted reasonably at the moment of dismissal, subsequently discovered facts will not render the dismissal unreasonable. However, it is apparent from *Chrystie v Rolls Royce (1971) Ltd* [1976] IRLR 336, that there will be a greater degree of flexibility where facts are discovered subsequent to the dismissal, in deciding whether the decision to dismiss, which was reasonable at the moment of dismissal, is shown by subsequently discovered facts to be unreasonable. The approach would still have to be as described *above* in *Stacey v Babcock Power Ltd.*

Procedural fairness (1): introduction

The tribunal is entitled to see whether the employer has followed a fair procedure. There may be an agreed procedure negotiated between the employer and the union, one which has been put forward by the employer unilaterally, or there may be no formal procedure. Guidance upon the fairness or otherwise of a procedure can be obtained from the current ACAS guidelines.

The original code of practice of 1972 was revoked on 1 June 1991. There is a code—Disciplinary Practice and Procedures in Employment (1977)—but in 1987 ACAS submitted a draft to replace it. The Secretary of State did not approve it. Its contents were developed into a handbook in 1988, published by ACAS as 'Discipline at Work'. Though it has no statutory force, it is a useful guideline and can be considered by a tribunal.

The Codes and Handbook are advisory only. The employer's failure to observe any of their provisions will not of itself render him liable to any proceedings, but when proceedings have been brought against him, the tribunal may take account of provisions. Although the 1977 Code and the Handbook differ from the 1972 Code, the reported cases under the 1972 Code are relevant to an examination of the way in which the tribunals and EAT will decide whether or not the dismissal was procedurally fair. In *Neefjes v Crystal Products Ltd* [1972] IRLR 118, the NIRC held: 'we do not think that a failure to observe the detailed provisions of the code of practice is fatal to the employer in a claim for unfair dismissal, provided that the procedure which has in fact been followed is fair and equitable in the circumstances and is one which enables the substantial merits of the case to be considered. That is the overall objective of the code . . .' As a guideline, the same is true of the 1977 Code, and the Handbook.

The importance of following a proper procedure has been reaffirmed by the House of Lords in two cases. In *West Midlands Co-operative Society Ltd v Tipton* [1986] IRLR 112, Lord Bridge, quoted from the judgment of Viscount Dilhorne in *W Devis and Sons Ltd v Atkins above*, where he said: 'It does not follow that non-compliance with the code necessarily renders a dismissal unfair, but . . . a failure to follow a procedure prescribed in the code may lead to the conclusion that a dismissal was unfair, which, if that procedure had been followed, would have been held to have been fair'.

See also the House of Lords' decision in *Polkey v AE Dayton Services Ltd* [1988] ICR 142. It is necessary briefly to consider the position before *Polkey*. As a result of cases such as *British Labour Pump Co Ltd v Byrne* [1979] ICR 347, the importance of following a proper procedure had been substantially undermined. The principle enunciated in *Byrne*'s case was as follows:

> even if, judged in the light of circumstances known at the time of dismissal, the employer's decision was not reasonable because of some failure to follow a fair procedure yet the dismissal can be held fair if, on the facts proved before the industrial tribunal, the industrial tribunal comes to the conclusion that the employer could reasonably have decided to dismiss if he had followed a fair procedure.

This decision was supported by the Court of Appeal in *W and J Wass Ltd v Binns* [1982] ICR 486. The decision was binding on tribunals. It was criticised in *Sillifant v Powell Duffryn Timber Ltd* [1983] IRLR 91. The judgment of Browne-Wilkinson J in *Sillifant*'s case was approved by the House of Lords in *Polkey*'s case, above. In *Sillifant*'s case Browne-Wilkinson J held:

> The only test of the fairness of a dismissal is the reasonableness of the employer's decision to dismiss judged at the time at which the dismissal takes effect. An industrial tribunal is not bound to hold that *any* procedural failure by the employer renders the dismissal unfair: it is one of the factors to be weighed by the industrial tribunal in deciding whether or not the dismissal was reasonable within s 57(3) of the EP(C)A 1978. The weight to be attached to such procedural failure should depend upon the circumstances known to the employer at the time of dismissal, not on the actual consequence of such failure. Thus in the case of a failure to give an opportunity to explain, except in the rare case where a reasonable employer could properly take the view on the facts known to him at the time of dismissal that no explanation or mitigation could alter his decision to dismiss, an industrial tribunal would be likely to hold that the lack of 'equity' inherent in the failure would render the dismissal unfair. But there may be cases where the offence is so heinous and the facts so manifestly clear that a reasonable employer could, on the facts known to him at the time of dismissal, take the view that whatever explanation the employee advanced it would make no difference: see the example referred to by Lawton LJ in *Bailey v BP Oil (Kent Refinery) Ltd* [1980] ICR 642. Where, in the circumstances known at the time of dismissal, it was not reasonable for the employer to dismiss without giving an opportunity to explain but facts subsequently discovered or proved before the industrial tribunal showed that the dismissal was in fact merited, compensation would be reduced to nil. Such an approach ensures that an employee who could have been fairly dismissed does not get compensation but would prevent the suggestion of 'double standards' inherent in the *British Labour Pump* principle. An employee dismissed for suspected dishonesty who is in fact innocent has no redress: if the employer acted fairly in dismissing him on the facts and in the circumstances known to him at the time of dismissal the employee's innocence is irrelevant. Why should an employer be entitled to a finding that he acted fairly when, on the facts known and in the circumstances existing at the time of dismissal, his actions were

unfair but which facts subsequently coming to light show did not cause any injustice?

In *Polkey*'s case Lord Bridge held:

> In the case of incapacity, the employer will normally not act reasonably unless he gives the employee fair warning and an opportunity to mend his ways and show that he can do the job; in the case of misconduct, the employer will normally not act reasonably unless he investigates the complaint of misconduct fully and fairly and hears whatever the employee wishes to say in his defence or in explanation or mitigation; in the case of redundancy, the employer will normally not act reasonably unless he warns and consults any employees affected or their representative, adopts a fair basis on which to select for redundancy and takes such steps as may be reasonable to avoid or minimise redundancy by redeployment within his own organisation. If an employer has failed to take the appropriate procedural steps in any particular case, the one question the industrial tribunal is *not* permitted to ask in applying the test of reasonableness posed by s 57(3) of the EP(C)A 1978 is the hypothetical question whether it would have made any difference to the outcome if the appropriate procedural steps had been taken. On the true construction of s 57(3) this question is simply irrelevant. It is quite a different matter if the tribunal is able to conclude that the employer himself, at the time of dismissal, acted reasonably in taking the view that, in the exceptional circumstances of the particular case, the procedural steps normally appropriate would have been futile, could not have altered the decison to dismiss and therefore could be dispensed with. In such a case the test of reasonableness under s 57(3) may be satisfied.

In *Hooper v British Railways Board* [1988] IRLR 517, the Court of Appeal followed *Polkey*'s case. It emphasised that it is for the tribunal to consider whether the employer acted reasonably notwithstanding the failure to follow a proper procedure and that depends upon the circumstances and the facts known to the employer at the time of making the decision. See also *McLaren v National Coal Board* [1987] ICR 370.

The tribunal may still need to consider what would have happened if a fair procedure had been followed. In *Polkey*'s case Lord Bridge held:

> If it is held that taking the appropriate steps which the employer failed to take before dismissing the employee would not have affected the outcome, this will often lead to the result that the employee, although unfairly dismissed, will recover no compensation or, in the case of redundancy, no compensation in excess of his redundancy payment.

If the tribunal is in doubt whether or not the employee would have been dismissed if a proper procedure had been followed, then that doubt can be reflected in reducing the amount of compensation by a percentage representing the chance that the employee would have still lost his employment.

Procedural fairness (2): the 1977 Code

General

The aim of the 1977 Code is to give practical guidance to both employers and trade unions as well as individual employees. It is concerned with three aspects of disciplinary practice and procedure: the disciplinary rules; the penalties for the breach of them; and the procedures for enforcing the rules and imposing the penalties. It is designed to apply regardless of the size of the business although the Code recognises that even in smaller establishments, although it may not be practicable to adopt all the provisions, most of the essential features of the disciplinary procedure could be adopted.

It may be impossible for a small employer to observe the code in the same way as a larger employer. For instance, an appeals procedure may be impracticable because there is nobody to whom the employee can appeal. Although the letter of the Code may not apply to a small employer the spirit of the Code will: see *Earl v Slater and Wheeler (Airlyne) Ltd* [1972] ICR 508. The EAT has suggested that the Code is drafted with industry and large enterprises in mind and it is not necessarily apt in the context of a small employer: *The Royal Naval School v Hughes* [1979] IRLR 383; and see also *MacKellar v Bolton* [1979] IRLR 59. However, the small size of the employer's undertaking will not be an excuse for the failure by the employer to carry out a proper procedure: see *Henderson v Granville Tours Ltd* [1982] IRLR 494. See also *De Grasse v Stockwell Tools Ltd* [1992] IRLR 269.

The Code provides that disciplinary rules and procedures are necessary for promoting fairness and order in the treatment of individuals and in the conduct of industrial relations. Rules set standards of conduct; procedure helps to ensure that standards are adhered to, and also provides a fair method of dealing with alleged failures to observe them. Management is responsible for maintaining discipline and ensuring that there are adequate disciplinary rules and procedures. To be fully effective the rules and procedures need to be accepted as reasonable by both management and employees. Management should therefore aim to secure the involvement of employees and all levels of management when formulating new or revising existing rules and procedures. Although trade union officials may not wish to participate in the formulation of the rules, ideally they should participate fully with management in agreeing the procedural arrangements which will apply to their members and in seeing that these arrangements are used consistently and fairly.

Where the employer reaches an agreement with the union, it is sensible for the employer to ensure that the agreement has been brought to the attention of the work force. In *Gray Dunn and Co Ltd v Edwards* [1980] IRLR 23, the Scottish division of the EAT held, *obiter*, that where the employer had negotiated an agreement with a recognised trade union they were entitled to assume that those employees who were members of the union knew of and were bound by its provisions. The rule related to conduct which any reasonable employee would realise would have as its consequence summary dismissal. In *W Brooks and Son v Skinner* [1984] IRLR 379, the English division of the EAT held that while the approach in *Edwards*'s case, *above*, may be a perfectly proper and reasonable approach in many cases, it did not follow that in every case an employer who reaches an agreement with the trade union will be justified in taking the view that the employees know what is agreed. In *Skinner*'s case there was clear evidence that Skinner did not know of the agreement, whereas in *Edwards*'s case no finding had been made as to whether or not the employee knew of the position. In *Skinner*'s case the agreement dealt with a specific occasion, namely that any employee who over-indulged at the Christmas party so that he was unable to attend for work would be instantly dismissed.

Where an employer can show that disciplinary rules, penalties and procedures have resulted from joint consultation then, where he dismisses an employee in reliance upon them, there is a greater chance of the dismissal being found fair.

Where a code is agreed between the parties, the employer cannot usually be accused of acting unreasonably if he follows the code and it is not for the tribunal to rewrite that code: *East Hertfordshire District Council v Boyten* [1977] IRLR 347, distinguished in *Vauxhall Motor Ltd v Ghafoor* [1993] ICR 376, where under the procedure an appeal from a disciplinary hearing could only be made with the consent of a trade union convenor, and only then if the employee were a member of the union. The EAT held, in criticising the procedure, that the right of appeal is that of the individual and he should not be deprived of it without express agreement. Where there is an agreed procedure which is fair, and has been properly developed and properly applied, it is not open to the tribunal to add a further step: *Donald Cook and Sons Ltd v Carter* [1977] IRLR 188.

Disciplinary rules and the proper penalty

Disciplinary rules may not cover all circumstances that arise. The rules required will vary according to particular circumstances. The aim should be to specify clearly and concisely those rules necessary for the efficient and safe performance of work, and for the maintenance of satisfactory relations within the workforce, and between employees and management. Rules should not be so general as to be meaningless. Rules and the consequences of breaking them should be readily available and management should make every effort to ensure that employees know and understand them. They should be given a clear indication of the type of conduct which may warrant summary dismissal.

Where the employer is unable to show a clear promulgation of the rule, or an amendment or variation of the rule, he will find himself in difficulty. In *Pringle v Lucas Industrial Equipment Ltd* [1975] IRLR 266, the variation of an older rule known to the employee had been agreed at a meeting of the shop stewards' committee and promulgated by the chief shop steward at a mass meeting at which Pringle had not been present. He was summarily dismissed for breach of the rule, but it was held that the informal promulgation of the rule in this manner was an abdication of the management's responsibility, and that the employer could not rely on the new rule to dismiss instantly. See also the cases of *Edwards* and *Skinner above*.

Where an employer wishes to be able to dismiss an employee without imposing warnings for a certain course of conduct there should be a clear rule brought to the attention of the employees, prohibiting that course of conduct and making it clear that the penalty will be dismissal.

Both the rule and the penalty should be known to the employee. In *Rigden-Murphy v Securicor Ltd* [1976] IRLR 106, Rigden-Murphy breached the employer's rules dealing with the transfer of money from a bank to the employer's vehicle. Although the rule was known to Rigden-Murphy, he was dismissed for the first breach. The dismissal was unfair because the employer had failed to make it clear what breaches would be regarded as sufficient to justify dismissal without prior warning.

In *Dairy Produce Packers Ltd v Beverstock* [1981] IRLR 265, Beverstock was dismissed because the company believed he had been drinking in a public house during the company's time. The tribunal accepted that he had been drinking while he should have been at work. However, other employees who were considered to be under the influence of drink while at work or had turned up late for work due to drink were only warned. The company argued that Beverstock had broken the duty of trust that existed because he worked away from the factory and so his conduct could not be monitored. It was held that, 'Where it is considered necessary to have specific penalties attached to the misuse of alcohol in a particular enterprise then it is proper . . . that this should be clearly laid down.'

A rule should be clear. If it is not the employer may not be able to rely upon it. In *Trusthouse Forte (Catering) Ltd v Adonis* [1984] IRLR 382, the company had a rule that anyone caught smoking in a no-smoking area would be dismissed for gross misconduct. However, in the employee's particulars of employment, under the section headed 'Disciplinary Rules', smoking in a non-designated area was included in the list of examples of misconduct in respect of which the employee would be warned and only dismissed if, after warning, his standard of conduct fell below a level which was acceptable. The particulars were reissued after a notice containing the rule had been posted on a board by the company. It was held that the particulars of terms of employment set out the terms and conditions of his employment, and that the employer could not rely upon the notice posted on the board to the effect that smoking in a no-smoking area would be treated as gross misconduct, and the dismissal was unfair.

Where both the rule and the penalty are known to the employee and the employer acts in reliance on the rule, his actions will usually be fair. See *Meyer Dunmore International Ltd v Rogers* [1978] IRLR 167, where the EAT considered a rule relating to fighting.

In *Rowe v Radio Rentals Ltd* [1982] IRLR 177, Rowe, a television engineer, repaired a TV set for a woman, who was not one of the company's customers, for his own benefit, in contravention of a rule in the company staff handbook, that private trading for gain was gross misconduct. His dismissal was fair. See also *Drym Fabricators Ltd v Johnson* [1981] ICR 274.

The employer's rules and penalties may not themselves be reasonable. In *Taylor v Parsons Peebles NEI Bruce Peebles Ltd* [1981] IRLR 119, the EAT held that Parsons' dismissal for fighting was unfair notwithstanding that the company operated a policy whereby any employee who deliberately hit another employee would be dismissed, because such a provision must always be considered in the light of how a reasonable employer would apply the rule and the penalty in the circumstances of each case. It considered that a reasonable employer having regard to the employee's 20 years' good conduct would not have applied the rigid sanction of automatic dismissal. See also *Ladbroke Racing Ltd v Arnott and Others* [1983] IRLR 154.

The employer may have been lax in enforcing the rule and the prescribed penalty. He may not then be able to rely on them in the future.

In *Rennie v Eric Bemrose Ltd* [1974] IRLR 334, the employer had an unwritten rule, which was generally known among the employees, that absence from the factory without leave constituted gross misconduct. Rennie absented himself without leave and was instantly dismissed. In the past the employer had not treated every absence without leave as gross misconduct warranting instant dismissal. The dismissal was unfair, *inter alia*, because the rule had not been treated as an absolute one in the past. The employee did not know what penalty would be applied because of the element of discretion.

In *Ayub v Vauxhall Motors Ltd* [1978] IRLR 428, the dismissal of an employee for sleeping on the night shift was unfair. An employee who had committed the same offence three days earlier was suspended for three days following his internal appeal against the dismissal. In *Post Office v Fennell* [1981] IRLR 221, the Court of Appeal found that the idea of equity in the phrase 'having regard to equity and the substantial merits of the case' involves 'the concept that employees who misbehave in much the same way should have meted out to them much the same punishment'. So an employer who is inconsistent, in imposing penalties, is likely to have a dismissal found unfair. See also *Eagle Star Insurance Co Ltd and Another v Hayward* [1981] ICR 860.

In *Cain v Leeds Western Health Authority* [1990] IRLR 168, the EAT held that the employer's lack of consistency was something which had to be considered in determining the reasonableness of the dismissal.

However, in *Hadjioannous v Coral Casinos Ltd* [1981] IRLR 352, the EAT found that the argument that a dismissed employee has not been treated in the same way as other employees is broadly relevant in determining the fairness of the dismissal in only three sets of circumstances:

> Firstly, it may be relevant if there is evidence that employees have been led by an employer to believe that certain categories of conduct will be either overlooked, or at least will not be dealt with by the sanction of dismissal. Secondly, there may be cases in which evidence about decisions made in relation to other cases supports an inference that the purported reason stated by the employers is not the real or genuine reason for a dismissal ... Thirdly ... evidence as to decisions made by the employer in truly parallel circumstances may be sufficient to support an argument in a particular case, that it was not reasonable on the part of the employer to visit the particular employee's conduct with the penalty of dismissal and that some lesser penalty would have been appropriate in the circumstances.

See also *Securicor Ltd v Smith* [1989] IRLR 356. In *Proctor v British Gypsum Ltd* [1992] IRLR 7, the EAT held that the employer should consider truly comparable cases of which he knew or ought reasonably to have known, but the overriding principle is that each case must be considered on its own facts. Also, the words 'liable to be' or 'may be' dismissed when used in employers' notices or rules do not mean that dismissal is not the likely consequence of misconduct.

Where the rule is known to the employee but the penalty is not prescribed, dismissal may be fair where the employee has been given an opportunity to comply with the rule and his failure to do so leaves the employer with no option but to dismiss him. In *Singh v Lyons Maid Ltd* [1975] IRLR 328, the employer had a rule 'Beards may not be worn by staff who work on the production line. Visitors must wear beard masks.' The rule was contained in a document that the employee acknowledged having received. He grew a beard in contravention of this rule, and although given an opportunity to comply, he failed to do so. The company had no work for him other than on the production line. This dismissal was fair. See also *Spiller v FJ Wallis Ltd* [1975] IRLR 362.

There may be exceptional cases where there is no rule and no penalty, but dismissal is nevertheless fair. In *CA Parsons and Co Ltd v McLoughlin* [1978] IRLR 65, the employer dismissed McLoughlin, a shop steward, for fighting with another employee. There was nothing in the employee's contract to prohibit fighting, but the dismissal was fair. The EAT found that the dangers of fighting in the workplace are so well known as to enable an employer to dismiss without having the need for a rule: 'it ought not to be necessary for anybody, let alone a shop steward, to have to have in black-and-white in the form of a rule that a fight is something which is going to be regarded very gravely by management'. Compare with *Meyer Dunmore International Ltd v Rogers* [1978] IRLR 167.

Disciplinary rules are not and cannot be exhaustive. 'A catalogue of offences which carry the potential sanction of dismissal contained in company rules may occasionally be useful in assessing the quality of an offence but it does not follow that no offence which does not fall within it can ever merit dismissal': *Distillers Company (Bottling Services) Ltd v Gardner* [1982] IRLR 47, where the offence could easily have been catalogued as a gross neglect of duty.

Other examples where the employer may succeed in dismissing fairly without a clear formal rule are theft, dishonesty and breach of safety rules.

Where there is a rule, the employer can only require the employee to do what is necessary under the rule.

If the employer does not have a clear rule and/or a penalty then (apart from exceptional cases) he will have to warn the employee to desist from that course of conduct and further warn the employee that a repetition of the same course of conduct will result in his dismissal. In effect the employer is creating a rule by warning the employee of the penalty to be imposed.

The penalty must fit the offence, and must not be disproportionate and excessive. The employer should consider the circumstances in which the offence has been committed and any mitigating circumstances which ought to be taken into account. There should be some discretion, but the discretion should be exercised in accordance with principles and within defined limits. A broad unfettered discretion may result in a finding of unfair dismissal: see *Lindsay v Fife Forge Co Ltd* [1976] IRLR 47.

In *Donson and Frudd v Conoco Ltd* [1973] IRLR 258, the tribunal concluded that a rule whereby an offence, whatever the degree of gravity, was punished by dismissal was too inflexible. Mitigating factors were not taken into account in the application of the rule. There was no provision enabling the employer to take into account the nature of the offence and whether it was grave or trivial.

In *Jones v London Co-operative Society* [1975] IRLR 110, the employer had a rule, which was known to the employee and agreed with the union of which she was a member, that 'incorrect recording of purchases for whatever reason would be treated as a serious offence and the employee will be summarily dismissed unless it can be proved that the employee was justified in such incorrect recording'. Jones had an impeccable record but on one occasion rang up a wrong amount. The employer, while not suggesting dishonesty, dismissed her. Her dismissal was unfair. The rule failed to 'distinguish between genuine error on one occasion on the one hand and either a calculated act or a persistent failure to maintain adequate cash control standards on the other'. See *Ladbroke Racing Ltd v Arnott and Others, above.*

It will be seen that many of the cases referred to *above* appear to take a somewhat legalistic view of 'rules'. These cases tend to be those decided in the comparatively early days of unfair dismissals. It is suggested that the employer's rules are but one factor, though an important, or weighted, factor for the tribunal to consider. They are but one of 'all the circumstances' referred to in s 57(3). The correct approach seems to be: what is the conduct? Bearing in mind the employer's rules, was dismissal within a reasonable band of responses? Use of the rules and consistency of treatment are matters to be weighed in the balance in dealing with the second question.

Procedural fairness (3): the 1977 Code in practice

There is some support for the view that the rules of natural justice have no application to internal disciplinary procedures: see *Malloch v Aberdeen Corporation* [1971] 2 All ER 1278, where the earlier authorities were reviewed. However, in *Khanum v Mid-Glamorgan Area Health Authority* [1978] IRLR 215 the EAT held:

> ... in our judgment as regards the sort of domestic tribunal with which we are concerned in this case the law is as it was expressed by Harman J in *Byrne v Kinematograph Renters Society Ltd* [[1958] 1 WLR 762] and approved and applied by the Privy Council to the context of a University Vice Chancellor's inquiry into cheating in examinations in ... [*University of Ceylon v Fernando* [1960] 1 WLR 223].
>
> What then are the requirements of natural justice in a case of this kind? First, I think that the person accused should know of the nature of the accusation made; secondly, that he should be given an opportunity to state his case; and thirdly, of course, that the Tribunal should act in good faith.

In *Bentley Engineering Co Ltd v Mistry* [1978] IRLR 437, the EAT held:

> natural justice does require not merely that a man shall have a chance to state his own case in detail; he must know in one way or another sufficiently what is being said against him. If he does not know sufficiently what is being said against him, he cannot properly put forward his own case. It may be, according to the facts, that what is said against him can be communicated to him in writing, or it may be that it is sufficient if he hears what the other protagonist is saying, or it may be that, in an

appropriate case, for matters which have been said by others to be put orally in sufficient detail is an adequate satisfaction of the requirements of natural justice . . . it is all a question of degree.

In *Louies v Coventry Hood and Seating Co Ltd* [1990] IRLR 324, it was held that where statements had been given by witnesses upon which the employer is going to rely almost entirely the employee should have a sight of them or be told very clearly exactly what is in them. A failure to do so will be a breach of the rules of natural justice. See also *Spink v Express Foods Group Ltd* [1990] IRLR 320. In *Fuller v Lloyds Bank Plc* [1991] IRLR 336, the Bank's failure to supply witness statements to the employee and his representative did not render his dismissal unfair. Although the tribunal was critical about the non-disclosure, in the particular circumstances 'failure to provide the witness statements did not go outside the band of reasonable procedures which should have been carried out. The allegation in essence was a simple one and the applicant knew exactly what was being alleged.' The EAT held that the employer's motivation in adopting the particular policy which led to the procedural defect was not relevant. The defect in the procedure was not serious enough to make the procedure unfair, and the process of dismissal was fair.

A failure by the employer to keep notes and to provide them to the employee during the disciplinary hearing can be a procedural defect: see *Vauxhall Motors Ltd v Ghafoor* [1993] ICR 376. It must be said, however, that this, of itself, is unlikely to cause a dismissal to be unfair.

The employee's absence from a hearing does not necessarily involve a breach of the rules of natural justice provided the employee's representative is present: see *Pirelli General Cable Works Ltd v Murray* [1979] IRLR 190 and *Gray Dunn and Co Ltd v Edwards* [1980] IRLR 23. In *Sartor v P & O European Ferries (Felixstowe) Ltd* [1992] IRLR 271, the Court of Appeal held there had been a breach of the rules of natural justice at the employee's disciplinary hearing in that the employee had not known in advance the case alleged against her and therefore had no opportunity to make representations. However, this was cured at an appeal where the procedure was not significantly defective.

It is apparent from these decisions of the EAT that the rules of natural justice apply to internal disciplinary procedures. The concept of fairness involves observance of the rules of natural justice.

In *Pritchett and Dyjasek v J McIntyre Ltd* [1986] IRLR 97, Waite J referring to the judgment of Sir Robert Megarry in *John v Rees and Others* [1969] 2 All ER 274, held that fairness and natural justice have a great deal in common.

In *Moyes v Hylton Castle Working Men's Social Club and Institute Ltd* [1986] IRLR 482, Moyes was dismissed because of his alleged sexual harassment of a female employee. Two of the employer's officials were both witnesses and judges. The EAT held that this was a breach of the rules of natural justice and any reasonable observer would conclude that 'justice did not appear to be done nor was it done'. It was not necessary for the two of them to be both witnesses and judges, and it was impossible for them to disassociate their role as witnesses from that as judges. While there might be cases where it was inevitable that the person who was a witness was also a judge this was not the position here. See *Hannam v Bradford City Council* [1970] 2 All ER 690.

Generally the person who conducts an inquiry must be seen to be impartial. However, in *Slater v Leicestershire Health Authority* [1989] IRLR 16, it was held that a nurse's dismissal was not unfair because the manager who carried out the preliminary investigation also conducted the disciplinary hearing and took the decision to dismiss. It was further held that the rules of natural justice do not form an independent ground upon which a decision to dismiss may be attacked, although a breach of the rules of natural justice will be an important matter for a tribunal to take into account when considering reasonableness.

Conduct

At the outset of the jurisdiction, the tribunals placed great emphasis on procedural matters, including the need to give warnings so that a dismissal without a warning was likely to be unfair. Following cases such as *British Labour Pump Co Ltd v Byrne* [1979] ICR 347, tribunals then looked to see what effect a failure to follow a proper procedure had, so that if it made no difference the dismissal might still be fair.

Greater importance now attaches to procedural matters since the decisions in *West Midlands Co-operative Society Ltd v Tipton* [1986] ICR 192 and *Polkey v AE Dayton Services Ltd* [1988] ICR 142, so that the employer will not be able to establish that he has acted reasonably unless he has taken the necessary procedural steps including the giving of warnings, save in exceptional circumstances. However, if the effect of the failure to follow such steps would have made no difference, whilst the dismissal will still be unfair the tribunal might decide not to make any compensatory award. Such a conclusion might, or might not, have an effect on the basic award (see Chapter 16).

Warnings
Warnings are separately considered under conduct which may be classed as gross misconduct and conduct which is not gross misconduct.

Gross misconduct The 1977 Code provides that a disciplinary procedure should 'ensure that, except for gross misconduct, no employees are dismissed for a breach of discipline': para 10(h). The disciplinary rules may provide that the employee will be dismissed with or without notice where he has breached certain rules. In cases of gross misconduct such a rule and penalty may be reasonable. It is not possible to provide any legal definition of gross misconduct which will fit every case. The NIRC refused to accept an invitation to attempt any legal definition of gross misconduct: *Connely v Liverpool Corporation* (1974) 9 ITR 51. While at common law the phrase 'gross misconduct' is usually used to describe conduct which is repudiatory of the contract, the tribunals and the EAT have, in cases of unfair dismissal, avoided this concept of gross misconduct for the purposes of the application of the disciplinary provisions of the former 1972 and of the 1977 Codes. The use of the phrase 'gross misconduct' in these cases may well not be an apt description of what is covered. The EAT has sounded a note of caution against becoming involved in an exposition of what is and what is not gross misconduct: *CA Parsons and Co Ltd v McLoughlin* [1978] IRLR 65. Whether conduct is gross misconduct for these purposes will depend upon the nature of the business, the position held by the employee and the circumstances of the case.

Tribunals have been prepared to find dismissals for severe misconduct which may be gross, fair notwithstanding the fact that the employee has been dismissed for a first breach without any prior warning, and even though the employer's own disciplinary procedure has not been observed. The basis of unfair dismissal cases is s 57. The word 'misconduct' does not appear there, nor, of course, do the words 'gross misconduct'. The section merely refers to the dismissal being 'related to the conduct of the employee'. In the light of *Connely*'s and *McLoughlin*'s cases *above*, the correct approach appears to be: what is the conduct? Bearing in mind the employer's rules or disciplinary procedure, was a dismissal within a band of reasonable responses?

In *Stevenson v Golden Wonder Ltd* [1977] IRLR 474, Stevenson was dismissed after he perpetrated a moderately serious and unprovoked assault on another employee at a social function held in the company's canteen, outside working hours. The employers failed to follow their own 'grievance procedure'. The EAT found the dismissal fair. The employer acted reasonably in dismissing Stevenson for blatant misconduct and the failure to follow the procedure was not fatal.

In some cases a dismissal has been held to be fair where the employer has no rule that the conduct for which the employee was dismissed would result in dismissal. See *McLoughlin*'s case *above* where the EAT held

> As the Court of Appeal pointed out [in *Retarded Children's Aid Society Ltd v Day* [1978] ICR 437], . . . the Industrial Relations Code of Practice is not to be ignored; but at the same time it is not necessarily a code which has the force of law. The Court of Appeal, moreover, said that

there were certain circumstances in which an employee could be dismissed without warning; in other words, that in some cases the employer is entitled to say, 'I cannot suspend, I cannot warn. This is in my view sufficiently serious for me to impose dismissal upon both the people who were involved in a fight in the factory.'

The EAT in *McLoughlin*'s case further held:

The mere fact of a fight, whoever starts it, is a very serious matter indeed . . . in *Greenwood v HJ Heinz and Co Ltd* [(1977) (unreported)] . . . the [EAT] said 'These are essentially matters for the employer to make up his mind about, not necessarily in the heat of the moment but after pause for reflection and after investigation'. We cannot do better than use some of the words of Mr Justice Bristow towards the end of that judgment:

It seems to us it is quite wrong to say that a management faced with fighting, even of a very modest nature, in a workplace where there is a large amount of machinery would be perverse in deciding that whoever started the fight must be dismissed . . . It is difficult enough sometimes to keep people who have to operate machines safe from hurting themselves in the machinery . . . Add some violence; the risk of serious injury to other people, let alone severe interference with the work, is clearly great. . . . in our judgment it certainly does not go without saying that to dismiss by reason of one blow, even by reason of the threat of a blow, is by itself plainly wrong. It may be in some circumstances wrong. It may well be a perfectly proper thing for management to do.

However, the foregoing approach is by no means universal. In *McPhail v Gibson* [1977] ICR 42, a farm manager was dismissed without warning where he gave an inaccurate reference about a farm labourer to a neighbouring farmer. The EAT considered that even in a case of gross misconduct a warning should usually be given. This case turned on its own facts and was before *McLoughlin*'s case.

A dismissal for a first offence of fighting may be unfair seen against 20 years' previous good service: see *Taylor v Parsons Peebles NEI Bruce Peebles Ltd* [1981] IRLR 119; see also *Dairy Produce Packers Ltd v Beverstock* [1981] IRLR 265. However, there is in such cases always the counter-argument that of all his employees, the employer should be able to trust such a long-serving employee not to indulge in such conduct.

Similar principles to those in *McLoughlin*'s case, *above*, may apply where the employee has been guilty of other acts which may be categorised as acts of gross misconduct: theft *Trust Houses Forte Hotels Ltd v Murphy* [1977] IRLR 186; or suspected dishonesty: *McCrory v Magee t/a Heatwell Heating Systems* [1983] ICR 414. In *Denco Ltd v Joinson* [1991] IRLR 63, Joinson, a shop steward, gained unauthorised access to information about a subsidiary company on the computer. The EAT held that 'if an employee deliberately uses an unauthorised password in order to enter or to attempt to enter a computer known to contain information to which he is not entitled, then that of itself is gross misconduct which *prima facie* will attract summary dismissal ... this ... can be compared with dishonesty. ... management should make it abundantly clear to its work force that interfering with it will carry severe penalties'. It considered the matter an extremely serious industrial offence, but it was obviously desirable to have written rules relating to access and use of computers posted up and also left near computers for reference.

In *Siraj-Eldin v Campbell Middleton Burness and Dickson* [1989] IRLR 208, the dismissal of an employee for taking alcohol on board an offshore rig justified dismissal for a first offence, even though the alcohol was kept in a locked suitcase. There was evidence that possession of alcohol on an oil rig was considered so serious that no mitigating circumstances could be accepted.

There may be no need to warn before dismissal in cases of severe misconduct where there is a clear and reasonable rule defining the conduct which will result in dismissal for the first offence.

A rule providing for dismissal where the conduct is regarded by the employer as gross misconduct may not be a reasonable rule when it is a first offence. In *Laws Stores Ltd v Oliphant* [1978] IRLR 251, Oliphant was guilty of a single lapse in operating the till. This fell within the definition of gross misconduct for which the penalty was instant dismissal under the company's agreed disciplinary procedure. However, the company did not act reasonably in dismissing her in the circumstances for a single lapse. See also *Ladbroke Racing Ltd v Arnott* [1979] IRLR 192.

The employer may not be able to argue that conduct warrants dismissal without warning in the absence of a clear rule. In *Meyer Dunmore International Ltd v Rogers* [1978] IRLR 167, the EAT held:

> if employers wish to have a rule that employees engaged in ... fighting are going to be summarily dismissed ... there is no reason why they should not have a rule, *provided* ... that it is plainly adopted, that it is plainly and clearly set out, and that great publicity is given to it so that every employee knows beyond any doubt whatever that if he gets involved in fighting in that sense, he will be dismissed.

See also *Trusthouse Forte (Catering) Ltd v Adonis* [1984] IRLR 382.

The employer should also ensure that the rule is made known to the employee, is fully understood by him and is consistently applied: *Richards v Bulpitt and Sons Ltd* [1975] IRLR 134. See also *Dairy Produce Packers Ltd v Beverstock* [1981] IRLR 265.

Where the employee has been guilty of gross misconduct, the employer may be entitled to dismiss him without prior warning, even if it is not clear whether that misconduct is a breach of the employer's rule. In *Martin v Yorkshire Imperial Metals Ltd* [1978] IRLR 440, Martin was dismissed after it was discovered he tied down a lever on an automatic lathe in the factory, in effect removing a safety device.

The EAT found that even though it was unclear whether the conduct was a breach of the employer's rule, the conduct was likely to endanger the safety of other employees and it was fair to dismiss for a first breach; compare *Trusthouse Forte (Catering) Ltd v Adonis, above.*

Even where there is a rule providing for dismissal for certain gross misconduct the employer should still investigate the circumstances and apply the rule reasonably so as to take into account any mitigating factors. See *Taylor*'s case, *above.* If the employer fails to apply the rule reasonably the tribunal may find the dismissal unfair and its discretion cannot be excluded: *Ladbroke Racing Ltd v Arnott, above.*

Misconduct which is not gross   Here the starting point is that it will be unfair to dismiss the employee in the absence of a clear and reasonable rule providing for dismissal for that offence, without prior warning. As it will appear there are qualifications to this premise.

In *MacKay v Robert Morton Temple Bakery* [1975] IRLR 57, MacKay's dismissal without warning was unfair where he failed to communicate with and send medical certificates to his employer over a period of ten days while he was away from work due to ill-health.

In *Greenslade v Hoveringham Gravels Ltd* [1975] IRLR 114, Greenslade's dismissal was unfair. He was told to wear a tie and have his hair cut. He did not comply and was told to go home. He discussed the matter further with the employer from home, but no conclusions were reached. Without warning he was dismissed.

In *Young v E Thomas and Co Ltd* [1972] IRLR 40, Young, a lorry driver, deviated from his prescribed route for his own purposes. His dismissal was unfair because at no stage had he been warned by the employer that he intended to dismiss employees for such conduct. See also *Newman v TH White Motors Ltd* [1972] IRLR 49.

Where employers have condoned a course of conduct, then a warning becomes particularly necessary before dismissing for that course of conduct. In *Hackwood v Seal (Marine) Ltd* [1973] IRLR 17, a manager dismissed an experienced machinist for refusing to assist an inexperienced machinist. The order was a lawful one. However, in the past the manager had taken a more lax attitude to the employee's refusal to obey orders, and before dismissing her he should have warned her that in the future he would not tolerate her attitude.

In *Ayub v Vauxhall Motors Ltd* [1978] IRLR 428, one offence of sleeping on the night shift did not justify dismissal. Where a clear warning or series of warnings have been given which the employee ignores, the employer is entitled to rely on the warnings and dismiss the employee: *Donald Cook and Sons Ltd v Carter* [1977] IRLR 188.

In *Hallett and Want v MAT Transport Ltd* [1976] IRLR 5, Want was given a second final warning that if he failed to improve his timekeeping significantly he would be dismissed. It was held that after the warning the employer was entitled to a substantial improvement and the dismissal was fair.

Conversely, where following a warning there has been an improvement in conduct, the employer may be acting unfairly if following that improvement he dismisses the employee. In *Hallett and Want v MAT Transport Ltd, above,* following the second final warning about lateness, Hallett was late on 7 days out of 77 and was dismissed. The tribunal found there was an improvement following the warning and it was necessary to look at the whole period between warning and dismissal to assess any improvement. It was held that the dismissal was unfair.

There are exceptions to the general principle. The first arises out of the purpose and nature of the warning. A warning is intended to give the employee a chance to improve. There may be cases where it is quite clear that a warning would not have made any difference. Thus, in *Farnborough v Governors of Edinburgh College of Art* [1974] IRLR 245, the employee, a lecturer, was dismissed without warning because he did not agree with a reorganisation. He became uncooperative and caused friction with the head of his department. He sought to involve the students and continually refused to carry out his employer's reasonable requirements. The dismissal was fair. He argued he would have improved if he had received a warning but it was clear from evidence this was not likely to happen. In *Retarded Children's Aid Society Ltd v Day* [1978] ICR 437, Day was employed at a home for retarded children and contrary to established practice required one of the children to do extra duties. When the employer discovered this, he was dismissed without warning. Day 'saw here an opportunity to apply his own methods. He thought he knew best. . . . [and] presented the risk of further transgression.' The dismissal was fair. Similarly, it may be clear that the employee will not improve where he is prickly and self-opinionated, and a difficult man to work with: *Henderson v Masson Scott Thrissell Engineering Ltd* [1974] IRLR 98, or where he refuses to accept a new wage agreement: *Tovey v F&F Robinson (Stockton-on-Tees) Ltd* [1975] IRLR 139.

The second exception arises where the employee knew or was in a position to know that by his act or conduct he was placing his job in jeopardy and ought not to have needed a warning. In *Newman v Alarmco Ltd* [1976] IRLR 45, Newman, the company's general manager, lived with his secretary. During office hours they showed affection for each other. The dismissal was fair. No warning was necessary because of his position. The conduct had persisted for some months, and he ought to have known that it was likely to discredit the company.

The third exception arises in cases where the interests of the business so dictate. In *James v Waltham Holy Cross UDC* [1973] ICR 398, Sir John Donaldson found the 'duty of fairness both to the employee and to the business is the only general rule. All else is but a particular application of that general rule'. The interests of the business must outweigh the interests of the employee for this exception to apply.

The fourth exception arises out of a recognition that the requirements of the 1977 Code must be applied to the circumstances of the particular case. They are not rules of law, but guidelines. Thus, what may be reasonable as between the foreman and the operative on the factory floor may not be reasonable in the case of a doctor and his receptionist, so a dismissal without warning may be fair: *MacKellar v Bolton* [1979] IRLR 59.

Overall, however, what is said on p 170 must be re-emphasised: the tribunal's duty is to apply s 57(2)(*b*) and (3) of the EP(C)A 1978. In s 57(2)(*b*) the word used is 'conduct', not misconduct, nor gross misconduct. In reality the tribunal's test is: bearing in mind the Code, the employer's disciplinary rules, any warnings, the conduct itself, the context in which it occurred, and any other circumstances, was dismissal within a band of reasonable responses for a reasonable employer?

(*b*) *Warnings generally*   A warning should be sufficiently clear, so that the employee knows what will happen if he does not improve. Circumlocutions like 'employment might be in jeopardy' should be avoided: *Wells v E&A West Ltd* [1975] IRLR 269. However, it can be unfair to dismiss an employee even where he has been told he was liable for dismissal: *Elliott Brothers (London) Ltd v Colverd* [1979] IRLR 92. In *Procter v British Gypsum Ltd* [1992] IRLR 7, the EAT held 'liable to' or 'may be' dismissed do not mean dismissal is not the likely consequence of misconduct.

Warnings should not be treated too technically: *Wood v Kettering Co-operative Chemists Ltd* [1978] IRLR 438. A warning may be sufficient even though it does not conform perfectly with the employer's disciplinary procedure. A written warning has no particular magic, except as evidential value: *McCall v Castleton Crafts* [1979] IRLR 218. To an intelligent man a verbal warning may be just as good.

Ideally, warnings should be given to individuals rather than generally. However, it will be fair to dismiss in reliance on a general warning; *Connely v Liverpool Corporation* (1974) 9 ITR 51: the employer had given a general warning to employees against drinking during their lunch hour. The employee broke this rule and was fairly dismissed.

There is no general rule as to how long a warning will remain in force. The disciplinary procedure may so provide, although that it not necessarily binding upon a tribunal. In the absence of a provision it is for the tribunal to decide if the employer can rely upon the warning.

Where warning is given to the employee requiring an improvement within a specified period, the warning will not automatically lapse at the end of the period so that the employer can no longer rely on it at a later date. Whether a warning has lapsed will depend on the circumstances of each case: *Kraft Foods Ltd v Fox* [1978] ICR 311.

Investigation

The employer should investigate any allegation of misconduct before taking steps against the employee. The employer has to show the tribunal the reason for the dismissal and he must also put forward evidence to enable the tribunal to decide whether or not he acted reasonably in all the circumstances. It has been seen that the tribunal has to ask itself the question 'Are we satisfied that the employers had, at the time of the dismissal, reasonable grounds for believing that the offence put against the applicant was in fact committed?': *Ferodo Ltd v Barnes* [1976] ICR 439. In *British Home Stores Ltd v Burchell* [1978] IRLR 379, the EAT found that in a case involving the employee's conduct the employer had to establish a genuine belief based on reasonable grounds. It held:

> First of all, there must be established by the employer the fact of that belief; that the employer did believe it. Secondly, that the employer had in his mind reasonable grounds upon which to sustain that belief. And thirdly, we think, that the employer, at the stage at which he formed that belief on those grounds, at any rate at the final stage at which he formed that belief on those grounds, had carried out as much investigation into the matter as was reasonable in all the circumstances of the case. It is the employer who manages to discharge the onus of demonstrating those three matters, we think, who must not be examined further.

This now well known 'Burchell test' was expressly approved by the Court of Appeal in *W Weddel and Co Ltd v Tepper* [1980] ICR 286.

See *Pritchett and Dyjasek v J McIntyre Ltd* [1987] IRLR 18, where the Court of Appeal reaffirmed the guidelines in *Burchell's* case and *Scottish Midland Co-operative Society Ltd v Cullion* [1991] IRLR 261.

The establishment of the employer's belief based on reasonable grounds and the need for reasonable investigation are inextricably entwined. The amount of investigation required will depend on the circumstances. At one extreme there may be a case where the employee is virtually caught in the act and at the other extreme where the issue is one of pure inference: *ILEA v Gravett* [1988] IRLR 497.

In *Linford Cash and Carry Ltd v Thomson and Others* [1989] ICR 518, where allegations were made by an informant whose name was not disclosed, the EAT laid down the following guidelines:

(1) The information given by the informant should be reduced into writing in one or more statements. Initially these statements should be taken without regard to the fact that in those cases where anonymity is to be preserved, it may subsequently prove to be necessary to omit or erase certain parts of the statements before submission to others in order to prevent identification.

(2) In taking statements the following seem important: (*a*) Date,

time and place of each or any observation or incident. (*b*) The opportunity and ability to observe clearly and with accuracy. (*c*) The circumstantial evidence such as knowledge of a system or arrangement, or the reason for the presence of the informer and why certain small details are memorable. (*d*) Whether the informant has suffered at the hands of the accused or has any other reason to fabricate, whether from personal grudge or any other reason or principle.

(3) Further investigation can then take place either to confirm or undermine the information given. Corroboration is clearly desirable.

(4) Tactful enquiries may well be thought suitable and advisable into the character and background of the informant or any other information which may tend to add to or detract from the value of the information.

(5) If the informant is prepared to attend a disciplinary hearing, no problem will arise, but if, as in the present case, the employer is satisfied that the fear is genuine then a decision will need to be made whether or not to continue with the disciplinary process.

(6) If it is to continue, then it seems to us desirable that at each stage of those procedures the member of management responsible for that hearing should himself interview the informant and satisfy himself what weight is to be given to the information.

(7) The written statement of the informant—if necessary with omissions to avoid identification—should be made available to the employee and his representatives.

(8) If the employee or his representative raises any particular and relevant issue which should be put to the informant, then it may be desirable to adjourn for the chairman to make further enquiries of that informant.

(9) Although it is always desirable for notes to be taken during disciplinary procedures, it seems to us to be particularly important that full and careful notes should be taken in these cases.

(10) Although not peculiar to cases where informants have been the cause or the initiation of an investigation, it seems to us important that if evidence from an investigating officer is to be taken at a hearing it should, where possible, be prepared in a written form.

Previous attempts by the EAT to lay down guidelines on various aspects, have (with the honourable exception of the Burchell test) frequently come to grief in the Court of Appeal or House of Lords. The Burchell test can be applied to all conduct dismissals (and its approach can be useful in many capability dismissals), but the *Linford Cash & Carry Ltd v Thompson* 'guidelines' are so detailed, and relevant to the special facts of the case, that they should be viewed with circumspection. After all the fundamental question for the tribunal is that in s 57(3): did the employer act reasonably in all the circumstances?

See also *Morgan v Electrolux Ltd* [1991] IRLR 89.

The employee must be given the opportunity to explain, which requires positive action by the employer. The fact there is a grievance procedure in existence is not the equivalent of the employer giving the opportunity. The two are quite different: *Clarke v Trimoco Group Ltd* [1993] IRLR 148.

In *W Devis and Sons Ltd v Atkins* [1977] ICR 662, Viscount Dilhorne held that an employer cannot be said to have acted reasonably if he reached his decision 'in consequence of ignoring matters which he ought reasonably to have known and which would have shown the reason was insufficient'. Again in *W Weddel and Co Ltd v Tepper* [1980] IRLR 96, Stephenson LJ held:

> [employers] must make reasonable enquiries appropriate to the circumstances. If they form their belief hastily and act hastily upon it, without making the appropriate enquiries or giving the employee a fair opportunity to explain himself, their belief is not based on reasonable grounds and they are certainly not acting reasonably.

A tribunal cannot conclude that the employer's investigations were not reasonable because they had failed to take account of facts or material at a disciplinary procedure, when that was not before them at that hearing, and was only introduced for the first time at the tribunal hearing: *Dick and Another v Glasgow University* [1993] IRLR 581.

Certainty on the part of the employer is not the test to be applied: see *AEI Cables Ltd v McLay* [1980] IRLR 84.

Although it has been said that the employer is under an obligation to carry out a real and thorough investigation of the facts and circumstances: *Johnson Matthey Metals Ltd v Harding* [1978] IRLR 248, in the light of the Court of Appeal's approval, two years later, of the Burchell test, it must be doubted whether the word 'thorough' is appropriate. The burden of s 57(3) is to act reasonably, not thoroughly. But in a case involving dishonesty or a similar offence, the employer is not expected to carry out the sort of investigation that a police officer might carry out: see *British Home Stores Ltd v Burchell, above*. See also *Royal Society for the Protection of Birds v Croucher* [1984] IRLR 425, where, dishonesty was admitted.

In establishing reasonable grounds for the employer's belief an admission made by the employee may constitute evidence upon which the employer is entitled to rely in forming his belief, notwithstanding the fact that it would not be admissible in a criminal trial because the confession was obtained contrary to the Judges' Rules: *Morleys of Brixton Ltd v Minott* [1982] IRLR 270.

A failure to carry out a proper investigation is not simply a procedural question (so that the dismissal will still be fair if the result would have been the same had a proper investigation been made), because in considering whether there has been an adequate investigation, the tribunal is concerned with the employer's state of mind at the moment of dismissal and the adequacy of the information to justify that state of mind: *Henderson v Granville Tours Ltd* [1982] IRLR 494.

Ideally any investigation should take place as quickly as possible as delay may be fatal. However, provided the delay is reasonable it will not necessarily be fatal to the employer: *Refund Rentals Ltd v McDermott* [1977] IRLR 59, where the delay was due to the company contacting customers as part of its investigation. In theory it is desirable that the investigatory procedure should be kept separate from the disciplinary procedure, but in practice this may not be possible. In exceptional circumstances following an investigation it may be that all the employer can establish is a reasonable suspicion short of actual belief. In *Monie v Coral Racing Ltd* [1980] IRLR 464, one or both of two employees were suspected of theft. The employer carried out an investigation but he was not able to establish whether one or both of the employees had been guilty of theft. It was held that it was fair for the employer to dismiss on the basis of a reasonable suspicion short of actual belief.

This approach was followed in *Whitbread and Co plc v Thomas and Others* [1988] ICR 135, where one or more of three persons was suspected of being responsible for stock losses. Despite extensive investigations the employer could not determine which and dismissed all three. The EAT concluded that the approach in *Monie*'s case could be followed in cases of capability. In *Parr v Whitbread and Co plc* [1990] ICR 427, a similar approach was followed where four employees were dismissed. The EAT held:

> In an attempt to analyse the *Monie* principles where dishonesty is involved together with the *Whitbread* principles where mere incapability was involved . . . a possible approach is as follows . . . If an Industrial Tribunal is able to find on the evidence before it: (1) that an act had been committed which if committed by an individual would justify dismissal; (2) that the employer had made a reasonable—sufficiently thorough—investigation into the matter and with appropriate procedures; (3) that as a result of that investigation the employer reasonably believed that more than one person could have committed the act; (4) that the employer had acted reasonably in identifying the group of employees who could have committed the act and that each member of the group was individually capable of so doing; (5) that as between the members of the group the employer could not reasonably identify the individual perpetrator; then provided that the beliefs were held on solid and sensible grounds at the date of dismissal, an employer is entitled to dismiss each member of that group.

See also *Whitbread and Co plc v Mills* [1988] IRLR 501. In cases involving a suspicion, a proper investigation is essential: see *Gravett*'s case *above*. In *Frames Snooker Centre v Boyce* [1992] IRLR 472, the EAT held the fact that one member of a group of employees who could have committed three burglaries was not dismissed did not in itself mean the dismissals of the others were unfair if the employer could show he had solid and sensible grounds for distinguishing between members of the group. 'There is no "all or none" situation.'

Opportunity for the employee to explain

In *Earl v Slater and Wheeler (Airlyne) Ltd* [1972] ICR 508, while Earl was away ill, the company discovered certain matters of an unsatisfactory nature connected with his work and decided to dismiss him. He was summoned to attend the office to see the works director. He was confronted by the works director and the managing director who gave him a letter advising him that he had been dismissed and a replacement found. The NIRC found the dismissal was unfair as Earl was not given an opportunity to explain his conduct and any deficiencies in his work. Although he was unable to offer any explanation, the employers had not taken steps to discover this. The NIRC held:

> Whilst we do not say that in all circumstances the employee must be given an opportunity of stating his case, the only exception can be the case where there *can* be no explanation which *could* cause the employers to refrain from dismissing the employee. This must be a very rare situation.

The NIRC took the view that if an employer knows the employee can offer no explanation then a dismissal without giving the employee a chance to explain would be fair. If at the time of the dismissal the employer does not know whether or not the employee can offer any explanation the dismissal will be unfair.

In *W Devis and Sons Ltd v Atkins* [1977] 3 WLR 214, Viscount Dilhorne considered that:

> It does not follow that non-compliance with the code [the 1972 Code] necessarily renders a dismissal unfair, but I agree with the view expressed by Sir John Donaldson in *Earl v Slater and Wheeler (Airlyne) Ltd* [1973] 1 WLR 51, that a failure to follow a procedure prescribed in the code may lead to the conclusion that a dismissal was unfair, which, if that procedure had been followed, would have been held to have been fair.

The above quotation was cited with approval by Lord Bridge in *West Midlands Co-operative Society Ltd v Tipton* [1986] IRLR 122; see also *UCATT v Brain* [1981] ICR 542. Recently, the importance of giving the employee an opportunity to put his side of the story has been re-emphasised. See *Polkey's* case *above*. In *McLaren v National Coal Board* [1988] ICR 370, McLaren assaulted another miner during the miners' strike. He was convicted and dismissed. The Court of Appeal held that the standards of fairness, including giving the employee an opportunity of explaining his conduct, are immutable and applied notwithstanding the exceptional circumstances of the strike, although in a particular case the employer might be justified in not seeking an explanation that was for the tribunal to investigate.

A number of cases illustrate the need to give the employee an opportunity to explain.

In *Lees v The Orchard* [1978] IRLR 20, Lees was suspected of dishonesty when money went missing. The employer dismissed her without giving her sufficient opportunity to explain. The EAT accepted that there were a number of ways in which the money could have gone missing without necessarily involving dishonesty by the employee. It held that the tribunal was entitled to find, on the evidence, that the employer had not given the employee a reasonable opportunity of explaining her alleged dishonesty before the dismissal, which was unfair. See also the decision of the EAT in *Laws Store Ltd v Oliphant* [1978] IRLR 251. There was no dishonesty involved but Oliphant was dismissed without being given a real opportunity to explain. The EAT held that in the circumstances the failure to give the employee a real opportunity to explain rendered the dismissal unfair. The EAT were clearly concerned that the employee was dismissed for a single lapse.

In *John Crawford and Co (Plumbers) Ltd v Donnelly* [1979] IRLR 9, Donnelly, was dismissed following a strike after he had been warned by the employer that a failure to return to work could result in his dismissal. He did not return to work because he was ill. Before he contacted the employer he was dismissed. The EAT held the dismissal was unfair. It found that if the company had given the employee an opportunity to explain his absence before they sent out the letter of dismissal, a satisfactory explanation might well have been given, and the employee would not have been dismissed.

Similarly in *Qualcast (Wolverhampton) Ltd v Ross* (1) and *Ross v Qualcast (Wolverhampton) Ltd* (2) [1979] IRLR 98, Ross was found asleep and was dismissed. He was given no opportunity to explain before the decision to dismiss was taken. The EAT found that this case was not an exceptional case where the gravity of the matter was such that no explanation could make any difference, and the dismissal was unfair.

The failure to give the employee an opportunity to explain will not inevitably render the dismissal unfair. There may be exceptional circumstances: see *Polkey's* and *McLaren's* cases, *above*, and *Hooper v British Railways Board* [1988] IRLR 517. Ideally, the employee should also be given the opportunity to explain before recollections fade. See *Marley Homecare Ltd v Dutton* [1981] IRLR 380 and *Royal Society for the Prevention of Cruelty to Animals v Cruden* [1986] IRLR 83.

See *below* for the employee's opportunity to explain where the employee has been engaged in criminal conduct and where the employee's capability is in question.

The nature of the opportunity

In *Khanum v Mid-Glamorgan Area Health Authority* [1978] IRLR 215, the EAT set out guidelines to be followed by an internal disciplinary body. See p 167, *above*. The employer was a large health authority with a relatively sophisticated set of procedures. While a small employer, and indeed a medium-sized employer, may not have a procedure which is in any way as sophisticated, nonetheless the employer is expected to avoid what has been described as the fundamental breach of the rules of natural justice in determining disciplinary issues. What is reasonable will depend upon the circumstances in any particular case.

Where the employer gives the employee an opportunity to explain, he must ensure that opportunity is capable of being used by the employee. It may be of little use if the employee is not in a fit state to give an explanation. In *Tesco Group of Companies (Holdings) Ltd v Hill* [1977] IRLR 63, Hill was under suspicion of dishonesty. She was asked for an explanation at a time when she was not well. The EAT held that the employer should have waited until she was better.

Where the police are present at a disciplinary hearing without the employee's prior knowledge and consent, that will be wholly improper. If the police are present and have administered a caution, then the employee cannot be said to have had an opportunity to explain. See *Read v Phoenix Preservation Ltd* [1985] IRLR 93.

The right to explain must be considered in a broad and common-sense way. In *Ayanlowo v Commissioners of Inland Revenue* [1975] IRLR 253, the employee was dismissed because of his poor work. He was told of his right to make written representations against dismissal and he did so. He received no further communication from the Board and was dismissed. He complained that the Board had breached the provisions of natural justice in not giving him a hearing. The Court of Appeal did not refer expressly to the Code, but made it clear that natural justice does not need 'an oral hearing of a complaint of this nature upon a matter of this kind'. The opportunity to make written representations was sufficient and the dismissal was fair.

The opportunity for the employee to explain involves knowing what is alleged against him and the factors being taken into account. He should be shown any documents or statements on which the employer intends to rely: *Bell v Devon and Cornwall Police Authority* [1978] IRLR 283. As an alternative to showing the employee a written state-ment the employer, before dismissing the employee, may ask those involved to outline to the employee the matters alleged against him. In either case the employee must know with sufficient certainty what is said against him. In addition it maybe that the employee should be given the opportunity of questioning any protagonist: *Bentley Engineer-ing Co Ltd v Mistry* [1979] ICR 47. However, the employee is probably not entitled to be given written statements and to have the right of oral evidence: *Khanum v Mid-Glamorgan Area Health Authority, above*.

Compare with *Louies v Coventry Hood and Seating Co Ltd, below*. There is no general obligation on an employer to carry out a quasi-judicial investigation, with confrontation of witnesses and cross-examination. There may be circumstances where it is necessary or desirable: *Ulsterbus Ltd v Henderson* [1989] IRLR 251. There is no absolute need for witnesses to be called if a procedure makes it optional whether or not to call them provided that justice is done: *East Hertfordshire District Council v Boyten* [1977] IRLR 347.

In *Louies v Coventry Hood and Seating Co Ltd* [1990] IRLR 324, the EAT held that where an employer relies almost entirely on witnesses' written statements the failure to make them available to the employee will be contrary to the rules of natural justice and so it will not be a fair procedure. It is difficult to reconcile the case with *Bentley Engineering Co Ltd v Mistry, above, Spink v Express Foods Group Ltd below*, and as mentioned *above*, with *Khanum v Mid-Glamorgan Area Health Authority*. It is suggested that the *dictum* in *Spink* is correct, although there may be cases on their own facts, where a more particular method would be needed before it could be said that the employer acted reasonably. In *Spink v Express Foods Group Ltd* [1990] IRLR 320, the EAT held that in general terms an employee should know the case he has to meet. He should hear or be told the important points of the evidence in support of that case and should have an opportunity to criticise or dispute the evidence, to adduce his own evidence and argue his case. See also *Vauxhall Motors Ltd v Ghafoor* [1993] ICR 376.

Where an employee fails to attend a disciplinary hearing and the employer proceeds in his absence this may well be fair: see *Mansard Precision Engineering Co Ltd v Taylor* [1978] ICR 44. However, when the employee is unable to participate because of ill-health then the employer, if he goes ahead on that basis, may be in difficulty: *Tesco Group of Companies (Holdings) Ltd v Hill, above*. If the employee fails to attend because of illness and writes to the employer explaining the position, the employer should consider the letter even though it arrives subsequently to the disciplinary hearing: *Chrystie v Rolls Royce (1971) Ltd* [1976] IRLR 336; see also *John Crawford and Co (Plumbers) Ltd v Donnelly* [1979] IRLR 9.

It has been held there is no rule of natural justice which requires the employee to be present at a disciplinary hearing where his representative is present throughout and the employee has been given a chance to explain: *Pirelli General Cable Works Ltd v Murray* [1979] IRLR 190. However, it is important that the rights of the employee are safeguarded by his duly accredited representatives: *Gray Dunn and Co Ltd v Edwards* [1980] IRLR 23.

Generally, the person who conducts an inquiry must be seen to be impartial. In *Slater v Leicestershire Health Authority* [1989] IRLR 16, a nurse's dismissal was not unfair because the manager who carried out the preliminary investigation also conducted the disciplinary hearing and took the decision to dismiss.

Capability

Warnings
It may be difficult to draw a clear distinction between dismissals by reason of conduct and capability. Where the lack of capability is due to fault on the employee's part such as carelessness or negligence, then the dismissal is probably better regarded as being a dismissal by reason of the employee's conduct rather than capability and so the need for warnings should be considered accordingly: *Sutton and Gates (Luton) Ltd v Boxall* [1979] ICR 67.

Both the former 1972 and the 1977 Codes in dealing with disciplinary procedures, rules and penalties refer only to conduct. Neither Code suggests that the same requirements should be observed when the reason for the dismissal is capability. Nonetheless, warnings are of relevance where the employee's lack of capability is in issue. See *Polkey*'s case *above*.

The NIRC held that the 'general concept of fair play inherent in the disciplinary procedure should also guide management in considering the dismissal for inefficiency': see *The Lewis Shops Group v Wiggins* [1973] IRLR 205; see also *Taylor v Alidair Ltd* [1978] ICR 445.

The approach to be followed in cases involving capability, including the need to give warnings, was set out by the NIRC in *James v Waltham Holy Cross UDC* [1973] 398. It held:

> If an employee is not measuring up to the job, it may be because he is not exerting himself sufficiently or it may be because he really lacks the capacity to do so. An employer should be very slow to dismiss upon the ground that the employee is incapable of performing the work which he is employed to do, without first telling the employee of the respects in which he is failing to do his job adequately, warning him of the possibility or likelihood of dismissal on this ground and giving him an opportunity of improving his performance.

The NIRC found there were two exceptions to this principle. The first arises where senior management 'may by the nature of their jobs be fully aware of what is required of them and fully capable of judging for themselves whether they are achieving that requirement. In such circumstances the need for warning and an opportunity for improvement is much less apparent.' The second exception arises where 'the inadequacy of performance is so extreme that there must be an irredeemable incapability. In such circumstances, exceptional though they no doubt are, a warning and opportunity for improvement are of no benefit to the employee and may constitute an unfair burden on the business.'

A similar approach was followed in *Winterhalter Gastronom Ltd v Webb* [1973] ICR 245, where a sales director was dismissed because of poor sales figures. The NIRC concluded 'many do not know they are capable of jumping the five-barred gate until the bull is close behind them'. The court differentiated between senior and junior personnel when considering the need for warnings.

In *Cook v Thomas Linnell and Sons Ltd* [1977] ICR 770, the EAT held:

> ... the rules of procedure ... may be of less importance when one is dealing with alleged incapacity, provided—and this is most important— that the complaint has been brought to the attention of the employee concerned over a period of time. This remains a requirement even where the employee holds a position in which he can, within reason, be expected to monitor his own performance.

A dismissal without a warning may be unfair if there is some possibility that the employee might improve, following a warning. Even though it is only a possibility, the employee should be given a chance to improve: see *Mansfield Hosiery Mills Ltd v Bromley* [1977] IRLR 301. What is a reasonable period to give the employee will depend upon the circumstances of the case: see *Sibun v Modern Telephones Ltd* [1976] IRLR 81.

The employee may receive a warning by implication about his capability. In *Judge International Ltd v Moss* [1973] IRLR 208, it was found that a failure to review a salary might be sufficient warning that the employee was not carrying out his functions adequately: see also *Coward v John Menzies (Holdings) Ltd* [1977] IRLR 428.

A warning may not be necessary and the dismissal therefore fair, eg where the employee is hopelessly incompetent so that no warning or suggestion to him that he should improve would alter the position. Similarly, a warning may not be necessary where the employee does not consider that he was performing badly and is not aware of any of his shortcomings so that a warning, even if given, would not have been heeded: see *Grant v Ampex Great Britain Ltd* [1980] IRLR 461.

In *AJ Dunning and Sons (Shop Fitters) Ltd v Jacomb* [1973] ICR 448, the employee who was a contracts manager was dismissed without warning. The NIRC considered whether a failure to give a warning was a matter of procedure or whether it was a matter of substance. They concluded that it was a matter of substance. In this case the tribunal had to ask itself:

> whether Mr Jacomb's incapacity as it existed at the time of dismissal was of such a nature and quality as to justify a dismissal, or whether it was of such a nature and quality that, were Mr Jacomb to receive a warning, he might or would be able to improve his performance. If the latter, then the mere fact that his performance had not been up to standard in the past would not, or might not, justify his dismissal.

The NIRC found that the lack of capability pointed to a constitutional inability on the employee's part so that a warning would have been of no use.

It may also be fair to dismiss an employee without a warning where the mistakes are serious. In *Lowndes v Specialist Heavy Engineering Ltd* [1977] ICR 1, the employee was dismissed after five costly mistakes without a warning or an opportunity to explain. The dismissal was fair, for the circumstances 'were so egregious that dismissal was justified, despite the failure in procedure, and no injustice was done'.

In *Taylor v Alidair Ltd* [1978] ICR 445, the Court of Appeal confirmed that it may be fair to dismiss an employee where his lack of capability is so serious that it is reasonable for the employer not to risk further serious errors, and approved the judgment of Bristow J in the EAT where he found:

> In our judgement there are activities in which the degree of professional skill which must be required is so high, and the potential consequences of the smallest departure of that high standard are so serious, that one failure to perform in accordance with those standards is enough to justify dismissal. The passenger-carrying airline pilot, the scientist operating the nuclear reactor . . . are . . . in the situation in which one failure to maintain the proper standard of professional skill can bring about a major disaster.

The EAT has also recognised that where there is a close personal relationship between employees as between a managing director and his personal secretary it may not be necessary specifically to warn the employee that unless there is an improvement dismissal will follow: *Brown v Hall Advertising Ltd* [1978] IRLR 246, where the EAT emphasised that the Code is not a mandatory document, the provisions of which fall to be applied rigidly to every employment situation. What is fair and good industrial practice for an employee on the shop floor will not apply in every situation. In this case the employee had at least been put on notice that her work was unsatisfactory and particular areas for improvement were pointed out to her.

As in the case of misconduct, a warning to the employee may be dispensed with when its need is outweighed by the interests of the business.

Where the employee has been taken on for a probationary or trial period a greater onus is placed on the employer to warn and aid the employee in his performance during that period: *Post Office v Mughal* [1977] IRLR 178. See also *Inner London Education Authority v Lloyd* [1981] IRLR 394. Similarly, in the case of young employees the employer's obligations may be greater. It has been suggested in the case of a young apprentice consideration should be given to consulting with his parents: *Small v Lex Mead Southampton* [1977] IRLR 48. However, compare *Finch v Betabake (Anglia) Ltd* [1977] IRLR 470. There is no general obligation on the employer to consult with the apprentice's parents.

There is no rule of law that an employer must attempt to fit the employee in elsewhere in the organisation. It will depend upon the circumstances in each case. It may be reasonable for a large employer but unreasonable for a small employer: see *Bevan Harris Ltd (t/a The Clyde Leather Co) v Gair* [1981] IRLR 520.

Warnings generally
The nature of the warning has already been considered in relation to conduct, see *'Warnings generally', above* at p 175.

The need for assessment and help
In cases involving substandard performance where the reason is a lack of skill in the broader sense on the employee's part, there is some obligation on the employer's part to assist the employee in reaching the required standard. That involves the employer in making an assessment.

It has already been seen that in cases involving probationary employees, there is an obligation on the employer to assess the employee's performance and to give advice and guidance: see *Post Office v Mughal* [1977] IRLR 178; *Inner London Education Authority v Lloyd* [1981] IRLR 394. Arguably similar guidelines apply where the employer has recently promoted the employee. In *Mansfield Hosiery Mills Ltd v Bromley* [1977] IRLR 301, the employee's dismissal was unfair where he had been promoted, because there had been insufficient supervision, warnings of his short-comings and a lack of encouragement to improve.

The reported cases involve in the main new and probationary employees and employees who have been newly promoted. However, similar steps should be taken where an existing employee's work becomes substandard due to factors other than the employee's capability. This may arise where there is a change in the level of the skill required, other demands made upon the employee by the employer, or problems away from the work place which affect his efficiency.

A failure to give appropriate guidance or training may lead or contribute to an unfair dismissal. In *Boobier v Johnsons Cleaners (Southern) Ltd* [1974] IRLR 329, complaints were made by the employer about the way in which Boobier managed the company's shop. He had never been given any advice or training on how the shop should be run. The tribunal found the dismissal was unfair. *Inter alia*, it found that the employer had not had regard to the guidance in para 35 of the then 1972 Code. Closely allied with the need for the employer to make the employee aware that his performance is not meeting the employer's requirements is the need for the employer to help the employee in achieving those requirements.

Tribunals have found an employee's dismissal substantively unfair where the employer has failed to give training and assistance. See 'Deficiencies in the employers organisation' *below* at p 203.

Investigation
The employer has to establish the reason for the employee's dismissal and that is a reason within s 57(1)(*b*) and (2) of the EP(C)A 1978. He must establish a genuine belief based on reasonable grounds that the employee is incapable: see *Taylor v Alidair Ltd, above*. In order to establish that belief he may need to carry out an investigation. See, generally, see '*Warnings generally*', *above* at p 175.

Opportunity for the employee to explain
In practice, the failure by the employer to give the employee an opportunity to explain may be less important than in the case of misconduct.

In *Sutton and Gates (Luton) Ltd v Boxall* [1979] ICR 67, Boxall, an electrician, was unfairly dismissed because of bad workmanship without being given the opportunity to explain. His lack of capability was affecting his employer's business. The EAT held that if the employee had been given an opportunity of explaining there was a possibility he would not have been dismissed, and the dismissal was unfair.

There are exceptions, one of which may arise where the offence is so heinous and the facts so manifestly clear that the employer could on the facts known to him at the time of dismissal conclude that whatever explanation was offered it could make no difference. In *Earl v Slater and Wheeler (Airlyne) Ltd* [1972] ICR 508, the NIRC held that the employee must be given an opportunity to explain, except where there can be no explanation which would cause the employers to refrain from dismissing the employee. This was a case where conduct and capability matters came to light during Earl's absence whilst sick. He was never asked for an explanation. The NIRC followed the same logic as later did the House of Lords in *Polkey v AE Dayton Services Ltd* [1987] IRLR 503, in deciding if the employer had acted reasonably. The conclusion was that the dismissal was unfair, but even with an explanation it would have been reasonable to dismiss, hence no compensation was awarded. See also *Lowndes v Specialist Heavy Engineering, above*.

Similarly, in *Taylor v Alidair Ltd* [1978] ICR 445, where an airline pilot made one single but serious mistake in landing his aircraft his dismissal was not unfair because he had been given no opportunity to explain prior to his dismissal.

Another exception may arise where the employee has already made known his views and giving him the opportunity to explain would simply result in them being reiterated: see *James v Waltham Holy Cross UDC* [1973] ICR 398.

Further exceptions may arise where there is a close relationship between the employer and the employee: consider *Brown v Hall Advertising Ltd* [1978] IRLR 246, and where giving the employee an opportunity to explain might impose an unfair burden on the business: see *James*'s case, *above*.

The nature of the opportunity
This has already been considered in relation to conduct. See '*The nature of the opportunity*', at p 180 *above*.

Criminal offences

Criminal offences inside employment
Exceptionally a criminal offence committed by the employee in his employment against the employer will not justify dismissal It depends on the circumstances. However, usually the commission of such a criminal offence will justify the employee's dismissal, if not the employee's summary dismissal. This will be particularly so where the employer has a rule providing for dismissal or summary dismissal in such cases. The employer will not, however, be absolved from following proper procedure: see *Fowler v Cammell Laird (Shipbuilders) Ltd* [1973] IRLR 72.

Where the criminal act is committed against a fellow employee as distinct from an employer, dismissal will usually be justified, although it must be remembered that whereas theft or some other act of dishonesty committed against the employer must almost inevitably involve a breach of the confidential relationship which exists between the employer and the employee, theft or some other act of dishonesty committed against another employee will not necessarily lead to such a breach: see *Johnson Matthey Metals Ltd v Harding* [1978] IRLR 248, where an employee with 15 years' service stole from a fellow employee and was dismissed. The dismissal was held to be unfair.

The onus is upon the employer to establish the reason. Even where the reason is the employee's alleged criminal conduct, the employer need only establish that at the time of the dismissal there were reasonable grounds for believing that the offence put against the employee was committed: *Ferodo v Barnes* [1976] ICR 439. In *British Home Stores Ltd v Burchell* [1978] IRLR 379, where Burchell was dismissed for dishonesty relating to staff purchases, the EAT held that where an employee is dismissed for misconduct the employer must show that he believed the employee to be guilty of that misconduct, he had reasonable grounds for his belief and, at the time he formed the belief on those grounds, he had investigated the matter to a reasonable extent in the circumstances. The employer must honestly or genuinely hold that belief. Where one, two or more employees are reasonably suspected of being guilty of misconduct but the employer cannot identify those responsible the employer may be entitled to rely upon a reasonable suspicion of dishonesty: see *Monie v Coral Racing Ltd* [1981] ICR 109; *Whitbread and Co plc v Thomas and Others* [1988] ICR 135, *Whitbread and Co plc v Mills* [1988] IRLR 501, and *Frames Snooker Centre v Boyce* [1992] IRLR 472, generally. It is obviously important for the employer to carry out a proper investigation, particularly where he seeks to rely upon a reasonable suspicion. The employer may be entitled to rely upon an employee's admission of guilt. In *British Gas plc v McCarrick* [1991] IRLR 305, a disciplinary hearing concluded that theft of petrol had not been proved, but McCarrick was subsequently convicted. The employers began fresh disciplinary proceedings, and despite McCarrick's maintenance that he was innocent and that he had been pressurised into pleading guilty, the disciplinary panel concluded 'the only reasonable response we can make to a guilty plea is to believe it'. The tribunal found the dismissal unfair and that a reasonable employer would have made enquiries from the employee's legal advisers and would not have taken the view that 'innocent people do not admit guilt'. The EAT allowed an appeal. The decision was confirmed by the Court of Appeal holding the tribunal had substituted its own view for that of a reasonable employer. It was for the employers to decide whether the employee's guilty plea was true or if it were an admission for the purpose of avoiding a prison sentence. They had reached the view that the employee was guilty and there were no grounds upon which the tribunal could interfere. To say that a reasonable employer would have made enquiries of the employee's legal advisers regarding the circumstances would impose too high a burden on employers.

Investigation   If an employee is found in possession of stolen property belonging to his employer it may be fair to dismiss without further investigation: *Scottish Special Housing Association v Linnen* [1979] IRLR 265.

However, where there is any doubt, the employer should carry out an investigation. While this investigation may be limited by the need not to prejudice criminal investigation, such inquiry may be necessary to establish the employer's belief that he had reasonable grounds for dismissal: *Scottish Special Housing Association v Cooke* [1979] IRLR 264, or indeed a reasonable suspicion.

In *Wm Low and Co Ltd v MacCuish* [1979] IRLR 458. MacCuish was dismissed for theft because she had taken pork chops from the employer without paying for them. She was not given a chance to explain and the employer, without having carried out an investigation and so without having reasonable grounds on which to base his belief that she was guilty, jumped to the conclusion that she was guilty. See also *McLaren v NCB* [1988] ICR 370.

It may not be possible to interview the employee suspected of a criminal offence. Here, the employer will have to consider whether he has sufficient material on which to form his belief that the employee is guilty of a criminal offence in accordance with the approach in *Burchell*'s case, or in *Monie*'s case, *above*, a reasonable suspicion. However, wherever possible, it is essential that the employer should afford the employee an opportunity of giving an explanation and the employee should know that the employer is contemplating dismissal. If the employee chooses or is advised not to tell the employer anything it does not mean that the employer in forming his beliefs or suspicion in the employee's guilt has failed to carry out as much investigation into the matter as was reasonable in all the circumstances. He may have done all he can. However, it maybe that in these circumstances where the employer cannot hear the employee's version of events, he will be unable to form a belief or suspicion as to the employee's guilt. The employer may have to wait until the outcome of any criminal proceedings: see *Harris and Shepherd v Courage (Eastern) Ltd* [1981] IRLR 153, upheld on appeal, see [1982] IRLR 509. In *Secretary of State for Scotland v Campbell* [1992] IRLR 263, Campbell, a prison officer and treasurer of the prison recreation club, was unable to explain a shortfall in club funds. He was convicted of embezzlement and subsequently warned he could be dismissed for gross misconduct. He then had an opportunity to explain at a disciplinary hearing and was dismissed. The EAT held the dismissal was fair. Embezzlement was a serious offence and even though that might itself be sufficient for the employer reasonably to dismiss an employee, the employers had made enquiries and given a further opportunity to explain before dismissing Campbell.

The importance of following a proper procedure, including giving the employee an opportunity of explaining or offering some mitigation has been emphasised by the House of Lords in *Polkey*'s case, *above*. By giving the employee the opportunity to explain, the employer can communicate to the employee the action which is proposed against him: see *Harris (Ipswich) Ltd v Harrison* [1978] ICR 1256. However, it is clear from the decision in *Polkey*'s case that there may be certain exceptions. The tribunal must consider whether the employer acted reasonably in not following a proper procedure. In rare cases an employer may act reasonably in taking the view that on the facts known to him at the time of the dismissal no explanation or mitigation could alter his decision to dismiss and so the failure to take this procedural step would not be fatal.

There are several early decisions where it has been held that the dismissal of an employee without an opportunity to explain was fair. In *Carr v Alexander Russell Ltd* [1976] IRLR 220, Carr, a labourer, was caught red-handed by the police in possession of his employer's property. He did not protest his innocence and did not exercise his rights under the employer's internal procedure. The police told the employer that he had been charged with theft of the employer's property. The employer dismissed him. Carr pleaded guilty to theft, he was convicted and fined. It was held that his dismissal was fair. The NIRC considered that Carr could offer no explanation and it would be unrealistic to expect the employer to accept any explanation offered. The decision was followed in *Conway v Matthew Wright and Nephew Ltd* [1977] IRLR 89. In *Parker v Clifford Dunn Ltd* [1979] IRLR 56, Parker admitted to the police that he had stolen goods from his employer. The police told the employer's managing director who dismissed him without giving him an opportunity of explaining his conduct. It was held that the dismissal was fair. The opportunity would have been of no use because it would not have made any difference to the employer's decision. He admitted having stolen his employer's property. He made no protestations of innocence to the employer although he had the chance to do so and did not follow the employer's grievance procedure.

In *Kingston v British Railways Board* [1984] IRLR 147, Kingston's dismissal was fair following his imprisonment for three months for an assault committed in the course of his employment, notwithstanding that the employer had not followed a proper procedure.

In each of these cases, arguably the result would have been the same if they had been decided after *Polkey*'s case because they fall within the exceptions envisaged in *Polkey*'s case.

However, the employer's failure to follow a proper procedure may mean the dismissal is unfair. In *Tesco Group of Companies (Holdings) Ltd v Hill* [1977] IRLR 63, a dismissal was unfair because at the time when Hill was asked to give an explanation of her conduct she was not fit to do so. It may be unfair because pressure is put on the employee to extract a confession: *Goodwin v Fred Hartley and Sons Ltd* (1978) (unreported). A dismissal may be unfair where the employer fails to organise the disciplinary procedure properly. In *Tesco Stores Ltd v Heap* (1978) 13 ITR 17, Heap was charged with five offences of dishonesty. Prior to the hearing he was called to a café and questioned about two of the five offences which he was alleged to have admitted. There was no warning of the purpose of the meeting, no real effort was made to obtain the employee's side of the story and the employer failed to draw the employee's attention to a right of appeal. The dismissal was unfair. In *Read v Phoenix Preservation Ltd* [1985] IRLR 93, the EAT held that where police officers are present at an internal disciplinary inquiry without the employee's knowledge and consent this will be wholly improper. The EAT also found that an employee will not have every opportunity of putting forward matters in his own defence where the police who are present at an internal inquiry were conducting a criminal inquiry, and had administered a caution to the employee.

A subsequent conviction   Since the employer need only show at most that he had reasonable grounds for believing that the employee was guilty of criminal conduct, it is not necessarily fatal that the employee is not subsequently convicted in criminal proceedings: *Davies v GKN Birwelco (Uskside) Ltd* [1976] IRLR 82. There is no general obligation on the employer to await the outcome of criminal proceedings: *Tesco Stores Ltd v Heap above*, or to suspend the employee on full pay while awaiting the result of any criminal proceedings: *Conway v Matthew Wright and Nephew Ltd* [1977] IRLR 89. See also *Harris and Shepherd v Courage (Eastern) Ltd* [1981] IRLR 153.

Fairness of the dismissal—general   The tribunal is not able to substitute its decision for that of the employer. It is concerned to see whether or not the employer has acted fairly in all the circumstances judged by the objective standard, what would a reasonable employer in that line of business have done in those circumstances?: see *Grundy (Teddington) Ltd v Willis* [1976] ICR 323 and *NC Watling and Co Ltd v Richardson* [1978] ICR 1049. It is for the tribunal to see whether or not the employer's response was within that range of reasonable responses: see *Rolls Royce Ltd v Walpole* [1980] IRLR 343.

The tribunal must look to see what the employer could reasonably have done where the employee is alleged to have committed a criminal offence. In *Parkers Bakeries Ltd v Palmer* [1977] IRLR 215, Palmer, a bread salesman, was 20 loaves of bread short in his deliveries to a particular customer on four consecutive days. The EAT found there was abundant evidence on which the employer could conclude that the employee was responsible. At an interview Palmer made no outright acknowledgement of guilt but did agree to pay back certain moneys. In the circumstances this was considered to be approaching a tacit acknowledgement of guilt and the employer had acted reasonably.

The employer must act swiftly. In *Allders International Ltd v Parkins* [1981] IRLR 68, an allegation of theft was made against Parkins, but nothing was done for nine days and he was allowed to work out the nine days. The dismissal was unfair.

Activity which may lead the employer to suspect criminal conduct can also be a breach of the employer's rules or a breach of an implied term in the contract. Although an employer may not be able to show criminal conduct, he may be able to show other conduct which might justify a dismissal.

Other factors for consideration   Where the employee is in custody the contract of employment may be frustrated. See generally Chapter 4. Even if the contract is not frustrated, the employee's imprisonment may be sufficient to justify dismissal. Where an employee is convicted of a criminal offence so that his continued employment in a particular position may involve a contravention of a statutory duty or restriction—for instance his inability to drive a vehicle on the public highway—it may justify dismissal. See, generally, Chapter 6.

Where the procedure cannot be carried out immediately Normally, when it is impossible or impracticable to follow the disciplinary procedure immediately, for whatever reason, the employee may be suspended with pay until the procedure can be followed.

Criminal offences outside employment

The 1977 Code provides that:

> [Criminal offences committed outside employment] . . . should not be treated as automatic reasons for dismissal regardless of whether the offence has any relevance to the duties of the individual as an employee. The main considerations should be whether the offence is one that makes the individual unsuitable for his or her type of work or unacceptable to other employees. Employees should not be dismissed solely because a charge against them is pending or because they are absent through having been remanded in custody. (Paragraph 15(*c*).)

As a general proposition, for a dismissal to be fair the offence must have some detrimental effect upon the employer's interests in the wider sense. In *Robb v Mersey Insulation Co Ltd* [1972] IRLR 18, Robb, a shipwright securing cargoes on board ships, was convicted of theft. He was dismissed and it was held the dismissal was fair. The tribunal found 'the reputation of [the employer's] business would have been adversely affected if it had come to the knowledge of their customers that employees with convictions of this nature were working among cargo'. See also *Richardson v City of Bradford Metropolitan Council* [1975] IRLR 296, a case involving the dismissal of a public servant after a conviction of theft. In *Gardiner v Newport CBC* [1974] IRLR 262, a lecturer was dismissed following a conviction for gross indecency with other men in a public toilet. He was in charge of male and female teenage students. The tribunal found the dismissal fair holding, 'Both on the ground that such a person either cannot or will not control himself in public and should not be trusted with young persons, with the opportunities that a teacher has, and also having some respect for the feelings of parents we think that the decision to dismiss . . . was reasonable'. In *Nottinghamshire CC v Bowly* [1978] IRLR 252, the EAT made it clear that while there is no rule that following a conviction of gross indecency the employee must be automatically dismissed or that dismissal in such circumstances is automatically unfair, provided the employer has considered the case fairly and properly and directed itself properly it cannot be faulted in doing what in their judgment is just and proper. In *Wiseman v Salford CC* [1981] IRLR 202, the EAT recognised that in cases involving teachers convicted of acts of gross indecency who come into contact with young male students, the tribunal has to assess the reasonableness of the employer's action in each case. There is no self-evident proposition that there is no risk attached to such an employee's continued employment. Wiseman's dismissal was fair.

In *Creffield v BBC* [1975] IRLR 23, the dismissal of a film camera-man following his conviction of indecently assaulting a 13-year-old girl was fair because the employer could not be selective in sending the employee on assignments and might be apprehensive about sending the employee on assignments in a responsible position in the future. In *P v Nottinghamshire County Council* [1992] IRLR 362, where a school groundsman was dismissed after his conviction for indecent assault on his daughter the Court of Appeal held that in an appropriate case it may be unfair to dismiss without considering the availability of alternative employment. There is nothing, however, in s 57(3) that states this must be investigated before the decision to dismiss is taken, rather than before the dismissal takes effect. The principle of alternative employment usually arises in cases of redundancy and ill-health. They also held that here the employer quite rightly took the view that they could not continue the employment which brought P into even casual contact with young girls.

If it can be shown that the employee's criminal conduct is not detrimental to the employer's interest in the wider sense then the dismissal will not necessarily be fair. In *Bradshaw v Rugby Portland Cement Co Ltd* [1972] IRLR 46, Bradshaw's dismissal following his conviction for incest was unfair. The tribunal found:

> This was an isolated incident, it had nothing to do with the applicant's work, his work did not bring him into contact with female staff, he was working with a gang of men, it did not, apparently, upset his relationships with his workmates in any way, it did not expose anyone to a moral danger from his presence in the works; and there must have been although we do not know what they were, very strong mitigating circumstances to enable a court to deal with the applicant in such a lenient manner [probation for three years].

See also *Norfolk County Council v Bernard* [1979] IRLR 220, where a teacher's dismissal after he was convicted of possession and cultivation of cannabis was unfair.

The employee may be fairly dismissed because he dishonestly conceals from his employer a criminal conviction which was imposed before he commenced employment with that employer: see *Torr v British Railways Board* [1977] ICR 785.

The employer need only satisfy himself at most that at the time of the dismissal he had reasonable grounds for believing that the offence put against the employee was committed, not that the employee in fact committed it: *Ferodo Ltd v Barnes* [1976] ICR 439; *British Home Stores Ltd v Burchell* [1978] IRLR 379. In exceptional circumstances a reasonable suspicion will be sufficient when the offence is committed outside the employment. See *Monie v Coral Racing Ltd* [1980] IRLR 464.

The employer should follow a proper procedure. Failure to do so is likely to result in the dismissal being unfair: see *Tesco Group of Companies (Holdings) Ltd v Hill* [1977] IRLR 63. See '*Criminal offences inside employment*', *above* at p 189. There will be exceptional cases where dismissal is not unfair: see *Carr v Alexander Russell Ltd* [1976] IRLR 220, and *Parker v Clifford Dunn Ltd* [1979] ICR 463. The employer must not do anything to prejudice any criminal proceedings or interfere with the course of justice: *Carr v Alexander Russell Ltd, above*.

Contravention of a statutory duty or restriction

The 1977 Code does not specifically deal with this reason for dismissal. However, there is no reason why the employer's obligations as to investigation, consultation or giving the employee an opportunity to explain should not apply when appropriate.

Where the continued employment would be in contravention of a statutory duty or restriction, the dismissal will not always be fair. It is clear from the decision in *Myeza v Avon Area Health Authority* (1977) (unreported), see Chapter 6, *Contravention of a statutory duty or restriction, above* at p 140, that the employer still has to act reasonably. In *Sutcliffe and Eaton Ltd v Pinney* [1977] IRLR 349, a trainee hearing-aid dispenser failed a Hearing Aid Council examination which meant the employer would commit an offence under the Hearing Aid Council Act 1968 by employing him to dispense hearing aids. If an extension of time to pass the examination had been obtained, then no action under the Act against the employer was likely. However, the employer did not ascertain the position but dismissed Pinney. The EAT held the dismissal unfair. The tribunal must consider reasonableness. The fact that continued employment would be in contravention of a statutory duty or restriction, does not necessarily mean dismissal is fair. However, compensation is likely to be the only remedy rather than reinstatement or re-engagement: *Sandhu v (1) Department of Education and Science, (2) London Borough of Hillingdon* [1978] IRLR 208.

In *O'Connor v Lothian Health Board* (1977) (unreported), a dentist who carried on private work without the Board's consent in breach of regulations which rendered the Board liable to prosecution by employing him was warned on several occasions to give up private practice, but did not, and his dismissal was fair.

Warnings are important where the employee is in breach of statute but could have remedied the situation. It would be different if the warning can be of no effect. The employer's genuine but erroneous belief that there has been a contravention is irrelevant in applying s 57(2)(*d*) of the EP(C)A 1978. The facts may provide the employer with 'some other substantial reason': *Bouchaala v Trust Houses Forte Hotels Ltd* [1980] IRLR 382.

For cases involving the contravention of a statutory duty or restriction under s 57(2)(*d*) of the EP(C)A 1978, see Chapter 6.

Some other substantial reason

Neither the former 1972 nor the 1977 Code make reference to the need for warnings, investigation, consultation or giving the employee an opportunity to explain before dismissing him for 'some other substantial reason'. Even though not required under either of those Codes, the employer should warn, investigate, consult with, and give the employee the opportunity to explain before dismissing him for 'some other substantial reason'. Exceptionally, failure to do so will not be fatal, the tribunal must consider the reasonableness of the employer's actions.

In *Hollister v National Farmers Union* [1979] ICR 542, Hollister was dismissed following a reorganisation of the employer's business. The Court of Appeal considered that consultation and negotiation were factors to be taken into account when considering the fairness of the dismissal, but in this case failure to do so did not mean that the dismissal was unfair. The tribunal had to look at all the circumstances and reach a proper conclusion. However, the lack of consultation may mean the employer is not aware of all the circumstances which, had he known them, would have led him to refrain from dismissing: *Ladbroke Courage Holidays Ltd v Asten* [1981] IRLR 59. See also *St John of God (Care Services) Ltd v Brooks and Others* [1992] IRLR 546.

Appeals

The 1977 Code provides that the disciplinary procedure should provide a right of appeal and specify the procedure to be followed: para 10(*k*). It is not confined to cases involving misconduct: *Lancaster v Anchor Hotels and Taverns Ltd* [1973] IRLR 13. The right is an important one and it should be brought to the attention of the employee or his representative: *Tesco Group of Companies (Holdings) Ltd v Hill* [1977] IRLR 63. Even if the employer's disciplinary procedure does not provide for a right of appeal, one should be given where possible: *Davison v Kent Meters Ltd* [1975] IRLR 145.

In *West Midlands Co-operative Society Ltd v Tipton* [1986] ICR 192, the House of Lords held that a failure to follow a proper procedure, including granting the employee a right of appeal may render the dismissal unfair. The nature and purpose of an appeal must be considered in determining the fairness of a dismissal where no appeal has been granted or the appeal procedure is defective. In *Post Office v*

Marney [1990] IRLR 170, a failure to consider on appeal whether dismissal was an appropriate remedy was not a breach of Marney's contractual appeal procedure. The EAT held that not every breach of a contractual right of appeal rendered the dismissal unfair. It held that the appeal is a process whereby what has been done by an inferior official or tribunal is investigated to see whether it is something which ought to be disturbed or not. It considered that the principle in *Tipton's* case that the employer's activities right down to the end of the appeal process have to be considered should not mean losing sight of the fundamental question which is, 'was the dismissal fair or unfair?' Only if an appeal procedure is defective in that it should or could have demonstrated a flaw in the decision at 'first instance' will the dismissal be unfair. If the process leading to the decision to dismiss was a proper one, then because on appeal the employer did not consider or review one of the parts of the process, it does not mean that the dismissal is unfair. Procedural defects may be remedied on an appeal where the appeal takes the form of a re-hearing and is comprehensive: see *Whitbread and Co plc v Mills* [1988] ICR 776.

It is more likely that a dismissal will be unfair where larger employers are involved and no right of appeal has been granted: see *Lloyd v Scottish Co-operative Wholesale Society Ltd* [1973] IRLR 93; and *McConvey v British Steel Corporation* [1974] IRLR 196. Where larger employers have been involved, the tribunals have looked to see whether there is a level of management above that which took the step of dismissing the employee to whom the appeal could have been made: see *Davison's* case, above, where the employer was a family concern with 250 employees and the failure to provide Davison with a right of appeal was found to contribute to a finding of unfair dismissal.

In practice, there may be difficulties in giving the employee a right to appeal in particular where small businesses are involved. In *Tiptools Ltd v Curtis* [1973] IRLR 276. Curtis was dismissed by the managing director of a family company with some 45 employees. In finding the dismissal unfair, the tribunal relied upon the fact that the employee had been given no right of appeal against the imposition of dismissal. The NIRC overturned the tribunal's decision. It found that the appeal provisions of the Code were designed for larger companies 'where the responsibility for dismissal may lie with a level of management below the top management'. Although it was desirable that there should be a right of appeal, in this case it was clearly impracticable since the decision to dismiss was taken by the highest level of management within the company. The tribunal's suggestion that the employer should provide a right of appeal to an outside body was not accepted.

Where there is an appeal procedure it should conform with the Code's guidance. In *Sewell and Francis v Ford Motor Co Ltd* [1975] IRLR 25, the appeal procedure provided that 'The appeal should be made in the first instance to the authority who administered the disciplinary action, rather than to any lower level of supervision.' The tribunal found this was not an appeal but rather a reconsideration of the decision by those who had taken it. It did not accord with the guidelines laid down in the Code and the provisions for appeal were sufficiently defective to make the dismissal unfair: but compare *Flude v Post Office* [1975] IRLR 330.

Where there is an appeal procedure, it should be followed and a failure to follow it may result in the dismissal being held unfair. In *Johnson Matthey Metals Ltd v Harding* [1978] IRLR 248, the EAT upheld the tribunal's criticism of the employer's appeals procedure. The manager, who considered an appeal, had already discussed the matter with other members of management who were involved and on a preliminary view decided on dismissal before the appeal was heard. In *Byrne v BOC Ltd* [1992] IRLR 505, a manager who investigated the employee's allegedly false overtime claims at the initial stages was held to be a judge in his own cause and disentitled from conducting a fair appeal, even though he took no part in the disciplinary hearing itself. In *Cabaj v Westminster City Council* [1994] IRLR 530, the dismissal was held to be unfair because it was heard by only two councillors, whereas the procedure agreed between the employer and the trade union prescribed three councillors.

Where the body hearing the appeal fails to consider the case properly, the dismissal may be unfair: *McCabe v Ninth District Council of the County of Lanark* [1973] IRLR 75. However, compare *Rowe v Radio Rentals* [1982] IRLR 177. The appeal process must be comprehensive if it is to overcome defects in the disciplinary process's earlier stages. There must be proper notice of the charges being brought against the employee and a full opportunity to explain: *Byrne v BOC Ltd, above.*

On appeal the employee should be given an opportunity to explain and, depending on the circumstances, either be given copies of statements, or when statements are not available have the case outlined orally to him: *Bentley Engineering Co Ltd v Mistry* [1979] ICR 47. On an appeal it is important that the employee knows what is alleged against him and the case he has to meet. In addition the employee may be given an opportunity to question any protagonist.

An employee does not acquiesce in his dismissal if he fails to exercise a right of appeal: see *Chrystie v Rolls Royce (1971) Ltd* [1976] IRLR 336 and *Hoover Ltd v Forde* [1980] ICR 239 (See also the latest view of the EAT on this point in *Lock v Connell Estate Agents* [1994] IRLR 444, and Chapter 16 under 'Failure to utilise the Employer's Disciplinary Procedure' at p 376 and 'Contributory Fault' at p 377). An employee must be allowed to exercise all the appeal rights to which he is contractually entitled: *Stokes v Lancashire County Council* [1992] IRLR 75, although in certain cases the right to appeal may be dispensed with where at the time of dismissal the employer reasonably decides there is no use in an appeal and it could not have altered the outcome: see *Polkey*'s case, *above*. In *Gardiner v Newport CBC* [1974] IRLR 262, a lecturer was dismissed following a conviction for gross indecency. The employee had no right of appeal. The tribunal found the procedure unsatisfactory because of this but in the circumstances the procedure was fair because any reasonable employer would have dismissed, even if a right of appeal had been given. In *Tovey v F and F Robinson (Stockton-on-Tees) Ltd* [1975] IRLR 139, the employee, a lorry driver, was dismissed because he refused to work overtime hours unless he was paid for them, although other lorry drivers had accepted this position. It was held that the employer's failure to give the employee a right of appeal where this was possible did not render the dismissal unfair because the employee was 'indicating that he was not prepared to abide by the terms ... which covered all the other employees at the respondent's place of work'.

In *Rowe v Radio Rentals Ltd* [1982] IRLR 177, the EAT held there was no conflict between the employer's disciplinary procedure and the rules of natural justice where the person who heard the appeal had been informed of the decision to dismiss before it took place, and further because the person who took the decision to dismiss was present at the appeal. He took no part in the appeal. Disciplinary bodies should not become entrammelled in the net of legal procedure; provided that they have acted fairly and justly there can be no complaints. It will often be difficult in practice to separate the 'dismisser' from the person hearing the appeal. Each case will depend on its own facts: cf *Johnson Matthey Metals Ltd v Harding* [1978] IRLR 248, and *above*.

Where the employer's disciplinary and dismissals procedure is agreed with the union and entitles either party to call witnesses although neither is obliged to do so, the dismissal will not be unfair merely because the employer does not call witnesses and the committee which hears the appeal does not insist on the relevant witnesses being called by the employer: *East Herts DC v Boyten* [1977] IRLR 347.

There is no rule of natural justice that an employee must be present at an appeal when his representative is present: see *Pirelli General Cable Works Ltd v Murray* [1979] IRLR 90.

The fact that the employee's post has been advertised before the appeal does not necessarily mean that the appeal has been prejudiced: *Lambsdale v Her Majesty's Stationery Office* [1975] IRLR 239.

The fact that the right of appeal arises after the effective date of termination does not mean that the tribunal is precluded from considering a failure to allow an appeal in deciding the reasonableness of the dismissal: *Rank Xerox (UK) Ltd v Goodchild* [1979] IRLR 185. See '*Reasonableness and subsequently discovered misconduct*', *above* at p 154.

The existence of an appeals procedure does not justify the employer in dispensing with the obligation to consult the employee and invite an explanation from him when contemplating dismissal: *Qualcast (Wolverhampton) Ltd v Ross (1); Ross v Qualcast (Wolverhampton) Ltd (2)* [1979] IRLR 98.

The right of representation

The 1977 Code provides that the employee should be given 'the right to be accompanied' either by a trade union representative or by a fellow employee of his choice: para 10(*g*).

The employer's procedure may provide for representation. If in such circumstances the employee is denied representation within the terms of the agreed procedure, this may be important, particularly where the employee is accused of a serious offence, in considering reasonableness: see *Rank Xerox (UK) Ltd v Goodchild, above.*

Where representation is allowed and the representative is present throughout the whole of the disciplinary hearing but the employee is not, and is only present when he gives his evidence, it is not contrary to the rules of natural justice if the employer proceeds in the absence of the employee, but in the presence of his representative: *Pirelli General Cable Works Ltd v Murray* [1979] IRLR 190; see also *Gray Dunn and Co Ltd v Edwards* [1980] IRLR 23.

Likewise, there is no rule of natural justice that the employee must be present at an appeal if his representative is present.

Where there has been a failure by the employer to allow the employee to be represented it does not necessarily mean that the dismissal will be unfair. The employer may reasonably decide representation would be futile and not alter the decision to dismiss. It is for the tribunal to consider reasonableness in all the circumstances.

Disciplinary action involving trade union officials

The 1977 Code provides 'disciplinary action against a trade union official can lead to a serious dispute if it is seen as an attack on the union's functions. Although normal disciplinary standards should apply to their conduct as employees, no disciplinary action beyond an oral warning should be taken until the circumstances of the case have been discussed with a senior trade union representative or full-time official': para 15(*b*). Cases decided under the former 1972 Code are of assistance.

In *Fowler v Cammell Laird (Shipbuilders) Ltd* [1973] IRLR 72, Fowler was convicted of theft from a fellow employee's car parked in the employer's car park in working hours. The employer's policy of instantly dismissing employees for dishonest acts, although not communicated to the employees in writing, had been made known to them. His summary dismissal was fair. The tribunal found: 'The requirement as to discussion with a full-time official of the union in the case of the shop steward who is the subject of disciplinary procedure obviously does not contemplate the type of case with which we are concerned—so the fact that the applicant was a shop steward is irrelevant in this context.'

Similarly, in *Donald Cook and Son Ltd v Carter* [1977] IRLR 88 a shop steward was dismissed in accordance with the employer's disciplinary procedure. He had been issued with warnings in connection with bad language on two occasions, poor performance on two occasions and with leaving his place of work. The dismissal was fair, even though there was no reference to a full-time union official.

In *CA Parsons and Co Ltd v McLoughlin* [1978] IRLR 65, a shop steward was dismissed following fighting with another employee. No reference was made to a full-time union official.

However, even where a dismissal is for a reason unconnected with the employee's union activities, it may well be advisable for the employer to consult with the full-time union official. In *Donnelly v London Brick Co Ltd* [1974] IRLR 331, the dismissal of a shop steward without consulting the full-time union official did not make the dismissal automatically unfair, however the tribunal held that if the full-time union official had been involved the decision to dismiss would not have been taken. The dismissal was unfair.

In *British Labour Pump Co Ltd v Byrne* [1979] IRLR 94, a shop steward was dismissed because of his involvement in theft from the employer. The dismissal was fair. A proper procedure had not been followed; there had not been sufficient regard to the employee's position as a shop steward, and a full-time official of the union had not been in attendance. The presence of the full-time union official might have resulted in representations being made on the employee's behalf which could have led to a lesser penalty.

However, the decision of the EAT upholding the tribunal's decision suggests that strict observance of the Code may not be essential in a case of this nature.

Other provisions of the former 1972 Code

Failure to follow other provisions of this Code may have contributed to a finding of unfair dismissal. Although the 1972 Code has been repealed the precedent of case law remains.

Under para 40 employers must use their best endeavours to ensure reasonable job security. Where the employee has been away ill for a short period and the employer dismisses him, and engages a replacement, the dismissal may be unfair because the employer has not had regard to the need for job security: see *Moore v Central Electricity Generating Board (Midland Region)* [1974] IRLR 296. Failure to follow the guidance on training contained in para 35 may have led to or contributed to an unfair dismissal: see *Boobier v Johnsons Cleaners (Southern) Ltd* [1974] IRLR 329. See '*The need for assessment and help' above* at p 187. However, the provisions of the 1972 Code, other than those dealing with redundancies, which are considered in Chapter 9, have figured only exceptionally in cases of unfair dismissal.

Substantive fairness

A dismissal may be unfair because no reasonable employer would have dismissed for that reason in all the circumstances, ie substantive unfairness. Substantive unfairness may result from a defect in the procedure where, for instance, the employer fails to give the employee an opportunity to explain before the dismissal and does not know all the facts and he would not have dismissed had he known these facts. Substantive unfairness may exist independently of a defect in the procedure.

The tribunal must consider what a reasonable employer would have done in the circumstances. If the employer had acted reasonably in all the circumstances the dismissal will be fair, notwithstanding the fact that the employee has also acted reasonably. The tribunal is not entitled to substitute its views as to what should have happened in a particular case for those of the employer where the employer has acted reasonably albeit that the tribunal would have reached a different conclusion. There may be a range of options open to the employer, several of which are reasonable: the question for the tribunal is 'was the employer's action within a band of reasonableness?' It is not possible to categorise the instances of substantive unfairness. It will depend upon the circumstances of each case. It is possible though to give some guidance.

Deficiencies in the employer's organisation

A dismissal may be substantively unfair because the employer has failed to provide the employee with adequate training: *Boobier v Johnsons Cleaners (Southern) Ltd* [1974] IRLR 329, see also *Welsh v Associated Steels and Tools Co Ltd* [1973] IRLR 111; or where the employer has failed to provide a trained assistant: *Woodward v Beeston Boiler* [1973] IRLR 7; or has failed to provide clerical help: *Cockcroft v Trendsetter Furniture Ltd* [1973] IRLR 6; or give proper instructions: *Newlands v J Howard and Co Ltd* [1973] IRLR 9; or has failed to define the management responsibilities: *Burrows v Ace Caravan Co (Hull) Ltd* [1972] IRLR 4.

Alternative vacancies

Where the reason for dismissal is conduct or capability the dismissal may be unfair if the employer fails to consider whether there is an alternative vacancy. This obligation may be particularly relevant if the dismissal is a borderline case: *Henderson v Masson Scott Thrissell Engineering Ltd* [1974] IRLR 98; where the employee has been convicted of a driving offence and has lost his licence, but there are other duties which he can perform: see *Fearn v Tayford Motor Co Ltd* [1975] IRLR 336; where the employee was unable to get on with customers: *Scott Packing and Warehousing Co Ltd v Paterson* [1978] IRLR 166; or where the employee has been over-promoted: *Kendrick v Concrete Pumping Ltd* [1975] IRLR 83. In the majority of cases the circumstances will be such that the employer is not under any obligation to offer the employee alternative employment: see *Fitzpatrick v Holbourn Eaton (Manufacturing) Co Ltd* [1973] IRLR 17, and *Bevan Harris Ltd (t/a The Clyde Leather Co) v Gair* [1981] IRLR 520, but see *Hamilton v Argyll & Clyde Health Board* [1993] IRLR 99, where the Board decided to consider re-employing the employee after she had been dismissed for gross misconduct and sent details of other posts to her. Gross misconduct does not automatically render an employee unsuitable for further employment within an employer's organisation.

Long service

The length of the employee's service and any past lapses should be taken into account: see *Johnson Matthey Metals Ltd v Harding* [1978] IRLR 248, where Harding's length of service contributed to a finding of unfair dismissal. It was coupled with a failure by the employer to give sufficient consideration to the employee's misconduct, and to carry out a proper investigation. Long service with an employer may lead to a finding that a dismissal which would otherwise be fair is substantively unfair. Although at first glance it may seem that an employee with a short period of service should be more leniently treated than one with a longer period of service who may be presumed to know better, there is support for the view that weight must be given to the employee's length of service—the longer the service the more favourable the treatment that should be given to the employee, especially if it is coupled with other factors: see *O'Brien v Boots Pure Drug Co* [1973] IRLR 261, and see also *Sewell and Francis v Ford Motor Co Ltd* [1975] IRLR 25. However, in *AEI Cables Ltd v McLay* [1980] IRLR 84, the Court of Session held:

> The length of service ... is ... in many cases a relevant consideration but ... The quality of the respondent's conduct was ... of such gravity that the length of his prior service was of no materiality.

See *British Leyland (UK) Ltd v Swift* [1981] IRLR 91. In *Tiptools Ltd v Curtis* [1973] IRLR 276, Curtis, who had 19 years' service was dismissed for a lack of capability. The NIRC found: 'One would surely have expected that some special consideration would have been given to a man who had been employed with the company from the age of

15.' See also *Scottish Midland Co-operative Society Ltd v Cullion* [1991] IRLR 261.

In the case of a probationary employee a higher onus is placed upon the employer to assess and help the employee before he is dismissed. However, because an employee is on probation it does not mean that the employer is not able to dismiss the employee. In marginal cases it is easier to dismiss an employee on probation than one who is not: see *Hamblin v London Borough of Ealing* [1975] IRLR 354; *Bowden v Post Office* [1976] IRLR 169.

Consistency of the employer

A dismissal may be unfair because the employer has not acted consistently. Substantive fairness is closely allied with following a proper procedure and the need to give the employee adequate warning of any new standard of conduct or capability required: see *Hackwood v Seal (Marine) Ltd* [1973] IRLR 17, where the dismissal was unfair because in the past the employer tolerated temperamental outbursts and the employee was entitled to be warned that there was a change in attitude. See also *Field v Leslie and Godwin Ltd* [1972] IRLR 12.

In *Haspell v Rostron and Johnson Ltd* [1976] IRLR 50, Haspell was dismissed because she lacked capability, was prone to lateness and used the employer's telephone for personal calls. The employer gave her a reference which said 'her work has been completely satisfactory' and referred to her 'pleasant nature' and continued 'at all times she has been an agreeable member of the staff'. The tribunal found that the employer could not 'blow hot and cold at one and the same time'.

Other instances

In *Morrish v Henlys (Folkestone) Ltd* [1973] ICR 482, Morrish's dismissal because he refused to follow a common practice of falsifying records to cover up any deficiencies was held not reasonable in all the circumstances.

In *Wicks v Charles A Smethurst Ltd* [1973] IRLR 327, Wicks's dismissal because he refused to go to Newry and Belfast unless his employer provided insurance against death or injury was unfair. The employer did not even examine the problem before dismissing.

In *Grace v Harehills Working Men's Club and Institute* [1974] IRLR 68, it was held not reasonable in all the circumstances to dismiss Grace who had left his wife and who had formed a sexual liaison with a young girl who was living with him in the employer's premises.

In *Kent County Council v Gilham and Others* [1985] IRLR 18, the employees were school-dinner ladies. Because of government restrictions on expenditure the local authority decided to effect savings in the education budget. Following negotiations the authority wrote to all the employees terminating their existing contracts of employment and offering them employment on the new terms and conditions contrary to a national agreement. The Court of Appeal held that the decision of the tribunal that the employees' dismissals were unfair was not perverse and the tribunal had to balance the economic difficulties faced by the council on the one hand against the fact that the council had departed from the terms of the national agreement and had not deferred a decision until the matter had been considered at national level on the other. Since it was important for good industrial relations that the national agreement should not be breached unilaterally, it could not be said that no reasonable tribunal could have found that the dismissals were unfair.

Conversely, dismissals have been found substantively fair in the following cases.

In *Whitlow v Alkanet Construction Ltd* [1975] IRLR 321, it was reasonable to dismiss Whitlow who had had sexual intercourse with the wife of the chief executive of the company when he had been invited to her home to work. This was so even though he had been subjected to temptation few men could resist.

In *James v Cory Distribution* [1977] IRLR 248, it was reasonable to dismiss an employee asked a fellow female employee, 'Is he shagging you or something?' because it was 'an imputation of promiscuity against [another employee] couched in offensive language'.

In *Saunders v Scottish National Camps Association Ltd* [1980] IRLR 174, the EAT held it was reasonable to dismiss a homosexual. The tribunal had not imposed their own criterion but had adopted that which they believed a reasonable employer would have adopted—that the employment of a homosexual should be restricted when required to work with children. This case was confirmed by the Court of Session [1981] IRLR 277.

In *Richmond Precision Engineering Ltd v Pearce* [1985] IRLR 179, the EAT held it was reasonable to dismiss Pearce when he refused to accept changes in his terms and conditions of employment which would bring him into line with other employees holding similar positions, notwithstanding the fact that he would be worse off under the new terms. Because there are disadvantages to the employee it does not mean that the employer has acted unreasonably. See also *Chubb Fire Security Ltd v Harper* [1983] IRLR 311, and *St John of God (Care Service) Ltd v Brooks and Others* [1992] IRLR 546, where the EAT held the tribunal had erred in holding that the crucial question was whether the new terms offered were those which a reasonable employer could offer. This excluded matters subsequent to the offer and consideration of whether or not other employees had accepted it (here 140 out of 170 staff had done so). Also, if there are sound business reasons for a reorganisation then the question of reasonableness has to be looked at in the light of the reorganisation. Regard cannot be given alone to the fact the employee might be acting reasonably in refusing the offer. In *Catamaran Cruisers Ltd v Williams and others* [1994] IRLR 386, the EAT held that there is no principle of law that an employer can only offer new terms of employment which are less or much less favourable than the old terms if the survival of the business depends on the employees accepting the new terms. However the tribunal must examine the motives for the change and satisfy itself they are not being imposed for arbitrary reasons.

Substantive reasonableness and the interests of the business

The interests and needs of the business may make a dismissal substantively fair. In *Treganowan v Robert Knee and Co Ltd* [1975] ICR 405, there was a clash of personalities involving Treganowan and the other girls in the office where she worked, for which she was to blame. 'The atmosphere in this office had become so tense that it was unbearable and was seriously affecting the respondent's business.' The dismissal was fair. The employer was entitled to have regard to the continued interests of the business. Contrast *Turner v Vestric Ltd* [1981] IRLR 23.

In *Pascoe v Hallen and Medway* [1975] IRLR 116, Pascoe, a registered disabled worker, suffered with asthma. She had considerable periods away from work, but more importantly her attacks of asthma caused disruption during working hours and made her temperamental, 'the consequences of her ill-health were having a disrupting effect on [the employer's] factory'. Her dismissal was fair.

In *Mordecai v Jacob Beatus Ltd* [1975] IRLR 170, Mordecai refused to accept a transfer to a neighbouring factory pursuant to the provisions of a flexibility agreement negotiated between the employer and the union. The employer considered that it was essential that employees should accept the need for flexibility. The dismissal was fair: 'the respondents were reasonably insisting on a term in the contract of employment, very necessary to them in running their business'.

In *Ali v Tillotsons Containers Ltd* [1975] IRLR 272, Ali was given an oral and written warnings advising him that if his attendance did not improve he would be dismissed. His absence was caused by poor health but although his attendance improved the employer dismissed him. The dismissal was fair, because the employer had to incur cost in hiring labour to replace Ali and such labour lacked the skills to achieve the output which would have resulted if Ali were more regularly present.

In *Hollister v National Farmers Union* [1979] ICR 542, Hollister, a group secretary, was given new contractual terms following a reorganisation. He objected to the new financial provisions because he believed they were inadequate. The Court of Appeal accepted the decision of the EAT that a dismissal might well be justified where there was some sound business reason for reorganisation as in this case. Since Hollister would not accept the new contract the only sensible thing to do was to terminate his contract. The Court of Appeal did not accept that it would only be sufficient to justify the dismissal of the employee where he does not agree to reorganisation if the effect of his failure to agree would bring the whole business to a standstill. *See Ellis v Brighton Co-operative Society Ltd* [1976] IRLR 419. *Hollister*'s case was followed by the EAT in *Genower v Ealing, Hammersmith and Hounslow Area Health Authority* [1980] IRLR 297. However, in *Evans v Elemeta Holdings Ltd* [1982] IRLR 143, the EAT held Evans's dismissal unfair because of his persistent refusal to accept a new contract of employment which involved new and substantial obligations to work overtime. The employer sought to impose the new contract because of the commercial need to rationalise the contract of employment. The EAT considered it was reasonable for Evans to have declined the new terms so that it was unreasonable for the employer to have dismissed him. It must be said that the EAT may well, in this case, have fallen into the trap they have pointed out to others. The question is whether the employer acted reasonably, not whether the employee did. If the EAT had described it as the employer acting unreasonably because of the effect on the employee of the new terms, the judgment accords with the other cases mentioned *above*.

An employee may work for a rival firm in his spare time or set up in competition with the employer either on his own account or with a competitor. The first problem was considered in *Nova Plastics Ltd v Froggatt* [1982] IRLR 146, where Froggatt was engaged by Nova Plastics Ltd as an odd-job man. He went to work for a rival company in his spare time. The EAT held his dismissal was unfair. The nature of the work which the employee did for the rival company did not contribute seriously to any competition. It did not accept that there is a general implied term that 'an employer is entitled to expect from an employee total involvement in his employer's business, even outside normal working hours, and that any form of work done for a competitor, however small, must be regarded as a breach of trust and contrary to the implied term of loyal service'. If employment in an employee's spare time is a breach of trust or of an implied term of loyalty then the dismissal might well be fair.

The second problem was considered by the EAT in *Laughton and Hawley v Bapp Industrial Supplies Ltd* [1986] IRLR 245. It referred to the decision of the NIRC in *Harris and Russell Ltd v Slingsby* [1973] IRLR 221. The NIRC held:

> This court ... would regard it as a wholly insufficient reason to dismiss a man, that he was merely seeking employment with a competitor, unless it could be shown that there were reasonably solid grounds for supposing that he was doing so in order to abuse his confidential position and information with his present employers. In the nature of things, when a

man changes employment, it is more likely he will be seeking fresh employment with someone in the same line of business and therefore, a competitor of his present employers.

In *Laughton and Hawley*'s case, the EAT found that the tribunal had erred in holding that the employees' intention to set up in competition with the employer was in breach of the implied contractual duty of loyalty to the employer and the employees were therefore guilty of gross misconduct. Compare *Marshall v Industrial Systems & Control Ltd* [1992] IRLR 294, where the employee managing director, together with another important manager, was planning to take away the company's best client. It had gone further than a plan to compete.

In *Cook v Thomas Linnell and Sons Ltd* [1977] ICR 770, the EAT commented, 'It is important that the operation of the legislation in relation to unfair dismissal should not impede employers unreasonably in the efficient management of their business, which must be in the interest of all.'

Chapter 8

Dismissal for Sickness or Injury

When an employee is absent because of sickness or injury, his employer may wish to dismiss him because the employee's absence is incompatible with the employer's operational requirements. The employee's ill-health may raise doubts in the employer's mind as to his suitability for continued employment. The now-repealed Code of Practice of 1972 and the 1977 Code, together with the Handbook issued by ACAS in 1988 'Discipline at Work', have been influential in formulating the tribunals' approach to sickness dismissals. It is desirable, if not essential, that in the employer's procedures there should be some provision for dealing with absences for sickness or injury, with reference to the employer's obligations and the employee's rights.

The dismissal

Frustration of the contract of employment has been considered in Chapter 4. In cases of sickness or injury it is relevant to enquire whether the contract still subsists so that there can be a dismissal. Under the doctrine of frustration, the contract of employment may be brought to an end by operation of law independently of any action or intention on the part of the employer or the employee.

Sickness may be long-term, or may be a series of unconnected short-term illnesses. The latter is considered under 'Frequent and persistent short-term absences (not necessarily connected)' *below* at p 219.

The reason

Sickness is a reason related to the employee's capability: s 57(2)(*a*) of the EP(C)A 1978. The onus is upon the employer to establish the reason.

In *Shook v London Borough of Ealing* [1986] IRLR 46, Shook, a residential care officer, had a history of back trouble but when she was medically examined for the position she was certified as being fit. Within a few weeks of starting work she suffered with back trouble. She was then appointed as a residential social worker and allocated to a home for handicapped children. After three years at the home she again suffered with back trouble and was away from work for some eight months and then her employment was terminated. It was contended on Shook's behalf that in deciding whether or not the reason was one relating to her capability the tribunal had to 'look at the whole range of work not only being performed by the employee under the employment contract but which . . . she might lawfully be required to do . . .' Since Shook might potentially have been required to carry out a very wide range of activities, it had to be shown that she was incapacitated from performing every such activity if the employer was to discharge the burden of establishing the reason for her dismissal. The EAT held:

> the reason must *relate* to the capability for performing the work of the relevant kind . . . The matter thus has to be looked at as an exercise in relation when one is dealing with questions of incapability. The Industrial Tribunal in the present case decided that the medical grounds leading to Miss Shook's dismissal constituted a reason which related to her capability for performing work of the kind which she was employed to do under her contract. However widely that contract is construed, her disabilities related to the performance of her duties thereunder even though it may not have affected her performance of all of them.

Therefore the tribunal's conclusion that the dismissal fell within s 57(2)(*a*) was correct in law.

However, in *Grootcon (UK) Ltd v Keld* [1984] IRLR 302, the employer was unable to establish that the reason for the employee's dismissal was a lack of capability. Keld, a plater on a North Sea Oil rig owned by British Petroleum Development Ltd, sustained a knee injury in the course of his work and was sent home three days before his tour of duty was to end. His own doctor advised him he would be fit for duty at the end of his normal period of leave. The company telephoned him and told him that he was being made redundant, but then wrote to him telling him that the medical department of British Petroleum Development Ltd considered that he was not fit for duty and he would not be allowed to return to the rig. The EAT accepted that there was no medical evidence, oral or written, as to the employee's condition and therefore the employer could not establish the reason.

Fairness

In addition where the dismissal is for sickness, as in the case of any other dismissal which is not automatically unfair, the tribunal must be satisfied that the dismissal is fair under s 57(3) of the EP(C)A 1978.

The general principles relating to reasonableness which are considered in Chapter 7 apply equally to dismissals by reason of ill-health.

This chapter considers those additional matters which are relevant to dismissals by reason of ill-health.

What is reasonable conduct on the part of the employer where the reason for the dismissal is ill-health depends upon the circumstances of each case: see *Harman v Flexible Lamps Ltd* [1980] IRLR 418. It is not possible to lay down a period after which it will be fair for the employer to dismiss the employee. In *Chadwick v Rochdale Brick Co (1929) Ltd* [1972] IRLR 52, Chadwick's dismissal after 16 years' service following an absence of 3 weeks coupled with a request to work fixed hours for 3 to 4 weeks following his absence was unfair. In *Taylor v CG Southcott & Co Ltd* [1972] IRLR 78, dismissal after 6 months' absence for sickness after a period of nearly 7 years' employment was unfair. Prior to this period of absence Taylor had been absent on several occasions through her ill-health and the ill-health of her husband. However, in *Bowden v Post Office* [1976] IRLR 169, 51½ days' absence in 1 year due mainly to illness where Bowden had been employed on a trial basis was held to be sufficient to justify dismissal. It was the employer's case that the employee's pattern of work is shown in the first 12 months of employment and that the absences were likely to continue, a view strengthened by the fact that he played rugby league and about half his absences were caused by injuries sustained in this sport.

It will not be fair to dismiss an employee because of a risk of illness in the future unless his employment is such that the risk makes it unsafe for the employee to continue in the job: see *Converfoam (Darwen) Ltd v Bell* [1981] IRLR 195. Where the ill-health of one employee is a source of danger to his fellow employees it may be reasonable for the employer to dismiss: see *Harper v National Coal Board* [1980] IRLR 260; see also *Jeffries v BP Tanker Co Ltd* [1974] IRLR 260 and *Singh-Deu v Chloride Metals Ltd* [1976] IRLR 56.

The employer's arrangements for sickness pay are not an indication of the length of time which an employee may be away from work due to ill-health. If the employer dismisses the employee during a period when, under his contract of employment, he is entitled to receive sickness pay, the dismissal will not necessarily be unfair. See *Coulson v Felixstowe Dock and Railway Co* [1975] IRLR 11. In *Hardwick v Leeds AHA* [1975] IRLR 319, it was found unfair to dismiss an employee whose entitlement to sick pay has been exhausted but where, at the time of dismissal there was every likelihood that she could return within 10 days. See also *Kerr v Atkinson Vehicles (Scotland) Ltd* [1974] IRLR 36.

In deciding whether it is reasonable in all circumstances to dismiss an employee because of sickness or injury the tribunal has to consider s 57(3) of the EP(C)A 1978. The law is contained in that section and nowhere else. It has to consider whether or not dismissal was within the parameters of reasonableness. It cannot substitute its view for that of the employer. Where the employee is absent from work due to sickness there may be a range of possible reasonable responses on the part of the employer, one of which may be to dismiss the employee. A failure to consider the factors enumerated in *Marshall v Harland and Wolff Ltd* [1972] ICR 101, which fall to be considered in deciding whether or not the contract has been frustrated does not mean that the tribunal has misdirected itself in reaching its decision. These factors are not necessarily relevant in deciding whether or not it is reasonable to dismiss an employee by reason of ill-health: see *Tan v Berry Bros and Rudd Ltd* [1974] ICR 586.

In *Spencer v Paragon Wallpapers Ltd* [1977] ICR 301, Spencer had been absent from work for two months and was likely to remain absent for another four to six weeks. He was dismissed and the tribunal found the dismissal was fair. On appeal, it was held that where an employee was dismissed through ill-health, the reasonableness of the dismissal will depend upon the circumstances of the case. 'The basic question which has to be determined in every case is whether, in all the circumstances, the employer can be expected to wait any longer and, if so, how much longer?' In deciding this, the tribunal has to consider the nature of the illness, the likely length of the continuing absence, the need of the employers to have the work done which the employee was engaged to do and the other circumstances generally. The tribunal has to maintain a balance between the need of the employer to carry on his business and the employee's need to return to work following a recovery. The EAT found that the questions as to whether the contract has been frustrated and whether dismissal for sickness is reasonable in the circumstances, are distinct. There may be an overlap between the criteria to be applied in answering these questions, but the criteria are not identical.

The more important the position held by the employee the more likely it will be that a dismissal will be fair, even after a short period of absence. Tribunals recognise that temporary replacements of key employees are not usually acceptable or suitable.

There may be a provision in the contract of employment which provides for the dismissal of an employee who is frequently absent because of ill-health or which provides for the dismissal of an employee after a relatively short spell of absence where the robust health of the employee is essential for the proper performance of the employer's business: see *Leonard v Fergus and Haynes Civil Engineering Ltd* [1979] IRLR 235 and *Taylorplan Catering (Scotland) Ltd v McInally* [1980] IRLR 53. Where good health is important for the employer's business it is sensible for the employer to make that abundantly clear to the employee. This may well help the employer when it comes to the question of reasonableness.

Where it is clear from the evidence that the employee will be unlikely to cope with the work in the future, dismissal, even after a short period of absence, is likely to be fair.

It may be reasonable to dismiss an employee where her illness has a disruptive effect upon other employees: see *Pascoe v Hallen and Medway* [1975] IRLR 116, where Pascoe was a registered disabled employee who suffered from severe asthma, and who required hospitalisation for asthma and depression. It may be fair to dismiss where absence imposes a considerable strain upon other employees: see *Ali v Tillotsons Containers Ltd* [1975] IRLR 272. Where at the time the employee is taken on it is known that he suffers with a disability, the employer can expect an increased level of absence. The obligations imposed upon the employer who takes on an employee in such circumstances may be increased: see *Kerr v Atkinson Vehicles (Scotland) Ltd* [1974] IRLR 36. Where the employee is a registered disabled worker the obligations imposed on the employer before dismissing the employee may be greater than in the case of an employee who is not disabled: see *Seymour v British Airways Board* [1983] IRLR 55 and s 9, Disabled Persons Employment Act 1944.

Illness arising out of the employee's employment
The employee's illness may result from his workplace. The employee's dismissal will not be unfair simply because ill-health results from the employment. This may arise out of an accident at work or where the employee is allergic to materials with which the employee comes into contact: see *Glitz v Watford Electric Co Ltd* [1979] IRLR 89. In *Jagdeo v Smiths Industries Ltd* [1982] ICR 47, Jagdeo was allergic to solder fumes. No other work was available and she was dismissed. However, as a result of negotiations attempts were made to overcome the allergy by the use of a mask and her dismissal was suspended. This proved to be unsuccessful and she was dismissed. However, before her dismissal took effect the employer was put on notice that the problem could have been overcome by the use of extractor fans. The tribunal found the dismissal was fair and the EAT remitted the case to the tribunal so that it could consider what response had been made by the company to that suggestion; it was a critical matter of fact which had not been considered by the tribunal in reaching its decision. While the case does not suggest that any greater burden is placed upon the employer not to dismiss the employee where the ill-health arises out of or in the course of the employee's employment, there is an obligation on the employer to ensure the health and safety of the employee and to act reasonably before dismissing the employee. See also the recent decision of the EAT in *London Fire & Civil Defence Authority v Betty* [1994] IRLR 384.

In *Rolls Royce Ltd v Walpole* [1980] IRLR 343, in the three years before Walpole's dismissal his absences averaged about 50 per cent. The company followed its internal procedure and since there was no reason to anticipate any improvement he was dismissed. The tribunal found the dismissal was unfair because the employee was not to blame as there was no up-to-date medical evidence. The EAT found that the decision of the tribunal was perverse and there was evidence upon which the tribunal could reach the conclusion that the dismissal fell within a range of reasonable responses on the part of the employer to Walpole's absenteeism record.

Warnings and consultations

In the early cases tribunals found that dismissal was unfair where the employer had not warned the employee that he was going to be dismissed because of his absence for sickness. The tribunals had in mind a warning akin to that given before the employee was dismissed for misconduct. They then expressed doubts about the need for warning. 'A warning would be irrelevant. The applicant could not help in that he was ill', held the tribunal in *Megennis v Stephen Austin and Sons Ltd* [1974] IRLR 357, and again 'persons cannot be warned to be well': *Case v Group 4 Total Security Ltd* [1974] IRLR 368. See also *Taylorplan Catering (Scotland) Ltd v McInally* [1980] IRLR 53.

In *Spencer v Paragon Wallpapers Ltd* [1977] ICR 301, the EAT commented:

> ... an employee ought not to be dismissed on the grounds of absence due to ill-health without some communication being established between the employer and the employee before he is dismissed. The word 'warning', perhaps is not appropriate, for by its association with cases of misconduct it carries with it [the] suggestion that the employee is being required to change or improve his conduct. That is not the case where the absence is due to ill-health, and it is possible to imagine cases of ill-health where some damage could be done by a written warning unaccompanied by a more personal touch.

It held that what is required is a discussion between the employer and the employee so that the employer can ascertain the position.

The EAT expanded upon the need for discussion and consultation in *Patterson v Messrs Bracketts* [1977] IRLR 137. Patterson had been ill with a heart complaint and was given three months' sick leave on half pay. During that period he attended an office party where his behaviour convinced his employer that he was acting without due regard to his health, and they decided to dismiss him. A tribunal found the dismissal fair, but the EAT reversed the finding. It found the dismissal unfair because before dismissing the employee the employer had neither given careful consideration to the employee's health nor taken steps to ascertain all the facts. The tribunal said two steps should be taken prior to a dismissal. First, there should be discussion with the employee to ascertain the position; and secondly other steps should be taken by the employer to enable him to form a balanced view about the employee's health. The EAT considered that the employer must, where appropriate (and it usually will be appropriate), seek the employee's assistance in finding out the true medical position. It may be necessary to consult the employee's doctor, and in such a case the employee's permission must be obtained. If he refuses, the employer may ask him to be examined by the employer's own doctor, but he cannot be compelled to do so. If the employee is unwilling to co-operate the employer will have to make his decision on the basis of the information available to him. The lack of medical evidence may be prejudicial to the employee, but if the employer has done all it can reasonably do the employer should not be prejudiced by the employee's failure to co-operate.

The decisions in the earlier cases were further considered by the EAT in *East Lindsey DC v Daubney* [1977] ICR 566. Daubney, who was employed as principal assistant (building) surveyor, was dismissed because of ill-health. The employer had relied on a report of a district community physician who had been asked to state whether Daubney's health was such that he should be retired prematurely. The physician replied that Daubney 'is unfit to carry out the duties of his post and should be retired on the grounds of permanent ill-health'. On the basis of this report, Daubney was dismissed. However, the district community physician's conclusions were based upon the report of another doctor, Dr O'Hagan of the Lincolnshire Area Health Authority. This report was never before the Council although they knew of it. The tribunal found the dismissal was unfair because the employer had replied upon the general conclusions of the district community physician and had never obtained a full medical report. Further, the employee was dismissed without any form of consultation or communication. He was given no opportunity to provide an independent opinion.

The EAT upheld the decision of the tribunal. It did not accept that the employer should be required to obtain a full medical report. While the report of the district community physician verged on the inadequate, the employer might have been entitled to rely on it if he had consulted with the employee and given him an opportunity of discussing the position. The employer's decision to dismiss is not a medical one, but a decision to be taken in the light of medical evidence. In seeking medical evidence, the employer should have regard to the circumstances and ensure that proper advice is sought. If the advice is inadequate the employer may not be entitled to rely on it. However, the failure by the Council to consult with Daubney was a fatal one.

The need for consultation was described as 'well established' and as 'an elementary requirement of fairness' by the EAT in *Williamson v Alcan (UK) Ltd* [1978] ICR 104.

Where the employer has a medical report on which he intends to rely, there is no obligation on him 'to evaluate it as a layman in terms of medical expertise'. The employer is entitled to rely on it unless it is plainly erroneous: *Liverpool Area Health Authority (Teaching) Central and Southern District v Edwards* [1977] IRLR 471.

The employer does not have to decide, if there are conflicting medical reports, which one he will rely upon, because the employer does not have the expertise to weigh up the respective merits of the reports. The employer can rely upon medical advice. If the employer relies upon the advice of a medical expert who fails to investigate the matter properly the employer will be saddled with that expert's lack of investigation. Although they may proceed on the basis that they had reasonable grounds for believing the employee was unfit for work that belief must be based upon a proper investigation. The employer may be in difficulty in establishing that belief if there has been no proper investigation: *Ford Motor Company Ltd v Nawaz* [1987] IRLR 163.

Where the employer has obtained a medical report and has carried out consultations with the employee, he still has to make a decision in the light of the evidence whether to dismiss the employee. Provided he acts fairly in the light of the medical evidence available, he will avoid a finding of unfair dismissal.

Medical examination

In cases where medical reports are obtained, the provisions of the Access to Medical Reports Act 1988 should be observed. Under this Act there are a number of rights and duties to be observed, including an obligation on the employer to obtain the consent of the employee for a medical report; a right of access to the report by the employee, a right of veto, and a right for the employee to seek an amendment of the report.

The employer's procedure or the employee's contract may provide for the employer or its doctor to obtain an independent medical report often from a specialist where there is doubt about the nature of the employee's illness or injury. Indeed from time to time employers have been criticised for relying upon a report of a general practitioner in reaching a decision to dismiss an employee particularly where there is doubt or uncertainty: see *Crampton v Dacorum Motors Ltd* [1975] IRLR 168. The employer may ask an employee to undergo a medical examination by a company doctor or a doctor or specialist nominated by the employer. Can an employer force an employee to submit to such an examination? In *Bliss v South East Thames Regional Health Authority* [1985] IRLR 308, Bliss was a consultant orthopaedic surgeon. The Court of Appeal held that in the absence of some relevant specific power in the employee's contract of employment, the employer has no general inherent power to require an employee to undergo a psychiatric examination. By analogy there is no general inherent power to require an employee to undergo any other form of examination. In *Bliss*'s case it was common ground that it was an implied term of his contract of employment that the employer was entitled to require him to undergo a medical examination if the employer had reasonable grounds for believing that he might be suffering from physical or mental disability which might cause harm to the patients, or adversely affect the quality of the treatment of the patients. This implied term depended very much upon the particular circumstances in *Bliss*'s case and it must not be taken as authority for the view that there is a general implied term in any employee's contract of employment that the employer can require the employee to undergo a medical examination. If the employee is asked by the employer to undergo a medical examination and unreasonably refuses, then the employer should point out to the employee the consequences of that refusal. If the employee still refuses to undergo a medical examination, then the employer who dismisses may well succeed in dismissing fairly if he has acted reasonably in all the circumstances on the evidence available to him, notwithstanding the fact that a further medical examination and the subsequent evidence in the form of a report, may have rendered it unfair for the employer to have dismissed.

Medical certificates

In *International Sports Co Ltd v Thompson* [1980] IRLR 340, it was held that there is no rule of law which requires the employer to investigate the *bona fides* of the medical certificates issued. However he is entitled to go behind the sick note to discover whether or not his employees are engaged in activities which suggest they are fit for work: *Hutchinson v Enfield Rolling Mills Ltd* [1981] IRLR 318.

The purpose of consultation with the employee must be borne in mind. It is to enable the situation to be assessed, to balance the employer's need to have the work done with the employee's need to recover his health, and to ensure that the employer takes proper steps to establish the true medical position.

The need for the employer to follow a proper procedure if the dismissal is to be fair has been emphasised in cases such as *Polkey v AE Dayton Services Ltd* [1988] ICR 142. See *A Links and Co Ltd v Rose* [1991] IRLR 353. However, if the tribunal is able to conclude that at the time of the dismissal the employer acted reasonably because of exceptional circumstances so that procedural steps which would normally have been appropriate would have been futile and could not have altered the decision to dismiss, and therefore could be dispensed with, the dismissal may be fair.

In *Eclipse Blinds Ltd v Wright* [1992] IRLR 133, the director who took the decision to dismiss wrote to the employee rather than see her personally, because he was genuinely concerned that if he saw her he might have to disclose information regarding her health, which he had obtained from her GP, about which she was unaware. The Court of Session confirmed the decision of the tribunal that the dismissal was fair, and referred to the decision of the Court of Session in *A Links & Co v Rose, above,* that the tribunal must determine as a matter of fact and judgment what consultation was necessary or desirable in a particular case. The instant case was exceptional. See also Chapter 7 concerning the fairness of the dismissal.

Frequent and persistent short-term absences (not necessarily connected)

In this situation it is always difficult for the employer to know whether the employee is genuinely ill or whether he is guilty of malingering or some other misconduct. Malingering would essentially be a matter of conduct.

Where the employee is persistently absent for minor ailments so that his level of attendance is unacceptable, the employer should first of all review the attendance record and the reasons for it and, secondly, after the employee has been given an opportunity to make representations, assuming it is justified, should give the employee a warning that his level of attendance is unacceptable. If there is no adequate improvement in his record dismissal will normally be justified: see *International Sports Co Ltd v Thompson, above* and *Rolls Royce Ltd v Walpole, above.* A medical report will not necessarily be appropriate for persistent unconnected short-term absences, although consultation may produce evidence of an underlying medical problem, and a medical report should then be obtained.

In *Lynock v Cereal Packaging Ltd* [1988] IRLR 510, the EAT held that where there is a poor attendance record due to intermittent periods of illness, each of which is unconnected, it is impossible to give a reasonable prognosis. While an employer may make enquiries there may be no obligation on him to do so because the results may produce nothing of assistance. Furthermore, the fact that at the time of dismissal the employee is fit will not render the dismissal unfair. In determining whether or not to dismiss an employee for intermittent periods of illness. Wood J, at p 512, stated:

> The approach of an employer in this situation is, . . . one to be based on . . . sympathy, understanding and compassion. There is no principle that the mere fact that an employee is fit at the time of dismissal makes his dismissal unfair; one has to look at the whole history and the whole picture. Secondly, every case must depend upon its own facts, and provided that the approach is right, the factors which may prove important to an employer in reaching . . . a difficult decision, include perhaps some of the following—the nature of the illness; the likelihood of recurring or some other illness arising; the length of various absences and the spaces of good health between them; the need of the employer for the work done by the particular employee; the impact of the absences on others who work with the employee; the adoption and the carrying out of the policy; the important emphasis on a personal assessment in the ultimate decision and of

course, the extent to which the difficulty of the situation and the position of the employer has been made clear to the employee so that the employee realises that the point of no return, the moment when the decision was ultimately being made may be approaching.

HIV/AIDS

Mere infection with the HIV virus would not normally be a reason for dismissal, and if the employee becomes ill as a result of the infection, the matter should be dealt with as a case of sickness in the ordinary way. Occasionally, there will be pressure either from fellow employees or from customers where an employee is infected with the virus. The employer should deal with this problem by means of education of the workforce or his customers, since an employer is under a duty to offer reasonable support to an employee, or otherwise the employee may be able to resign and claim constructive dismissal. On the other hand, where a customer does threaten to withdraw custom, there could be the possibility of dismissal of the infected employee for 'some other substantial reason'.

Employer's further obligations

There are two further problems for employers. First, are they obliged to find the employee a job elsewhere, and secondly, do they have to create a special job for the sick employee which he can manage to do?

In *Megennis v Stephen Austin & Sons Ltd* [1974] IRLR 357, it had been agreed with Megennis, a compositor's auxiliary, that on his return to work following a period of illness, he should be employed as a storeman. However, before he returned to work, it was decided to dispense with the position of storeman, and he was dismissed. It was held that the dismissal was not unfair. There was no obligation on the employer to keep open another job for a sick employee which was outside the employee's contract of employment and which would not otherwise exist.

In *Case v Group 4 Total Security Ltd* [1974] IRLR 368, Case was absent from work with a heart condition. He was then certified as being 'perfectly fit for all ordinary office work or supervisory work but obviously shouldn't be expected to run after criminals, carry heavy weights or be exposed to sudden excessive physical strain'. The employer found these were vital elements in his job and he was dismissed. The tribunal found the dismissal fair because the employer was under no obligation to find other work for a sick employee. Even if there were such a requirement, on the facts of this particular case there was no job that Case could fill. Certainly the employer was not obliged to restructure the job which he was doing so that he could manage it, nor was he obliged to promote him to a higher position where he had more administration to carry out, nor to appoint him to a position for which he was not qualified. Equally, where the employee was required to have special physical and mental qualities for the job he was employed to do, there was no obligation on the employer to find the employee alternative employment suited to the employee's new state of health when that work was not available, in the sense of not being already in existence: *Leonard v Fergus and Haynes Civil Engineering Ltd* [1979] IRLR 235; *Taylorplan Catering (Scotland) Ltd v McInally* [1980] IRLR 53.

In *Merseyside and North Wales Electricity Board v Taylor* [1975] IRLR 185, the High Court held that there is no rule of law that an employer is obliged to create a job for a sick employee; conversely, neither is there a rule of law that the employer is not obliged to find alternative work for the employee. Each case depends on its circumstances so that if the employer has a light job available which the employer can do, it may be unreasonable if the employer fails to offer him the job even though it is at a lesser rate of pay than his old job. On the facts of this case it is apparent that the job must actually be available.

In *Spencer v Paragon Wallpapers Ltd* [1977] ICR 301, the EAT accepted that there was no obligation on the employer to create a job for the employee, but where there is an alternative suitable position for him which could await the employee's availability, it might be unfair to dismiss him. Where another vacancy does exist, it might not be reasonable for the employer to keep that vacancy open until the employee is capable of doing the work. The basic question is whether, in all the circumstances, the employer can be expected to wait any longer, and, if so, how much longer.

The tribunal will consider whether the employer has sought to place the employee in any alternative available work as at the date of dismissal. In *Todd v North Eastern Electricity Board* [1975] IRLR 130, the tribunal, accepting there was no obligation on the employer to create a job for a sick employee, found that the dismissal was unfair because the employer did not offer the employee a suitable job which was in existence and available. In *Garricks (Caterers) Ltd v Nolan* [1980] IRLR 259, Nolan was employed as a maintenance fitter on shifts. He suffered heart trouble, following which he was certified as fit for days but not for shifts. The company dismissed him because he refused to work shifts. The tribunal found that a day job could have been made available and rejected the employer's argument that it involved heavy lifting. It found that the employer could have reorganised matters without inconvenience to itself so that the employee could have been accommodated. The tribunal's decision was upheld on appeal.

Inactive registers and holding departments

Some employers operate an inactive register or holding department to which sick employees are transferred in accordance with the procedures thereof. Consideration has been given to the nature of these arrangements in the following cases.

In *O'Reilly v Hotpoint Ltd* [1970] 5 ITR 68, the tribunal and the High Court found that where an employee was transferred to a holding department, the contract of employment continued so that the rights and obligations of the parties were suspended, and the transfer did not operate as a dismissal.

In *Marshall v Harland and Wolff Ltd* [1972] ICR 101, the NIRC held that the effect of a transfer to a holding department was that the employee 'ceases to be employed in any legal sense', but is on a list of men with whom there is a voluntary arrangement that the employers will do their best to provide them with work as soon as they are fit again. The court envisaged that such an agreement might be reached between the employer and the union or with the employees direct. Such a transfer was applicable to long-term sickness. In the case of short-term sickness, the employees should 'be maintained in employment whether or not [they are] in receipt of full wages or sick pay'.

In *Normanton v Southalls (Birmingham) Ltd* [1975] IRLR 74, the tribunal found that where there is an inactive register or holding list, an employee can be transferred, particularly where he holds a key position and needs replacing, so that the employer will keep him on the list rather than dismiss him; and further found that where an employee is transferred to an inactive register or holding list, he will have those rights conferred on him under a scheme which will generally be negotiated with the union. The rights should be clearly defined. Normally the transfer will operate after a specified period. It does not preserve the employee's right on immediate recovery from illness to have his old job back, but the effect of an inactive register is to suspend the contract of employment so that the employee is retained and is not dismissed and his continuity of employment is preserved without interruption. During the period of sickness the employer is able to make arrangements for the work to be carried on without incurring any liability for unfair dismissal. Whether the employee is paid and has insurance contributions deducted during this period is a matter for agreement. There may be some limit on the length of time that the employee can remain on an inactive register or holding list. Where the employee reports back to work and the employer is not able to find him a job, the employee may then be dismissed for redundancy depending on the circumstances.

Other tribunals have reached different conclusions on the effect of the transfer to the inactive register or holding list in the circumstances of the particular cases. In *Burton v Boneham and Turner Ltd* (1976) (unreported), the employee was transferred to the holding department after receiving three warnings that he would be transferred unless he improved his record of absence for sickness. Once in the holding department his terms of contract were changed fundamentally. It was held that there was a termination of the existing contract of employment and a dismissal.

In *Parker v Westland Helicopters Ltd* (1976) (unreported), there were two holding departments. Employees transferred to one department continued in insurable employment and pension contributions were paid; on recovery, by custom and practice, they returned to their old jobs. Employees in the other department were out of benefit with the company and had to wait for a suitable vacancy before restarting work. It was held that employees transferred to the first holding department continued in employment. Those who were transferred to the second holding department did not, and the transfer constituted a dismissal.

The employee's position on a transfer to a holding department or an inactive register should be defined. Where the matter is contractual, there can be little room for doubt. Transfers of sick employees to a holding department or an inactive register where the contract continues within defined time limits are beneficial for the employer.

The employee's obligations

Where the employee is absent from work due to ill-health there has to be some term implied in the contract limiting the employee's obligation to perform all the terms of his contract of employment during such time as he is sick. However as the EAT has held:

> one does not imply into any contract any term wider than is necessary to give it business effect. In our view, business commonsense does not require that *all* obligations of an employee are suspended during sickness. The commonsense implication is that the employee is relieved of the obligation to perform such services as the sickness from which he is suffering prevent[s] him from carrying out.

Thus, in this particular case, the EAT upheld the decision of the tribunal that the employer was entitled to require the employee to remove merchandise from her car standing on the public highway in accordance with the terms of her contract notwithstanding that she was away from work through ill-health at the time the request was made to her: *Marshall v Alexander Sloan and Co Ltd* [1981] IRLR 264.

It is important in cases where the employee is absent through sickness or injury that he should keep in touch with and inform the employer of developments. It may involve the need to provide the employee with medical certificates. Where the employee fails to do so, the employer should warn the employee of the consequences. However, in *Mitchell v Arkwood Plastics (Engineering) Ltd* [1993] ICR 471, where there had been a series of doctor's certificates to the employers setting out the position, the EAT held that while *East Lindsey District Council v Daubney* [1977] IRLR 181, suggests that in the absence of exceptional circumstances enquiries should be made by the employer regarding the employee's health and prospects of returning to work, there is no equivalent duty on the employee to indicate to the employer his prospects of recovery.

Chapter 9

Dismissal for Redundancy

An employee may be able to claim unfair dismissal where he has been dismissed for redundancy. Under s 81(2) of the EP(C)A 1978, an employee is dismissed for redundancy where the dismissal is wholly or mainly due to the fact that:

(*a*) his employer has ceased, or intends to cease, to carry on the business for the purposes of which the employee was employed by him, or has ceased, or intends to cease, to carry on that business in the place where the employee was so employed; or

(*b*) the requirements of that business for employees to carry out work of a particular kind, or for employees to carry out work of a particular kind in the place where he was so employed, have ceased or diminished or are expected to cease or diminish.

Redundancy for unfair dismissal purposes has the same technical meaning set out *above* and the question as to whether any dismissal is for redundancy will be decided in accordance with these provisions: see *Chapman v Goonvean and Rostowrack China Clay Co Ltd* [1973] ICR 310; and also *O'Hare and Rutherford v Rotaprint Ltd* [1980] ICR 94. To claim a redundancy payment, the employee must have completed two years' continuous employment ending with the relevant date: s 81(4) of the EP(C)A 1978. To claim unfair dismissal, the employee must usually show that he has been continuously employed for a period of not less than two years at the effective date of termination: s 64(1)(*a*) of the EP(C)A 1978, but this does not apply where the reason or principal reason that the employee was selected for redundancy is an inadmissible reason rendering the dismissal automatically unfair. See 'Automatically unfair dismissal' *below* at p 226. Where the employee is dismissed for redundancy, the dismissal may be automatically unfair because it contravenes s 59 of the EP(C)A 1978 or s 153 of the TULR(C)A 1992, or it may be unfair because it is not reasonable in the circumstances (contrary to s 57(3) of the EP(C)A 1978). The fact that an employee has accepted a redundancy payment from the employer is not to be taken as an indication that he accepts that his dismissal is fair: see *Clarkson International Tools Ltd v Short* [1973] ICR 191.

Automatically unfair dismissal

Section 59 of the EP(C)A 1978 and s 153 of the TULR(C)A 1992 provide that dismissal for redundancy will be automatically unfair. Both sections relate to the reason why he was selected for redundancy. Where a dismissal is automatically unfair it is not necessary to consider reasonableness under s 57(3) of the EP(C)A 1978.

Under s 59(a) the dismissal will be automatically unfair if the reason for selection (or, if more than one, the principal reason), is that:

(1) the employee had acted in connection with health and safety issues: s 57A of the EP(C)A 1978;

(2) it was in connection with the employee's pregnancy: s 60(a)–(e) of the EP(C)A 1978;

(3) the employee had asserted a statutory right: s 60A of the EP(C)A 1978.

Under s 153 of the TULR(C)A 1992 the dismissal will be automatically unfair if the reason for selection (or, if more than one, the principal reason) is that under s 152(1) of the TULR(C)A 1992 the employee:

(a) was, or proposed to become, a member of an independent trade union; or

(b) had taken part, or proposed to take part, in the activities of an independent trade union at an appropriate time; or

(c) had refused or proposed to refuse to become or remain a member of *any* trade union. Section 152 of the TULR(C)A 1992 re-enacts the repealed s 58 of the EP(C)A 1978.

Under s 59(b) of the EP(C)A 1978 a dismissal of an employee is also automatically unfair if the reason or principal reason for his selection for redundancy is in breach of a customary arrangement or agreed procedure for selection and there were no special reasons justifying a departure from the arrangement or procedure. The Deregulation Bill proposes to repeal s 59 (b).

Both s 59 of the EP(C)A 1978 and s 153 of the TULR(C)A 1992 contain a limitation on the extent of the provisions so that the dismissal will only be automatically unfair where the circumstances constituting the redundancy applied equally to one or more other employees in the same undertaking who held positions similar to that held by the employee and who have not been dismissed.

Where the dismissal is not automatically unfair then reasonableness will have to be considered under s 57(3) of the EP(C)A 1978.

In practice it has been difficult for the employee to establish that he has been selected for redundancy on the *above* grounds (although there have not yet been any reported cases under ss 57A, 60(a)—(e) and 60A of the EP(C)A 1978).

For an example of an automatically unfair dismissal under what was then s 58(1), see *Port of London Authority v Payne and others* [1992] IRLR 447, and on appeal [1994] IRLR 9.

The unit of selection

The statutory unit of selection is 'one or more other employees in the same undertaking'. The tribunal is left to decide whether the word 'undertaking' means the whole of the employer's business or particular departments or sections or just the department or section in which the employee was working. There are few cases and it is difficult to lay down clear guidelines.

In *Kapur v Shields* [1976] 1 All ER 873, it was suggested that some evidence of organisational unity is probably necessary to indicate that activities of separate persons constitute an undertaking.

In *Heathcote v North Western Electricity Board* [1974] IRLR 34, a driver's mate was dismissed for redundancy because the Board decided there was no longer any need for drivers' mates. Selection for dismissal was made on the basis of last in, first out, but in making its selection, the Board looked only in the transport section and not in the whole of its business. This was not the correct approach. If there were employees with specialist attributes within a department, they might form a group of persons who would form the unit of selection without reference elsewhere, but generally the selection should not be considered within specific departments or sections but throughout the whole concern, particularly where, as in this case, the employee involved was a labourer. This case supports the proposition that the less skilled the employee, the wider the field which forms the unit of selection.

In *Simpson v Roneo Ltd* [1972] IRLR 5, the inspectors in one department only were considered as the unit of selection. The tribunal accepted that the test only applied in relation to the one department and not on the basis of the whole concern. See also *Dorrell and Ardis v Engineering Developments (Farnborough) Ltd* [1975] IRLR 234, *Oxley v Tarmac Roadstone Holdings Ltd* [1975] IRLR 100, and *Gargrave v Hotel and Catering Industry Training Board* [1974] IRLR 85. The only conclusion that can be drawn is that it is a question of fact in each case. The unit of selection might be constituted by a place, by more than one place, by a trade or grade, or perhaps some other distinguishing feature, or by any combination of them.

No help in the definition of 'undertaking' is afforded by s 188 of the TULR(C)A 1992 (previously s 99 of the EPA 1975) dealing with the procedure for handling redundancies. Here 'establishment' is the relevant unit, but it is not defined and it is for the tribunal to decide: see *Barratt Developments (Bradford) Ltd v UCATT* [1978] ICR 319.

Positions similar

Comparison can only be made with employees who held positions similar to that held by the employee. 'Position' in relation to an employee means the following matters taken as a whole: 'his status as an employee, the nature of his work and his terms and conditions of employment': s 153(1) of the EP(C)A 1978.

In *Heathcote's* case, *above* the tribunal accepted that employees who were interchangeable and who did almost the same jobs were employed in similar positions, even though they were employed in different departments. In *Gargrave's* case, *above* the NIRC considered that comparison could only be made with employees in 'the department or field of activity directly affected by the redundancy situation and who are engaged in the same type or category of work'.

Different skills may mean that employees hold different positions. In *Simpson v Roneo Ltd* [1972] IRLR 5, there were five inspectors in one department. Four did the same work and the other did a more specialised job. It was held that the position held by that inspector was not the same as the others since he was engaged in more specialised work. Similarly, in *Selby and Teese v Plessey Company Ltd* [1972] IRLR 36, there were detail and assembly fitters. Detail fitters were more versatile than the assembly fitters who were declared redundant. The differences in skill justified selection from the one group only. In *Powers and Villiers v A Clarke and Co (Smethwick) Ltd* [1981] IRLR 483, it was held that Class 1 drivers and Class 3 drivers did not hold similar positions because of differences in lorry driving skills.

Inadmissible reasons—ss 57A, 60 (a)–(e) and 60A of the EP(C)A 1978

The selection of an employee for dismissal for redundancy for any of these reasons is automatically unfair and the question of reasonableness under s 57(3) of the EP(C)A 1978 is irrelevant.

These sections were introduced by TURERA 1993. Sections 57A and 60A came into force on 30 August 1993: s 60(a)–(e) on 10 June 1994. There are not yet any reported cases on these sections.

For full details of s 57A (on health and safety issues) see Chapter 13, s 60 (a)–(e) (on pregnancy or childbirth) see Chapter 10, and s 60A (on assertion of a statutory right, either by bringing proceedings to enforce such a right, or alleging the employer has infringed such a right) see Chapter 14.

Inadmissible reasons—s 153 of the TULR(C)A 1992

The dismissal of an employee is regarded as automatically unfair under s 153 of the TULR(C)A 1992 if the reason or principal reason is that the employee was, or proposed to become, a member of an independent trade union; or had taken part, or proposed to take part, in the activities of an independent trade union at an appropriate time; or was not a member of any trade union, or of a particular trade union, or of one of a number of particular trade unions, or had refused or proposed to refuse to become or remain a member.

Most of the reported cases were decided under earlier legislation (when the reason was an 'inadmissible reason' which although similar to, was wider then s 153 of the TULR(C)A 1992, but they are still of assistance. In addition, as to when trade union activities can be connected with a strike, see *Britool Ltd v Roberts* [1993] IRLR 481.

Boorman and Kemp v Pickard and Beale Ltd [1973] IRLR 135, is a case where it was held that the dismissal was unfair because the employees had been selected on the grounds of their employer's opposition to their trade union membership and activities. However, inevitably, it will be a question of fact in each case.

It may be difficult to decide whether the employee was dismissed in a redundancy situation for one of the reasons contained in s 152 of the TULR(C)A 1992, or whether he had been selected for redundancy because of such a reason. *Taylor v Butler Machine Tool Co Ltd* [1976] IRLR 113 illustrates the point. The tribunal found that the dismissal was not wholly or mainly attributable to redundancy but, on the balance of probabilities, was attributable to union membership or activities which would now be a reason or reasons within s 152 of the TULR(C)A 1992. The distinction is, of course, academic in most cases.

The relationship between a dismissal for one of the reasons contained in s 152 and selection for such a reason in a redundancy situation under s 153 was considered in *Farmeary v Veterinary Drug Co Ltd* [1976] IRLR 222. The tribunal used the illustration of the employer who was antipathetic to trade union membership. Such an employer might dismiss an employee for becoming a member of a union or engaging in union activities. The dismissal will be for a reason within s 152 irrespective of the existence of a redundancy situation. Such a dismissal will be an automatically unfair dismissal under s 152. Section 153 covers the same employer, who in a redundancy situation selects one employee in preference to another because the one was a trade union member and the other was not. In such a case, the principal reason for dismissal will be redundancy, not a dismissal for a reason within s 152, but the method of selection (which is for such a reason) renders the dismissal automatically unfair under s 153.

There is no presumption in such cases. Although the onus of showing the reason for dismissal is on the employer, if the employer alleges that the reason is, for instance, misconduct, it is for the employee to show that he was selected for one of those reasons specified in s 153 (and presumably where the point is in issue, in contravention of a customary arrangement or agreed procedure) at least on the balance of probabilities: *Bristol Channel Ship Repairers Ltd v O'Keefe and Lewis* [1978] ICR 691.

Contravention of customary arrangement or agreed procedure

The Deregulation Bill proposes to amend the law on this aspect. It is not possible to forecast the effect of the amendment if, indeed, it is passed. What is set out *below* is the current position.

Where there is a customary arrangement or an agreed procedure, the onus is on the employer to show that he has observed it. Failure to discharge the onus may lead to a finding of unfair dismissal. Tribunals should not take too technical or too objective a view of the matter: *Wailes Dove Bitumastic Ltd v Woolcocks* [1977] ICR 817. Section 59(*b*) is concerned with the cases where the selection of the employee is in contravention of a customary arrangement or an agreed procedure. It does not apply where the employer has failed to comply with the procedure requiring consultation with the union concerned or to consider volunteers for redundancy: *McDowell and Others v Eastern British Road Services Ltd* [1981] IRLR 482.

Customary arrangement

This is not defined in the legislation. In *Bessenden Properties Ltd v Corness* [1973] IRLR 365, the tribunal considered that 'the normal customary arrangement in industry in general proceeds on the principle of "last in, first out".' The NIRC found that this conclusion was erroneous. The tribunal had 'decided that what, within their knowledge, was a normal custom in industry amounted to a "customary arrangement".' The court concluded that what is contemplated by 'customary arrangement' (although the court was at pains to make it clear that it was not defining the phrase) 'is something which is so well known, so certain and so clear as to amount in effect to an implied "agreed procedure", as contrasted with the express "agreed procedure" which is the alternative contemplated by [s 59(*b*)]'. The Court of Appeal upheld the decision of the NIRC: *Bessenden Properties Ltd v Corness* [1974] IRLR 338.

In *Henry v Ellerman City Liners plc* [1984] ICR 57, the Court of Appeal considered the decision of Sir John Donaldson in *Bessenden's* case *above*. It concluded that an agreed procedure could be one that is made either expressly or by implication. Therefore, an implied agreed procedure was not a customary arrangement. Regrettably the Court of Appeal did not consider what was meant by customary arrangement. In *Bessenden's* case *above*, the NIRC had to consider whether or not there was a customary arrangement. It is open to argument that an arrangement which while not amounting to an implied agreed procedure may be a customary arrangement, even though it may have some of the characteristics of an implied agreed procedure.

In *Kyle Stewart Contractors Ltd v Stainrod* (1977) (unreported), the EAT found that a 'customary arrangement' may exist, provided it is supported by suitable evidence even though there is only 'a measure of notoriety among the workforce'. The fact that it is not universally known will not defeat the customary arrangement. However, what is suitable evidence and what is sufficient notoriety are questions of fact which the tribunals will have to decide in each case.

Where there is a last in, first out principle, as part of a customary arrangement, it is important that the employer is clear which employees are to be dismissed and, in computing the length of employment, only those weeks which will count for continuity of employment in the legal sense will probably be considered unless there is some clear arrangement that the selection will be based upon cumulative service: *Dorrell and Ardis v Engineering Developments (Farnborough) Ltd* [1975] IRLR 234; and see *Sudders v Prestige Group Ltd* [1975] IRLR 367.

Agreed procedure

The 'agreed procedure' for the purposes of s 59(*b*) of the EP(C)A 1978 may be oral or in writing. It may be express or implied: see *Henry v Ellerman City Liners plc, above.* No particular form is required. Usually the procedure will be agreed between the employer and the employees, or their representatives. It should lay down criteria to be followed in the selection of employees in the event of redundancies.

There must be a clear morally or legally binding agreement. In *Jackson v General Accident Fire and Life Assurance Co Ltd* [1976] IRLR 338, the company undertook, in a letter sent to the union, that there would be no redundancies but a gradual run-down of staff over two years. The tribunal found that there was no agreed procedure between the employer and the employees, or their representatives. The EAT agreed. The letter was an expression of intent and was not intended to create a binding agreement. The EAT did not point out that, even if the letter were an agreement, it did not provide a means of selection in the true sense, and may, therefore, have been outside the scope of s 59.

An agreement between an employer and a union which is an *ad hoc* agreement covering a particular set of circumstances may be an agreed procedure: see *Evans and Morgan v A B Electronic Components Ltd* [1981] IRLR 111. It cannot, of course, be a customary arrangement.

In *Camper and Nicholson Ltd v Shaw* [1978] ICR 520, the tribunal found that the employers had operated an agreed procedure of 'last in, first out, all other things being equal'. It was held by the EAT to have erred in substituting its own view of what was equal for that of the employers. The EAT said that 'equal' meant equal in the eyes of a fair and reasonable employer applying proper industrial considerations.

An agreed procedure may apply to the whole of the employer's concern or, alternatively, it may be negotiated with unions covering certain sections of the employer's labour force or certain departments in the employer's undertaking.

It was not unusual for an employer and a union to reach an agreement under which in the event of a redundancy non-union members would be selected for redundancy in preference to union members. See *Bygott v Woodall-Duckham Ltd* [1976] IRLR 168; and *Evans and Morgan v A B Electronic Components Ltd, above*. When an employee is selected for redundancy because he is not a member of the union, the dismissal will now be automatically unfair. See Chapter 11.

It is possible to amend an agreed procedure. However, where it is intended to modify well-established and understood industrial procedures, that should clearly be made known by the employer to all concerned: see *International Paint Co Ltd v Cameron* [1979] ICR 429. A belief by one party to an agreed procedure that there has been some alteration will be insufficient unless the alteration has been agreed to by both sides either expressly or impliedly: *Tilgate Pallets Ltd v Barras and Others* [1983] IRLR 231.

Special reasons justifying a departure
Where an employer seeks to argue that there are special reasons justifying a departure from a customary arrangement or agreed procedure the onus is upon the employer to establish those reasons. This will usually involve the employer establishing that he used objective criteria: *Tilgate Pallets Ltd, above*.

In *Wailes Dove Bitumastic Ltd v Woolcocks* [1977] ICR 817, the EAT suggested that in deciding whether there has been a departure from the procedure, the matter should not be looked at too rigidly but 'in the light of both sides trying to operate an agreed procedure as best they can'. Presumably, the same approach is to be adopted in the case of customary arrangements. It is for the tribunal acting as an industrial jury to decide whether or not there were special reasons justifying a departure from an agreed procedure. Therefore the decision of the tribunal cannot be overturned unless its decision is perverse: *Cross International v Reid and Others* [1985] IRLR 387.

Customary arrangements   In *Best v Taylor Woodrow Construction Ltd* [1975] IRLR 177, the tribunal accepted that the employer is entitled to depart from the normal practice and select an employee with longer service where that employee's record is worse than one with shorter service. In *Briers v ARC Marine Ltd* (1975) (unreported), the employee's incapacity was a special reason justifying a departure from the customary arrangement. In *Axe v British Domestic Appliances Ltd* [1972] IRLR 8, the selection for retention of employees on compassionate grounds put forward by the union was a special reason justifying a departure.

Agreed procedures In *Weston v Bentley Engineering Co Ltd* (1977) (unreported), the employer refused to dismiss one of the volunteers because of his experience, and instead dismissed a non-volunteer. The tribunal held the dismissal was fair. The company was entitled to retain an employee with experience in the interest of the business. It was a special reason justifying a departure. See also *Green v Commercial Cable Co Ltd* (1976) (unreported), where the employee's fluency in Spanish (the employer trading in South America) was a special reason for retaining him in preference to the dismissed employee. See also *Crump v Chubb and Sons Lock and Safe Co Ltd* [1975] IRLR 293, and *International Paint Co Ltd v Cameron* [1979] IRLR 62.

Where under an agreed procedure, selection is an act of unlawful sex discrimination, this will be a good reason for departing from the agreed procedure: see *Clark and Powell v Eley (IMI) Kynoch Ltd* [1982] IRLR 131. See further comment on this case *below* at p 234.

In *Cross International v Reid and Others* [1985] IRLR 387, Neill LJ in the Court of Appeal found that the employers could not argue that provided their decision was within a range of reasonable options of the employer in the particular situation then the dismissal could not be unfair. He held:

> The Industrial Tribunal acting as an industrial jury had to apply to the facts ... the words '... and there were no special reasons justifying a departure from that procedure'. They had to consider and evaluate the 'reasons' which the parties put before them. I see no ground for putting a gloss on the words in the section [s 59(*b*) EP(C)A] so as to introduce the concept of a range of possible options. The section [s 59(*b*)] does not say 'which could justify a departure'; the words are 'special reasons justifying a departure'.

In *Rolls Royce Motor Cars Ltd v Price and others* [1993] IRLR 203, the EAT held that the employer had established a special reason for departing from the agreed procedure of 'last in first out' because applying that criteria alone could 'defeat the objective of carrying forward the business in difficult times'.

Reasonableness

Where an employee is selected in accordance with a customary arrangement or agreed procedure, then his dismissal will usually be fair. However, tribunals have from time to time examined customary arrangements to see that the arrangement in itself is fair. See *Norton v Chemidus Wavin Ltd* [1975] IRLR 294. The fact that the customary arrangement results in personal hardship does not mean that the employer is acting unreasonably: *Forman Construction Ltd v Kelly* [1977] IRLR 468. It is less likely that an agreed procedure will be found unreasonable than will a customary arrangement, except where the procedure discloses some manifest injustice: *Boothby v Kingston Craftsmen Ltd* [1975] IRLR 138.

An important decision is that of the EAT in *Clarke and Powell v Eley (IMI) Kynoch Ltd* [1982] IRLR 131. The employer had an agreed procedure, whereby in a redundancy part-time employees would be dismissed before full-time employees and full-time employees would then be selected on the basis of last in, first out. Selection was on a unit basis. There was a proviso giving the employer some discretion as to selection where the agreed selection procedure would be harmful to the needs of the business. Powell could not work full time because of domestic commitments, whereas Clarke had been in a position to work full time in the years before the dismissal and the requirement to be a full-time worker was not to her detriment. The employer, in operating the procedure, had been guilty of unlawful indirect sex discrimination against Powell and the requirement or condition could not be shown to be justifiable irrespective of the sex of the person to whom it applied. Therefore, under s 57(3) the dismissal of Powell, since it was an unlawful discriminatory selection under the SDA 1975, was not a fair selection. The tribunal considered that Powell should be taken back into employment. It accepted that this might necessitate the dismissal of a full-time employee with less service which would be in breach of an agreed procedure but none the less considered that it might well be a special reason justifying a departure from the agreed procedure.

In the case of Clarke, it held that the time at which the ability or inability of an employee to comply with a requirement or condition has to be shown is the date on which she suffered the detriment. This is the same point in time at which the requirement or condition has to be fulfilled. Clarke had shown that she suffered the detriment on dismissal because when she was dismissed she could not comply with the condition that she should be a full-time worker. It did not matter that at an earlier date she could have avoided the detriment by becoming a full-time worker. The implication of the judgment seems to be that the agreed procedure may, of itself, be unlawful. Correctly analysed, however, that would make the dismissal unfair under s 57(3) rather than under s 59, for the employee was not selected in breach of the procedure. The EAT expressed the view, *obiter*, that the tribunal had erred in holding that a dismissal which is discriminatory is necessarily unfair under s 57(3) of the EP(C)A 1978, although the circumstances when such a dismissal could be fair are difficult to imagine and would, in any event, give rise to a claim of unlawful discrimination.

Where there is an agreed procedure the fact that it causes hardship for an individual will not mean that the dismissal in accordance with the agreed procedure is unfair. There may be circumstances where an agreed procedure is fair to the majority of employees but an individual suffers. It is for the tribunal to consider whether or not either side has manipulated a situation unfairly to an individual: see *Wailes Dove Bitumastic Ltd v Woolcocks* [1977] ICR 817.

Reasonableness

Where the employee has been selected in contravention of s 59 of the EP(C)A 1978 or s 153 of the TULR(C)A 1992, the dismissal is automatically unfair and there is therefore no defence in this situation available to the employer. However, the employee may not be able to bring himself within the scope of this section and in this situation the dismissal falls to be considered under s 57(3) of the EP(C)A 1978 which provides that the fairness or otherwise shall depend on whether in the circumstances (including the size and administrative resources of the employer's undertaking) the employer acted reasonably or unreasonably in treating redundancy as a sufficient reason for dismissing the employee; and that question shall be determined in accordance with equity and the substantial merits of the case.

It was suggested by the Scottish division of the EAT in *Jackson v General Accident Fire and Life Assurance Co Ltd* [1976] IRLR 338, that where a redundancy dismissal passes the hurdle of s 59 of the EP(C)A 1978, it was difficult to envisage a case where it would be unreasonable in the terms of s 57(3). See also *Robinson v Ulster Carpet Mills Ltd* [1991] IRLR 348, and *Atkinson v George Lindsay and Co* [1980] IRLR 196.

More recently, however, the ratio of reported appeal cases indicates that dismissals for redundancy may still be unfair. They may be unfair on a number of different bases which are considered *below*.

Reasonableness—general principles

In *Williams and Others v Compair Maxam Ltd* [1982] ICR 156, the EAT sought to lay down certain guidelines for tribunals in cases involving unfair dismissal in a redundancy. The case and the guidelines must, however, be regarded now as lightweight. Not only has it not always been followed by the EAT (eg *A Simpson and Son (Motors) v Reid and Findlater* [1983] IRLR 401 and *Gray v Shetland Norse Preserving Co Ltd* [1985] IRLR 53), but there are two Court of Appeal cases which are directly in point, and a further EAT case which adds to the argument. In *Hollister v National Farmers' Union* [1979] ICR 542, the Court of Appeal pointed out that reasonableness must be judged in the light of all the circumstances. In *Bailey v BP Oil (Kent Refinery) Ltd* [1980] ICR 642, Lawton LJ said:

> In our judgment it is unwise for this court, or the Employment Appeal Tribunal to set out guidelines, and wrong to make rules and establish presumptions for Industrial Tribunals to follow or take into account when applying . . . [s 57(3)].

In *Rolls-Royce Motors Ltd v Dewhurst* [1985] IRLR 184, the EAT held:

To direct themselves, as the Tribunal has done—namely, that an act contrary to *any* of the principles enunciated in *Compair Maxam* leads to conclusion, even *prima facie*, that the dismissals are unfair—is not, in our judgment, a proper direction.

There is, however, one important part of the *Compair Maxam* judgment which has not been subject to either adverse comment, or criticism, and which seems to accord with a number of other cases. The EAT held:

> ... it is not the function of the industrial tribunal to decide whether they would have thought it fairer to act in some other way: the question is whether the dismissal lay within the range of conduct which a reasonable employer could have adopted. The second point of law, particularly relevant in the field of dismissal for redundancy, is that the tribunal must be satisfied that it was reasonable to dismiss each of the applicants on the ground of redundancy. It is not enough to show simply that it was reasonable to dismiss *an* employee; it must be shown that the employer acted reasonably in treating redundancy 'as a sufficient reason for dismissing *the* employee', ie the employee complaining of dismissal. Therefore, if the circumstances of the employer make it inevitable that some employee must be dismissed, it is still necessary to consider the means whereby the applicant was selected to be the employee to be dismissed and the reasonableness of the steps taken by the employer to choose the applicant, rather than some other employee, for dismissal.
>
> In law, therefore, the question we have to decide is whether a reasonable tribunal could have reached the conclusion that the dismissal of the applicants in this case lay within the range of conduct which a reasonable employer could have adopted.

The EAT cited with approval the headnote in *Greig v Sir Alfred McAlpine and Son (Northern) Ltd* [1979] IRLR 372. In that case the tribunal found:

> When so many employees are involved, and a basis of selection is to be used which is open to the possibility of being influenced by over-subjective assessments, or even sheer prejudice, on the part of the person making the choice, it is important that management be able to show that they took sufficient steps to make their decision as objective and unbiased as possible.

One helpful approach to the test of reasonableness was set out in *Dyke and Others v Hereford and Worcester County Council* [1989] ICR 800, see *below* at p 245.

In the light of these general guidelines there will now be considered substantive and procedural unfairness.

Substantive unfairness

The necessity for redundancies

As a first step the tribunal will decide whether or not the dismissal is for redundancy. It must be satisfied that the employee is redundant within the provisions of s 81(2) of the EP(C)A 1978. The tribunal cannot demand an 'excessively high standard of proof' of a redundancy. The employer is not obliged to produce 'accounts or figures to show the loss referred to, how it was sustained and how much it came to', nor does the employer have to show 'that the redundancy situation was so bad as to cause the dismissal'; nor is there any 'obligation on the employers to establish the existence of some economic or accountancy state of affairs which would, as it were, justify the declaration of a state of redundancy' in order to establish the necessary facts to show that the dismissal was because of redundancy: *H Goodwin Ltd v Fitzmaurice* [1977] IRLR 393.

Once a redundancy has been established then it is not open to the tribunal to consider the actions of the employer which led to the redundancy situation. Tribunals are not there to make findings about the way in which the employer has conducted the business: *Moon v Homeworthy Furniture (Northern) Ltd* [1977] ICR 117. In *Guy v Delanair (Car Heater) Ltd* [1975] IRLR 73, the company decided to do away with the whole of the night shift as a method of reducing production in a redundancy situation. The tribunal found it 'is not in a position to criticise the manner in which an employer decides its work must be cut down'. The tribunal was not prepared to consider whether the redundancies were necessary.

In *Lloyd v The Standard Pulverised Fuel Co Ltd* [1976] IRLR 115, the company operated two shifts. It dismissed one shift and left the other shift doing overtime. The tribunal found the dismissal unfair because there would have been no dismissals for redundancy if the company had considered eliminating overtime and introducing a limited amount of short-time working. This case comes dangerously close to the tribunal substituting its own view of a commercial decision. For anyone in commerce or industry, the commercial and financial advantages of what the employer did are obvious. Even so, it is not for the tribunal to say that the genuine commercial decision of the employer was wrong.

The tribunal may also find the dismissal unfair where it is likely that the employees could have been absorbed elsewhere within a short time. In *Allwood v William Hill (North East) Ltd* [1974] IRLR 258, there was a redundancy and the company decided to dismiss 12 of its betting-shop managers. The tribunal was not satisfied that the position was as desperate as the company thought. In the industry there was a high wastage of managers, and the employers had a large number of betting shops. The tribunal found that the company could have transferred employees, even temporarily, to other establishments until vacancies had occurred within the company through natural wastage or the expansion of the larger offices. Since the dismissals, vacancies had occurred. Additionally, the decision to dismiss had been taken with

great haste; there was no warning or consultation. The dismissal was
unfair.

Selection

Selection may be seen as either a matter of substance or procedure.
Inevitably there will be many cases where selection is irretrievably
bound up with the need for consultations. Although the onus of establishing reasonableness is no longer on the employer, when there is
selection between employees, the employer will have to show the
information he took into account and the criteria used for selection.
He will have to go into some detail to satisfy the tribunal: *Bristol
Channel Ship Repairers Ltd v O'Keefe and Lewis* [1978] ICR 691. In
Cox v Wildt Mellor Bromley Ltd [1978] ICR 736, the EAT considered
that this might be discharged by calling witnesses to explain the circumstances of the redundancy. Only the employer will know the reasons
for the selection and he must ensure that there is evidence before the
tribunal.

In *Buchanan v Tilcon Ltd* [1983] IRLR 417, the Court of Session
following the decision in *Cox's* case held:

> it is quite unrealistic and unreasonable for an industrial tribunal, which is
> prepared to accept that the senior official who made the selection reached
> his decision fairly upon the basis of company information, the reliability
> of which he had no reason to question, to demand of the employer for
> the purposes of s 57(3) that he should set up the accuracy of that infor-
> mation by direct evidence of other witnesses speaking, perhaps, to records
> for which they had responsibility. The industrial tribunal, in our opinion,
> set for the respondents in this case a standard which was much too high.

The way in which the tribunal is to consider the reasonableness
of the employer's selection of the employee has given rise to some
difficulty.

In *Bessenden Properties Ltd v Corness* [1974] IRLR 338, there was
no agreed procedure or customary arrangement. The Court of Appeal
held that the tribunal was entitled to find the selection unfair because
a last in, first out, procedure was not used. The tribunal, in deciding
the issue of fair selection, was entitled to take everything into account
and to act as 'an industrial jury'.

In *Grundy (Teddington) Ltd v Willis* [1976] ICR 323, the tribunal
found that the dismissal was unfair. The High Court upheld the company's appeal. The tribunal has to decide 'not what they would have
done had they been the management', but whether or not management
acted reasonably, so, 'provided the employers have applied their minds
to the problem and acted from genuine motives, they cannot really be
faulted, or be said to have acted unreasonably, in choosing one in
preference to another'.

It would seem that there was a difference in approach between the
two courts. In *Grundy's* case the High Court did not accept that

the judgment in *Bessenden*'s case meant that 'the decision as to who should be selected . . . is one ultimately to be left to the industrial tribunal'.

Clearly, if in *Bessenden*'s case the Court of Appeal was indicating that the tribunal was entitled to substitute its decision for that of the employer, *Bessenden* is wrong in law. However, if it is simply recognising that the tribunal in reaching its decision whether the employer has acted reasonably, is sitting as an industrial jury, then that is a correct interpretation of the law, and there is no difference between the decisions in *Grundy*'s case and *Bessenden*'s case. However, *Bessenden*'s case is now over twenty years' old, and was decided at a time when 'last in first out' was almost a golden rule. Decisions have developed since then and 'last in first out' has, if not fallen into disrepute, certainly fallen into disuse, except perhaps as a form of 'tie-breaker'. It is unlikely that *Bessenden* would have been decided in the same way in the modern economic environment.

In *NC Watling and Co Ltd v Richardson* [1978] IRLR 255, the EAT found that in deciding whether the dismissal was fair, the tribunal had to consider s 57(3) of the EP(C)A 1978 as a starting point, and that a dismissal for redundancy will be fair unless the case is one where the employer has acted in a way in which no reasonable employer would have done.

In *Iceland Frozen Foods Ltd v Jones* [1982] IRLR 439, the EAT considered the earlier decisions and held:

> Since the present state of the law can only be found by going through a number of different authorities, it may be convenient if we should seek to summarise the present law. We consider that the authorities establish that in law the correct approach for the Industrial Tribunal to adopt in answering the question posed by s 57(3) of the 1978 Act is as follows.
> (1) the starting point should always be the words of s 57(3) themselves;
> (2) in applying the section an Industrial Tribunal must consider reasonableness of the employer's conduct, not simply whether they (the members of the Industrial Tribunal) consider dismissal to be fair;
> (3) in judging the reasonableness of the employer's conduct an Industrial Tribunal must not substitute its decision as to what was the right course to adopt for that of the employer;
> (4) in many (though not all) cases there is a band of reasonable responses to the employee's conduct within which one employer might reasonably take one view, another quite reasonably take another;
> (5) the function of the Industrial Tribunal, as an industrial jury, is to determine whether in the particular circumstances of each case the decision to dismiss the employee fell within the band of reasonable responses which a reasonable employer might have adopted. If the dismissal falls within the band the dismissal is fair: if the dismissal falls outside the band it is unfair.

> Although the statement of principle in *Vickers Ltd v Smith* is entirely accurate in law, for the reasons given in *Watling v Richardson* we think Industrial Tribunals would do well not to direct themselves by reference

to it. The statement in *Vickers Ltd v Smith* is capable of being misunderstood so as to require such a high degree of unreasonableness to be shown that nothing short of a perverse decision to dismiss can be held to be unfair within the section. This is how the Industrial Tribunal in the present case seems to have read *Vickers v Smith*. That is not the law. The question in each case is whether the Industrial Tribunal considers the employer's conduct to fall within the band of reasonable responses, and Industrial Tribunals would be well advised to follow the formulation of the principle in *Watling v Richardson* or *Rolls-Royce v Walpole.*

The EAT had decided in *Vickers Ltd v Smith* [1977] IRLR 11, that if the tribunal thought the management's decision was wrong, it has to go on to ask whether it was so wrong that no sensible or reasonable management could have arrived at that decision. See also *Rolls Royce Ltd v Walpole* [1980] IRLR 343.

In *Williams and Others v Compair Maxam Ltd above*, the EAT emphasised the need to use objective criteria in selecting that employee, so that the employer can demonstrate the reasonableness of choosing that employee rather than some other.

In *Buchanan v Tilcon Ltd* [1983] IRLR 417, the Court of Session following the decision in *Atkinson v George Lindsay and Co, above*, found that where the issue was the employees' selection, all that the employer had to do was 'to prove that their method of selection was fair in general terms and that it had been applied reasonably in the case of the appellant by the senior official responsible for taking the decision'. This emphasises that the test is contained in s 57(3). It is not open to the tribunal to substitute its own decision for that of the employer, the tribunal must simply be satisfied that the employer's decision was within the band of reasonable responses.

The process of selection
Under s 59 of the EP(C)A 1978 the dismissed employee is only entitled to plead in his aid employees holding similar positions. There is no such restriction under s 57(3): *Thomas and Betts Manufacturing Co Ltd v Harding* [1980] IRLR 255. However, in that case the Court of Appeal was not laying down a general principle that in selecting for redundancy the employer may not confine himself to an examination of employees holding similar positions in the same undertaking. There may be cases where it is not reasonable for the employer simply to restrict his attention to those employees who hold similar positions. In *Green v A and I Fraser (Wholesale Fish Merchants) Ltd* [1985] IRLR 55, it was held that Green was fairly selected as the driver to be made redundant on the basis of last in, first out, although there was another employee, a mechanic, who occasionally did some driving and had less service than Green. Where the work is unskilled it may be easier to fit in an employee of long standing at the expense of an employee who has been recently recruited. As *Green's* case makes clear there is

no obligation to bump. It may be unfair to dismiss an employee for redundancy simply because there was a diminution in the employer's requirements for work which the employee was actually doing, if there is other work which the employee can be required to do under the terms of his contract. See *Cowen v Haden Carrier Ltd* [1982] IRLR 225; and *NC Watling and Co Ltd v Richardson, above.*

Length of service may be an important factor to be taken into account in determining the fairness of selection, but it is not a principle of law that selection must be on a last in, first out basis.

The employer must be able to show that the criteria are reasonable, and that they have been applied rationally and effectively where large numbers are involved. Selection should be on a structured and comparative basis and over-subjective assessments or bias should be avoided: *Grieg v Sir Alfred McAlpine and Son (Northern) Ltd* [1979] IRLR 372. This approach was confirmed in *Williams and Others v Compair Maxam Ltd* [1982] IRLR 83. The EAT recognised in the latter case that the burden is for the employer to show what criteria have been used and why he considered that these criteria are reasonable, as these are matters within his knowledge.

In *Graham v ABF Ltd* [1986] IRLR 90, the EAT found it was open to a tribunal to uphold a selection for redundancy based on the employee's attitude to his work, his quality of work, and his efficiency in carrying it out. The EAT recognised that while an assessment of the employee's attitude involved personal and subjective judgments, and was dangerously vague, it was not so inherently nebulous and subjective a concept that it could play no part in any fair basis for redundancy selection. It found that the more vague and the more subjective the test used by the employer the greater should be the opportunity for personal consultation before the employee is judged by it.

Whilst length of service may in most cases be a factor, there are many other factors which it may be reasonable for an employer to take into account. Examples are better management potential, administrative ability, stronger personality, more drive and greater cost-consciousness: *Lovie v Hugh Macrae and Co (Builders) Ltd* (1977) (unreported); or lesser expense: *Joines v B and S (Burknall) Ltd* [1977] IRLR 83, or greater skill and efficiency: see *Shaw v Garden King Frozen Foods Ltd* [1975] IRLR 98; a greater degree of experience in the operation of a particular piece of machinery: *(1) Abbotts and (2) Standley v Wesson-Glynwed Steels Ltd* [1982] IRLR 51; but it may not be fair to select a bachelor in preference to a married man who has less service: *Pickering v Kingston Mobile Units* [1978] IRLR 102. That would in any event be contrary to s 3 of the SDA 1975—but to select the married man in preference to the bachelor is not unlawful!

In *BL Cars Ltd v Lewis* [1983] IRLR 59, it was held that there was no justification for attaching 'priority' to the employee's length of service so that there had to be major shortcomings in the employee's performance if this were to outweigh the length of service. Here, the employer's need was to retain a balanced workforce and in making the selection the employers were entitled to take into account length of service, occupation and skill without giving priority to length of service.

In *Noble and Others v David Gold and Son (Holdings) Ltd* [1980] IRLR 253, female employees were employed in a warehouse to do light work and men were employed to do heavy work. There was a reduction in the employer's need for the lighter work and six women were dismissed even though some had longer service than the men. There was a division in the work, based not on sex but on practical experience. The employer regarded the men's work as different. The Court of Appeal held the selection was fair.

In *Forman Construction Ltd v Kelly* [1977] IRLR 468, the EAT held that employers should take into account personal circumstances. It was unfair to select Kelly because he was a member of a particular squad of building workers whose work had run out without regard to his length of service compared with other employees and the fact that Kelly was disabled.

However, the definition of redundancy in s 81 must be borne in mind in cases of this nature, in particular the words in s 81(*a*): '. . . in the place where the employee was so employed'. The tribunal can, therefore, find itself being asked whether or not it was reasonable for the employer to 'bump'. In practice, very often the conclusion is that whichever step the employer took, he would find himself before the tribunal, albeit that the applicant may differ. It may be difficult, if not impossible, for the tribunal, in those circumstances, to say that the employer had not acted reasonably. If the employer takes one of a number of reasonable routes, the dismissal cannot be unfair.

In *Paine and Moore v Grundy (Teddington) Ltd* [1981] IRLR 267, the employer selected employees for redundancy on the basis of their attendance records without looking at the reasons why they had been absent. The EAT held that the selection was not reasonable because the employer should have ascertained the reason for the absences before selecting the employees for redundancy. Similarly, a failure to distinguish in an attendance record between authorised and unauthorised absence, may make the dismissal unfair, especially where the agreed criteria indicated such a distinction: *Boulton and Paul Ltd v Arnold* [1994] IRLR 532.

In *Gray v Shetland Norse Preserving Co Ltd* [1985] IRLR 53, it was held that it was not incumbent upon an employer to warn an employee whose attendance record was unsatisfactory that in the event of redundancies he would be selected. It was necessary to distinguish a case where an employee was selected for redundancy because of a bad attendance record and the case where he was dismissed by reason of that bad attendance record. None the less if it is made clear to employees that a poor disciplinary record will affect selection, it may assist the employer in defending a claim for unfair dismissal based on selection for such a reason.

In selecting employees for redundancy, it seems that the employer is entitled to take into account the fact that the employees have been on strike. In *Cruickshank v Hobbs* [1977] ICR 725, six Newmarket stable lads went on strike. After the strike, five of these were selected for redundancy. It was held that the dismissal was fair. In selecting the employees the employer was entitled to rely on the fact that he would lose the loyalty of his remaining stable lads if he dismissed non-strikers. The EAT found that the particular factors of this case made the decision reasonable. (Note that a strike does not fall within the definition of 'trade union activities' in s 152 of the TULR(C)A 1992. It is just conceivable that it might be within the definition of 'trade union membership', especially if the non-union staff did not go on strike).

In establishing the fairness of selection the employer may show that the method of selection has been discussed with the union representative: see *Clyde Pipeworks Ltd v Foster* [1978] IRLR 313; and *Dutton v Hawker Siddeley Aviation Ltd* [1978] ICR 1057. See *De Grasse v Stockwell Tools Ltd* [1992] IRLR 269, where the EAT held that although the small size of a business might affect the type and formality of the consultation process it cannot be the excuse for a complete lack of warning and consultation.

Where the employee is registered as disabled, special consideration must be given to him in the event of his prospective selection for redundancy: see *Seymour v British Airways Board* [1983] ICR 148 and *Hobson v GEC Telecommunications Ltd* [1985] ICR 777. See also s 9(5) of the Disabled Persons (Employment) Act 1944, which provides that an employer who employs a person registered as handicapped by a disablement shall not, unless he has reasonable cause for doing so, discontinue the employment of that person.

Procedural unfairness

Warning and consultation
In *Short v Clarkson International Tools Ltd* [1973] IRLR 49, the tribunal found that Short's dismissal was unfair because of the 'unnecessarily abrupt and perfunctory manner' of the dismissal. There had been no warning and no consultation. The decision was upheld by the NIRC which found that warnings and consultation might only be dispensed with where 'the situation was truly exceptional'. The NIRC had in mind cases where 'a premature announcement of redundancy may shake confidence in the product and excessively long notice . . . may be very damaging to morale'; *Clarkson International Tools Ltd v Short* [1973] IRLR 90. See also *Rigby v British Steel Corporation* [1973] ICR

160. Following these cases, tribunals were ready to find that a dismissal for redundancy was unfair where the former 1972 Code of Practice had not been observed. Where the employee had suffered no loss thereby, a nil award of compensation might result, as in *Short's* case *above*.

There then followed a series of cases which placed less emphasis on the need for warnings and consultation. See *George M Whiley Ltd v Anderson* [1977] ICR 167; *Quinton Hazell Ltd v Earl* [1976] IRLR 296, and *Delanair Ltd v Mead* [1976] ICR 522. In *British United Shoe Machinery Co Ltd v Clarke* [1978] ICR 70, the EAT found that where there had been a lack of consultation it was necessary to consider what would have been the likely result if the employer had done what should have been done. If it would not have made the slightest difference it was open to a tribunal to find either that the dismissal was not unfair or that it was unfair, but there should be no compensation. See also *British Labour Pump Co Ltd v Byrne* [1979] ICR 347. Since the decision is *Polkey v AE Dayton Services Ltd* [1988] ICR 142, this approach can no longer be followed. See also *Duffy v Yeomans and Partners Ltd* (1994) *The Times* 26 July *below*, and *Heron v Citylink— Nottingham* [1993] IRLR 372.

In *Freud v Bentalls Ltd* [1982] IRLR 443, the EAT held:

> In the particular sphere of redundancy, good industrial relations practice in the ordinary case requires consultation with the redundant employee so that the employer may find out whether the needs of the business can be met in some way other than by dismissal and, if not, what other steps the employer can take to ameliorate the blow to the employee. In some cases (though not this one) the employee may be able to suggest some re-organisation which will obviate the need for dismissal; in virtually all cases the employer, if he consults, will find out what steps he can take to find the employee alternative employment within the company or outside it. For example, in present day conditions when so many people are unemployed, many employees facing redundancy by reason of the disappearance of their existing job are prepared to take other jobs of lower status and commanding less pay. Only by consulting the employee can the employer discover whether such an option is open in any given case. Therefore good industrial relations practice requires that, unless there are special circumstances which render such consultation impossible or unnecessary, a fair employer will consult with the employee before dismissing him.
>
> We must emphasise that we are not saying that good industrial relations practice *invariably* requires such consultation. There may well be circumstances (for example a catastrophic cash flow problem making it essential to take immediate steps to reduce the wages bill) which render consultation impracticable. We are only saying that we would expect a reasonable employer, if he has not consulted the employee prior to dismissal for redundancy in any given case, to be able to show some special reason why he had not done so.

Whilst *Freud* and a number of the earlier cases relied rather heavily on what was the Code of Practice, and on 'good industrial relations', in fact they are to a great extent synonymous with reasonableness, and thus are of, at the very least, persuasive authority.

In *F Lafferty Construction Ltd v Duthie* [1985] IRLR 487, the Scottish division of the EAT also emphasised the importance of consultation. In *Graham v ABF Ltd* [1986] IRLR 90, the EAT held that in this case the failure to consult rendered the dismissal unfair and found that because of the nebulous nature of the criterion adopted in selection 'the more powerful . . . becomes the need that the employee should be given an opportunity of personal consultation', before he is selected in accordance with that criterion. It has already been seen that where a failure to warn and consult would have made no difference the dismissal may either be fair or unfair but nil compensation is awarded.

In *Polkey*'s case, [1988] ICR 142, the importance of following a proper procedure was reiterated. Lord Bridge held:

> . . . in the case of redundancy, the employer will normally not act reasonably unless he warns and consults any employees affected or their representative, adopts a fair basis on which to select for redundancy and takes such steps as may be reasonable to avoid or minimise redundancy by redeployment within his own organisation. If an employer has failed to take the appropriate procedural steps in any particular case, the one question the industrial tribunal is *not* permitted to ask in applying the test of reasonableness posed by section 57(3) is the hypothetical question whether it would have made any difference to the outcome if the appropriate procedural steps had been taken. On the true construction of section 57(3) this question is simply irrelevant. It is quite a different matter if the tribunal is able to conclude that the employer himself, at the time of dismissal, acted reasonably in taking the view that, in the exceptional circumstances of the particular case, the procedural steps normally appropriate would have been futile, could not have altered the decision to dismiss and therefore could be dispensed with. In such a case the test of reasonableness under section 57(3) may be satisfied.

Thus the fairness of the dismissal must be scrutinised at the moment of dismissal. In *Walls Meat Co Ltd v Selby* [1989] ICR 601, the Court of Appeal approved the criteria in *William*'s case, *above*, and followed the approach in *Polkey*'s case.

In *Dyke and Others v Hereford and Worcester County Council* [1989] ICR 800, the EAT held:

> The phases of redundancy would seem to be as follows: first, the consideration of the overall necessity for redundancies; secondly, the issuing of [what was then] the section 99 notice; thirdly, the selection of individuals whom it is proposed to dismiss for redundancy; fourthly, the actual issue of the dismissal notice, action taken on the decisions earlier reached, and lastly, the period of notice before the employment is terminated. At each of the four stages, it is important that consultation should take place either with the trade union and (if the trade union will permit it—which it did not in the present case) with the employees individually or with both, and the importance of such consultation cannot be over-emphasised. Such

consultation must necessarily be based upon sufficient information for them to be sensible.

It held that in a redundancy case the tribunal should examine the procedures up to the moment when the notice of dismissal was issued and decide on the facts whether the employer had acted reasonably. Then it should examine what had occurred during the period of notice for two purposes, first, if the employer had acted reasonably up to the issue of the notice to see whether he continued to do so up to the date of termination and, secondly, if he had acted unreasonably at the date of the issue of the notice to see whether that part of the procedure which had been criticised had, if it was capable of rectification had been rectified before the date of termination.

In *Selby*'s case, *above*, the Court of Appeal held that while in an appropriate case there should be a two-stage consultation, first with the union and then with the employees selected for redundancy, it was not always necessary to enter into such a two-stage process. Dismissal was held to be unfair because of the failure to consult with the individual even though the union had been consulted. In *Duffy v Yeomans and Partners Ltd* [1993] IRLR 368, the EAT held that Lord Bridge in *Polkey's* case did not intend the test to be whether the employer in question had considered consultation and taken the view it could be dispensed with but rather that the test is an objective one, ie 'could a reasonable employer in the light of the facts known to him at the time have dismissed the employee without consultation?' The Court of Appeal at (1994) *The Times* 26 July, held that 'There was no warrant for the proposition that there had to be a deliberate decision by the employers that consultation would be useless, with the corollary that in the absence of evidence that such a decision had been made, a finding by an industrial tribunal that a dismissal for redundancy was reasonable was necessarily wrong in law'. See also *Heron v Citylink-Nottingham* [1993] IRLR 372.

For a general discussion of procedural issues see Chapter 7.

Where the dismissal is unfair because the employer has failed to warn and consult with the employee, it may be that if the employer had warned and consulted, the employee would still have been dismissed. This may mean that the employee, though unfairly dismissed, will recover no compensation (other than a redundancy payment). However, as *(1) Abbotts and (2) Standley v Wesson-Glynwed Steels Ltd* [1982] IRLR 51, illustrates, even if there had been warnings and consultations but the employee would still have been dismissed there may still be a loss. The EAT found that had there been consultations with Abbotts he would have remained in employment for a longer period to enable consultations to take place, and awarded 14 days' remuneration as compensation. If, as a result of a failure to warn and consult the employee, he has been deprived of the opportunity of filling another vacancy, the losses will be more substantial. It is for the tribunal to assess the loss. It must compensate the employee for the financial loss suffered and should not award compensation out of benevolence or as a mark of disapproval of the employer's actions: *Lifeguard Assurance Ltd v Zadrozny* [1977] IRLR 56, or indeed as a topping up of the employee's redundancy payments. In *Polkey's* case Lord Bridge, quoting the judgment of Browne-Wilkinson J, in *Sillifant v Powell Duffryn Timber Ltd* [1983] IRLR 91, held that:

> There is no need for an 'all or nothing' decision. If the industrial tribunal thinks there is a doubt whether or not the employee would have been dismissed, this element can be reflected by reducing the normal amount of compensation by a percentage representing the chance that the employee would still have lost his employment.
>
> The second consideration is perhaps of particular importance in redundancy cases. An industrial tribunal may conclude, as in the instant case, that the appropriate procedural steps would not have avoided the employee's dismissal as redundant ... if ... that conclusion does not defeat his claim for unfair dismissal, the industrial tribunal, apart from any question of compensation, will also have to consider whether to make any order under section 69 of the Act of 1978. It is noteworthy that an industrial tribunal may, if it thinks fit, make an order for re-engagement under that section and in so doing exercise a very wide discretion as to the terms of the order. In a case where an industrial tribunal held that dismissal on the ground of redundancy would have been inevitable at the time when it took place even if the appropriate procedural steps had been taken, I do not, as at present advised, think this would necessarily preclude a discretionary order for re-engagement on suitable terms, if the altered circumstances considered by the tribunal at the date of the hearing were thought to justify it.

Once unfair dismissal has been established, the onus of proof is on the employee to show his losses. The tribunal must not speculate, or guess, or top up, a redundancy payment. Equally, it must not attempt to apply the onus of proof 'so strictly that no claimant can hope to discharge it': *Barley v Amey Roadstone Corporation Ltd (No 2)* [1978] ICR 190. Once the employee puts forward some coherent, sensible suggestion as to what the loss is likely to be through the employer's failure the evidential burden will usually shift to the employer: see *Rolls-Royce Motor Cars Ltd v Price and others* [1993] IRLR 203.

There may be situations where the employer has exceptional reasons why he did not warn and consult. Possible reasons may be in the interests of the other employees or the continuance of the business. In such exceptional circumstances the dismissal may be found fair: see *Polkey's* case, *above*. The employer need not, however, specifically have considered whether or not to consult, and then concluded not to do so: *Duffy v Yeomans and Partners Ltd, above*. However, what the employer may believe to be an exceptional reason may not be well founded: see *Heron v City Link-Nottingham* [1993] IRLR 372, and

Ferguson and another v Prestwick Circuits Ltd [1992] IRLR 266, where the fact that the employer had taken a deliberate decision not to consult prior to announcing redundancies, because on a previous occasion they had been told by the work force they would have preferred to have been told on the day they were to be made redundant, was held to be insufficient. There was no evidence that the employees in this case had waived any right to consultation or warning. Consultation with the employee's union without consulting the employee may be insufficient. See *below*.

The statutory obligation to consult and unfair dismissal

Section 188 the TULR(C)A 1992 requires the employer before dismissing for redundancy an employee of a description in respect of which an independent trade union is recognised, to consult with the representatives of that union. Consultation must start at the earliest opportunity, and must include consultation about ways of avoiding dismissals, reducing the number of employees to be dismissed and mitigating the consequences of dismissals, and is to be undertaken by the employer with a view to reaching agreement with the union representatives: s 188(6) of the TULR(C)A 1992. There are minimum prescribed periods depending upon the number of employees it is proposed to dismiss by reason of redundancy within certain periods. Where, due to special circumstances, it is not reasonably practicable for the employer to comply with his statutory obligations, he need only take such steps as are reasonably practicable in the circumstances. However, where the decision leading to the proposed dismissals is that of a person controlling the employer (directly or indirectly), a failure on the part of that person to provide information to the employer shall not constitute special circumstances rendering it not reasonably practicable for the employer to comply with such a requirement: s 188(7) of the TULR(C)A 1992. The employer's failure to carry out his statutory obligations may result in proceedings under s 189 of the TULR(C)A 1992 for a protective award. Only the appropriate trade union is entitled to make a complaint which is heard by a tribunal. The question which arises is, to what extent is the individual employee entitled to rely upon the employer's failure to consult under s 188?

At first it seemed that the employee could rely upon the employer's failure to consult with the representatives of the union when claiming unfair dismissal. In *Kelly v Upholstery and Cabinet Workers (Amesbury) Ltd* [1977] IRLR 91, the employee was dismissed without any warning or consultation either under the former 1972 Code or the former s 99 of the EPA 1975. There was a recognised union. The EAT found the dismissal was unfair. There should have been consultation under the 1972 code and also under s 99. The employer's failure under s 99 was something the employee could rely upon in claiming unfair dismissal.

In *Gorman v London Computer Training Centre Ltd* [1978] ICR 394, the EAT found that the approach in *Kelly's* case *above*, needed to be applied with care. This view was confirmed by the Court of Session in *Atkinson v George Lindsay and Co* [1980] IRLR 196.

In *Forman Construction Ltd v Kelly* [1977] IRLR 468, the Scottish division of the EAT found that the right conferred by s 99 of the EPA 1975 was a limited one. The remedy was provided by s 101 of the EPA 1975, and no other rights are conferred on either the union or the employee for failure to follow the prescribed procedure. It is considered that this is the correct approach. See *Williams and Others v Compair Maxam Ltd* [1982] 83, *below*. Indeed s 188(8) of the TULR(C)A 1992 states that the section does not confer any rights on an employee except as provided in ss 189–192 of the TULR(C)A 1992.

None the less a failure to consult with the recognised union may have a considerable bearing upon a claim for unfair dismissal. Thus in *Williams and Others v Compair Maxam Ltd*, the EAT considered that if there had been consultation reasonable management would not have insisted on the criteria that were followed. Furthermore, consultation with the recognised union might also have been relevant to the question of transfers within the organisation. These factors, *inter alia*, influenced the finding of the tribunal that the dismissals were unfair. See also *Grundy (Teddington) Ltd v Plummer and Salt* [1983] IRLR 98 and *Tilgate Pallets Ltd v Barras* [1983] IRLR 231.

Even where the employer has consulted with a recognised union it is not open to him to infer that an individual employee is privy to the negotiations. Notwithstanding that consultation has taken place with a recognised union, a failure to consult with an individual may lead to the dismissal being unfair: see *Huddersfield Parcels Ltd v Sykes* [1981] IRLR 115. In *Pink v (1) White and (2) White and Co (Earls Barton) Ltd* [1985] IRLR 489, the EAT emphasised 'that it is not desirable for an employer to seek to discharge his duty by referring questions of redundancy solely to a trade union instead of consulting the employee as well'. The EAT found that the tribunal was justified in concluding that individual consultation would have made no difference. See also the guidance given in *Dyke and Others v Hereford and Worcester County Council, above*. In *Rolls Royce Motor Cars v Price and others* [1993] IRLR 203, the EAT held dismissals were unfair under s 57(3) of the EP(C)A 1978 because there had been insufficient consultation both with the union and the employees affected regarding the application of the criteria used for selecting those to be made redundant. Just because consultation with the union on the criteria to be applied has been taken as far as it can does not mean there ceases to be any obligation on the employer to consult with the union or the employees concerned about the application of the criteria to individual employees. There is no rule of law that the employer's obligation is only to consult either the union or the employees about the application of the criteria. The tribunal correctly held that an employer acting reasonably would have seen each individual employee affected and disclosed their assessments on the criteria applying to that individual.

Alternative employment
Under the former 1972 code employers were obliged to consider transferring employees to other work or to other establishments within the undertaking.

In *Vokes Ltd v Bear* [1974] ICR 1, Bear was employed as a works manager by the company which was taken over by the Tilling Group and Bear was told that he was to be made redundant and was asked to leave forthwith. The tribunal found that the dismissal was unfair because no attempt had been made to see whether Bear could have been employed elsewhere within the group, which consisted of some 300 companies. Shortly after the dismissal another company within the group was advertising for persons to fill senior management positions. For the company it was argued that there was no centralised personnel system which could provide the information as to vacancies. The tribunal considered that it was practicable for the company to make enquiries to help Bear. The NIRC upheld the decision.

Following the decision in *Bear*'s case, in *Perks v Geest Industries Ltd* [1974] IRLR 228, the tribunal found that the employer was required to look not only at the transportation division of the company where the employee was employed, but throughout the company. In *Smith v Collinsons Precision Screw Co Ltd* [1975] IRLR 196, the tribunal held that the company should have looked not only at companies within the same division but also at companies in other divisions.

Later decisions of the EAT have suggested that the employer's obligations are not so strict as were suggested in *Bear*'s case. In *Cliff v Reed Building Products Ltd* (1977) (unreported), the EAT applied the test of company law, holding that the company was under no obligation to look at separate companies within the group.

In *Quinton Hazell Ltd v Earl* [1976] IRLR 296, it was held that employers are required to take reasonable steps to look for other employment but it may well be that they are not required to search for other employment. This obligation exists independently of any request by the employee: *Modern Injection Moulds Ltd v Price* [1976] ICR 370.

There may be an obligation on the employer to retain the employee if he would be able to relocate him in the near future: *Allwood v William Hill (North East) Ltd* [1974] IRLR 258.

In *Avonmouth Construction Co Ltd v Shipway* [1979] IRLR 14, the EAT held that the company had a duty to consider carefully whether they could transfer the employee to another vacancy within the undertaking but added that whether the vacant position involved demotion was something for the employee to worry about. Shipway's dismissal was unfair because the employer had not offered him a job which would have involved demotion for him.

Where the employee is employed under a fixed-term contract and his employment is brought to an end through redundancy during the continuance of the fixed term it may be fair to dismiss the employee if there is no other work for him to do. However the tribunal must be satisfied on the basis of credible evidence that reasonable enquiries about alternative work have been made without success: *Holliday Concrete (Testing) Ltd v Woods* [1979] IRLR 301. The fact that the dismissal is not unfair does not deprive the employee of his common law right to claim wrongful dismissal. The employer's obligation may probably be best described as an obligation to take such steps as a reasonable employer would consider important in an effort to find alternative employment: *Cox v Wildt Mellor, Bromley Ltd* [1978] ICR 736.

In *Thomas and Betts Manufacturing Co Ltd v Harding* [1980] IRLR 255, the employee, a packer, was dismissed by reason of redundancy. The Court of Appeal rejected a contention that the employer is under no obligation to look among his other employees, other than those employed in similar positions to the dismissed employee to see if there were any alternative employment. However, the Court of Appeal held that a tribunal was entitled to conclude that the employer should have found work for the employee as a packer, notwithstanding the fact that that would have necessitated dismissing a recently recruited packer. It could be said that had the original tribunal concluded that the dismissal was fair, on the basis that it was open to a reasonable employer to have refrained from 'bumping', the decision might still have been upheld by the Court of Appeal. The Court of Appeal approved the decision in *Vokes Ltd v Bear*, above.

In *Barratt Construction Ltd v Dalrymple* [1984] IRLR 385, the EAT found that the reasonable employer will not dismiss an employee by reason of redundancy if he can employ him elsewhere.

Since the decision in *Polkey*'s case, *above*, if the employer fails to follow a fair procedure which Lord Bridge considered included taking reasonable steps to avoid or minimise redundancy in the organisation, the dismissal may be fair if, per Lord Mackay of Clashfern, 'the employer could reasonably have concluded in the light of the circumstances known to him at the time of dismissal that consultation or warning would be utterly useless. . . .'

Finally, in *MDH Ltd v Sussex* [1986] IRLR 123, the EAT found that the tribunal had erred in law in finding an employee's dismissal for redundancy unfair primarily because the employers had failed to look for alternative employment amongst other companies within the same group. (MDH Ltd was in fact part of a much larger group of companies than Tilling, which by chance had even absorbed the Tilling Group itself. Of course, in *Vokes Ltd v Bear* the employer was part of the

Tilling Group.) The EAT found that the decision in *Vokes Ltd v Bear*, above, did not lay down any principle of law.

Where, shortly after the dismissal, a job becomes available, then it is open to argument that since it was not available at the time of the dismissal, the failure subsequently to offer that job could not affect the fairness of the dismissal. Consider *Octavius Atkinson and Sons Ltd v Morris* [1989] IRLR 158, and *Labour Party v Oakley* [1987] ICR 178 (overturned on different grounds [1988] ICR 403).

Where the employer makes an offer of alternative employment on unreasonable terms that may result in the dismissal being unfair: see *Elliot v Richard Stump Ltd* [1987] ICR 579, where the employer had acted unreasonably in refusing the employee a trial period to which the employee was entitled as a matter of law.

Employer's other obligations

The former 1972 code provided that the employer should consider short-time working to cover a temporary fluctuation in manpower needs. It also suggested that a scheme should be introduced by the employer for voluntary redundancies. When an employer is considering dismissals for redundancy there is still an obligation upon him to consider these matters. Failure to do so will not necessarily result in the dismissal being held unfair, but the tribunal may still take account of this factor. It has to be weighed with any other factors in deciding whether, in all the circumstances, the employer has acted reasonably. It may be sufficient to defeat any argument that the employer should have considered a shorter working week if such a proposal is incompatible with his business requirements: *Atkinson v George Lindsay and Co* [1980] IRLR 196.

Chapter 10

Dismissal and Maternity

General

As a result of the adoption of the EC Directive on the Protection of Pregnant Women at Work 92/85, the TURERA 1993 contains provisions which radically change the employment rights of pregnant women. Sections 23–25 of the TURERA 1993 deal with the necessary alterations to the EP(C)A 1978. By virtue of the TURERA 1993 (Commencement No 3 and Transitional Provisions) Order (SI 1994 No 1365) the maternity provisions of the TURERA 1993 are brought into effect in relation to women whose expected week of childbirth begins on or after 16 October 1994, and the provisions relating to dismissal apply to any dismissal where the effective date of termination falls on or after 10 June 1994.

The following is a summary of the various employment rights applicable to pregnant women, and they are dealt with in more detail in the subsequent sections of this chapter.

(1) *Maternity leave* There is a right to a period of 14 weeks' maternity leave for all employees, irrespective of their length of service or hours of work.

(2) *Maternity absence and the right to return* This is a right for those employees who have two years' service to return after 29 weeks' absence.

(3) *Automatic unfair dismissal* This occurs on certain specified grounds when the reason or principal reason is pregnancy or childbirth.

(4) *Written reasons for dismissal* These must be given, irrespective of length of service, whenever a women is dismissed while pregnant or during maternity leave.

(5) *Rights in relation to suspension on maternity grounds* These rights are to be offered suitable alternative work if available, and to be paid normal remuneration while suspended.

The Government has introduced, under the sponsorship of the Department of Social Security, new provisions for maternity pay. They are the Maternity Allowance and Statutory Maternity Pay Regulations

1994 (SI 1994 No 1230) and the Social Security Maternity Benefits and Statutory Sick Pay (Amendment) Regulations 1994 (SI 1994 No 1367). This chapter deals only with the employment aspects of maternity rights.

Maternity leave

This is a new right to 14 weeks' maternity leave for all employees, irrespective of their hours of work or length of service. It is introduced by s 23 of the TURERA 1993 which inserts new ss 33–44 of the EP(C)A 1978.

During the maternity leave period the employee is entitled to the benefit of the terms and conditions of employment, apart from remuneration: s 33. This means that benefits, such as the provision of a company car and pension contributions, would continue during the maternity leave. The conditions applicable to maternity leave are contained in ss 34–38A of the EP(C)A 1978.

Commencement—s 34

The maternity leave period begins either with
(1) the date which, in accordance with s 36 of the EP(C)A 1978, the employee notifies to her employer as the date on which she intends her period of absence from work in exercise of her right to maternity leave to begin; or
(2) if earlier, the first day on which she is absent from work wholly or partly because of pregnancy or childbirth after the beginning of the sixth week before the expected week of childbirth: s 34(1) of the EP(C)A 1978.

Where childbirth occurs before the day on which the employees' maternity leave period would otherwise commence the leave commences on the day of childbirth: s 34(2) of the EP(C)A 1978.

'Childbirth' is defined in s 153 of the EP(C)A 1978, as amended by TURERA 1993, as either the birth of a living child or the birth of a child whether living or dead after 24 weeks of pregnancy (this amendment follows the changes in the abortion laws).

The combined effect of these provisions is that any absence (except for the birth of a live child) prior to six weeks before the expected week of childbirth would be for sickness, and would not be for maternity leave.

The 'expected week of childbirth' means the week, beginning with midnight between Saturday and Sunday, in which it is expected that childbirth will occur: s 153(1) of the EP(C)A 1978.

Since maternity leave commences automatically (even if the employee does not want it to) on an absence due to pregnancy, it is open to an employer and employee to agree that the maternity leave would not commence in this way (eg where the absence was of short duration and the employee was still fit to carry on work).

Duration—s 35

The maternity leave period shall continue for 14 weeks from the date it begins or until the birth of the child, if that is later: s 35(1) of the EP(C)A 1978. This means that if birth occurs more than 14 weeks after the leave has begun, the employee's leave would end on the day after the birth.

The EC Directive 92/85 provides for a compulsory two-week period of leave either before or after the birth. The Government has introduced The Maternity (Compulsory Leave) Regulations 1994 (SI 1994 No 2479) which provide for a two-week compulsory period of leave after the birth, thus ensuring that whenever the maternity leave expires, there will always be a two-week period of leave after the birth. The regulations came into force on 19 October 1994. This is the effect of s 35(2) of the EP(C)A 1978. Normally, of course, this compulsory two-week leave would be within the 14-week leave period, but it could lengthen the 14 weeks' leave by up to two weeks if the maternity leave expires at the time of the birth.

When an employee is dismissed during the maternity leave period, the leave ends at the time of the dismissal: s 35(3) of the EP(C)A 1978. Therefore, the employee has no further right to the continuation of the benefit of the terms and conditions of employment from the time of dismissal, but must rely on the remedies provided for breach of contract, or unfair dismissal under s 60 of the EP(C)A 1978 (see *below*).

Notice

An employee will not have the right to maternity leave unless she complies with the various notice provisions contained in ss 36, 37 and 37A of the EP(C)A 1978.

The first notice is that contained in s 37 which is as follows. An employee must inform her employer in writing at least 21 days before her maternity leave period begins, or if that is not reasonably practicable, as soon as is reasonably practicable (a) that she is pregnant, and (b) of the expected week of childbirth or, if the childbirth has occurred, the date on which it did occur: s 37(1) of the EP(C)A 1978. An employee must, if her employer so requires, produce for his inspection a certificate from a registered medical practitioner or a registered midwife stating the expected week of childbirth.

Secondly, under s 36 an employee must (a) notify her employer of the date (called the notified leave date) on which she intends her maternity leave to begin not less than twenty-one days before that date or, if that is not reasonably practicable, as soon as is reasonably practicable; or (b) where she is first absent from work wholly or partly because of pregnancy or childbirth before the notified leave date or before she has notified such a date and after the beginning of the sixth week before the expected week of childbirth, notify her employer as soon as is reasonably practicable that she is absent for that reason; or (c) where childbirth occurs before the notified leave date or before she has notified such a date notify her employer that she has given birth as soon as is reasonably practicable after the birth.

She may not notify a date under s 36(1)(a) which occurs before the beginning of the eleventh week before the expected week of childbirth: s 36(2) of the EP(C)A 1978. This second notice does not have to be in writing, unless her employer so requests (s 36(1)), but quite likely both the first notice (under s 37) and the second notice (under s 36) would be given together, ie she would notify her employer of the fact of her pregnancy, her expected week of childbirth and the date she intends her leave to start.

Return during the maternity leave period

If an employee intends to return to work earlier than the end of her maternity leave period, she must give her employer not less than seven days' notice of the date on which she intends to return: s 37A(1) of the EP(C)A 1978.

If she returns to work without having notified her employer of her intention to do so or without giving him the seven days' notice required under s 37A(1), the employer shall be entitled to postpone her return to a date which will ensure that he has seven days' notice of her return: s 37A(2) of the EP(C)A 1978. However, he cannot postpone her return to work to a date after the end of her maternity leave period: s 37A(3) of the EP(C)A 1978, except presumably by agreement with the employee.

Where an employee returns to work despite a notification of postponement under s 37A(2) the employer is under no contractual obligation to pay her remuneration until the date he has specified as the date on which she may return: s 37A(4) of the EP(C)A 1978. The benefit of the other terms and conditions of employment still apply though: see s 33 of the EP(C)A 1978.

The difference between the return to work under the maternity leave provisions and the right to return under s 39 (see *below*) is that, subject to satisfying certain conditions under s 39, an employee can extend her period of absence up to 29 weeks after the beginning of the week in which childbirth occurs if she qualifies for the right to return under s 39.

It appears that the employee has the right to resume working in exactly the same job on exactly the same terms and conditions as before the commencement of the maternity leave period, subject to any variation of the contract of employment by agreement with the employer. Any unilateral variation of the contract by the employer could entitle the employee to leave and claim constructive dismissal and/or breach of contract.

Redundancy

If during an employee's maternity leave period it is not practicable by reason of redundancy for the employer to continue to employ her under her existing contract of employment he must, where there is a suitable available vacancy, and before the ending of her employment under the original contract, offer her alternative employment either with himself or his successor or an associated employer under a new contract of employment which will take effect immediately on the ending of the employment under the previous contract: s 38(1) of the EP(C)A 1978. The new contract must be such that (a) the work to be done under it is of a kind which is both suitable in relation to the employee and appropriate for her to do in the circumstances; and (b) the provisions as to the capacity and the place in which she is to be employed and the other terms and conditions of her employment are not substantially less favourable to her than if she had continued to be employed under the previous contract: s 38(2) of the EP(C)A 1978. The cases decided prior to the new provisions are still relevant.

'Suitable available vacancy'

In *Martin v BSC Footwear (Supplies) Ltd* [1978] IRLR 95, a case involving a pregnant employee, the tribunal held that the dismissal was unfair because the employer had not discharged the burden of proving that there was no suitable available vacancy. Martin could have been kept on to do a job of display packaging until a sick employee returned or Martin left, whichever was earlier. The tribunal accepted that 'suitable available vacancy' (in what was then s 60(2) of the EP(C)A 1978) is different from 'suitable alternative vacancy'. There is no obligation on an employer to create a job or modify a job description. 'Suitable' meant 'suitable to the lady's pregnant condition and health and, in relation to any vacancy, to her particular skill, experience and qualifications'. 'Available' meant 'the suitable job should exist or can be made to exist within the given complement of the employer's staffing and the employer's layout and organisation of operations'. 'Vacancy' meant 'a job vacancy existing in the organisation, structure and layout of the work and operations of and in the employer's business as they were at the effective date of termination'.

The employer must make reasonable attempts to see if there is a suitable available vacancy for an employee made redundant during her maternity leave period.

Contractual maternity leave

An employee who has the statutory right to maternity leave under s 33 of the EP(C)A 1978 and also a right to maternity leave under a contract of employment or otherwise may not exercise the two rights separately but may take advantage of whichever right is in any particular respect the more favourable: s 38A(1) of the EP(C)A 1978. See the earlier cases on the exercise of the composite right under Maternity absence and the right to return *below*.

Constructive dismissal

In the case of pregnant employees, or those absent on maternity leave, employers must ensure that changes, such as a change in the employee's hours, intended to be for the employee's benefit, are not in fact breaches of the employee's contract entitling the employee to resign and claim a constructive dismissal. Whether pregnancy or child-birth gives rise to new implied terms in the contract to be observed by an employer, breach of which will entitle the employee to claim constructive dismissal is unresolved.

Continuity

Any period of absence under the maternity leave provisions will not break continuity of employment and will count in accordance with s 33 of and Sched 13 to the EP(C)A 1978. See Chapter 3.

Maternity absence and the right to return

General

There is a right for those women who have been continuously employed for over two years at the beginning of the eleventh week before the expected week of childbirth to return to work at any time up to 29 weeks from the week in which childbirth occurs (see s 39 of the EP(C)A 1978). Amendments have been made so as to make this right fit into the scheme by which all pregnant employees can have 14 weeks' maternity leave (see under 'Maternity leave' *above*).

Unless caught by s 60 of the EP(C)A 1978, when the dismissal will be automatically unfair, an employee may claim unfair dismissal where she is dismissed during a period of absence, (*a*) provided that she has the right to return to work under s 39 of the EP(C)A 1978 and (*b*) either her maternity leave period ends by reason of dismissal, or (*c*) she is dismissed after her maternity leave period: para 6(1) of Sched 2 to the EP(C)A 1978.

An employee is not to be taken as dismissed after her maternity leave period if the dismissal occurs in the course of the employee attempting to return to work in accordance with her contract in circumstances in which s 44 of the EP(C)A 1978 applies: para 6(2) of Sched 2 of the EP(C)A 1978.

Section 44 states that where an employee has both a statutory right to return to work (under s 39 of the EP(C)A 1978) and also a contractual right to return to work after absence because of pregnancy or childbirth, she may not exercise the two rights separately but may, in returning to work, take advantage of whichever right is, in any particular respect, the more favourable: s 44 (1) of the EP(C)A 1978.

During the period of maternity absence the employee may claim that she is dismissed for redundancy and/or unfair dismissal. The onus of proving dismissal is on her. The onus of proving the reason for dismissal will be on the employer. In cases of unfair dismissal the tribunal will have to be satisfied that the dismissal is reasonable in all the circumstances: s 57(3) of the EP(C)A 1978. The dismissal during the employee's maternity absence does not affect her right to return to work: para 6(4) of Sched 2 to the EP(C)A 1978. If the tribunal finds the dismissal unfair it may make an order for reinstatement or re-engagement, but any such order may have to be modified to take into account the employee's statutory right to return to work. If the tribunal awards compensation, that compensation shall be assessed without regard to the employee's right to return to work: para 6(4)(a) of Sched 2 to the EP(C)A 1978.

Further, her right to return to work is exercisable only on her repaying any redundancy payment or compensation for unfair dismissal paid in respect of that dismissal if the employer requests such repayment: para 6(4)(b) of Sched 2 to the EP(C)A 1978.

Where the employee is dismissed during her maternity absence she is entitled to notice equivalent to the statutory minimum under s 49 of the EP(C)A 1978.

If the dismissal during absence is fair it seems that the employee is still not precluded from exercising her right to return to work: ss 39–42 of the EP(C)A 1978. The employer may refuse to have the employee back. Such refusal amounts to a dismissal (see ss 56 and 86 of the EP(C)A 1978), unless the circumstances come within the provisions contained in s 56A of the EP(C)A 1978. Where there is a refusal within s 56 the tribunal will have to consider whether this dismissal is for redundancy and, if so, whether it is fair or unfair. In practice if the dismissal during absence is fair it will be difficult to envisage the circumstances in which an employee can claim that a dismissal because of a refusal to allow her to return can be unfair.

Where the employee has a contractual right to return to work, dismissal during the maternity absence may be a breach of that contract. This may be in addition to any rights which she has in respect of unfair dismissal.

Part V of the EP(C)A 1978 (the unfair dismissal provisions) is modified by para 6(3) of Sched 2 to the EP(C)A 1978, in that in cases of dismissal during a period of maternity leave the following provisions do not apply:

(a) s 64—qualifying period and upper age limit;

(b) s 65—exclusion of the statutory protection against unfair dismissal when there is a dismissal procedure agreement;

(c) s 66—revocation of exclusion order under s 65;

(d) s 141(2)—employment ordinarily outside Great Britain;

(e) s 144(2)—employment as master or crew member of a fishing vessel remunerated by a share in profits or gross earnings.

The right to return to work applies whether or not a contract of employment subsists during the period of absence after the end of the maternity leave period (as to the continued existence of the contract, see *Hilton International Hotels (UK) Ltd v Kaissi* [1994] IRLR 270.) The employee's statutory right to return comes into existence as soon as she has given notice prior to her leave. Thus, the employer is obliged to offer her any suitable vacancy that arises if her job becomes redundant, even though that vacancy arises before she notifies her employer of her intended date of return: *Philip Hodges & Co v Kell* [1994] ICR 656. Provided that the employee fulfils the conditions contained in ss 39 and 40 and 42 it does not matter that the employee resigns where the absence is wholly or partly because of pregnancy or childbirth: see *Mitchell v British Legion Club* [1980] IRLR 425.

Under s 39 it is not necessary that the employee should work until immediately before the beginning of the eleventh week before the expected week of childbirth. The question is whether or not she is employed. See *Satchwell Sunvic Ltd v Secretary of State for Employment* [1979] IRLR 455, and *Secretary of State for Employment v Doulton Sanitaryware Ltd* [1981] IRLR 365. Compare *J W Williams & Co Ltd v Secretary of State for Employment* [1978] IRLR 235. Although they are all cases on maternity pay they involve an interpretation of what is now s39(1)(b) of the EP(C)A 1978.

Continuous employment until immediately before the beginning of the eleventh week before the expected week of childbirth requires continuity of employment throughout the twelfth week before the expected week of childbirth. The requirement is strict. If the employee leaves before the beginning of the eleventh week she will lose her right, even though she leaves early because of a miscalculation: see *Hepworth v Teesside High School* (1978) (unreported).

The right to return to work is the right to return to work with the person who was the employee's employer before the end of the maternity absence period, or his successor, in the job in which she was then employed. This must be:

(a) on terms and conditions as to remuneration not less favourable than those which would have been applicable to her had she not been absent from work at any time since the beginning of her maternity leave period;

(b) with her seniority, pension rights and similar rights as they would have been if the period or periods of her employment prior to the end of her maternity leave period were continuous with her employment following her return to work (but subject to the requirements of para 5 of Sched 5 to the Social Security Act 1989 (credit for the period of absence in certain cases)); and

(c) otherwise, on terms and conditions no less favourable than those which would have been applicable to her had she not been absent from work after the end of her maternity leave period: s 39(2) of the EP(C)A 1978.

'Job', in relation to an employee, means the nature of the work she is employed to do in accordance with her contract, and the capacity and place in which she is so employed: s 153(1). 'Terms and conditions not less favourable than those which would have been applicable to her if she had not been absent from work at any time since the commencement of her maternity leave period' means, as regards seniority, pension rights and other similar rights, that the period or periods of employment prior to the end of the maternity leave period are to be regarded as continuous with her employment following her absence: s 39(2)(b) of the EP(C)A 1978.

In *Edgell v Lloyd's Register of Shipping* [1977] IRLR 463, the tribunal found that the employee's right to return to work is not a right to return to exactly the same job. She is entitled to return to a job of the same nature and capacity at the same place. During the period of maternity leave there may be a reorganisation or change in the employer's business. This may result in a change in the employee's job, but provided this change is not fundamental, the employer will have complied with what is now s 39.

In *McFadden v Greater Glasgow Passenger Transport Executive* [1977] IRLR 327, the employee, before her maternity leave, was employed in an established clerical position. On her return to work she was given a non-established, supernumerary, clerical post. As a supernumerary, her terms and conditions of employment were less favourable and if, for instance, there were redundancy dismissals in the future, she would be more at risk than an established employee. Therefore, she had not been allowed to return on terms and conditions which were not less favourable to her than she had previously enjoyed.

Where in *Edgell's* case there was no dismissal, in *McFadden's* case the employee had not been permitted to return to work in accordance with what is now s 39 and so under s 56 of the EP(C)A 1978 there was a dismissal which was held to be unfair.

Under the former s 45 it was the job under the original contract to which the employee was entitled to return, not any job which was given to her during her pregnancy, for instance, because that was a lighter job and she was more able to do it. Under s 39(2) it is the job in which she was employed before the end of her maternity absence.

Notice

In order to qualify for the right to return, an employee has to give the notice required for the maternity leave under s 37(1) (see *above*) and in addition, has to include the information that she intends to exercise the right to return: (see s 40(1) of the EP(C)A 1978.

Where an employee, other than in pursuance of her statutory obligations, makes a general statement that she will not be returning to work, this will not necessarily amount to a resignation disentitling her from claiming the statutory right to return. It may prevent the employee substantiating a claim for unfair dismissal if she allows the employer to act on this statement to his detriment (eg by engaging a replacement) before the employee notifies the employer that she wants to return: See *Hughes v Gwynedd Area Health Authority* [1978] ICR 161.

Where, after childbirth, the employer makes further enquiry of the employee about whether or not she intends to return, such a general statement may disentitle her from claiming the statutory right of return. The employee loses the right to return to work under s 39 where, not earlier than 21 days before the end of the maternity leave period, her employer, or his successor, requests the employee in writing to give him written confirmation that she intends to exercise her right to return, unless she gives the requested confirmation within fourteen days of receiving the employer's request, or if that is not reasonably practicable as soon as is reasonably practicable. The employer's request must be accompanied by a written statement that she will lose the right to return unless she complies with the request: s 40(2) and (3) of the EP(C)A 1978.

The tribunal may have to consider the meaning of 'reasonably practicable'. In *Nu-Swift International Ltd v Mallinson* [1978] IRLR 537, an employee who knew of her rights and the obligation to give notice did not do so because she was concerned about the health of her baby. The EAT held it was reasonably practicable for her to have given notice. They took the view that the legislation is intended to cover someone who intended to resume working, but not someone who did not intend to return and subsequently changes her mind, nor an employee who is not really sure. Where there are matters which make it doubtful that the employee will return then she should talk to her employer at the outset and clarify the position with him.

In deciding what was reasonably practicable the EAT had regard to the Court of Appeal and EAT decisions in deciding what was reasonably practicable for the purposes of s 67(2) of the EP(C)A 1978 (where the complaint of unfair dismissal is not presented to the tribunal within three months of the effective date of termination). The importance of complying with the statutory provision is illustrated by the NICA decision in *McKnight v Adlestones (Jewellers) Ltd* [1984] IRLR 453, where *McKnight* had no contractual right to return to work. She failed to give at least 21 days' notice in writing before her absence began that she intended to return to work. It was held that the only inference to be drawn from the parties' intention was that the contract of employment was to be suspended during the employee's absence and could only be revived if the employee complied with her statutory right to return. Since *McKnight* had no contractual right to return, her failure to comply with the statutory requirements resulted in her losing her statutory right to return and the employer's refusal to have her back was not a dismissal in law. See also *F W Woolworth plc v Smith* [1990] ICR 45. In *Lucas v Norton of London Ltd* [1984] IRLR 86, Lucas failed to give the prescribed notice and lost her statutory right. Since the contract subsisted the refusal to allow her back was a dismissal. See also *Hilton International Hotels (UK) Ltd v Kaissi, above.*

Right to return and redundancy

Where an employee is entitled to return to work, but it is not practicable by reason of redundancy (for the meaning of redundancy see s 81 of the EP(C)A 1978 and Chapter 9) for the employer to permit her to return to work she is entitled, where there is a suitable available vacancy, to be offered alternative employment with her employer or his successor or an associated employer: s 41(1) of the EP(C)A 1978. The new contract of employment must comply with certain conditions:
  (*a*) the work to be done under the contract must be a kind which is both suitable in relation to the employee and appropriate for her to do in the circumstances; and
  (*b*) the provisions of the new contract as to the capacity and place in which she is to be employed and as to the other terms and conditions of her employment must not be substantially less favourable to her than if she had returned to work pursuant to her right to return: s 41(2) of the EP(C)A 1978.

In *Community Task Force v Rimmer* [1986] IRLR 203, the EAT held that the test of availability in what is now s 41(1) is not expressed to be qualified by considerations of what is economic or reasonable. If a suitable vacancy is available the consequences of the employer offering the job to the employee are not relevant to the consideration of s 41(1).

Suitability to the employee presupposes the application of the same tests as in the case of a dismissal for redundancy. This is a concept borrowed from the redundancy payments provisions where there is an offer of alternative employment. It is reasonable to assume this provision will be interpreted in broadly the same way. 'Appropriate for her to do in the circumstances' does not have its origin in the redundancy payments provisions. The phrase suggests that the tribunal can consider the particular problems of the employee following childbirth. Greater protection is therefore given to the redundant employee who is seeking to return to work following a pregnancy and/or childbirth. The phrase 'not substantially less favourable' is also different from the corresponding provisions relating to redundancy payments: see s 82(6) of the EP(C)A 1978. It may well have the effect of extending the range of jobs that can be offered to the employee over and above the original contract as well as over and above what could have been offered to her were it a redundancy in the ordinary course of events without the intervention of a period of absence for pregnancy or childbirth.

If the employee declines work which is suitable and appropriate for her to do she will not be entitled to a redundancy payment.

Where the employee has the right to return under s 39 and has exercised it in accordance with s 42 of the EP(C)A 1978 and is not permitted to return because of redundancy, she is treated as dismissed (see s 86 of the EP(C)A 1978) and she may have a claim under Part VI of the EP(C)A 1978, ie for redundancy.

She may also be able to claim unfair dismissal. Where the employer fails to offer her alternative employment within s 41(1) of the EP(C)A 1978 where there is a suitable available vacancy, that failure shall be treated as an automatically unfair dismissal: para 2(2) of Sched 2 to the EP(C)A 1978.

Where the employee is not allowed to return to work because of a redundancy following an absence for pregnancy and/or childbirth, the dismissal may also be automatically unfair under s 59 of the EP(C)A 1978 or it may be unfair where the employer has not acted reasonably: s 57(3) of the EP(C)A 1978.

Unless it is a case falling within para 5 of Sched 2, the employee will be regarded as having been continuously employed up to the notified day of return and her redundancy entitlement will be calculated accordingly, and as if she had been dismissed from the notified day of return for the reason for which she was not permitted to return: s 86 of the EP(C)A 1978.

Exercise of the right to return

An employee must exercise her right to return to work under s 39 of the EP(C)A 1978 by giving written notice to her employer, (who may be her employer before the end of her maternity leave period or a successor of that employer), at least 21 days before the date on which she proposes to return, of her proposal to return on that day, which is referred to as the notified day of return: s 42(1) of the EP(C)A 1978. The requirement is mandatory. The giving of the notice is of critical importance, since all the employee's other rights flow from it. Unless 21 days' notice has been given which comply with the provisions of s 42(1), the employee cannot claim unfair dismissal under s 56 of the EP(C)A 1978 because the right only arises where the employee has exercised her right to return in accordance with s 42. It is also clear that the employee must also comply with the provisions of s 42(1), even where the employee's contract of employment subsists during the period of absence for maternity. By virtue of s 44 of the EP(C)A 1978, where an employee relies on a contractual right to return following a maternity leave period she is treated as exercising a composite right. However that right is subject to the provisions of s 42 and s 56 of the EP(C)A 1978. A failure to allow the employee to return where the employee exercises or seeks to exercise her composite right gives rise to a claim under s 56 for unfair dismissal. Once again the right to claim unfair dismissal under s 56 depends, *inter alia*, upon the employee having complied with the requirements of s 42(1). It might be different if the contract contained some express provisions dealing with the right to return: see *Lavery v Plessey Telecommunications Ltd* [1982] IRLR 180, upheld on appeal [1983] IRLR 202; and *Kolfor Plant Ltd v Wright* [1982] IRLR 311, where the EAT held that if the employee cannot bring herself within the provisions of s 56, s 55 does not apply. See *Lucas, above.* Section 55 can only apply if the employee was dismissed otherwise than in the course of exercising her right to return.

An employer may postpone an employee's return to work until a date not more than four weeks after the notified day of return if he notifies her before that day that for specified reasons he is postponing her return until that date, and accordingly she will be entitled to return to work with him on that date: s 42(2) of the EP(C)A 1978.

The employee may:

(a) postpone her return to work until a date not exceeding 4 weeks from the notified day of return, notwithstanding that the date falls after the end of the period of 29 weeks beginning with the week in which childbirth occurred; and

(b) where no day of return has been notified to the employer, extend the time during which she may exercise her right to return so that she returns to work not later than 4 weeks from the expiration of the said period of 29 weeks;

if before the notified day of return or, as the case may be, the expiration of the period of 29 weeks, she gives the employer a certificate from a registered medical practitioner stating that by reason of disease or bodily or mental disablement (not necessarily disease or disablement because of the pregnancy or childbirth) she will be incapable of work on the notified day of return or the expiration of the period as the case may be: s 42(3) of the EP(C)A 1978. The employee may only once exercise a right of postponement or extension in respect of the same return to work: s 42(4) of the EP(C)A 1978. Again these pro-

visions will be strictly interpreted. See *Dowuona v John Lewis plc*
[1987] IRLR 310 and *Kelly v Liverpool Maritime Terminals* [1988]
IRLR 310. If the employee does not comply with the statutory provisions the employment terminates.

If the employee has notified a day of return, but there is an interruption of work, whether due to industrial action or otherwise, which
renders it unreasonable to expect her to return to work on the notified
day of return, she may instead return to work when work resumes
after the interruption, or as soon as reasonably practicable thereafter:
s 42(5) of the EP(C)A 1978.

If no day of return has been notified and there is such an interruption of work, whether due to industrial action or otherwise, which
renders it unreasonable to expect her to return before the expiration
of the 29 weeks, or which appears likely to have that effect, and in
consequence she does not notify a day of return, she may exercise her
right of return so that she returns to work at any time before the end
of the period of 28 days from the end of the interruption, notwithstanding that she returns to work outside the period of 29 weeks: s 42(6) of
the EP(C)A 1978.

Where the employee has either exercised her right under s 42(3)(*b*)
to extend the period during which she may exercise her right to
return to work, or has refrained from notifying the day of return under
s 42(6), the other of those subsections shall apply as if for the reference
to the end of the period of 29 weeks there were substituted a
reference to the end of the further period of 4 weeks or, as the case
may be, 28 days from the end of the interruption of the work: s 42(7)
of the EP(C)A 1978.

Where an employee's return to work is postponed by her employer
under s 42(2) or by her under s 42(3)(*a*), *above*, or where the employee
returns to work on a day later than the notified day of return in
accordance with s 42(5), then references to the 'notified day of return'
are construed as references to the day to which the return is postponed
or, as the case may be, that later day: s 43(4) of the EP(C)A 1978.

Right to return and unfair dismissal

Refusal to permit a woman to return to work when she has exercised
her right under s 42 is deemed to be a dismissal with effect from the
notified date of return. The reason for the dismissal will be the reason
for which she is not permitted to return to work. This is the effect of
s 56 of the EP(C)A 1978 and a similar provision applies where the
woman is claiming a redundancy payment (s 86 of the EP(C)A 1978).

The refusal is deemed to be a dismissal (not necessarily unfair—
that will still have to be investigated). It is necessary for there to be a
'deemed dismissal,' since the employee's contract may not have sub-

sisted during her absence, and therefore her employer could not have ended it by dismissal.

The employer will be in breach of s 56, where he allows the employee to return to work, but she does not return to the job which she was employed to do under the contract in which she was employed before the end of the maternity leave period: see s 39(2); *above*. The failure to permit the employee to return to work may enable her to claim redundancy and unfair dismissal in a redundancy situation, where the reason for the failure is redundancy (see 'Right to return and redundancy', at p 263) or to claim unfair dismissal. The employee must have tried to exercise her right to return even though she may have been dismissed during her maternity leave. Certain dismissals will be automatically unfair.

In *Institute of the Motor Industry v Harvey* [1992] IRLR 343, the EAT held that where an employee had failed to give the requisite notice under what was s 47 (but will in future be s 40 of the EP(C)A 1978), since there was no obligation on the employer to permit the employee to return, there could be no breach of that obligation for the purpose of claiming constructive dismissal. They did, however, hold that there was a continuing contract after the employee left on maternity leave (or absence).

This was also found to be the case on the particular facts of the case in *Hilton International Hotels (UK) Ltd v Kaissi* [1994] IRLR 270.

In a claim for unfair dismissal, where there is a failure to permit an employee to return to work after childbirth, the provisions of s 57(3) of the EP(C)A 1978 are modified. Thus, determination of the question whether the dismissal was fair or unfair having regard to the reasons shown by the employer shall depend upon whether in the circumstances (including the size and administrative resources of the employer's undertaking) the employer would have been acting reasonably or unreasonably in treating it as a sufficient reason for dismissing the employee if she had not been absent from work; and that question shall be determined in accordance with equity and the substantial merits of the case: para 2(1) of Sched 2 to the EP(C)A 1978.

Section 56A of the EP(C)A 1978 provides for the exclusion of s 56 in certain cases. The first exclusion arises where immediately before the end of the maternity leave period (or if it ends by reason of dismissal, immediately before the dismissal), the number of employees employed by the employer added to the number employed by any associated employer of his did not exceed five, and it is not reasonably practicable for the employer or his successor to permit the employee to return to work in accordance with s 39 of the EP(C)A 1978 or for him or an associated employer to offer her employment under a contract of employment fulfilling the conditions set out in s 39(2): s 56A(1) of the EP(C)A 1978.

Secondly, s 56 shall not apply to an employee if it is not reasonably

practicable, for a reason other than redundancy, for the employer or
his successor to permit her return to work in accordance with s 39 and
he or an associated employer offers her employment under a contract
which satisfies certain conditions specified in s 56A(3), and she accepts
or unreasonably refuses that offer: s 56A(2). The conditions are that
the work to be done under the contract is of a kind which is both
suitable in relation to the employee and appropriate for her to do in
the circumstances, and that the provisions of the contract as to the
capacity and place in which she is to be employed and as to the other
terms and conditions of the employment are not substantially less
favourable to her than if she had returned to work in accordance with
s 39: s 56A(2) and (3) of the EP(C)A 1978. These latter provisions
follow the provisions of s 39(2) (see 'Maternity absence and the right
to return, General' at p 258).

Where in a claim for unfair dismissal the question arises as to
whether or not the operation of s 56 is excluded by s 56A(1) and (2),
the onus is upon the employer to show that the provisions of those
subsections were satisfied in relation to the employee: s 56A(4) of the
EP(C)A 1978.

In a claim for unfair dismissal in relation to the failure to permit
an employee to return to work after childbirth, the provisions of
EP(C)A are modified by paras 2(1) and 2(4) of Sched 2. The following
provisions do not apply, with the exception of (b) which applies in a
modified form:

   (a) Section 55—the meaning of unfair dismissal and the effective
       date of termination. There is substituted therefor s 56 of the
       EP(C)A 1978 which deals with the question of dismissal where
       the employee is not permitted to return to work after confine-
       ment. Section 56 is subject to s 56A.
   (b) Section 57(3)—the test of fairness. See *above*.
   (c) Section 64(1)—the qualifying period and upper age limit.
   (d) Section 65—exclusion of the statutory protection against unfair
       dismissal where there is a dismissal procedure agreement.
   (e) Section 66—revocation of an exclusion order under s 65.
   (f) Section 73(5) and (6)—the provisions relating to the upper age
       limit for the purposes of the basic award of compensation.
   (g) Section 141(2)—employment ordinarily outside Great Britain.
   (h) Section 142(1) as amended—exclusion of the statutory protec-
       tion against unfair dismissal in contracts for one year or more.
   (i) Section 144(2)—employment as master or crew member of a
       fishing vessel remunerated by a share in the profits or by gross
       earnings.

There are also consequential amendments for the purpose of computing the period of employment in that para 11(1) of Sched 13 to the
EP(C)A 1978 does not apply, and for the purpose of calculating normal
working hours and a week's pay in that paras 7(1)(f) to (i) and (2) and

8(3) of Sched 14, do not apply. Paragraph 10 of Sched 15 does not apply. This paragraph deals with the exclusions from protection against unfair dismissal where there are certain fixed-term contracts.

References to the effective date of termination in Part V of the EP(C)A 1978 and to the date of termination of employment in ss 69 and 70 are construed as references to the notified day of return: para 2(3) of Sched 2 to the EP(C)A 1978. Part II of Sched 14, in relation to ss 71 and 73, is also amended: see para 2(5) of Sched 2 to the EP(C)A 1978.

Contractual right to return

An employee who has a right both under the EP(C)A 1978 and under a contract of employment, or otherwise, to return to work, may not exercise the two rights separately, but may in returning to work take advantage of whichever right is, in any particular respect, the more favourable: s 44(1) of the EP(C)A 1978.

In *Bovey v Board of Governors of the Hospital for Sick Children* [1978] ICR 934, Bovey had a statutory right to resume full-time working in her original job but she wanted to return on a part-time basis. Her employers gave her the option of returning either to the previous position full-time or of taking a part-time position on a lower grade. Bovey claimed that the two rights could be composited to give her the right to return to her original job on a part-time basis. The EAT held that she could not form a composite right to return to work after maternity absence under what was then s 48(1) of the EP(C)A 1978, by claiming that the offer of a part-time post on a lower grade allowed her to exercise her statutory right to return to her original job on a part-time basis in accordance with a contractual right. The legislation referred only to the contract of employment under which she is employed when she departs on maternity leave. It is under that contract that the right to return to work arises. It does not arise under an agreement under which she may have acquired a right to return to work on a part-time basis. She could not accept the offer and add to it her statutory right. Her claim for unfair dismissal therefore failed. Where the employee's contract subsists during a period of absence for maternity leave and the employee exercises her contractual right to return, then by virtue of s 44 she is treated as exercising a composite right. That right is subject to the provisions of ss 42 and 56 of the EP(C)A 1978. The only way in which the employee can claim unfair dismissal is in accordance with s 56 which involves the employee having to comply, *inter alia*, with the provisions of s 42(1). If the employee fails to comply with the latter provisions by not giving the appropriate length of notice then she can have no claim for unfair dismissal under the provisions of s 56. See s 44(2) of the EP(C)A 1978 and *Lavery v Plessey Telecommunications Ltd* [1982] IRLR 180, upheld on appeal [1983] IRLR 202, *Kolfor Plant Ltd v Wright* [1982] IRLR 311, *Lucas v Norton of London Ltd* [1984] IRLR 86, and *Institute of the Motor Industry v Harvey* [1992] IRLR 343. Likewise, if she fails to comply with s 42 of the EP(C)A 1978, she will have lost her right to return: see the cases of *Dowuona* and *Kelly, above.*

Sections 39, 41 to 43, 56 and 86 of and paras 1, 2, 3, 4 and 6 of Sched 2 to the EP(C)A 1978 apply subject to any modifications necessary to give effect to any more favourable terms, to the exercise of this composite right as they apply to the right to return to work under s 39: s 44(2) of the EP(C)A 1978.

Replacements

Where an employee is taking maternity leave the employer may engage a replacement. If on doing so he informs that replacement in writing that his or her employment will be terminated on the resumption of work by another employee who is, or will be, absent wholly or partly because of pregnancy or childbirth and he dismisses the replacement employee to make it possible for the other employee to resume her work, then for purposes of s 57(1)(*b*) of the EP(C)A 1978 (see Chapter 6) the dismissal is regarded as having been for a substantial reason of a kind such as to justify the dismissal of an employee holding the position which the replacement held: s 61(1) of the EP(C)A 1978. The reasonableness of the dismissal will be considered under s 57(3) of the EP(C)A 1978: s 61 of the EP (C)A 1978. However, the dismissal of a replacement who herself becomes aware that she is pregnant during the course of her employment as a replacement will be automatically unfair under s 60(*a*) of the EP(C)A 1978. Any attempt to contract out of the maternity provisions would be void by virtue of s 140 of the EP(C)A 1978.

Automatically unfair dismissal on the ground of pregnancy and childbirth

General

A dismissal will be automatically unfair where the reason or principal reason is that the employee is pregnant, or is any other reason connected with the employee's pregnancy. This is the effect of the new s 60 introduced into the EP(C)A 1978 by the TURERA 1993.

The detail of s 60 is as follows: an employee is automatically unfairly dismissed if:

(*a*) the reason or principal reason for her dismissal is that she is pregnant or any other reason connected with her pregnancy;

(*b*) her maternity leave period is ended by the dismissal and the reason or principal reason for her dismissal is that she has given birth to a child or any other reason connected with her having given birth to a child;

(c) the reason or principal reason for her dismissal, where her contract of employment was terminated after the end of her maternity leave period, is that she took, or availed herself of the benefits of, maternity leave. For the purposes of this paragraph a woman 'takes maternity leave' if she is absent from work during her maternity leave period and a woman 'avails herself of the benefits of maternity leave', if, during her maternity leave period, she avails herself of the benefit of any of the terms and conditions of her employment preserved by s 33 of the EP(C)A 1978 during that period;

(d) the reason or principal reason for her dismissal, where:

(i) before the end of her maternity leave period, she gave to her employer a certificate from a registered medical practitioner stating that by reason of disease or bodily or mental disablement she would be incapable of work after the end of that period, and

(ii) her contract of employment was terminated within the four-week period following the end of her maternity leave period in circumstances where she continued to be incapable of work and the certificate relating to her incapacity remained current,

is that she has given birth to a child or any other reason connected with her having given birth to a child;

(e) the reason or principal reason for her dismissal is a requirement or recommendation such as is referred to in s 45(1) of the EP(C)A 1978 (ie suspension on maternity grounds); or

(f) her maternity leave period is ended by the dismissal and the reason or principal reason for her dismissal is that she is redundant and s 38 of the EP(C)A 1978 has not been complied with.

Where the employee is dismissed for any of the above reasons the dismissal is automatically unfair and it is not necessary for the tribunal to consider whether the employer acted reasonably or unreasonably under s 57(3) of the EP(C)A 1978.

There is no qualifying period required before the employee can bring a claim where it is shown the reason for the dismissal was an inadmissible reason, which includes one of those specified in s 60(a)–(e), above; s 64(3) and (4) of the EP(C)A 1978.

Section 60(a) of the EP(C)A 1978—'Pregnancy or any other reason connected with pregnancy'

Section 60(a) covers both the pre-natal and post-natal position. However, the pregnancy may be coincidental. It is not automatically unfair to dismiss a pregnant woman if the employer can show that she would have been dismissed even if she had not been pregnant. In such cases, the fairness of the dismissal will be considered in accordance with s 57(3) of the EP(C)A 1978. Where the employee is pregnant, and establishes a *prima facie* case that her dismissal was because of her pregnancy or a reason connected with it, the onus is on the employer to show that the dismissal is not automatically unfair within s 60(*a*) of the EP(C)A 1978. This may be difficult because poor attendance, illness or lack of capability may all stem from the pregnancy or by some other reason connected with the pregnancy.

In *George v Beecham Group* [1977] IRLR 43, George had been given a final warning, following frequent absences, that if she was absent again in the next six months she would be dismissed. She became pregnant, suffered a miscarriage and entered hospital. She was dismissed. It was held that the reason for her dismissal was the absence caused by her miscarriage—a reason connected with her pregnancy. The tribunal held that under s 60 of the EP(C)A 1978 there has to be a distinction between ill-health which is and ill-health which is not connected with the pregnancy.

If the employer did not know or believe that the employee was pregnant when he dismissed her the reason for the dismissal cannot be that the employee was pregnant nor can it be some other reason connected with her pregnancy. In *Del Monte Foods Ltd v Mundon* [1980] IRLR 224, Mundon had been away from work on several occasions because of gastro-enteritis or some other form of intestinal upset. She was again away from work due to some intestinal upset. The employer decided to dismiss her because of gastro-enteritis, although before they dismissed her they learned that she was pregnant. It was found that the reason for the dismissal was the gastro-enteritis.

The phrase 'or any other reason connected with her pregnancy' has been broadly interpreted. In *Stockton-on-Tees Borough Council v Brown* [1988] ICR 410, Brown was employed on a temporary contract as a care supervisor, but funding for the post was to be withdrawn. Three vacancies had arisen for the post of supervisor/instructor under a revised scheme. There were four applicants for the new post from among the staff who were to be made redundant and the employers applied selection criteria which included the applicants' ability to undertake their duties. Brown was pregnant. The employer considered that since she would require maternity leave and would be away from work for between six to eight weeks, she would be unable to fulfil the contract and was not offered a position as a supervisor/instructor.

The House of Lords held that the selection of a woman for redundancy because she is pregnant and will require maternity leave is a dismissal for a reason connected with her pregnancy within s 60 of the EP(C)A 1978. Her pregnancy was the reason why she is selected for dismissal on the grounds of redundancy. The reason for her dismissal was directly and intimately connected with her pregnancy. The House of Lords held that if an employer dismisses a woman because she is pregnant the dismissal is automatically unfair. The same principle should apply where the employee is selected for redundancy. The matter is now covered in s 59(1) and (2) of the EP(C)A 1978 which states that where the reason or principal reason for which the employee was selected for dismissal was an inadmissible reason, which includes any reason specified in s 60(*a*)–(*e*), then the dismissal shall be automatically unfair. In *Clayton v Vigers* [1989] ICR 713, Vigers was dismissed after the birth because the employer had been unable to employ a temporary assistant and had engaged a permanent replacement. It was held that her dismissal was automatically unfair under s 60 of the EP(C)A 1978. Following the decision in *Brown's* case, the EAT found that the background to the dismissal was the pregnancy or its after-effects. It considered that the words 'any other reason connected with her pregnancy', ought to be read widely so as to give full effect to the statute.

Section 60(*b*) of the EP(C)A 1978—Maternity leave ended by dismissal

'Childbirth' is defined in s 153(1) of the EP(C)A 1978 as the birth of a living child, or the birth of a child whether living or dead, after 24 weeks of pregnancy. This section will apply if the reason for dismissal is that quite simply an employee has had a baby, and even where an employee is taking maternity leave after giving birth to a dead child, or where she has given birth to a living child which subsequently dies during the maternity leave period. It will also apply if a woman is ill after childbirth, because of the birth of the child, but not if she is ill for any other reason, where the reason for the dismissal would fall under s 57(1) of the EP(C)A 1978—and reasonableness would have to be considered in the normal way. See Chapters 7 and 8.

Section 60 (*c*) of the EP(C)A 1978—Dismissal because she availed herself of maternity leave

For this section to apply a contract of employment must exist after the end of the maternity leave period, this being either a continuation of the contract under which she was employed prior to taking maternity leave and which contract continued during maternity leave by virtue of s 33, or a new contract under s 38A, or the contract which subsists under s 39(2) or s 44(1) of the EP(C)A 1978. There could be a new contract entered into during, or at the end of, the maternity leave period. The new contract could be any new contract for any job after the end of the maternity leave period.

A woman 'takes maternity leave' if she is absent from work during her maternity leave period. She avails herself of the benefits of maternity leave if during her maternity leave period she avails herself of the benefit of any of the terms and conditions of her employment preserved by s 33 during that period. It will be recalled that s 33 gives an employee who is absent from work at any time during her maternity leave, subject to giving the required notices and information to her employer, the benefit of the terms and conditions of employment which would have been applicable to her if she had not been absent and had not been pregnant or given birth to a child, excepting any entitlement to remuneration.

Section 60(*d*) of the EP(C)A 1978—dismissal while under doctor's certificate

This section applies where a contract of employment subsists after the end of the maternity leave period and that contract is terminated within four weeks following the end of the maternity leave period. The doctor's certificate must have been given to the employer before the end of the maternity leave period and the dismissal must have taken place while the certificate was still current at the time of the dismissal during the four-week period after the end of the maternity leave period. The certificate merely has to state that by reason of disease or bodily or mental disablement the employee would be incapable of work after the end of the maternity leave period. The certificate does not appear to have to specify that the disease or disablement has to be caused by the pregnancy or childbirth or any other reason connected with either of them. However, the reason for dismissal has to be that the employee has given birth to a child or any other reason connected with her having given birth to a child.

If it is not established that the reason for dismissal in these circumstances is that the employee has given birth to a child or is any other reason connected with her having given birth to a child then the dismissal will be potentially fair and reasonableness will be assessed in accordance with the provisions of s 57(3) of the EP(C)A 1978.

Section 60(*e*) of the EP(C)A 1978—suspension on maternity grounds

Sections 45–47 of the EP(C)A 1978 deal with suspension from work on maternity grounds. Section 60(*e*) states that the employee shall be automatically unfairly dismissed if the reason or principal reason for her dismissal is a requirement or recommendation such as is referred to in s 45(1), being (*a*) any requirement imposed by or under any relevant provision of any enactment or of any instrument made under any enactment, or (*b*) any recommendation in any relevant provision of a code of practice issued or approved under s 16 of the Health and Safety at Work etc Act 1974.

For the suspension provisions to operate the employee must continue to be employed by her employer.

Section 60(f) of the EP(C)A 1978—redundancy and s 38 of the EP(C)A 1978

The dismissal will be automatically unfair where the employee's maternity leave period is ended by the dismissal and the reason is that she is redundant and s 38 has not been complied with. For the meaning of redundancy see s 81 of the EP(C)A 1978 and Chapter 9. Also see 'Maternity Leave', 'Redundancy' at p 257 for s 38.

Written reasons for dismissal

In support of the amendments to the law concerning dismissal on the grounds of pregnancy, s 53 is amended. Employers who dismiss an employee while pregnant or during maternity leave will have to provide written reasons for the dismissal, whether or not they are requested, and irrespective of the employee's length of service.

Section 53(2A) of the EP(C)A 1978 provides that an employee shall be entitled (without making any request and irrespective of whether or not she has been employed for any period) to be provided by her employer with a written statement giving particulars of the reasons for her dismissal if she is dismissed (a) at any time while she is pregnant, or (b) after childbirth in circumstances in which her maternity leave period ends by reason of dismissal.

A complaint may be presented under s 53 to a tribunal by an employee on the ground that the employer unreasonably failed to provide a written statement.

See also Chapter 6, p 121 for further explanation of s 53.

Remedies

An employee who is unfairly dismissed under any of the *above* provisions has the same remedies available to her as in the case of any other employee who is unfairly dismissed: see s 68 of the EP(C)A 1978 and Chapter 16 (ie reinstatement, re-engagement, basic award and compensatory award).

A compensatory award has to be assessed without regard to the employee's right to return (ie as if she did not have such a possibility): para 6(4)(a) of Sched 2 to the EP(C)A 1978. However, if she exercises her right to return, she must refund any compensatory award or redundancy pay awarded to her, if the employer requests such repayment: para 6(4)(b).

If she returns to work the continuity of her employment will be preserved: para 10 of Sched 13 to the EP(C)A 1978. Since continuity of employment is preserved, then arguably in the event of a further unfair dismissal the employee would be entitled to a basic award based on the then period of continuous employment, although the employee has already claimed one basic award in respect of all or part of that period of continuous employment.

Rights in relation to suspension on maternity grounds

These rights, contained in ss 45, 46 and 47 of the EP(C)A 1978 are the rights to be offered suitable alternative work, if available, and to be paid normal remuneration while suspended. Such rights are outside the scope of this volume, but the reader's attention is drawn to them for completeness.

Sex discrimination

Until the changes brought about by TURERA 1993, a woman claiming the protection of s 60 (dismissal on ground of pregnancy) had to have two years' qualifying service. This has encouraged employees to allege sex discrimination, where no qualifying period is required. The new s 60, which does not require any qualifying period, was brought into force on 10 June 1994 (SI 1994 No 1365). There should not now be the same necessity to rely on sex discrimination, although some may still wish to bring such claims in order to obtain compensation for hurt feelings, which is not available in claims for unfair dismissal.

Difficulty has arisen in English law because of the need for a comparator under the SDA 1975. Since pregnancy is unique to women, it is argued that there is no such need. However, until recently the English courts have kept to the comparative approach, and required a pregnant women to be compared with a hypothetical man away from work for sickness. This was the approach in such cases as *Hayes v Malleable Working Men's Club and Institute* [1985] ICR 703. The position of the European Court of Justice has been more straightforward. The two leading European cases are *Dekker* and *Hertz*.

In *Dekker v Stichting Vormingscentrum Voor Jonge Volwassenen (VJV-Centrum) Plus* [1991] IRLR 27, the European Court of Justice held that to refuse to employ a woman or to dismiss her because she is pregnant was a breach of Directive 76/207 (the Equal Treatment Directive), since it was direct discrimination on the grounds of sex. It was not necessary to compare the treatment of a pregnant woman with that of a hypothetical man. The case involved a Directive and is as such enforceable by employees of the state. In applying national law a tribunal is required to interpret national law in the light of the wording and purpose of the Directive that the law was passed to implement. Although the SDA 1975 was not passed to implement the Equal Treatment Directive and the House of Lords has held in *Duke v GEC Reliance Ltd* [1988] ICR 339, that it has no obligation to distort the meaning of the SDA 1975 in order to enforce the Directive against an individual, there would be no distortion of the SDA 1975 Act as far as the provisions relating to pregnancy are concerned. First, the Act does not stipulate that there must be a comparator and secondly, the Act allows positive discrimination in connection with pregnancy or childbirth. Arguably, national courts should interpret national law so as to give effect to the wording and purpose of any directive: see *Marleasing SA v LA Comercial International de Alimentacion SA* [1992] CMLR 305.

In *Handels-Og Kontorfunktionaererrnes Forbund i Danmark (acting for Hertz) v Dansk Arbejdsgiverforening (acting for Aldi Marked K/S)* [1991] IRLR 31, the European Court of Justice found that a woman is protected from dismissal because of absence for a reason connected with the pregnancy or confinement during pregnancy and any maternity leave to which she has a right under national law. If she is ill after her maternity leave there is no distinction under the Directive between illness which arises out of pregnancy or childbirth and any other illness. There is some protection under s 60 of the EP(C)A 1978.

In *Webb v EMO Air Cargo (UK) Ltd* [1993] IRLR 27, the House of Lords referred to the European Court of Justice the following questions:

> Is it discrimination on grounds of sex contrary to Directive 76/207 for an employer to dismiss a female employee ('the appellant'):
>
> (a) whom he engaged for the specific purpose of replacing (after training) another female employee during the latter's forthcoming maternity leave,
> (b) when, very shortly after appointment, the employer discovers that the appellant herself will be absent on maternity leave during the maternity leave of the other employee, and the employer dismisses her because he needs the job holder to be at work during that period,
> (c) had the employer known of the pregnancy of the appellant at the date of appointment, she would not have been appointed, and
> (d) the employer would similarly have dismissed a male employee engaged for this purpose who required leave of absence at the relevant time for medical or other reasons?'

The European Court of Justice has now ((1994) *The Times* 15 July) given the answer as follows: 'The Equal Treatment Directive precludes dismissal of an emloyee who is recruited for an unlimited term with a view, initially, to replacing another employee during the latter's maternity leave and who cannot do so because shortly after recruitment she is herself found to be pregnant.'

If Webb had been dismissed after the introduction of the new maternity leave period provisions she would have had a claim for an automatically unfair dismissal under s 60(*a*) of the EP(C)A 1978.

Chapter 11

Dismissal and the Trade Union Member

This chapter considers the dismissed employee's position as against his employer where the issues involved are the membership of an independent trade union or the non-membership of a trade union or taking part in the activities of an independent trade union.

General

Section 152(1) of the TULR(C)A 1992 (re-enacting s 58(1) of the EP(C)A 1978) provides that the dismissal of an employee shall be automatically unfair if the reason or, if more than one, the principal reason was that the employee:

    (a) was, or proposed to become, a member of an independent trade union, or

    (b) had taken part, or proposed to take part, in the activities of an independent trade union at an appropriate time, or

    (c) was not a member of any trade union, or of a particular trade union, or of one of a number of particular trade unions, or had refused or proposed to refuse to become or remain a member.

The tribunal does not have to consider whether the dismissal was reasonable in all the circumstances under s 57(3) of the EP(C)A 1978. The employer is given no opportunity of putting forward a potential defence under that sub-section.

It must be noted that paras (a) and (b) refer to 'an independent trade union', but there is no such limitation in para (c). The definition of 'an independent trade union' is contained in s 5 of the TULR(C)A 1992. For an example of a dismissal under the former s 58(1)(c), see *Transport and General Workers' Union v Howard* [1992] ICR 106.

Section 152(1) (a) and (b) will be interpreted strictly. In *Carrington and Others v Therm-A-Stor Ltd* [1983] ICR 208, the TGWU wrote to the company requesting recognition of the union. Shortly thereafter the company decided to make 20 employees, all TGWU members, redundant. The selection of the employees was carried out by charge hands who were given no instructions as to the method of selection. Union membership played no part in selection by the charge hands.

The Court of Appeal found that the employees were dismissed by the company because of the union's request for recognition. It did not accept the submission put forward on behalf of the employees that s 152 should be construed so as to recognise a collective dimension; nor did it accept the contention that since the employees were members of the union and the reason for the dismissal was the activities of that union (the request for recognition), the reason for the dismissals was the employees' union membership or activities, albeit with others. The Court of Appeal held that s 152(1)(*a*) and (*b*):

> is concerned solely with the dismissal of *an* employee and provides that it shall be regarded as unfair if the reason was that the (ie *that*) employee had done or proposed to do one or more specified things. The reason why each of the . . . employees was dismissed had nothing to do with anything which the employee concerned had personally done or proposed to do.

In *Crosville Motor Services Ltd v Ashfield* [1986] IRLR 475, Ashfield, a bus driver, was dismissed ostensibly because of a ticket irregularity. However, he had made it clear that unless there were changes in union policy and organisation he would leave the union, the TGWU, which had sole bargaining rights with the company. The tribunal held that the reason for his dismissal was his proposed refusal to remain a member of the union. The EAT upheld the decision of the tribunal and held that s 152(1)(*c*) could apply where the proposed refusal to remain a member of the union was conditional or contingent.

It is not necessary that the trade union should be one recognised by the employer: *Lyon v St James Press Ltd* [1976] ICR 413. Nor is it material that the employee has not made up his mind which trade union to join: *Cotter v Lynch Bros* [1972] ICR 263.

Onus of proof

The onus is placed upon the employer to show the reason for the employee's dismissal. Where the employee alleges that his dismissal was for one of the reasons set out in s 152(1) of the TULR(C)A 1992 the burden of proof is not reversed. The onus is still upon the employer to establish the reason for the dismissal. If the employer produces evidence to show a reason for dismissal then the burden passes to the employee to show that there is a real issue as to whether that was the true reason. The burden is a lighter burden than that imposed upon the employer, but the employee cannot simply assert that the reason put forward by the employer was not the true reason. The evidential burden upon him is to produce some evidence that casts doubt upon the employer's reason. The graver the allegation by the employee, the heavier will be the burden: *Maund v Penwith DC* [1984] ICR 143; see also *Shannon v Michelin (Belfast) Ltd* [1981] IRLR 505.

However, where the employee does not have the necessary qualifying period of employment to bring a claim for unfair dismissal and argues that the reason for his dismissal is one falling within s 152(1), the onus is upon him to prove the reason for his dismissal: *Smith v The Chairman and Other Councillors of Hayle Town Council* [1978] IRLR 413. The dissenting judgment of Lord Denning in this case recognises the difficulties facing the employee in successfully proving that the reason or principal reason is one falling within s 152(1). Where there is more than one reason, a reason within s 152(1) has to be the principal reason so that, for instance, anti-union sentiment, which is not the principal reason would not be sufficient. See *Smith*'s case, *above*. See also *The Marley Tile Co Ltd v Shaw* [1980] IRLR 25.

Once the employee has presented his case, (where the onus is on him because he does not have the qualifying period of employment), the employer has to present his case. It has been suggested that it will only be in exceptional circumstances that the tribunal will be justified in not hearing the employer's evidence because, although the employee's allegations may at first instance appear weak, the evidence of the employer may also be weak and so bolster the employee's case: *H Goodwin Ltd v Fitzmaurice* [1977] IRLR 393. This was a view in the early days of the legislation. The onus is on the employee. If he does not show a *prima facie* case, it is quite likely that the tribunal will accede to a submission on behalf of the employer.

In deciding whether or not the reason or principal reason for the dismissal is within s 152(1)(*b*), the Court of Appeal, in *The Marley Tile Co Ltd v Shaw*, *above* suggested that the tribunal should determine the following:

(*a*) For what reason or reasons did the company dismiss the employee and, if more than one, what was the principal reason?

(*b*) Was the conduct of the employee which formed the only or principal reason for his dismissal, trade union activities?

(*c*) If so, was it with the consent, express or implied, of the company . . .?

(*d*) If with implied consent only, then as a matter of construction of [s 152(2)(*b*) of the TULR(C)A 1992] does consent include an implied consent or must it be express?

In *CGB Publishing v Killey* [1993] 520, the tribunal found that if Killey 'had not been a trade union member he would not have been dismissed'. However, the EAT held that this 'but for' test was wrong because it did not raise any question as to the employer's state of mind at the time of the dismissal, nor does the 'but for' principle approach the question of causation. Some further guidance can be gained from *Driver v Cleveland Structural Engineering Co Ltd* [1994] ICR 372.

The statutory provisions

Trade union

A trade union means an organisation (whether permanent or temporary) which either—

    (*a*) consists wholly or mainly of workers of one or more descriptions and whose principal purposes include the regulation of relations between workers of that description or those descriptions and employers or employers' associations; or

    (*b*) consists wholly or mainly of—

        (i) constituent or affiliated organisations which fulfil the conditions specified in para (*a*) *above* (or themselves consist wholly or mainly of constituent or affiliated organisations which fulfil those conditions) or,

        (ii) representatives of such constituent or affiliated organisations,

and whose principal purposes include the regulation of relations between workers and employers or between workers and employers' associations, or the regulation of relations between its constituent or affiliated organisations: s 1 of the TULR(C)A 1992.

'Independent trade union'

An 'independent trade union' means a trade union which:

    (*a*) is not under the domination or control of an employer or group of employers or of one or more employers' associations, and

    (*b*) is not liable to interference by an employer or any such group or association (arising out of the provision of financial or material support or by any other means whatsoever) tending towards such control;

and, in relation to a trade union, 'independence' is to be construed accordingly: s 5 of the TULR(C)A 1992.

The phrase 'liable to interference by an employer ... tending towards such control' has been interpreted as having the meaning 'vulnerable to interference' in that the union is exposed to the risk of interference. In deciding whether or not the union is independent it may be relevant to enquire whether there is a possibility of interference by the employer tending towards control of the union. If there is a risk which is recognisable and not insignificant, then it is likely that the union is not independent: *The Certification Officer v Squibb UK Staff Association* [1979] IRLR 75. See also *A Monk & Co Staff Association v Certification Officer* [1980] IRLR 431.

Membership of an independent trade union

Where an employee is dismissed because he refuses to transfer from one independent trade union to another independent trade union, this is not a reason within s 152(1): *Rath v Cruden Construction Ltd* [1982] ICR 60. In *Discount Tobacco and Confectionery Ltd v Armitage* [1990] IRLR 15, (approved by Dillon LJ in *Palmer v Associated British Ports* and *Wilson v Associated Newspapers Ltd* [1993] IRLR 336. However, in both these cases leave has been given to appeal to the House of Lords), Armitage enlisted the help of her union official to obtain a written statement of her terms and conditions of employment. The tribunal found that the reason she was dismissed was her union membership. The EAT held that the activities of the trade union officer in elucidating the terms of employment was simply the visible manifestation of trade union membership. It is an incident of union membership and no distinction should be drawn between membership of the union on the one hand and making use of the essential services of the union on the other. If such a distinction were drawn then s 152(1)(*a*) would have to be construed without regard to the consequences of union membership. To construe it so narrowly would be to emasculate the provision. Armitage's dismissal would now be automatically unfair under s 60A of the EP(C)A 1978 as she was asserting a statutory right.

Activities of an independent trade union

'Activities' are not defined in the legislation. Guidance can be obtained from reported cases which, although involving an interpretation of earlier legislation, are still relevant. Activities in s 152(1)(*b*) of the TULR(C)A 1992 means activities of a particular or specific union, not activities of trade unions generally: *Fitzpatrick v British Railways Board* [1990] ICR 674, following *National Coal Board v Ridgway and Another* [1987] ICR 641. The contrast, on this feature, with membership and non-membership cases must be noted.

In *Brennan and Ging v Ellward (Lancs) Ltd* [1976] IRLR 378, the EAT held that in deciding whether an employee is taking part in the activities of a trade union the tribunal should make a list of all the acts and facts relied upon as constituting the activities and whether the employee is a union representative. If the common-sense view is that these factors constitute the activities of an independent trade union, then the tribunal must so find. It is not fatal that these acts are also for the employee's own benefit. The EAT did not accept that the activities must be those of a member of the union authorised to carry out those acts. A union member who during his lunch-break sought to recruit further employees as members, would be engaged in the activities of a trade union.

In *Lyon v St James Press Ltd* [1976] ICR 413, Lyon and another secretly organised the formation of a chapel of the National Union of Journalists among the company's employees. Not all the employees were invited to join, which led to unrest. The EAT held that the acts done by Lyon and his associate were done in the course of taking part in the activities of a trade union, and their dismissal was unfair. However, the EAT commented that not 'every such act is protected. For example, wholly unreasonable, extraneous or malicious acts done in support of trade union activities might be a ground for dismissal which would not be unfair.'

In *Dixon and Shaw v West Ella Developments Ltd* [1978] ICR 856, the EAT held that the interpretation of activities was not restricted 'to such matters as membership meetings and activities involving status as trade unionists'. The words are 'activities of an independent trade union' not 'trade union activities'. The EAT found that 'the words "trade union" are not being used in an adjectival sense; what is being looked for are the activities of a trade union'. It agreed with an example given in *Brennan and Ging*'s case *above*: 'if a man were dismissed because he had sought the advice of a union representative on the shop floor, and had sought to apply approved union practice, such conduct could we think, in some circumstances, arguably at least fall within [s 152(1)(*b*) of the TULR(C)A 1992]'. The EAT further found that 'arguably at least' could be expressed as 'strongly arguably'. Criticism of union policy by a group of union members can constitute an activity of a trade union: *British Airways Engine Overhaul Ltd v Francis* [1981] IRLR 9.

In *Chant v Aquaboats Ltd* [1978] ICR 643, it was held that organising a petition on safety standards which was the act of a single trade unionist was not within the phrase 'activities of an independent trade union'. The EAT held:

> It is, of course, open to employees in any firm to make representations . . . to their employers about machinery which is unsafe. The mere fact that one or two of the employees making representations happen to be trade unionists, and the mere fact that the spokesman of the men happens to be a trade unionist does not make such representations a trade union activity.

In *Drew v St Edmundsbury BC* [1980] ICR 513, it was held that an individual's complaints about matters of health and safety were not activities of a trade union. The employee was carrying out his own activities and not the activities of a trade union. See also the *obiter* remarks of Eveleigh LJ and Stephenson LJ in *The Marley Tile Co Ltd v Shaw* [1980] IRLR 25, where they doubted whether an accredited shop steward calling a meeting in working hours was engaging in the activities of a trade union. Again, where two chapel officers were engaged in concerted resistance to management culminating in a breach of a collective agreement incorporated as a term of their contract they were not engaged in the activities of a trade union. They were acting on their own initiative without the endorsement of a chapel meeting. It was questionable whether their actions had the support of the majority of the chapel members and it was just as likely that they were representing only themselves in the action they took: *Stokes and Roberts v Wheeler-Green Ltd* [1979] IRLR 211; see also *Carrington and Others v Therm-A-Stor* [1983] ICR 208, from which it is clear the activities must be the activities of the employee who is dismissed.

Occasionally the question has arisen as to whether the employee who is taking part in a strike or other industrial action is taking part or proposing to take part in the activities of an independent trade union. In *Winnett v Seamarks Brothers Ltd* [1978] ICR 1240, it was considered that the industrial action in this case was not synonymous with the activities of a trade union. Where the employee is dismissed because he is on strike the facts may show that he is dismissed for taking part in a strike rather than taking part or proposing to take part in the activities of a trade union. In *Drew*'s case *above*, the EAT went further and emphasised the difference parliament intended between cases where the employee is dismissed because he takes part in activities of a trade union and cases where he is dismissed while he is engaged in a strike or other industrial action. See s 238 of the TULR(C)A 1992 (previously s 62 EP(C)A) and Chapter 12 which deals with dismissal during a strike or other industrial action. The EAT considered it would be impossible for an employee to be both within s 152(1) and s 238.

In *Rasool v Hepworth Pipe Co Ltd (No 2)* [1980] IRLR 137, it was held that while an unauthorised meeting at the employer's premises in working hours to discuss wage negotiations, interrupting the manufacturing process of the employer, was not industrial action, it might be regarded as taking part in the activities of a trade union.

In *Fitzpatrick v British Railways Board* [1992] IRLR 221, the Court of Appeal held that s 152(1) could apply to trade union activities which occurred before the employment commenced, because an employer who dismisses an employee having become aware of previous trade union activities will almost inevitably be dismissing him because he fears the employee will take part in trade union activities while in his employment. Compare this with *Birmingham DC v Beyer* [1978] 1 All ER 910, where it was held that deceit in obtaining employment by covering up previous trade union activities may not fall within the section.

In *Britool Limited v Roberts* [1993] IRLR 481, the EAT held that a tribunal had not erred by concluding that a union officer was unfairly selected for redundancy by reason of trade union membership and activities where he had been an important and influential member in leading a strike. Although actual participation in a strike, whether as a leader or otherwise, will rarely, if ever, constitute an activity, leading a strike embraces not only the activities of strike leaders, while the strike is in operation, but also the preliminary planning and consultation stage. It is the latter which formed the basis of the tribunal decision which was approved by the EAT.

In practice, while action taken by a trade union official may fall within the definition of activities of an independent trade union, the same action taken by an individual member may not.

In determining what is meant by activities of a trade union, some assistance may be gained from s 146 of the TULR(C)A 1992 (previously s 23 of the EP(C)A 1978). This section provides that every employee shall have the right not to have action short of dismissal taken against him by the employer for the purposes of preventing or deterring him from being, or seeking to become, a member of an independent trade union or penalising him for doing so; or preventing or deterring him from taking part in activities of an independent trade union at any appropriate time, or penalising him for doing so; or compelling him to be or become a member of any trade union or of a particular trade union or of one of a number of particular trade unions. In *Dixon and Shaw v West Ella Developments Ltd, above*, the EAT interpreted s 146 as pertaining to activities 'of a fairly varied kind'. See also s 168 of the TULR(C)A 1992 which deals with the trade union official's right to time off for carrying out trade union duties and s 170 of the TULR(C)A 1992 which deals with the employee's right to time off for trade union activities, as well as the Code of Practice, Time Off for Trade Union Duties and Activities, (SI 1991 No 968) which came into force on 13 May 1991. In *Luce v Bexley London Borough Council* [1990] ICR 591, it was held that time off to attend a lobby of parliament to convey political or ideological objections to legislation was not taking part in trade union activities under what is now s 170.

Appropriate time

The 'appropriate time', in relation to an employee taking part in the activities of a trade union, means time which either:

(*a*) is outside his working hours; or

(*b*) is a time within his working hours at which, in accordance with arrangements agreed with or consent given by his employer, it is permissible for him to take part in those activities;

and 'working hours', in relation to an employee, means any time when, in accordance with his contract of employment, he is required to be at work: s 152(2) of the TULR(C)A 1992.

The employee's right to take part in the activities of a trade union may be a contractual right: *Miller v Rafique* [1975] IRLR 70.

'Working hours' do not include lunch, tea or other breaks during which, by contract or custom, the employee is not required to be actually at work. Nor do they include the pre-start time, or post-finish time presence on the premises: '... at work' means 'actually at work ...', ie actually working: per Lord Reid in *Post Office v Union of Post Office Workers* [1974] 9 ITR 136.

The arrangements or the consent under s 152(2)(*b*) will usually be express. Depending upon the facts of the case it seems there may be circumstances where consent is implied. In *Zucker v Astrid Jewels Ltd* [1978] ICR 1088, the EAT found that conversation about trade union matters during working hours may be trade union activities within working hours undertaken in accordance with arrangements agreed with or consent given by the employer, since these might be informal and the employer had permitted employees to converse during working hours. Further it found, following the decision of the House of Lords in *Post Office v Union of Post Office Workers above*, that meal breaks might be times during which an employee although paid was not required to be at work and was not doing what she did during working hours. Thus meal breaks might be an appropriate time even if there were no arrangement or consent.

However, in *The Marley Tile Co Ltd v Shaw* [1980] IRLR 25, the Court of Appeal, reversing the decision of the tribunal and the EAT, held that a tribunal must be careful before finding that consent is implied. While recognising there may be circumstances where on the facts consent is implied, consent could not be implied in this case where an unaccredited shop steward called a meeting of the maintenance men in working hours to consider a problem which did not call for a desperately urgent solution. The employer remained silent; by so doing he was not deemed to have given consent. Nor could consent be implied by extension from other factories in the group, nor by custom and practice. The suggested exclusion of custom and practice appears to conflict with *Post Office v Union of Post Office Workers, above*. It is suggested that custom and practice must be some evidence, at least, of implied consent.

'Time' is not restricted to time with that employer. See *Fitzpatrick's* case *above*, but fraud in covering up earlier activities may be outside s 152(1). See *Beyer's* case *above* and see generally s 137 of the TULR(C)A 1992 (formerly s 1 of the EA 1990).

If the activities have not taken place at an appropriate time or where it was proposed that they would not take place at an appropriate time, an employee's dismissal in such circumstances will be outside s 152(1), and the reason for and the reasonableness of the dismissal will be considered in the normal way.

The employees' objection

Section 152(3) of the TULR(C)A 1992 provides that where the reason or one of the reasons for the dismissal of an employee was:

(a) his refusal, or proposed refusal, to comply with a requirement (whether or not imposed by his contract of employment or in writing) that, in the event of his not being a member of any trade union or of a particular trade union or of one of a number of particular trade unions, he must make one or more payments; or

(b) his objection, or proposed objection (however expressed) to the operation of a provision (whether or not forming part of his contract of employment or in writing) under which, in the event mentioned in para (a), his employer is entitled to deduct one or more sums from the remuneration payable to him in respect of his employment;

that reason shall be treated as falling within s 152(1)(c) of the TULR(C)A 1992.

References in s 152 of the TULR(C)A 1992 to a trade union include references to a particular branch or section of the union.

There are two features of s 152(3) that need emphasising: (a) it applies to any trade union, and is not restricted to an independent trade union, and (b) it applies if the refusal or objection is one of the reasons for dismissal—it need not be the principal reason.

Interim relief

See also Chapter 16, 'Remedies' and Chapter 18, 'Time Limits'.

An employee who presents a claim to a tribunal for unfair dismissal under 152(1) of the TULR(C)A 1992 may apply for interim relief: s 161 of the TULR(C)A 1992. A certificate supporting the application is required and must contain the information set out in s 161(3)(a) and (b) of the TULR(C)A 1992. Unlike every other time limit in connection with presenting complaints, this one commences 'immediately following' the effective date of termination, and not 'beginning with' it. However, there is no power whatsoever for the time to be extended, either for the presentation of the application, or the certificate, although the tribunal may, in certain circumstances, in its discretion allow amendments after the expiration of the period: *Barley v Amey Roadstone Corporation Ltd* [1987] ICR 546. An authorised official is one authorised by the union to act in these cases: s 161(4) of the TULR(C)A 1992.

No form of certificate is prescribed and it appears that provided there is substantial compliance with the statutory provisions this will be sufficient. The certificate must clearly set out the reasons which must relate to trade union membership or activities: *Stone v Charrington and*

Co [1977] ICR 248. A loosely worded application and certificate may not comply with the relevant provisions: *Farmeary v Veterinary Drug Co Ltd* [1976] IRLR 322. However, the EAT has warned against too great a concentration on technicality: *Bradley v Edward Ryde and Sons* [1979] ICR 488. The signatory need not state that he is an authorised official. In the absence of a challenge, the tribunal is entitled to proceed on the basis that he is authorised. If the signatory's authority is challenged the onus is on him to establish his authority: *Sulemany v Habib Bank Ltd* [1983] ICR 60. Documents purporting to be an authorisation of an official by a trade union to act for these purposes shall be taken to be such an authorisation unless the contrary is proved: s 161(5) of the TULR(C)A 1992.

No application can be made under this provision where it is contended that the employee has been unfairly selected for dismissal in a redundancy situation for one of those reasons specified in s 152(1) of the TULR(C)A 1992: *Farmeary v Veterinary Drug Co Ltd, above.*

The onus is upon the employer to establish the reason for dismissal, unless (as happens in many interim relief cases) the employee has less than two years' service. The onus is on the employee in a claim for interim relief. It is sufficient for the employee to discharge the onus of proof in a claim for interim relief if he can show the tribunal that it is likely that the reason for his dismissal is trade union membership or activities. 'Likely' means that he has quite a good chance of succeeding in a claim for unfair dismissal. It is necessary for the employee to achieve a higher degree of certainty than showing that he has a reasonable chance of success. It has been described (rather unjudicially) as having a 'pretty good chance': *Taplin v C Shippam Ltd* [1978] IRLR 450. Where the employee seeks to show that the reason for his dismissal is his union membership or activities, the employer, to defeat a claim for interim relief, must show a reason or principal reason for the dismissal other than trade union membership or activities. Where he alleges some other reason he must produce evidence to support it. It is not sufficient to show that the evidence was such that he could have dismissed for that reason.

Pressure on employer to dismiss

In determining the reason, or principal reason, why the employee was dismissed or whether the reason or principal reason is within s 57(1)(*b*) of the EP(C)A 1978 or whether the employer acted reasonably in dismissing the employee, no account should be taken of certain pressure put upon the employer: s 63 of the EP(C)A 1978. The tribunal is not entitled to take into account any pressure put on the employer by the calling, organising, procuring or financing of a strike or other industrial action, or threatening to do so: s 63(*a*) of the EP(C)A 1978, and any such question shall be determined as if no such pressure had been exercised: s 63(*b*) of the EP(C)A 1978. The effect may be a fiction. The employer may dismiss because of a threatened strike and for no other reason. The tribunal is precluded from taking this into account in deciding the reason and so the employer will fail. In *McColm v Agnew and Lithgow Ltd* [1976] IRLR 13, the tribunal was unhappy with this fiction. However, in *Hazells Offset Ltd v Luckett* [1977] IRLR 430, the EAT found that although s 63 might produce a fiction, nonetheless it was bound by it and could not take into account industrial pressure.

Although the employer is not entitled to plead in his aid pressure placed upon him to dismiss, it may be open to him to argue that the pressure placed on him was due in part to the employee's fault and that he had contributed to his dismissal, for the purposes of a reduction in compensation: *Hazells Offset Ltd v Luckett, above.*

In *Ford Motor Co Ltd v Hudson* [1978] IRLR 66, the EAT in considering s 63, said that it was not necessary for the employee to show that those exerting pressure on the employers explicitly sought the employee's dismissal, but that conduct short of that might amount to pressure to dismiss. It suggested as an appropriate test:

> Was the pressure exerted on the employers such that it could be foreseen that it would be likely to result in the dismissal of those employees in respect of whom the pressure was being brought?

It may be that the pressure exerted upon the employer results in the employer unilaterally changing the terms of the employee's contract: *Colwyn Borough Council v Dutton* [1980] IRLR 420.

Section 160 of the TULR(C)A 1992 allows the employer who dismisses an employee because of pressure placed on him by a trade union or other person, to join that trade union or other person as a party to the proceedings. The pressure envisaged is referred to in s 160 and must have been exercised because the employee was not a member of any trade union, or of a particular trade union, or of one of a number of particular trade unions. Where the employer is ordered to pay compensation to an employee he may recover a contribution or indemnity from the third party: s 160 of the TULR(C)A 1992.

In addition to the employer's rights the employee is given the power to join a trade union or other person as a party to proceedings where he alleges that the trade union or other person put pressure on the employer to dismiss him because he was not a member of any trade union or of a particular trade union or of one of a number of particular trade unions. The pressure is that referred to in s 160. The third party may be ordered to pay the whole of any award, or part of any award, with the employer paying the other part, as the tribunal may consider just and equitable in the circumstances. For a more detailed consideration of these provisions see Chapter 16.

Chapter 12

Dismissals During Strikes and Lock-outs

General

Under the TULR(C)A 1992, where an employee, who is referred to as the complainant, claims that he has been unfairly dismissed by his employer and at the date of dismissal the employer was conducting or instituting a lock-out, or the complainant was taking part in a strike or other industrial action, a tribunal has no jurisdiction to determine whether the dismissal was fair or unfair, unless it is shown that one or more relevant employees of the same employer have not been dismissed, or that any such employee has, before the expiry of the period of three months beginning with that employee's date of dismissal, been offered re-engagement and that the complainant has not been offered re-engagement: s 238(1) and (2) of the TULR(C)A 1992.

If the reason, or the principal reason for the dismissal, or in a redundancy case, for selecting the employee for dismissal was one of those specified in s 57(A) or s 60 of the EP(C)A 1978 (dismissal in health and safety and maternity cases) then a tribunal does have jurisdiction unrestricted by the conditions in s 238(2): s 238(2A) of the TULR(C)A 1992. Section 60 was brought into force on 10 June 1994 (SI 1994 No 1365). Section 238(3) confirms that nothing in s 237 (dismissal of those taking part in unofficial industrial action) affects the question 'who are relevant employees?' for the purposes of s 238. The effect of this provision is that if the employee takes unofficial action and is dismissed he cannot bring an action for unfair dismissal even if he is selectively dismissed or if there is selective re-engagement.

Where the complainant claims unfair dismissal and shows that he has not been offered re-engagement where one or more other relevant employees have been offered re-engagement (see s 238(2)(*b*), ss 57–61 of the EP(C)A 1978, and ss 152 and 153 of the TULR(C)A 1992 take effect as if instead of referring to the reason or principal reason for which the complainant was dismissed they refer to the reason or principal reason for which the complainant has not been offered re-engagement: 239(3) of the TULR(C)A 1992.

For the purposes of s 238 'date of dismissal' means, where the employee's contract of employment was terminated by notice, the date on which the employer's notice was given, and in any other case the effective date of termination: s 238(5) of the TULR(C)A 1992.

For the purposes of s 238 'relevant employees' means in relation to a lock-out, employees who were directly interested in the dispute in contemplation or furtherance of which the lock-out occurred, and in relation to a strike or other industrial action, those employees at the establishment who were taking part in the action at the complainant's date of dismissal. 'Establishment' means the establishment of the employer at or from which the complainant works: s 238(3) of the TULR(C)A 1992.

The employer may treat each establishment as a separate unit thereby overcoming the problem where the employer has several establishments. Where there are different establishments it may be difficult for the employer to identify accurately which employees are taking part in a strike or other industrial action and who have to be dismissed.

No definition of establishment has been laid down in the TULR(C)A 1992 or the EP(C)A 1978, but s 188 of the TULR(C)A 1992 (duty of employer to consult trade union representatives) (formerly s 99 of the EPA 1975) does refer to an establishment. The definition of establishment under this section has been considered: see *Barratt Developments (Bradford) Ltd v UCATT* [1978] ICR 319, but it is clear from this decision that it is difficult to lay down guidelines for what is essentially a question of fact and the meaning of establishment must be left to the tribunal to decide in the particular case.

Any reference to an offer of re-engagement is a reference to an offer made either by the original employer, his successor or an associated employer to re-engage an employee either in the job which he held immediately before the date of dismissal or in a different job which would be reasonably suitable in his case: s 238(4) of the TULR(C)A 1992.

The effect of s 238 is that a tribunal can only consider a dismissal where the employee is locked out, or is engaged in a strike or other industrial action, if it can be shown that the employee has been subjected to discriminatory treatment in the matter of dismissal or re-engagement: see *Heath v JF Longman (Meat Salesmen) Ltd* [1973] 2 All ER 1228 and *Faust and Others v Power Packing Casemakers Ltd* [1983] IRLR 117.

Definitions

Although many of the following cases were decided under earlier legislation, they are none the less relevant in considering s 238.

'Lock-out'

Paragraph 24(1) of Sched 13 to the EP(C)A 1978 defines a 'lock-out' as the closing of a place of employment, or the suspension of work, or the refusal by an employer to continue to employ any number of persons employed by him in consequence of a dispute, done with a view to compelling those persons, or to aid another employer in compelling persons employed by him, to accept terms and conditions of or affecting employment. It should be noted that this definition is applied by statute only to Sched 13. However, the statutory definition was applied in *Fisher v York Trailer Co Ltd* [1979] ICR 834. In this case the company sought an undertaking from 34 employees that they would work normally. They were told that if they did not sign the undertaking they would be suspended from the start of the next shift. They did not sign, but the following day held a meeting to discuss the matter. All but seven of the employees signed. The seven were treated as suspended, and although they attended the factory they were not permitted to work. They were given another opportunity to sign an undertaking; they refused, and were dismissed. The EAT held that the dismissals had occurred during a lock-out. In *Express and Star Ltd v Bunday and Others* [1988] ICR 379, the majority of the Court of Appeal held that whether there has been a lock-out or a strike is a question of fact. Whether the presence of a particular element is necessary before there can be a lock-out may be a mixed question of law and fact or a question of pure fact. The Court of Appeal held that the definition of a lock-out contained in para 24(1) of Sched 13 affords guidance in determining what is meant by a lock-out. It is not a statutory definition of a lock-out to be applied generally. Whether the employer has breached the contract of employment is a relevant consideration in determining whether there has been a lock-out, but a breach is not an essential ingredient for there to be a lock-out. The statutory definition presupposes the continuance of the contract of employment between the parties. For earlier cases where the statutory definition contained in para 24(1) of Sched 13 was not followed: see *Rasool v Hepworth Pipe Co Ltd (No 2)* [1980] IRLR 137 and *McCormick v Horsepower Ltd* [1980] IRLR 182. See also the definition of a strike *below*.

In *Brown v William Press and Son Ltd* [1975] IRLR 8, a tribunal having regard to the *Shorter Oxford English Dictionary* found a lock-out to mean 'a refusal on the part of an employer, or employers acting in concert, to furnish work to their operatives except on conditions accepted by the latter collectively'. A dictionary definition may be a useful indication of what is a lock-out, but it is not incorporated in the statute: see *Bunday's* case, *above*.

'Dispute'

Under s 238 of the TULR(C)A 1992, relevant employees in relation
to a lock-out means employees who were directly interested in the
dispute in contemplation or furtherance of which the lock-out occurred.

'Dispute' is not defined in s 238, but this section falls within Part V
which is headed *'Protection of acts in contemplation or furtherance of
trade dispute'* and s 244 defines a trade dispute. It appears that 'dispute'
would be wider than 'trade dispute' and would include it. Section
244(1) defines a 'trade dispute' as a dispute between workers and their
employer which relates wholly or mainly to terms and conditions of
employment or the physical conditions of work; engagement, non-
engagement or termination or suspension of employment or duties of
workers; allocation of work or duties; discipline; membership or non-
membership of a trade union; facilities for officials of a trade union;
and negotiating or consulting machinery or other procedures for dealing with the foregoing or with recognition issues. A worker in relation
to a dispute with an employer means a worker employed by that
employer, or a person who has ceased to be employed by that
employer, where his employment was terminated in connection with
the dispute, or the termination of his employment was one of the
circumstances giving rise to the dispute: s 244(5). A 'worker' means an
employee, including the employees of government departments other
than naval, military or air force personnel (or the police service: see
s 280 of the TULR(C)A 1992), as well as any person who undertakes
to perform personally any work or services for another party to the
contract where the other party is not his professional client: s 296(1)
of the TULR(C)A 1992.

Strike and industrial action

Strike

This is defined in s 246 of the TULR(C)A 1992 as 'any concerted
stoppage of work'. Lord Denning used the same description in *Tramp
Shipping Corporation v Greenwich Marine Inc* [1975] 2 All ER 989.
Thus, a strike must be more than a one-man withdrawal of labour. The
essence of a strike is its collectivity. It is arguable that as in the case
of a lock-out, a strike is not restricted to a strike in contemplation or
furtherance of a trade dispute. It extends to any dispute.

In *Hindle Gears Ltd v McGinty and Others* [1984] IRLR 477, the
EAT held that the tribunals are sole arbiters of what does or does not
amount to taking part in strike action. While the question whether or
not the employer was aware of any particular conduct on the part of
an employee would be relevant to determining whether that conduct
amounted to taking part in a strike, it was not a principle of law that

the employee's participation in strike action had to be known to the employer before it could be capable of constituting conduct amounting to taking part in the action, for the purposes of what is now s 238(3)(*b*) of the TULR(C)A 1992.

Although s 238 does not make it clear whether or not the strike must be in breach of the employee's contract of employment the provisions of s 238 will operate when a strike is not in breach of the employee's contract of employment: *Power Packing Casemakers v Faust and Others* [1981] IRLR 120 (upheld on appeal [1983] IRLR 117). In most cases a strike would be in breach of the employee's contract of employment but it will not operate to terminate the contract unless the repudiation is accepted by the employer: *Simmons v Hoover Ltd* [1976] IRLR 266, and see generally Chapter 4.

Other industrial action

It may be difficult to decide whether particular action amounts to a strike. However, the phrase in s 238(3)(*b*) is 'strike or other industrial action' and where there is doubt the tribunal is likely to find in the alternative.

Industrial action may include the following: preventing the employer from installing and using a new machine: *Thompson v Eaton Ltd* [1976] ICR 336; an overtime ban: see *Power Packing Casemakers v Faust and Others, above*; a decision to impose an immediate overtime ban: see *Naylor and Others v (1) Orton and Smith Ltd (2) MD Tweddell Engineering Ltd* [1983] IRLR 233; a go-slow: see *Drew v St Edmundsbury BC* [1980] IRLR 459; a work to rule: see *Secretary of State for Employment v ASLEF (No 2)* [1972] ICR 19; as well as picketing: *Thompson v Eaton Ltd, above* and possibly sit-ins, but in *Rasool and Others v Hepworth Pipe Co Ltd (No 2)* [1980] IRLR 137, it was held that where employees attended an unauthorised mass meeting at the employer's premises during working hours, such action did not constitute 'other industrial action'.

In *Power Packing Casemakers v Faust and Others, above*, the EAT found that the industrial action did not have to be in breach of contract. This was upheld by the Court of Appeal, Stephenson LJ posing the question 'why ... should the ... tribunal have to embark on an enquiry into the terms of a claimant's contract of employment, express and implied, in order to decide whether he was taking part in industrial action when he was dismissed?' Whether or not action amounted to 'other industrial action' was a matter for a tribunal to decide. The words must be given their plain and ordinary meaning. In this case the employees were dismissed for refusing to work overtime hours at a time when wage negotiations were in progress. When the employees were threatened with dismissal all but three agreed to work overtime hours. The three who refused to work overtime hours were dismissed. The tribunal held that they were not in breach of their contracts of employment and were therefore unfairly dismissed. The EAT held that they were engaging in 'other industrial action' and therefore the tribunal had no jurisdiction to hear the claim.

In *Winnett v Seamarks Brothers Ltd* [1978] ICR 1240, it was held that employees who agreed at a meeting to stop work from the time of the meeting may be engaging in 'other industrial action' from the time of the decision, notwithstanding that at the time of the decision they are not contractually due to work, but they have made it clear that when asked to work they will not do so: see *Naylor*'s case, *above.*

In *Midland Plastics v Till and Others* [1983] IRLR 9, the employees advised their employer that they were going to engage in industrial action at 11 o'clock. Before they engaged in industrial action they were dismissed. It was held that they were not engaging in other industrial action at the time of dismissal.

It may not be clear whether employees are engaging in a strike or other industrial action or whether they are taking part or proposing to take part in the activities of an independent trade union. The difference is important as the EAT emphasised in *Drew v St Edmundsbury BC* [1980] IRLR 459. If the employee is dismissed for taking part or proposing to take part in the activities of a trade union then the dismissal is automatically unfair. See Chapter 11, and consider s 152 of the TULR(C)A 1992. However, if the employee is taking part in a strike or other industrial action then the tribunal does not have jurisdiction to hear the claim under s 238 of the TULR(C)A 1992, unless the employee can prove that the employer has been selective in dismissing or re-engaging.

Strikes or other industrial action 'engineered' by the employer
The legislation draws no distinction between a strike or other industrial action which is initiated by the employees of their own volition and a strike or other industrial action which results from conduct on the part of the employer, for instance where the employer seeks unilaterally to alter working conditions. In *Wilkins v Cantrell and Cochrane (GB) Ltd* [1978] IRLR 483, the employers on a number of occasions sent out lorries in an overloaded condition. Following the dismissal of employees who went on strike because of this, the EAT found that the tribunal was entitled to conclude that the instances of overloading which occurred were insufficient to constitute a fundamental breach. It added that even if the employers had been in breach of contract by requiring the employees to drive overloaded vehicles, the act of going out on strike could not be held to be a sufficient indication by the employee that he was treating the contract as not only capable of being repudiated, but as one which has been broken and which he regarded as at an end. The employee was therefore dismissed whilst on strike since the contract still continued. Further, there was no jurisdiction to hear the claim even though the strike was caused by

the employer's actions. This case was followed by the EAT in *Marsden v Fairey Stainless Ltd* [1979] IRLR 103, in which it was held that where a strike is 'engineered' by the employers, the provisions of what is now s 238 of the TULR(C)A 1992 will continue to operate. Consider also *Faust and Others v Power Packing Casemakers Ltd* [1983] IRLR 117, where the Court of Appeal held that motive on the part of the employer in dismissing the workers is entirely irrelevant.

Date of dismissal

Where the employee's contract of employment is terminated by notice, the date of dismissal is the date on which the employer's notice was given: s 238(5)(*a*) of the TULR(C)A 1992. In any other case the date of dismissal is the effective date of termination: s 238(5)(*b*).

For s 238 to apply, the employer must have been conducting a lock-out or the employee must have been taking part in a strike or other industrial action at the date of dismissal. In both cases 'date', in effect, means 'time': *Heath v JF Longman (Meat Salesmen) Ltd* [1973] 2 All ER 1228. For example, if a strike takes place in the morning and finishes at noon, an employee who was on strike and who was dismissed at 2 o'clock is not on strike at the date of the dismissal. The tribunal has jurisdiction to hear his claim. If the employer does not know that the strike or industrial action has been called off, and could not have known other than by a communication from those involved, it is open to argument whether the tribunal has jurisdiction under s 238: *Heath v JF Longman (Meat Salesmen) Ltd, above.* However, to claim the benefit of this argument it is likely that the employer must honestly believe and have good grounds for believing that the strike or other industrial action is still continuing. Thus, if the employees act in a manner consistent with the discontinuance of the strike, the employer may be unable to rely on this argument.

In *Midland Plastics v Till and Others* [1983] IRLR 9, the employees told their employer that they were going to take part in a strike at 11 o'clock. They were dismissed before 11 o'clock. It was held that they were not taking part in a strike at the date of the dismissal, see *above*. A warning of possible dismissal when industrial action ceases is not a notice of dismissal: *Bolton Roadways Ltd v Edwards and Others* [1987] IRLR 392.

Taking part in a strike or other industrial action

On this issue the case of *Britool Ltd v Roberts and others* [1993] IRLR 481, illustrates the problem of when a dismissal is because the employee is dismissed for trade union activities, when he is the leader of a strike. The case emphasises the need to analyse carefully the true reason for the dismissal where there is a strike.

In *Coates and Venables v Modern Methods and Materials Ltd* [1982] IRLR 318, the Court of Appeal held that a tribunal was entitled to find that an employee who went to her place of work but who was unwilling to pass the picket line because she did not wish to suffer abuse, and who stayed for an hour at the gate and then went home, was taking part in the strike. The Court of Appeal considered that an employee's participation in a strike had to be judged by what the employee did and not by what he thought or why he did it. Since the employee did not say or do anything to make plain any disagreement with the strikers, or anything which could amount to a refusal to join them, she was held to be on strike in this case.

Eveleigh LJ, in a dissenting judgment, held that for a person to be participating in a strike he must act jointly or in concert with those who withdrew their labour and that this was not the position here.

The majority of the Court of Appeal held that whether or not an employee was taking part in a strike or other industrial action was a matter of fact for the tribunal to decide.

This approach (ie that it is a matter of fact for the tribunal) was the subject of criticism by the EAT in *Naylor and Others v (1) Orton and Smith Ltd and (2) MD Tweddell Engineering Ltd* [1983] IRLR 233. The EAT found that since the question whether or not an employee was taking part in a strike or other industrial action was not a point of law, they could not interfere with the decision of the tribunal. The EAT held:

> in our judgment a decision to impose an immediate overtime ban could reasonably be considered as not constituting taking industrial action, as the Industrial Tribunal held: it could also reasonably be considered to constitute industrial action. Since both views are reasonable, we cannot interfere with the industrial tribunal decision . . . In cases to which [what is now s 238 of the TULR(C)A 1992 applies], it is of great importance to employers that they should, so far as possible, know the consequences of their acts before they decide who to dismiss and who to retain or re-engage. If both views can properly be held, an employer confronted with an overtime ban who asks for advice can only be advised to dismiss everyone who could conceivably have taken part in the industrial action. If he follows that advice, the consequences to the employees who might be considered not to be taking part are that they lose their jobs. Whether such employees have a claim for unfair dismissal will depend on whether or not the Industrial Tribunal they chance to come before takes the view that they were taking part in industrial action. The present case illustrates the quandary facing employers. These employers are small companies. If the Industrial Tribunal had reached the opposite conclusion, the employers' liability to pay compensation for unfair dismissal to those dismissed could easily reach six figures, a sum which would effectively put them out of business. In our view it is not in the best interests of orderly industrial relations that such severe consequences to both employers and employees should depend on which of two, equally correct but diametri-

cally opposite, views is subsequently adopted by the Industrial Tribunal before which the case may come.

The approach of the majority of the Court of Appeal in *Coates's* case has been followed more recently by EAT in *Lewis and Britton v E Mason & Sons* [1994] IRLR 4, where the EAT confirmed the tribunal's decision that Britton was taking part in industrial action by refusing to drive a vehicle from Wales to Scotland unless he was given five pounds for overnight accommodation. He was refusing to obey a lawful order in order to coerce the employer to improve his terms and conditions of employment. It was not necessary that others had to be involved. He could take industrial action on his own and the tribunal correctly concluded they had no jurisdiction to hear his claim. Lewis and other staff were dismissed when they informed the employer that if he did not reinstate Britton that they would not come into work the next day. The EAT confirmed that the tribunal could conclude that at the time Lewis was dismissed he was taking part in industrial action; '. . . a definite threat was made at the time when further negotiation could not have been expected to take place, where the work for the following day had already been allocated by the employer. Before the dismissal the employer felt that the situation had not changed and there was therefore no realistic prospect of further negotiation'.

In reaching their decision, EAT relied on the approach of the Court of Appeal in *Coates's* case and stated that the Court of Appeal '. . . have made it perfectly clear that the question of whether an employee is participating in "other industrial action" is the sort of question which an industrial jury is best fitted to decide and is accordingly a question of fact and fact alone'.

If the employee is away from work on holiday at the time of the strike, the employer cannot claim the benefit of s 238 of the TULR(C)A 1992. Where the employee is on strike and then becomes sick the employer is protected if the employee would have been on strike in such circumstances unless he expressly notifies the employer that he is no longer on strike but is away sick and would return if he was not sick: *Craig v JD Welding Construction and Engineering Co* (1975) (unreported). In *Williams v Western Mail and Echo Ltd* [1980] ICR 366, the employee, with others, had taken part in industrial action. He then went on a one-day strike. All the employees were told that unless they resumed normal working they would be dismissed. Notwithstanding this ultimatum the other industrial action continued. Williams did not attend work following the strike due to ill-health. He was dismissed. The tribunal found that since he had not indicated to his employers that he no longer intended to take part in industrial action, he was still taking part in the industrial action and what is now s 238 applied. The EAT, upholding the decision of the tribunal, found:

> once men have stated that they will apply sanctions and do so they may

be regarded as applying the sanctions either until they are discontinued or until they indicate or state an intention of stopping them.

Indeed, were it to be otherwise it would cause immense problems for the employer. In *Hindle Gears Ltd v McGinty and Others* [1984] IRLR 477, Smith had been away from work due to ill-health when his colleagues were engaged in strike action. He visited the factory regularly for the sole purpose of handing in medical certificates. In the course of those visits he spent time with his colleagues who were pickets at the factory gate and talked to them. The tribunal found that he was participating in the strike. The EAT found that the tribunal's decision was perverse and that no reasonable tribunal could have found that such fleeting encounters between a sick employee and his striking colleagues was participation in strike action. Whereas Williams had been engaged in industrial action and had then become ill, Smith had never engaged in industrial action and had been away during the whole of the period when his colleagues were on strike. For a similar situation see *Rogers v Chloride Systems Ltd* [1992] ICR 198, where the EAT remitted the case for a re-hearing because there had been insufficient finding of fact upon which a proper inference could be drawn that the applicant, while sick, had taken part in a strike or other industrial action.

Whether an employee is taking part in a strike is to be determined by evidence. If his actions and omissions justify an inference that he was participating in a strike that cannot be invalidated simply because his employer was unaware of his actions or omissions: *Bolton Roadways Ltd v Edwards* [1987] IRLR 392. The emphasis placed on the employer's knowledge by Waite J in *McGinty's* case, *above*, was not accepted.

Later cases have confirmed that the approach in *Edwards's* case is to be preferred, ie it is an objective test.

In *Manifold Industries Ltd v Sims* [1991] IRLR 242 at p 245 Knox J, delivering the decision of EAT, said:

> '... the question whether an employee is or is not taking part in a strike is to be determined by evidence of what in fact he is in fact (sic) doing or omitting to do. If his actions and omissions do not justify the conclusion that he was participating in the strike action, then that settles the matter. If his actions and omissions are such as to justify the inference that he was participating in the strike action it does not seem to us that the inference can be invalidated by the circumstances that his employer was unaware of his actions and omissions.;

He specifically approved the approach in *Edwards's* case and disapproved of the approach of Wood J in *McKenzie v Crosville Motor Services* [1989] IRLR 516, where he had suggested that the test was a subjective one depending on the state of mind of the employer.

Indeed, Wood J himself acknowledged that the approach in

Edwards' and *Sims'* cases was the correct one when he delivered his judgment in *Jenkins v P & O European Ferries (Dover) Ltd* [1991] ICR 652.

If the employee leaves the place of employment not because he is on strike but because he is afraid for his health or safety during the strike then it may well be that he is participating in the strike: see *Coates and Venables v Modern Methods and Materials Ltd* [1982] IRLR 318, *above*. However, it may always be that the employee has been dismissed for a reason specified in s 57A (health and safety) or s 60 (pregnancy) of the EP(C)A 1978, and the dismissal will be automatically unfair.

Relevant employees

A tribunal has no jurisdiction where the complainant was locked out or was engaging in a strike or other industrial action unless it can be shown that relevant employees of the same employer have not been dismissed or a relevant employee has been offered re-engagement and the complainant has not been offered re-engagement: s 238 of the TULR(C)A 1992. The definition of 'relevant employees' is in s 238(3).

In the case of a lock-out relevant employees are those employees who were directly interested in the dispute in contemplation or furtherance of which the lock-out occurred: s 238(3)(*a*). The definition is not confined to employees locked out to the end. The question, 'Which employees are directly interested in the dispute in contemplation or furtherance of which the lock-out occurred?' involves enquiry as to 'when the lock-out occurred and what was the ... dispute in contemplation or furtherance of which the lock-out was put into effect': *Fisher and Others v York Trailer Co Ltd* [1979] IRLR 386.

In deciding who were 'relevant employees' for the purposes of s 238(3)(*a*), the test is a retrospective one. What the tribunal has to consider is who, at the date at which the lock-out occurred, were the employees directly interested in the dispute in contemplation or furtherance of which the lock-out occurred. Employees who return to work before the lock-out ceases may also be relevant employees: *H Campey and Sons Ltd v Bellwood and Others* [1987] ICR 311.

In *Presho v DHSS* [1984] ICR 463, a case involving the interpretation of the Social Security Act 1975, as amended, it was held that the words 'directly interested' in relation to a trade dispute meant that whatever the outcome of the trade dispute, it would be applied to all employees whether or not they were members of the union in dispute. They were directly interested.

In the case of a strike or other industrial action relevant employees are the employees at the establishment who are taking part in the action at the complainant's date of dismissal: s 238(3)(*b*). In *Hindle Gears Ltd v McGinty and Others* [1984] IRLR 477, employees were on strike. The employer wrote to each of the employees dismissing them with immediate effect. Before the letter had been received two employees returned to work. The employer only took them back once it had obtained their assurances that they had not received the letters. The EAT held that the dismissal could not take effect until the employees had been told of the decision to dismiss them. Since the employees were not dismissed and they were no longer taking part in the strike when the other employees were dismissed they were not relevant employees for the purposes of s 238(3)(*b*). Thus, only those employees who are on strike or are engaging in other industrial action will have to be examined in determining whether or not there has been any discrimination, and not those who have returned to work. Selective dismissal or re-engagement in the case of a strike or other industrial action is easier than in the case of a lock-out.

In *P and O European Ferries (Dover) Ltd v Byrne* [1989] ICR 779, the Court of Appeal held that the words 'unless it is shown' in what is now s 238(2) means unless it is proved on the evidence and shown to the satisfaction of the tribunal. These words unambiguously direct attention to the conclusion of the relevant hearing before the tribunal. This may be the substantive hearing or the preliminary hearing at which the jurisdictional point is considered. See *Sims's* case *above*. *Obiter* remarks contained in *McCormick*'s case, *above*, which suggest the words mean the beginning of the hearing, were not applied.

This was confirmed in *Sims's* case, *above*, when Knox J held at p 246, that 'the material time for testing whether or not a relevant employee has not been dismissed is the conclusion of the hearing determining jurisdiction to hear the complainant's application to the Industrial Tribunal ... Those who are dead, have retired or have voluntarily resigned all fall to be disregarded.'

Section 238(2)(*b*) provides that a tribunal shall not have jurisdiction unless it is shown that a relevant employee has, before the expiry of the period of three months beginning with the relevant employee's date of dismissal, been offered re-engagement and that the complainant has not been offered re-engagement. After three months have elapsed from the date of the last dismissal of any relevant employee the employer can start to re-engage selectively the former employees without affecting the protection afforded by s 238. This applies if it is the employer conducting or instituting a lock-out, or if it is the employee who is engaging in a strike or other industrial action.

There is no obligation to offer re-engagement to all the employees at the same time. In *Highlands Fabricators Ltd v McLaughlin* [1984] IRLR 482, 2,000 employees went on strike. On 17 August they were dismissed. On 21 August 1,600 employees were offered re-engagement. McLaughlin was not one of them. On 16 September the remaining 400, including McLaughlin, were offered re-engagement. The chairman of the tribunal found that since all the striking employees, including

McLaughlin, had been offered re-engagement within the appropriate period, neither of the exceptions in s 238(2) applied and the tribunal had no jurisdiction to entertain the application. The EAT upheld the decision of the tribunal chairman. It found:

> For a variety of reasons offers of re-engagement may be made to striking employees in differing numbers and at different times. It would wreck all chance of negotiation in what is frequently a delicate and tense industrial situation if a limited offer of re-engagement were to confer immediately on employees to whom the offer was not directed a vested right to complain of unfair dismissal. Certainly if at the date of the Tribunal hearing such an employee can show that the terms of [s 238(2)(a) or (b)] have been complied with, the Tribunal will have jurisdiction to entertain the application. We regard the three month period . . . as something of a 'cooling off' period, designed to achieve the very objective which was reached in the present case, viz settlement of a strike on terms acceptable to management and workforce alike, on sensible and honourable terms. To interpret s 238(2)(b) in the manner in which the majority of the Tribunal have done would make it impossible to attain this objective and we do not consider it was the intention of Parliament that it should be construed in this way.

The reason for dismissing or not re-engaging a relevant employee

What is the position of a relevant employee who has been dismissed or not offered re-engagement, not because he was participating in a strike or other industrial action, but for some other reason? In *McCormick v Horsepower Ltd* [1980] IRLR 182, B was employed as a fitter's mate. The boilermakers, of whom McCormick was one, employed at the employer's premises, went on strike. B refused to cross a boilermaker's picket line, although subsequently he did cross the picket line. After he had recommenced work and while the strike was continuing, B was dismissed for redundancy. It found that B had withdrawn his labour to aid the strikers against their common employer so he was a relevant employee. The EAT also held that an employee who took part in a strike and was dismissed for whatever reason could not be a relevant employee who took part in the strike and was not dismissed. It did not matter that he was not dismissed for taking part in the strike or other industrial action and that the reason for his dismissal was, for instance, redundancy. The Court of Appeal (see [1981] IRLR 217) disagreed with the EAT's view that B took part in the strike. Although he refused to cross the picket line he did not have any common purpose with the strikers or any interest in their dispute and was not acting in concert with them, and therefore was not a relevant employee. The Court of Appeal, however, held that there was no requirement that a relevant employee had to be dismissed while he was taking part in the strike and he could be dismissed for other reasons.

This proved an important factor in *Britool Ltd v Roberts and others, above,* where the employees were not offered re-engagement because of their trade union activities in the planning and consultation stage of the strike.

Re-engagement

Where following a lock-out, strike or other industrial action one or more relevant employees have been offered re-engagement within the prescribed period and the complainant has not been offered re-engagement, the unfair dismissal provisions contained in ss 57–61 of the EP(C)A 1978 and ss 152–153 of the TULR(C)A 1992 must be interpreted as if for any reference to the reason or principal reason for which the employee was dismissed there were substituted a reference to the reason or principal reason for which he has not been offered re-engagement: s 239(3) of the TULR(C)A 1992.

It may be that following a strike or other act of industrial action all the relevant employees are dismissed but subsequently one or more are offered re-engagement. If a claim for unfair dismissal is brought by one or more employees who have not been offered re-engagement the test of reasonableness under s 57(3) of the EP(C)A 1978 is whether in the circumstances (including the size and administrative resources of the employer's undertaking), the employer acted reasonably or unreasonably in treating the reason for which the applicant has not been re-engaged as a sufficient reason for not offering re-engagement; and that question shall be determined in accordance with equity and the substantial merits of the case. The tribunal must look at the situation which exists at the time of the failure to offer re-engagement; the facts at the time of the initial dismissal may well be relevant, but the question of reasonableness cannot be restricted to them. See *Edwards v Cardiff City Council* [1979] IRLR 303.

Any reference to an offer of re-engagement is construed as a reference to an offer made either by the original employer, or by a successor of that employer or an associated employer to re-engage an employee, either in the job which he held immediately before the date of dismissal or in a different job which would be reasonably suitable in his case: s 238(4) of the TULR(C)A 1992.

In *Williams and Others v National Theatre Board Ltd* [1981] IRLR 5, the EAT had to consider the position where some employees on strike were offered re-engagement on condition they would be treated as being on a second warning under the employer's disciplinary procedure, whereas another employee had been offered re-engagement without any such condition. It held that what is now s 238(4) defines an offer of re-engagement as an offer to re-engage an employee either in the job which he held immediately before the date of dismissal or in a different job which would be reasonably suitable in his case. Section

153 of the EP(C)A 1978 defines job to mean 'the nature of the work which he is employed to do in accordance with his contract and the capacity and place in which he is so employed'. The EAT did not accept that a change in capacity was the same thing as a change in the security of employment so that the offer was not the offer of the employees' jobs. The jobs which they were offered were those which they held immediately before the dismissal. This decision was upheld by the Court of Appeal: see [1982] IRLR 377. An offer of re-engagement need not be in writing. Nor is there any need for a communication to each individual employee: *Marsden v Fairey Stainless Ltd* [1979] IRLR 103. An offer of re-engagement does not require some positive offer; a tacit acceptance of continuity of employment may be sufficient: *Bolton Roadways Ltd v Edwards* [1987] IRLR 392.

In *Bigham and Keogh v GKN Kwikform Ltd* [1992] IRLR 4, Bigham, who had been dismissed whilst on strike, obtained employment at one of the company's other sites within three months of his dismissal. He had revealed on his application form that he had previously been employed by GKN but gave no further details. The EAT held that for there to be an offer of re-engagement the employer must have had actual knowledge of the job from which he was dismissed and the reason why he was dismissed or constructive knowledge that what is being offered is re-engagement within what is now s 238 of the TULR(C)A 1992. Here the employer had constructive knowledge. The employee had revealed he had previously worked for GKN but the employer had failed to make any further enquiry. The contract could not be void because no fraudulent application had been made. The employer took Bigham on in a hurry. This was 'a risk which employers of that kind who organise their businesses in that way have to run unless they take steps to avoid it'.

In *Crosville Wales Ltd v Tracey and Others* [1993] IRLR 60, the EAT held that a general recruitment policy including notices in the depot, press and local radio announcements and advertisements in local job centres did not amount to an offer of re-engagement to the complainants even though they were aware of the employer's recruitment policy and the fact that employees were being taken on.

Fairness of selection

Where an employer selectively dismisses or fails to re-engage some employees but not others the tribunal will consider the fairness of the selection—the employer's reasons for selecting those who were dismissed or not re-engaged, and those who were retained or re-engaged. The tribunal must be satisfied that the employer acted reasonably in making the selection. It follows that in practice the employer must be able to show the tribunal the criteria which he used in making the selection for dismissal or the failure to offer re-engagement. Thus, if during the course of the strike or other industrial action some employees are re-engaged but others are not because of redundancy, the relevant criteria for the employer to consider are those which would have applied in a redundancy situation: *Laffin and Callaghan v Fashion Industries (Hartlepool) Ltd* [1978] IRLR 448; see also *Cruickshank v Hobbs* [1977] ICR 725. The reasonableness must be judged at the time of the dismissal or the failure to offer re-engagement: *Edwards v Cardiff City Council, above.*

Where selection for redundancy is made after the date of the strike, s 238 will not apply and either s 59 of the EP(C)A 1978 will apply, or the fairness or otherwise of the dismissal will have to be considered under s 57(3) of the EP(C)A 1978.

The limitation period

Section 239(2) of the TULR(C)A 1992 provides that s 67(2) of the EP(C)A 1978 (the usual time limit of three months for bringing a complaint) does not apply, but a tribunal shall not consider the complaint unless it is presented to the tribunal before the end of the period of six months beginning with the date of the complainant's dismissal (as defined by s 238(5)) or, where the tribunal is satisfied that it was not reasonably practicable for the complaint to be presented before the end of that period, within such further period as the tribunal considers reasonable.

Where s 237 applies (dismissal of those taking part in unofficial industrial action) then s 67(2) will apply. See *below*.

Dismissal and unofficial industrial action

The TULR(C)A 1992 draws no distinction between an employee taking part in official and unofficial industrial action. Section 237(1) provides that an employee has no right to complain of unfair dismissal if at the time of the dismissal he was taking part in an unofficial strike or other industrial action.

A strike or other industrial action is unofficial in relation to an employee unless:

(*a*) he is a member of a trade union and the action is authorised or endorsed by that union; or

(*b*) he is not a member of a trade union but there are among those taking part in the industrial action members of a trade union by which the action has been authorised or endorsed,

provided that a strike or other industrial action shall not be regarded as unofficial if none of those taking part in it are members of a trade union: s 237(2) of the TULR(C)A 1992.

Whether industrial action is taken or has been authorised or endorsed by a trade union shall be determined in accordance with s 20(2)–(4) TULR(C)A 1992. Section 20(2) provides that an act shall be authorised or endorsed by a trade union if it was done, authorised or endorsed by any person who had the power under the rules to do, authorise or endorse acts of the kind in question; or by the principal executive committee, president or general secretary of the union; or by any committee of the union being a group of persons constituted in accordance with the rules of the union or any other official (whether employed or otherwise) of the union.

An act shall be deemed to have been done, authorised or endorsed by an official if it was done, authorised or endorsed by, or by any member of any group of persons of which he was at the material time a member and the purposes of which include organising or co-ordinating industrial action: 20(3)(b). It does not matter that the principal executive committee, president, general secretary or other committee or official were acting contrary to any union rules, contract or rule of law. However, the actions of a committee or official of the union may be repudiated by the principal executive committee, president or general secretary, provided that it is done as soon as reasonably practicable after coming to their knowledge: s 21(1). If the repudiation is to be effective, written notice of the repudiation must be given to the committee or official without delay and the union must do its best to give individual written notice of the repudiation and the date thereof without delay to every member of the union who the union has reason to believe is taking part or might take part in industrial action, and to the employer of every such member: s 21(2). The notice, which must contain a statement in a prescribed form, shall inform members that the union has repudiated the call for industrial action and is not supporting such action so that any member dismissed while taking part in such action will have no right to complain of unfair dismissal: s 21(3). An action will not be treated as repudiated if, after the purported repudiation, the principal executive committee, president or general secretary has behaved in a way which is inconsistent with the purported repudiation: s 21(5). Behaviour is to be regarded as inconsistent if upon a request made to any of them within three months of the purported repudiation by a person who is a party to a commercial contract which has been or may be interfered with as a result of the action and who has not been given written notice by the union of repudiation, does not have written confirmation forthwith that the action has been repudiated: s 21(6).

Thus, where a strike has been called by a shop steward, it does not matter that the action is unsupported by a ballot, it is still official action. Even if the action is repudiated by the union it does not become unofficial immediately. Industrial action shall not be treated as unofficial before the end of the next working day after the day on which the repudiation takes place: s 237(4). A working day means any day which is not a Saturday or a Sunday, Christmas Day, Good Friday or a bank holiday under the Banking and Financial Dealings Act 1971: s 237(5). Whether industrial action is official or unofficial is a question of fact to be determined at the time of the dismissal: s 237(4).

Time of dismissal means:

(a) where the employee's contract of employment is terminated by notice, when the notice is given;

(b) where the employee's contract of employment is terminated without notice, when the termination takes effect, and

(c) where the employee is employed under a contract for a fixed term which expires without being renewed under the same contract, when that term expires: s 237(5).

The interrelationship of s 237(4) and (5) means that it is possible for an employee to be dismissed before he has been told that the industrial action has become unofficial and thereby protection removed.

Membership of a trade union for purposes unconnected with the employment in question is disregarded. However, an employee who is a member of a trade union when he began to take part in industrial action continues to be treated as a member for the purpose of determining whether that action is unofficial in relation to him or another, notwithstanding that he may in fact have ceased to be a member: s 237(6).

Chapter 13

Dismissal for Health and Safety

General

Section 28 of Sched 5 to the TURERA 1993 introduce new rights in respect of dismissal in health and safety cases, inserting s 57A(1)–(3) in the EP(C)A 1978.

The dismissal of an employee shall be automatically unfair if the reason (or if more than one, the principal reason) for the dismissal was that the employee:

(*a*) having been designated by the employer to carry out activities in connection with preventing or reducing risks to health and safety at work, carried out, or proposed to carry out any such activities.

(*b*) being a representative of workers on matters of health and safety at work or a member of a safety committee—

(i) in accordance with arrangements established under or by virtue of any enactment, or

(ii) by reason of being acknowledged as such by the employer, performed, or proposed to perform, any functions as such a representative or a member of such a committee,

(*c*) being an employee at a place where—

(i) there was no such representative or safety committee, or

(ii) there was such a representative or safety committee but it was not reasonably practicable for the employee to raise the matter by those means,

brought to his employer's attention, by reasonable means, circumstances connected with his work which he reasonably believed were harmful or potentially harmful to health or safety,

(*d*) in circumstances of danger which he reasonably believed to be serious and imminent and which he could not reasonably have been expected to avert, left, or proposed to leave, or (while the danger persisted,) refused to return to, his place of work or any dangerous part of his place of work, or

(*e*) in circumstances of danger which he reasonably believed to be serious and imminent, took, or proposed to take, appropriate

308

steps to protect himself or other persons from danger: s 57A(1) of the EP(C)A 1978.

Whether the steps which an employee took, or proposed to take, were 'appropriate' has to be decided taking into account all the circumstances including in particular the employee's knowledge and the facilities and advice available to him at the time when he took those steps under s 57A(1)(e): s 57A (2) of the EP(C)A 1978.

The employee's dismissal under s 57A(1)(e) will not be automatically unfair if the employer can show that it was or would have been so negligent for the employee to take the steps which he took, or proposed to take, that a reasonable employer might have dismissed him for taking, or proposing to take those steps: s 57A(3) of the EP(C)A 1978.

A selection for redundancy on the *above* grounds is also automatically unfair: s 59(2) of the EP(C)A 1978. There is no qualifying period of employment required before a claim can be made under this section: s 64 of the EP(C)A 1978.

See Chapter 16 as to remedies and interim relief.

Chapter 14

Dismissal for Assertion of Statutory Right

General

An employee is automatically unfairly dismissed if the reason or principal reason was that the employee—
  (*a*) brought proceedings against the employer to enforce a right of his which is a relevant statutory right; or
  (*b*) alleged that the employer had infringed a right of his which is a relevant statutory right: s 60A(1) of the EP(C)A 1978.

It does not matter whether the employee, in fact, has the right or not, or whether it has been infringed or not, but only that the claim to the right and its infringement must be made in good faith: s 60A(2) of the EP(C)A 1978.

For s 60A(1) to apply the employee only has to make it reasonably clear to the employer what the right claimed to have been infringed was. He does not have to name or specify the right accurately.

The rights

For the purposes of s 60A(1) the following statutory rights are relevant—
  (*a*) any right conferred by the EP(C)A 1978 (as set out *below*) or the Wages Act 1986, for which the remedy for infringement is by way of complaint or reference to an industrial tribunal;
  (*b*) the right conferred by s 49 of the EP(C)A 1978 (minimum period of notice);
  (*c*) the rights conferred by ss 68, 86, 146, 168, 169 and 170 of the TULR(C)A 1992 (as set out *below*);
  (*d*) the rights conferred by Sched 4 to the STA 1994 (as set out *below*).

The rights conferred by the EP(C)A 1978 are as follows:

s 1:   right to statement of employment particulars
s 4(1):   right to statement of changes of employment particulars

s 8:	right to itemised pay statement
s 9(1):	right to standing statement of fixed deductions from pay
s 12:	right to guarantee payment
s 19:	right to remuneration on suspension on medical grounds
s 22A:	right not to suffer detriment in health and safety cases
s 29:	right to time off for public duties
s 31:	right to time off for work or making arrangements for training
s 31A:	right to time off for ante-natal care
s 33:	right to maternity leave
s 39:	right to return to work
s 49:	right to minimum period of notice (see s 60A(4)(*b*))
s 50:	rights of employee in period of notice
s 53:	right to written statement of reasons for dismissal
s 54:	right not to be unfairly dismissed (see generally Part V), including
s 60A:	(assertion of statutory right)
s 81:	right to redundancy payment (see generally Part VI)

Note The last six rights *above* will rarely arise in practice. It is conceivable that in respect of a prospective dismissal, the employee might assert that he has such rights and would then be dismissed for the assertion.

Wages Act 1986

The rights conferred by the Wages Act 1986 are those in respect of deductions from wages.

The rights conferred by the TULR(C)A 1992 are as follows:

s 68:	right not to suffer deduction of unauthorised or excessive subscriptions
s 86:	right to object to contribution to political fund
s 146:	right not to have action short of dismissal taken against employee in respect of trade union membership or activities
s 168:	right to time off for carrying out trade union duties
s 169:	right to payment for time off under s 168
s 170:	right to time off for trade union activities

Where the reason or principal reason for the dismissal of an employee was redundancy, but it is shown that the circumstances constituting the redundancy applied equally to one or more other employees in the same undertaking, holding positions similar to that held by the employee and who have not been dismissed by the employer, and the reason or principal reason for selecting the employee for dismissal was an inadmissible reason, including assertion of a statutory right under s 60A(1) read with (2) and (3), then the dismissal is automatically unfair. There is no qualifying period of employment required before the employee can present a complaint to a tribunal under these provisions.

These provisions came into force on 30 August 1993. So far there have been no reported cases though it is known that some have been decided by the tribunals.

The rights conferred by the STA 1994

The rights conferred on protected shop workers and opted-out shopworkers by Sched 4 to the STA 1994 are as follows:

para 7(1): right not to be dismissed for refusing to work on a Sunday or proposing to opt out.

para 10(1): right not to suffer a detriment for refusing to work on a Sunday or proposing to opt out.

para 8(1): right not to be selected for redundancy for refusing to work on a Sunday or proposing to opt out.

These provisions came into force on 26 August 1994. There is no qualifying period required for the employee to bring an action under these provisions.

It will be noticed that there is a certain amount of duplication between s 60(A) of the EP(C)A 1978 and Sched 4 to the STA 1994.

Chapter 15

The Transfer of Undertakings and the Employee

General

The Transfer of Undertakings (Protection of Employment) Regulations 1981 (SI 1981 No 1794) safeguard the employee's rights in the event of the transfer of an undertaking. The regulations were made to implement the EEC Council Directive 77/187 (the Business Transfers Directive 77/187, known in the UK as the Acquired Rights Directive). They have been amended by s 33 of the TURERA 1993 in order to bring the regulations further into line with Directive 77/187, which had not been fully implemented by the 1981 regulations, and because enforcement action was issued by the European Community.

Tribunals and courts have recently given a more purposive construction to the interpretation of the regulations in order to bring the regulations into line with the wording and intended effect of directives and English judgments. The UK law must be looked at in the light of recent decisions of the European Court of Justice. See *Webb* v *EMO Air Cargo (UK) Ltd* [1993] IRLR 27, where the House of Lords held that a UK court must construe domestic law to accord with the European Court of Justice's interpretation of directives if it is possible to do so, ie without distorting the meaning of the domestic law, and if the domestic law is open to an interpretation consistent with the directive. Where an individual is an employee of the State or an emanation of the State he or she can bring an action against the employer relying directly upon the directive in question.

Under the regulations an employee is defined as any individual who works for another person whether under a contract of service or apprenticeship or otherwise but does not include anyone who provides services under a contract for services. A contract of employment means any agreement between an employee and his employer determining the terms and conditions of his employment: reg 2(1). The definition of an employee is wider than under the EP(C)A 1978. It does not include an equity partner: see *Cowell* v *Quilter Goodison Co Ltd and QG Management Services Ltd* [1989] IRLR 392.

A transfer within the regulations is a relevant transfer: reg 2(1).

The regulations apply to a transfer from one person to another of an undertaking situated immediately before the transfer in the UK or a part of one which is so situated: reg 3(1). They apply whether the transfer is effected by sale or by some other disposition or by operation of law: reg 3(2).

'Undertaking' includes any trade or business: reg 2(1) (prior to amendment by s 33 of the TURERA 1993, there was excluded any undertaking or part which was not in the nature of a commercial venture). Local government is not excluded, and nationalised industries would appear to be within the regulations. The regulations apply to the transfer of part of an undertaking provided that it is being transferred as a business. The transfer of a ship without more is expressly excluded: reg 2(2).

The regulations apply notwithstanding that the transfer is governed or effected by the law of a country or territory outside the UK, that persons employed in the undertaking or part transferred ordinarily work outside the UK (but see Chapter 1, *above*), or that the employment of any of those persons is governed by any such law: reg 3(3).

A transfer of an undertaking or part thereof may be effected by a series of two or more transactions, and may take place whether or not any property is transferred to the transferee by the transferor, eg the forfeiture of leases, franchises and other instances where no property is transferred. In deciding whether or not such a series of transactions constitutes a single transfer regard must be had to the extent to which the undertaking or part thereof was controlled by the transferor and transferee respectively before the last transaction, to the lapse of time between each of the transactions, to the intention of the parties and to all other circumstances: reg 3(4). For the position of seamen on the transfer of a UK registered ship: see reg 3(5).

The meaning of an undertaking

The regulations apply only where there is a change in the legal identity of the employer. They do not apply where what is transferred is the share capital of a company, so that the sale and purchase of shares is not a transfer within the regulations. See *Barclays Insurance and Finance Union* v *Barclays Bank plc* [1987] ICR 495. Whether or not there has been a relevant transfer of an undertaking is a question of fact for the tribunal to determine.

The regulations do not apply where there is merely a sale and purchase of the physical assets of an undertaking or part thereof without anything more, unless, of course, it puts the purchaser in the position of carrying on the business of the vendor without interruption (see *Lloyd v Brassey* [1969] 1 All ER 382). In determining whether or not there has been a transfer of an undertaking as distinct from a pure asset sale the earlier cases involving redundancy or continuity of employment (see Chapter 3) are of assistance. In *Woodhouse and Another v Peter Brotherhood Ltd* [1972] 2 QB 520, there was a transfer of the factory and some of the plant, machinery, equipment, fixtures and fittings in the factory. However, the transferor and transferee carried on different businesses and there was no transfer of the goodwill. The Court of Appeal held that there was no transfer of the ownership of the business or undertaking, in that the transferee had not become the proprietor of the business or undertaking in succession to the transferor. In *Kenmir Ltd v Frizzell* (1968) 3 ITR 159, there was no transfer of the stock in trade and goodwill of the business. The Divisional Court held that in deciding whether the transaction amounted to a transfer of a business:

> the vital consideration is whether the effect of the transaction was to put [the] transferee in possession of a going concern the activities of which he could carry on without interruption. Many factors may be relevant to this decision though few will be conclusive in themselves.

It was held that although the assignment of goodwill is strong evidence of the transfer of a business it is not conclusive and found that there had been a transfer of a business.

In *Melon and Others v Hector Powe Ltd* [1981] 1 All ER 313, Lord Fraser referring to the criteria applied by Lord Denning in *Lloyd v Brassey* [1969] 2 QB 98, held that where a business (rather than physical assets) is transferred it is transferred as a going concern 'so that the business remains the same business but in different hands' whereas where assets are transferred to the new owner they are to be used in whatever business he chooses. Individuals may not actually realise they are working in a different business.

The existence of a workforce is not vital to the existence of an undertaking and there may be a transfer of an undertaking within the regulations even though at the time of the transfer there was no workforce: see *Secretary of State for Employment v Spence and Others* [1986] IRLR 248.

The following may be transfers of an undertaking: the transfer of land and farm buildings: see *Lloyd v Brassey* [1969] 2 QB 98; the surrender of the lease of a public house by the tenant to the brewery which then carried on the business: see *Young v Daniel Thwaites and Co Ltd* [1977] ICR 877; where the licensee of a petrol station gives up the licence to the petrol company: see *Premier Motors (Medway) Ltd v Total Oil Great Britain Ltd and Others* [1984] ICR 58. There was a sale of the business of a petrol station by Premier Motors to Total Oil. Premier Motors continued to run the business as licensees. When they gave up the licence there was a transfer of a business as a going concern to Total Oil. Total Oil then granted a licence to a third party. It appears that it was accepted there was a further transfer of a business as a going concern to the third party.

In *Norris (t/a Littlebrickhill Service Station) v Bedwell* EAT (1983) (unreported), the EAT found that there was a transfer of a business as a going concern between the outgoing tenant of a petrol station and the incoming tenant. The fixtures and fittings, and stock-in-trade were sold by the outgoing tenant to the incoming tenant. Under the terms of the lease the outgoing tenant could not assign the lease to the incoming tenant and had to surrender it to the petrol company which then in turn granted a new lease to the incoming tenant. The transfer of a franchise may not be the transfer of an undertaking: see *Robert Seligman Corporation v Baker and Another* [1983] ICR 770. Robert Seligman Corporation had a concession to carry on the business of a ladies' hairdresser in a store belonging to Debenhams plc. Debenhams terminated Seligman's concession and granted it to Roband Investments Ltd with effect from 21 June. Baker was employed by Seligman. On 29 June Baker was told there was no job with Roband. Under the terms of the concession Seligman was responsible for installing shop fittings. On the termination of the concession the position was obscure but it was found that Debenhams reimbursed Seligman for the cost of the fixtures and made them available to Roband. A crucial question in deciding whether there had been a transfer of a business was whether or not the goodwill belonging to Seligman had been transferred to Roband. The essential element of goodwill attributable to the skills of Seligman's staff was not transferred to Roband. It was open to Seligman to set up in competition next door using the same staff. It was held that there had been a transfer of physical assets and not the transfer of a business. Therefore, Baker's contract of employment was not transferred to Roband under the regulations.

In other cases the transfer of a business which involves a franchise may be a transfer of an undertaking as a going concern, eg 'a Wimpey': see *Lane v Dyno Rod* (1985) (unreported).

Cases heard by the European Court of Justice illustrate the scope of the Directive upon which the 1981 Regulations are based and the decisions of the UK courts and tribunals must now be read in the light of the European Court of Justice's decisions, and also now in the light of the amendments made to the regulations by s 33 TURERA 1993. In *Foreningen af Arbejdsledere i Danmark v Daddy's Dance Hall A/S* [1988] IRLR 315, it was held that the Directive applied where, after the termination of a non-transferable lease of a restaurant and bars, the owner leased the restaurant and bars to a new lessee who continued to run the business without any interruption using the same staff. It was held that the Directive applied as soon as there was a change of the natural or legal person responsible for operating the undertaking. In *Landsorganisationen i Danmark v Ny Mølle Kro* [1989] IRLR 37, it was held that the Directive applied where the owner took back the running of a leased business following a breach of the lease by the lessee. It was held the objective of the Directive is to safeguard the rights of workers in the event of a change of employer and it applies whenever, as a result of a legal transfer or merger, there is a change in the natural or legal person responsible for running the undertaking and who because of this enters into contractual obligations as an employer towards the employees in the undertaking regardless of whether ownership of the undertaking has been transferred. In *P Bork International A/S v Foreningen af Arbejdsledere i Danmark* [1989] IRLR 41, it was held that the Directive applied where the owner of an undertaking, after giving notice terminating the lease or after forfeiting the same, retakes possession of the undertaking and then sells it to a third party who thereafter continues operations which had ceased on the termination of the lease with one-half of the staff previously employed in the undertaking by the former lessee, provided the undertaking retained its identity. There had to be an economic entity still in existence which was continued by the new employer carrying on the same or a similar business. This was a question of fact which depended upon whether the tangible and intangible assets had been transferred as well as the major part of the staff, the degree of similarity between the activities before and after the transfer, and the period of interruption. In *Berg and Busschers v Besselsen* [1989] IRLR 447, it was held that the Directive applied to the transfer of an undertaking under a lease purchase agreement as well as to the re-transfer of the undertaking where the lease purchase arrangement had been dissolved. In *Curling and Others v Securicor Ltd* [1992] IRLR 549, the EAT held that where successive contractors are engaged by a person who owns premises from which a business is carried on, whether or not there is a transfer of an undertaking, depends on whether an economic unit is transferred to the transferee. The fact that the same work is carried out by the employees before and after the transfer is not conclusive. Here the economic unit belonged to the Home Office who entered into successive contracts for the management of a detention centre, which did not belong to the respondents or Group Four Total Security who replaced them. The EAT referred to *Expro Services Ltd v Smith* [1991] IRLR 156. However, in *Dr Sophie Redmond Stichting v Bartol and others* [1992] IRLR 366, the European Court of Justice held that where a public body decides to terminate a grant to one legal person and to transfer it to another legal person then there is a legal transfer within art 1(1) of Directive 77/187. The Directive applies wherever there is a change in the legal or natural person responsible for carrying on the business and who incurs the obligations of the employer towards employees of the undertaking. The community law test is whether the unit has retained its identity—see *Spijkers v Gebroeders Benedick Abattoir CV* [1986] CMLR 296, and *Ny Mølle Kro, above*, where it was held that this was a decisive criterion.

In *Rask and Christensen v ISS Kantineservice A/S* [1993] IRLR 133, the European Court of Justice held that the contracting out of a staff canteen by Philips was a transfer of an undertaking under art 1(1) of Directive 77/187. The decisive criterion for deciding whether there has been a transfer is whether the business in question retains its identity and this is indicated by whether the operations are continued or resumed. The European Court of Justice held the Directive can apply even if the activity transferred is only ancillary or the services provided are solely for the benefit of the transferor in return for a fixed fee. Whether there is a transfer of an undertaking depends on the facts and whether there is merely a transfer of a contract for services or the transfer of a business. In *Wren v Eastbourne Borough Council and UK Waste Control Ltd* [1993] IRLR 425, the EAT held that a transfer of services only was capable of being a transfer of an undertaking, with the definition of a recognisable economic entity including the provision of services.

In *Kenny and others v South Manchester College* [1993] IRLR 265, a case brought directly under art 1(1) of Directive 77/187, the High Court held that the transfer of prison education services from a local education authority to the college would be a transfer under art 1(1) even though there was no direct relationship between the two, no transfers of assets, clients or customers, and the continuing function of providing education would be carried out in a different manner. The education department would retain its identity and the operation would continue as a going concern. A declaration would be made that when the transfers took place the employees would become employees of the defendants. The High Court stated that a clear pattern was emerging from the decision of the European Court of Justice cases in such instances.

In *Porter and Nanayakkara v Queen's Medical Centre (Nottingham University Hospital)* [1993] IRLR 486, the High Court held (again in a case brought directly under art 1(1) of the Directive) that the transfer of the supply of paediatric and neo-natal services from two district health authorities to an NHS Trust was a legal transfer within art 1(1). The court followed the reasoning in the *Dr Sophie Redmond Stichting* case, *above*. The undertaking of providing the services had retained its identity through the change of the provider. The provision of medical services is a type of undertaking in which it is likely that different ways of carrying on the undertaking may be adopted without destroying its identity.

However, in *Dines and Others v (1) Initial Health Care Services Ltd and (2) Pall Mall Services Group Ltd* [1994] IRLR 336, the tribunal had held that there was no transfer of an undertaking where Allsett Hospital awarded a cleaning contract to new contractors after compulsory competitive tendering. When Pall Mall took over they provided their own equipment, management, tools and materials and there was no transfer of goodwill from Initial to Pall Mall and no transfer of an undertaking or economic unit to which the regulations could apply. The EAT held that two questions had to be asked: (*a*) whether there is an identifiable economic unit ie a going concern and, (*b*) whether there has been a transfer of that unit. The EAT concluded that these are difficult to prove where there are three parties involved. It was suggested that the existence of a transfer was a question of cause rather than effect. The tribunal had taken the view that when 'a different company wins the contract from the company that was previously providing the services then this is a cessation of the business of the first contractor . . . and the commencement of a new business by [Pall Mall], when they were awarded the contract.', but the Court of Appeal stated this view did not accord with decisions of the European Court of Justice. A transfer could and did take place in two phases, the first being the handing back by Initial of the cleaning services on 30 April 1991, and the grant or handing over to Pall Mall of the cleaning services on 1 May 1991, which as from that date were operated by substantially the same labour force.

Recent decisions of the European Court of Justice have emphasised the result of the transfer. In the *Dr Sophie Redmond Stitching* and *Rask* cases the European Court of Justice ruled 'the decisive criterion . . . is whether the business in question retains its identity . . . by the fact its operation was actually continued or resumed'. These two decisions do not refer to 'going concerns'.

In *Christel Schmidt v Spar-und Leihkasse der früheren Ämter Bordesholm, Kiel und Cronshagen* [1994] IRLR 302, the European Court of Justice gave a preliminary ruling that art 1(1) of Directive 77/187 was to be interpreted as covering the situation where the activity transferred did not involve the transfer of tangible assets, was only an ancillary activity of the transferor and not necessarily connected with its objects, and covered only one employee. In this case, Mrs Schmidt, the cleaner of one branch of a bank, was dismissed when its cleaning services were granted to the bank's main cleaning firm, which offered to employ Mrs Schmidt, who refused the offer. The European Court of Justice ruled that the Directive did not depend on the number of employees assigned to that part of the undertaking which was the subject of the transfer, nor did the absence of tangible assets preclude the existence of a transfer.

The transfer of part of an undertaking is covered by the regulations if it is being transferred as a business. It is a question of fact whether or not what is being transferred is part of a business. It need not be self-contained: *GD Ault Ltd v Gregory* (1976) 2 ITR 301. In *Melon and Others v Hector Powe Ltd, above*, Lord Fraser held 'a change in the ownership of part of a business will, I think, seldom occur, except when that part is to some extent separate and severable from the rest of the business, either geographically or by reference to the products, or in some other way'. See the decision in *Rask, above*, where the activity was ancillary.

However, where staff are redeployed and there is no transfer of assets or goodwill then the regulations will not apply: *Banking*

Insurance and Finance Union v Barclays Bank plc and Others [1987] ICR 495. Staff were redeployed from subsidiaries of Barclays Bank to a service company established to provide staff for an international investment bank which was to be formed.

Regulation 3(4) provides that a transfer of an undertaking may be effected by a series of two or more transactions. Whether or not such a series constitutes a single transfer is a question of fact. Regard must be had to the extent to which the undertaking or part of it was controlled by the transferor and transferee respectively before the last transaction, to the lapse of time between each of the transactions, to the intention of the parties and to all the other circumstances. In *Forth Estuary Engineering Ltd v Litster and Others* [1986] IRLR 59, decided before the amendment excluding the words 'between the same parties' was made by s 33(3) of the TURERA 1993 the EAT, *obiter*, considered that reg 3(4) was declaratory and permissive. It did not make it essential that the transaction must be between the same parties. It merely declared that where there is a series of transactions between the same parties that may amount to a relevant transfer.

Transfers by receivers and liquidators

Where the receiver of the property or part of the property of a company or the administrator of a company appointed under Part II of the Insolvency Act 1986 or, in the case of a creditors' voluntary winding up, the liquidator of the company, transfers the company's undertaking, or part of the company's undertaking (the relevant undertaking) to a wholly owned subsidiary of the company, the transfer shall be deemed not to have been effected until immediately before:

(*a*) the transferee company ceases (otherwise than by reason of its being wound up) to be a wholly owned subsidiary of the transferor company; or

(*b*) the relevant undertaking is transferred by the transferee company to another person;

whichever first occurs, and, for the purposes of the regulations, the transfer of the relevant undertaking shall be taken to have been effected immediately before that date by one transaction only: reg 4(1). For these purposes 'creditors', 'winding up' and 'wholly owned subsidiary' have the same meaning as in the Companies Act 1985: reg 4(2).

The Transfer of Undertakings (Protection of Employment) (Amendment) Regulations 1987 (SI 1987 No 442) amend reg 4 of the 1981 Regulations to reflect changes in the law made by the Insolvency Act 1986.

This regulation is intended to deal with a hiving-down operation. Before the regulations became law it was frequently the practice where a receiver or liquidator contemplated a sale of an undertaking for the receiver or the liquidator to separate the business from the employees.

To achieve this the receiver or liquidator would transfer the 'undertaking' or part of the 'undertaking' to a wholly owned subsidiary. The purchaser would either acquire the wholly owned subsidiary or the purchase would be made from the wholly owned subsidiary. The employees would not become employees of the subsidiary, although their services would be made available. Often it was essential that the business was hived off as quickly as possible. The purchaser would be relieved of the obligation to make a decision immediately, whether or not he would take on some or all of the employees and could make a decision at a later date. If he did take some of these employees on he could do so after the transfer of the 'undertaking' and in the meantime the employees remained employees of the original employer. The original employer became liable for any claim to notice and/or redundancy pay. The purchaser thereby avoided liability for any claims for redundancy and/or unfair dismissal. Regulation 4 is designed to preserve the flexibility of a hive down, but to protect the employees in such circumstances.

Regulation 5 provides that on a relevant transfer the employees become the employees of the transferee. The effect of reg 4 is that the transfer of the employees' employment is delayed until immediately before the transferee company ceases to be a wholly owned subsidiary of the transferor company or the undertaking is transferred by the transferee company to another person.

Under reg 4(1)(a) the number of shares acquired by the transferee is therefore irrelevant. The transfer takes place when the subsidiary is no longer wholly owned. There is deemed to have been only one transaction and the work-force will be transferred to the ultimate purchaser via the subsidiary at the time that the real transfer takes place.

If the transferee insists that the employees are dismissed then the liability may pass to the transferee if the employees were employed immediately prior to the transfer. See *below*. If they were not employed immediately prior to the transfer, the liability will of course remain with the transferor. In practice this will mean that the Secretary of State will become liable for any redundancy payment or basic award.

Automatic transfer of the contract of employment

A transfer within the regulations shall not operate so as to terminate the contract of employment of any person employed by the transferor in the undertaking or part transferred, but any such contract which would otherwise have been terminated by the transfer shall have effect after the transfer as if originally made between the person so employed and the transferee: reg 5(1), except where objection is made under reg 5 (4A), (see *below*). See *Morris Angel and Son Ltd v Hollande*

[1993] ICR 71, a case where a transferee company sought to rely on reg 5(1) in asserting the transferor's rights under the contract.

Without prejudice to reg 5(1), on the completion of the relevant transfer all the transferor's rights, powers, duties and liabilities under or in connection with any such contract will be transferred to the transferee, and anything done before the transfer is completed by or in relation to the transferor in respect of that contract for a person employed in that undertaking or part shall be deemed to have been done by or in relation to the transferee: reg 5(2). However, this is subject to reg 5(4A) which provides that reg 5(1) and (2) shall not operate to transfer the employee's contract of employment and the rights, duties and liabilities under or in connection with it if the employee informs the transferor or the transferee that he objects to becoming employed by the transferee. In these circumstances, the contract of employment with the transferor shall be deemed to have been terminated and the employee shall not be treated for any purposes as having been dismissed by the transferor. Regulation 5(4A) and (4B) were introduced into the regulations by s 33 of the TURERA 1993 as a result of *Katsikas v Konstantinidis* [1993] IRLR 179, where the European Court of Justice held that Directive 77/187 did not prevent an employee from refusing the transfer of his contract of employment. The Directive cannot oblige the employee to continue in employment with the transferee, nor does it have the purpose of continuing the employment with the transferor where the employee does not want to remain with the transferee. In *Newns v British Airways plc* [1992] IRLR 575, the Court of Appeal held that there is no implied right in a contract of employment which enables an employee to restrain a proposed transfer of a business in which he is employed and in particular he has no right to restrain the transfer of an undertaking merely because the effect of reg 5 will mean that there will be a transfer of the employment. Since the regulations, the transfer of a business does not *per se* mean there is a repudiation resulting in a breach of contract entitling an employee to terminate his contract. Regulation 5 provides for a statutory novation of the contract. An employee cannot prevent an employer from divesting himself of his business.

Any reference in reg 5(1) or (2) to a person employed in an undertaking or in part of one, transferred by a transfer within the regulations, is a reference to a person so employed immediately before the transfer, including, where the transfer is effected by a series of two or more transactions, a person so employed immediately before any of those transactions: reg 5(3).

Regulation 5(2) shall not transfer or otherwise affect the liability of any person to be prosecuted for, convicted of and sentenced for any offence: reg 5(4).

Regulation 5(1) and (4A) are without prejudice to any right of an employee arising apart from the regulations to terminate his contract of employment without notice if a substantial change is made in his working conditions to his detriment; but no such right shall arise by reason only that, under reg 5(1), the identity of his employer changes unless the employee shows that, in all the circumstances, the change is a significant change and to his detriment: reg 5(5). See p 327.

At common law the effect of a transfer of a business was to bring the employee's contract of employment to an end with the transferring employer. Where this was without notice the employee was wrongfully dismissed by the employer. The common law position was set out in *Nokes v Doncaster Amalgamated Collieries Ltd* [1940] AC 1014, where it was held that an employee is entitled to choose the employer whom he promises to serve, so that the right to his services cannot be transferred from on employer to another without his assent.

There is nothing in the regulations which prevents the employer from terminating the employee's contract. However, such a termination may have certain consequences for the employer which are considered later. The regulations also confirm the employee's right to resign and claim a constructive dismissal, except perhaps in very exceptional circumstances. This will be considered later.

Regulation 5 has given rise to difficulties. In the main the difficulties have surrounded the interpretation of the phrase 'immediately before the transfer'. What was meant by 'immediately before'? Was it to be interpreted literally or was the employee employed immediately before the transfer where there was a gap between his dismissal and the transfer? In *Apex Leisure Hire v Barratt* [1984] IRLR 224, it was held that the employee was employed by the transferor immediately before the transfer, notwithstanding that he was dismissed on a Friday and the business was not transferred until a Monday. See also *Secretary of State for Employment v Anchor Hotel (Kippford) Ltd* [1985] ICR 724, *Fenton v Stablegold Ltd (t/a Chiswick Court Hotel)* [1986] IRLR 64 and *Bullard v Marchant* [1986] ICR 389, where the decision in *Apex Leisure Hire v Barratt*, above, was followed.

Other decisions of both the tribunals and the EAT suggested a different approach. In *Premier Motors (Medway) Ltd v Total Oil Great Britain Ltd and Others* [1984] ICR 58, the EAT held that 'immediately before' meant at the time of, or moment of the transfer. In *Bullard's* case, above, the EAT felt obliged to follow *Barratt's* case, above, but recognised the problems of the conflicting interpretations.

In *Secretary of State for Employment v Spence and Others* [1986] IRLR 248, the Court of Appeal considered reg 5. Spence and Sons (Market Harborough) Ltd went into receivership on 16 November. On Monday 28 November at 11.00am the workforce was told that they were dismissed with immediate effect. At 2.00pm on the same day there was a transfer by the receiver. The Secretary of State refused to pay a redundancy payment on the basis that there had been a transfer of the undertaking and that the employees had been employed immediately before the transfer. Therefore there was no redundancy. The effect of reg 5 was to transfer their employment to the transferee.

The Court of Appeal held that there was no contract in existence at the time of the transfer. Since there was no contract, there was nothing on which the regulations could bite. Balcombe LJ held:

> [reg 5(1)] has two effects: first, that a relevant transfer does not terminate a contract of employment; and the second effect ... is that there is a statutory novation of the contract. That provision can clearly only relate to a contract of employment which is subsisting at the moment of transfer; otherwise there is nothing on which the regulation can operate.

Balcombe LJ concurred with the judgment of Browne-Wilkinson J in *Premier Motors (Medway) Ltd v Total Oil Great Britain Ltd and Others, above.* He accepted that immediately before meant at the time or moment of transfer. Conversely, he found *Apex Leisure Hire v Barratt,* and *Secretary of State for Employment v Anchor Hotel (Kippford) Ltd v Marchant, above,* were wrongly decided.

Although the decision in *Spence*'s case, *above,* clarified the law, it has meant a loss of protection of continuity of employment for an employee whose contract is brought to an end before the business is transferred because of the transfer. (It may give rise to a claim for unfair dismissal, see *below*).

In *Bork*'s case, *above,* see p 317, the European Court of Justice held that where the employment relationship has been terminated before the transfer in breach of art 4(1) of the Directive (which provides that the transfer of an undertaking shall not itself constitute grounds for dismissal by the transferor or transferee), the employee must be considered as still employed at the date of the transfer so that the obligations of the employer are transferred from the transferor to the transferee. Regulation 8 gives effect to art 4(1) of the Directive.

The matter was put beyond doubt in *Litster v Forth Dry Dock and Engineering Co Ltd* [1989] ICR 341. The company went into receivership. At 3.30pm on 6 February the entire workforce was dismissed with immediate effect. At 4.30pm the business was transferred by the receivers. Within 48 hours the transferee was recruiting employees. Three former employees were re-engaged. The House of Lords held that the purpose of the Directive and the regulations was to protect employees where there was a transfer of the business in which they were employed. If the words 'immediately before a transfer' were read literally it was possible to circumvent the purpose of the Directive and the regulations by dismissing the employees a short time before the transfer took effect. Following the decision in *Bork*'s case, *above,* the House of Lords held that the regulations had to be construed to give effect to the UK's obligations under the Directive and that the words 'a person employed immediately prior to the transfer' in reg 5(3) must be construed as meaning a person employed immediately prior to the transfer or who would have been so employed if he had not been unfairly dismissed within reg 8(1). Regulation 8(1) (which provides where the reason or principal reason for a dismissal is the transfer, or a reason connected with it, the dismissal shall be automatically unfair), gives effect to art 4 of the Directive in that the transfer is not to be a good ground for dismissal. If it is possible to show that the employee has been dismissed for an economic, technical or organisational reason entailing changes in the workforce within the meaning of reg 8(2), then the dismissal is not automatically unfair under reg 8(1) and if such an economic, technical or organisational reason can be shown then *Spence*'s case, above, will apply. Thus, if it can be shown that the reason is an economic, technical or organisational reason and the employee is not employed immediately prior to the transfer, his contract of employment will not transfer. The House of Lords held that the expression 'immediately before' takes its meaning from the context, but ordinarily it involves the notion that between the two relevant events there is no intervening space, lapse of time or event of any significance. Where an employee has been dismissed prior to the transfer, but is deemed to have been employed immediately prior to the transfer is the dismissal ineffective or does it simply pass the liabilities to the transferee? It is submitted that the liabilities pass but the dismissal remains effective. Where *Litster*'s case, above, applies then arguably all the liabilities, not just the liability for unfair dismissal, become the liabilities of the transferee. However, where the dismissal is not automatically unfair under reg 8(1) it may be unfair under s 57(3) of the EP(C)A 1978. Following *Litster*'s case, *above*, the liability would in that case be that of the transferor.

The EAT has held recently that there is nothing in reg 5 (2) to prevent the liability for a dismissal carried out by a transferor which taken effect before or simultaneously with a transfer, remaining with the transferor: see *Allan and others v Stirling District Council* [1994] IRLR 208. Article 3(1) of Directive 77/187 states that member states may provide that the transferor will continue to be liable in respect of obligations arising from the employment contract, and the EAT took the view in the present case that because there is no wording in reg 5(2) specifically excluding liability on the transferor then the Council remained liable. This is a startling decision. It holds that, where a member state is empowered by the Directive to include in its domestic legislation a provision that the liability remains with the transferor, because the UK Government did not expressly state that it was not so providing, it has been deemed to have so provided. It not only puts gloss on the Regulation, but actually adds a provision to it which is not required by the Directive. It conflicts with the House of Lords' decision in *Litster's* case *above*, and directly with the wording of regs 5(1) and 5(2). It is clearly an unsafe decision.

Although the cases of *Spence* and *Litster*, *above* support the view that employment must exist at the time or moment of the transfer, the Directive refers to the date of the transfer: see also *Wendelboe v LJ Music ApS* [1985] ECR 457.

Under reg 5(4) the transferee is not liable for the criminal offences of the transferor. However, he would appear to be liable for most civil as distinct from criminal wrongs, including tortious liability: see *Spence*'s case, *above*.

In *Angus Jowett and Co Ltd v National Union of Tailors and Garment Workers* [1985] ICR 646, it was held that liability under a protective award where an employer has failed to consult with a recognised trade union under s 99 of the Employment Act 1975 (now s 188 of the TULR(C)A 1992), would not transfer from the transferor to the transferee. Regulation 5(2)(*a*) provides that on a transfer all the transferor's rights, powers, duties and liabilities under, or in connection with, any such contract shall be transferred to the transferee. The EAT held that although the words 'in connection with' were extremely wide, the employer's duties or liabilities which lead to the making of a declaration that the employer has not complied with the requirements of s 99 of the 1975 Act, arise under the Act and not in connection with any contract with an individual employee but by reason of the failure to consult a recognised union. However, the position may be different where terms of a collective agreement have been incorporated into the individual's contract of employment.

The transfer of the business may take place at a single moment. or it may be spread over a period of time as, for instance, where there is an exchange of contracts with completion taking place at a later date. In *Kestongate Ltd v Miller* [1986] ICR 672, the EAT thought that transfer could be on exchange of contracts where completion took place later. However, in *Spence*'s case, above, the Court of Appeal appeared to assume that transfer meant completion. In *Wheeler v Patel* [1987] ICR 631, doubt was cast upon whether the decision in *Kestongate* was right, particularly since it was decided before *Spence*'s case. In *Brook Lane Finance Co Ltd v Bradley* [1988] IRLR 283, further support was given to the view that transfer takes place on completion. However, in *Macer v Abafast Ltd* [1990] IRLR 137, the EAT seems to have assumed that exchange could be a transfer, or indeed that possibly an offer and acceptance prior to exchange could be a linked transaction and therefore a transfer. Regulation 3(4) provides that linked transactions may be regarded as one. In *Wheeler*'s case, *above*, it was held that exchange and completion could not be construed as a linked transaction. It is suggested that exchange and completion should be regarded as two separate parts of the same transaction. They are only the method of carrying out the transaction: see *Longden and another v Ferrari and another* [1994] IRLR 157. In *A & G Tuck Ltd v Bartlett and A & G Tuck (Slough) Ltd* [1994] IRLR 162, the EAT held that even where the employee remained in the employment of the transferor until two weeks after the transfer, continuity was not affected. Paragraph 17(2) of Sched 13 to the 1978 Act appears to apply where the employee is employed by the transferee in connection with the transfer after a gap which related to the machinery of the transfer.

In *Justfern Ltd v D'Ingerthorpe and others* [1994] IRLR 164, the EAT held that para 17(2) operated where a lecturer's employment with a college terminated due to its insolvency, and he was re-employed by the new management over a week later. This was so even though he had received unemployment benefit—he was available for work. The approach in *Macer's* case was held not to be limited to deliberate avoidance schemes and para 17(2) operated where the termination was by virtue of the employer' insolvency, rather than as a step in the transfer of a business.

A further issue which remains to be determined is whether or not continuity of employment is preserved under the regulations. Even if it is not, it is preserved under para 17. The problem was considered in *Keabeech Ltd v Mulcahy* [1985] ICR 79. One view is that continuity is preserved under para 17 rather than the regulations. Continuous employment is neither a right nor liability. It is simply a question of calculation based upon facts: see *Macer's* case, *above*. It is open to argument that the transfer of an undertaking within the regulations is wider than the transfer of a business within the EP(C)A 1978. The other view is that reg 5(1) provides for statutory novation so that the employee is deemed to have been employed by the transferee from the commencement of the contract of employment under which he is serving immediately before the transfer. Hence continuity is preserved.

There may be a transfer of a business, notwithstanding that a proposed merger is subsequently called off: *Dabell v Vale Industrial Services (Nottingham) Ltd* [1988] IRLR 439. Dabell was employed by the company which became technically insolvent. An agreement was reached in principle to transfer the business to Nofotec. Orders, machines and other items or materials were transferred, together with a list of the company's debtors. Dabell and others were sent to premises under Nofotec's control. Subsequently negotiations between the respondent and Nofotec failed and the merger did not take place. Nonetheless there was a transfer.

Regulation 5(5) provides that the transfer of the contract of employment is without prejudice to any right of an employee arising other than by virtue of the regulations to terminate his contract of employment without notice if a substantial change is made in his working conditions to his detriment. This regulation provides that no right shall arise by reason only that under this regulation the identity of the employer changes unless the employee can show that in the circumstances the change is a significant change and is to his detriment. The first part of the regulation confirms the employee's right to resign and claim a constructive dismissal where there is a substantial change in his working conditions to his detriment. The second part deals with the change in the identity of the employer. The change in identity of the employer of itself is not sufficient to enable the employee to terminate his contract without notice and claim a constructive dismissal, unless the change is a significant change and is to the employee's detriment. It is difficult to envisage circumstances in which a change of employer's identity is likely to be a significant change and to be to the employee's detriment. Where the employee can bring himself within this provision it seems that he can claim a constructive dismissal. Presumably, the use of the word detriment is intended to suggest a change which strikes at the root of the contract and so is fundamental. See also now reg 5(4A) and (4B) *above*.

Collective agreements

Regulation 6 provides that where at the time of a relevant transfer there is a collective agreement made by or on behalf of the transferor with a recognised union (not necessarily an independent trade union) covering an employee whose contract is automatically transferred under reg 5(1), then broadly the effect is to transfer the obligations arising out of the collective agreement to the transferee. Regulation 6 is without prejudice to s 18 of the TULRA 1974 (now s 179 of the TULR(C)A 1992) which provides that collective agreements are conclusively presumed to be unenforceable, unless the agreement is in writing and contains a proviso that it is intended to be legally enforceable. Where the terms of a collective agreement have been incorporated into the individual's contract of employment, reg 5 will apply. Regulation 6 is concerned with the transferee's liability under a collective agreement. A collective agreement will cover terms such as disputes procedures, collective grievance procedures or redundancy procedures. It may provide for union recognition. Regulation 6, however, does not meet the requirements of art 3.2 of the Directive. That requires collective agreements to remain in force for at least one year. Where the transferee is an emanation of the State, the Directive can be relied upon by an individual.

Where a collective agreement is 'transferred' the transferee is not obligated to observe the terms in respect of employees who are not in the undertaking at the time it was transferred: *Ny Mølle Kro, above*. Where, after a relevant transfer, the undertaking, or part thereof, maintains an identity distinct from the remainder of the transferee's undertaking, reg 9 applies. Where before such a transfer an independent trade union is recognised to any extent by the transferor in respect of employees of any description who in consequence of the transfer become employees of the transferee, then, after the transfer, the union shall be deemed to have been recognised by the transferee to the same extent in respect of employees of that description and any agreement for recognition may be varied or rescinded accordingly.

There is a potential overlap between regs 6 and 9. A collective agreement may provide for union recognition. Under reg 6 this obligation will pass to the transferee even though the undertaking does not maintain a separate identity in the hands of the transferee. If the agreement is not legally enforceable it is open to the transferee to terminate the same. The transferee may enter into negotiations with the union after the transfer.

A collective agreement has the same meaning as in the TULR(C)A 1992 and a recognised trade union has the same meaning as in the EP(C)A 1978: see reg 2(1).

Exclusion of occupational pension schemes

Regulations 5 and 6 do not apply to a contract of employment or collective agreement which relates to an occupational pension scheme or to any rights, powers, duties or liabilities under or in connection with any such contract, or subsisting by virtue of any such agreement and relating to such a scheme or otherwise arising in connection with the person's employment and relating to such scheme. An occupational pension scheme is one within the meaning of the Social Security Pensions Act 1975: reg 7(1).

However, any provisions of an occupational pension scheme which do not relate to benefits for old age, invalidity or survivors shall be treated as not being part of the scheme: reg 7(2). See *Perry v Intec Colleges Ltd* [1993] IRLR 56, decided before reg 7(2) was inserted into the regulations by s 33 of the TURERA 1993. Here the tribunal held that the regulations did not comply with Directive 77/187 which requires member states to protect the interests of employees in respect of rights conferring on them immediate or prospective entitlement to old age benefits, including survivors' benefits, under supplementary schemes. The tribunal adopted a purposive construction of the regulations to accord with the intentions of the Directive. It held it was entitled to imply further wording into the regulations to ensure that they complied with the Directive. Compare this with the decision of the EAT in *Walden Engineering Co Ltd v Warrener* [1993] IRLR 420, where it was held that the pension scheme in question fell within the exclusion from the transfer regulations (before amendment) so that the new owner was not obliged to provide a pension no less beneficial than provided by the previous employer. Here the EAT did not feel they could insert the wording as in *Perry*.

Dismissal of an employee because of a transfer

Regulation 8(1) provides that where either before or after a relevant transfer any employee of the transferor or transferee is dismissed that employee shall be treated for the purposes of Part V of the EP(C)A 1978 as unfairly dismissed if the transfer or a reason connected with it is the reason or principal reason for his dismissal. A dismissal can be in connection with a transfer of an undertaking even though at the moment of the dismissal there is no identifiable transferee: see *Harrison Bowden Ltd v Bowden* [1994] ICR 186. However, in *Ibex Trading Co Ltd (in administration) v Walton & Others and Alpine (Double Glazing) Ltd* (1994) (unreported), the EAT found that where employees were dismissed in an attempt to make the business saleable, they were not dismissed for a reason connected with the transfer. Doubtless the Court of Appeal will eventually decide between the two apparently conflicting approaches. Under reg 8(1) a dismissal is automatically unfair. However reg 8(2) provides that where an economic, technical or organisational reason entailing changes in the workforce of either the transferor or the transferee before or after a relevant transfer is the reason or principal reason for dismissing an employee, reg 8(1) shall not apply. In such case the dismissal shall for the purposes of s 57(1)(*b*) of the EP(C)A 1978 be regarded as having been for a substantial reason of a kind such as to justify the dismissal of an employee holding the position which that employee held. It will then be for the tribunal to determine whether the employer acted reasonably in dismissing the employee under s 57(3) of the EP(C)A 1978: see *McGrath v Rank Leisure Ltd* [1985] ICR 527.

Regulation 8(3) provides that the regulations apply whether or not the employee in question is employed in the undertaking or part thereof transferred or to be transferred.

Regulation 8(4) provides that reg 8(1) shall not apply where the dismissal of an employee was by reason of the application of s 5 of the Aliens Restriction (Amendment) Act 1919 to his employment.

The onus is upon the dismissing employer to establish an economic technical or organisational reason entailing changes in the workforce: see *Forth Estuary Engineering Ltd v Litster*, above.

In *Anderson and Another v Dalkeith Engineering Ltd* [1985] ICR 66, the EAT held that the words 'economic', 'technical', and 'organisational' were not mutually exclusive and a reason may 'at the same time be economic and organisational, technical and organisational, or all three together'. In *Wheeler's* case the EAT held that economic had to be construed *ejusdem generis* with the adjectives technical and organisational. This justified giving a limited meaning to the word economic.

One issue involving reg 8(2) is its impact upon the employee's entitlement to a redundancy payment. There is a division of opinion between the Scottish EAT and the English EAT. In *Meikle v McPhail (Charleston Arms)* [1983] IRLR 351, the Scottish division of the EAT held that where a dismissal is for an economic, technical or organisational reason, it is treated as a substantial reason of a kind such as to justify the dismissal of the employee holding the position which that employee held under s 57(1)(*b*) of the EP(C)A 1978. Therefore, the dismissal cannot be described as being a dismissal by reason of redundancy because that is a reason within s 57(2)(*c*). This approach was followed in *Canning v (1) Niaz (2) McLoughlin* [1983] IRLR 431. However, in *Gorictree Ltd v Jenkinson* [1985] ICR 51, the English division of the EAT held:

> we are unable to accept that regulation 8(2) creates, for the purposes of s 57 of the EP(C)A 1978 a category of reasons from which redundancy is necessarily excluded. As a matter of fact, we suppose that redundancy is one of the most common of the economic, technical or organisation reasons entailing changes in the workforce to which regulation 8(2) applies. If the reasons comprised in regulation 8(2) commonly include redundancy as a matter of fact, we feel that clear words would be required to exclude redundancy as a matter of law; and the words used do not appear to us to satisfy that requirement ... the position would be different if reg 8(2) required the reasons to which it applied to be regarded as falling within the category of some 'other' substantial reason, for that would imply that it had to be regarded as a reason other than redundancy.
>   ... we attach much importance to the fact that regulation 8(2)(*b*) applies for the purposes of s 57(1)(*b*). The function of s 57(1) is to determine 'for the purposes of this Part'—that is, Part V of the Act—whether the dismissal of an employee was fair or unfair. The right to a redundancy payment, on the other hand, is created by s 81 which introduces Part VI of the Act.

In *Anderson*'s case, *above*, the Scottish division of the EAT preferred the decision in *Gorictree Ltd v Jenkinson*, *above*, to that in *Canning v (1) Niaz (2) McLoughlin*, *above*, and suggested that it was open to tribunals to follow the reasoning in *Gorictree Ltd v Jenkinson*, if they preferred it to that in *Canning v (1) Niaz (2) McLoughlin*.

Another issue arising out of reg 8(2) is whether or not a pre-transfer dismissal can be for an economic, technical or organisational reason. A pre-transfer dismissal may be at the request of the transferee. There may be a contractual obligation to that effect in the agreement. In *Anderson*'s case the Scottish division of the EAT came to the conclusion that a contractual stipulation that the transferor should dismiss the employees prior to the transfer was for an economic reason and in this case the dismissal was unfair. In *Litster*'s case, the EAT also appeared to accept that a pre-transfer dismissal could be for an economic technical or organisational reason. However, more recent cases throw doubts on this.

Thus, in *Wheeler v Patel, above*, the EAT held that the word economic had to be construed *ejusdem generis* with the words technical and organisational. Economic had to be given a limited meaning relating to the conduct of the business. It did not include broader economic reasons, eg the achievement of a sale, or sale at an enhanced price. In *Gateway Hotels Ltd v Stewart* [1988] IRLR 287, the hotel was sold by Gateway to Lytpark. Lytpark insisted as a condition of the sale that the employees should be dismissed before the sale. The employees were dismissed by reason of redundancy prior to the sale. Some were subsequently taken on by the purchaser. It was argued that the reason for the dismissal was redundancy and that that was a reason within reg 8(2). The EAT, upholding the decision of the tribunal, found that the principal reason for the dismissal was the condition in the contract of sale and this did not amount to an economic, technical or organisational reason. Thus, following this case, any agreement between the parties that the employees should be dismissed prior to the transfer will not be a reason within reg 8(2). Likewise, some tribunals have found that where a receiver dismisses employees prior to the transfer simply to gain an enhanced price even though not expressly asked by the purchaser, the reason is not one in reg 8(2).

Regulation 8(2) will apply if the reason for the dismissal is an economic reason relating to the conduct of the business. A genuine redundancy unconnected with the transfer will fall within reg 8(2).

Liability for automatically unfair pre-transfer dismissals will pass to the transferee under the principle in *Litster*'s case, *above*. Regulation 5(2) provides that any action taken by the transferor, in relation to the transfer, shall be deemed to have been done by the transferee. It appears quite clear, therefore, that a dismissal before the transfer, by the transferor is deemed to be by the transferee. Similarly, the regulation provides that the transferor's liabilities shall be transferred to the transferee. There have been a number of cases where the liability has been placed on the transferee. However, in *Allan v Stirling District Council* [1994] IRLR 208, the Scottish EAT decided that the regulation does not exclude the liability of the transferor. It has to be said that this is a generous addition to the wording of the Regulation. It is suggested that the earlier cases are safer authorities. See p 322 *above*.

The economic, technical or organisational reason must entail changes in the workforce: reg 8(2). In *Berriman v Delabole Slate Ltd* [1985] ICR 546, Berriman was a quarryman. He had a guaranteed weekly wage of £100. The undertaking in which he was employed was transferred. After the transfer the transferee told Berriman that his remuneration would be altered to an hourly rate of £1.94 (£77.60 a week) with an anticipated weekly bonus of around £22.00. The transferee wished to ensure that the employees transferred enjoyed standard rates of pay with existing employees. Berriman resigned and claimed a constructive dismissal. The EAT found that the dismissal was unfair. There were no changes in the workforce, the only change was in terms and conditions of employment—the rate of pay. The fact that Berriman had been constructively dismissed was not sufficient to constitute a change in the workforce for the purposes of reg 8(2). The Court of Appeal affirmed the decision of the EAT and held:

> First, the phrase 'economic, technical or organisational reason entailing changes in the workforce' in our judgment requires that the change in the workforce is part of the economic, technical or organisational reason. The

employers' plan must be to achieve changes in the workforce. It must be an objective of the plan, not just a possible consequence of it.

Secondly, we do not think that the dismissal of one employee followed by the engagement of another in his place constitutes a change in the 'workforce'. To our minds, the word 'workforce' connotes the whole body of employees as an entity: it corresponds to the 'strength' or the 'establishment'. Changes in the identity of the individuals who make up the workforce do not constitute changes in the workforce itself so long as the overall numbers and functions of the employees looked at as a whole remain unchanged.

The Court of Appeal was not persuaded by the argument that if this construction was adopted it would mean that after a transfer of an undertaking the employer would not be able to impose on the employees taken over changes in the terms and conditions of employment which, if the transfer had not taken place, they could have imposed upon the existing workforce. See *Hollister v National Farmers Union* [1979] ICR 542, where it had been recognised that employers may be able to make changes in the terms and conditions of employment where commercial considerations so dictate. The Court of Appeal recognised that one of the intentions of the regulations was to safeguard employee's rights. Among the employees' most important rights are the existing terms and conditions of service. See also *Bullard and Another v Marchant and Another* [1986] ICR 389.

In practice the transferee who wishes to change the terms and conditions of employment may be better off in dismissing the employees, and then offering new terms and conditions to such of the employees as are prepared to return on those new terms and conditions. This would appear to be within reg 8(2).

In *Crawford v Swinton Insurance Brokers Ltd* [1990] ICR 85, Crawford was told that after the transfer of the business the nature of her job would change from secretarial work to selling insurance. Instead of working from home she would have to attend the office and work normal office hours, and would lose the use of her company car. She resigned and claimed a constructive dismissal. The tribunal found that she had been constructively dismissed, but that the dismissal was not automatically unfair under reg 8(1) because the reason was an organisational one entailing changes in the workforce within reg 8(2). The tribunal found the dismissal was fair. The EAT held that there could be a change in the workforce under reg 8(2) where the same people are retained but undertake different job functions. In *Porter and Nanayakkara v Queen's Medical Centre (Nottingham University Hospital)* [1993] IRLR 486, a case brought directly under the provisions of the Directive, the High Court found that the changed methods which the defendants intended to introduce were a reorganisation entailing changes in the workforce. The defendants were introducing a new organisation which called for a different kind of doctor. The plaintiffs were redundant because the employer's alteration to the requirement to do work of a particular kind, and the change in the work force for organisational reasons, was the termination of the existing contracts.

Once the employer has been able to establish that reg 8(2) applies, it is then necessary for the tribunal to consider the test of reasonableness in the normal way: *McGrath v Rank Leisure Ltd* [1985] ICR 527.

Where the dismissal is held to be unfair then the tribunal must assess compensation in the normal way. However, where the employer seeks to limit his liability by arguing that even if the employees had not been dismissed at the time when they were, they would have been dismissed within a short time thereafter, the onus is upon the employer to establish the evidence limiting its liability.

Duty to inform and consult trade union representatives

Regulation 10 imposes a duty on the employer of 'any affected employees' to inform and consult a recognised trade union. It also imposes on a transferee the duty to provide the transferor with information to enable the latter to comply with his obligations. The recognised trade union may complain to a tribunal concerning a breach. Regulation 11 empowers the tribunal to award compensation not exceeding 4 weeks' pay. There is, however, no right to claim unfair dismissal for a breach of reg 10.

Restrictions on contracting out

Regulation 12 provides that any provision of any agreement whether a contract of employment or not shall be void in so far as it purports to exclude or limit the operation of regs 5, 8 or 10, or to preclude any person presenting a complaint to a tribunal under reg 11.

Exclusions

Regulations 8, 10 and 11 do not apply to employment where under his contract of employment the employee ordinarily works outside the UK. A person employed to work on board a ship registered in the UK shall, unless the employment is wholly outside the UK or he is not ordinarily resident in the UK, be regarded as a person who under his contract ordinarily works in the UK: reg 13. See Chapter 1.

Coming into force of the regulations

Amendments to the 1977 Regulations made by s 33 of the TURERA 1993 have effect in relation to any transfer of an undertaking taking place on or after 30 August 1993 and the related repeal of s 94 of the EP(C)A 1978, and so those cases will have to be decided in relation to the law as amended.

Chapter 16

Remedies

Where the tribunal makes a finding of unfair dismissal it may make an order for reinstatement or re-engagement, or it may make an award of compensation: s 68 of the EP(C)A 1978. An order for either reinstatement or re-engagement is the principal remedy.

The tribunal must explain to the employee that it can make an order for reinstatement or re-engagement, and explain the circumstances in which these orders can be made. It must also ask him whether he wishes to be reinstated or re-engaged: s 68(1) of the EP(C)A 1978. See also *Pirelli General Cable Works Ltd v Murray* [1979] IRLR 190, where it was held that the tribunal's obligation to explain its power to the employee is mandatory even if the employee is professionally represented. If the employee is not seeking reinstatement or re-engagement the tribunal must consider compensation: s 68(2) of the EP(C)A 1978.

Reinstatement

An order for reinstatement has the effect of putting the employee in the same position which he would have enjoyed had he not been dismissed: s 69(2) of the EP(C)A 1978. The tribunal, under s 69(5) of the EP(C)A 1978, has to take into account the following considerations:

(a) Does the employee wish to be reinstated?
(b) Is is practicable for the employer to comply with an order for reinstatement?
(c) Where the employee has caused or contributed to some extent to the dismissal, would it be just to order his reinstatement?

The tribunal must, under s 70(1) of the EP(C)A 1978, ignore the fact that the employer has engaged a permanent replacement for the dismissed employee unless the employer can show:

(a) that it was not practicable for him to arrange for the dismissed employee's work to be done without engaging a permanent replacement; or
(b) that he engaged the replacement after the lapse of a reasonable

period, without having heard from the dismissed employee that he wished to be reinstated or re-engaged, and that when the employer engaged the replacement it was no longer reasonable for him to arrange for the dismissed employee's work to be done except by a permanent replacement.

On making the order the tribunal must, under s 69(2) of the EP(C)A 1978, specify:

(a) any amount payable by the employer in respect of any benefit which the employee might reasonably be expected to have had but for the dismissal, including arrears of pay, for the period between the date of termination of employment and the date of reinstatement;

(b) any rights and privileges, including seniority and pension rights, which must be restored to the employee; and

(c) the date by which the order must be complied with.

In addition, the order must reflect any improvement in the terms and conditions which the employee would have enjoyed but for the dismissal: s 69(3) of the EP(C)A 1978.

If the employee has a contractual right to be promoted then that is something which the tribunal must take into account in making an order: *O'Laoire v Jackel International Ltd* [1991] IRLR 170.

The amount of any benefit payable by the employer to the employee under para (a), *above*, is to be reduced by any sums received by the employee between the date of termination and the date of reinstatement by way of:

(a) wages in lieu of notice or *ex gratia* payments paid by the employer; and

(b) remuneration paid in respect of employment with another employer.

The tribunal also must take into account, so as to reduce the amount, any other benefits it thinks appropriate in the circumstances: s 70(2) of the EP(C)A 1978. There is no limit to the amount of any benefit which the tribunal may order to be deducted under this provision.

Where the employee has been guilty of any contributory fault the tribunal must consider whether it is just to order reinstatement: s 69(5)(c) of the EP(C)A 1978. However, the order cannot reflect any element of contributory fault because of the effect of s 69(2) of the EP(C)A 1978.

In *Boots Company plc v Lees-Collier* [1986] IRLR 485, the employee was dismissed because his employers believed that he was guilty of theft. The dismissal was unfair and the tribunal ordered him to be reinstated. The employers appealed and the EAT found that the wording of s 69(5)(c) echoed the words of s 74(6) of the EP(C)A 1978 which provides that where the tribunal finds that the dismissal was to any extent caused or contributed to by any action of the employee, it shall reduce the amount of the compensatory award by such proportion as it considers just and equitable having regard to that finding. Thus, once the tribunal had reached the conclusion that the employee's conduct had not caused or contributed to his dismissal, in the sense that it would justify a reduction in the compensatory award, there was no rule for finding that he had caused or contributed to some extent to his dismissal for the purposes of s 69(5)(c) of the EP(C)A 1978.

Re-engagement

The tribunal may make an order that the employee should be re-engaged by the employer or by a successor of the employer or by an associated employer in employment comparable to that from which he was dismissed, or other suitable employment: s 69(4) of the EP(C)A 1978. In deciding whether to make an order for re-engagement the tribunal, under s 69(6) of the EP(C)A 1978, has to take into account the following considerations:

(a) What are the employee's wishes as to the nature of the order to be made?

(b) Is it practicable for the employer, successor, or associated employer to comply with an order for re-engagement?

(c) Where the employee caused or contributed to some extent to the dismissal, would it be just to order his re-engagement and if so on what terms?

Except where the tribunal takes into account contributory fault, where it orders re-engagement it must do so on terms which are, so far as is reasonably practicable, as favourable as an order for reinstatement: s 69(6) of the EP(C)A 1978.

In deciding whether it is practicable for the employer to comply with an order for re-engagement the tribunal has to ignore a permanent replacement, except in the same limited circumstances as in the case of reinstatement: s 70(1) of the EP(C)A 1978. See under 'Reinstatement', at p 335.

Where the tribunal makes an order for re-engagement it must specify the terms on which re-engagement is to take place including:

(a) the identity of the employer:

(b) the nature of the employment;

(c) the remuneration for the employment;

(d) any amount payable by the employer in respect of any benefit which the employee might reasonably be expected to have had but for the dismissal, including arrears of pay, for the period between the date of termination of employment and the date of re-engagement;

(e) any rights and privileges, including seniority and pension rights, which must be restored to the employee; and

(f) the date by which the order must be complied with: s 69(4) of the EP(C)A 1978.

Section 70(2) applies to computing (*d*), *above*. Again, there is no limit on the amount the tribunal can deduct. See under 'Reinstatement' at p 335.

Where the tribunal makes an order for re-engagement it writes a new contract for the parties. Sometimes a tribunal directs the employer to offer re-engagement within a stated period upon terms specified by the tribunal (which is called an 'offer direction'), without specifying as to whether and if so in what circumstances or upon what terms the employee should be bound in law to accept it. An offer direction does not discharge the obligations of the tribunal under s 69(4) of the EP(C)A 1978 and is to be discouraged: *Lilley Construction Ltd v Dunn* [1984] IRLR 483.

Where the tribunal finds that the employee has contributed to his dismissal by as much as 75 per cent, an order for re-engagement would probably not be appropriate: see *Nairne v Highland and Islands Fire Brigade* [1989] IRLR 366.

There is no power to reduce the arrears of pay for the period between the date of termination of employment and the date of re-engagement because a tribunal considers that if the employee had pursued her complaint more vigorously or expeditiously she would probably have been re-engaged at an earlier date. An order for reinstatement requires the employer to treat the employee in all respects as if she had not been dismissed and an order for re-engagement must be on terms which are, so far as is reasonably practicable, as favourable as an order for reinstatement: see s 69(6) of the EP(C)A 1978. The discretion given to the tribunal in s 69(1) of the EP(C)A 1978 is not capable of overriding these mandatory provisions. The reference in s 69(2)(*a*) and (4)(*d*) to a benefit which the employee might have had but for the dismissal does not confer a discretion on the tribunal to increase or decrease what the employee would otherwise have had: *City and Hackney Health Authority v Crisp* [1990] IRLR 47.

Where a tribunal orders re-engagement at a lower salary, in assessing arrears of pay up to the date of re-engagement, the relevant salary is the salary at the date of dismissal and not the new salary: see *Electronic Data Processing Ltd v Wright* [1986] IRLR 8.

Non-compliance with order for reinstatement or re-engagement

Tribunals have no power to enforce orders for reinstatement or re-engagement. Where an employer fails to comply with an order the matter must be dealt with under s 71(2) of the EP(C)A 1978. The tribunal will make an award of compensation calculated in the usual way together with an additional award or special award. Only one order can be made under s 69 of the EP(C)A 1978 and an applicant cannot try all over again for a further order under s 69: see *Mabirizi v National Hospital for Nervous Diseases* [1990] IRLR 133.

It used to be the case that the monetary provisions of a reinstatement or re-engagement order did not create a cause of action enforceable through the county courts: *O'Laoire v Jackel International Ltd* [1990] IRLR 70. Section 71 of the EP(C)A 1978 has been amended by s 30(1) and (2)(*b*) of the TURERA 1993 by the addition of s 71(1A) which provides that the statutory limit on a compensatory award (at present £11,000) may be exceeded by the amount necessary to enable the award to reflect fully a monetary award under s 69. Before this amendment there was no incentive on an employer to comply with a reinstatement order, whereas now, if he fails to implement it, he will still have to pay the arrears under the reinstatement order as well as the compensatory award.

Partial compliance

Where the employee is reinstated or re-engaged, as the case may be, but the terms of the order are not fully complied with, the tribunal must make an award of compensation to be paid by the employer to the employee of the amount the tribunal thinks fit, having regard to the loss sustained by the employee through the employer's failure to comply fully with the order: s 71(1) of the EP(C)A 1978. The provision is a compensatory one and follows the wording of the section providing for the compensatory award. An award under this heading is based upon the employee's loss subject to a maximum of £11,000, except for the provisions of s 71(1A) *above*. See under 'Compensatory award' at p 348.

Non-compliance

Where the employee is not reinstated or re-engaged, the tribunal must make an award of compensation for unfair dismissal calculated on the same principles which apply where the tribunal awards compensation only (see *below*). Except in a case in which the dismissal is unfair by virtue of s 57A(1)(*a*) and (*b*) (dismissal of or selection for redundancy of employer-appointed health and safety officers or employee health and safety representatives in health and safety cases—see Chapter 13), or in which the employer is able to satisfy the tribunal that it was not practicable to comply with the order, the tribunal must make an additional award of compensation the amount of which will be (i) not less than 26 weeks' pay nor more than 52 weeks' pay, or (ii) not less than 13 weeks' pay nor more than 26 week's pay: s 71(2) of the EP(C)A 1978. Under s 71(3), the higher band will only apply where the employer has dismissed the employee:

(a) where the dismissal is an unlawful act of discrimination within the meaning of SDA 1975, or

(b) where the dismissal is an unlawful act of discrimination within the meaning of RRA 1976.

Where the additional award is not available in health and safety cases to those categories of employee specified in s 57A(1)(a) and (b) then these employees may be eligible for a special award. The remaining categories of employee set out in s 57A(c)–(e) are eligible for the additional award in the normal way.

Again there is no additional award for non-compliance with an order for reinstatement or re-engagement where the dismissal was on union grounds, but the employee may be eligible for a special award. See s 72(2) of the EP(C)A 1978, s 157(1) of the TULR(C)A 1992, and under 'Special award' at p 370.

There is no additional award or special award available where an order is partially complied with, but only where it is not complied with at all. The award in the former case is one for compensation of such amount as the tribunal thinks fit having regard to the loss sustained by the employee in consequence of the failure to comply fully with the order: see s 71(1) of the EP(C)A 1978.

Additional award

Although the additional award is referred to as an award of 'compensation' it is not compensation in the sense that it compensates the employee for specific losses suffered by him. The tribunal has a discretion as to what award it should make within the limits set out *above* and no reference is made to assessing losses. It is impossible to see how it could be argued that these limits reflect the employee's losses. The view that an additional award is a penalty is strengthened by a comparison between the wording of s 71(1) and (2)(b) of the EP(C)A 1978. Subsection (1), which deals with assessment of compensation where the employer has not fully complied with the order for reinstatement or re-engagement, refers to 'loss' and has it origins in the compensatory provision. Subsection (2)(b) makes no reference to 'loss'.

Where a week's wages exceed £205, the excess is ignored: para 8(1)(a) of Sched 14 to the EP(C)A 1978, which applies where the date by which an order for reinstatement or re-engagement must be complied with is a date after 1 April 1992. Previously the limit was £198. A week's pay for the purposes of an additional award is a week's pay gross; a week's pay net is the basis for assessment for the compensatory award: *George v Beecham Group* [1977] IRLR 43.

Tribunals have a wide discretion as to the matters which can be taken into account in deciding where in the range the additional award should fall. The tribunal is entitled to have regard to the conduct of the employer in refusing to comply with the order: see *Morganite*

Electrical Carbon Ltd v Donne [1988] ICR 18, followed in *Motherwell Railway Club v McQueen and Another* [1989] ICR 418. See also *George*'s case, *above*, where the tribunal found it regrettable that a national employer of the size and responsibility of the respondent should be unable to comply with an order for reinstatement of a modest production line employee. It may be material for the tribunal to take into account, where the statutory limit results in compensation being reduced (see *below*), the extent to which the compensatory award has met the actual loss suffered by the employee: see *Donne*'s case, *above*. It may also reflect the fact that the employer's failure to reinstate was neither a wilful refusal nor a device to save money, although culpability attached to the employer's non-compliance: see *Mabirizi*'s case, *above*. See *Darr and another v LRC Products Ltd* [1993] IRLR 257, where the EAT held that the amount of the additional award could be reduced in certain circumstances.

In making an additional award it is incumbent on the tribunal to act with care and scrupulous fairness: *Enessy Co SA (t/a The Tulchan Estate) v Minoprio* [1978] IRLR 489.

Practicability and orders for reinstatement or re-engagement

Practicability must be considered by the tribunal first in deciding whether to make an order for reinstatement or re-engagement and, secondly, where it has made an order which has not been complied with, whether it was practicable for the employer to comply with it.

In *Freemans plc v Flynn* [1984] ICR 874, the EAT held that under s 69(6)(*b*) the tribunal has to take practicability of compliance as a 'consideration' into account, but under s 71(2)(*b*) the employer is under a burden of proof to show that it was not practicable to comply with the order. The EAT followed the reasoning in *Timex Corporation v Thompson* [1981] IRLR 522 (see *below* at p 342), that under s 69(6)(*b*) the tribunal does not have to conclude whether or not it would be practicable to comply with an order for re-engagement, but under s 71(2)(*b*) they do have to make a definite finding.

Making the order

In deciding whether or not to make an order for reinstatement or re-engagement the tribunal is exercising an independent discretion. See s 69 of the EP(C)A 1978. What is practicable depends upon the context.

In *Meridian Ltd v Gomersall* [1977] ICR 597, where two employees were unfairly dismissed for clocking offences, and reinstatement was ordered, the EAT, in deciding whether reinstatement was practicable, referred to *Dedman v British Building and Engineering Appliances Ltd*

[1974] ICR 53, where Scarman LJ found the word 'practicable' to be a word of great flexibility, its application involving common sense and compromise. A broad common sense view is required. In this case reinstatement was not practicable because a redundancy situation had overtaken the company.

Expediency has nothing to do with what is practicable. It describes the state of things which is favourable to the fulfilment of some objective which is in mind and is not a relevant matter for consideration by the tribunal when exercising its discretion as to whether to order reinstatement or re-engagement: (1) *Qualcast (Wolverhampton) Ltd v Ross* and (2) *Ross v Qualcast (Wolverhampton) Ltd* [1979] IRLR 98. 'This legislation is not designed to enable complainants to re-establish ... or vindicate their reputation'. Once a finding of unfair dismissal has been made the tribunal must see 'how reasonably and most sensibly to compensate the ... employee': *Nothman v London Borough of Barnet (No 2)* [1980] IRLR 65 at p 66.

In *Timex Corporation v Thomson* [1981] IRLR 522, the EAT held that the tribunal must only 'have regard' to practicability under s 69(6), and only under s 71(2)(*b*) of the EP(C)A 1978 need it make a definite finding on the question. In *Rao v Civil Aviation Authority* [1992] IRLR 203, confirmed by the Court of Appeal on other grounds, the EAT held the word practicable in s 69(5)(*b*) and s 69(6)(*b*) of the EP(C)A 1978 does not mean possible or capable and the test is not whether or not reinstatement or re-engagement is 'capable' of being put into effect. In deciding whether or not to make the order for reinstatement or re-engagement it is not necessary for the tribunal to reach a conclusion on practicability, but it must look at past and anticipated future events, maintaining a fair, just and reasonable balance between the parties.

In *Cold Drawn Tubes Ltd v Middleton* [1992] IRLR 160, the EAT held that under s 71(2)(*b*) of the EP(C)A 1978 reinstatement is not a practicable course of action open to the employer if it would result in redundancies or overmanning. Each case has to be decided in the context of all the circumstances taking a broad common sense view and in this case it was not practicable for the employer to reinstate the employee, because there was insufficient work for him to do.

In *Port of London Authority v Payne* [1994] IRLR 9, the Court of Appeal held that, while under s 69 of the EP(C)A 1978 the tribunal must consider practicability, this is only a provisional assessment, the matter being finally decided under s 71(2)(*b*) of the EP(C)A 1978.

The employer can rely on facts occurring after the order has been made and it is under s 71(2)(*b*), that the employer must satisfy the tribunal it was not practicable to comply with the order. The test is of practicability, not possibility, and although the employer's reasons should be scrutinised the tribunal should give due weight to management's commercial judgment. See also *Boots Company plc v Lees-Collier* [1986] IRLR 485.

In looking at the practicability the tribunal is entitled to consider the industrial reality. In *Coleman v Magnet Joinery Ltd* [1974] ICR 25, affirmed by the Court of Appeal [1975] ICR 46, Coleman and another employee had stopped paying union dues. The union and company sought to persuade them to continue payment but failed. A stoppage of work resulted and the company was threatened with a strike if nothing was done about the employees. The company therefore dismissed the employees and the tribunal, finding the dismissal unfair, held that re-engagement was not practicable. Before the NIRC it was argued for the employees that 'practicable' had to be given 'a very restricted construction closely equated to "possible" '. The court considered that such an interpretation could lead to unfortunate results, and there is little point in making decisions which cannot be acted upon, which might lead to industrial strife, and which would lose the tribunal credibility. In this case the order was likely to lead to industrial unrest and so it was not practicable.

In *Bateman v British Leyland (UK) Ltd* [1974] ICR 403, Bateman refused to join a union and was dismissed following consequent industrial unrest and the threat of a stoppage of work. Before the NIRC it was argued on Bateman's behalf that since he was not to blame and was anxious to be re-employed an order should be made for re-engagement. It was further argued that the tribunal had erroneously held that because a recommendation for re-engagement would have been resented on the shop floor it would not be practicable; the tribunal should have assumed that its recommendations would be complied with. The NIRC upheld the view of the tribunal emphasising the importance of preserving tribunals' discretion in deciding whether re-engagement was practicable. See also *Langston v Amalgamated Union of Engineering Workers (No 2)* [1974] ICR 510.

Friction may arise because a reinstatement or re-engagement would cause dissension within the place of employment either generally: *see Coleman v Tolemans Delivery Service Ltd* [1973] IRLR 67, or with a particular person or persons: see *Wood v Louis C Edwards and Sons (Manchester) Ltd* [1972] IRLR 18; *Thornton v SJ Kitchin Ltd* [1972] IRLR 46.

It may not be practicable to order re-engagement because the employee has made allegations during the course of the proceedings about her fellow employees: see *Nothman v London Borough of Barnet (No 2)* [1980] IRLR 65, where Nothman alleged that her fellow employees had conspired to oust her from her employment.

In *Goodbody v British Railways Board* [1977] IRLR 84, the tribunal considered that reinstatement was practicable. Goodbody had refused to join a union because of his membership of 'The Brethren'. The tribunal found the dismissal unfair and ordered reinstatement because

both parties to the application accepted that there would be no difficulty in a reinstatement and were able to agree the terms.

In addition to the industrial realities the tribunal is also entitled,
when considering re-engagement, to look and see if there is a suitable
vacancy. It may not be possible to make an order for reinstatement or
re-engagement where at the time of the hearing the place of work had
closed: *Mawson v Leadgate Engineering Ltd* [1972] IRLR 105, or where
a redundancy situation has arisen at the place of employment: *Trusler
v Lummus Co Ltd* [1972] IRLR 35. An order for reinstatement or re-
engagement may place an undue burden upon the employer: *Perks v
Geest Industries Ltd* [1974] IRLR 228 or the employee himself may
not be able to return because he is no longer fit: *McAulay v Cemen-
tation Chemicals Ltd* [1972] IRLR 71.

Reinstatement or re-engagement will be difficult where there was a
close personal relationship between the employer and the employee,
as in the case of a small employer. It is probable that an order for
reinstatement or re-engagement in such circumstances will be exceptional and should only be made where the tribunal is clear that there
is powerful evidence that it will succeed: *Enessy Co SA (t/a The Tulchan Estate) v Minoprio* [1978] IRLR 489.

Enforcing the order

Where an employer fails to comply with an order for reinstatement or
re-engagement he will only escape an additional award if he can show
that it was not practicable to implement the order: s 71(2)(*b*) of the
EP(C)A 1978. In *George v Beecham Group, above,* the tribunal did
not accept that reinstatement was not practicable because of the long
history of the affair and the effect on other employees, and the result-
ant undermining of management's authority. In its view these were all
exaggerated fears which, although bound to arise to some extent,
should be overcome by competent management. Redundancy arising
after the tribunal hearing may be an example of where it is not
practicable to implement the order.

Where the tribunal makes an order for reinstatement or re-engagement which the employer does not follow, the tribunal may still make
an additional award of compensation, even though, following the order,
the employee decides not to return, if the employer has reached his
decision in ignorance of the employee's change of heart: *Cullen v
Neilly* (1977) (unreported).

Other awards of compensation

Where the tribunal makes an order for reinstatement or re-engagement
which is not complied with, then in addition to any additional award
of compensation (see 'Additional award' at p 339 *et seq*), it must make

a basic award and a compensatory award. In certain circumstances it will also make a special award. See under 'Special award' at p 370. Where it finds the dismissal unfair but makes no order for reinstatement or re-engagement it must make a basic award and a compensatory award.

Basic award

A basic award will be made even though the employee has suffered no financial loss other than his accrued rights, eg redundancy entitlement: see *Cadbury Ltd v Doddington* [1977] ICR 982. The amount of the basic award depends upon the length of continuous employment. Starting with the effective date of termination and working backwards, the number of complete years of continuous employment is calculated: s 73(3) of the EP(C)A 1978. Under this section the employee is entitled to:

    (*a*) $1\frac{1}{2}$ weeks' pay for each year of employment in which the employee was not below the age of 41;

    (*b*) 1 week's pay for each year of employment not falling within para (*a*) above in which the employee was not below the age of 22; and

    (*c*) $\frac{1}{2}$ week's pay for each such year of employment not falling within either of paras (*a*) and (*b*).

The effect of para (*c*) is that an employee who at the effective date of termination is aged between 16 and 18 can claim a basic award calculated in accordance with that paragraph. Employees who have a year of employment in which their 41st or 22nd birthdays fall may count that year in the higher bracket for the purpose of calculating the basic award.

Where the effective date of termination is after the 64th birthday, the amount of the basic award will be reduced by $\frac{1}{12}$ for each complete calendar month after the 64th birthday, and before the effective date of termination: s 73(5) and (6) of the EP(C)A 1978. An employee whose contractual age of retirement is in excess of 65 may claim unfair dismissal: *London Borough of Barnet v Nothman* [1979] IRLR 35. However he cannot recover a basic award.

Where by virtue of s 55(5) to (7) of the EP(C)A 1978, a date is treated as the effective date of termination which is later than the effective date of termination as defined by s 55(4) the period falling between the two dates counts as a period of employment for the purposes of computing the basic award: para 11(1) of Sched 13 to the EP(C)A 1978. Section 55(5) to (7) of the EP(C)A 1978 has the effect of extending the effective date of termination as defined in s 55(4) by the length of notice prescribed in s 49 in cases where the employee is dismissed without the notice prescribed by s 49 or is constructively dismissed.

In reckoning back the number of years of continuous employment no account is to be taken of years of employment prior to 20 years from the effective date of termination: s 73(4) of the EP(C)A 1978.

The amount of the basic award is limited to two weeks' pay (s 73(2) of the EP(C)A 1978) where the reason, or principal reason, for dismissal is redundancy and the employee:

(a) unreasonably refuses to accept a renewal of the contract or suitable alternative employment or where the employee during a trial period unreasonably terminates the contract under s 82(5) or (6); or

(b) is not dismissed on the ending of his employment under the old contract under s 84(1) (on a renewal of employment or re-engagement).

Section 73 (6A) of the EP(C)A 1978 provides that where the reason or principal reason for dismissal, or for selecting the employee for dismissal for redundancy was a reason specified in s 57A(1)(a) and (b) (dismissal of employer appointed safety representatives, or worker appointed safety representatives or committee members) (see also Chapter 13), then the amount of the basic award must not be less than £2,700. The Secretary of State may by order increase the sum: s 73(6C) of the EP(C)A 1978. There is a corresponding provision in s 156(1) of the TULR(C)A 1992 where a dismissal is unfair by virtue of s 152(1) or s 153 TULR(C)A 1992 (dismissal on union grounds or selection for redundancy on union grounds).

The basic award may be reduced where the employee has unreasonably refused an offer by the employer which if accepted would have had the effect of reinstating him in his employment in all respects as if he had not been dismissed. Here the tribunal must reduce the amount of the basic award to such extent as it considers just and equitable having regard to the finding: s 73(7A) of the EP(C)A 1978. See also s 156(1) of the TULR(C)A 1992.

There are certain matters to be disregarded in assessing contributory fault in cases coming within ss 152 or 153 TULR(C)A 1992 when the tribunal considers whether it would be just and equitable to reduce or further reduce the amount of the award: s 155(1) of the TULR(C)A 1992.

The employee's conduct or action is to be disregarded insofar as it constitutes a breach or proposed breach of a requirement:

(a) to be or become a member of any trade union or of a particular trade union or one of a number of particular trade unions,

(b) to cease to be, or refrain from becoming, a member of any trade union or of a particular trade union or of one of a number of particular trade unions, or

(c) not to take part in the activities of any trade union or of a particular trade union or of one of a number of particular trade unions.

A requirement is a requirement imposed upon the employee by or under any arrangement or contract of employment or other agreement: s 155(2). The employee's conduct or action must not be taken into account where he refuses to make payments in lieu of union membership or to agree to a deduction from pay in lieu of membership. Under s 156 there must the age reduction before the statutory minimum is imposed. In a redundancy case there is to be no reduction for contributory fault (where union grounds are not involved) but only in health and safety cases. See Chapter 13 for the reduction.

The basic award cannot be reduced because of a failure to mitigate but it may be reduced because of contributory fault on the part of the employee: see Mitigation and Contributory Fault *below* at p 373 and p 377 and *Lock v Connell Estate Agents* [1994] IRLR 444. The amount of the basic award is reduced or further reduced by the amount of any redundancy payment awarded by the tribunal under Part VI of the EP(C)A 1978 for the same dismissal or any payment made by the employer on the ground that the dismissal was by reason of redundancy whether in pursuance of Part VI or otherwise: s 73(9) of the EP(C)A 1978 and see s 156(1) of the TULR(C)A 1992.

Section 73(1)(*e*) of the EP(C)A 1978 provides that the calculation of the basic award shall be subject to s 76 which prohibits compensation being awarded under the EP(C)A 1978 for unfair dismissal and the SDA 1975 or the RRA 1976 in respect of the same matter.

For the purposes of the basic award a week's pay is the gross amount: *George v Beecham Group* [1977] IRLR 43. Nevertheless, moneys emanating from someone other than the employer should be excluded in calculating the basic award: *Palmanor (t/a Chaplins Night Club) v Cedron* [1978] ICR 1008 (tips). Payment in excess of £205 is ignored: para 8(1)(*b*) of Sched 14 to the EP(C)A 1978, where the effective date of termination falls on or after 1 April 1992. Previously the limit was £198. Pay for voluntary overtime should not be included in the calculation of the basic award, though net overtime pay should be included when the compensatory award is calculated: *Brownson v Hire Service Shops Ltd* [1978] ICR 517. See Chapter 17.

Where an employer makes an *ex gratia* payment in excess of the total of the maximum compensatory award and the appropriate basic award, the employer is entitled to set off the *ex gratia* payment against the basic award. The tribunal is not obliged to order a further basic award. Although the amount of a basic award can only be reduced in the manner prescribed by statute, where the employer has paid an *ex gratia* payment, including an amount in respect of the basic award, a defence of payment is not reducing the amount of the basic award; it is accepting the amount and putting forward payment as an answer. This is the position whether or not the employer admits liability: *Chelsea Football Club and Athletic Co Ltd v Heath* [1981] IRLR 73.

Whereas the payment in full of a statutory redundancy payment breaks the continuity of employment for the purpose of a later redundancy payment, (see para 1(1) and (2) of Sched 13 to the EP(C)A 1978, there is no corresponding provision relating to basic awards. If the employer is, or becomes, insolvent as defined by s 127 of the EP(C)A 1978, any basic award to which the employee is entitled on (*a*) the date of insolvency, (*b*) the date of termination of employment or (*c*) the date of the award, is recoverable from the National Insurance Fund under the provisions of s 122 of the EP(C)A 1978.

Compensatory award

The amount of a compensatory award is the amount the tribunal considers just and equitable in all the circumstances having regard to the loss sustained by the employee in consequence of the dismissal in so far as that loss is attributable to the action taken by the employer: s 74(1) of the EP(C)A 1978. This is subject to the proviso that the amount of the compensation should not exceed £11,000: s 75(1) of the EP(C)A 1978 where the effective date of termination is on or after 1 June 1993. Previously the limit was £10,000. However, the limit may be exceeded under s 71(1A) and s 74(8) of the EP(C)A 1978 where compensation is payable in circumstances where an additional award is made for reinstatement or re-engagement and is not fully complied with to the extent that it is necessary that the award reflects an amount which would otherwise have been payable under s 69(2)(*a*) or s 69(4)(*d*) of the EP(C)A 1978, where the tribunal on making the order for reinstatement or re-engagement specifies the amount payable in respect of benefits the employee would have had but for the dismissal: s 75(1) of the EP(C)A 1978 (see also under 'Partial compliance' at p 339). For the operation of this limit see s 75(3) which provides that the limit applies to the amount which the tribunal would, apart from this section, award after taking into account any payment made by the employer in respect of the dismissal and any reduction required by statute. The loss referred to in s 74(1) includes any expenses reasonably incurred by the employee in consequence of the dismissal and (subject as *below*) any loss of benefit that he might reasonably be expected to have had but for the dismissal: s 74(2) of the EP(C)A 1978.

The loss in so far as it is a loss of any entitlement, potential entitlement or expectation of, a payment on account of dismissal by reason of redundancy, whether under Part VI of the EP(C)A 1978 or otherwise, includes only the loss by which the amount of that payment exceeds the amount of the basic award for that dismissal; any reduction in the basic award under s 73(7A) to (9) of the EP(C)A 1978 in respect of the same dismissal is ignored for these purposes: s 74(3) of the EP(C)A 1978. Thus any deduction from the basic award cannot be added back in to the entitlement to the compensatory award.

If the amount of any payment made by the employer to the

employee on the grounds that dismissal was by reason of redundancy, whether under Part VI of the EP(C)A 1978 or otherwise, exceeds the basic award which would be payable but for s 73(9), the excess goes to reduce the amount of the compensatory award: s 74(7) of the EP(C)A 1978. Thus, the payment for redundancy is first set off against the basic award and any excess is then set off against the amount of the compensatory award. In *Rushton v Harcros Timber & Building Supplies Ltd* [1993] IRLR 254, the EAT held that Rushton who was unfairly dismissed on the ground of redundancy, was not entitled to compensation for loss of pay during the period of prior warning of redundancy because an *ex gratia* payment of £5,320 had to be credited against the compensatory award with the result in this case that no compensation was payable. The amount of the basic award was reduced to nil under s 73(9). Hague J held the meaning and intent of s 74(7) is 'reasonably plain'. The employer should receive credit for any redundancy payment made and the purpose of s 74(7) is to encourage employers to be generous in making *ex gratia* payments in redundancy situations, which they would not do if they were likely to find tribunals made awards over and above the *ex gratia* payments, however generous they may have been. *Ex gratia* payments would therefore be reduced and detrimental to the interests of employees generally. Section 74(7) applied to the facts of this case. There was no evidence Rushton would have had the *ex gratia* payment in any event if he had been given proper prior warning of his dismissal.

In *Darr and another v LRC Products Ltd* [1993] IRLR 257, the EAT confirmed the correct way to calculate the compensatory award is to assess the employee's loss and then deduct the amount of any severance payment, over and above that which has been appropriated to the basic award and to wages in lieu of notice. The statutory maximum is then applied to the final sum. If it can be established that a severance payment made by an employer is offered and accepted in satisfaction of or in contribution towards any additional award under s 71(2), should such an award be made, then if the severance payment at least satisfies the compensatory award, the tribunal would have to consider in all the circumstances if the additional award should be reduced by the excess.

The employee is under an obligation to mitigate his loss. See s 74(4) of the EP(C)A 1978 and under 'Mitigation' at p 373. The amount of the compensatory award may be reduced because of contributory fault on the part of the employee. See under 'Contributory fault' at p 377.

Calculation of compensatory award

In *Norton Tool Co Ltd v Tewson* [1972] ICR 501, the NIRC rejected the application of the common law principles, holding that the measure of compensation for unfair dismissal was to be found in statute law and nowhere else. A tribunal has an element of discretion in assessing compensation in that it is not necessary to adopt 'the approach of a conscientious and skilled cost accountant or actuary', but the tribunal has to exercise its discretion judicially on the basis of principle. Compensation must be assessed in an amount which is just and equitable and 'there is neither justice nor equity in a failure to act in accordance with principle'. The court recognised that tribunals are often faced with unaided litigants who cannot be expected to prepare precise details of their losses. If any other approach were adopted it would burden the parties with the expense of 'adducing evidence... which is disproportionate to the sums in issue'.

Where the compensatory award has been calculated on the basis of principle, nonetheless the tribunal may reduce the amount of the compensatory award where it would not be just and equitable for the employee to receive either the whole or part of the compensatory award. See *W Devis and Sons Ltd v Atkins* [1977] ICR 662.

In *Townson v The Northgate Group Ltd* [1981] IRLR 382, the EAT held that when assessing the compensatory award, the tribunal must calculate the actual losses and must then consider all the circumstances. Then acting as an industrial jury it must decide what is just and equitable compensation in all the circumstances. The circumstances include a consideration of the employee's conduct and how unfair the dismissal was, although, it is submitted that the employee's conduct is not a proper consideration under s 74(1) of the EP(C)A 1978 and is a matter for the tribunal to take into account in assessing contributory fault on the part of the employee under s 74(6) of the EP(C)A 1978, otherwise the compensatory award will be reduced twice: see *Morris v Acco Co Ltd* [1985] ICR 306. Indeed it has been held recently in *Soros and Soros v Davison and Davison* [1994] IRLR 264, that post-dismissal conduct is not relevant in determining the amount of compensatory award which is just and equitable in all the circumstances in the terms of s 74(1) of the EP(C)A 1978.

Tribunals cannot make an award of compensation to express disapproval of any industrial relations policies: *Clarkson International Tools Ltd v Short* [1973] ICR 191; *British United Shoe Machinery Co Ltd v Clarke* [1978] ICR 70. They must not act in 'a general, benevolent manner according to their conception of what they think would be fair in the circumstances': *Lifeguard Assurance Ltd v Zadrozny* [1977] IRLR 56.

It may be just and equitable for the employee to receive compensation where she has been unfairly dismissed notwithstanding that the employer could have dismissed her fairly for another reason: see *Trico-Folberth Ltd v Devonshire* [1989] IRLR 396.

In *Tewson's* case, *above*, the NIRC considered loss under the following heads:

(*a*) immediate loss of wages;

(*b*) manner of dismissal;
(*c*) future loss of wages;
(*d*) loss of protection in respect of unfair dismissal and dismissal by reason of redundancy.

These categories are not exhaustive. If necessary, the tribunal should itself raise each of these heads: *Tidman v Aveling Marshall Ltd* [1977] ICR 506. The tribunal should set out its reasoning when awarding compensation so that, as Phillips J held in *Blackwell v GEC Elliott Process Automation Ltd* [1976] IRLR 144, the parties can see if the amounts awarded are correct, they can decide if it is an appropriate case to appeal, the EAT can see whether the compensation order was correct, and the setting out in detail of the award together with reasons reduces the possibility of error in arriving at a reasonable figure. Depending on the circumstances the tribunal may also have to consider loss of fringe benefits, loss of pension and expenses incurred in seeking other employment.

Immediate loss of wages
This is the loss suffered between the date of dismissal and the date of the tribunal hearing. The tribunal must look to see what has actually occurred between the two dates. In *Gilham and Others v Kent CC* [1986] IRLR 56, the tribunal imposed an arbitrary cut-off point of 12 months in assessing dinner ladies' losses, regardless of what actually had happened and found that if the county council had not terminated the existing contracts of employment and offered ones on less advantageous terms, the school meals service would have closed down within a year. The EAT held that the tribunal had fallen into an error of law in examining the future prospects of the school meals service instead of looking at what had actually happened.

Thus, in assessing this loss the tribunal must make its assessment in the lights of facts known to it at the date of the assessment. Where the employee has obtained other employment between the date of dismissal and the date when compensation falls to be assessed, the earnings of that employment will normally have to be brought into account either to reduce or to extinguish any ongoing losses of the employee: see *Ging v Ellward Lancs Ltd* reported [1991] ICR 222, although decided in 1978 by EAT. However, it may be that the employer's liability for compensation terminates once the employee has found other employment, even though the employee subsequently loses that job before compensation falls to be assessed: *Courtaulds Northern Spinning Ltd v Moosa* [1984] IRLR 43. Moosa's dismissal by the new employer was not attributable to action taken by Courtaulds and therefore they were not liable after the date when he obtained employment with a new employer. In *Lytlarch v Reid* [1991] ICR 216, a case of constructive dismissal, the tribunal assessed compensation from the date of the dismissal to the date of commencement of new employment, which was prior to the date of the tribunal hearing. The EAT held that although it was normal to assess compensation up to the date of the hearing, setting off earnings in new employment during that period, there could be exceptions, eg a lengthy delay in a case coming to hearing, or it could be just and equitable under s 74(1) to award compensation to the start of new employment only. Where the employee earns a higher wage in new employment obtained prior to the tribunal hearing it may not be just and equitable to take into account the higher wage and reduce the award to a small amount: *Fentiman v Fluid Engineering Products Ltd* [1991] ICR 570. Here the employee successfully appealed to the EAT that his compensatory award should be calculated from dismissal to the date of new employment, and his award was therefore increased.

Wages in lieu of notice

In an action for wrongful dismissal the employee has to give credit for anything which he earned or could have earned during the period of notice with another employer. In *Norton Tool Co Ltd v Tewson, above*, the NIRC held that the employee need not give credit for any sums which he earned or could have earned elsewhere during the notice period.

In *J Stepek Ltd v Hough* (1973) 8 ITR 516, it was held that an employee who receives some wages in lieu of notice, but not his full entitlement, may claim the balance without deduction even though he works elsewhere for that part of the notice period for which he seeks to claim from his former employer.

In *Hilti (Great Britain) Ltd v Windridge* [1974] ICR 352, it was held that where the employer makes a payment in lieu of notice but bases this on gross pay rather than net and makes a payment which is short of the number of weeks' entitlement, the excess of the gross pay over the net pay can be set off against the liability of the employer to make payment for the weeks of the notice for which no payment was made. In *Everwear Candlewick Ltd v Isaac* [1974] ICR 525, it was held that any sums over and above the net pay for the notice period must be brought into account. See also *Blackwell v GEC Elliott Process Automation Ltd* [1976] IRLR 144.

In *Vaughan v Weighpack Ltd* [1974] ICR 261, the NIRC held:

> [The tribunal shall] bring into the equation on one side the wages and other benefits the employee would have received had he not been dismissed and on the other side all sums which he has received as a direct consequence of the dismissal, including any sums paid in lieu of notice, any wages earned since the dismissal, unemployment benefits, training grants and so forth. It may occasionally happen that the result of this arithmetic will produce a figure lower than the wages he should have received in lieu of notice. If this be the case the compensation assessed should be equivalent to wages in lieu of notice. If, however, as will

probably more often be the case, it produces a larger figure, then that is the figure to which he is entitled.

However, in *Tradewinds Airways Ltd v Fletcher* [1981] IRLR 272, the EAT refused to accept that where an employee finds another job during the notice period, wages in lieu of notice was the irreducible minimum to which the unfairly dismissed employee is entitled.

However, in *TBA Industrial Products Ltd v Locke* [1984] IRLR 48, the EAT held that an employee dismissed with pay in lieu of notice does not have to give credit to his former employer for any earnings from a new employer during the period covered by the payment in lieu of notice.

In *Babcock FATA Ltd v Addison* [1987] IRLR 173, the Court of Appeal upheld the principle established in *Norton*'s case. Gibson LJ held that the reasoning was: an employee should not have to make repayment of wages in lieu of notice on finding new employment in the notice period and good industrial relations practice requires either notice or wages in lieu. If he receives neither, the employee should not have to give credit for wages earned elsewhere, despite the duty to mitigate. The principle of good industrial relations practice gives the employee the opportunity to earn wages during the notice period without giving credit, and if the employee does not find alternative employment then he is not entitled to anything over and above wages in lieu. The effect of this decision is to give tribunals considerable discretion to decide what good industrial practice demands.

However, in *Isleworth Studios Ltd v Rickard* [1988] ICR 432, Rickard, who had a fixed-term contract, was unfairly dismissed. He earned more in his new business than he would have done had he continued to work under the fixed-term contract. The EAT reduced the compensatory award to nil. It held that to provide compensation where there was no loss was inconsistent with s 74 of the EP(C)A 1978. Contrary to the view in *Addison*'s case, it found that *Norton*'s case was laying down a rule of law of limited scope. From the judgment it was difficult to see when *Norton*'s case might apply. *Rickard*'s case should be regarded as confined to its own facts in the light of the decision in *Addison*.

Apart from wages in lieu of notice the employee is entitled to claim compensation for the loss of other benefits which he has suffered. Since these losses may fall to be considered under both this and the next heading, they are for convenience considered under the next heading.

Since tribunals are concerned with assessing loss in calculating the loss of wages, whether past or future, the tribunal should work on the difference between the net wage enjoyed by the employee in his former employment and the net wage in the new employment: *Tradewinds Airways Ltd v Fletcher, above.*

Future loss of earnings

'[T]here must be some evidence of future loss and the scale of future loss to enable the tribunal to make any award under [this] head': *Adda International Ltd v Curcio* [1976] IRLR 425.

Whereas the calculation of the immediate loss of wages is based upon fact, the calculation of future loss of wages must be speculative. Where, at the date of the hearing before the tribunal, the employee has obtained other employment at a wage equal to or higher than that which he earned with his former employer there is no future loss; however, where the employee has obtained other employment at a wage less than that enjoyed with his former employer, the tribunal has to consider when it is likely that the employee will be restored to the position which he held with his former employer.

Where the employee has not secured new employment at the date of the hearing the calculation of future loss becomes even more speculative. There is no specific period as to the length of future loss that should be allowed, nor is there any normal period despite a suggestion to this effect in *Tidman v Aveling Marshall Ltd* [1977] ICR 506. Parties may or may not lead evidence as to when the employee is likely to obtain other employment. If the employee wishes to adduce evidence as to the period of future loss he should do so, otherwise he will have no cause for complaint about the period of future loss fixed by the tribunal, provided that it acts properly: *UBAF Bank Ltd v Davis* [1978] IRLR 442. Tribunals in reaching their conclusions are entitled to draw on their knowledge of local conditions and their knowledge of the local employment situation and common sense in assessing future loss. Where the tribunals exercise their discretion properly it is unlikely that an appellate body will interfere with their decision: *Moncur v International Paint Co Ltd* [1978] IRLR 223. The uncertainties and the imponderables which surround the assessment of future loss may be reflected in the multiplier chosen by the tribunal to assess future loss: *Cartiers Superfoods Ltd v Laws* [1978] IRLR 315.

Where the tribunal allows future loss over a period of time it must make clear its reasoning behind the period chosen: (1) *Qualcast (Wolverhampton) Ltd v Ross* (2) *Ross v Qualcast (Wolverhampton) Ltd* [1979] IRLR 98.

The tribunal must consider the circumstances of the employee as well as the current employment position and the availability of particular jobs. In *Fougère v Phoenix Motor Co Ltd* [1976] ICR 495, Fougère, 58, and in poor health was unfairly dismissed. The tribunal in calculating future loss ignored his age and health. Instead they considered the length of time it would take a man of average health to find other employment. The EAT held that the employer must take the employee as he finds him. The personal characteristics of the employee are important in deciding the future loss. In this case 'they unfairly dismissed an employee who, at the date of his dismissal and before, was elderly and in poor health'. The tribunal had to look at that employee and decide how long it would take for him to find employment elsewhere. Compensation is for the loss sustained by the individual employee.

Where, at the date of the dismissal, although it is not the reason for dismissal, the employee suffers from an illness or disability the tribunal must take that into account in assessing future loss and the likelihood of him obtaining other employment. It must also consider whether the employer would have been entitled to dismiss the employee in the future because of that illness or disability and whether the employer instead of dismissing the employee for illness or disability in the future would have kept the employee on in some alternative position, possibly at a reduced wage: *Brittains Arborfield Ltd v Van Uden* [1977] ICR 211.

Another factor is the proximity of pension age. In *Penprase v Mander Bros Ltd* [1973] IRLR 167, Penprase was 3½ years from retirement when he was unfairly dismissed. The tribunal found that but for the dismissal he would have continued to be employed until he was 65. They assessed his losses over 3½ years, taking the view that it was unlikely that he would obtain other employment. See also *Isle of Wight Tourist Board v Coombes* [1976] IRLR 413.

Normally compensation will not be awarded for losses occurring after the employee has attained the age of 65 or, if in that employment there is a normal retiring age, that age. However, if the employee can establish that but for the dismissal he would have continued in employment after 65 or the normal retiring age as the case may be, then compensation for such losses may be awarded.

In *Wood v Louis C Edwards and Sons (Manchester) Ltd* [1972] IRLR 18, it was held there was nothing in the legislation which limited the loss of earnings to those accruing before the 65th birthday. See also *Barrel Plating and Phosphating Co Ltd v Danks* [1976] ICR 503.

Redundancy may also affect the assessment of future loss. In *Marcus v George Wimpey and Co Ltd* [1974] IRLR 356, Marcus was unfairly dismissed for redundancy. Between the date of the dismissal and the date of the tribunal hearing, four months had elapsed. During this period there had been a worsening of the employment situation and the employer's work had further reduced. Dismissal at the time of the hearing would have been fair. Thus, the employee was not entitled to any future loss. A similar decision was reached in *Costello v United Asphalt Co Ltd* [1975] IRLR 194. The burden is on the employer to show that even if the employee had not been dismissed then, he would have been dismissed in the future for redundancy. The tribunal must not speculate and should not calculate that the employee was likely to be redundant in the future unless there is evidence to support that conclusion: *Young's of Gosport Ltd v Kendell* [1977] ICR 907; but compare *Tidman v Aveling Marshall Ltd* [1977] ICR 506.

If a future redundancy provides a cut-off point for compensation, the tribunal may award as compensation the amount equivalent to a redundancy payment to which the employee would at that time have been entitled.

It is not open to a tribunal to award compensation for an 'unfair declaration' of redundancy unless the dismissal is unfair, for instance, because an employee has been unfairly selected or a proper procedure has not been followed. Although a tribunal is entitled to consider whether the closure of a business is genuine it is not open to it to investigate the commercial and economic reasons for a closure. Where the closure is genuine compensation cannot be awarded beyond that date: *James W Cook and Co (Wivenhoe) Ltd (in liquidation) v Tipper and Others* [1990] IRLR 386.

The issue of future redundancy being a cut-off point for compensation is one which must be raised by the employer before the tribunal and cannot be introduced *de novo* on an appeal: *Kunz Engineering Ltd v Santi* [1979] IRLR 459.

Another factor affecting the assessment of future loss may arise when following the dismissal, the employee decides to undertake a course of training or study: *Pagano v HGS* [1976] IRLR 9. In *Justfern Ltd v D'Ingerthorpe and Others* [1994] IRLR 164, the EAT held that in calculating the compensatory award it was not necessary to make a deduction for an educational grant which the employee had received in connection with a degree course he started after his dismissal. The employer should not have the benefit of the efforts the employee had made to improve himself. However, remuneration received from part-time working should be taken into account in calculating the employee's losses.

A problem which may fall to be considered in relation to both present and future loss is what losses should be allowed when the dismissal is unfair because the employer has failed to follow a proper procedure. In *(1) Abbotts and (2) Standley v Wesson-Glynwed Steels Ltd* [1982] IRLR 51, Abbotts was dismissed without consultation. The tribunal considered that consultation would have made no difference and the employee would still have been dismissed. However the EAT reversed the decision of the tribunal that Abbotts was not entitled to any compensation and instead awarded two weeks' pay. It considered that if there had been consultation it would have resulted in Abbotts remaining in employment for a further two weeks.

This case was followed in *Mining Supplies (Longwall) Ltd v Baker* [1988] IRLR 417.

In *Red Bank Manufacturing Co Ltd v Meadows* [1992] IRLR 209, the EAT held that the tribunal must specifically refer to what might have happened if a fair procedure had been followed, when assessing compensation. Where a redundancy dismissal is unfair because of the failure to follow a procedure *Polkey's* case requires the tribunal to ask:

(i) if the procedure had been followed would it have resulted in an offer of employment;

(ii) if so what would the employment have been and what wage would have been paid in respect of it.

In *Britool Ltd v Roberts and Others* [1993] IRLR 481, the compensatory award was not reduced to reflect the chance the employee would have been dismissed if a fair procedure had been followed. Where a dismissal is unfair through lack of consultation or warning the employee has a *prima facie* loss, being the loss of his job, and the evidential burden shifts to the employer to show that the dismissal could or would be likely to have occurred in any event, and in this case the employer had not discharged that burden.

In *Campbell and Others v Dunnoon and Cowal Housing Association Ltd* [1993] 496, the whole of the office and administrative staff of the Association were dismissed for redundancy. The tribunal found the dismissals unfair because of lack of consultation prior to dismissal. However, the tribunal reduced all the awards of compensation by 75 per cent. The Court of Session upheld the decision. Relying on *Polkey's* case the tribunal had reduced compensation on the basis that if consultation had taken place it was likely the employees would still have been dismissed. The tribunal had not erred in refusing to consider the commercial merits of their decision. *Polkey's* case establishes that commercial merits of employer's decision are not matters for the tribunal.

In *Steel Stockholders (Birmingham) Ltd v Kirkwood* [1993] IRLR 515, the EAT held that the principle laid down in *Polkey's* case only applied where the dismissal was unfair because of a procedural shortcoming, and it did not apply in this case where the dismissal was substantively unfair. An unfair selection procedure was held to be a substantive matter. Compare *Dunlop v Farrell* [1993] ICR 885, where the EAT held that where there was a failure to consult the employees in a redundancy situation the tribunal is under an obligation to apply the *Polkey* test and where the answer is uncertain they must make a percentage assessment of the likelihood of the employee being retained. In *Rao v Civil Aviation Authority* [1994] IRLR 240, the tribunal had reduced the basic and compensatory awards on account of Rao's blameworthy conduct, and reduced the compensatory award by a further 80 per cent to reflect the fact if a fair procedure had been followed he would still have been dismissed. The Court of Appeal held that the compensatory award may be reduced twice, under s 74(1) and s 74(6) and if there has been a large reduction under s 74(1) then the percentage reductions under both s 74(6) and s 73(7B) might well be different.

The tribunal acting as an industrial jury has considerable discretion over what period it will allow future losses. It will have regard not only to the circumstances of the individual employee, but also to the economic climate: see *Perks v Geest Industries Ltd* [1974] IRLR 228;

and *MacNeilage v Arthur Roye (Turf Accountants) Ltd* [1976] IRLR 88.

The tribunal may assess compensation on the basis that the employee will be unable to obtain another job for a considerable time. However, after the tribunal hearing the employee may obtain another job. The compensation may be well in excess of the loss which the employee has suffered. In such circumstances what redress has the employer? Where the tribunal has erred in law the employer may appeal against its decision. This must be done within 42 days from the date of the decision: r 2 of the EAT Rules 1993 (SI 1993 No 2854). If there is no error in law the employer may ask the tribunal to review its decision on the grounds that a review is necessary in the interests of justice. The application must be made not later than 14 days from the date the decision was sent to the parties: r 11 of the Industrial Tribunals (Constitution and Rules of Procedure) Regulations 1993 (SI 1993 No 2687). In deciding whether to allow a review:

> The tribunal must ask itself whether the forecasts which were the basis of its decision have been falsified to a sufficiently substantial extent to invalidate the assessment and whether this occurred so soon after the decision, that a review was necessary in the interests of justice. There must be some finality ... but ... if very shortly after a tribunal has reached a decision it comes to its notice, upon an application for review, that the facts are so different from those which it had assumed, that the whole substratum of its award has gone, then, subject to such consideration as whether the party applying could have obtained that evidence before the hearing, there is manifestly a case for review: *Yorkshire Engineering and Welding Co Ltd v Burnham* [1974] ICR 77.

In *Help the Aged Housing Association (Scotland) Ltd v Vidler* [1977] IRLR 104, the tribunal assumed that Vidler, who was 60, would be unlikely to find new employment. It awarded £4,700 compensation. Thirteen days after the hearing he obtained new employment and the Association asked for a review. The tribunal refused and the Association appealed. The EAT accepted that the tribunal's assumption was a reasonable one to make, but found that because Vidler had obtained other employment so quickly the substratum of the award had gone. It reduced the compensation to £3,000.

Future loss where the employee starts his own business   The employee must act reasonably and try to mitigate his loss: see s 74(4) of the EP(C)A 1978. If he has made a reasonable attempt to find other employment but has been unsuccessful, the tribunal may find that he then acted reasonably in setting up in business on his own account. However, if he has not sought other employment then he may not be able to hold his former employer responsible for the losses flowing from the dismissal. The employer may argue that compensation should be restricted to the loss which the employee would have incurred had he made reasonable attempts to obtain comparable employment: *York Trailer Co Ltd v Sparkes* [1973] ICR 518.

In *Gardiner-Hill v Roland Berger Technics Ltd* [1982] IRLR 498, it was held that the employee who became self-employed had not failed to mitigate his loss simply because he did not look for salaried employment. He had acted reasonably in setting up his own business and was entitled to compensation, including the cost of setting up.

In *Lee v IPC Business Press Ltd* [1984] ICR 306, it was held that Lee, who became self-employed, was entitled to compensation for any losses he suffered following his unfair dismissal. He had an obligation to mitigate his losses but simply because he became self-employed he was not thereby prevented from claiming compensation. There was no finding that he had not mitigated his losses.

The period which the tribunal allows will depend on how long it thinks it will be before the employee can make the new venture viable. The tribunal may take into account that the compensation for those losses which may make up the deficit between the first year's trading and the employee's former salary is an accelerated receipt of capital: *York Trailer Co Ltd v Sparkes, above.* However, the fact that the employee may have a capital asset in the business which he is establishing will usually be ignored.

In *Lee*'s case, *above*, Lee was entitled to a contractual redundancy payment from his employer in the event of his dismissal by reason of redundancy. This was something which he lost as a result of the unfair dismissal. If Lee took another job he would have to requalify for the right not to be unfairly dismissed and also the right not to be made redundant and, if he were dismissed by reason of redundancy, the chances were that he would not have been entitled to an enhanced redundancy payment under the terms of his new contract. The EAT held that in assessing compensation, these were matters for the tribunal to consider. Compare *Sparke*'s case and *Gardiner-Hill*'s case, *above*, where it was held that the employee was not entitled to compensation for the loss of his accrued statutory employment rights. However, see '*Loss of statutory rights*' below at p 360.

Manner of dismissal

Generally an award will be made under this head only in exceptional circumstances. The manner and circumstances of the dismissal must give rise to a risk of loss in the future, as for instance, where the employee is less acceptable to a potential employer or likely to be selected for dismissal in the future. There must be cogent evidence that the manner of the dismissal caused financial loss: *Vaughan v Weighpack Ltd* [1974] ICR 261, (confirmed in *Brittains Arborfield Ltd v Van Uden* [1977] ICR 211). The fact that Vaughan lived in a small community and was dismissed on a Sunday did not warrant any increase in compensation.

In *Wiggins v Lewis Shops Group* [1973] IRLR 114, Wiggins, a manageress, had been dismissed in distressing circumstances without a reference. This resulted in her being unable to obtain another management job. The tribunal took this into account in assessing future loss. The circumstances of the dismissal had contributed to the loss. The case was overturned on other grounds.

However, in *John Miller and Sons v Quinn* [1974] IRLR 107, the NIRC confirmed that nothing should be awarded for emotional upset on its own. Distress following dismissal could only be taken into account if it were likely to affect the employee's chances of securing other employment. However, in *Devine v Designer Flowers Wholesale Florist Sundries Ltd* [1993] IRLR 517, the EAT held that where the employee had become unfit for work, wholly or partly as a direct result of the dismissal, then she was entitled to compensation for loss of earnings for at least a reasonable period following dismissal until she could have been expected to have found other employment. In ascertaining the amount of compensation, there was no reason why her personal circumstances could not be taken into account, including the effect of dismissal on her health. The tribunal must arrive at a sum which is just and equitable though an employee may not be entitled to loss of earnings for the whole period of unfitness for work, because the whole period of unfitness may not necessarily be attributable to the action of the employer in dismissing the employee.

Loss of statutory rights
In *Norton Tool Co Ltd v Tewson* [1972] ICR 501, the sum of £20 was awarded to the employee to compensate him for the loss of his accrued statutory rights. The loss of the employee's statutory rights includes his loss of protection against unfair dismissal. He will have to be employed for a continuous period of two years before he will be able to claim unfair dismissal in the future.

Tribunals award a nominal sum for loss of accrued statutory rights, (for instance, to claim unfair dismissal), because the employee has to requalify for those rights. In *SH Muffett Ltd v Head* [1986] IRLR 488, the EAT held that the sum of £20 was now inappropriate and that the sum of £100 should be regarded as appropriate in all the circumstances. It rejected the view that the sum of £20 was fixed and immutable. The sum of £100 had been reached after consultation with the President of the EAT and the EAT commented that this figure would need to be reconsidered in three to four years' time. Although there has been no reported decision increasing this sum, in fact tribunals have been awarding up to £200 under this heading.

In addition, the tribunal may make an award because the employee has lost his entitlement to a longer period of notice under Part IV of the EP(C)A 1978. Again, the employee has to requalify for this right. This may be a speculative matter although in principle it is a permissible head of loss. In *Hilti (GB) Ltd v Windridge* [1974] IRLR 53, it was held that it should not attract other than a very small award in the average case. However in *Daley v AE Dorset (Almar Dolls Ltd)* [1981] IRLR 385, the EAT suggested that the loss of entitlement to a longer period of notice may now be more valuable in view of the economic conditions than previously. In this case a sum of half the employee's statutory notice entitlement was awarded.

Some tribunals award the sum of £100 for this element. See also *Lee v IPC Business Press Ltd* [1984] ICR 306.

However, as the EAT pointed out in *SH Muffett Ltd v Head, above*, compensation for loss of the longer period of notice depended upon a double contingency, first that the dismissed employee will get a new job and secondly that he will be dismissed from that job before building up the same entitlement to the period of notice applicable to the first job. The EAT accepted that this was a matter for the tribunal to consider, but a tribunal will not err simply because it makes no award where it considers the double contingency is extremely unlikely.

In *Arthur Guinness Son and Co (GB) Ltd v Green* [1989] IRLR 288, the EAT found that while it is the practice in a proper case to award a sum calculated by multiplying net take home pay by a fraction of the statutory maximum period of 12 weeks' notice, the multiplier should not be more than 6 weeks.

Fringe benefits, past and future

The employee is entitled to claim compensation for the loss of fringe benefits, pension and expenses. These losses form part of past or future losses but for convenience are dealt with separately.

Remuneration   Where commission and other payments in the nature of commission form part of the employee's emoluments, he will receive compensation for the loss. He may also lose bonuses and gratuities. Where these are part of his remuneration, he will be compensated for their loss. Allowances which are chargeable to tax and therefore form part of the remuneration will be compensated. Allowances which are paid to reimburse expenses actually incurred and which are tax free will not be remuneration, so no compensation will be received: see *Tradewinds Airways Ltd v Fletcher* [1981] IRLR 272.

Loss of car   If the employee was only entitled to use the car for business purposes, he will have suffered no loss on that account from the dismissal. However, contractually he may be entitled to use the car for his own purposes. Where the employee has made contributions towards the purchase of the car either by a lump sum payment or by hire-purchase contributions, he is entitled to compensation for the loss of capital involved. However, he may have made no capital contribution but be contractually entitled to use the car for his own purposes, with or without the obligation to provide petrol. Here the tribunal will have to assess the loss to the employee of the use of the car.

Usually a tribunal will award a specific sum per week. It will also have to decide the number of weeks for which the loss will continue. This need not be the date when the employee obtains other employment since he may not have a car in that employment, or the terms upon which the vehicle is made available to him may not be so advantageous. Instead of awarding a weekly payment for loss, the tribunal may award a capital sum as in *Sparks v ET Barwick Mills Ltd* (1977) (unreported), where the employee had to make a down payment on a new car of £1,000. The tribunal allowed this sum as his loss. Tribunals may have regard to guidance on the value of a car obtained from figures produced by the AA. These figures give a breakdown between the fixed costs of a car and the running costs of a car.

Housing   The tribunal will have to assess the value of free housing lost on dismissal: *Butler v J Wendon and Sons* [1972] IRLR 15. Where the employee has found other accommodation for which he has to pay rent, the loss will be the new rent: *Scottish Co-operative Wholesale Society Ltd v Lloyd* [1973] ICR 137. Where he has not obtained other accommodation, the tribunal will have to consider what it will cost him to obtain premises which are suitable for him.

Where the housing which the employee enjoyed through his job was not free but subsidised, the difference will be the difference between the payment which he made and the rent which he will have to pay in the future. The employee may decide not to rent accommodation but to purchase his own with a mortgage. The tribunal may award the difference between the payments he was making for the property occupied by virtue of his employment and any weekly mortgage payment on a similar property, or it may award the difference between the actual rent (if any) which he paid and the open market rent for the former property.

Food and board   The employee may be entitled to free food or board and accommodation, as in the case of farm workers. The employee is entitled to compensation for such losses. Compensation will be assessed on the basis of the loss to him. The tribunal will have to determine the length of the continuing loss.

Stock options
The employee may be entitled to be compensated for the loss of stock options; see *O'Laoire*'s case, *above*.

Holiday leave
Loss of holiday leave may also be a loss for which the employee can be compensated: *Tradewinds Airways Ltd v Fletcher* [1981] IRLR 272.

Removal expenses
In looking for new employment the employee may be able to show that he was unable to find new work in the area and that he is moving elsewhere where he will be able to find employment. In such cases the tribunal may allow the costs of removal, legal costs and estate agents' fees. In *Co-operative Wholesale Society v Squirrell* (1974) 9 ITR 191, Squirrell decided that his prospects of employment were better in an urban area rather than in the rural area where he had been employed. He moved house incurring legal fees and removal expenses of £800. The tribunal allowed these sums and the decision was upheld by the NIRC. See also *Yeats v Fairey Winches Ltd* [1974] IRLR 362.

Tribunals may assess compensation on the basis that the employee will have to move in the future to obtain other employment thus restricting the period of future loss which it would otherwise award if the employee did not move but awarding in lieu the costs of moving to another area.

The assessment of loss and tax
Where the employee has been dismissed and has not obtained new employment, he is likely to receive a repayment of income tax. Where he obtains other employment at a lesser wage his liability to tax for the remainder of the year may be reduced and result in a repayment. In assessing the loss a tribunal may take this repayment into account, particularly where the loss is large. Tribunals have deducted it from the total amount of the compensatory award. However, it is clear from the decision in *Norton Tool Co Ltd v Tewson*, above, that where the sums involved are small such calculations may be inappropriate to the broad common-sense assessment of the compensation. This approach was confirmed by the EAT in *Adda International Ltd v Curcio* [1976] ICR 407.

However, in *Lucas and Others v Laurence Scott and Electromotors Ltd* [1983] IRLR 61, it was held that a compensatory award could include a sum to represent a loss of income tax rebates. In this case the employer had failed to follow a redundancy procedure which, if used, would have resulted in the employees being dismissed on 14 July rather than 27 March. If the employees had continued in employment up to 14 July they would have received their wages less tax. In the ensuing financial year each of the employees was totally unemployed. At the end of that financial year, bearing in mind the tax allowances and the notional earnings from 27 March to 14 July, the employees would probably have received a tax rebate. The EAT held that this was an element of loss of wages which the employees should recover.

However, in *MBS Ltd v Calo* [1983] ICR 459, the EAT held that the tribunal was correct in ignoring a tax rebate. It recognised that the assessment of future earnings is based upon the employee's net wage rather than gross wage. Certain assumptions are made which may prove to be false, for instance, that the employee will be taxed in the future at the same rate as he has been in the past. It is the obligation of the tribunal to assess compensation in such amounts as it considers just and equitable in all the circumstances.

Pension

Guidelines as to the way in which tribunals should assess compensation for loss of pension rights is contained in a booklet (Industrial Tribunals: Loss of Pension Rights) prepared by a committee of chairmen of tribunals in consultation with the Government Actuary's Department (Second Edition published by HMSO 1991). The burden of proof is on the employee: see *Copson & Another v Eversure Accessories Ltd* [1974] ICR 636. It is the duty of the tribunal to enquire into possible heads of compensation and raise the question of pension rights. Although the burden of proof of loss rests on the applicant, tribunals should do what they can to assist unrepresented applicants: see *Tidman v Aveling Marshall Ltd* [1977] IRLR 218. There is no right way of assessing the loss. A broad common-sense approach should be adopted. The tribunal has to award a just and equitable sum. It is open to the tribunal to use a rough and ready system if necessary: *Manpower Ltd v Hearne* [1983] IRLR 281.

In *Bingham v Hobourn Engineering Ltd* [1992] IRLR 298, the EAT held there was no duty on a tribunal to follow the guidelines laid down in the booklet and there is no error of law by the tribunal if they do not give precise effect to the guidelines. It may be that in a particular case the guidelines should not be relied upon at all.

The retirement pension payable by the State can be made up of a basic pension, a graduated pension (based on contributions paid between April 1961 and April 1975) and an additional pension payable pursuant to the State Earnings Related Pension Scheme (SERPS) which varies according to an individual's earnings since April 1978. It is possible to contract out of SERPS where there is an occupational pension scheme, provided certain criteria are fulfilled. The guidelines recommend that the assumption should be made that there is no loss where an employee is unfairly dismissed if he is not in an occupational pension scheme. That assumption is, of course, capable of being rebutted by evidence.

An occupational pension scheme may be either a final salary scheme (ie defined benefit) or a money purchase scheme (ie defined contribution). A final salary scheme is where the amount of the employee's pension is based not on the contributions made but on a proportion of the salary when he retires—eg 1/60 of his final salary for each year of service. Occupational pension schemes differ as to the fraction. Some schemes take an average of the employee's salary over a number of years. Some schemes use the best of a number of years' salary. In a final salary scheme the employer's contributions are not earmarked for a particular employee. They are a contribution to the fund. What the employee receives is not necessarily proportionate to the contributions that he and his employer have made. It is usually possible to ascertain the contributions made by the employer as a percentage of the total pay roll, although this may depend on what is required for funding the scheme. The guidelines suggest that where there is a lack of accurate evidence, or when the pension contribution position is anomalous, on average the overall contribution for a good scheme is 15 per cent of the pay roll made up in a contributory scheme, as to 10 per cent from the employer and 5 per cent from the employee. In a final salary scheme which is non-funded (such as is found in the public sector), there are no contributions as such. However, the notional contributions are fixed by the scheme's actuary and should be easily attainable. Non-funded schemes should be treated in the same way as other final salary schemes. Some publicly financed schemes do have the advantage in that they are index-linked to the cost of living index, both from the date of leaving until retirement and after retirement without any top limit.

Where additional voluntary contributions (AVCs) are made they usually operate on a money purchase basis (see below), even though the main scheme is a final salary scheme and they should be treated as an employer's money purchase scheme. Where a scheme allows an employee to purchase extra years, those years should be put into the equation as if the employee had actually worked those years. AVCs which are made by the employee alone must be distinguished from 'free standing additional voluntary contributions', which are in effect separate money purchase plans and should be dealt with as personalised plans.

A money purchase scheme is where the pension is directly related to contributions made by the employer and employee. These have the advantage that the employer knows exactly how much he will have to pay in each year. They do not have the open-ended commitment of a final salary scheme. Closely allied with the money purchase scheme is a personalised plan where the employer and the employee pay a contribution to a pension policy in the name of the individual employee. On retirement the employee receives an annuity based on the value of his personal fund. The employee decides where the money should be invested.

The employee who leaves pensionable employment before retirement is known as an early leaver. This expression will include an employee who is unfairly dismissed. The tribunal has to consider his position, depending upon whether he is in a final salary scheme or money purchase scheme. Where the employee is a member of a final salary scheme he will be entitled to a pension payable as from what would have been his retirement date as an annuity for the rest of his life. In the guidelines this is referred to as a deferred position. Usually when an employee retires he will receive 1/60 of his final salary for each year he has worked. For an employee retiring at 60 there is a maximum 40/60ths. The early leaver will receive a deferred pension representing 1/60th of his final salary for each year that he worked. It follows that if he had worked until his retiring age the final salary would be more than the salary which he actually receives at the date he left (unless this was close to his retirement age). The Social Security Act (SSA) 1985 provides that in respect of service after 1 January 1985 the deferred pension should increase by 5 per cent per annum up to retirement or by the annual price rises if lower than 5 per cent. The SSA 1990 provides that as from 1 January 1992 all preserved pension rights will be increased in accordance with this formula, and it will not be necessary to distinguish between pre- and post-1985 service.

The unfairly dismissed employee might not have remained in the employment until retirement. Equally if he had not been unfairly dismissed he might have remained in the employment but in a better position earning more and with a better pension. These are factors which have to be taken into account. Under the SSA 1985 an ex-employer can be required to transfer the value of his accrued pension either to a similar scheme run by a new employer or the employee can make other arrangements meeting the statutory requirements. The transfer value is calculated in accordance with the Occupational Pensional Schemes (Transfer Values) Regulations 1985 (SI 1985 No 1931).

The employee's losses will depend upon the nature of the pension scheme. While many schemes have a degree of commonality there are considerable variations, but the broad approach to the way the employee's losses are to be calculated are now considered.

Loss of pension rights from the date of dismissal to the date of hearing
If the employee had not been dismissed, and he and his employer had continued to make contributions to the pension fund, this would have secured additional pension benefits. Although there is a difference between a final salary scheme and a money purchase scheme the guidelines suggest that in both cases the tribunal should include a sum to represent what the employer would have contributed notionally to the employee's pension, had he still been employed. Although it recognises that in a final salary scheme this is not strictly the correct method of assessing the employee's loss, since the benefit which accrues to the employee by remaining in employment does not necessarily correspond to the figure, it is fair to both parties. In a money purchase scheme or personalised plan it will be easy to ascertain the employer's contribution and calculate it on a weekly basis. In a final salary scheme, the guidelines suggest that the normal cost of the scheme to the employer is usually given as a percentage in the actuary's report. This percentage should be applied to the employee's gross pensionable pay to produce a weekly figure for loss of pension rights. It may be necessary to adjust

this sum to take account of the circumstances, for instance if the pension fund is over-funded and the employer is having a pension contribution holiday. In the case of a non-contributory pension scheme, then it may be necessary to impute a notional contribution. If the figure for the employer's contribution is not readily ascertainable, then the guidelines suggest that the tribunal should assume the employer's contribution is 10 per cent (or 15 per cent in the case of non-contributory schemes). In each case the employer's contribution should be treated as a weekly loss in the same manner as a weekly loss of earnings. If the employee has obtained other employment with a scheme which provides the same or better benefits the date when he joined that scheme will be the date up to which losses will be calculated.

Loss of future pension rights   This is the loss of benefits which the employee would have had if he had continued in employment beyond the date of the hearing. The guidelines suggest that the same principles should apply as in the case of the loss of pension rights from the date of dismissal to the hearing. It is for the tribunal to decide what multiplier to use, reflecting the time when the employee will be in the position in which he would have been if he had not been dismissed. The guidelines suggest that the multiplier should be the same as the assessment for future loss of earnings, so if the tribunal assumes that the employee will obtain fresh employment in one year and his earnings in the new employment are likely to be comparable with the old, then it is reasonable to assume that the pension scheme will also be comparable. However, it may be that that is not appropriate, where the employee gains employment and there is no loss of earnings but simply a loss of pension rights. The guidelines recognise that it is unlikely that there will be a substantial qualifying period before an employee can benefit from the new employer's pension scheme. If there is a qualifying period benefits may be backdated once the qualifying period has been met. The guidelines suggest that if the qualification period is two years or less and if once the qualification period has been met the entitlement is backdated to the beginning of the employment, there is no loss.

Where the pension scheme in the new employment is as beneficial as in the old employment there will be no loss, but if it is not as beneficial the guidelines suggest that the difference in contributions can be regarded as the weekly loss of future pension rights and the tribunal should apply the appropriate multiplier.

If in the new employment there is no pension scheme the loss of the employer's contributions will be assessed as a weekly or other periodic loss and the employee will be included in SERPS. Any contribution made to SERPS by the new employer should be deducted. If the SERPS contribution is now known then it can be assumed that the employer is contributing 3 per cent of the employee's gross pay to SERPS.

Loss of enhancement of accrued pension rights If the employee had not been unfairly dismissed there might have been further enhancement of the rights which have already been secured. In some cases accrued rights may be forfeited. The guidelines suggest that the tribunal should assume there is no loss of enhancement of accrued pension rights unless the contrary is proved in money purchase schemes or personalised plans. Similar principles apply to public sector schemes, both funded and non-funded, and also to private sector final salary schemes where the employee has less than five years to go until retirement and where all the service is after 1 January 1985, or the trustees of the pension fund indicate that service prior to 1 January 1985 is to be index-linked in the same way as service after 1 January 1985.

Where there is a final salary scheme in ascertaining the loss of enhancement of accrued pension rights the guidelines suggest that the tribunal should ascertain the deferred pension the employee will receive. Any anticipated increases or additional benefits should be ignored. The employee's age and his anticipated date of retirement should be ascertained. An appropriate multiplier should be applied. The multipliers are set out in Appendix 4 to the guidelines. The figure obtained should be reduced, if appropriate, by a percentage representing the likelihood that the employee would have lost his job before retirement even if he had not been unfairly dismissed.

It is up to the tribunal to make a reasonable assessment of the appropriate reduction.

The guidelines can be no more than guidelines. The facts of a particular case may indicate that they are not appropriate. The starting point is the statute.

Compensation may be reduced because there is a high degree of probability that the employee would have been dismissed due either to a continuation of his unsatisfactory performance or to redundancy, and further reduced because his poor performance contributed to his dismissal. In *TBA Industrial Products Ltd v Locke* [1984] IRLR 48, the tribunal reduced the compensation for loss of pension rights by 70 per cent because of the employee's unsatisfactory performance to reflect the fact that he might have been dismissed fairly for this reason in the future or by reason of redundancy and then reduced the compensation again by a further 70 per cent, because by his poor performance he had contributed to his dismissal. Locke was not being penalised twice for the same reason, the poor performance was taken into account twice for different reasons.

Expenses
The employee is under an obligation to mitigate his loss and look for other employment. He may have to take additional newspapers or trade journals or professional papers where jobs are advertised, to write to or to telephone employers, or to travel for interviews. This is a loss for which compensation can be recovered: *Mathieson v Noble and Son Ltd* [1972] IRLR 76. Credit will have to be given for anything received from employers by way of expenses for interviews or from the Department of Employment. Generally, these expenses will be small, but they can be considerable where the employee has been out of work for some time and has made substantial efforts to obtain other employment. Legal costs are not included. To award compensation to cover such costs would be to circumvent r 12 of the 1993 Regulations (SI 1993 No 2687): see *Raynor v Remploy Ltd* [1973] IRLR 3; and *Nohar v Granitstone (Galloway) Ltd* [1974] ICR 273.

Ex gratia payments
Ex gratia or similar payments made by the employer will normally be set off against the compensatory award: see *Finnie v Top Hat Frozen Foods* [1985] ICR 433; *Addison v Babcock FATA Ltd* [1987] ICR 805; and *Horizon Holidays v Grassi* [1987] ICR 851. In certain cases however an *ex gratia* payment may not be deducted if the employee would have received it in any event: see *Roadchef Ltd v Hastings* [1988] ICR 142.

Where the compensation award exceeds the statutory maximum of (what is now) £11,000, the EAT held in *McCarthy v British Insulated Callenders Cables plc* [1985] IRLR 94, that s 75(3) of the EP(C)A 1978 makes it clear that the amount of *ex gratia* payments must be deducted from the compensatory award before the statutory maximum for compensatory awards is applied: see *Morris v Gestetner Ltd* [1973] ICR 587; but compare *Powermatic Ltd v Bull* [1977] ICR 469.

Where the employer makes an *ex gratia* payment, that *ex gratia* payment may be set off against any basic award for which the employer is liable: see *Chelsea Football Club and Athletic Co Ltd v Heath* [1981] IRLR 73.

Industrial pressure
In assessing the compensatory award and determining how far the loss sustained by the employee was attributable to action taken by the employer, no account is to be taken of any pressure which, by calling, organising, procuring or financing a strike or other industrial action, or threatening to do so, was exercised on the employer to dismiss the employee: s 74(5) of the EP(C)A 1978. The employer may be able to recover the whole or part of any compensation awarded from the person exercising the pressure; see more particularly 'Contribution and pressure on the employer' at p 372.

In such circumstances the employee could have contributed to the dismissal. However, such a finding is more likely where there are factors other than the pressure to dismiss which the tribunal may take into account: *Ford Motor Co Ltd v Hudson* [1978] ICR 482. In this case it was held:

> No doubt there are many cases where if the pressure is put out of mind as the result of a compliance with . . . [s 63 of the EP(C)A 1978 which directs a tribunal where an employer dismisses an employee because of a threat of industrial action to determine the fairness or otherwise of the dismissal as if there had been no such industrial pressure] it will be found that the pressure so excluded was the sole cause of the dismissal, and in such a case no doubt a contribution by the employee to the dismissal is out of the question. We do not think that such is necessarily the case. For example, assuming that the Industrial Tribunal came to the conclusion that this case was one to which . . . [s 63] applied, and further came to the conclusion that the dismissal was unfair, it would be open to them to find (if they thought it was the fact) that the applicants had been unduly unco-operative in a difficult situation, and not wholly reasonable in refusing to move.

In *Sulemanji v Toughened Glass Ltd* [1979] ICR 799, following indus-trial action with which Sulemanji did not agree, he ceased paying his union subscriptions. When he started work he knew he would have to be a member of the appropriate union. His colleagues refused to work with him. Despite attempts to persuade him to pay the subscriptions he refused to do so and was dismissed. The tribunal concluded that the dismissal was unfair and it was not entitled to take account of the pressure put upon the employer. However, because the dismissal was solely the result of the employee's own conduct the tribunal reduced the compensatory award by 100 per cent and this was upheld by the EAT. The compensatory award and the basic award may be reduced: see *Colwyn BC v Dutton* [1980] IRLR 420. Dutton was a dustcart driver. His colleagues refused to work with him because they believed that he was a dangerous driver. Industrial action was threatened if they were disciplined for refusing to travel with him. He was dismissed. His driving had contributed to his dismissal and the EAT held that therefore Dutton's compensation should be reduced.

Special award

This is available where the dismissal is automatically unfair, either because of trade union reasons, or health and safety reasons. It will be in addition to the normal basic and compensatory awards, but only where the employee has asked the tribunal to make an order for reinstatement or re-engagement, whether or not the tribunal actually makes such an order. This is the effect of s 72(2) of the EP(C)A 1978 and s 57A(1)(*a*) and (*b*) of the EP(C)A 1978 (dismissal or selection for redundancy for health and safety reasons) and ss 152 or 153 of the TULR(C)A 1992 (dismissal because of trade union membership, non-membership, or trade union activities, or selection for redundancy for any such reason).

A special award is not payable at all under s 73(2) of the EP(C)A 1978; that is where the reason for dismissal is redundancy and the employee unreasonably refuses to accept a renewal of the contract or suitable alternative employment or where the employee during a trial period unreasonably terminates the contract under s 82(5) or (6) of the EP(C)A 1978; or is not treated as dismissed on the ending of his employment under the old contract under s 84(1) of the EP(C)A 1978 (on a renewal of employment or re-engagement): s 72 of the EP(C)A 1978.

The levels of special award are different, according to whether the tribunal has made an order for reinstatement or re-engagement or not.

If there has been no order for reinstatement or re-engagement the amount of the special award shall be either

(a) one week's pay multiplied by 104 or
(b) £13,400 whichever is the greater, but shall not exceed £26,800: s 75A(1) of the EP(C)A 1978 and s 158(1) of the TULR(C)A 1992.

If there has been an order for reinstatement or re-engagement and the employer has failed to comply with it the amount of the special award shall be increased to

(a) one week's pay multiplied by 156 or
(b) £20,100 whichever is the greater: s 75A(2) of the EP(C)A 1978 and s 158(2) of the TULR(C)A 1992.

Where the employer can show that it was not practicable to comply with an order for reinstatement or re-engagement a special award shall still be made under s 75A(1) of the EP(C)A 1978 or s 158(1) of the TULR(C)A 1992. The amount will be either one week's pay multiplied by 104 or £13,400 whichever is the greater, but shall not exceed £26,800.

An award under s 75A(2) of the EP(C)A 1978 or s 158(2) of the TULR(C)A 1992 is made instead of an additional award of compensation in those circumstances where an additional award would otherwise be made. The cases in which a special award of compensation can be made are wider than those in which an additional award can be made. For the circumstances in which an additional award can be made see 'Additional award' at p 339 et seq.

Section 75A(2) of the EP(C)A 1978 and s 158(2) of the TULR(C)A 1992 are subject to the following provisions.

Where the amount of the basic award is reduced under s 73(5) of the EP(C)A 1978 (where the effective date of termination is after the employee's 64th birthday) the amount of the special award shall be reduced by the same fraction. That fraction is $\frac{1}{12}$ for each complete calendar month after the 64th birthday and before the effective date of termination: s 75A(3) of the EP(C)A 1978 and s 158(3) of the TULR(C)A 1992.

Where the employer has engaged a permanent replacement for the employee the tribunal shall not take that fact into account in determining for the purposes of s 75A(2) of the EP(C)A 1978 or s 158(2) of the TULR(C)A 1992 whether it was practicable to comply with an order for reinstatement or re-engagement unless the employer shows that it was not practicable for him to arrange for the employee's work to be done without engaging a permanent replacement: s 75A(6) of the EP(C)A 1978: s 158(6) of the TULR(C)A 1992.

The Secretary of State is given power to increase the sums of £13,400, £26,800 and £20,100 respectively. The sums apply where the effective date of termination falls on or after 1 April 1992. Previously the limits were £13,180, £26,290 and £19,735: see s 75A(7) of the EP(C)A 1978 and s 159 of the TULR(C)A 1992.

There is no limit on the amount of a week's pay that can be taken into account in calculating the special award under the EP(C)A 1978 or the TULR(C)A 1992. By virtue of s 158(7) of the TULR(C)A 1992, Sched 14 to the EP(C)A 1978 applies for the purposes of calculating a week's pay under s 158 of the TULR(C)A 1992 with an amendment relating to the calculation date. See Chapter 17.

The special award, although referred to as an award of compensation, is not compensation in the sense that it compensates the employee for a specific loss suffered by him.

The amount of the special award can be reduced by the employee's contributory conduct; see under 'Mitigation' at p 373, and Contributory fault at p 377.

Contribution and pressure on the employer

Section 160 of the TULR(C)A 1992 provides that if in proceedings for unfair dismissal the employer or the employee claims that the employer was induced to dismiss the employee because of pressure which a trade union or other person exercised on the employer, either the employer or the employee may request the tribunal to direct that the person who he claims exercised the pressure be joined as a party to the proceedings. The pressure is pressure which is exercised on the employer by calling, organising, procuring or financing a strike or other industrial action, or by threatening to do so, and which is exercised because the employee was not a member of any trade union, or of a particular trade union or of one of a number of particular trade unions: s 160(1) of the TULR(C)A 1992.

A request to join a person exercising the pressure as a party to the proceedings must be granted if it is made before the hearing of the complaint of unfair dismissal begins, but it may be refused if it is made thereafter. No request may be made after the tribunal has made an award under s 68(2) of the EP(C)A 1978 (an award of compensation for unfair dismissal) or under s 69 of the EP(C)A 1978 (an order for reinstatement or re-engagement): s 160(2) of the TULR(C)A 1992. Where any person has been joined as a party to the proceedings and the tribunal makes an award of compensation under ss 68(2) or 71(2)(a) of the EP(C)A 1978 or ss 156 or 157 of the TULR(C)A 1992, (ie whether a compensatory award, basic award, additional award or special award), but the tribunal also finds that such pressure has been exercised against the employer, the tribunal may make an award against that person instead of the employer, or partly against that person and partly against the employer, as the tribunal may consider just and equitable in the circumstances: s 160(3) of the TULR(C)A 1992. In assessing the employee's losses, no account however is to be taken of any such pressure put upon the employer to dismiss the employee: s 74(5) of the EP(C)A 1978.

Mitigation

The tribunal must apply the same rule concerning the duty of the person to mitigate his loss as applies to damages recoverable under the common law: s 74(4) of the EP(C)A 1978. There is a statutory obligation to consider mitigation in relation to both past and future loss: *Morganite Electrical Carbon Ltd v Donne* [1987] ICR 18.

The obligation to mitigate at common law was considered in *Yetton v Eastwoods Froy Ltd* [1966] 3 All ER 353. Yetton was a joint managing director of a company under a five-year contract. After he had completed just over a year's service he was offered a post as assistant managing director at the same salary but with loss of status. He refused. Blain J held that 'the basic principle of damages is *restitutio in integrum*'. The employee should seek and take alternative employment unless in the particular instance it is reasonable to refuse it. He referred to *Payzu Ltd v Saunders* [1919] 2 KB 581, where Bankes LJ held that the question of reasonableness is one of fact taking into account the circumstances of each case, and Scrutton LJ held that 'in certain cases of personal service it may be unreasonable to expect a plaintiff to consider an offer from the other party who has grossly injured him.' The court held that Yetton had not unreasonably refused the offer of alternative employment.

Section 71(5) of the EP(C)A 1978 provides that in making an award of compensation where the tribunal finds that the employee has unreasonably prevented an order of reinstatement or re-engagement being complied with, it shall take that conduct into account as a failure by the employee to mitigate his loss. This is without prejudice to the generality of s 74(4) of the EP(C)A 1978.

The duty to mitigate arises when the employee has been dismissed. The employee cannot be expected to suspect in advance that his employment will come to an end. An employee who has been unfairly dismissed does not have to show that he took steps in mitigation before he was actually dismissed: *Savoia v Chiltern Herb Farms Ltd* [1981] IRLR 65, and on appeal [1982] IRLR 166, where this point was not considered. See also *Prestwick Circuits Ltd v McAndrew* [1990] IRLR 191.

Alternative employment

The essence of mitigation is that the employee cannot recover losses which he could have avoided by taking reasonable steps. The employee must seek suitable alternative employment. If the employee mitigates him loss by taking such reasonable steps he cannot recover any of the losses which he has avoided, even though the steps which he has taken have been more than were reasonably required of him. If in looking for other employment he incurs any expense or cost in taking reasonable steps, he can recover this expense or cost from the employer. The employee cannot recover compensation for losses arising because he failed to mitigate his loss by seeking other employment.

In *AG Bracey Ltd v Iles* [1973] IRLR 210, the NIRC held that although the employee has a duty to act reasonably in mitigating his loss it is not necessarily reasonable to take the first job which he is offered. See also *McKinney v Bieganek* [1973] IRLR 311.

In *Bessenden Properties Ltd v Corness* [1973] IRLR 365, confirmed on appeal [1974] IRLR 338, the NIRC found that the question is one of reasonableness in all the circumstances. If, apart from the fact he could look for compensation from the employer, it would have been reasonable to have accepted a particular job, he should have done so.

The approach was followed in *Archbold Freightage Ltd v Wilson* [1974] IRLR 10. The onus is on the employer to show that the employee ought reasonably to have mitigated his loss by taking certain steps: *Fyfe v Scientific Furnishings Ltd* [1989] ICR 648; see also *Corness*'s case, *above*.

It may be in the interests of both the employer and the employee that the employee should wait until a better job is offered, provided that the employee is making efforts to secure a better job. Conversely, it may be reasonable for the employee to suffer a drop in status and to accept less pay; and any failure to do so may be regarded as a failure to mitigate. This may arise because of the difficulties of obtaining suitable employment due to the economic situation or due to the employee's age. It would probably not be reasonable to make only one application for a job in a period of eight weeks: *O'Reilly v Welwyn and Hatfield DC* [1975] IRLR 334.

Although it should be slow in so finding, it is open to the tribunal to find that an employee has acted reasonably in failing to accept subsequent employment where the remuneration he would receive would be less than any benefit he was receiving from the State. The employer would therefore be liable for compensation even after the date when the employee could have accepted such other employment: see *Daley v AE Dorsett (Almar Dolls Ltd)* [1981] IRLR 385.

Regard must be had to all the surrounding circumstances: see *Fyfe's* case, *above*, where it was held that Fyfe's failure to accept an offer of early retirement the benefit of which outweighed unfair dismissal compensation was not a failure to mitigate.

Following the dismissal, the employee may obtain other employment which he subsequently loses. He will not have failed to mitigate his loss if he has not been culpable in losing the second job: *Barrel Plating and Phosphating Co Ltd v Danks* [1976] ICR 503, but see *Moosa's* case, and 'Calculation of compensatory award', '*Immediate loss of wages*' at p 351.

Where an employee following his dismissal chooses to set up his own business rather than looking for employment he will not necessarily have failed to mitigate his loss. While there is an onus on the employee to take reasonable steps to mitigate his loss becoming self-employed may be reasonable in all the circumstances. See *Gardiner-Hill v Roland Berger Technics Ltd* [1982] IRLR 498; *Lee v IPC Business Press Ltd* [1984] ICR 306, and see 'Calculaton of compensatory award', '*Future loss of earnings*' at p 354.

Reinstatement or re-engagement

The EAT has held that an employee's failure to accept an offer of employment made by the employer during the notice period may be a failure by the employee to mitigate his loss if he has not acted reasonably: *Gallear v JF Watson and Son Ltd* [1979] IRLR 306; *Kendrick v Aerduct Productions* [1974] IRLR 322; and *Sweetlove v Redbridge and Waltham Forest Area Health Authority* [1979] IRLR 195, but this will not be so in every case: see *How v Tesco Stores Ltd* [1974] IRLR 194. Where the tribunal makes an order for reinstatement or re-engagement, it must consider the employee's unreasonable refusal to comply with the order as a failure on the part of the employee to mitigate his loss. This is without prejudice to the generality of s 74(4) of the EP(C)A 1978: see s 71(5) of the EP(C)A 1978.

Where the tribunal finds that the employee has unreasonably refused an offer by the employer which if accepted would have had the effect of reinstating the employee, the tribunal shall reduce or further reduce the amount of the basic award to such extent as it considers just and equitable having regard to its findings: s 73(7A) of the EP(C)A 1978. The provision appears to envisage the situation where the employer of his own volition makes an offer, rather than where he is ordered to reinstate by the tribunal. The provision applies only to reinstatement and not re-engagement. Although this provision applies only to the basic award the tribunal can still reduce the compensatory award under s 74(4) EP(C)A: see for example *Gallear v JF Watson and Son Ltd above*. The tribunal's power to make a reduction under s 73(7A) is in addition to its power to make a reduction under any other provisions.

Where a special award is payable under s 72(2) of the EP(C)A 1978 (dismissal or selection for redudancy of certain employees for health and safety reasons) s 75A(5) of the EP(C)A 1978 provides that where the employee has unreasonably prevented an order of reinstatement or re-engagement from being complied with the tribunal shall reduce or further reduce the amount of the special award to such an extent as it considers just and equitable. This is similar to the provision contained in s 71(5) of the EP(C)A 1978 (a failure to mitigate his loss). Section 75A(5) of the EP(C)A 1978 further provides that if an employee unreasonably refuses an offer by the employer made otherwise than in compliance with an order of the tribunal which, if accepted, would have had the effect of reinstating the employee in his employment in all respects as if he had not been dismissed, the tribunal shall reduce or further reduce the amount of the special award to such an extent as it considers just and equitable having regard to that finding. This is similar to the provision contained in s 73(7A) of the EP(C)A 1978 (reduction of basic award). The only difference is that s 75A(5) makes it quite clear that the offer is an offer made by the employer of his own volition and not made pursuant to an order of the tribunal. Section 158(5) contains the equivalent provisions in respect of dismissals unfair on union grounds by virtue of ss 152(1) and 153 of the TULR(C)A 1992.

Failure to utilise the employer's disciplinary procedure

In *Seligman and Latz Ltd v McHugh* [1979] IRLR 130, McHugh was constructively dismissed. She did not utilise the employer's 'grievance procedure'. It was held that the fundamental breach of contract by the employer brought the contract to an end and it was not open to the employer to claim that the employee had failed to mitigate her loss by not following the 'grievance procedure'.

In *Hoover Ltd v Forde* [1980] ICR 239, the EAT found that the failure by an employee to appeal internally against his dismissal might amount to a failure to mitigate. However, in *William Muir (Bond 9) Ltd v Lamb* [1985] IRLR 95, the EAT held that a dismissed employee is not obliged to use an internal appeal procedure before bringing a claim and it would be 'wrong in our view to penalise an employee who has been unfairly dismissed by reducing her compensation because she did not follow through whatever internal appeal procedure may have existed'. The approach in *Lamb's* case has now been approved by the EAT in *Lock v Connell Estate Agents* [1994] IRLR 444, where it was held that the failure of an employee to operate the internal appeals procedure after dismissal cannot as a matter of law amount to a failure to mitigate under s 74(4) of the EP(C)A 1978. Also s 74(4) only applies to the compensatory award, and there is no corresponding provision in s 73 of the EP(C)A 1978 relating to the calculation of the basic award. Therefore, the basic award cannot be reduced because of a failure to mitigate.

Mitigation and compensation

In assessing the deduction to be made from the employee's compensation because of his failure to mitigate his loss, tribunals usually disallow any claim beyond the time when they think the employee could reasonably have secured other employment.

In *Gardiner-Hill v Roland Berger Technics Ltd* [1982] IRLR 498, the EAT held that where a tribunal finds that an employee has failed to mitigate his loss it is not open to the tribunal to make a percentage reduction in the compensation. It held that the tribunal should '. . . identify what steps should have been taken: the date on which that step would have produced an alternative income and, thereafter, to reduce the amount of compensation by the amount of the alternative income which would have been earned'.

In *Sturdy Finance Ltd v Bardsley* [1979] IRLR 65, it was held that Bardsley who took a refund of his pension contributions rather than taking a deferred pension, did not fail to mitigate his loss of pension rights. There is no rule of law that an employee must take a deferred pension rather than a refund of contributions, and the onus was on the employer to establish that it was wholly unreasonable for the employee to elect to take a refund of his pension contributions.

One exception to the principle of mitigation in claims for unfair dismissal arises in that no deductions may be made from sums awarded for wages in lieu of notice when the employee has obtained, or could have obtained, other employment during the notice period. See '*Wages in lieu of notice*' at p 352.

Contributory fault

The doctrine of contributory fault applies to each of the basic, compensatory and special awards.

Basic award

Section 73(7B) of the EP(C)A 1978 provides that where the tribunal considers that any conduct of the employee before the dismissal or, where the dismissal was with notice, before the notice was given, was such that it would be just and equitable to reduce or further reduce the amount of the basic award to any extent the tribunal shall reduce or further reduce that amount accordingly. This section specifically refers to conduct and not to capability. Only the conduct of the employee dismissed (and not that of a fellow employee) may be taken into account: see *Parker Foundry Ltd v Slack* [1992] IRLR 11 and 'Conduct of the employee' at p 380.

Subsequently discovered conduct may make it neither just nor equitable that the employee should receive the whole or part of the basic award. This section would also appear to allow the employer to adduce before the tribunal evidence of the employee's conduct generally, even where it was known to the employer at the time of the dismissal, although that conduct may not have been relied upon by the employer as the reason or principal reason for the dismissal.

Section 73(7C) of the EP(C)A 1978 provides that s 73(7B) shall not apply where the reason or principal reason for the dismissal was that the employee was redundant unless the dismissal is unfair under s 57A(1) (*a*) and (*b*) of the EP(C)A 1978—dismissal or selection for redundancy of certain employees on health and safety grounds, or s 153 of the TULR(C)A 1992—dismissal or selection for redundancy on union grounds—and in that event shall apply only to so much of the basic award as is payable because of s 73(6A). Section 73(6A) of the EP(C)A 1978, where the effective date of termination falls on or after 1 April 1992, provides, *inter alia*, that in such cases the amount of the basic award before reduction under the other provisions of s 73 of the EP(C)A 1978 shall not be less than £2,700, so that the reduction will in effect only apply to the excess of the basic award over what would otherwise be the basic award, which will usually be the same as the redundancy payment.

Where a tribunal reduces the amount of the compensatory award to take account of the employee's contributory conduct must it make the same reduction in the basic award as in the compensatory award? In *G McFall and Co Ltd v Curran* [1981] IRLR 455, the NICA held that the same deduction ought to be made in respect of both compensatory and basic awards to take account of the employee's contributory conduct. However, in *Les Ambassadeurs Club v Bainda* [1982] IRLR 5, the EAT held that it was open to the tribunal to reduce the compensatory award by 70 per cent while leaving the basic award untouched.

This difference in approach was considered in *RSPCA v Cruden* [1986] ICR 205. The EAT held that it would only be in exceptional circumstances that a tribunal should treat a reduction in the basic award differently from the reduction in the compensatory award to reflect the employee's contributory conduct. It held that s 73(7B) of the EP(C)A 1978 specifically refers to the employee's conduct, whereas a s 74(6) refers to any action of the employee. 'Just and equitable' are words common to both subsections. However s 73(7B) refers to 'conduct' and states ' . . . shall reduce . . . that amount accordingly', whereas s 74(6) refers to any action and states ' ... such proportion as it considers just and equitable having regard to that finding.' The tribunal has a discretion under both subsections and although a differentiation can be made, the EAT thought that it would only be in exceptional cases that it would be justified. In the present case the employee had been 'guilty of grave neglect of duty. They were amply justified in reducing the compensatory claim to nothing, and on the facts '... we cannot see how a proper exercise of their discretion would have enabled them to take any different course in relation to the basic award'.

See *Chaplin v H J Rawlinson Ltd* [1991] ICR 553, and *Polentarutti v Autokraft Ltd* [1991] ICR 757, *below*, where both the basic and compensatory awards were reduced by the same percentages.

Special award

Dismissal on health and safety grounds

Under s 75A(4) of the EP(C)A 1978, where the tribunal considers that any conduct of the employee before the dismissal, or where the dismissal was with notice, before the notice was given, was such that it would be just and equitable to reduce or further reduce the amount of the special award to any extent the tribunal shall reduce or further reduce that amount accordingly. This provision follows s 73(7B) of the EP(C)A 1978. For a consideration of s 73(7B) see under 'Basic award', *above* at p 345.

Dismissal on union grounds

The corresponding provision to s 75A(4) of the EP(C)A 1978 is s 158(4) of the TULR(C)A 1992. See also s 73(7B) *above*.

Compensatory award

Under s 74(6) of the EP(C)A 1978 where the tribunal finds that the dismissal was to any extent caused or contributed to by any action of the employee, then it shall reduce the amount of the compensatory award by such proportion as it considers just and equitable having regard to that finding.

In deciding whether the dismissal is fair or unfair the tribunal is not entitled to take into account reasons which only came to the employer's knowledge after dismissal. It is clear from the judgment of the House of Lords in *W Devis and Son Ltd v Atkins* [1977] ICR 662, that the employer cannot rely on s 74(6) to reduce the assessment of the compensatory award to take account of reasons discovered after the dismissal. The tribunal has to find that the dismissal was to some extent caused or contributed to by the actions of the employee. Where these actions were not known until after the dismissal, they cannot have been factors relevant to the dismissal. It is equally clear from the judgment that the assessment of the compensatory award must be just and equitable in the circumstances: see s 74(1) of the EP(C)A 1978. However, the EAT held in *Soros and Soros v Davison and Davison* [1994] IRLR 264, that in their view s 74(1) is only concerned with events which existed during and not subsequent to the contract of employment.

In *Tele-Trading Ltd v Jenkins* [1990] IRLR 430, Jenkins's compensation was not reduced under s 74(6) where his dismissal for alleged dishonesty was found to be unfair, because at the time of the dismissal the employer did not have reasonable grounds for believing that he was guilty. The Court of Appeal accepted the argument that the compensatory award could be reduced under s 74(1) if a thorough investigation would or might have resulted in the employee still being dismissed.

General

The onus of proving contributory fault is upon the employer. Whether or not the employee has contributed to his dismissal and to what extent are questions of fact for the tribunal: *Associated Tyre Specialists (Easter) Ltd v Waterhouse* [1977] ICR 218. In *Hollier v Plysu Ltd* [1983] IRLR 260, the Court of Appeal held that the apportionment of responsibility 'is so obviously a matter of impression, opinion and discretion' that the EAT is not entitled to interfere with the decision of the tribunal unless there is 'either a plain error of law, or something like perversity'. In *Warrilow v Robert Walker Ltd* [1984] IRLR 304, the EAT held that in deciding whether or not the tribunal's findings as to the apportionment of contributory fault can stand, the principles of law to be applied are precisely the same as the principles which apply and which bind an appellate court in relation to appeals under the Law Reform (Contributory Negligence) Act 1945, ie that the proportion of culpability is a matter for the tribunal of fact and can be interfered with only where there has been some failure by that tribunal to appreciate some material aspect of fact. In *Maris v Rotherham County BC* [1974] IRLR 147, the NIRC held that in exercising its discretion the tribunal should ignore technicalities. The tribunal had to look at all the circumstances and take a broad commonsense view.

Conduct of the employee

Section 73(7B) (reduction of the basic award) and s 75A(4) of the EP(C)A 1978 (reduction of the special award in health and safety cases), and s 158 (4) (reduction of the special award in cases of dismissal on union grounds) expressly refer to the employee's conduct. It is doubtful whether conduct will include a lack of capability. Section 74(6) of the EP(C)A 1978 refers merely to the employee's action. In *Polentarutti v Autokraft Ltd* [1991] ICR 757, the EAT held that even where there has been a constructive dismissal there can still be a deduction in compensation for contributory fault. It was not necessary there should be exceptional circumstances. Here the employee was held 66⅔ per cent to blame and the basic and compensatory awards were reduced.

Only where the employee has by his fault caused or contributed to his dismissal will there be any reduction; otherwise it would not be just and equitable: see *Morrish v Henlys (Folkestone) Ltd* [1973] 2 All ER 137, where an employee was dismissed because he failed to falsify certain records. Although there is no reference in the statute to culpability or blameworthiness the conduct on the part of the employee must be culpable or blameworthy.

In *Nelson v BBC (No 2)* [1980] ICR 110, Brandon LJ held that he 'would approach the application of ... [s 74(6) of the EP(C)A 1978] on the basis ... it could never be just or equitable to reduce a successful complainant's compensation unless the conduct on his part relied on as contributory was culpable or blameworthy ...' He thought culpability or blameworthiness, although involving conduct amounting to a breach of contract or a tort, also includes conduct, which, while not amounting to a breach of contract or a tort, is perverse or foolish.

In *Morrison v Amalgamated Transport and General Workers Union* [1989] IRLR 361, it was held that in determining contributory fault the tribunal must take a broad, common-sense approach, which should not necessarily be confined to a particular moment, even the terminal moment of employment. What the tribunal has to look for over a period is conduct on the part of the employee which is culpable, blameworthy or otherwise unreasonable, which contributed to or played a part in the dismissal.

In *Gibson and Others v British Transport Docks Board* [1982] IRLR 228, the EAT held that where an employee has been guilty of improper conduct of a blameworthy nature which led to his dismissal, the tribunal may find that the conduct contributed to the dismissal.

The action or conduct of the employee must have caused or contributed to the dismissal and the amount of the reduction is the amount which is just and equitable having regard to that finding. For the purposes of s 74(6) of the EP(C)A 1978 there must be a causal link between the actions or conduct of the employee and the dismissal: *Hutchinson v Enfield Rolling Mills Ltd* [1981] IRLR 318, but general bad behaviour may result in a reduction: see s 73(7B) and s 75(A)(4) of the EP(C)A 1978, and s 158(4) of the TULR(C)A 1992.

It is the employee's conduct alone which is relevant: *Allders International Ltd v Parkins* [1981] IRLR 68. In *Parker Foundry Ltd v Slack* [1992] IRLR 11, Slack, who had been involved in a fight with a fellow employee at work, was found to have been unfairly dismissed because of procedural irregularities. He was held 50 per cent to blame and his compensation reduced by the same percentage. The Court of Appeal held that even though the other person involved had only been given a two-week suspension, by virtue of s 73(7B) and s 74(6) of the EP(C)A 1978 the tribunal could only take into account Slack's conduct and what had happened to the other employee was not relevant. Although by virtue of s 74(1) of the EP(C)A 1978 the compensatory award must be such amount as the tribunal considers just and equitable 'in all the circumstances', those latter words are not included in s 73(7B) or s 74(6) and therefore only the complainant employee's conduct could be taken into account.

However, blameworthy conduct of a person acting on behalf of the employee as his agent may be taken into account. In *Allen v Hammett* [1982] IRLR 89, the employee's solicitor's actions were contributory to the dismissal, and his compensation was reduced accordingly.

In the somewhat unusual case of *Ladup Ltd v Barnes* [1982] IRLR 7, an employee was dismissed after being arrested and charged with growing and possession of cannabis. It was held that the dismissal was unfair because a proper investigation had not been carried out. Compensation was awarded. After the hearing he was convicted. On a review the tribunal refused to reduce the compensation because of the employee's conduct. On appeal the EAT reduced the compensation by 100 per cent because of the employee's conduct.

Failure by an employee to disclose a spent criminal conviction under the Rehabilitation of Offenders Act 1974 will not mean he has contributed to his dismissal because there is no obligation upon him to disclose a spent conviction and therefore there is no blameworthy conduct: *Property Guards Ltd v Taylor and Kershaw* [1982] IRLR 175.

Where the employee is dismissed because of lack of capability rather than misconduct it may be difficult to argue that he has caused or contributed to his dismissal. In *Kraft Foods Ltd v Fox* [1978] ICR 311, the EAT held that while an employee has control over his conduct he does not have control where he is incompetent or incapable, ie 'if he is doing his best and his best is not good enough.'

In *Slaughter v C Brewer and Sons Ltd* [1990] IRLR 426, it was held that in cases of ill-health there will rarely be a reduction in the compensatory award on the grounds of contributory fault because there will be no act or omission on the part of the employee which was culpable or blameworthy. In a case of ill-health it may be possible to reduce the amount of compensation under s 74(1) of the EP(C)A 1978 where, for instance, a dismissal is unfair on procedural grounds, but the employee is incapable of doing the job: see *Nelson*'s case, *above*.

The approach in *Fox*'s case is by no means one of universal application. In *Patterson v Messrs Bracketts* [1977] IRLR 137, the EAT found the tribunal was entitled to take into account in assessing contributory fault not only the employee's conduct but 'the whole of [the employee's] work record ... to the extent that his dismissal was contributed to by his lack of ability at work.' Similarly, in *Moncur v International Paint Co Ltd* [1978] IRLR 223, another division of the EAT doubted whether the decision in *Fox*'s case, *above*, was attempting to lay down a proposition of law. See also *Finnie v Top Hat Frozen Foods* [1985] ICR 433.

In *Sutton and Gates (Luton) Ltd v Boxall* [1978] IRLR 486, the EAT found that it was necessary to distinguish between the case where the employee's lack of capability was due to his own fault in the sense that he was lazy, negligent or idle, or did not try to improve, as distinct from the case where the employee tries desperately hard but cannot cope. In the first case the degree of contribution would be considerable.

Where an unfair dismissal involves the selective re-engagement of employees who have taken part in a strike or other industrial action, the issue of contributory fault must be considered in relation to the dismissal. Did the employee contribute to his dismissal? It is neither necessary nor proper to consider whether he has contributed to his failure to be re-engaged. Where the employee is dismissed because he took part in a strike or other industrial action can the taking part in such strike or other industrial action be characterised as contributory fault? It has been held that:

> it is not possible for an Industrial Tribunal to hold under s 74(6) ... that the industrial action in which the employee was taking part (whether or not it was in breach of contract) in itself justifies a reduction in compensation, since an Industrial Tribunal is unable to determine whether or not, and to what extent, it is just and equitable to make such reduction (*Courtaulds Northern Spinning Ltd v Moosa* [1984] IRLR 43).

However, the EAT held in *TNT Express (UK) Ltd v Downes and Others* [1993] IRLR 432, that where a tribunal has jurisdiction under [what is now s 238 of the TULR(C)A 1992] it can take into account the circumstances surrounding the industrial action itself, when considering s 73(7B) or s 74(1) or (6), and considered the decision in *Moosa's* case was unsound. If the tribunal has jurisdiction under s 238 'then it must carry out its statutory function and seek to do that which is fair, just and reasonable between the parties. All the surrounding circumstances will be examined as in any other case'.

Amount of deduction

The tribunal has to decide whether or not there should be a reduction because of contributory fault. Any reduction will be expressed in percentage terms. In assessing the degree of contribution it is the gravity of the action rather than the state of mind of the employee which is relevant: *Ladbroke Racing Ltd v Mason* [1978] ICR 49. The tribunal must first ascertain the extent to which the employee's action brought about his dismissal; and secondly it must decide by what proportion the award should be reduced considering justice and equity. Justice and equity means justice to both sides and fair treatment of both sides: *Parker and Farr Ltd v Shelvey* [1979] IRLR 434.

The reduction may not be from the whole of the award. The tribunal must examine what the employee would have received by way of earnings if he had not been dismissed, and must then take into account any wages in lieu of notice or *ex gratia* payment which has been paid to the employee by the employer. These sums will be deducted before applying the appropriate proportion for contributory fault. Thus, if the employee has a net loss of wages of £2,000 but has been paid £1,500 wages in lieu of notice and has contributed to his dismissal by 25 per cent, a 25 per cent reduction will be made from the £500 which remains after deducting £1,500 from £2,000 and not by applying it to the £2,000 leaving £1,500 and then reducing this to a nil figure by deducting the £1,500: *UBAF Bank Ltd v Davis* [1978] IRLR 442; *Clement-Clarke International Ltd v Manley* [1979] ICR 74; *Parker and Farr Ltd v Shelvey, above.*

In *TBA Industrial Products Ltd v Locke* [1984] IRLR 48, Locke suffered a reduction of 70 per cent in the assessment of his compensation for loss of pension rights because there was a very high degree of probability that he would have left the employment, either due to a continuation of his unsatisfactory work performance, or because of a redundancy. He suffered a further 70 per cent reduction of his total compensation, including the compensation for loss of pension rights, because his unsatisfactory work had contributed to his dismissal. The EAT held that he had not been improperly penalised twice.

The contributory fault deduction will be made from total losses awarded and not from the maximum permitted by statute. Thus, if the employee has a compensatory award of £12,000 and is found 25 per cent to blame, £3,000 will be deducted from the £12,000 and not from the statutory maximum of £11,000: see *Morris v Gestetner Ltd* [1973] ICR 587 and *Walter Braund (London) Ltd v Murray* [1991] IRLR 100. Confirmation of this approach is provided by s 75(3) of the EP(C)A 1978.

There is nothing incompatible with a finding of unfair dismissal by making a nil award of compensation or an award of nominal compensation: *W Devis and Sons Ltd v Atkins* [1977] ICR 662; see also *Allders International Ltd v Parkins* [1981] IRLR 68. In *Chaplin v H J Rawlinson Ltd* [1991] ICR 553, the employee, a lorry driver, had worked for 26 years but was summarily dismissed for breaches which threatened the loss of two customers. He had deliberately blocked a road on one occasion, and was discovered to have urinated over wheat he had just delivered on another. The tribunal awarded nil basic and compensatory awards on the ground he was wholly responsible for his own dismissal. The EAT upheld the decision on the basis that it would not be just and equitable to give financial compensation where he was 100 per cent to blame. In *Rao v Civil Aviation Authority* [1994] IRLR 240, the tribunal had reduced the basic and compensatory awards on account of Rao's blameworthy conduct, and reduced the compensatory award by a further 80 per cent to reflect the fact that if a fair procedure had been followed he would still have been dismissed. The Court of Appeal held that the compensatory award may be reduced twice, under s 74(1) and s 74(6) and if there has been a large reduction under s 74(1), then the percentage reductions under both s 74(6) and s 73(7B) might well be different.

A reduction by 100 per cent may be logical where the only reason the dismissal is unfair is due to a procedural irregularity: *Nairne v Highland and Islands Fire Brigade* [1989] IRLR 366.

In *Hollier v Plysu Ltd* [1983] IRLR 260, the EAT suggested that there should be a tariff for contributory conduct of 25 per cent, 50 per cent, 75 per cent or 100 per cent. In *Yorke v Brown* (1982) (unreported), it was suggested that a reduction of 10 per cent on account of the employee's contribution was almost *de minimis*.

Constructive dismissal

There may be a deduction for contributory conduct where the employee has been constructively dismissed: *Western Excavating (ECC) Ltd v Sharp* [1977] IRLR 25, overruled by the Court of Appeal on other grounds at [1978] ICR 221. See also *Polentarutti v Autokraft Ltd* [1991] ICR 757, *above*.

It is for the tribunal to decide whether the employer's actions amount to a constructive dismissal. Where the employer has repudiated the contract the behaviour of the employee must be examined in deciding upon contributory conduct. The tribunal is entitled to take into account the circumstances of the dismissal, but these may be completely or largely irrelevant in assessing compensation or any reduction. The proper approach is for the tribunal to look broadly over the whole period of time prior to the dismissal: *Garner v Grange Furnishing Ltd* [1977] IRLR 206. See *Morrison*'s case, *above*.

In *Holroyd v Gravure Cylinders Ltd* [1984] IRLR 259, the EAT distinguished the case of *Garner v Grange Furnishing Ltd*, *above*, on the grounds that it was 'a last-straw incident' following a course of conduct which gave rise to the fundamental breach of contract by the employer. Although it held that it was 'exceptional to have a situation where there is a genuine constructive dismissal due to the employer's breach of contract which at the same time has been contributed to by the employee', there may be such cases.

Failure to appeal

Where an employee fails to appeal against his dismissal under an internal procedure he is not thereby guilty of contributory fault: *Hoover Ltd v Forde* [1980] ICR 239. The EAT held that where the employee has no duty in law to make use of an appeal procedure after his dismissal, he could not be said to have contributed to his own dismissal by failing to use the appeal procedure. See also *William Muir (Bond 9) Ltd v Lamb* [1985] IRLR 95; the latest view of the EAT in *Lock v Connell Estate Agents* [1944] IRLR 444, and under Mitigation, Failure to utilise the employer's disciplinary procedure at p 376.

Factors which cannot be taken into account

Section 155 of the TULR(C)A 1992 restricts the power of the tribunal in determining contributory fault by providing that certain conduct of the employee shall be ignored. This section applies where the tribunal makes an award of compensation under s 68(2) of the EP(C)A 1978 (where an order for reinstatement or re-engagement is not made but there is an award of compensation), or under s 71(2)(*a*) of the EP(C)A 1978 (where an order for reinstatement or re-engagement is made but the order is not complied with) and the dismissal is regarded as unfair under s 152 or s 153 of the TULR(C)A 1992, that is where the employee is unfairly dismissed or selected for redundancy on union grounds.

In such a case the tribunal in considering whether it would be just and equitable to reduce or further reduce the amount of any part of the award, shall disregard any conduct or action of the employee in so far as it constitutes:

(*a*) a breach or proposed breach of any requirement falling within s 155(2) of the TULR(C)A 1992.

(*b*) a refusal or proposed refusal, to comply with the requirement of a kind mentioned in s 152(3)(*a*) of the TULR(C)A 1992 (a refusal or proposed refusal to comply with a requirement (whether or not imposed by his contract of employment or in writing) that in the event of the employee not being a member of any trade union, or a particular trade union or one of a number of particular trade unions he must make one or more payments), or

(*c*) an objection or proposed objection however expressed to the operation of a provision of a kind mentioned in s 152(3)(*b*) (an objection or proposed objection to a provision (whether or not forming part of his contract of employment or in writing) enabling the employer to deduct money from remuneration in the event of the employee failing to be a member of any trade union, or a particular trade union or one of a number of particular trade unions): s 155(3) of the TULR(C)A 1992 (*sic*). This section provides that there may be a reduction in the basic award (see s 73(7B) of the EP(C)A 1978), the compensatory award (see s 74(6) of the EP(C)A 1978) or the special award (see s 158(4) of the TULR(C)A 1992).

A requirement for the purposes of s 155(2) of the TULR(C)A 1992 is one imposed upon the employee by or under any arrangement, or contract of employment, or other agreement and requires him:

(*a*) to be or become a member of any trade union or of a particular trade union or of one of a number of particular trade unions;

(*b*) to cease to be, or refrain from becoming a member of any trade union or of a particular trade union or of one of a number of particular trade unions; or

(*c*) not to take part in the activities of any trade union or of a particular trade union or of one of a number of particular trade unions: s 155(2) of the TULR(C)A 1992.

In *TGWU v Howard* [1992] IRLR 170, Miss Howard's dismissal was automatically unfair under what is now s 152(*c*) of the TULR(C)A 1992. The EAT distinguished between what was done by the employee and the way it was done, and if the conduct of the employee prior to dismissal deserved to be criticised, then the tribunal was at liberty to reduce the award. Howard had been employed at TGWU but resigned as a member of the union and the tribunal found that her conduct in so resigning without seeking prior discussion was confrontational and 'if not bloody-minded was certainly unreasonable'. The case was remitted to the tribunal for consideration as to whether the award should be reduced in respect of her conduct before dismissal.

Section 155 has been inserted to prevent the employer relying upon any contractual arrangement entered into by the employee for reducing the amount of the award of compensation on the grounds of contributory fault.

Compensation and state benefit

Past benefit—recoupment

Unemployment benefit or income support paid to the employee by the State between the date of the dismissal and the date of the tribunal hearing are not deducted from the immediate loss of earnings: reg 5(1) of the Employment Protection (Recoupment of Unemployment Benefit and Supplementary Benefit) Regulations 1977 (SI 1977 No 674) as amended. Instead, when giving a decision, the tribunal must, under reg 5(3), set out the following particulars:

(*a*) the monetary award;

(*b*) the amount of the prescribed element, if any;

(c) The dates of the period to which the prescribed element is attributable; and

(d) the amount, if any, by which the monetary award exceeds the prescribed element.

The monetary award is the total amount of the compensation awarded. The prescribed element is the immediate loss of wages. Where the monetary award is reduced to take account of the employee's contributory fault or because it exceeds the statutory maximum, a proportionate reduction has to be made in the amount of the prescribed element: reg 5(2).

Where the tribunal makes a monetary award at the hearing it must then (and in any case in the written decision) explain to the parties the amount of the prescribed element and the provisions as to recoupment: reg 5(4). The prescribed element is not payable by the employer until the Department of Employment has either notified the employer that it does not intend to serve a recoupment notice or serves a recoupment notice. The Department of Employment must serve either of these notices, where the tribunal announces its decision at the hearing, 21 days after the hearing, or 9 days after the decision has been sent to the parties, whichever is the later; or in any other case 21 days after the decision has been sent to the parties: reg 9(5) and (6). A recoupment notice requires the employer to pay the Department of Employment the lesser of the following sums: either the amount of the prescribed element; or the amount paid as on account of unemployment benefit or supplementary benefit to the employee for any period that coincides with the period for which the prescribed element is attributable: reg 9(1) and (2).

Payment to the Department of Employment is a complete discharge for the employer in favour of the employee, although the employee is not prejudiced thereby in appealing against the recoupment notice: reg 9(10). Where the employer pays the recoupable amount to the employee before the time for serving the recoupment notice he will still be liable to the Department of Employment: reg 9(9). In *Hilton International Hotels v Faraji* [1994] ICR 259, the EAT held there need be no reduction from the calculation of the compensatory award for invalidity benefit received between dismissal and the tribunal hearing. The benefit was an insurance benefit, and not covered by the Regulations.

In cases where the employer and employee settle a case without going to the tribunal, there is no liability to recoupment unless the agreement identifies the amount of the immediate loss of wages. Further, in such circumstances, the employee will not necessarily be disentitled to unemployment benefit in the future. Where the employee receives a capital sum there may be a re-determination of his entitlement to benefit.

Future benefit

The position of future benefits is governed by the Social Security (Unemployment, Sickness and Invalidity Benefit) Regulations 1983 (SI 1983 No 1598) as amended. Reference is to those regulations as amended.

The employee is not treated as being unemployed and so is not entitled to benefit for any day where a tribunal following an order for reinstatement or re-engagement awards an amount for non-compliance with such an order of reinstatement or re-engagement or as compensation for unfair dismissal and the payment represents remuneration which the tribunal considers the employee might have earned for that day but for the dismissal: reg 7(1)(k)(iii).

These provisions only apply within a year from the date of registration of the tribunal's decision: reg 7(1)(k)(iii). The compensation awarded by the tribunal must be payable to the employee. Payable means due and owing rather than has been or will be paid so it is immaterial that the employer does not or cannot pay: *Marton v Chief Adjudication Officer* [1988] IRLR 444.

Death of the employee

Where the employee has died tribunal proceedings for unfair dismissal may be instituted or continued by a personal representative of the deceased employee. If the employer has died proceedings for unfair dismissal may be defended by a personal representative of the deceased employer: para 2 of Sched 12 to the EP(C)A 1978. Where there are no personal representatives of a deceased employee the claim for unfair dismissal may be instituted or continued on behalf of the estate of the deceased employee by such person as the tribunal may appoint, being either a person authorised by the employee before his death to act or a close relative: see para 3(1) of Sched 12.

If either the employee or the employer dies during the notice period the unfair dismissal provisions shall apply as if the contract had been terminated by the employer by notice expiring on the date of death: para 8 of Sched 12.

Paragraph 9 of Sched 12 applies where, by virtue of s 55(5) and (6) of the EP(C)A 1978, the notice period has been extended so that if either the employer or the employee dies before the later date s 55(5) and (6) take effect as if the notice would have expired on the date of death. Where an employee has died and no order for reinstatement or re-engagement had already been made, the tribunal can award compensation only: para 10 of Sched 12. It follows that the award of compensation will be circumscribed by the date of the employee's death. If an order for reinstatement or re-engagement has been made and the employee dies before the order is complied with, but the employer before the employee's death has refused to carry out the order, the tribunal will assess compensation in the normal way and an additional award will become payable unless the employer can show that it was not practicable at the time of the refusal to comply with the order: para 11(a) of Sched 12. Because of the wording of para 11 of Sched 12 it is doubtful if a special award can be made. If there has been no refusal by the employer to comply with the order but the employer fails to comply with any ancillary terms of the order which remain capable of fulfilment after the employee's death the tribunal shall assess compensation as if the employee had been reinstated or re-engaged, but the employer has not fully complied with the terms of the order (see s 71(1) of the EP(C)A 1978): para 11(b) of Sched 12.

Discrimination

Where compensation is awarded for an act both under the Sex Discrimination Act (SDA 1975) and/or the Race Relations Act 1976, (RRA 1976) and under the EP(C)A 1978 for unfair dismissal, compensation in respect of any loss can only be awarded once for that act: s 76(1) of the EP(C)A 1978.

There is now no limit to the awards which can be made under the SDA 1975 and the RRA 1976. The Sex Discrimination and Equal Pay (Remedies) Regulations 1993 (SI 1993 No 2798) abolish the limit on compensation relating to sex discrimination and equal pay with effect from 22 November 1993, and the Race Relations (Remedies) Act 1994 abolishes the limit on compensation for race discrimination with effect from the end of two months beginning with 3 May 1994. Thus, where an unfair dismissal is also an act of discrimination under the SDA 1975 or the RRA 1976 there can be unlimited compensation together with the usual basic award and, if appropriate, additional or special awards.

Interest

Awards relating to unfair dismissal

Under the Industrial Tribunals (Interest) Order 1990 (SI 1990 No. 479) where the whole or any part of a sum of money awarded by a tribunal remains unpaid, the sum of money remaining unpaid on the calculation day carries interest. The calculation day is the day immediately following the expiry of the period of 42 days, beginning with the relevant decision day. The decision day is the day signified by the date recording the sending of the document to the parties recording an award or other determination of a tribunal (ie promulgation). There are separate definitions where the decision of a tribunal is reviewed, an appellate court remits a matter to the tribunal for reassessment or if there is an appeal from the decision of the tribunal. The rate of interest is the rate specified in s 17 of the Judgements Act 1838 on the decision day. The order came into force on 1 April 1990. The rate of interest is currently 8 per cent (as at June 1994).

Awards relating to discrimination

As a result of the decision of the European Court of Justice in *Marshall v Southampton and South West Hampshire Area Health Authority* (No 2) [1993] IRLR 445, interest is now payable on awards relating to sex discrimination. Under the Sex Discrimination and Equal Pay (Remedies) Regulations 1993 (SI 1993 No 2798), as from 22 November 1993 interest (currently 8 per cent) is payable differently from that on unfair dismissal awards. It runs from the day after promulgation, but no interest is payable if the full amount of the award is paid within 14 days of promulgation.

In addition, there is provision for calculation of interest from the date of the act of discrimination to be included in the award for injury to feelings, and from the mid-point date (as defined) to be included in the rest of the award for discrimination. Reference should be made to the Statutory Instrument for the details which are outside the scope of this book.

The Race Relations (Interest on Awards) Regulations 1994 (SI 1994 No 1748) provide for interest on awards for race discrimination similar to the interest provisions for sex discrimination as from 1 August 1994.

Interim Relief

General

Where an employee presents an application alleging unfair dismissal on the ground that the reason, or principal reason, for his dismissal was one of those mentioned in either:

(a) s 57A(1(a) or (b) of the EP(C)A 1978—health and safety reasons—(but not s 59(2), ie selection for redundancy on those grounds), or

(b) s 152(1) of the TULR(C)A 1992—trade union membership, non-membership, or activities—(but not s 153, ie selection for redundancy on those grounds),

he is entitled to apply to the tribunal for interim relief: s 77(1) of the EP(C)A 1978 and s 161 of the TULR(C)A 1992 respectively.

There are strict time limits (see Chapter 18). The tribunal must give the employer at least seven days' notice of the hearing of the application for interim relief but, subject to that, must determine the application as soon as practicable: s 77(3) and (4) of the EP(C)A 1978 and s 162 of the TULR(C)A 1992. The hearing can only be postponed where the tribunal is satisfied that there are special circumstances: s 77(5) of the EP(C)A 1978 and s 162(4) of the TULR(C)A 1992.

At the interim relief hearing, if the tribunal considers that it is likely, at the unfair dismissal hearing, to find that the dismissal was for the reason alleged, it shall announce its findings.

If the parties are present, the tribunal must explain what remedies are available, and must ask the employer if he is willing to reinstate or re-engage the employee pending the unfair dismissal hearing: s 77A(1) and (2) of the EP(C)A 1978 and s 163(1) and (2) of the TULR(C)A 1992. If the employer is willing to reinstate the employee, the tribunal must make an order to that effect: s 77A(4) of the EP(C)A 1978 and s 163(4) of the TULR(C)A 1992.

Where the employer is willing to re-engage the employee, then, if the employee is willing to accept the job, the tribunal must make an order to that effect; but if the employee reasonably refuses the job, the tribunal must make an order for the continuation of the contract. If the employee unreasonably refuses the job, the tribunal will not make any order at all: s 77A(5)(b) of the EP(C)A 1978 and s 163(5) of the TULR(C)A 1992. If the employer fails to attend the hearing, or is unwilling to reinstate or re-engage the employee, the tribunal must make an order for the continuation of the contract: s 77A(6) of the EP(C)A 1978 and s 163(6) of the TULR(C)A 1992.

An order for the continuation of the contract, is an order that the contract of employment continues in force:

(a) for the purposes of pay or any other benefit derived from the employment, seniority, pension rights, and other similar matters, and

(b) for determining for any purpose the period for which the employee has been continuously employed,

from the date of its termination (whether before or after the date of the order) until the hearing, or settlement of the unfair dismissal application: s 78(1) of the EP(C)A 1978 and s 164(1) of the TULR(C)A 1992. Thus, it does not require the employee to work.

As to what should be included in the order, and the amounts due to the employee, see s 78(2)–(7) of the EP(C)A 1978 and s 164(2)–(7) of the TULR(C)A 1992. Either the employer or the employee can apply to the tribunal for revocation or variation of the order (on the ground that there has been a relevant change of circumstances since the making of the order) at any time before the hearing, or settlement, of the unfair dismissal application: s 78A(1) of the EP(C)A 1978 and s 165(1) of the TULR(C)A 1992.

Failure to comply with order for reinstatement or re-engagement

If the employer fails to comply with the order for reinstatement or re-engagement, the tribunal must:

(*a*) make an order for the continuation of the contract, and

(*b*) order the employer to pay to the employee such compensation as the tribunal considers just and equitable in all the circumstances, having regard to:

  (i) the infringement of the employee's right to be reinstated or re-engaged in pursuance of the order,

  and

  (ii) any loss suffered by the employee in consequence of the non-compliance.

See s 79(1) of the EP(C)A 1978 and s 166(1) of the TULR(C)A 1992. The provisions of s 78 EP(C)A 1978 and s 164 of the TULR(C)A 1992 also apply to orders made under s 79(1) and 166(1) respectively.

Failure to comply with order for continuation of a contract

The employee can apply to the tribunal if the employer does not comply with the terms of an order for continuation. If the failure is to make any payment specified in the order, the tribunal must decide the amount owed by the employer at the date of *this* hearing. If the unfair dismissal hearing takes place on that same date, and if the tribunal finds that the employee has been unfairly dismissed, it shall specify the amount owed separately from any other sum awarded. In any other case, the tribunal must order the employer to pay to the employee such compensation as it considers just and equitable having regard to any loss suffered by the employee in consequence of the non-compliance: s 79(3)–(6) of the EP(C)A 1978 and s 166(3)–(5) of the TULR(C)A 1992.

Chapter 17

Normal Working Hours and a Week's Pay

In calculating the amount of the employee's basic and any additional or special award, the tribunal must ascertain the amount of a week's pay: see ss 72(2)(*b*), 73 and 75A of the EP(C)A 1978. As a preliminary the tribunal must decide whether or not the employee has any normal working hours.

Normal working hours

The employee's normal working hours may be ascertained from collective agreements, national or local, the written contract of employment, the statutory statement served pursuant to ss 1 or 4 of the EP(C)A 1978 or an oral agreement and the conduct of the parties.

The express terms of the contract of employment may be varied expressly or impliedly: see *Armstrong Whitworth Rolls Ltd v Mustard* [1971] 1 All ER 598. However, the evidence must establish that there has been a variation. In *Friend v PMA Holdings Ltd* [1976] ICR 330, the EAT held that there had been no variation in the employees' contracts. A temporary arrangement did not operate to vary the existing contracts. But compare *Lowe v East Lancashire Paper Mill Ltd* (1970) 5 ITR 132.

Where an employee signs a contract of employment which clearly sets out the normal working hours that agreement will be conclusive evidence of the terms of the contract as to normal working hours in the absence of any variation or waiver of its terms: see *Gascol Conversions Ltd v Mercer* [1974] ICR 420. In this case the Court of Appeal was not prepared to accept that the national agreement which was reflected in the contract of employment had been varied by a local agreement. Whether or not the national agreement incorporated into the employees' contracts can be varied by a local agreement, depends upon the circumstances, and whether or not the local agreement has become incorporated into the contracts: see *Barrett v NCB* [1978] ICR 1101.

Paragraph 2 of Sched 14 to the EP(C)A 1978 provides that where the contract of employment fixes the number, or the minimum number

394

of hours in a week or other period, whether or not those hours can be reduced in certain circumstances, and even though those hours exceed the number of hours without overtime pay, those hours are the normal working hours. Thus in practice, it does not matter that some of those hours are regarded as overtime hours, nor that they are remunerated at overtime rates. If the employer has contracted to provide a fixed number of hours' overtime and the employee to work it, so that the overtime is compulsory on both sides, those fixed hours form part of the normal working hours. Conversely, where the employee works additional hours to those which are fixed by the contract, and the additional hours are voluntary on both sides, those hours do not form part of the normal working hours. Where, under the contract, overtime hours are compulsory for the employee only, as where the employer is entitled but not bound to call on the employee to work overtime, but the employee is bound to work overtime when called upon by the employer to do so, those hours are not normal working hours: *Tarmac Roadstone Holdings Ltd v Peacock* [1973] ICR 273; *Gascol Conversions Ltd v Mercer* [1974] ICR 420; and *Lotus Cars Ltd v Sutcliffe and Stratton* [1982] IRLR 381.

A week's pay

The legislation specifies four categories of employee, who may be classified as: employees on time work (ie those with normal working hours whose pay does not vary with the amount of work done); employees with normal working hours whose pay does vary with the work done; employees on a rota or shift; and employees who have no normal hours of work. Each category of employee is treated separately and each section of the legislation dealing with these separate categories has its own peculiar wording. However, in each case it is necessary to ascertain what is meant by the word 'remuneration' for the purposes of computing a week's pay. There is no statutory definition of remuneration. Guidance is available from the reported cases. Although it was at one stage considered that remuneration might differ for each of the categories of employee (consider *S and U Stores Ltd v Lee* [1969] 2 All ER 417), the practice among tribunals is to interpret the word 'remuneration' in the same way for each of the four categories of employees.

In *S and U Stores Ltd v Wilkes* [1974] ICR 645, the NIRC held:

> In our judgment the test for determining the 'average' weekly rate of 'remuneration' is as follows:
> (i)   any sum which is paid as a wage or salary without qualification is part of the employee's remuneration;
> (ii)   the value of any benefit in kind (eg free accommodation) or paid in cash by someone other than the employer (eg the Easter offering) is to be disregarded as not forming part of the remuneration;

(iii) any sum which is agreed to be paid by way of reimbursement or on account of expenditure incurred by the employee has to be examined to see whether in broad terms the whole or any part of the sum represents a profit or surplus in the hands of the employee. To the extent that it does represent such a profit or surplus it is part of the employee's remuneration.

This is not a matter which calls for an involved accountancy exercise. It is for the tribunal of fact to form a broad common sense view of the realities of the situation as revealed by the evidence assessed in the light of their expert knowledge and experience.

Remuneration includes wages and salaries. It is the wage or salary payable under the contract of employment in force on the calculation date. Therefore, if the employee has agreed to a reduction in his wage or salary before the calculation date, it is that reduced wage which must be taken into account: see *Valentine v Great Lever Spinning Co* (1966) 1 ITR 71. Any future increase cannot be taken into account. It is doubtful that any future increase awarded under an agreement made after the calculation date, but having retrospective effect, can be taken into account: see *Leyland Vehicles Ltd v Reston and Others* [1981] ICR 403, where such an increase was discounted; but compare *Carrod v Pullman Spring Filled Co Ltd* (1967) 2 ITR 650; see also *Tsoukka v Potomac Restaurants Ltd* (1968) 3 ITR 259, and *Cooner v P S Doal & Sons* [1988] ICR 495. Both concerned Wages Council Orders, where the 'week's pay' was held to be the contractual pay, or the minimum under the Order, whichever was the greater.

Where an employee is entitled under his contract to a basic wage together with commission, remuneration will include commission: see *Weevsmay Ltd v Kings* [1977] ICR 244. Where commission is payable at the end of an accounting period it may be apportionable under the employee's contract of employment: *J and S Bickley Ltd v Washer* [1977] ICR 425. This case is some support for the proposition that commission can be apportioned similarly under the statutory provisions. Remuneration includes a contractual bonus: see *Mole Mining Ltd v Jenkins* [1972] ICR 282, and a regular bonus: see *A and B Marcusfield Ltd v Melhuish* [1977] IRLR 484. A site bonus may also be included where it is an implied term of the contract that the employee shall receive the same: see *Donelan v Kerrby Constructions Ltd* [1983] ICR 237.

Remuneration will not include payments in kind, for instance the provision of a car including maintenance and petrol: see *Skillen v Eastwoods Froy Ltd* (1966) 2 ITR 112; board and lodging: *British Transport Hotels Ltd v Minister of Labour* (1966) 2 ITR 165. Nor will it include a lodging allowance: *AM Carmichael Ltd v Laing* (1972) 7 ITR 1.

Remuneration will not include any payment made by a third party. Thus, a waiter cannot claim tips or gratuities as part of his remuneration for statutory purposes: see *Palmanor Ltd t/a Chaplins Night Club v Cedron* [1978] IRLR 303; although where customers of a restaurant were contractually obliged to pay a 10 per cent service charge, which was then distributed to employees in fixed proportions, the payment (known as tronc) to an employee did form part of remuneration for statutory purposes: *Tsoukka and Others v Potomac Restaurants Ltd* (1968) 3 ITR 259. See also *Keywest Club Ltd v Choudhury* [1988] IRLR 51.

A week's pay for the purposes of Sched 14 is a week's pay gross: see *Secretary of State for Employment v John Woodrow and Sons (Builders) Ltd* [1983] IRLR 11. The case of *Secretary of State for Employment v Jobling* [1980] ICR 380, which held that a week's pay was net of tax is wrong in law.

Employees on time work

If an employee's remuneration for employment in normal working hours, whether by the hour or week or other period, does not vary with the amount of work done in the period, the amount of a week's pay is the amount which is payable by the employer under the contract in force on the calculation date if the employee works throughout his normal working hours in a week: para 3(2) of Sched 14.

Employees whose pay varies with work done

Where the employee has normal working hours, but the pay varies with the amount of work done in the period (eg piece work, or production bonus), the amount of a week's pay is the amount of remuneration for the number of normal working hours in a week, calculated at the average hourly rate of remuneration payable in respect of the period of 12 weeks ending, where the calculation date is the last day of the week, with that week or, in any other case, with the last complete week before the calculation date: para 3(3) of Sched 14. References to remuneration varying with the amount of work done include references to remuneration which may include any commission or similar payment which varies in amount: para 3(4) of Sched 14; see also para 5 of Sched 14. (See 'Employees on shifts or rotas', *below*.)

Employees on shifts or rotas

Where there are normal working hours for an employee, and he is required under that contract to work during those hours on days of the week, or at times of the day, which differ from week to week or over a longer period so that the remuneration payable for or apportionable to any week varies according to the incidence of those days or times, the amount of a week's pay is the amount of remuneration for the average weekly number of normal working hours at the average hourly rate of remuneration: para 4(1) and (2) of Sched 14.

The average number of weekly hours is calculated by dividing by 12 the total number of the employee's normal working hours during the period of 12 weeks ending, where the calculation date is the last day of the week, with that week, or, in any other case, with the last complete week before the calculation date: para 4(3) of Sched 14. The average hourly rate of remuneration is the average hourly rate of remuneration payable by the employer to the employee for the same 12 weeks: para 4(4) of Sched 14.

In computing the average hourly rate of remuneration (for the purposes of paras 3 or 4) only hours worked and only payment made for those hours can be considered. This may cause hardship for the employees, hence the averaging formula. If in some of the 12 weeks no remuneration was payable, those weeks are ignored and the next preceding weeks are taken into account: para 5(1) of Sched 14. See also para 5(2) of Sched 14 which provides for work done other than in normal working hours at a greater remuneration than work done in normal working hours to be treated as work done in normal working hours at a rate of remuneration adjusted accordingly. See *British Coal Corporation v Cheesborough* [1990] ICR 317. No account is to be taken of any overtime premium even if the overtime hours are compulsory: see para 5(3) of Sched 14.

Employees with no normal working hours

If there are no normal working hours for an employee, the amount of a week's pay is the amount of the employee's average weekly remuneration in the period of 12 weeks ending, where the calculation date is the last day of the week, with that week or, in any other case, with the last complete week before the calculation date: para 6(1) and (2) of Sched 14.

No account is taken of a week in which no remuneration was payable. Those weeks are ignored and the next preceding weeks are taken into account so as to bring the number of weeks up to 12: para 6(3) of Sched 14.

The calculation date

The calculation date for the purposes of determining a week's pay varies according to the circumstances.

Failure to give a written statement of the reasons for dismissal under s 53 of the EP(C)A 1978
Where the dismissal was with notice the calculation date is the date on which the employer's notice was given: para 7(1)(f) of Sched 14. In

any other case, the calculation date is the effective date of termination: para 7(1)(*g*) of Sched 14. Note that the limit on a week's pay in para 8(1) of Sched 14 (currently £205) does not apply to awards under s 53.

The basic or additional award for the employee who is unfairly dismissed in breach of her right to return after maternity
The calculation date is the last day on which she worked under the original contract of employment: para 2(5) of Sched 2.

Where s 55(5) or (6) of the EPC(A) 1978 applies (ie where the employer gives no notice, or a notice shorter than that prescribed by s 49, or in a constructive dismissal case), so that a later date is treated as the effective date of termination, the calculation date is the earlier effective date of termination as defined by s 55(4): see para 7(1)(*h*) of Sched 14.

Where neither s 55(5) nor (6) applies (ie where the employer gives the notice prescribed by s 49 or greater, or a fixed-term contract expires), the calculation date is the date upon which notice would have been given had certain conditions been fulfilled, even if, in fact, they were not fulfilled: see para 7(1)(*i*) of Sched 14.

Those conditions are in para 7(2). It has to be deemed that the employer gave the s 49 notice to expire on the effective date of termination. This can have unexpected results. If, for example, an employee of four years' service is given a three-month contractual notice, the calculation date is four weeks back from the date upon which the three-months' notice expires. It is difficult to explain or comprehend the logic of this provision.

Additional award for compensation where there is a failure to comply with an order for reinstatement or re-engagement
Where the dismissal was with notice the calculation date is the date on which the notice was given. In any other case, it is the effective date of termination: para 7(1)(*f*) and (*g*) of Sched 14.

The special award
Where there is a special award under s 72 of the EP(C)A 1978 or s 158 of the TULR(C)A 1992 then, where the dismissal was with notice, the calculation date is the date on which the notice was given, and in any other case, it is the effective date of termination: para 7(*a*), (*ia*) and (*ib*) of Sched 14; s 158(7) of the TULR(C)A 1992.

The calculation date for the basic award can cause problems in certain cases of constructive dismissal or where a fixed-term contract expires without being renewed. The calculation date has to be determined by ascertaining the date when the employment actually ended— the effective date of termination—and, when the actual date has been found, it is necessary to take away the number of weeks' notice to which the employee is entitled under the statutory provisions. The date which is then reached is the calculation date. Where the employee is dismissed with notice which is less than the statutory minimum, the employee is credited with the additional weeks and the effective date of termination is later than the date when the employment actually ended. Were there no provision for calculating a week's wages, since the effective date of termination will be later than the actual date when the employment terminated, weeks would be taken into account when the employee had not worked. To overcome this difficulty the calculation date for these purposes is the effective date of termination—ie when the contract actually ends and not the date when the contract would have ended if proper notice had been given.

Supplemental

Where the employee has not been employed for a sufficient period to enable a calculation to be made, the amount of a week's pay is the amount which fairly represents a week's pay. In ascertaining this, the tribunal must apply as nearly as possible the provisions contained in Sched 14: para 9 of Sched 14. It may have regard to remuneration offered by the employer to the employee and the amount received by the employee for the work. It may also have regard to remuneration received by other persons engaged by the same employer, or other employers for relevant comparable employment: para 9(*a*)–(*d*) of Sched 14.

Account may be taken of remuneration earned by the employee with a former employer, where that counts as part of the employee's continuous employment: para 10 of Sched 14.

The tribunal has power to make apportionments in computing the rate of remuneration: para 11 of Sched 14.

Twelve weeks means the last 12 calendar weeks. It does not mean the last 12 working weeks or the last 12 weeks of employment: see *Sylvester v Standard Upholstery Co Ltd* (1966) 2 ITR 507.

For the purposes of this chapter, a week means, in relation to an employee whose remuneration is calculated weekly by a week ending with a day other than Saturday, a week ending with that other day; and in relation to any other employee, a week ending with Saturday: s 153 of the EP(C)A 1978.

Paragraph 8(1) of Sched 14 provides that for the purposes of an additional award under s 71(2)(*b*), and a basic award under s 72, there is a limit on a 'week's pay.' The limit is reviewable annually by the Secretary of State of Employment. Currently, it is £205.

For the purposes of the special award payable under s 75A of the EP(C)A 1978 or s 158 of the TULR(C)A 1992 there is no limit on the amount of a week's pay which can be taken into account.

Chapter 18

Time Limits, Reviews and Appeals

In respect of unfair dismissal claims, there are four time limits to be considered for:
 (a) presenting the originating application;
 (b) making an application for interim relief;
 (c) making an application for review;
 (d) lodging an appeal.

Presenting the originating application

The relevant provisions can be found in s 67(2) and (4) of the EP(C)A and the Industrial Tribunals (Constitution and Rules of Procedure) Regulations 1993 (SI 1993 No 2687). An industrial tribunal cannot hear a complaint unless it is presented within three months *beginning with* the effective date of termination. The tribunal can, however, extend that time if it is satisfied that it was not reasonably practicable for the application to have been presented within the time: s 67(2).

Where the employer dismisses by notice, the application can be presented at any time after the notice has been received, even if it is before the effective date of termination: s 67(4). In *Presley v Llanelli Borough Council* [1979] IRLR 381, the EAT concluded that s 67(4) applied where the employee terminated by notice under s 55(2)(c). In the light of s 67(4)(a) this seems impossible. The time limit is jurisdictional not procedural. It cannot, therefore, be waived and the tribunal itself must take the point if it arises. It can arise at any time during the proceedings: see *Westward Circuits Ltd v G W S Read* [1973] IRLR 138 and *Rogers v Bodfari (Transport) Ltd* [1973] ICR 325.

Presentation consists of the application arriving at the Central Office of the Industrial Tribunals at Bury St Edmunds. This can be achieved by three methods: by post, fax or delivery. If an application is received at a regional office the regional secretary is deemed to accept it under IT r 12(6) which amounts to 'presentation': *Bengey v North Devon District Council* [1976] 11 ITR 211. Each application is date-stamped on the day of arrival, and the envelope in which it arrives is retained, so that the postmark can be checked if needed.

Presentation can be effected by hand delivery to the office or by placing it in the tribunal letter box: *Hetton Victory Club v Swainston* [1983] ICR 341. If the tribunal office has no letter box, then a Bank Holiday will be a *dies non*: *Ford v Stakis Hotels & Inns Ltd* [1987] ICR 943. It should be noted that this case was decided before the tribunal offices had fax equipment. The position may possibly be different now, as the fax is available at all times.

As has been stated *above*, the three-month period commences with the effective date of termination: *Hammond v Haigh Castle & Co Ltd* [1973] IRLR 91. Month means calendar month, so that the corresponding day rule applies. Thus, if the effective date of termination is the 10 January, the last date for presentation is the 9 April. If the effective date of termination is the 29 or 30 November, the last date for presentation is the 28 February: *Pruden v Cunard Ellerman Ltd* [1993] IRLR 317. Similarly, termination on, eg 31 January, March and August give a last presentation date of the thirtieth of the appropriate month.

The effective date of termination

This is dealt with in Chapter 5. The only matter which must be stressed is that for the purposes of the time limit, there is no 'extension' by the period of notice.

Extension of time

The tribunal can extend the three-month period, but only if it is satisfied that it was 'not reasonably practicable' for the application to have been presented within the time limit, and then only to a limited degree (see para (*d*), below). This provision has engendered a disproportionate amount of litigation since 1971. From the cases, and in particular *Dedman v British Building and Engineering Appliances Ltd* [1973] IRLR 379 and *Trevelyans (Birmingham) Ltd v Norton* [1991] ICR 488, certain basic principles can be distilled:

(*a*) It is now more difficult to persuade tribunals that an applicant was unaware of the right to claim that he was unfairly dismissed. This was an argument which was frequently put in the early days of unfair dismissal.

(*b*) An applicant who is aware of the right is obliged to seek information and advice on its enforcement.

(*c*) The failure of advisers to give proper advice is no excuse. This applies to all advisers: lawyers, the CAB, trade union officers and other advisers. If, however, the applicant has been given wrong information or advice by an employee at the Job Centre, or a tribunal office, this may provide an escape from the time limit.

(*d*) To wait for the outcome of either an internal appeal or criminal proceedings is no excuse.

(*e*) Solicitors in criminal proceedings have a duty to advise an applicant of the need to issue an application, and that he should not wait the outcome of the criminal proceedings.

(*f*) The time limit is strict. The test is whether it was reasonably practicable for the application to be presented within time, *not* whether there was some good reason why it was not presented within time.

(*g*) If it was not reasonably practicable, the tribunal can only extend the time limit by such period as would have made it reasonably practicable for the application to have been presented. Further delay will be fatal.

The situation under para (*g*), *above*, has been considered in the light of what may be called 'after acquired knowledge'. In *The Machine Tool Industry Research Association v Simpson* [1988] ICR 558, the applicant had been dismissed for a reason which seemed to her to be proper. After the three month time limit had expired, she learned of facts that indicated that the reason for her dismissal had not been both what she had been told and believed. The time was held by the Court of Appeal to have been properly extended. A similar state of affairs, though rather more complex (because it involved a late amendment to the application), can be seen in *Marley (UK) Ltd and another v Anderson* [1994] IRLR 152. Paragraph (*g*) *above*, applies to both sets of circumstances.

Interim relief

This is an application for an order that the applicant's employment shall be continued until the hearing of the applicant's complaint of unfair dismissal. It can be made under either s 77 of the EP(C)A 1978 or s 161 of the TULR(C)A 1992. The former relates to cases where the reason for the dismissal is alleged to be because the applicant had carried out activities as a safety representative, or as a member of a safety committee, under s 57A(1)(*a*) or (*b*) of the EP(C)A 1978; the latter because of the applicant's trade union membership, non-membership or activities under s 152(1) of the TULR(C)A 1992. Both provisions have very strict requirements and time limits. An application for unfair dismissal on the grounds *above* must be lodged. There must be an application for interim relief (they can be in the same document). The application must be presented within seven days *following* the effective date of termination. If the claim is under s 161 of the TULR(C)A 1992, a certificate under s 161(3), signed by an authorised trade union official, must also be lodged within the same period. There is no provision for extending the time. See Chapter 11 for a full discussion on interim relief.

Application for review

An application may be made at the hearing. If not, it must be made to the tribunal office in writing within 14 days after the date upon which the decision was sent to the parties. The grounds must be stated in full: IT r 11(4).

A chairman can extend that time under the general power contained in IT r 15(1). It is wise to seek the extension before the 14 days has expired.

Appeals to the EAT

The time limit is specified in r 3(2) of the Employment Appeal Tribunal Rules 1993 (SI 1993 No 2687). It is 42 days from the date upon which the extended reasons for the tribunal's decision were sent to the parties. This rule is enforced by the EAT with some rigidity. Any application for an extension should be made to the EAT within the period and be for good cause. As extended reasons are necessary, these must be requested from the tribunal (if they have not already been supplied – they are obligatory in discrimination cases). If they have not been requested at the hearing, the request must be in writing and must be made before the end of the period of 21 days of the date on which the decision was sent to the parties: IT r 10(4). A chairman can extend that time under the general power contained in IT r 15(1). It is possible that the EAT may be asked to deal with an appeal without extended reasons by waiving the need under EAT r 32(2).

Where the registrar of the EAT notifies an appellant that the notice of appeal does not give the EAT the jurisdiction to entertain the appeal, the appellant may serve a fresh notice of appeal. That must be done either within the original 42 days or within 21 days of the notification, whichever is the longer period: EAT r 3(4). The respondent to the appeal is notified by the registrar of the date by which any answer should be delivered to the EAT. Any cross-appeal should be lodged within the same period: EAT r 6(2) and (3).

Appeals to the Divisional Court

If any party before (*inter alia*) an industrial tribunal is dissatisfied on a point of law with a decision, they may either appeal to the High Court, or require the tribunal to state a case for the opinion of the High Court: s 11(1) of the Tribunals and Inquiries Act 1992. However, s 11(2) excludes that provision in respect of matters before an industrial tribunal under any of the enactments mentioned in s 136(1) of the EP(C)A 1978. That includes unfair dismissal. A similar exclusion is in s 291(3) of the TULR(C)A 1992, in respect of matters under that Act.

Review or appeal?

There is an important distinction between the two, but it must be noted that an application for review does not extend the time limit for appeal. The grounds for a review are strictly limited; they are contained in IT r 11(1):

    (a) the decision was wrongly made as a result of an error on the part of the tribunal staff;

    (b) a party did not receive notice of the proceedings leading to the decision;

    (c) the decision was made in the absence of a party;

    (d) new evidence has become available since the conclusion of the hearing to which the decision relates, provided that its existence could not have been reasonably known of or foreseen at the time of the hearing; or

    (e) the interests of justice require such a review.

An application for review may be refused by a chairman. That refusal is itself susceptible of appeal. If it is not so refused, it must be heard by a tribunal which may confirm, vary, or revoke the original decision. A decision on the review will be sent to the parties, which again is susceptible of appeal. Thus, it is possible to have an appeal against a decision, and an appeal against a review decision on the same case.

An appeal can only be on a point of law. For this purpose, the lack of evidence to support the tribunal's findings of fact, is a point of law; so also is a perverse decision, ie one that no reasonable tribunal could reach.

Appeals are also possible against interlocutory orders. Thus, a refusal to postpone the hearing, the grant or refusal of witness orders, orders for discovery, etc are all issues on which an appeal can be made provided always that there is a point of law involved. The time limit will run from the date on which the party was notified of the matter concerned. Requests are frequently made to, and granted by, the EAT for an expedited hearing of an appeal on an interlocutory matter.

Judicial review

Theoretically, the decisions of industrial tribunals can be the subject of judicial review. The most recent example occurred at an early stage of *Enderby v Frenchay Health Authority and Another* [1993] IRLR 591. That aspect of the case was unreported. It is somewhat surprising that the Divisional Court did not take the view that judicial review was inappropriate when there is a perfectly satisfactory method of judicial appeal. That point was not argued before the Divisional Court. Although, therefore, such a step may be pursued, its prospect of success is far from certain.

The Court of Justice of the European Community

It is not possible to appeal to the European Court of Justice, nor for parties to commence litigation there. A tribunal, the EAT, the Court of Appeal or the House of Lords, have a discretion to refer a question to the European Court of Justice for a ruling at any stage. This can be done at the request of one or more of the parties, or of the tribunal's or court's own motion. Obviously, this will only be done where there is a point of Community law involved.

Any rights conferred on individuals by the Treaty of Rome or a directive must be pursued in the national courts.

Index